W9-CAW-124

Also by Hunter S. Thompson

Hell's Angels
Fear and Loathing in Las Vegas
Fear and Loathing: On the Campaign Trail '72
The Great Shark Hunt
The Curse of Lono
Generation of Swine
Songs of the Doomed
Screwjack
Better Than Sex
The Proud Highway
The Rum Diary

FEAR AND LOATHING IN AMERICA

SIMON & SCHUSTER

New York London Toronto Sydney Singapore

The Brutal Odyssey of an Outlaw Journalist

1968–1976

HUNTER S. THOMPSON

Foreword by David Halberstam
Edited by Douglas Brinkley

SIMON & SCHUSTER
Rockefeller Center
1230 Avenue of the Americas
New York, NY 10020

Copyright © 2000 by Gonzo International Corp.
All rights reserved,
including the right of reproduction
in whole or in part in any form.

SIMON & SCHUSTER and colophon are registered trademarks
of Simon & Schuster, Inc.

Designed by Katy Riegel
Manufactured in the United States of America
10 9 8 7 6 5 4 3 2 1

Library of Congress Cataloging-in-Publication Data

Thompson, Hunter S.
Fear and loathing in America : the brutal odyssey of an outlaw journalist, 1968–1976/
Hunter S. Thompson ; foreword by David Halberstam ; edited by Douglas Brinkley.
p. cm.
1. Thompson, Hunter S.—Correspondence. 2. Journalists—United
States—Correspondence. I. Brinkley, Douglas. II. Title.

PN4874.T444 A3 2000
070'.92—dc21
[B]

00-047012

ISBN 0-684-87315-X

To Oliver Treibick and Bob Braudis

May you live in interesting times

—ancient Chinese curse

Contents

Foreword by David Halberstam

I was both delighted and surprised by the request to write the Foreword to this collection of Hunter Thompson's letters. Delighted because I am an unabashed fan of the Doctor, and I think his work is touched by genius and transcends mere journalism. Surprised because I am the ultimate literal reporter who comes from the opposite end of the spectrum, and my work could not be more different than his. I go where my interviews, my facts, and my anecdotes take me. Hunter, by contrast, goes where his instincts take him, and his instincts, as his work has proved to us over the years, have a certain brilliance to them.

His truths are, I suspect, larger than the truths of most of the rest of us and allow him to be a man of Gonzo and yet have such a great resonance with the non-Gonzoists among us. He helps fill an immense vacuum in the world of journalism. For in America these days print journalism is in sharp decline, significantly more anemic than it was thirty-five years ago, and television journalism, more often than not, is a mockery of itself. We live in a communications society where image is more important than truth and spinning is our great new growth industry; even television reporters now have their own personal public relations people, the better, if not to spin their viewers and the ever admiring celebrity magazines, then at least to spin themselves on the value of what they do. Therefore in a culture like ours Hunter's truths seem like laser beams cutting through the fog of lies and obfuscations, an industrialized man-made fog that is now so easily manufactured, bought, and paid for in the wealth of contemporary America. Hunter is fog immune. Or at least man-made fog immune.

The moment when he wrote these letters is important. It is not the best of times in America. It is post-Tet, the Vietnam War is winding down, the Democratic Party is badly divided, the backlash against a more optimistic liberalism that marked the Civil Rights movement is growing. Watergate is just taking place and the violations of constitutional rights that it represents, violations of the rights of ordinary citizens at the order of the president of the United States, will not come as any great surprise to many people. Tensions in society abound, over the war, over race, and over class. Literal journalism often seems inadequate, facts seem futile to many people. All in all, it is fertile time for someone with a sensibility like Hunter's. Not surprisingly, his work is becoming more widely admired and his truths often seem more real than the facts accumulated by most traditional reporters. He is working on a mother lode that he is sure is out there, a darkness of the spirit.

There are endless letters going back and forth between him and his loving and admiring book editor, Jim Silberman, on something that he wants to do but cannot quite get his hands on, a book on the Death of the American Dream. It was a book that somehow eluded him, though of course, it is there in almost everything he wrote before, during, and after that time. But for the moment it is hard going. In December 1969, he writes a friend named Steve Geller about how hard it all is: "All of which reminds me that I'm many months overdue with that wonderful Random House offering called 'The Death of the American Dream.' I hate to spend 3 yrs writing a pile of worthless shit, but that's what I'm into—a sophomore jinx on all fronts. I've done everything I can to put it off, but now—stone broke again—I don't see any way out. Just write the fucker and clear the decks . . . take the beating and play counter-puncher. Fuck them . . . This is really a stinking way to have to make a living."

This collection of letters is instructive in a number of ways. I think the first is the passion of the young Hunter Thompson to be someone, his absolute certainty of the value of his talent, his unyielding faith in himself in a world whose editors had not always deigned to recognize his talents. He knows that he is gifted, he is sure that he knows things about reporting that they do not, he knows he cannot do it any other way. He is absolutely sure that he has a right to be published, and that they have an obligation to publish him. Besides, there is no other way to go. To one of his favorite editors, a gifted young man at *Playboy* named David Butler, who had made suggestions about how to make a piece more publishable (and salable), he wrote: "I'm pretty well hooked on my own style—for good or for ill—and the chances of changing it now are pretty dim. A journalist into Gonzo is like a junkie or an egg-sucking dog; there is no known cure."

Looking back at what he did, reading these letters now (and the previous volume, *The Proud Highway*), I think there is a certain invincibility to Hunter that shows in both collections. Even when no one else yet realized it, he always knew he was the Great Hunter Thompson. That faith, it seems to me, is at the core of his work and his success.

His voice is sui generis. He is who he is. No one created Hunter other than Hunter. Somehow he found his voice, and he knew, before anyone else, that it was special. It is not to be imitated, and I can't think of anything worse than for any young journalist to try to imitate Hunter. That's the price of being an original. There's room for only one on the ark. The other thing these letters reveal is how hard it is to be an original. He could not be anything else, not like some of his would-be successors, who came and tried to do what he did for a brief once-around-the-track tour and then ventured out to Hollywood for their just reward as screenwriters. There was no easy niche for him, not then, not now. Hunter is many things but one thing he is not is a cynic. He had to do it his way. The financial rewards were and are minimal. His work does not bring Hollywood courting. In the period covered here, his constituency is just beginning to grow—in time he will be something of a cult figure, but hardcover readers are not exactly storming the barricades and pumping his books onto the best-seller lists. When you are an original, the way is often lonely, and the rewards come slowly. In those days he was doing wonderful work and getting very little back for it financially. Jim Silberman is endlessly patient and Jann Wenner to his credit was relatively good to Hunter, but the times were always hard, he was always fighting for a little more money and a little more respect from most editors. The IRS seems to be in constant pursuit, and he is always arguing with editors for his last check and for his expense accounts. If there is a melancholy series of letters in this book, it is a group that he wrote to a very wealthy man named Max Palevsky who had once loaned him $10,000 and was calling the loan in—with the use of lawyers. In these letters Hunter's voice changes—it is not the feigned put-in-mock-combat, death-to-the-pigfuckers that is his normal manner; instead the words are those of a man truly pained by the unkindness of someone else.

His taste is good and what he is always looking for in the work of others is the essential truth of their work. There is a letter in here to Selma Shapiro, the Random House publicity chief, in praise of an as yet unknown writer named Fred Exley who has just written a book called *A Fan's Notes*, eventually to be designated a cult classic. Exley's work, like much of Hunter's writing, is iconic and hard to categorize. "There is something very good and right about it, hard to define," Hunter writes of *A Fan's Notes*. He debates with himself the pros and cons of Exley's writing and then comes up with the reason he likes it: "I suppose it's the truth-level, a demented kind of honesty." Then he goes on a small riff about other writers who deal with class and racial tensions. "I've never paid much attention to the Black/Jew/Wasp problem; it strikes me as a waste of time and energy. My prejudice is pretty general, far too broad and sweeping for any racial limitations. It's clear to me—and has been since the age of 10 or so—that most people are bastards, thieves and yes—even pigfuckers."

That is, I think, a very important passage, and perhaps the most revealing in the book—it shows what he is really about and what he is searching for, and why his work is so powerful. It's all in the truths.

David Halberstam
New York
August 9, 2000

Editor's Note by Douglas Brinkley

Gentlemen, nature works in a mysterious way. When a new truth comes upon the earth, or a great idea necessary for mankind is born, where does it come from? Not from the police force or the prosecuting attorneys or the judges or the lawyers or the doctors; not there. It comes from the despised and the outcast; it comes perhaps from jails and prisons; it comes from men who have dared to be rebels and think their thoughts; and their fate has been the fate of rebels. This generation gives them graves while another builds them monuments; and there is no exception to it. It has been true since the world began, and it will be true no doubt forever.

Clarence Darrow, 1920

It was March 1967 and freelance journalist Hunter S. Thompson was in New York City on tour for Random House, which had published his first book, *Hell's Angels: A Strange and Terrible Saga*, a brutal and eloquent account of the year he spent riding with the notorious biker gang, then a symbol of everything that made Middle America nervous. Overnight Thompson had become a literary *enfant terrible,* his book climbing onto best-seller lists. After appearing on NBC's *Today Show* with host Hugh Downs, the chain-smoking Thompson had a singular request of his publicist, Selma Shapiro. "I insisted that we take a break from the grueling schedule for a few minutes," Thompson recalled. "I was desperate to hear the just-released Jefferson Airplane album."

Together they found a record store on Madison Avenue that carried *Surrealistic Pillow*, a soaring soundtrack from the carnival-like streets of San Francisco's Haight-Ashbury, where Thompson had written *Hell's Angels* and befriended the psychedelic band. While writing the book, he would often zoom through North Beach on his BSA Lightning motorcycle, park in front of The Matrix, and listen to the Airplane's lead vocalist, Grace Slick, belt out rock classics like "White Rabbit." It was Thompson, in fact, who had introduced *The San Francisco Chronicle*'s music critic, Ralph J. Gleason, to the Jefferson

Airplane, insisting that they were as good as, if not better than, the Grateful Dead. Now, with Shapiro at his side, Thompson went into the store's listening booth and spun the disk.

"Upon hearing the first note I smiled," Thompson recalled years later. "This was the triumph of the San Francisco people. We were all making it, riding a magical wave which we didn't think would break." Thompson kept dropping the stylus onto every track, anxious to hear a sampling of each cut. When he got to the fourth song—"Today"—he could no longer control his enthusiasm: "'Hot damn, Selma,' I remember saying. 'You've been asking me pesky questions about what I think. Listen to this. Wow! I could have written these lyrics myself. Today *is* my time.'"

The letters published in *Fear and Loathing in America*—the second volume in a projected trilogy—cover the eight frenetic years from 1968 to 1976 when Thompson was at the glorious height of his literary powers. As documented in the first collection, *The Proud Highway: Saga of a Desperate Southern Gentleman*, the Kentucky-bred Thompson had slowly risen in the world of journalism, writing for such newspapers and journals as *The New York Herald Tribune*, *The National Observer*, *The Nation*, *The Reporter*, and *The New York Times Magazine*. While working continually on two novels—"Prince Jellyfish" (unpublished), set in New York City, and *The Rum Diary* (1998), based in Puerto Rico—Thompson garnered a formidable reputation in newsrooms for his reportage on the bizarre. In his freelance journalism he wrote profiles of Butte hobos, Caribbean smugglers, Beat poets, nude dancers, Sacramento politicians, Oregon drifters, flower children, riverboat gamblers, bluegrass pickers, San Joaquin migrant workers, and Sioux activists. As critic Richard Elman noted in *The New Republic*, Thompson was asserting a "kind of Rimbaud delirium of spirit" in his writing, which "only the rarest of geniuses" could pull off. Such well-known American chroniclers as Studs Terkel, Tom Wolfe, William Kennedy, and Charles Kuralt were the first reporters to recognize that Thompson was a masterful prose stylist, imbued with a strange gift for comic despair and sledgehammer humor. They saw him as a hilarious schemer, an attack dog like H. L. Mencken, an outrageous outsider like novelist J. D. Salinger's Holden Caulfield. Meanwhile, mainstream editors also learned to respect Thompson's well-honed instinct for accurately reporting on the fringe characters of the tumultuous 1960s. "He became our official crazy," John Leonard claimed in *The New York Times*, "patrolling the edge." Now, with the wild success of *Hell's Angels*, the first printing selling out within days of publication, Thompson had the freedom to explore "the edge" in new modes of journalism that borrowed from fiction writing.

Almost overnight, assignment offers came pouring in from *Esquire*, *Harper's*, *The Saturday Evening Post*, and a dozen other periodicals, all anxious for an offbeat piece from the celebrated thirty-year-old author of *Hell's Angels*. It soon became apparent, however, that Thompson's fiercely subjective style just wasn't for editors with weak stomachs or nervous advertisers. *Playboy*, for example, had assigned Thompson to write a profile of Jean-Claude Killy, a handsome Olympic skier turned Chevrolet pitchman. "On balance, it seems unfair to dismiss him as a witless greedhead, despite all the evidence," Thompson concluded. "Somewhere behind that wistful programmed smile I suspect there is something akin to what Norman Mailer once called (speaking of James Jones) 'an animal sense of who has the power.'" This was too unhinged for *Playboy*, too honest. In rejecting what literary historians now deem the first pure example of Gonzo journalism—the piece eventually ran as "The Temptations of Jean-Claude Killy" in the March 1970 *Scanlan's Monthly*—*Playboy*'s editor composed an internal memo denouncing "Thompson's ugly, stupid arrogance" as "an insult to everything we stand for."

What becomes clear in *Fear and Loathing in America* is how important a role the editor of *Scanlan's Monthly*, Warren Hinckle, played in the development of Thompson's infamous Gonzo style. The two first met in San Francisco in 1967 when Hinckle was running the leftist magazine *Ramparts*. As a pure literary art form, Gonzo requires virtually no rewriting: the reporter and his quest for information are central to the story, told via a fusion of bedrock reality and stark fantasy in a way that is meant to amuse both the author and the reader. Stream-of-consciousness, article excerpts, transcribed interviews, telephone conversations—these are the elements of a piece of aggressively subjective Gonzo journalism. "It is a style of reporting based on William Faulkner's idea that the best fiction is far more true than any kind of journalism," Thompson has noted. Today the term "Gonzo" appears in the Webster's and Random House dictionaries—with Thompson given credit as its coiner—but when Hinckle first published the Killy piece in *Scanlan's*, he was taking a huge risk. His editorial gamble would soon pay off handsomely, however, when Thompson returned to his hometown of Louisville—with British illustrator Ralph Steadman at his side—to cover America's premier Thoroughbred horse race.

The story of how Thompson and Steadman first teamed up to take on the Kentucky Derby is revealed for the first time through the letters in this collection. One evening in May 1970, Hunter and his wife, Sandy, were dining at the Aspen home of James Salter, a dear friend whose novel *A Sport and a Pastime* is considered a modern classic. Salter, knowing that Thompson was raised along the Ohio River, casually asked him if he was going to attend the Derby. "I told him 'no,'" Thompson remembered. "But I immediately seized upon the idea that I should cover it." At 3:30 the next morning, Thompson telephoned Hinckle and got the assignment. Refusing a photographer, Thompson suggested that editorial cartoonist Pat Oliphant from *The Denver Post* accompany him to the mint-julep spectacle. Oliphant was unavailable, so Hinckle hired the thirty-four-year-old Steadman, a Welsh illustrator renowned for his hideous and hilarious caricatures of British politicians in *Private Eye* magazine. The combustible pairing changed the face of modern journalism: they produced

"The Kentucky Derby Is Decadent and Depraved," in which Thompson's traditional reportage was skewed in favor of a viciously funny, first-person, Gonzo perspective while Steadman's perversely exact illustrations were drawn in lipstick to shock the unprepared reader. The outrageous, ribald result won immediate acclaim. "The Derby story had pointed the way toward the great mother lode," novelist and friend William Kennedy recalled. "Hunter had discovered that confounding sums of money could be had by writing what seemed to be journalism, while actually you were developing your fictional oeuvre."

But as we learn at the outset of *Fear and Loathing in America*, it was the 1968 presidential election that jarred Thompson to unleash his vitriolic prose on the leading politicians of the day. It all began with his first weird encounter with Richard Nixon, the Republican nominee, whom he interviewed that February in New Hampshire. Thompson had considered Nixon "just another sad old geek limping back into politics for another beating." But the new Nixon—full of football stories and the "V" for victory sign—startled him. "He was brighter and therefore more dangerous than I had surmised," Thompson recalled. "He was a brute in need of extermination."

That July, *Pageant* published Thompson's "Presenting: The Richard Nixon Doll." The piece marked the beginning of Thompson's relentless stalking of Nixon, his all-purpose arch-nemesis. This book, in fact, could easily have been subtitled *The Age of Nixon.* Two of Thompson's most enduring works—the incomparable *Fear and Loathing: On the Campaign Trail '72,* published by Straight Arrow Books in 1973, and the cogent "Fear and Loathing at the Watergate: Mr. Nixon Has Cashed His Check," a lengthy article that appeared in the September 27, 1973, *Rolling Stone*—were inspired by Thompson's insatiable distrust of Richard Nixon. When the president resigned under the dark cloud of Watergate, Thompson's first instinct was to throw a sack of dead rats over the wrought iron White House fence in celebration. Thompson acknowledged his debt to "Tricky Dick" by dedicating his 1979 anthology, *The Great Shark Hunt,* "To Richard Milhous Nixon, who never let me down." And his merciless obituary of Nixon, published in 1994 in *Rolling Stone*, stands as the most devastating critique of a politician since H. L. Mencken set out to destroy the populist reputation of Nebraska's William Jennings Bryan shortly after the 1925 *Scopes* "monkey" trial.

Yet perhaps even more than the dark specter of Nixon, it was the brutish actions of the Chicago police force at the Democratic National Convention in 1968 that gave Thompson the fear. Somewhat foolishly, Thompson had signed a contract with Random House to write a nonfiction book on "The Death of the American Dream." He had journeyed from his ranch in Woody Creek, Colorado, which remains his home, to the Windy City in hopes of gathering material for the book. While waiting with other members of the press to get into the convention hall, he witnessed a mob of demonstrators marching toward a flank of policemen at the corner of Michigan and Balboa. Seconds later, the police charged the protestors with billy clubs waving. Ignoring the press credentials that hung around his neck, the police shoved Thompson against a plate glass window as chaos and violence erupted all around him. "I went to the Democratic Convention as a journalist," Thompson wrote of the encounter, "and returned a cold-blooded revolutionary."

Chicago proved to be the political awakening of Hunter S. Thompson. No longer would he simply write about politics, he would personally enter the fray. Believing that "politics was the art of controlling your environment," Thompson soon found himself in the unlikely role of leader of the Freak Power Movement in the Rocky Mountains. Many of the letters published here center on Thompson's hubristic run for sheriff of Pitkin County, Colorado, in 1970. "The die is already cast in my race," he wrote. "And the only remaining question is how many freaks, heads, criminals, anarchists, beatniks, poachers, Wobblies, bikers and persons of weird persuasion will come out of their holes and vote for me." With his head shaved clean, a bright-red fist with two thumbs clasping a peyote button as his campaign poster, jazz artist Herbie Mann's spirited "Battle Hymn of the Republic" as his anthem, and a party platform that included changing Aspen's name to "Fat City" to slow down development, Thompson's savage campaign attracted considerable national attention.

Other celebrated American writers have run for political office—Upton Sinclair in California and Norman Mailer in New York, for example—but none with the surreal flair with which Thompson conducted his 1970 campaign for sheriff. *The New York Times* assessed him favorably in a profile featuring a photograph of Thompson in front of a large portrait of FBI Director J. Edgar Hoover, while *Harper's* commissioned a lengthy essay on his dark horse run. "In the ominous, ugly-splintered context of what is happening in 1970 Amerika a lot of people are beginning to understand that to be a freak is an honorable way to go," Thompson wrote on one of the eight *Wallposters* he produced for the campaign. "This is the real point: that we are not really freaks at all—not in the literal sense—but the twisted realities of the world we are trying to live in have somehow combined to make us feel like freaks. We argue, we protest, we petition—but nothing changes.

"So now, with the rest of the nation erupting in a firestorm of bombings and political killings, a handful of 'freaks' are running a final, perhaps atavistic experiment with the idea of forcing change by voting." Astonishingly, Thompson lost by only four hundred–odd votes of more than twenty-five hundred cast. In fact, he carried three of the four city precincts, but was massively rejected by voters in the populous down-county suburbs and ski centers.

More than any other periodical it was *Rolling Stone*, a rock 'n' roll magazine published in San Francisco, that embraced Thompson's wildcat run for sheriff. Brazen owner and editor Jann Wenner had become a principal spokesman for the so-called "Love Generation," and his magazine—its name taken from the title of a Muddy Waters blues song—was setting the tone for counterculture art and fashion in America. The first piece Thompson wrote for *Rolling Stone,* published in the October 1, 1970, issue, was "The Battle of Aspen," an autobiographical account of the Freak Power Movement in Colorado. Like Hinckle, whose *Scanlan's Monthly* soon folded because of financial mismanagement, Wenner understood that Thompson was a rock 'n' roll mix of Ernest Hemingway, F. Scott Fitzgerald, and H. L. Mencken—a sort of literary wild man running amok on speed and insolence, yet with a controlled grace and unreal precision to his hallucinatory prose, and in the end his trenchant and sober-minded critiques of modern society were perhaps, as Nelson Algren put it, "the sanest of all." By 1970, what Bob Dylan had become to electric music, Hunter Thompson had become to cutting-edge journalism.

Sidetracked by Aspen politics and freelance assignments, Thompson, as revealed in this volume, was having a hard time with his book on "The Death of the American Dream" for Random House. Deadlines came and went. Debts piled up and frustration grew. Stone broke was a way of life. It was under this intense duress that—while working on a serious investigative piece for *Rolling Stone* on Ruben Salazar, a Chicano activist who had been shot and killed by a member of the Los Angeles County Sheriff's Department—Thompson stumbled on the answer to his three-year-old quest in the glitzy gambling emporiums of Nevada.

The appearance of *Fear and Loathing in Las Vegas* in two issues of *Rolling Stone* in 1971, under the pseudonym Raoul Duke, sealed Thompson's reputation as an outlaw genius. As the subtitle warns, the work takes readers on "a savage journey to the heart of the American Dream." *The New York Times* review said, "What goes on in these pages makes Lenny Bruce seem angelic. . . . The whole book boils down to a kind of mad, corrosive poetry." Tom Wolfe pronounced it "a scorching, epochal sensation." Essentially, the narrative follows Duke and his three-hundred-pound Samoan attorney, Dr. Gonzo, to Las Vegas, ostensibly to cover a motorcycle race and then a convention of district attorneys. How did Thompson and his accomplice prepare for the trip? As Duke wrote: "We had two bags of grass, seventy-five pellets of mescaline, five sheets of high-powered blotter acid, a salt shaker half full of cocaine, and a whole galaxy of multi-colored uppers, downers, screamers, laughers . . . and also a quart of tequila, a quart of rum, a case of Budweiser, a pint of raw ether and two dozen amyls."

The primary question that readers of *Fear and Loathing in Las Vegas* ask is: Was it all true? Did he really gobble up all those drugs? Was his attorney—a thinly disguised portrayal of Chicano activist Oscar Zeta Acosta—really that demented? The correspondence included in this volume between Thompson and his Random House editor, Jim Silberman, addresses this speculation in a frank, candid, and surprising fashion. An unexpected image emerges of Thompson as clever wordsmith, completely coherent and purposeful as he tries to puncture the hypocrisy of Rotarian America and fulfill his contractual obligation to boot. Self-editing throughout the process of completing the book at Owl Farm in Colorado and a Ramada Inn in California, Thompson knew he had a bizarre classic on his hands, a book that only he could have written.

Also included in *Fear and Loathing in America* are several of the outlandish letters that Acosta, the legendary Brown Buffalo, wrote to Thompson from California and Mexico during the 1970s. A nearly full-blooded Aztec Indian obsessed with the violent legacy of Cortés the Killer in the New World, Acosta is now considered one of the most influential "Chicano Power" playwrights, defense attorneys, and intractable activists of his era. Raised by Mexican parents in El Paso, Texas, as a strict Catholic, Acosta received formal religious training in Panama. Blessed and afflicted with a hyperkinetic disposition and forever craving the limelight, Acosta loved to preach like an Old Testament prophet one minute, then eat LSD like a deranged drug offender on the run the next. But one historical observation from the period is certain: a synergy developed between Thompson and Acosta during the winter of 1967–1968 that benefited both artists. "There were times—all too often, I felt—when Oscar would show up in front of the courthouse at nine in the morning with a stench of fresh gasoline on his hands and a green crust of charred soap-flakes on the toes of his $300 snakeskin cowboy boots," Thompson wrote in his memorable *Rolling Stone* obituary of Acosta, who died mysteriously in 1977 somewhere in Mexico. "He would pause outside the courtroom just long enough to give the TV press five minutes of crazed rhetoric for the Evening News, then he would shepherd his equally crazed 'clients' into the courtroom for their daily war-circus with the Judge. When you get into bear baiting on that level, paranoia is just another word for ignorance. . . . They really *are* out to get you."

Paranoia is a central theme on nearly every page of this book. Deep suspicions of the FBI, the CIA, and the Secret Service abound. Doom is always looming down; financial ruin is always on the horizon like a thundercloud about to break. In Thompson's distrustful world, agents are thieves, editors are swine, and politicians, with occasional exceptions like former South Dakota senator George McGovern, are charlatans. While writing the series of articles for *Rolling Stone* that became *Fear and Loathing: On the Campaign Trail '72,* Thompson excoriated George Wallace, Hubert Humphrey, Edmund Muskie, Henry "Scoop" Jackson, Richard Nixon—the whole phalanx of candidates. But unlike other sharp-tongued critics of the American political process, there was a Jeffersonian idealism in Thompson's writing that transcended mere cynicism. "Hunter was a patriot," McGovern recalls of the Gonzo journalist who crisscrossed the nation with him in 1972. "He thought in universal terms. He was not a jingoist. He hated that war in Vietnam with a passion. And he hated the hypocrisy of the establishment. Basically, I think he wanted to see this country live up to his ideals. And he wanted us to do better. There is no doubt that what he wrote in 1972 was the most valuable book on the campaign."

Fear and Loathing in America holds many surprises for the political junkie. We learn of Thompson's wild-eyed ambition to run for the U.S. Senate from Colorado, his retention of lawyer Sandy Berger to sue cartoonist Garry Trudeau for the potentially libelous portrayal of him as "Uncle Duke" in the *Doonesbury* comic strip, his strange friendship with Nixon man Patrick Buchanan, and his unexpected embrace of Jimmy Carter during the 1976 presidential election. There are feuds with journalists Sidney Zion and Sally Quinn, denunciations of Timothy Leary and Abbie Hoffman, and bitter disappointment when even McGovern turned to the pols. Experimentation—and overindulgence—in drugs such as mescaline, hashish, and LSD are also commonplace occurrences in these letters. For a while, in fact, Thompson considered titling this book "Confessions of a Mescaline Eater" or "The Jimson Weed Chronicles," in tribute to narcotics enthusiasts Thomas DeQuincey and William S. Burroughs.

In the pages that follow are largely unedited letters documenting eight years in the high-speed life and times of Hunter S. Thompson. As in *The Proud Highway,* the dilemma was choosing which letters to include, which to excise. At a party to celebrate the twenty-fifth anniversary of the publication of *Fear and Loathing in Las Vegas*, a reporter from *Entertainment Weekly* asked Jann Wenner what Thompson would have been without drugs and guns. "An accountant," Wenner answered without hesitation. "No doubt about it." When asked about this, Thompson replied: "Well, Jann says a lot of stupid things. He used to be smart, but now he's just another bean-counter."

For every letter included in this volume, five others were cut. Some of the axed missives were of an intense personal nature regarding Thompson's wife, Sandy, and son, Juan. Others were rejected because of repetition or their financial nature. Many of the letters dealing with Aspen politics were left out due to their obsolete "inside baseball" content. An effort was made, however, to include letters that showcase Thompson's struggles as an aspiring writer, the difficult task he confronted waking up every day with a sheet of snow-white paper in his typewriter, seemingly demanding that first-rate prose come to grace it.

At times Thompson's uncompromising perfectionism overwhelmed his editors. But it must be remembered that he was a self-made, rugged individualist living in the wilds of Colorado, thousands of miles from Madison Avenue. Worried that treacherous New Yorkers were going to take advantage of his high-country isolation and rip him off, Thompson assiduously stayed on top of his business affairs, threatening lawsuits over late checks and sloppy bookkeeping. There is a legalistic quality to many of these letters, with Thompson playing the righteous Clarence Darrow dueling fraudulent and churlish confidence men of every stripe. Over the years, in fact, Thompson has worked on a book he calls "Hey Rube," a wicked manifesto that lampoons the white-collar criminals and New Age astrologers who take advantage of the hardworking, honest folks in the provinces that John Steinbeck wrote about with such tender awareness. Filled with an avenger's rhetoric and idiopathic outrage, "Hey

Rube" is Thompson's all-seasons scorecard against the world of fast-talking money manipulators, used-car salesmen, and TV evangelists.

Behind the complex personality of Hunter S. Thompson—the Gonzo journalist cranked up on Chivas Regal, Dunhill cigarettes, and LSD—lurks a trenchant humorist with a sharp moral sensibility. For Thompson understands that against the assault of laughter nothing can stand, at least not for long. His exaggerated style may defy easy categorization, but his career-long autopsy on the death of the American Dream places him among the twentieth century's most iconoclastic writers. Outsized truths are Thompson's stock-in-trade, and the comic savagery of his best work will continue to electrify readers for generations to come. Perhaps novelist Tom Robbins comes closest to explaining the enduring high-octane appeal of Thompson's work: "His prose style reads like he's careening down a mountain highway at 110 miles an hour, steering with his knees."

It would be a mistake to claim that *Fear and Loathing in America* answers the question of whether Thompson writes fiction or nonfiction. But we do learn what a literary workhorse he was during the chaotic era of Woodstock and Watergate. Like Mark Twain, he believed that the difference between the nearly right word and the right word was a large matter, the difference between the lightning bug and the lightning. An aspiring Gonzo journalist working for some alternative newspaper like the *Boulder Planet* or an Associated Press stringer anxious to insert invective into his copy would be wise to take note of the supreme discipline Thompson devoted toward perfecting every word in every line. As with Hemingway, many young writers ache to imitate Thompson's hyperbolic style and maverick attitude; they nearly all fail miserably. There is only one Hunter S. Thompson: an incorrigible, doom-haunted observer whose dazzling prose and outlaw persona have made a distinctive mark on our times.

Douglas Brinkley
New Orleans
July 15, 2000

**Special thanks to Shelby Sadler for researching/writing the footnotes and many of the letter introductions and contributing editorially to the entire volume; Marysue Rucci for brilliantly overseeing the entire Simon & Schuster editorial process; Deborah Fuller for managing the Thompson Archive in Woody Creek, Colorado; Erica Whittington of the Eisenhower Center at the University of New Orleans for manuscript preparation and superb editorial assistance; Anita Bejmuk for her heroic all-night proofreading sessions; Curtis Robinson for brainstorming with Dr. Thompson and creating subheads; and Wayne Ewing for his ceaseless intellectual input into how to improve* Fear and Loathing in America.

Author's Note by Hunter S. Thompson

The Form calls for me to write a few words of wisdom at this point—but I am not feeling wise tonight, so I will leave that job to Mr. Halberstam, who is better at it than I am.

These letters are not the work of a wise man, but only a player and a scribe with a dangerous gambling habit. . . . That is a risky mix that will sooner or later lead you to cross the wrong wires and get shocked, or even burned to a cinder. On some days you will be lucky and only break your fingers and make a fool of yourself. But luck is a very thin wire between survival and disaster, and not many people can keep their balance on it.

I have never believed much in luck, and my sense of humor has tended to walk on the dark side. Muhammad Ali, one of my very few heroes, once took the time to explain to me that "there *are* no jokes. The truth is the funniest joke of all."

Ho ho. It takes a special kind of mind-set to believe that & still have smart people call you Funny. I have never quite understood it.

But there are many things that I have never quite understood—and these letters, to me, are a sort of berserk historical record of my efforts to grope & flail & occasionally crawl along in the darkness and try to make functional sense of it. That is the best we can do, I think, and Luck has little to do with it. The real keys are timing, and balance, and the learned ability to know a hot wire when you see one.

People who count on luck don't last long in the business of defusing bombs and disarming land mines, and that is what my business seems to be. It helps to know these things. Muhammad Ali was not lucky. He was fast, very fast.

The period covered in these letters (1968–1976) was like riding on top of a bullet train for eight years with no sleep and no wires to hang on to. (Is that a dangling participle?) Never end a sentence with a preposition. Never get off a train while it's moving. These are only a few of the rules I have learned & carefully broken in my time.

"Beer on whiskey, mighty risky—Whiskey on beer, never fear." That is a rule I learned early, and it has always served me well. I don't take credit for it, but I will pass it along as truth. It has stood the test of experience.

So that's about it for my wisdom tonight. (I guess I lied. Or maybe I just changed my mind. So what?) Right now I am focused on going out in my dark front yard and shooting a bear who weighs five hundred pounds and is into a feeding frenzy. . . . I don't want to *kill* the bear, I just want to sting it in the ass & make it move along. I am a territorial man, and I have been here longer than the bear has.

I don't mind *sharing* with him, in principle—but the bear is rude, and he makes a mess when he eats. I have plenty of food, and if the bear wants to act right, I will feed him. If he has interesting things to say, I will offer him whiskey & shrimp & snow-peas. I am a good listener. But I don't have time for guests who compel me to keep a loaded .44 Magnum on my side of the table because they might go wild & get into a feeding frenzy.

If that happens, I will quickly shoot the beast, but that would bring its own strange problems, and I don't need them.

And so much for that, eh? Fuck bears. I will deal with them soon enough. . . . Right now we are talking about Letters, many letters, and my job is to find some meaning in them, which is not an easy assignment.

All I can see, for sure, is that I got what they call an "adult dose" of American political reality in an era when the nation seemed to be going up in flames every day of every week. There was no relief from it, and no place to hide. You didn't have to be a "revolutionary" to be part of the Revolution—and even if you were innocent, you could be beaten & gassed just for watching. In a four-year span I was tear-gassed or beaten or chased like a rat by police about two hundred times in at least twenty states, from Key Biscayne to the Olympic Peninsula, from Gainesville & Miami to Montreal & Austin & the gates of Beverly Hills. I had such a steady diet of riot-control gas that I became a junkie, & I still get nostalgic for it on slow nights.

I came to know gunfire and panic and the sight of my own blood on the streets. I knew every airport in the country before they had metal-detectors & you could still smoke on planes. Pilots knew me by name and stewardesses took me home when my flights were grounded by snow. I made many new friends & many powerful enemies from coast to coast. I went without sleep for seventy or eighty hours at a time & often wrote five thousand words in one sitting. It was a brutal life, and I loved it.

My main luxury in those years—a necessary luxury, in fact—was the ability to work in and out of my home-base fortress in Woody Creek. It was a very important psychic anchor for me, a crucial grounding point where I always knew I had love, friends, & good neighbors. It was like my personal Lighthouse that I could see from anywhere in the world—no matter where I was, or how weird

& crazy & dangerous it got, everything would be okay if I could just make it home. When I made that hairpin turn up the hill onto Woody Creek Road, I knew I was safe.

Or at least I was safe from my enemies. Nobody is safe from their friends, and especially not me. I have never really worried about my enemies—not even when they included the president, the director of the FBI, or the district attorneys in five states. . . . I am generally proud of my enemies. The list is long & I still hate every one of them. I have forgiven a lot of the minor sins, but the major ones will still get me cranked up in a matter of seconds, on a hot rainy day in the wrong town.

Jesus. This riff could go on & on, so let's leave it for now—except to add, in boldface, thanks to Sandy Thompson and Juan Thompson, who had to Live with the whole bizarre saga and kept the home fires burning at all times. . . . You bet, we *need* those fires, bubba, and we need that place to laugh. So, thanks again. And may the right gods fall in love with you, like I did.

Hunter S. Thompson
Woody Creek, Colorado
August 20, 2000

1968

CHICAGO: THE GREAT AMERICAN SLAUGHTER-HOUSE . . . PUBLIC MURDERS & PRIVATE BEATINGS . . . WHIPPED LIKE A DOG WITH THE WHOLE WORLD WATCHING . . . WHICH SIDE ARE YOU ON? . . . CLANDESTINE MEETING WITH NIXON, COUP DE GRÂCE FOR THE SIXTIES . . .

Thompson's press pass for
the 1968 Democratic National
Convention in Chicago.
(Courtesy of HST Archives)

Self-portrait,
Woody Creek, 1968.
(Photo courtesy of HST Archives)

Juan Thompson, age four, views a
bullet-riddled portrait of FBI director
J. Edgar Hoover, summer 1968.
(Photo courtesy of HST Archives)

The Gamekeeper, summer 1968.
(PHOTO BY BURK UZZLE)

OWL FARM—WINTER OF '68:

1967 was the year of the hippy. As this is the last meditation I intend to write on that subject, I decided, while composing it, to have the proper background. So, in the same small room with me and my typewriter, I have two huge speakers and a 100 watt music amplifier booming out Bob Dylan's "Mr. Tambourine Man." This, to me, is the Hippy National Anthem. It's an acid or LSD song—and like much of the hippy music, its lyrics don't make much sense to anyone not "cool" or "with it" or "into the drug scene." I was living in San Francisco's Haight-Ashbury district when the word "hippy" was coined by *San Francisco Chronicle* columnist Herb Caen—who also came up with "beatnik," in the late 1950s—so I figure I'm entitled to lean on personal experience in these things. To anyone who was part of that (post-beat) scene before the word "hippy" became a national publicity landmark (in 1966 and 1967), "Mr. Tambourine Man" is both an epitaph and a swan-song for the lifestyle and the instincts that led, eventually, to the hugely-advertised "hippy phenomenon."

Bob Dylan was the original hippy, and anyone curious about the style and tone of the "younger generation's" thinking in the early 1960s has only to play his albums in chronological order. They move from folk-whimsy to weird humor to harsh social protest during the time of the civil rights marches and the Mississippi summer protests of 1963 and '64. Then, in the months after the death of President Kennedy, Dylan switched from the hard commitments of social realism to the more abstract "realities" of neo-protest and disengagement. His style became one of eloquent despair and personal anarchism. His lyrics became increasingly drug-oriented, with double-entendres and dual meanings that were more and more obvious, until his "Rainy Day Women #12 & 35" was banned by radio stations from coast to coast . . . mainly because of the chorus line saying "Everybody must get stoned. . . ."

By this time he was a folk hero to the "under thirty generation" that seemed to be in total revolt against everything their elders were trying to believe in. By this time, too, Dylan was flying around the country—from one sold-out concert to another—in his private jet plane, worth about $500,000. His rare press conferences were jammed by reporters who treated them more like an audience with a Wizard than a question and answer session with an accidental public figure. At the same time, Dylan's appearance became more and more bizarre. When he began singing in Greenwich Village about 1960 his name was Bob Zimmerman and he looked like a teen-age hobo in the Huck Finn tradition . . . or like the Nick Adams of the early Hemingway stories. But by 1965 he had changed his last name to Dylan & was wearing shoulder-length hair and rubber-tight, pin-stripe suits that reflected the colorful & sarcastically bisexual image that was, even then, becoming the universal style of a sub-culture called "hippies."

This focus on Dylan is no accident. Any culture—and especially any sub-culture—can be at least tentatively defined by its heroes . . . and of all the hippy heroes, Bob Dylan was first and foremost. He appeared at a time when Joan Baez was the Queen Bee of that world of the young and alienated . . . but unlike Joanie, who wrote none of her own songs and preferred wistful ballads to contemporary drug anthems, Dylan moved on to become the voice of an anguished and half-desperate generation. Or at least that part of a generation that saw itself as doomed and useless in terms of the status-quo, business-as-usual kind of atmosphere that prevailed in this country as the war in Vietnam went from bad to worse and the United States, in the eyes of the whole world's "under thirty generation," seemed to be drifting toward a stance of vengeful, uncontrolled militarism.

The fact that this viewpoint wasn't (and still isn't) universal deserves a prominent mention, but it has little to do with the hippies. They are a product of a growing disillusion with the military/industrial realities of life in these United States, and in terms of sheer numbers, they represent a minority that doubles and triples its numbers every year. By 1967 this minority viewpoint had emerged, full-blown, in the American mass media . . . and it obviously had a powerful appeal—at least to the publishers, editors and reporters who measured the public taste and found it overwhelmingly ready for a dose of hippy articles. The reason for this is the reason the hippies exist—not necessarily because of any inherent worth of their own, but because they emphasize, by their very existence, the same uneasy vacuum in American life that also gave birth to the beatniks some ten years earlier. Not even the people who think all hippies should be put in jail or sent to the front-lines in Vietnam will quarrel with what is usually accepted as the Hippy Ethic—Peace, Love, and Every Man for Himself in a Free-Wheeling Orgy of Live and Let Live.

The hippies threatened the establishment by dis-interring some of the most basic and original "American values," and trying to apply them to life in a sprawling, high-pressure technocracy that has come a long way, in nearly 200 years, from the simple agrarian values that prevailed at the time of the Boston Tea Party. The hippies are a menace in the form of an anachronism, a noisy reminder of values gone sour and warped . . . of the painful contradictions in a society conceived as a monument to "human freedom" and "individual rights," a nation in which all men are supposedly "created free and equal" . . . a nation that any thinking hippy will insist has become a fear-oriented "warfare state" that can no longer afford to tolerate even the minor aberrations that go along with "individual freedom."

I remember that pre-hippy era in San Francisco as a good, wild-eyed, free-falling time when everything seemed to be coming out right. I had an exciting book to write, and a publisher to pay for it, and a big chrome-red motorcycle to boom around the midnight streets wearing a sweatshirt and cut-off levis and wellington boots, running from angry cop cars on the uphill blocks of Ashbury st, doubling back suddenly and running 90 miles an hour up Masonic toward the Presidio . . . then gearing down, laughing, on the twisting black curves with the white line leading through the middle of that woodsy fortress, past the MP shack out to the crowded lights on Lombard st, with the cold Bay and the yacht club and Alcatraz off to the left and all the steep postcards of cable car San Francisco looking down from the other side. Getting off Lombard to avoid the lights and roaring down Union st, past the apartment where that girl used to live and wondering who's up there now, then around the corner by the dentist's office (and I still owe that man two hundred and eleven dollars. Pay him off, pay all those old debts . . . who else do I owe? Send a bill, you bastards. I want to flush those beggar memories . . .).

Around the corner and down a few blocks on Union to the Matrix, a blank-looking place on the right, up on the sidewalk and park between those two small trees, knowing the cops will come around yelling and trying to ticket the bike for being off the street (Park that motorcycle in the gutter, boy . . .). Maybe seeing Pete Knell's orange chopper parked in that gutter. Pete was then the talking spirit of the Frisco Angels and later president of that doomed and graceless chapter . . . sometimes he played a banjo in the Drinking Gourd up on Union, but that was before he became a fanatic.

The Matrix, womb of the Jefferson Airplane. They owned part of the club when it still served booze, and maybe they own it all now. They've rolled up a lot of points since that night when I reeled through the door with no money, muttering "Jerry Anderson invited me," and then found Jerry somewhere in back, listening to his wife Signe wailing out in front of the Airplane's half-formed sound. Signe with the trombone voice, and Marty Balin polishing his eternal signature song that he titled, for some wrong reason, "And I Like It." I recall telling Jerry, while he paid for my beer, that this Jefferson Airplane thing was a surefire famous money bomb for everybody connected with it . . . and later calling Ralph Gleason, the *Chronicle*'s special pleader, to tell him the Airplane was something worth hearing. "Yeah, sure," he said. "People keep telling me about these groups; I try to check em out—you know how it is." Sure, Ralph . . . not knowing if he remembered that about a year earlier I'd pushed another group on him, a group that almost immediately got a record contract without help and then exploded into oblivion when Davy, the lead singer, choked to death on his own vomit in an elegant house on the beach in Carmel.

But about a year after the Airplane opened at the Matrix, Gleason wrote the notes for their first record jacket.

The Jefferson Airplane is another key sound from that era—like Dylan and the Grateful Dead. And Grace Slick, who made even the worst Matrix nights worth sitting through. In that era she was carrying a hopeless group called The Great Society, which eventually made it by croaking the group and going off in different directions. But Grace Slick was always my best reason for going to the Matrix. I would sit back in the corner by the projection booth and watch her do all those things that she later did with the Airplane and for *LOOK* magazine, but which seemed so much better then, because she was her own White Rabbit. . . . I was shocked to learn she was married to the drummer. But I got a lot of shocks in that era . . . my nerves were pretty close to the surface and everything registered. It's hard to understand now, why "things seemed to be coming out right." But I remember that feeling, that we were all making it somehow. And the only one around who had already made it was Ken Kesey, who seemed to be working overtime to find the downhill tube. Which he eventually did, and I recall some waterhead creep accusing me (in the *L.A. Free Press*) of "giving away" Kesey's secret address in Paraguay when he fled the country to avoid a marijuana rap. That was about the time I kissed off the hippies as just another failed lifestyle.

All these veteran heads keep telling me to get off the speed because it's dangerous, but every time I have something to say to them late at night they're passed out. And I'm sitting up alone with the music and my own raw nerves hearing Balin or Butterfield[1] yelling in every corner of my head and feeling the sounds run up my spine like the skin of my own back was stretched across a drumhead and some burning-eyed freak with the Great American knot swelling up in his head was using my shoulderblades for a set of kettledrums. So I guess I should quit this speed. It tends to make me impotent, and that can be a horrible bummer when it comes with no warning. Like a broken guitar string. A gritting of teeth and thinking, Holy shit not NOW, you bastard. Why? Why?

Speed freaks are unpredictable when the great whistle blows. And boozers are worse. But put it all together with

1. Lead singer in the Chicago-based Paul Butterfield Blues Band.

maybe sixty-six milligrams and nine jolts of gin on ice and maybe two joints . . . and you get the kind of desperate loser who used to crawl into the woods on the edge of Kesey's La Honda compound and drop some acid for no real reason except that the only part of his body that would still work was his mouth and his swallowing muscle. And the ears, the goddamn ears, which never quit . . . the terrible consistency of the music mocked the failures of the flesh. That too-bright hour when you know it's time for breakfast except that only the pure grassmasters are hungry and you want to come alive again because it's a new sunshiny day, but the goddamn speed is doubling back on you now, and although you're not going down, you can't go up either, but just Out, and stupid. An electric eel with a blown fuse. Nada.

So maybe the heads are right. Forswear that alcohol and no more speed . . . just wail on the weed and go under with a smile. Then get up healthy and drive up the road for breakfast at the Knotty Pine Cafe.

But despite the nature-healthy prospect of a legal grass-culture just around tomorrow's corner, I think I'll stay with the speed . . . even with the certain knowledge of burning out a lot sooner than if I played healthy. Speed freaks are probably the junkies of the marijuana generation. There is something perverse and even suicidal about speed. Like "The Devil and Daniel Webster."[2] Buy high and sell low . . . ignoring that inevitable day when there's no more high except maybe a final freakout with cocaine and then down the tube. A burned out case, drunk and brain-crippled, a bad example for Youth. The walking, babbling dead.

And why not. Speed is like sandpaper on the nerves. When all the normal energy is down to dead ash and even the adrenaline starts to vaporize in the dull heat of fatigue . . . there's a rare kind of brightness, a weird and giddy sensitivity that registers every sound and smile and stoplight as if every moment might be the next to last, memories carved with a chisel. . . .

That's what I see and hear when I look back on those pre-hippy days in San Francisco. I remember a constant

2. Stephen Vincent Benét's 1937 short story about a mid-nineteenth-century New Hampshire farmer who sells his soul for earthly gain—then gets out of the contract by convincing legendary lawyer and statesman Daniel Webster to take the devil on in court.

excitement about something happening, but only the fake priests and dingos called it the wave of the future. The excitement, for that matter, was all done in by the time the big-league press got hold of those "hippy" spokesmen and guru caricatures like Tim Leary and the press-conference Diggers.[3] By that time the Haight-Ashbury had become a commercial freak show and everybody on the street was selling either sandals or hamburgers or dope. The whole area was controlled by "hippy businessmen" who wore beards and beads to disguise the sad fact that they were actually carbon copies of the bourgeois merchant fathers whom they'd spent so much time and wrath rejecting.

But despite all that, and probably because of it—a sense of doom generates a weird, intense kind of light—that whole pre-hippy scene lent a special kind of élan to everybody who blundered into being a part of it. And the root of the excitement was the black certainty of a time limit, a euphoric, half-wild fatalism about the whole thing coming to a bad end at almost any moment. But this was the special light, and it was good while it lasted.

TO U.S. SENATOR EUGENE McCARTHY:

Although he admired Lyndon Johnson's Great Society programs, Thompson had turned on the President for escalating America's military involvement in Southeast Asia. By 1968 Thompson was so drawn to Senator Eugene McCarthy's anti–Vietnam War candidacy that he offered his services to the Minnesota Democrat's long-shot presidential campaign.

January 3, 1968
Woody Creek, CO

Dear Senator McCarthy:

I just read William S. White's comments on your potential candidacy—your "grandiose design," as it were—and I thought I'd send a note to offer any possible help I could lend to this hideous plot you're unfolding.

I'm not sure how I could help, but given the fact that I make my living as a writer, it would have to be in that area. I see your efforts more as a tactical—and not a determining—factor in the '68 elections, so I don't feel any real compulsion to volunteer for Ward duty.

Any ideas about how I could be of help would have to come from you . . . but if you have any, I assure you I'll go out of my way to deal with

3. The Diggers were a group of benignly radical Haight-Ashbury street performers and pamphleteers.

them. At the moment I'm fairly loose, in terms of assignments, etc.—but that changes weekly and even daily. I move around quite a bit, but I can always be reached here in Woody Creek (Aspen), Colo., at (303) 925-2250 . . . or via Random House in New York (Selma Shapiro).

For your own information and perspective, I'm enclosing a copy of a book I wrote more or less recently. It might help you to know more about what—if anything—I might be able to do. In any case, good luck. . . .

Sincerely,
Hunter S. Thompson

TO GERALD WALKER, *THE NEW YORK TIMES:*

The success of Hell's Angels *had brought Thompson numerous high-profile free-lance assignments, including "The 'Hashbury' Is the Capital of Hippies," which he wrote in May 1967 for* The New York Times Magazine. *Walker, the assigning editor, next commissioned a piece from Thompson on the Nevada state prisons' new "therapy retreats," designed to teach guards and inmates to coexist more agreeably.*

January 3, 1968
Woody Creek, CO

Dear Gerald . . .

Like I've been saying for months, this is a bad year all around. 1967 is the Year of the Overall Freak-Out. Which is neither here nor there . . . for now.

Anyway, I found out what my trouble was. I had a serious case of flu and I was trying to cure it with what those in the trade call "speed." This does not mean methedrine, despite what you read in *Newsweek* . . . and I suspect there are people over there who know better.

But back to the general badness. . . . I talked to Paul Semonin[4] the other night and he said the *Times* refused to publish the "Hell No, We Won't Pay" ad. I'm a bit surprised, for reasons I should probably examine . . . desperation makes for strange bed-fellows and a few strange prickteasers in the bargain. And how's that for a head on the *Times'* editorial page: "Desperation Makes for Strange Prickteasers."

And so much for that. You can apply the $10 I sent against the $366 expense money you sent me. It came on the same day, and in the same mail, with a letter from one of the NSP convicts, asking when the article would be published. That thing has become a terrible albatross around my neck . . . not a day goes by without somebody claiming that I let them down, and of course they're all right. That expense check from you was close to the final straw. I told my wife I was going to send it back and she began screaming. She handles

4. An upper-middle-class, self-styled Marxist, Paul Semonin had been a year ahead of Thompson at Louisville Male High School.

the finances and knows our treacherous score. I sense it, but I'd rather not know the details. Things have been rather tense here since the Tahoe article crisis and my simultaneous derailing of two other projects totaling $3700. We are into another one of those nightmarish pregnancy scenes—whacking God in the teeth again—and that helps. Life should be made as difficult as possible . . . so that the victims might develop more character.

(. . . Jesus, I just went outside to piss and got whacked in the eyes by the results of what looks like a 7–8 inch all-nite snow, the first of the year . . . it's 6:45 a.m. here, with the sun just coming up . . . everything is fat white, even the sky is white. Dead silence, no color . . . this is what should happen in Vietnam. It gives you a sense of mortality . . . like if anybody was unnatural enough to drop a bomb in my clean white front yard this morning, I'd natcherly blow his head off with a 12 gauge shotgun. And then I'd eat all the flesh off his bones, just to teach him a lesson.)

Christ, it feels good to be out of the flu funk. I'd like to go out in the snow and fuck some corpse in the neck. I'm sure there's one out there. [Outgoing U.S. Secretary of Defense] Robert McNamara came last week to check on his new house; he arrived in a black car with six Secret Service men—acting like some humanoid from another planet—and since he had to drive through an area of dope-smoking construction workers who once tried to burn his house to the ground, I'm sure he created some corpses—if for no other reason than to take them back to LBJ, who likes his erotic brunch.

And so much for that, too. The point of all this, I guess, is that those dirty bastards from Tahoe have loaded me with so much guilt about that failed article that I might, despite my better judgement, attempt to resurrect it. I don't know exactly how, because it's obviously no longer a news item and in fact it never was. But I still think it's one of the best subjects I've dealt with in several years. It reminded me of the first article I did, somewhat reluctantly, on the Hell's Angels—which gave me an incredible amount of trouble because of all the confusing action it kicked off in my head—which wouldn't fit into an easy 20-page article, and which eventually wound up as an 800-or-so-page manuscript that had to be cut in half (by me) to fit into book covers.

But . . . back to the point: How do we deal if I actually do a rewrite on that article? I assume you should have first reject rights . . . and I also assume it'll be rejected, since I don't have the vaguest idea how to make the thing work as an acceptably contemporary news item. But I *might* try, and I stress that word "might." Probably I will, so give me a guideline about how to proceed diplomatically. The only other markets that seem even possible right now are *Ramparts* and *The Nation,* but considering the circumstances and the onus that settled on me, I'd much prefer that any resurrected article appear in the *Times*—if only because that's how I represented myself in the first place.

In any case, send a word or two as to etiquette. And obligations. And possibilities. My agent used to handle these things, but he's now suing me or at least forcing me to sue him for not leaving me alone. That's Scott Meredith, in case you're curious and even if you're not . . . that evil pigfucking skunk. For the past year he's been hounding me like some sort of cop out of [nineteenth-century Russian novelist Feodor] Dostoyevsky. It's a nightmarish story—maybe even a book. Yeah: "Only You, HST—Or, How to Make a Million Dollars by Taking Scott Meredith's Advice and Identifying with Norman Mailer, the Only Meredith Client Who Lives in the Black—And Any Punk Who Don't Like It Can Sue." There's another good title for you. Maybe I should get a job with *Time,* eh?

Yours in deep snow,
Hunter

TO VIRGINIA THOMPSON:

A few days into the New Year Thompson flew to New York to negotiate a deal with Random House for a book on "The Death of the American Dream." At this early stage Thompson envisioned it as a scathing exposé of the U.S. armed forces' Joint Chiefs of Staff.

January 5, 1968
Delmonico's Hotel
Park Avenue at 59th Street
New York

Dear Mom . . .

I've just about finished here—& things seem to have gone as well as possible—although no contracts are signed yet. Wednesday night I had a five-hour dinner with the Vice-President of Random House, the editor-in-chief of Ballantine (& my lawyer) at the Four Seasons, the most expensive restaurant in N.Y. That's a good omen. Especially since nobody blinked when I wore my boots & my shooting jacket. I'm still being sued for $5.5 million in Calif.—I thought that had collapsed. But the other legal problems seem manageable, at least for the moment.

In all, I have a hell of a busy year ahead of me—three & possibly four books. The big one is being referred to as "The Death of the American Dream"—which makes me nervous because it's so vast & weighty. *Hell's Angels* is past the 500,000 mark in printing, not sales—but if they all sell, that's a lot of nickels for your black-sheep son. I keep borrowing against earnings—to the point where I stay about even—but after April I should be able to send Jim[5] a few dollars if he gets in trouble.

The Xmas visit was good—sorry my nerves were so edgy, but the miscarriage thing had me worried ever since we left Aspen—that's why I decided at

5. Thompson's youngest brother, Jim, was thirteen years his junior.

the last moment to go to Florida—I didn't want Sandy to be alone in planes & airports if the thing was going to happen any moment.

Anyway, it was good seeing all of you—I enjoyed the stay more than I expected to—& it was good getting to know Jim again. It was even better to see that you've got the drinking under control. I'm proud of you.

That's it for now. I still have to re-write that *N.Y. Times* article.

Love
H

TO BERNARD SHIR-CLIFF, BALLANTINE BOOKS:

While in New York, Thompson pitched his idea for a savage fictional attack on President Johnson to Bernard Shir-Cliff, who had edited the paperback of Hell's Angels *for Ballantine Books. Shir-Cliff asked to see a written proposal.*

January 12, 1968
Woody Creek, CO

Bernard . . .

Here's a Lyndon Johnson idea. I was talking to Peter Collier at *Ramparts* tonight, trying to buck him in on a Super Bowl bet . . . and somewhere along the line I mentioned our Johnson project. He suggested a serious, non-fantasy preview of the Demo convention, based on his "certain knowledge" that all manner of hell is going to break loose in terms of critical protests, demonstrations. *Ramparts* has numerous connections with SDS[6] and other radical types, and Collier says they're going to freak out the convention. At first I said no, but then I added the fantasy element and saw a possibility . . . which is fading almost as fast as I can type. Maybe a good pamphlet, but probably not a book . . . unless you can figure out a new twist.

What I came up with, and this was just a few minutes ago, was a very straight-faced—and very night-marish—handbook for convention delegates. Like when the 10,000 rats are going to be released on the convention floor, and which organization is planning to kidnap an entire state delegation in order to degrade and humiliate them for the purpose of making an underground film. We have to keep in mind that various outrages are in fact being planned, and that I probably wouldn't have much trouble getting a vague battle plan . . . but of course that wouldn't be enough. I'd have to mix up fact and fantasy so totally that nobody could be sure which was which. We could bill it as a fantastic piece of root-hog journalism—The Thompson Report, as it were. This courageous journalist crept into the sewers of the American underground and emerged with a stinking heap of enemy battle plans—and just in time, by god,

6. Students for a Democratic Society.

to warn the good guys what to watch out for. Oh, I could have a rattling good time with it. . . . I could even compose a fictitious interview with Guru Bailey, the Demo chieftain, during which I try to warn him of this impending disaster and he reacts first in anger, then with tears, throwing down hooker after hooker of gin during our conversation. And a private chat with Johnson, who heard of my dread information and summoned me to the White House for a toilet-side interview with two recording secretaries—a prancing fag and nervous old lady from New Orleans—taking notes on a voice-writer(s)—echoing my words, and Lyndon's, for the private record.

Yes indeed, I'm beginning to hear the music. Did you ever see the Walter Jenkins,[7] Dean Rusk,[8] drugs and leather cults section that I had, at one point, in the *H.A.* [*Hell's Angels*] manuscript? I don't think I ever sent it in. Some of the best parts of the H.A. book never made it past the first-draft because they wandered too far afield. (The Case of the Naked Colonel . . . did you ever see that? A fantastic story, and absolutely true . . . a Pentagon colonel found naked in his car, passed out on the steering wheel with a pistol in each hand . . . no explanation.)

The music, yes. I hear the sound of drums now . . . an interview with Richard Nixon, who calls me at my Chicago hotel, during the course of my research, and offers me $20,000 for my information . . . then a meeting with Nixon and his advisors, they want to exploit the freak-out . . . but an argument erupts when one of Nixon's aides makes a crude remark about his daughter—undertones of drugs and nymphomania, Julie caught on the 14th green at Palm Springs with a negro caddy at midnight, the caddy now in prison, framed on a buggery count.

Well, I guess you have the drift by now. Sort of a "Report from Iron Mountain," as rewritten by Paul Krassner.[9] I see it as a ding-dong seller, given adequate promotion, at least until the convention. But I'm not sure what kind of staying power it would have unless we could come up with a longevity gimmick. The key, I think, would be pre-convention publicity—the existence of this frightful report by the well-respected, hard-digging author of *Hell's Angels,* a known confidant of all undergrounds, a man with his ear to the sewer at all times. But if we couldn't promote it fast and fat enough to sell 100,000 copies, I'm not sure I could work up the superhead of steam that I'd need to get the thing done. The idea of writing against a fiendish deadline, with $10,000 at stake, gets me high and wild just thinking about it. I hear gongs and drums and whistles all around me . . . not even the Green Bay Packers roll that high. The SuperBowl stake is only $7,500 per man.

7. Walter Jenkins, a longtime aide to Lyndon B. Johnson, had been arrested on a "morals charge" involving a homosexual act in a men's room on federal property shortly before the 1964 presidential campaign season.

8. Dean Rusk was U.S. secretary of state from 1961 to 1968.

9. Paul Krassner edited *The Realist*, a Los Angeles counterculture magazine.

What do you think? Any ideas for keeping the book alive beyond the convention? Needless to say, most of the fantasy content would be based on fact . . . and for that I'll need the 1964 Theodore White book, Nixon's Crises[10] bullshit, and the Iron Mountain thing that I asked for quite a while ago. The more I think about this, the more I think in terms of fictitious interviews and bogus secret meetings with the principals. What about lawsuits there? If it rings any bells at all, let's ponder it on the phone . . . or if this idea kicks off any others in your head, let's talk about those too. Send word, make contact, etc. . . .

Ciao,
Hunter

TO ROBERT CRAIG:

Thompson rented his house in Woody Creek, ten miles outside Aspen, from a good-humored friend—fortunately for both.

January 13, 1968
Woody Creek, CO

Bob . . .

I came by the house twice last week and called tonight, so I assume you're off somewhere, and for god knows how long.

Anyway, in lieu of rent money, I'm sending another mean bitch about foul-smelling water backing up in the basement. This isn't directed at you, but I figure you can use my complaint as reason for refusing to pay those incompetent fucks a penny until they finish the job they agreed to do. I was going to call Holub tonight, but he disregards everything I tell him until you vouch for it, so I don't see any sense in calling him a lying pigfucker for nothing. In any case, this goddamn water scene is going to have to be cured eventually—no matter who is, or isn't, living in the house. I've been waiting for months to make something out of that big room in the basement, but with all of Springer's gear in the way, and a flood of shit-water every night, it's impossible to do any work down there. Even the lumber I bought is getting wet and warped (the lumber for building in the room).

All this brings me to ponder a much longer view—which includes the fact that I'm due, sometime this spring, for a fat royalty on the paperback *Hell's Angels* sales and I intend to spend it on some kind of real estate. So if you're at all inclined to think about selling either this property or the (east) mesa or any

10. Theodore White's campaign book *The Making of the President, 1964,* and Richard Nixon's 1962 memoir, *Six Crises.*

combination, we should probably talk seriously about it sometime soon. Because I've never been known to hang onto money—and this next check will be no exception. So let's get together, when you get back, for a serious rumble about money, acreage, etc. And water rights. Which brings to mind that you still owe me a bottle of Old Fitz. But I might let you off the hook for some blue-chip ski instruction. I suspect we can work out a deal. Which leads me to the point of the whole rude note, to wit: give a ring when you get back; among other things, I have a Lord Buckley[11] record for you.

Ciao . . .
Hunter

TO JIM SILBERMAN, RANDOM HOUSE:

Silberman had edited Hell's Angels *for Random House, and would continue to provide Thompson with editorial guidance.*

January 13, 1968
Woody Creek, CO

Dear Jim . . .

A late-rising thought: What happened to my *Hell's Angels* manuscript? I asked Margaret [Harrell] about it several times last spring, but it was always "somewhere else." I just read where D. H. Lawrence traded the ms. of *Sons and Lovers* for a ranch in Taos, so I'm naturally concerned about mine. I'm land-hungry right now, and maybe the ms. will come in handy if I want to buy a ranch from a dirty old rich woman. Which I might. Half the land around Aspen is owned by dirty old rich women who are also cousins of Paul Nitze[12]—and friends of McNamara. I suspect that my probing of the Joint Chiefs will reveal that one of them is the real owner of the house I live in. Anyway, send word on my manuscript—or, better still, send the manuscript.

Thanx . . .
Hunter

TO KELLY VARNER:

In its first year in print, Hell's Angels *sold nearly half a million copies and generated a torrent of fan mail. Thompson occasionally replied to the most thoughtful letters.*

11. Richard M. "Lord" Buckley, a wild-living nightclub comedian who had been doing a hilariously boozy aristocrat act since the 1930s, became a Beat Generation favorite and an influence on Lenny Bruce and Bob Dylan, among others.

12. Paul Nitze was a well-known U.S. diplomat and a major investor in the Aspen Ski Corporation.

January 15, 1968
Woody Creek, CO

Dear Kelly . . .

I just got back from New York and found your letter . . . and for a moment I was going to throw it in the fire because I found it depressing, but on second thought I decided to answer it.

First, thanks for the good words on the book. One of the best things about writing for publication is getting letters from people who read what you tried to put down . . . I think the shrinks call it "communication." Anyway, it's a good feeling to know that somebody in Herrin, Ill. is hearing my music, however weird or warped it might sound at that range.

But I'll be flat goddamned if I can understand how a guy like you, who sounds pretty bright and on top of things, can take the Angels seriously enough to want to go to all that trouble to Join Them. What the fuck would you want to do that for? You sound like you have enough going for you, as an individual, so that you wouldn't need some kind of bogus identity like a H.A. jacket. Do you really need Sonny Barger's O.K. to do what you feel like doing? If so, here's the last address I have for him, which is at least a year old: 9847 Stanley, Oakland Calif. I doubt that he still lives there, but he might. You can try.

As far as I know, Sonny is still pres. of the Oakland chapter, but I haven't followed that scene for a long time. As for the rest of your questions, Sonny could answer them better than I could . . . especially since I view your whole notion of getting "approval" from the Angels as a bad joke. I'm not trying to put you down here; if that was the idea, I wouldn't have bothered to answer your letter, so don't take it that way.

The thing is that you sound like you have more sense than any six Angels I can think of, and I can't quite understand why you want to defer to them. But that's obviously none of my business, and that's why I'm sending the only address I have for Sonny. But I'm also sending my own ideas on the subject—which you didn't ask for, but which you can't keep me from laying on you anyway—and the main one is, "Play your own game, be your own man, and don't ask anybody for a stamp of approval." For the past two years the Angels have been creatures of their own publicity; I wouldn't get fucked up with them any more than I would with the FBI or the Lyndon Johnson Fan Club. To hell with organizations. There's a lot of things wrong with this country, but one of the few things still right with it is that a man can steer clear of the organized bullshit if he really wants to. It's a goddamn luxury, and if I were you, I'd take advantage of it while you can.

Ciao,
Hunter S. Thompson

TO GERALD WALKER, *THE NEW YORK TIMES:*

Walker had been pressuring Thompson to revise his article on the Nevada state prison system.

January 15, 1968
Woody Creek, CO

Dear Gerald . . .

Here's a better response to your telegram. I sent a rude card earlier tonight, but it didn't say much. Anyway, I'm struggling *now* with the goddamn new lead . . . and fighting the overwhelming temptation to write a new article. I don't want to, and in truth I don't think I should. What I probably didn't make clear in NY is my feeling, based on your suggested revisions, that you're asking me to write the kind of article that you should have assigned to [Amherst College historian] Henry Steele Commager or some of that ilk. If I wanted to write in the wire-service or Five W's style, I'd have sent in my original manuscript with an application for a job on *The NY Times*. . . .

. . . and maybe that sounds worse than I mean it to sound; the point is that I don't really have any heart for changing the article (except for the obviously necessary new lead), and especially not in terms of putting it into a "cool, straightforward chronology." In those terms, you're asking for an account of something that didn't happen. The conference was chaotic; the participants destroyed the planned chronology on the second day; nobody knew, from one day to the next, if the whole thing might be cancelled to prevent a riot . . . and I'll be fucked if I'm going to try to pass it off as a 1, 2 , 3, 4 . . . sort of a thing. If anything, it was 3, 2, 4, 1 . . . and that's the way I tried to write it, because that's the way I saw it.

On the other hand, I'll admit that my lead—as it stands now—is perhaps a bit dull and confusing. Or at least confusing. But I can't get over the feeling that you're asking me for an article that you never should have assigned me to in the first place . . . some sort of legally logical exercise in straight-grey journalism, which is what I'm trying to do right now, if for no other reason than a deadweight sense of obligation all around. Frankly, I wish I'd never heard of the goddamn article, or the conference, or anything connected with it. OK for now; I just thought I'd get that off my head . . . and thanks for the good lunch.

Ciao,
Hunter

TO CAREY MCWILLIAMS, *THE NATION:*

McWilliams, editor of the left-leaning Nation, *had "discovered" Thompson in 1964 after reading his articles on South America in* The National Observer. *They became friends, and the next year Thompson wrote two notable pieces for McWilliams's magazine: "Motorcycle Gangs: Losers and Outsiders" (May 17, 1965) and "Nonstudent Left" (September 27, 1965).*

January 20, 1968
Woody Creek, CO

Dear Carey . . .

It's always good to hear from you, so no sense commenting on your note of Jan. 11. As it happens, I left NYC on Jan. 10, after a short, very intense, whirl on the contract/lawsuit circuit. I'm being sued on both coasts—for $5.5 million in Calif. and for 10% of my total earnings in NY. The catch is that the bastards have to come to Colorado to get me into court . . . so I spent my time in NY slinking around like a weasel.

You asked about the Joint Chiefs book . . . which is what all the contract talk was about. Scott Meredith apparently had me in a legal limbo until Dec. 15 of last year, but I didn't find that out until I got there. I now have a lawyer, instead of an agent. Leon Friedman, by name. He seems ok and I left all my dealing in his hands. As far as I can tell, I've settled with Random and Ballantine for a book that I still call the "Joint Chiefs," but which they refer to as 1) "Hunter Thompson's America," and/or 2) "The Death of the American Dream." Which is all the same thing, I guess . . . but it's hard to adjust to the idea that somebody wants to pay me for writing an epitaph for three generations. Or maybe five. I don't know yet. The only thing certain about the book is that it's going to kick off with a gaggle of profiles, or sketches, of the Joint Chiefs of Staff. That's the first chapter . . . but after that, I'm open. And, frankly, I don't have the vaguest idea as to what kind of narrative thread I'll use to hang the whole thing together.

What I'll really be writing, I think, is a sort of Prosecutor's Brief, demanding a fitting penalty for the killers of the "American Dream." Whatever that is, or was, or might have been. I suspect I could have found an easier book to write . . . especially since I've come to see myself as a sort of hoodlum-writer. I'm not sure how I feel about taking on the whole Establishment in one swack. But that's what I've agreed to do, and—as I've said in the past—if you have any good article leads for me, I'll be more than happy to work on them. The catch—as I've also noted in the past—is that I've never had a saleable article idea of my own, and at this stage of the game I don't expect to. In other words, don't expect me to sell you anything in embryo. And I say this to you in particular, because our whole editor-writer history has been a monument to the notion. You've rejected every idea I've sent, and the two articles I did on your specific request are among the best things I've ever done.

But I guess that doesn't take into account your ideas for a book, which in fact are very much at the root of the Joint Chiefs thing. So if you feel like adding anything specific to a prosecution brief, by all means let me know. Ideally, I'd like to use some article-assignments as springboards for this book project . . . and you're the best idea-man I know.

My entire output for 1967, by the way, consisted of three articles—all three on hippies and all written last spring . . . for a total of less than $1500. It was, as they say, a bad year. In any case, I'm sorry I didn't get by to see you in NY, but after three weeks in Florida and Kentucky, I was in no mood to socialize when I got to the Big Money Graveyard on the Hudson. I just wanted to get my legal bullshit straight, and get out. Or, more specifically, back here to Woody Creek. I'm beginning to wonder how in hell anybody can live in New York and still consider himself human. It's the meanest goddamn place in the world, and I think it's a damn good thing that they have the Sullivan Law.[13] Without it, half the population of the island would be killed overnight. And maybe that's the answer.

But not for me. I'm sitting out here waiting for contracts to arrive in the mail and wondering what I'm going to write after I sign them. If you have any ideas, be my guest.

Ciao . . .
Hunter

TO JIM SILBERMAN, RANDOM HOUSE:

Thompson's memo on his book tracing "The Death of the American Dream" follows the letter.

January 29, 1968
Woody Creek, CO

Jim . . .

The enclosed is something I ripped off just before dawn on Sunday . . . and a few hours later I had a scene in my front yard that scared even me. Gun freaks; it looked like a Minuteman meeting. And weird conversation. Birchers.[14] I think I told you once that these private army people were a bunch of "demented gas station attendants," but the first two on the scene were far from that: the assistant D.A. and the local dentist; then came a pilot and a ski patrolman and a reporter for one of the papers. There was another guy who looked so wild and evil that I couldn't bring myself to inquire about his line of work. All these people arrived just as my stone-hippy Montana friends were leaving, gathering their water-pipes and acid for the trip north. My world is becoming a zoo.

Anyway, I hope the enclosed is coherent. If any one thing seems unclear, as

13. Tammany Hall leader "Big Tim" Sullivan had pushed an early-1900s bill through Albany limiting women to a fifty-four-hour workweek, because "we ought to help these gals by giving 'em a law which will prevent 'em from being broken down while they're still young."
14. Members of the far-right John Birch Society.

I wrote it, I think it's my own idea of how to create the "bone-structure." So let's try again: I want to take all those things you mentioned in your letter, along with several others, and *illustrate* them. Maybe I'll want to go to a pro football game with a ranking Marine general, and then talk about the Super Bowl mentality in terms of the Pentagon . . . but letting the general talk, thus making him a character in the narrative.

During that talk I may find out that he's been married four times, so that would lead to another phase . . . maybe a talk with one of his ex-wives, now married to a "peace freak." That's unlikely, considering the very special nature of military wives, but it points up to the fact that I want to have *people* in this book, and I want to make them real. The editorializing will come in my choice of people, and how I treat them in print. I want them to introduce themselves, as it were . . . instead of being introduced by the author, as archetypes.

The bone-structure, then, will be made up of existing individuals—not necessarily named—whose lives, words, actions, fears, hatreds, etc. best illuminate the various keys we need to show *how and why* the American Dream is dead. Consider, for instance, a self-educated, multi-millionaire businessman who is now, at the age of 50, a Democratic National Committeeman, a power in both state and national politics. What kind of power is he exercising, and how does it relate, for that matter, to Abe Lincoln? What does he say about him? And what does he say about Eichmann?[15]

Maybe this should clarify what I mean about "bone-structure." I want to search out specific people to illustrate specific points, and on this score I'll welcome any help or suggestions I can get. Billy Graham,[16] for instance; how does he fit in the American Dream? Is he a rose or a thorn? And what is he really saying?

OK for now. This, plus the enclosed three pages, should give you something of an answer to your questions . . . or maybe I should say, "your letter."

Ciao,
Hunter

***

MEMO TO JIM SILBERMAN:

Thanks for the good letter of Jan. 16 and sorry I didn't reply sooner. I've had people here ever since I got back, and more coming. The rising tide, as it were. I'm trying to learn how to write in this situation. When I was doing the *Hell's Angels* book nobody came to see me because they were afraid I'd ask for a

15. Nazi Lieutenant Colonel Adolf Eichmann headed the Gestapo's "Jewish Division."
16. Internationally renowned Baptist evangelist Billy Graham has been befriended by U.S. presidents from Eisenhower on.

loan . . . but now I've paid back all those loans, and the scene has changed by 180 degrees. At the moment I'm grateful to the supplicants who only write, instead of making personal appearances. I am also the victim of a momentary confusion in the national-action polarity; not even the front-runners know if the center of gravity is on the east or west coasts, so everyone's in flux. I have one friend coming through from NY, with all his furniture, driving a rented van en route to L.A. Another, a musician, is coming from L.A. en route to Boston. Right now I have two potters from Montana in the house. Next week it's a musician from Calgary. These are the ones I've confirmed. On Feb. 15 I get the Tangier shipment, coming to pick up the motorcycle they left in my basement. And then my brother, looking for a scent of the West. Selah.

And now . . . for the root of your letter. I like your clutch of ideas; as a matter of fact I'm both amused and pleasantly surprised at some of the connections you make . . . but I *don't* think it all sounds like a good way to open another book by Hunter S. Thompson. Probably this explains why we had trouble talking about the *bones* of the book in NY; we all know what the meat's going to taste like, but the bone-structure is still a bit hazy on the screen . . . and the last way I want to clarify it is in terms of an *essay.*

I don't think that's my gig at all. I write essays by accident, by injecting my own bias into the material even when I try to avoid it. This is what I meant when I said I'd write the same book, no matter what we decided to call it. But coming up with a title and a vague subject is not quite the same as structuring a book that I necessarily approach as a sort of major document. And I say "necessarily" because I'll need that "big book" notion to keep me working. I could say a lot more about this, but by this time I figure you should know me well enough to understand the drift. I have no interest in writing a book that won't be read . . . and I think the surest way down that tube is to lead off with an essay. Any essay, however brilliant. This is the age of scare-headlines—not essays, and the only way to suck the readers in is to jolt them off their rails so far that they'll need an explanation for what jolted them. The "latent essay," if you will. Some examples that come to mind: *The Fire Next Time, The Other America*, most of Oscar Lewis' stuff[17] . . . well, to hell with that list . . . it doesn't seem to be proving my point.

Which is, for good or ill, that I think this American Dream thing needs a *narrative structure* to hold it together. *Hell's Angels* had that by accident, or because my involvement served as a narrative . . . and that's all we'll need for the next one. I can't sit out here in Woody Creek and ruminate on the Death of the American Dream. That's why I tried to impress on you—as subtly as possible, since Leon was handling the details—the importance of providing, in the con-

17. James Baldwin's 1963 essay collection on the civil rights movement, *The Fire Next Time,* warned of coming violence; Michael Harrington's passionate 1962 book, *The Other America,* used statistics to paint a bitter portrait of poverty in an affluent nation; and anthropologist Oscar

tract, for adequate expense money to let me get *involved.* Otherwise, I'll sit out here and serve up a bundle of pompous bullshit.

As a start, my involvement will have to serve as the beginning of a narrative. But, once I get into the thing, I suspect I'll find something tougher and not so Plimptonesque.[18] In any case, I'll want to zero in on *details* and *action* . . . and let the essays happen as they will. And that's the least of our worries. I just delivered, standing in front of my own fireplace, what was probably a 40,000 word screed on "Why I Won't Shoot Lyndon Johnson." My mind is going so fast these days, and working on so many brutal edges, that it's no trouble at all to rap off a verbal essay. The problem will be in lining it all out, so that every nervous bastard who reads five pages of the book will be compelled to read it all. And I don't see a "lead-essay" as the fuse we're looking for in that area.

That's a good concept: *The Fuse;* the reader lights it by becoming initially involved in the book—the first few pages—and then he has to be dragged (reluctantly, if possible, so as to traumatize his memory) all the way to the end . . . at which point he may or may not realize that he's been forced, or duped, into reading an essay. Which hardly matters . . .

The point is that I want at least a dim notion, in my own head, of a story line that will jerk reluctant readers from Beginning to End. On another level, I think the phrase for that is "render." The story should be "rendered," or maybe it would be more honest to say "the bullshit should be rendered."

The gig I have in mind is an opening research shot at the Pentagon, featuring attempts to interview the Joint Chiefs . . . by a man who got tired, many months ago, of seeing them referred to as a nameless, yet ominous, cabal that seemed to be in charge of almost everything crucial. I don't really expect these worthies to indulge me, but I think their lack of indulgence will be the beginning of my narrative, to wit: "Who are these people who won't talk to me? Where did they come from and why are they in charge? How far does their power extend? Where does their power originate? Why them, and not me?" And—once we've established some answers in the form of a pattern (or historical framework)—"Where now?"

If you disagree with this, the overall tentative approach, I urge you to make yourself as clear as possible NOW. Because there's no sense in my getting started on something you might not want or agree with. I've had enough arguments and bullshit, in the past year, to last me a lifetime . . . so I don't want to court another accidental war by my failure to explain what I intend to do for $20,000 plus expenses. I assumed, after that friendly-elegant dinner at the Four Seasons, that we all understood that I was going to use the Joint Chiefs as a *tool* for getting at "The Death of the American Dream." I don't want to just

Lewis decried the "culture of poverty" in studies of poor Latin Americans, such as his 1961 analysis, *The Children of Sanchez.*

18. George Plimpton, now editor of the *Paris Review,* was known for his participatory, first-person New Journalism.

comment on it; I want to *show* it, and show it in terms of a narrative that will also be an exercise in selective judgement . . . so that even people who disagree with my triumphantly subjective thesis will have to come to grips with the book in order to quarrel with it. In a nut, I want to hold up a mirror and let the bastards argue with *that,* not *me.*

Which boils down to the simple, flat and absolute fact that I have no intention of writing an Essay. That's what critics are for, so let's give them something to chew on. Details, madness, action . . . all leading, inevitably, to the theme of the book. But not in terms of just another well- (or ill-) qualified opinion; let's do up a massive indictment, focusing on the murderers of the so-called "American Dream." Let's name these swine, and perhaps even turn the indictment around to zap the false prophets of a new world that never existed except as a gaggle of slogans. Or maybe not; I don't know enough right now to say anything, for sure, about what I'll finally write.

I *am* sure, however, that I want at least a general agreement—between you and me and Shir-Cliff—before I gear down. So if anything I've said in this jangled and 6:05 a.m. letter seems like something we should talk about, let's do it. And on that note, I'm hanging it up; four local Minutemen-types are due here in five hours for a shotgun orgy, and I'll need some rest in order to shoot well enough to keep them nervous. OK for now . . .

Hunter

TO THE ALASKA SLEEPING BAG CO.:

Thompson never could tolerate shoddy merchandise.

January 29, 1968
Woody Creek, CO

Alaska Sleeping Bag Co.
334 NW 11th Ave.
Portland, Oregon 97209

Gentlemen:

I am returning the navy blue Everest Parka that I received from you two days ago. Your guarantee notes that "I may return merchandise within 10 days after delivery and my full purchase price will be refunded." So that is the purpose of this letter, and the carton to which it's attached. In the carton you'll find the parka, never worn and in absolutely new condition.

I'm returning it for a very simple reason: I don't think it feels or looks right on me, and I don't think it's as good a value as several other parkas I could buy here in Aspen for the same price. This is no fault of yours—except that your catalogue description led me to believe that I was ordering a much tougher and heavier parka than the one I received. But I suspect this was a matter of misinterpretation on my part, and for that reason I offer my apologies.

In any case, I'm returning the parka and requesting a full refund, inre: your guarantee. Thanks.

As you know, I ordered three other items when I sent the check that covered the parka: a canvas hunting coat, a leather vest, and a pair of leather moccasins. I trust these will be sent as soon as possible . . . but if there's any problem, please send me a refund on these items also. My check, #253, was for $121.35.

Sincerely,
Hunter S. Thompson

TO THE OVERSEAS PRESS CLUB:

The Overseas Press Club offered its members group health insurance at good rates.

January 30, 1968
Woody Creek, CO

Business Office
Overseas Press Club
54 W. 40th
NYC 18

Gentlemen . . .

I seem to have lost contact with the OPC, which is par for the course except that I want to keep track of my Blue Cross group plan insurance. One of the bad aspects of the club was brought home to me recently, when I spent about two weeks in New York and had to spend about $700 on a hotel where the only other guest I knew was [TV variety-show host] Ed Sullivan. The point, of course, is that I'd have stayed at the OPC if it still offered rooms . . . and the secondary point is that I never even found time to get to the club, where my presence would have shown up very powerfully at the bar ledger.

In any case, I wonder why I haven't received any Blue Cross bills for awhile . . . and, for that matter, any bills for club dues. The last dues bill I got was for some massive amount—about five times what I've been paying for the past two or three years. Naturally, I discarded it. But since I'd like to retain my Blue Cross policy, I thought I'd write and inquire. Please bring me up to date. Thanks . . .

Hunter S. Thompson

TO SUE GRAFTON:

Now one of America's best-known mystery novelists, Grafton grew up in Thompson's Louisville, Kentucky, neighborhood, three years behind him in school.

January 31, 1968
Woody Creek, CO

Dear Sue . . .

Your very elegant mash note arrived today, and although I'm not sure how to answer it, I thought I'd at least say "thanks." I don't get many letters like that, and probably it's a good thing. . . . I wouldn't get much work done. I don't, anyway, for a lot of good reasons that range from simple diversions like drinking and skiing to other, murkier things that would probably be ominous if I gave them enough thought. Like my reasons for answering this letter. . . .

. . . aside from that one sentence, in yours, that would be reason enough for answering any letter, to wit: "It seems to me that we have vital business to conduct on a level that should threaten neither of our households."

Well . . . if that's true, I guess we might as well have at it. But first you'll have to be a little more specific. I'm not sure exactly what level of engagement would threaten your household, and I'm not particularly worried about mine—but from what you say about yourself, I get the impression that we might tend to misinterpret each other. I am not given to mysticism, for instance, or astrology. I smoke and drink constantly . . . but I guess I don't have to make a list, since you've already read the book.

Which reminds me that you were very recently "impressed on my consciousness," as you put it, when my mother told me the library had just received your (first?) novel. I was curious, but I wasn't in Louisville long enough to see it. It was my first visit in four years and, considering the possibilities, it was fairly pleasant. My mother still lives in the same house on Ransdell . . . and it just occurs to me that I remember almost exactly where you lived, but not the name of the street, although I think it was up a hill from Willow, just off the park. I can't imagine why I remember that . . . or do I? Maybe I'm wrong. For that matter, I barely remember you, except as Ann's little sister. Your description of me as a lurking, sinister figure, menacing young girls on Longest . . . well, I *did* have a cracked brown leather jacket, army surplus with broken zippers on the slanted chest pockets . . . but most of those worthies you mentioned were among my brother's gang. I ran with an older gang, more wicked; we sold dope at the Oatey-Forbes magazine counter, to finance our candy bar habits. At least that was the word on Longest, and it probably still is. My youngest brother, Jim, told me the word at Atherton was that I'd *joined* the Hell's Angels; the book was only an afterthought.

Anyway, I got to Louisville on Christmas eve and left a few days later for New York. Ever since the book came out I've been involved in fantastic legal hassles: breaking contracts, trying to fire an agent who wouldn't quit, haggling endlessly about new contracts for new books . . . but I think it's finally settled. I have two books to deliver by June 1—the novel, and a paperback quickie aimed at LBJ. Then I have another to deliver about a year and a half from now.

Random House calls it "The Death of the American Dream," and I call it "The Joint Chiefs." Which hardly matters. It's going to take a vast amount of travel and brain-twisting; I have no idea what I'm going to write, but if nothing else I expect to learn a lot, and that's the only part of writing I enjoy. The actual work—the typewriter horrors—I approach with fear and loathing. Maybe that's why I've written almost nothing for the past year; I wasn't broke enough, I didn't need the money, so all I did was a few articles on hippies.

And so much for all that . . . except for your question about the novel *The Rum Diary.* I wrote it a long time ago, but after it bounced once or twice I put it away. Then, after I'd agreed to write a book on the Angels, I sold the novel to Pantheon almost by accident. But Pantheon is a division of Random House, so RH took the novel, and about that time I decided to completely rewrite it. But I didn't have time until I finished the HA book, and after that I got involved in the contract fight. So it's still un-rewritten. I'm not sure how easy it's going to be to get back to fiction, but I'll know more about it when I get started. Right now I'm not thinking about it.

You said you're "writing" your sixth book. Have you published five? That would be fairly incredible. In any case, why don't you send me a copy of whichever one you like best. Or tell me the title, and I'll order it here. Or I'll trade you straight across for a graffiti-laden copy of mine.

OK for now. Is this what you expected from the wicked wizard of Longest? I'm getting meaner and my hair is falling out, exposing numerous scars. I doubt that you'll ever find out who I am, but I'm flattered that you're curious and your letter was the best thing I've read in months. Thanks again . . .

Hunter

FROM OSCAR ACOSTA:

El Paso, Texas, native Oscar "Zeta" Acosta was a radical East Los Angeles lawyer known for representing poor Chicanos and challenging race-based exclusions from California's grand juries. Thompson had met Acosta in Aspen in 1967, and would make him notorious as the restless and brutish "300-pound Samoan attorney" of Fear and Loathing in Las Vegas. *This letter was the first in their long, strange, and sometimes serious correspondence.*

January 31, 1968
Woody Creek, CO

Grand Hotel
10th S. El Paso St.
El Paso, Texas

Hunter,

True that most men live lives of quiet desperation, with the emphasis on "most." Then there's the freakheads, flopouts, flamethrowers and narcs.

Christ, three days in Mexico and I've been screwed several times (broads), drunked up, doped up, in jail, fights, blah blah! In that order.

But my head is good and my spirits never in better shape.

My friend wasn't home when I arrived late Friday. Checked into a cheap hotel in Juarez with roaches for room mates. I had $185 with me so I put $150 of it in the "safe." Went out and did the town. Returned next morning to check out. Asked the clerk for my loot. What loot? Señor. Here's the receipt, Señor. Sorry, Señor, there is no money of yours in the safe. You mother fucker, Señor, where's my *dinero*?

Turned out the guy who took my money was not THE clerk, but a "mere" acquaintance who was watching the store while the REAL clerk was out eating. So I cussed the bastard out and went into my room to pack. Five minutes later the inevitable knock of the narc knocks on my door . . . Señor, this man claims you have insulted him. You goddamn right I insulted him, the stupid shit! Blahblah, argue, spit, cuss, Señor. I was arrested for insulting the dignity of the man and using obscene language in the presence of others, mainly two old farts sitting in the lobby.

I wasn't thinking. I could have bought them off for five bucks each, there were two of them. But my dander was up so I flounced into jail knowing that justice would prevail.

I had heard of Mexican jails and Mexican justice before but since those telling the stories were gringos I always believed that it was a combination of prejudice and unfamiliarity with the language . . . nope!

I don't have time to describe it justly, suffice it to say crud, crap, cold, stupidity, stench, barf, ugliness . . . dilapidated is too nice a word. Sixty ugly poor drunks in a room 8 × 40. Since I was late I had to stand. I had maybe two cubic feet to myself. There was no roof and we had a cup of beans for breakfast and a cup of beans with a slice of bread for dinner. What you think this is, a hotel, Señor? The cold here, when it is, is worse than in Aspen. My balls ached, no sleep for two days, dirty, grubby and still shit faced I suffered for 24 hours. Until my trial.

My arguments were well prepared. Had all day to think it over. Here I come, Juez, ready or not, I will blow your mind, Señor Juez.[19]

I peek in the door and see a lady! Voilà! A lady, I can win over easier than a Señor . . . Enter Oscar into a room not unlike the cell.

Lady: (Reading) It says here you insulted a man and used obscene words in front of others, is that true?

Oscar: If the court please . . .

Lady: Is that true!

Cop: Just answer the question, Señor! (threatening)

Oscar: Your honor, I would like to explain that I am an attorney and . . .

19. *Juez* is Spanish for "judge."

Lady: One more time, Señor. Is it true that you insulted this man in the hotel! (eyes a'blaring now cause I've taken too much time for my trial . . . delay of justice and all that.)

Oscar: We had an argument over this matter . . .

Lady: It also says you insulted the policeman, the arresting officer. Is that true also?

Oscar: (nods, cause he's smart by now and knows he should admit everything to hurry things up.)

Lady: That'll be $1200 pesos. Or thirty days.

Oscar: I'm sorry, I don't understand.

Lady: The *multa*[20] is $1200 pesos; $300 pesos for each offense.

Oscar: (figures quickly) But your honor, that only amounts to $900 pesos.

Lady: (thinks for a moment) Didn't you use obscene language in the presence of the arresting officers also, Señor?

Oscar: (Smiling humbly) Oh, that's correct, your honor. It is my error. Forgive me.

In round figures, that's about $100 (American).

Then a man directs me into a cubelike thing about 6 × 4 and offers me coffee and cigarettes and is very, very nice, Señor. After an hour of pleasant chitchat he asks if I'd like to get out. Or do I intend to put in the thirty days.

Out, man, out, now! Well, we can fix this matter up, don't worry, I'll help you. I am your friend. Maybe the only friend you have in all of Mexico, is that not true? Yes, si, Señor, you are my benefactor, my only salvation. Help me, please.

Well, we got a message to my friend here in Juarez, sold my record player, pawned my clarinet, radio and camera and I was finally called, ten hours later, to the front. I had put about $25 in the bag when I checked in. They gave me a receipt. They took me into another room and searched me again. The first guy had let me keep my cigs, matches, gum and the receipt. The second guy took it all. He'd take care of my receipt for me, Señor.

I'm five feet from freedom and the money is not in the sack.

Fat Cop: Is everything in order, Señor?

Oscar: No, Señor, the money is missing.

Fat Cop: Money, Señor?

Oscar: Yes, Señor, I had $25 dollars, American, when I came in.

Fat Cop: (Ostentatiously looks over list, checks it against contents.) No, Señor, you must be mistaken, there is no money in here. The receipt says nothing of any money except for those coins.

Oscar: (Five feet from freedom) The receipt I had said . . .

Fat Cop: (Smiling like a bastard) Let me see your receipt, Señor.

Oscar: (Five feet from freedom, smiles) I lost it, Señor.

20. *Multa* is Spanish for "fine."

Fat Cop: (the mark of the victor, smiles) Ah, then you have no proof, is that correct, Señor?

Oscar: (Five feet from freedom) No, Señor.

Fat Cop: And had you had your drinks that night, Señor?

Oscar: (Five feet from freedom) Yes, Señor, I was drunk as hell. I probably gave it to the whore.

Fat Cop: Yes, that is probably what happened. These things happen. (philosophically) Many times they happen to those who come here to drink and sleep with our women . . . it happens, you know.

Upon leaving I found out that the benefactor, the guy who got the messages across, etc., *he is a prisoner,* doing ten for dope. He had asked me for my clothes but I convinced him I'd send him a fiver when I got out. I wondered why he was so trustworthy. Now I know.

I've paid for a week to stay here in El Paso. Got a few deals going (not the smuggling, Adrian has spent all his money building his house, he's returning to Aspen to work at Tico's) but I won't know for a few days what I'll do; as usual, everything depends on Him, in His good time; but I do know that all things work together for good, to those who love the Lord, to those who are the called according to his purpose . . . a fifth of tequila costs 96 cents so I got no worries.

Yours in Christ,
Oscar Acosta
Attorney At Large

TO DOROTHY DAVIDSON, AMERICAN CIVIL LIBERTIES UNION:

Thompson, a proud lifelong member of the ACLU, had been asked to help out at the Aspen chapter.

February 1, 1968
Woody Creek, CO

Mrs. Dorothy Davidson
American Civil Liberties Union
1452 Pennsylvania St. Room 22
Colorado Branch
Denver, Colorado 80203

Dear Mrs. Davidson . . .

Thanks for your 1/31 letter, the information and the suggestions. I'd be happy to *assist* you in reorganizing the chapter . . . and there's not much doubt that it needs a shot of something. Or maybe not; I say this mainly because a friend of mine, rather desperately needing legal help in what I considered a good case, couldn't locate anybody in Aspen who claimed to even be a member of the ACLU, much less a legal representative.

I notice, however, that Bil Dunaway (of the *Aspen Times*) is listed on your stationery as a member of the State Committee. I know Bil, and I'll talk to him about getting the local chapter at least active enough to be visible.

I don't, however, think that I'd be the right person to represent the ACLU locally. The Aspen guru should be somebody with local leverage, such as Dunaway or a local attorney. My reputation as the author of a book on the Hell's Angels, a Woody Creek recluse, gun freak and friend of known criminals is not the image the ACLU needs to be most effective. I'm listed as a columnist for *Ramparts,* I've signed the Editors & Writers Vietnam tax protest, and I've admitted in print—*The New York Times,* no less—that I smoke marijuana. This is not the man to deal with local judges and juries.

Besides that, I'm travelling about half the time and after June 1st, I'll probably be gone all summer. I'm writing a book on the Joint Chiefs of Staff, so I won't have much time to devote to local affairs. I tell you all this to explain that I can't maintain the degree of availability and effectiveness that I'd like to see in a local chapter-head.

But I'll talk to Dunaway and let you know what happens. I'll also check with [local ACLU members] Janet Gaylord and Banker. Thanks again for writing.

Sincerely . . .
Hunter S. Thompson

TO CHARLES KURALT, CBS NEWS:

Charles Kuralt, who died in 1997 after a distinguished forty-year career at CBS News, had been a correspondent for the network in South America and one of Thompson's favorite drinking buddies when they both lived in Rio de Janeiro in 1962 and 1963.

February 5, 1968
Woody Creek, CO

Charley . . .

I assume you're still there, stomach boils and all. And I thought I recognized your off-camera voice asking a question of Gene McCarthy in N.H. the other night. Are you up there?

If so, I'll probably see you very soon. I just got a fluff assignment to do a piece on Nixon for *Pageant*—but what it really is, or hopefully will be, is a chance to get material for the Johnson campaign book, which will naturally feature Nixon in a triple-cameo role. I've agreed to do that one and also agreed to gamble a bag of money and time on it. That's one book that came out of the NY visit; two others, *The Rum Diary* and the Joint Chiefs, are now also scheduled. It's an even bet now as to whether my hair will turn white before it falls out, or vice-versa. Anyway, I'll try to find you in the east if you're still there. I'd guess around mid-Feb, or whenever Nixon is in N.H.

Otherwise, give me some warning about your DOA here. I have numerous transients on my hands, so if you'll want to bring anyone with you I'll need advance word. But there's no problem if it's only you. Send word, and hello to Petey.[21] . . .

Hunter

TO BILL, ASPEN DENTIST:

February 8, 1968
Woody Creek, CO

Bill . . .

I'm here, but not for long—leaving for New Hampshire and Nixon tomorrow, just got back from NY to find your bill and desperate search note. The idea of me sending anyone $277 in one shot is sheer madness—unless the supplicant can prove great and urgent need—but here's $100 to maintain good faith, etc. Don't worry about the rest; I'll get it to you, but don't forget to send periodic reminders. I doubt, quite frankly, that I'll be needing any further dental assistance; I just read today in the *Underground Press* that frequent inhalation of marijuana smoke prevents rot and heals cavities, in addition to making the teeth sparkle and the soul smile. I may have to try the stuff, but only under strict supervision. Keep this to yourself. . . .

Hunter

Check #286
$100—sent 2/8/68
1/3 payment

TO THE ALASKA SLEEPING BAG CO.:

Thompson took "satisfaction-or-your-money-back" guarantees at their word.

February 8, 1968
Woody Creek, CO 81656

Alaska Sleeping Bag Co.
334 N.W. 11th Ave.
Portland, Oregon

Gentlemen:

I am returning the "Alaska Hunting Coat"—for which I recently paid you $24.95—for a full refund, as noted in your standard guarantee. The "Cadiz, Kentucky" coat I received bears only a vague resemblance to the coat pictured

21. Petey was Charles Kuralt's wife.

in your catalogue. The most flagrant misrepresentation has to do with the "leather-lined" pockets and "leather shoulder-patches." If the garbage on this coat is leather, I'll eat it.

In a nut, the coat is far below the standards I've come to expect from quality mail-order suppliers . . . such as Eddie Bauer and L.L. Bean, from whom I buy consistently. On the other hand, I'm quite satisfied with the Russell Oneidas you sent, and also the Jokay shooting vest.

So I'm willing to write this off as inconsistency, rather than fraud . . . but I suggest, in the meantime, that you be more careful about the wording of your catalogue.

I look forward to receiving your check for $79.90. This represents $54.96 for the "Everest Down Parka" that I returned last week, and $24.95 for the enclosed hunting coat.

Thanks,
Hunter S. Thompson

P.S. . . . I see, in the *new* catalogue that came with my order, that you've dropped the word "leather" from the description of the hunting coat's shoulder patches and pocket edgings. This is an admirable move, but it's not much help to me—since I was using your not-so-new catalogue.

HST

TO OSCAR ACOSTA:

"The thing I liked about Oscar," Thompson says, "was that he was always willing to go further than I was." This included burning a judge's lawn.

February 9, 1968
Woody Creek, CO

Dear Oscar . . .

My knee is ripped, my crotch is broken, I hurt all over and about two hours from now I have to go out to the fucking airport and wait around—on standby—for a crucial flight to Denver & NYC, and then to New Hampshire for a week with Nixon. A quick article for *Pageant* & also fat research for a bogus book I've signed to do almost instantly, by Apr. 1. On the Johnson-Nixon campaign . . . the only problem is that it has to come out before either party holds its convention . . . a hideous fantasy.

Anyway, your book came in today's mail and I figured the best thing to do was send it along before I lose it in my mushrooming paper-mass. I'm enclosing a letter from one Margaret Harrell, my copy editor for the *Hell's Angels* book. You'll note that she says I shouldn't let you "get hold" of the letter, but the tone of the letter indicated that it was written more to you than me—with a formal disclaimer at the end. So I'm sending it along, with a request that you do me the favor of compounding the fiction in case you ever talk or write to

Margaret. In other words, just remember that *I told you what she said* in the letter; I didn't send you the letter itself. OK? She'd be embarrassed if she knew you had the original . . . for reasons I'm sure you'll understand.

Life here is a zoo of false and impossible promises. I have the Campaign book to deliver by Apr. 1 . . . *The Rum Diary* by July 1 . . . and the massive Joint Chiefs thing by July 1 of '69. So gone are the freaked and lazy days of 1967. This is the year of the Monkey, which for me means work. I have already become very ugly about guests and visitors. A friend named McGarr[22] just left today for L.A. and may look you up. He's ok, but don't let him near the wives of any friends you value. I suspect you'll like him.

Your own action sounds like you're a few months ahead of me in terms of getting back on the rails. I don't know how the hell you managed it—in light of your special trials in Juarez—but I guess you wetback freaks have a special god. (Which reminds me—it's sitting out on the window shelf right now, gathering evil spirits like god's own vacuum cleaner—thanks.) I haven't read the novel and couldn't possibly get to it until late April or May; I've over-extended myself so badly that whatever hair I have left at the end of this year will be stone white. Besides that, I've refused to pay my War Taxes, and I'm a sitting duck for the IRS so look forward to massive trouble in that area. I've also agreed to put my little brother through at least enough college-time to keep him from being killed. This looks to be a hairy year all around.

In terms of your political action, I might be checking with you this summer about writing something about "Brown Power," or whatever term is stylish at that time. I don't like that term any more than I do the Black equivalent, but it's a sure winner on the editorial front. I no longer plan to work on random articles, but my research on the Joint Chiefs book will take me into a lot of things I can write about and publish as side-effects of the book, and your gig may be one of them. We'll see . . . but in any case I'll probably be in L.A. this spring and looking for a shortdog or two. Let me know if your phone or address changes.

On your car: if you want me to get it running and rolling, send me some sort of notarized letter or signed pink slip so I can deal with it legally. I figure $300 will get it running about as well as it was before, but I'd only get involved in it if you sent me some sort of official or neo-legal authorization and agreed to repay me when you re-claim the car. In other words, I'll get it running at my expense if you'll give me enough paperwork to get it even temporarily licensed until you reimburse me for the repair bill and take it away. It's crazy to junk a car that needs so little work, and which could be a good machine for 2 or 3 years once the work is done. So let me know. I don't need it for wheels, so don't do me any favors. But it offends my sense of survival to see a good life-tool abandoned for want of a few horseshoes, as it were.

22. Eugene McGarr had been Thompson's fellow copyboy at *Time* magazine a decade earlier.

Your last letter wasn't very optimistic about the novel, but if you change your mind and put any rewrite work into it—and want me to read it a few months from now—send it along and I'll say whatever comes to mind. Keep in mind—while you're fucking around with "short stories"—that your chances of selling a short novel are far better than they are in any short story market. My offhand suggestion would be to cut the novel down to the bare bones, which means about 50,000 words, and then write a book on Brown Power which will give you a launching platform for the novel. If the idea of writing anything (book length) on the BP theme interests you, let me know and I'll try to interest somebody. Your problem there is that your club hand is dialogue, which used to mean fiction—but if you can teach yourself to use dialogue to tell a topical, non-fiction story you'll sell it. I guarantee that—but only if you get that goddamn missionary instinct out of your narrative. Let the people tell their own stories; they may surprise you.

OK for now. I have to pack and flee. Sandy is as pleased as I am with your new gig. Maybe by summer we'll be ready to invite you and Marco[23] out for a visit. Where is he now? Anyway, you're one of the few people I can think of right now that I'd enjoy seeing . . . for whatever that's worth. Send word. . . .

Hunter

TO JUAN THOMPSON:

Homesick in a Sunset Strip hotel while in Los Angeles to explore a possible movie deal for Hell's Angels, *Thompson vented to his three-year-old son back in Woody Creek.*

February 13, 1968
Hyatt House Hotels
Los Angeles, CA

Dear Juan . . .

I thought I'd write you a letter on this weird typewriter I borrowed from Oscar. I'm just learning to use it, so I'll make a few mistakes before I get straightened out. It's raining outside on my balcony and the news is on. It's been raining all day. I'm on the 11th floor of this hotel on the Sunset Strip in Hollywood. I haven't been outside all day. I slept until two, then went down to the coffee shop and had a club sandwich. Now I have some beer and a bucket of ice, getting ready to work for awhile on the test pilot article . . . ah, damnit, my package of carbon paper slipped into a puddle of eucalyptus oil. I . . . I just went out on the balcony to get my last beer. I keep them out there, where it's cold. Very cold here, rotten weather. In about two hours I'll go down to the coffee shop again and have another club sandwich. Then I'll come back up

23. Marco was Oscar Acosta's young son.

here and work on the article. I don't know what's on TV because I don't have a newspaper.

Tomorrow I'll call John Smith[24] and maybe go out to see Nicholas and Emily. McGarr is moving this weekend and his phone is disconnected, so I can't get hold of him. I met Oscar's new wife last night, a pretty little Mexican girl. I have to mail this article on Monday, so I'll have to spend most of tomorrow working on it. The Air Force visit was interesting; I saw a lot of strange planes and talked to a lot of dull people. For entertainment, I drove around at high speeds in a rented Mustang, going ninety miles an hour across the desert. There is no snow out there, just sand and dry bushes. And you can see for twenty miles in all directions. There are no grizzly bears on the desert, but people say there are a lot of wild pigs. I didn't see any. As a matter of fact, I didn't see much of anything.

Well, there's more news coming on. Still raining outside, I have the sliding glass door open, to cool the room. When the news is over I'll call Sandy and find out how things are going.

Love
Hunter

FROM OSCAR ACOSTA:

At this point Acosta was winning more cases for Mexican clients than any other defense attorney in California. He often asked Thompson to critique his writing, then objected to what he heard back.

February 20, 1968
Los Angeles, CA

THE DESTRUCTIBILITY OF CONTINGENT REMAINDERS . . .
AND OTHER SUCH NONSENSE

Hunter,

You've got to be mad. How the fuck you gonna do all that stuff? And what's the Rum Diary? Your memoirs at so early an age? I've thought of that. Seems everyone waits until they're old farts and got nothing much left to say . . . but the whole truth. And since, as it's now been established by you and Miss Harrell now that I'm honest abe in brown, maybe I should start working on my biography now. I once made a deal with a poet buddy that he'd write mine and I his. Until he fell for my ex and felt too guilty to talk to me anymore. It was funny because I wanted him, I encouraged him, I even encouraged her, to take up together. I only got pissed off when they *both* cut out on me. Anyway, per-

24. John Macauley Smith was an old friend of Thompson's from Louisville.

haps if we're still around in, say, 2000 a.d., perhaps you can make a few bucks off me and I one or two off you.

I wrote a letter to your friend. I thanked her and explained a few things about myself and the mss. And I asked her if she'd read "Perla" in exchange for some California sun. I also told her you were nuts:

1. Oscar writes a short novel.
2. Hunter says it should be a short story.
3. Oscar writes a short story.
4. Hunter says it should be a short novel.
5. Oscar says Hunter is a novel short story.

I *have* thought about doing non/fiction. In fact, just yesterday I decided to do a long letter to the editor type thing for/to the *Free Press.* A little one about their constant reference to Mexican/Americans and Spanish/Americans. Any stupid fucker who thinks he knows where it's at now'a days and uses terms like that, euphemistic, insulting shit, needs to have a few lessons in the art of semantics. For christ sake that's what the okies used to do with us. You see, *to them,* the word "Mexican" was like "nigger." So *to us*, we got all screwed up about it, too. So, when they "liked" you, (uncle tom, where are you?) they'd say, "Hey, bud, you Spanish?" Now the only Spaniard in Riverbank was the owner of the grocery store and *everyone* knew damn good and well the rest of us brownos weren't anything like old man Bordona. So we all got in the habit of saying, Yes. Even my cousin Becky, who married an okie kid named Billie who raises pigs, who once told me when she was *six* years old, "Me italiana" . . . Okay, that was in the forties and fifties.

So in the later years when the politicos started asking for the brown vote they started calling us Mexican/Americans. (my hyphen is broken.) Because, you see, they too thought Mexican was a bad word. Did you know the only other significant group that is still commonly hyphenated are the Japanese/Americans? Why? WW2, that's why. How come there ain't no Negro/Americans, Irish/Americans, Aspen/Americans? Et cetera.

So one would expect these leftwingrags to know this sort of stuff. One would expect the highest Mexican elected representative to know this, too? Wouldn't you think? So I went to see congressman Roybal[25] and talked to his field secretary. The secretary kept on using the word. Over and over. Mr. Roybal has done this and that for his people, the Mexican/American . . . blahblahblah. Finally, I said, Yes, but what's he done for us? Who's that, sir? (I think at that moment he thought I was Indian.) Us, sir. What's Mr. Roybal done for the Mexicans?

Also, I want to write a studied article on what to do to protect your right of privacy. I've had about 25 dope cases in the past three weeks and could possi-

25. Democrat Edward R. Roybal was a U.S. congressman from California.

bly have won twice as many as I did if people would remember a few rules of the road. (Trip?) Main thing: Don't open the fuckin door. Let them break it down. It's better to pay for a broken lock which gives you a better chance to beat it than go to jail. Second: Don't say a fucking word. Nothing! If you feel compelled to talk, if you're the gabby sort of uptight guy, then just say nonono to everything. Third: If you're selling, for god sake don't keep all the *paraphernalia* around the house. Fourth: Keep the stash hidden.

Now everyone knows this, but I want to show from actual cases that were won or lost on appeal why it is imperative. Also, in advance of any retort about, "Well, man, that's being too uptight," I want to say a few words about you fucking A john it's uptight. I've yet to see anyone cool in the cooler. (In fact, why not, A Cooler Is Not Cool, for a title?) In other words, better to be uptight a few minutes while you're hiding your shit than spend a couple of years in CYA or Big Q.[26]

Had this nazi bastard on the stand the other day. He had qualified as an "expert witness" to testify that he could give an expert opinion to the fact that this single two inch joint was marijuana. (The chemist had done the test, but I refused to stipulate to that, which is a story in itself, but they couldn't find him and the judge and the D.A. were determined to finish the case that day so they put the cop on the stand.) He testified that he had seen and smelled dope over a hundred times and that in his opinion, by smelling it and looking at it there on the stand, that it was dope. So I asked the following questions to which he answered "I don't know."

Is that a California joint or an Eastern joint? Is that Acapulco gold or Bangkok gold?

How much, if any, hash does that contain? Is it rolled in sugar?

Well, is it cut with anything?

You ever smelled clover?

How would you define that "unique" smell?

Are you sure it isn't dried banana?

Have you smelled dried banana skins?

Is oregano a narcotic?

Have you ever smelled a mixture of oregano, banana and dried clover?

Are young kids using that combination to turn on?

Needless to say the judge struck his testimony on the grounds that the cop was not an expert. Off [the record] the judge asked me, no it was the sheriff, if that was true. I told him that kids nowadays were turned on by almost anything.

I'm still wearing my boots to court every day and the rumor has spread that the D.A.s are out to "get me." Don't you think I'm having one swell time. I am. Not since my first year of preaching has it been so good.

26. The California Youth Administration or the state penitentiary at San Quentin.

You never answered the letter about the short story (23 pages) and Sandy was vague. I don't care nothin for that stinkin greaser novel. Had a bit of dope and booze in S.F. last weekend. I'm staying clean in L.A. because I seriously believe the cops might be after me because of my success and my bugging them in court. And because I got no need for it.

Oscar

TO BOB SEMPLE, *THE NEW YORK TIMES:*

Robert B. Semple, Jr., a New York Times *editor who would win the 1996 Pulitzer Prize for Editorial Writing, helped set up interviews for Thompson's* Pageant *magazine article on ominous Republican presidential candidate Richard M. Nixon.*

February 20, 1968
Woody Creek, CO

Dear Bob . . .

Thanks again for the help in Manchester.[27] I kept after Ray Price[28] all day Friday (the day you took off from Boston), and just about the time I gave up I found myself in Nixon's car, with the great man himself bending my ear about pro football. The bastard really knows it; I figured his claiming to be a fan was just another one of his hypes, a pitch for the violence-vote. You're right, I think, in saying he's not a *conscious* phoney. That complicates my story considerably. I'm not sure what I'll write, but I'll send you a copy if and when it comes out.

Meanwhile, if you see Ray Price, tell him I did my "homework," based on the lesson he gave me, and now I'm *sure* he was bullshitting me. He should have quit while he was ahead.

And convey my thanks to Don Irwin.[29] He's a good example of my theory that journalism, despite all its faults, is still flexible enough to give people like Irwin enough elbow room to redeem the other 90%.

OK for now. Stop by Owl Farm on your way out to Oregon. Ciao . . .

Hunter

TO VIRGINIA THOMPSON:

Hunter Thompson wrote to his mother often until the day she died in 1998. His concern for his brothers was always apparent, even on less serious matters than how to keep Jim, the youngest, out of Vietnam.

27. New Hampshire held 1968's first presidential primary on March 12.
28. Nixon campaign speechwriter Raymond K. Price.
29. Don Irwin was a national political reporter for the *Los Angeles Times.*

February 22, 1968
Woody Creek, CO

Dear Mom . . .

Now that you mention it, I guess you know how *I* feel about thank you notes, too—so yours is a bit embarrassing, and especially so when I thought I wrote that check for $25. But what the hell? Money-talk is always embarrassing—like "thank you" notes.

I didn't answer Jim's very good letter because I had to go to New Hampshire right after I received it. Sandy wrote him a letter while I was gone. I just got back and now have to write 4000 words on the meaning of the "new, new, new Nixon." The trip was fun, but grueling—very little sleep and expensive confusion trying to deal with Nixon, Romney[30] and McCarthy all at the same time. McCarthy is the only human being in the race, so he's naturally doomed. But he's fun to travel with. Nixon is a nightmare of bullshit, intrigue and suspicion. Romney is a circus. I was there about nine days, then I spent a day or two in New York to argue about contracts. Things are *almost* settled—but the difference between "almost" and "settled" is vast and treacherous.

As for Jim and college, I'll do everything I can to keep him out of the draft, but my income is so irregular and uncertain that I can't promise anything in advance. If we're lucky, I'll have what he needs when he needs it. If not, we'll have to kite some checks. OK for now.

Love,
Hunter

TO SUE GRAFTON:

Again Grafton asked Thompson to "reveal himself" to her.

February 23, 1968
Woody Creek, CO

Dear Sue . . .

Sorry to be so late, short-worded and useless, but I just got back from New Hampshire and ten days with Nixon—and now I have to make sense of it all, very quickly. Who is Nixon? And why? In 4000 words by the end of the month. I've also just signed (tonight) the contract for a book on Johnson, so I won't be geared for letter-writing for awhile.

Yours was vaguely unsettling; I'm not sure why . . . except that I've always been leery of people who want to know "who I am." Most of them seem to be probing for some kind of response, from me, to confirm an uncertain image they have of themselves. So I never know what's expected of me—except that I'm expected to respond, for good or ill. Don't take this personally; I'm talking

30. GOP presidential candidate George Romney was governor of Michigan.

in half-remembered generalities and besides that, it's 4:42 a.m. here and my head's not working as well as it should. I shouldn't be writing this at all; I'm way behind schedule on the article and it still hasn't jelled in my head. I have visitors here, as always, and my water-pipes are freezing. The basement is flooded, one of my cars is dying and the tax man is after me for explanations I don't have. Send me your book and I'll write again after I read it.

Ciao . . .
Hunter

TO OSCAR ACOSTA:

February 23, 1968
Woody Creek, CO

Dear Abe . . .

I don't recall telling you to rewrite that story as a short novel; I was merely trying to brief you on the current word market, where books sell much faster than stories. This is a weird situation and it won't last, so if I were you I'd try to ride it. Believe it or not, your chances of getting a $5000 guarantee for a "brown power" non-fiction book are far better than your chances of getting $500 for "Perla." It's also true that your chances of getting $5000 for the book depend on its being *unwritten* at the time of negotiations. Don't write a word until you get at least $1000 and a firm contract for the rest. I'm not kidding.

Your comments on Mexican-Americans strike me as a good book-seed; send me *two* double-spaced pages, describing whatever kind of book you'd like to write, and I'll send it on to Ballantine with a recommendation. Keep it loose, loud and menacing—with *details.* I don't recall getting your letter about the short story, but let me look. Meanwhile, keep whacking on the bastards. I just got back from 10 days with Nixon & now I have to write something. Ciao . . .

HST

TO TOM WOLFE:

Thompson had quit his job at The National Observer *in 1965 when the editor refused to run his glowing review of Tom Wolfe's* The Kandy-Kolored Tangerine-Flake Streamline Baby. *Later, he lent the author some tape recordings he had made at novelist Ken Kesey's California ranch, which Wolfe would put to good use in his 1968 book on the Merry Pranksters,* The Electric Kool-Aid Acid Test.

February 26, 1968
Woody Creek, CO

Dear Tom . . .

I just got back from a quick shot in the East, and called from the airport but you weren't home again. Who are these old crones who answer your telephone?

I have a picture of some gout-riddled old slattern on her knees in your hallway, waxing the floor when the phone rings and rising slowly, painfully, resentfully, to answer it and snarl "He ain't here." Anyway, I called. The quick shot was New Hampshire for a look at the new, etc. Nixon. I'm not sure what I found, but since the article is due in two days I'll shut this off and get back to it.

Did you, by the way, hear about the death of Neal Cassady?[31] The *Berkeley Barb* says he died of unknown causes while walking along some railroad tracks in Mexico. I offer that, for the moment, without comment.

What stage is the Kesey book in? I finally came to terms with Ballantine (after coming to terms with Lynn Nesbit[32]) for a fantasy book on Johnson, to be finished at once.

Did you ever deal with those tapes? Don't lose them.

Ciao . . .
Hunter

TO JIM SILBERMAN, RANDOM HOUSE:

Thompson had come to rely on Silberman's editorial judgment, and together they would spend two years searching for the right approach to a book on "The Death of the American Dream."

March 3, 1968
Woody Creek, CO

Dear Jim . . .

Thanks for the good letter. It arrived just as two of my houseguests returned from taking two others to the train station in Glenwood Springs. Tomorrow I plan to dynamite my cesspool, which will blow up my driveway and perhaps even the county road—in order to get the sewage out of my basement. Things are happening here. I insist on drainage, and if the landlord won't provide it, then Alfred Nobel[33] will. (Alfred? Is that right?)

I'm glad we all agree on the *active,* rather than *abstract* nature of the Joint Chiefs book. I don't see the narrative idea as an ego trip on my part, but as the only possible way to make the book an *original* document. The essays have already been written and I'll probably steal from a lot of them, but I think we need a participant's point of view, not an observer's. My overdue article on Nixon should give you an idea what I mean; I'll send you a copy if it ever gets finished.

31. Neal Cassady was the model for the Dean Moriarty character in Jack Kerouac's novel *On the Road*.

32. Lynn Nesbit was Thompson's literary agent.

33. Alfred B. Nobel was the Swedish chemist who invented dynamite in 1866 and founded the Nobel Prizes, first awarded in 1901.

Probably I'll need a lot more help on this book than I did on the other, at least in the formative stages. What I'm looking for right now is a long list of "joint chiefs," which I can narrow down to about a dozen. The first, of course, will be the Joint Chiefs of Staff—the real ones. But after that I want to select the ten most prominent suspects in this investigation of the murder of the American dream. I've already settled firmly on the Oil Industry and the Press, but I'm not sure exactly where I'll focus on either one of those. Maybe the *ChiTrib/NYNews* combine would be a good starter for the Press section. As I've said before, this is a far extension of Faulkner's idea of "seeing the world in a grain of sand."[34] Except that I need at least ten grains of sand. I want to concentrate on ten specific people or institutions who represent the ten most obvious suspects in this case. The Police? Perhaps even the new Negro leadership. Maybe the gun freaks. Mailer had the right idea in his last book.[35] Why, indeed?

So if you come up with any ideas, please send them along. Maybe just newspaper clippings, or somebody's column. I can't read everything, and this is a crucial first stage. Thanks,

Hunter

TO THE EDITOR, *ASPEN TIMES* AND *ASPEN NEWS:*

Outraged that Sheriff Earl Whitmire had ordered riot gear for tiny, mostly rural Pitkin County's police force, Thompson wrote a satirical letter to the editor of the local paper praising Aspen's move toward law and order the Gestapo way.

March 9, 1968
Woody Creek, CO

Herr Editor . . .

I am writing this letter for my friend Martin Bormann,[36] who has finally arrived—in one piece, as it were—but who has not yet mastered the language. We were warming ourselves around the furnace the other night, chatting about discipline, when I pointed out the newspaper article on Sheriff Whitmire's request for riot-control weapons. We both agreed that the sheriff would certainly make a name for himself if he ever got his hands on a full arsenal of riot-control devices and that the town would reap untold benefits if a local boy made good in the national press . . . but we also wondered if weapons alone would do the trick.

34. Quoted from English poet William Blake's 1804 "Auguries of Innocence."

35. Norman Mailer, in his 1967 book *Why Are We in Vietnam?*

36. Martin Bormann, Adolf Hitler's chief personal assistant, is believed to have fled to South America before his conviction as a war criminal at the 1946 Nuremberg Trials. He was sentenced to death in absentia.

What we really need is a riot. This would not only justify the purchase of gas, firebombs, electric zappers and various armored equipment—it would also give Aspen the modern, up-to-date image that it vitally needs. We are fortunate in having people like the sheriff and Guido and Bugsy around, if only to keep a rein on dangerous waterheads like Tom Benton.[37]

Now I realize that a lot of people know about the bad blood between me and Benton because he crossed up my plans to build a fourteen story bamboo and styro-foam turkey barracks on top of the Paragon. Mr. Bormann and I had commitments for Argentine financing on this project, and it cost us a lot of money . . . but the big loser was the city of Aspen and one or two local architects whom we naturally refused to pay when the gig turned sour. Most of the locals were in favor of this project; I overheard numerous conversations at the Tower, the Refactory and the Leather Jug, and everybody was asking the same question: "What happened to the turkey barracks?"

But no matter. The thing we need now is a powerful symbolic display of Aspen's willingness to come to grips with the 20th Century . . . and by this I mean a flat-out, ding-dong riot. Mr. Bormann and I have offered, on numerous occasions, to furnish the necessary ingredients on a cost-plus basis. Sheriff Whitmire, in his wisdom, has anticipated our project and is already pushing it. Aspen needs more men like this: far-sighted men who are willing to invest in the future. Martin Bormann and I can do business with people like this; we can turn Aspen into a paying proposition.

To the others I say only "Beware." They will be driven, like the *schwein*[38] they are, from the money-changing temple. The future is on us, and in closing I can only offer my condolences.

Sincerely,
Hunter S. Thompson
(For Martin Bormann)

TO BERNARD SHIR-CLIFF, BALLANTINE BOOKS:

March 25, 1968
Woody Creek, CO

Bernard . . .

I'm enclosing a few words on a book idea by a friend of mine named Oscar Acosta. Brown Power, as it were. Be the first on your block to have the definitive text on this new and growing menace to the white man's peace of mind. *Après les blaques, les brownes* . . . once more, Zapata,[39] looting and rapine, throw the rascals out.

37. Thompson's friend Tom Benton was a local Aspen artist.
38. *Schwein* is German for "pigs."
39. Mexican Indian revolutionary leader Emiliano Zapata.

Yeah . . . and if I seem a bit flippy from being threatened at every corner of my consciousness, you'll have to pardon it at least long enough to remember your job . . . which is, they say, to publish saleable books—and in that context I think I'm doing you a favor by putting you onto a potential inside view of the "brown power" thing. Somebody's going to do it; that's obvious. And it's going to make money—especially when the first Negro governor of California is burned at the stake on a Big Sur beach by Brown Nationalists.

Oscar is very much into this scene, as I think you'll see by his letters. The two pages marked "outline" are intentionally limited—at my suggestion—so don't blame Oscar if you'd have preferred to get more. I told him two pages would do for an opener, but after reading these two I suspect five or ten would have been a better vehicle. Anyway, I think Oscar is eminently capable of writing a book on this thing, despite the fact that he seems to have approached the outline as an adversary proceeding. He has a pretty good eye for most things, and I suspect he'll regain his focus once the initial excitement of this new scene breaks down into mean tangibles. As a "Chicano lawyer," he'll be forced to see "brown power" for whatever it is, in terms of day-to-day reality.

Anyway, I recommend it. Check with Oscar and see what you think. His address is on the outline, and I'm enclosing his card. He has, by the way, written a full-length (unpublished) novel and several other things, so he won't go blank at the notion of turning out 75,000 words. Call me if this letter doesn't tell you all it should. OK. . . .

Hunter

TO OSCAR ACOSTA:

March 26, 1968
Woody Creek, CO

Oscar . . .

I sent your "outline" and four other pages to Bernard Shir-Cliff at Ballantine. Probably you'll hear from him soon, but in the meantime I suggest you pay your rent by conventional means. (This is not to say I've paid mine—at the moment I owe Craig for Feb. and March, but I'll have to pay him soon or he won't introduce me to McNamara.) Yeah . . .

Anyway, I was not impressed with your presentation on "Brown Power Through the Vengeful Eyes of Oscar A." The subject itself will sell a book by somebody, but damn few publishers are going to want a flat-out piece of bugle-blast propaganda. You're asking for some serious beatings—both as a writer and a lawyer—if you persist in your notion that all Mexicans are doomed heroes. Some Mexicans, as I recall, actually drive their own cars off of cliffs for no reason at all, or stall in the middle of highways and piss on themselves . . . right?

And we all know what the world can expect from Kentucky booze-freaks, so don't bother with that indictment—it's a matter of public record. My point is that you're going to have to figure out some way to reconcile your roles as a Chicano lawyer and a Chicano writer—which might also involve some weird juggling of the lawyer-client relationships, eh? Or maybe not. But if you want to write propaganda tracts about how all the brown and black brothers sing TRUTH AT ALL TIMES AND FUCK ANYBODY WHO CAN'T UNDERSTAND IT, then I submit that you'll probably wind up publishing your own book. Yeah . . . the whole publishing world is a gang of evil racist swine: they won't give Nelson Algren[40] a Guggenheim Fellowship because they're saving the money for LeRoi Jones.[41] Back-scratchers. But not racists. They don't have the balls for that. They talk about Jesus, but they pay dues to the Grand Inquisitor. . . . Jesus is the favorite son, but on the second ballot the smart money will be on the G.I. Selah.

Obviously, it's late here. Your letters and outlines are sealed in a fat envelope, so I can't answer anything in detail—which hardly matters because the only question you asked had to do with the book-notes you sent me. And this letter should settle all that. As for prospects, I suspect you'll have to outline your ideas again for Shir-Cliff, and in far more detail; your problem is going to be in convincing any publisher that you're capable of deciding, in your own head, whether you want to write as a reporter or an advocate. I'm not sure, myself, what you have in mind, but since most of the stuff you've sent me was biased to the point of dementia, I felt an obligation to tell Shir-Cliff that your head is really pretty good.

Ciao, HST

TO TED SORENSEN:

JFK's gifted wordsmith Theodore Sorensen was working on New York senator Robert F. Kennedy's just-announced presidential bid when Thompson volunteered his speechwriting services—just as he had three months earlier to Eugene McCarthy's rival Democratic campaign.

March 28, 1968
Woody Creek, CO

Ted Sorensen
c/o Sen. Robert Kennedy
Senate Office Building
Washington D.C.

40. Nelson Algren was the author of *The Man with the Golden Arm*, a 1949 novel about a heroin addict.

41. LeRoi Jones was a New York Beat turned black nationalist poet of the 1950s and '60s.

Dear Mr. Sorensen:

I understand that you and the Senator are casting about for human assistance in this strange and whimsical gig you're into. Perhaps I can help in some way; I'm not sure how, but if you have any ideas by all means let me know. I met you several years ago at the Aspen Institute. You were one of the gurus at that session, along with Walter Reuther, Lionel Trilling and Justice Brennan.[42] I was writing a piece on the Institute for *The National Observer,* my employer at the time. The article appeared, in gutted form, some weeks later—spring of '63, as I recall. But what the hell?

Shortly after that I moved to California and continued to work for the *Observer* until the 1964 GOP convention, which I covered as part of the Dow Jones "team" and blew my cover, as it were, in the process. That scene, plus my coverage of the first Berkeley uprising, caused the *Observer* to question my objectivity . . . which led to my reclassification as a book reviewer and eventually as a non-person.

At that point I began writing for *The Nation,* which led almost instantly to a book project—the results of which I'm enclosing, along with a review of the book and an article I did last year on hippies. All I can tell you about the book is that it's about a hell of a lot more than the Hell's Angels; they are a logical product of a society that created them just as inevitably as it also created McDonald's Golden Arch. And The President, our leader and millstone.

With the lone exception of the 1960 presidential campaign, I've gone out of my way to avoid any personal involvement in politics . . . but I have the feeling that we're down to bedrock again, and if that's the case I guess I want a piece of the action.

Like I say, I'm not sure what I'm offering. I live in Woody Creek, about 10 miles out of Aspen, but I think that's immaterial. I move around a lot, and right now my schedule is pure politics. I spent about two weeks in New Hampshire, for instance, following Nixon around with the idea of finding out if he really existed. I'm still not sure, but the article is already written and now I have to finish a quick paperback for Ballantine by June 1 called "The Johnson File." Your friend and mine. It's a fantasy book, a rude parody of the Iron Mountain thing, but this time with all the fangs showing.

No sense explaining it here, but I'll tell you about it in Oregon if you have time for a beer up there. I'll be there in connection with another book that I'm writing for Random House on "The Joint Chiefs," and/or "who killed the American dream." If Nixon wins (or, "if the boss gets in," as Pat Buchanan[43] says), he'll qualify for canonization as one of Thompson's "joint chiefs." Actu-

42. Walter Reuther was president of the United Automobile Workers, Lionel Trilling an author and literary critic, and William J. Brennan a leading liberal justice on the U.S. Supreme Court.
43. Nixon campaign aide and later White House speechwriter Patrick J. Buchanan would mount archconservative presidential bids of his own in 1992, 1996, and 2000.

ally, he's already qualified: Nixon is a monument to all the bad genes and broken chromosomes that have queered the reality of the "American Dream." Nixon is the Dorian Gray[44] of our time, the twisted echo of Jay Gatsby[45]—the candidate from almost–Los Angeles.

And so much for all that. I think I'm rambling. It's late here—almost dawn, in fact—and in looking back over this letter I don't think I've made myself clear. So I'll try to strip it all down, to wit: I'm not volunteering to ring doorbells or hassle the 500 or so registered voters of Aspen, many of whom are already worried about my houseguest, Martin Bormann, who writes letters to the local papers about McNamara. So precinct-work is out; I'm not looking for a career in politics or even a dam for Woody Creek. All I really want to do is get that evil pigfucker out of the White House and not let Nixon in . . . and the only real hope I see right now is your friend Robert. So maybe I can write something for you; that's the only thing I do better than most people, so I guess that's what I should offer. This *Hell's Angels* book, by the way, has sold about 500,000 in paperback, mainly in college-type bookstores. I'm not sure how relevant that is to your interests, but perhaps you can do something with it.

If you think I could help in some way, by all means write or call ASAP so I can adjust. My phone here is (303) 925-2250. Or you can reach me through Jim Silberman at Random House or my agent, Lynn Nesbit at 1271 Sixth ave. OK for now . . .

Hunter S. Thompson

TO JIM THOMPSON:

Thompson's youngest brother was now a sophomore at the University of Kentucky.

April 3, 1968
Woody Creek, CO

Dear Jim . . .

Sorry, very sorry, to be so late with a letter. I've more or less given up writing them. Ever since Xmas I seem to have been either traveling somewhere, or just getting ready to leave, or just getting back. And in between all that, I've been plagued with visitors. My nerves are shot and my temper is raw . . . and last Sunday night Johnson's cop-out cost me $10,000. That's what I was going to get for a book on the bastard. I really hated to see him quit; he deserved to be destroyed on his feet.

44. The doomed antihero of Oscar Wilde's 1891 novel *The Picture of Dorian Gray,* whose portrait ages and decays while he does not.
45. The doomed antihero of F. Scott Fitzgerald's 1925 masterpiece *The Great Gatsby,* which Thompson considers the Great American Novel.

Speaking of all that, how is it going at UK? I think you'll have it made if you can hold out another year; it's going to take us that long to admit that we've lost this war in Vietnam. I say this without losing sight of the chance that Johnson might provoke something totally unforeseen . . . and if that happens it's every man for himself. But I don't think it's going to happen that way; I traveled around with McCarthy in New Hampshire long enough to realize that a lot of people are very disturbed about this war and its implications. I went there to write about Nixon, but McCarthy was a lot more fun to travel with, so I switched off whenever I got the chance. My Nixon article should be in the June or July issue of *Pageant*. Another article just came out in the *Collier's Encyclopedia 1967–68 Yearbook*. Check in the library if you get a chance. The photo in the front of the book is a horror.

I've checked with the local radio station about the possibility of hiring you this summer, and it doesn't seem too promising. There's a chance, but it's damn slim. Keep looking around on your own and don't count on this thing; I'll let you know if anything breaks. Sandy's mother says she might be able to get something for you with a new station in Deland, Florida. I'll have Sandy check on that and let you know.

The enclosed check is something I've had on my desk for a few weeks, so I thought I'd put it to good use. Maybe it's a birthday present. I don't know how you're fixed for money in terms of tuition, etc., but let me know if you get seriously strapped. The sudden death of this Johnson book has jolted the shit out of me in terms of this year's money, but if things get hairy on your end I can probably come up with something. In any case, let me know. Like I said, I think you can ease off after the elections. But hang on until then. It would be a rotten goddamn thing to get drafted out and killed for no damn reason at all . . . and don't kid yourself about that; draftees your age are going to be killed right up until the last hour of this stinking war. So be cool about it. I assume you're in good shape, but I haven't heard anything for awhile and if your status has changed any since Xmas, let me know.

I thought I'd have a chance to stop and see Davison[46] on the trip to New Hampshire, but it didn't work. I haven't heard from him at all in a few months. I haven't heard anything, for that matter, so send a line when you have time. I feel like a pure bastard for not writing in so long, but there aren't enough hours in my day to even keep up with the basic action. Right now, for instance, it's 8:15 on a Thursday morning and I'm going to bed just as soon as I finish this letter. Juan is already up, banging around in the kitchen and watching *Captain Kangaroo* or something like that on the TV. Sandy is still asleep. The dogs are outside, fighting over a deer-hide that turned up yesterday and terrorizing a

46. Davison was the middle Thompson brother.

strange dog that turned up on the porch last night and won't leave. It's a fine bright day, for a change. Still a lot of snow on the hills, but there's already grass in the yard and I have my motorcycle running—that's a sure sign of spring.

Juan and Sandy say hello. We'll let you know about the slim chance of a radio job here, but even if it doesn't work out, plan to come for a visit sometime this summer. The phone here is (303) 925-2250; call collect some night and bring us up to date. OK for now,

Love . . .
Hunter

FROM OSCAR ACOSTA:

Civil rights leader Martin Luther King, Jr., had been assassinated on the balcony outside his room at the Lorraine Motel in Memphis on April 4, 1968.

A day or two after they shot King . . . or,
a day or two before we burn.
[April 6, 1968]
Los Angeles, California

Hunter,

One thing the movement does to you is [it] takes away your sense of humor. Once upon a time I was a liberal, yesterday I was a militant, today I am a revolutionary, trying like hell not to become uptight.

By their own admission, four of us have "wrecked the educational system of six million." An inside joke amongst ourselves. Today East LA, tomorrow the world. Outside agitators arise!

One tries like hell not to take one's self so seriously, the awesome responsibility of the rabble rouser matures you; when you suddenly realize you could raise the people to take arms against his neighbor, to burn the city, to murder the fascist pigs, Christ that makes you grow up overnight.

TV cameras, reporters, electronic equipment, suffocating white lights, Bastards from the Dolce Vita jamming those mikes in your all too tired face, Your Thing becomes headlines, and suddenly the newsprint becomes The Event. And all the time you get this sickening feeling that they (the fourth estate) want you to burn the fucking town, all for a bigger and better circulation.

What has happened in ELA to this day from the time of my arrival, depending on what happens to us within the next week or two, could be an historic thing. Even on paper it looks like a man carried away with his own rhetoric, doesn't it?

Look at it this way: The mayor, through millionaires, wants to meet with me in private; we have, in our pocket, a telegram of support ending with the words

"*Viva La Raza!*"[47] signed by Bobbie [Kennedy]; large sums of money are being dangled in our brown hungry faces; and the sex thing . . .

Hunter, I came here to blow minds, as usual, and as a secondary thing to stir the Mexican-American Liberation. It has happened all too fast. The slogans have become reality. And now with the King thing fucking our heads it is not inconceivable that this largest of cities could be on fire before this letter reaches you. I'm scared shitless because the anger within me looks forward to seeing the fear in their faces . . . and the burning.

Oscar

TO KAREN SAMPSON:

Thompson could be extraordinarily generous with his time and thoughts in responding to young Hell's Angels *fans such as Sampson, a high school student who had written him for advice on her term paper about the biker gang.*

April 14, 1968
Woody Creek, CO

Dear Karen . . .

Thanks for your good letter and comments on my Hell's Angels book. I wish I could send you a bundle of ripe information that wasn't included in the book, but unfortunately I didn't anticipate this market, so I went ahead and put most of what I knew about the Angels into the book. Sorry. The only thing I can think of that might help you with your term paper is an aspect of the story I couldn't put in print for the same reasons I can't tell it to you in a letter. This is the fact that I was as careful as possible to leave out of the book any piece of specific information that might have been used as evidence, in a criminal case, against any of the people I was writing about. This is something that might help you, if you ever pursue sociology as a means of income. It took maybe five or six months of drifting around with the Angels to convince most of them that I wasn't going to write something that would get them all arrested. This is a problem that every honest "street-level" sociologist runs into sooner or later: if the people you're interested in are living in any sort of conflict with the law, they won't tell you the truth until they're sure they can trust you. And that's when your work really begins, because then you have to decide if they're really capable of telling you the truth. Some of the Angels, for instance, were so much in the grip of their own myth that they really believed some of the ridicu-

47. *La Raza* is Spanish for "The Race."

lous lies they told me. So I had to keep cross-checking, sifting, comparing versions, etc.

This is the sort of thing I mean, and it's very involved. The point I mean to make is that any book like this is written in a web of "additional" information that can't be published. [Ernest] Hemingway referred to it, in a different sense, as that part of the iceberg that floats beneath the surface, or something more or less in those words.

As for your note on my "courage for spending a year with them," I think you miss the point by focusing on the word "courage." I never thought of it that way, at the time—it was simply an assignment: to write a true book, and to write the truth I had to get close to it. Right now, tonight, there are photographers and reporters in Vietnam doing far more dangerous things than arguing with Hell's Angels. If you're looking for an example of Courage this year, try a name like Martin Luther King.

OK for now. I hope this helps your paper a bit.

Good luck,
Hunter S. Thompson

TO TOM WOLFE:

Thompson admired Tom Wolfe's sociological term "behavioral sink," and offered up his own word jewel: "atavistic endeavor."

April 21, 1968
Woody Creek, CO

Dear Tom . . .

I was talking to a friend in L.A. the other day & when he asked what I was doing I replied that I was into a "behavioral sink." And I'm only putting quote marks on the term because he advised me that you've already written about it. He lived in New York until about two months ago; claims he read your "sink" stuff in the *Tribune*. Did he? If so, could you send me a copy?

The term itself is a flat-out winner, no question about it. Every now and then I stumble on a word-jewel; they have a special dimension, like penetrating oil. Right? "Behavioral Sink" is up in that league with my all-time, oft-used champ, the "Atavistic Endeavor." I picked that up in a Ketchum, Idaho, bar about five years ago and I suspect it's appeared in every article since then. Or almost. Even Kesey: his whole problem in La Honda was that he didn't understand that his whole gig was an atavistic endeavor. How about that for a zapper? Yessir, penetrating oil. To queer the lubricant and bring us back to zero. Oh, it's a good life here; meanness and terror on the land, the tax man just bit me with nine-league fangs. If you can send me a copy of that thing you wrote I might be able to get out of the . . . yes . . . and thanx.

Hunter

TO LARRY SHULTZ:

Another Hell's Angels *fan got a pointed answer to his question about Christianity among bikers.*

April 21, 1968
Woody Creek, CO

Dear Mr. Shultz . . .

. . . in response to your query about the Hell's Angels and Christianity—which I note you spelled with a capital "C." In that context, I'd have to say that the Hell's Angels have no attitude at all toward Christianity; this is one of the few redeeming facets of their collective personality. Through no fault of their own, they have been spared the millstone of one of history's greatest lies.

. . . the answer to your second question should be self-evident by now: the notion that capital C christianity might reach anybody who's in touch with the reality of this world strikes me as a hopeless joke. Those bastards have done enough damage with their hypocritical, dues-paying, soul-rotting cage of a mean religion. If any one of those hired swine had a decent impulse in him, he'd get the hell out of the way and make room for some christians.

I trust this answers your question.

Sincerely,
Hunter S. Thompson

TO OSCAR ACOSTA:

April 22, 1968
Woody Creek, CO

Dear Oscar . . .

. . . you rotten brown freak, thanx for the clips that give me at least a distant notion about what you're into. You forgot to explain it, in those other letters, so I didn't know what the fuck you were talking about. I hadn't seen the *Time* clip, for instance, or anything in the *L.A. Times*. All I had was a shoddy, amateurish story in the *Free Press* about a school walkout—and it didn't mention you. Try to keep in mind that all your truth and passion and fiery brown baptist absolutes aren't worth a hoot in hell out of context—or when you're railing at a dumb anglo mutherfucker who doesn't know Brown Power from Brown & Root.

This is the bitch I had with the book-stuff you sent me, and it's also why I didn't send it back. I knew you'd call me a dirty anglo hack if I told you that you have to at least pretend to be objective when you're trying to sell a book to a New York publisher. I didn't see any sense in telling you to back off and get un-involved . . . because you'd have told me to fuck off, right? I figured that the book idea would stand a better chance if I passed it along to the dirty white hack in New York, and tacked on a few explanatory notes of my own. To wit: "Oscar's excited now, but believe it or not he can actually say what he means now and then—he has a weird instinct for dialogue: he can make it carry a whole narrative. There's a good book in this, if you can get Oscar calm enough to write it . . . I suggest you offer him some money."

Those aren't exact quotes, but they're the main tone of a long letter. And if Shir-Cliff hasn't answered yet, keep in mind that he hasn't answered me either—and he owes me a fat bag of money that I want NOW, AT ONCE to buy some Woody Creek acres. So at least he hasn't burned you: that's more than I can say. I just paid a New York lawyer $436 to deal with this shit (the $36 is for phone calls), and I can't get anything out of him either. One of these days you brown and black radical blowhards will figure out that money is power in this country, and that money is colorblind. That bullshit about color is for the sheep—keep em squabbling, stabbing each other. And then lock em up, teach the scum a lesson.

Maybe I'm wrong, maybe this is just another dose of gringo bullshit, but it seems to me that this color bag is so limited that it has to be self-defeating. I had this same argument a few years ago with a guy named Clyde Warrior, a wild-eyed beautifully articulate Indian freak from Oklahoma who is now raising some headlines by telling the tribesmen to use their rifles because that's all the white bastards can understand. But Clyde can't tolerate niggers, or at least he couldn't then. Maybe he's figured things out by now. I just wrote him at his old address, and if he's up to anything active I might drive over there sometime soon and have some serious drink-talk with him. You'd like the bastard; if I can locate him, maybe the CP will pay your way out here for an eyeball-to-eyeball chat with him. He's a natural ally, and he wails first-class at the podium. But he needs to be jerked out of that narrow pure-indian gig he's into . . . or maybe he's already out of it; I haven't seen him in two years—for all I know he's tight with Tijeria by now. Anyway, I should know pretty soon. Would you be interested in getting together with him if I can work it out? Send word.

As for your "book," I think I made myself clear to McGarr when he called the other day. My objection will obviously be the publisher's—*any* publisher's—and it dwells on the brutally partisan nature of your stance. It's like [if I had] joined the Angels before writing the book—so that everything I said would be suspect, in terms of which axe I was grinding. And that's all fine if we're talking about biography—but neither of us is famous enough at this point to sell our life history and viewpoints to the evil anglo press lords. At least not in those terms. The thing for you to do, I think, is to write about a 3000 word article for *The Nation* . . . and send it to Carey McWilliams, the editor, with a note saying I thought he should have a look at it. Then, if he puts it in print, you'll be in a leverage position on a book contract.

I'm not saying this is something you *have* to do; it's just a ripe and proven way to get a book contract. All this talk ignores my obvious doubt that you're capable, right now, of writing anything less partisan than a bazooka shot on this subject. There is a shale hassle, and after that I may or may not pick up that dormant thing I was doing on Aspen. These pigfuckers should all be boiled in oil. If I can find my latest Marty Bormann letter I'll enclose it along with a clip on Diaz Ordaz, which I think you'll like. If you can think of any central happening that I could peg a story on (in connection with the chicano action), let me know and SEND a CLIPPING—which I can use to convince some editor to pay my ticket to LA or wherever. Your signed voucher won't make the nut. Sorry.

As for here, it's 6:37 now and the grey light of dawn is bubbling up on yesterday's heavy snow. No sun, just stinking wet warm snow. Yesterday afternoon I stumbled into the living room and found Juan talking very straight and seriously to your wooden man with the necklace. He has served his purpose, at least to the extent of keeping evil spirits away. What I need now is a man to keep well-meaning people away.

Juan and Sandy both speak well of you, which is more than I can say for myself. And I'm about to go to the mat with the local greedheads. As for your car, it's not a question of my *wanting* you to sign it over—I HAVEN'T seen it since you left, but unless you want it towed off to the Pitkin County dump, you'll have to authorize *somebody* to cope with it. I can get it repaired—if it isn't already stripped—but if I do, you'll have to pay the repair bills before I sign it back over to you. If you send me the pink slip I'll do something about the car; if you don't, I'll forget it. OK for now . . .

Hunter

TO SELMA SHAPIRO, RANDOM HOUSE:

In New York after visiting Thompson in Woody Creek, former Richmond, California, mayor David Pierce was supposed to hand-deliver a gift from the writer to Selma Shapiro, the Random House publicist for Hell's Angels.

April 24, 1968
Woody Creek, CO

Dear Selma . . .

I was expecting a letter from you, but not the kind you sent—the *LOOK*/Mailer review, which I appreciated immensely, due to my crippled self-image as an actual working writer. Any mention like that reminds me of what I should be doing. And it also reminds me that people expect me to do it—although I'm not sure I need any more reminders on that score than I get every day in the mail.

But now . . . back to why I was expecting to hear from you this week: Pierce left my house about 10 days ago with your "present" (the long-lost totem) in his possession. He was en route to NY by train, which made him the first available human carrier I've managed to come up with in a year or so. He left the house about five in the morning and was due to catch the train a few hours later; the totem was all wrapped and tied with notes, addresses, etc., and all he had to do was get it to the train. But a few days ago I stopped at the hotel he stayed in here—and there was the goddamn totem, forgotten and abandoned on top of a disconnected bathtub full of firewood. I raised all manner of snarling hell with the tenants, whose responsibility it was to get him and all his baggage to the train station some 45 miles away . . . which they did, except for the totem . . . but they said he was pained and distraught from a flesh wound sustained the night before his departure while operating a tape recorder (and attempting to steal a tape) in my living room. He was shot in the base of the spine, he said, by a plastic target bullet of a .44 Magnum caliber—causing him extreme fear at the moment of contact, and prolonged pain thereafter. . . . Ho, ho, hee . . . the giddy bastard thought, for an instant, that I'd laid a genuine .44 Magnum round on him. He thought he was dead, he said, but when he realized he could still walk, he fled from the house at great speed—abandoning the tape he was trying to get off with when I caught him in the act and nailed him on the coccyx bone with my trusty .44.

So I guess we can't really wonder why good old Pierce, the prophet of non-violent theft, was not entirely straight when he gathered his baggage together a few hours after being shot. I just got a card from him today—from the boat. He said he wished I were there—100 yards off the starboard bow, floundering in the water, so he could shoot at me & hopefully teach me a lesson.

Anyway, that's why I didn't get a letter from you last week, either thanking me or cursing me for my present. It's sitting on the porch right now, covered with stinking evil snow. The weather has gone mad here—fine spring days laced with blizzards and freezing sleet. And last week I got swacked with a $2800 tax bill.

I told Gerald Walker of *The New York Times* this would happen. His circular said he wanted the signatures of "respectable, law-abiding (and presumably tax-paying) writers." I tried to explain that I was none of these, and that any tie to me would compromise the high liberal masochism that he seemed to favor. What is the position of the tax protest right now? Is Wilbur Mills[48] running it? I suspect I'll be locked up for egregious non-payment before I have to decide whether to withhold 10% or 23%. I think that's the last one of those white-collar protest gigs I'll get involved with. Or maybe not. I was going to say that the whole tax protest was a bad joke, but I guess that's not fair.

And it's not fair to grapple with anything that complicated at this hour of the morning, which is late and getting light. For the moment I'll just say goodnight. Send a decent letter, when you have time, and tell me what's happening there. As for here, I just focused back on *The Rum Diary*—after losing the Johnson

48. Arkansas Democrat Wilbur Mills was chairman of the U.S. House Ways and Means Committee from 1958 to 1974.

fantasy book and the easiest $10,000 I ever thought I'd see—so maybe I'll get off something human and interesting before I have to get into that stinking fat compendium on the American Dream/Power and Reality. In the meantime, I have to go over to Denver on May 1, for a conference on the Oil Shale menace—an article for the *LA Times.* Call if you feel like talking; I'll be at the Brown Palace Hotel from May 1 to May 4. Wheeling and dealing with the oil moguls. Drunk and oily . . . and quite faithfully yours in half-light . . .

Hunter

TO BERNARD SHIR-CLIFF, BALLANTINE BOOKS:

Thompson responded to his editor about the possibility of writing a short book on American violence.

April 26, 1968
Woody Creek, CO

Dear Bernard . . .

Two days have gone by since I talked to you by Bell telephone regarding the commercial withering of my Johnson File and the new possibility that you mentioned—a quick book hung somehow on the title: "Violence in America, Does it have a future?"

Well . . . . I'll bite. Does it?

This is a really fascinating question, Bernard, but I'm damned if I can see any way to make a book out of it unless you want to roll high and wild . . . and make it a sort of essay question for me. This could produce almost anything: 40,000 words of mad drivel, perhaps. Or a strange manifesto of some kind. I've thought about your question long enough to know I can't give you a quick answer.

As you probably suspect, I think that Violence in America has a Fat and Happy future. I have before me at this moment in space and time—a printed advertisement from the *Shotgun News,* which I'd otherwise enclose for your amusement except that I want to order several of these items, to wit: One tube of Mace Gas, complete with "top grain belt holster," and maybe a GR3 "All chrome, lowest priced .38 Special on the market—$32.95."

There is a touch of fine humor in this gunpowder game these right-wing all-american waterheads are said to be loading up like young oxen . . . 40 feet of running room and a cheap, unreliable, overpriced weapon in every loser's pot. They are due for an awful surprise when the go-horn sounds . . . sort of like Batista.[49] They are courting some weird echoes. Which is neither here nor there, except to stress the peculiar and potentially biased tone of my own involvement. Any realistic appraisal of the next few years of history and action

49. Former Cuban president Fulgencio Batista had been driven off the island by Fidel Castro's rebels on New Year's Day, 1959.

in this country would have to be weighted heavily on the side of tearful, mind-bending violence. It will come to the point of martial law and a non-elected "emergency" regime, headed by god knows what sort of monster—but a military man, choked up from the ranks of that faceless, soulless, hopeless power tribe that Mendel Rivers[50] has helped us make for ourselves.

Maybe Pat Nugent.[51] Or where is Dave Schine[52] these days?

Well . . . I had to let that rest for a few days; I can't handle too much of my own bullshit at any one sitting. What's fun in two sentences becomes rancid in two paragraphs. I get tired of whipping on the same old freaks; we need some new villains or at least some new names. Anyway, I've drawn a blank when it comes to thinking of specific forms, shapes and contexts for a Violence in America book. The more I think about it, the more it sounds like my Joint Chiefs idea. Hell, it's all the same subject—the one we've been haggling about for more than a year. Let's assume this and get down to the narrow, finite focus we need for a beginning. It's the same subject; what we're looking for is that opening that newspaper freaks call a "peg." And that, as I see it, is more your province than mine. You're an editor, right? I'm only a writer . . . and maybe we're both on the skids if you overprinted the H.A. book by 400,000, which is what I have to assume if I have only $10,000 on account with 600,000 copies in print. Why don't you put your sales & distribution guru in a heavy canvas bag and send him to me—COD, Woody Creek. I think I could use some instruction in The Basics: windsprints with Doberman pursuit, etc.

Sincerely,
Hunter

TO RUST HILLS, *ESQUIRE:*

Thompson had enrolled in Rust Hills's creative writing course at Columbia University in 1958. Now he let the critic know what he thought of Esquire's *kid-gloves review of* Making It, *the latest neoconservative screed from* Commentary *magazine founder Norman Podhoretz. A decade earlier—in his December 1958* Esquire *article "Where Is the Beat Generation Going?"—Podhoretz had proclaimed that "what juvenile delinquency is to life, the San Francisco [Beat] writers are to literature."*

50. In September 1966, South Carolina Democrat and U.S. House Armed Services Committee chairman Mendel Rivers had urged that the United States "flatten Hanoi if necessary" and "let world opinion go fly a kite."
51. Pat Nugent was a celebrated dealer in psychedelic narcotics.
52. G. David Schine and Roy M. Cohn, aides to Wisconsin Republican senator Joseph McCarthy, had been sent abroad by their red-baiting boss in the mid-1950s to look for possible communists at the State Department's precursor to the U.S. Information Agency.

April 29, 1968
Woody Creek, CO

Dear Rust . . .

I liked the zap and spirit of your *Esquire* piece on Norman Podhoretz, but I suspect you walked right into his snare. You gave him another billboard; the book deserved one of those hard, one-page shots you were always talking about at Columbia. Jesus, what a really horrible and degrading book . . . and what a horrible and degrading way of life it describes. I didn't sense much emphasis on that connection in your piece . . . but, shit, I guess a man has to be careful. Norman's harmless, but some people in that family, well . . . they have a bit of clout, right?

I'll be interested to see your new book. The last I heard, you were driving a cab in Stamford and writing radio spots for Nixon as a sideline. And growing a neck-beard. It just goes to show that some folks will lie about a man.

Anyway, I liked the tone of the article. The best line was in Part III, to wit: "But the impulse and motive seem to have come first." I thought you were moving in for a critic-type kill, there, but you backed off and only hinted at it. I think you lack the killer-instinct, Rust . . . that's a very mean gig that Norman is into, and he seems to be pretty good at it. Which side are you on? Viva la Raza and pie in the sky buy American, right?

Hunter S. Thompson

TO BUD PALMER, KREX-TV:

Located 150 miles away in Grand Junction, Colorado, KREX was the only station Thompson's TV could receive in pre-satellite-dish Woody Creek.

April 30, 1968
Woody Creek, CO

Bud Palmer
KREX-TV
Grand Junction, Colo.

Dear Mr. Palmer:

I've been meaning to write you ever since that night you made the statement on the death of Martin Luther King. I couldn't quite believe what I was seeing on KREX; it was a hell of a fine thing.

Since then, however, KREX-TV has appeared to be under the direction of Eric Starvo Galt. You may have taken a cheap, outback station and made it even cheaper and more provincial than it was under that freak who is now working for Nixon. I've had about all I can stomach of Chinchillas, Cushman golf carts, Smoky Mountain travelogues, *Insight, Romp* and Walter Cronkite at mid-afternoon. Somebody told me in Aspen the other day that you'd scheduled the Smothers Brothers at noon on Sunday, and I believed it. That's a very bad atmosphere to have to live in—especially when Bil Dunaway's *Aspen Times* cable is only 10 miles away. It's a nightmare to confront your (my) TV set and know that the programming is 20 years behind reality.

Yeah, I know all about the advertisers and the local culture and the rest of that Madison Avenue bullshit. And it all made sense in the context of [Palmer's predecessor] Rex Howe. But how did you come out from Chicago, with all your liberal credentials, just to perpetuate a cheap carnival? Are you that contemptuous of the people you've come out here to "entertain"? You know some of us can actually spell and read . . . like I get *The New York Times* every day including the sabbath; and I get the *San Francisco Chronicle* every day excepting the sabbath, and I get all the local papers too . . . but the curse of my life, on a day to day basis, is the total abdication of responsibility in broadcasting that I find in the programming of KREX-TV. This is understandable, to some extent, in that you brought some waterhead from small-town Pennsylvania to whip us yokels into line for the sponsors. I notice you even have your newscasters reading commercials for the camera . . . and, man, you can't get much cheaper than that.

I've heard—from Dunaway—that you're the bright young man from the big city who's supposed to be getting this crippled station back on its feet . . . but I'll be damned if I've seen any evidence that you're doing anything but whipping it down to its knees. You've done a spectacular job of mangling the *sequence* of your programming—to the point where it's impossible to know what's coming at any given hour or any day—but the overall *level* of programming is noticeably lower than it was in the Howe era. Not much lower . . . but that shouldn't be the point.

What I see, when I look at my one-channel set, is an unctuous liberal who came out here for some fresh air and a good investment and to give the local folks what he thinks they want. But what are your credentials for deciding that the KREX audience is so goddamn eager to watch half-hour advertisements in prime weekend time? Do you really believe we're all so dense and primitive that we don't realize that all that garbage about chinchillas and golf carts and Smoky Mountain tourist delights doesn't cost you a penny? Whereas a good movie or a decent network special would cost you something? There's plenty of good, interesting stuff available on TV this year—the Denver listings are evidence of that—and as an independent station, KREX should be able to pick and choose for a first-class format. But you've apparently chosen to go with Whatever's Cheapest. I guess I'll have to take your word for your claim that you knew "Doc" King, but if the KREX programming is any indication of the way you think, I can't believe you ever had the faintest understanding of what Martin Luther King was talking about.

Regardless of what you (or I, or we) thought about the man, there was no denying his courage or his faith in the ultimate goodness of even the people who hurled rocks and eggs and insults at him. Dr. King didn't patronize anybody; he was wrong at times, and even foolish, but I think he believed what he preached and I envy him for his faith in men who gave him damn little reason for it. The style of his death was a testament to his ignorance. He felt he was an honest man, and that even potential murderers would be neutralized by this honesty . . . but of course he was wrong, and in retrospect his faith in this country seems like a tragic delusion.

Your personal eulogy, on the night of his assassination, would have been more appreciated by Dr. King, I think, if it had not been such a rare and startling departure from the normal run of crude, cheap and degrading commercialism that KREX-TV dumps on its captive audience night after night. To my mind it's unfortunate—like you get to get off with one-shot hypocritical weepings that, in the context of those other 364 days of the year, are more a mockery of the living than a tribute to the dead.

Most sincerely,
Hunter S. Thompson

TO JIM BELLOWS, *LOS ANGELES TIMES:*

Because of legal concerns, Thompson's long article for the Los Angeles Times *on oil shale development in the West was never published.*

May 7, 1968
Woody Creek, CO

Dear Jim . . .

I just got back from Denver & the Oil Shale Symposium—which turned out to be an oil company pep rally, instead of the free-wheeling dialogue that I naively expected to fall into . . . on the basis of a small notice I saw in *The Denver Post* . . . which turns out to have been a press release from the Colorado School of Mines . . . which is to the oil and mining industries what CalTech and MIT are to the defense industry[53] . . . so I spent three days and about $150 in the grip of one of the most high-powered lobbies in this nation or any other . . . jesus, you should have heard them talking about the student-action at Columbia; they wanted to make soap out of the faculty, lampshades out of "the niggers," and a corpse out of Bobby Kennedy. These are weird people, Jim . . . and after listening to them for three days I think I'm inclined to take

53. Caltech and MIT are the California and Massachusetts Institutes of Technology, respectively.

Garrison's New Orleans action[54] a bit more seriously than I have in the past. I drank with some of the more articulate of these oil freaks for two straight nights, and I haven't had conversations like that since I was hanging around with the Hell's Angels. Strange, dehumanized concepts, highly technical one moment and insanely callous the next. When I was an hour late for dinner on Saturday I explained that I'd been haggling over the purchase of a shotgun, and they thought that was fine.

The point of all this is to advise you that we're into a very heavy subject, involving some very heavy people and some very heavy investments (like $7 million in one case that I know of, and $10 million in another) that are hanging, right now, in a Udall[55]-created limbo . . . and the investors are highly sensitive to the possibility of uncontrolled exposure in such press as the *L.A. Times*. The enclosed postcard, for instance, is from the Jim Smith who was assistant secy. of the Navy under Ike and is now a prime mover of some sort in the oil shale gig. He lives in Aspen, but he doesn't know me and I don't know him. Nevertheless, this card was in my mailbox on Monday, and I got back from Denver late Sunday night. When I called him today I asked how he knew I was writing something on oil shale, and he said "somebody from the Oil Shale Symposium told me." The odd thing about that is that I told the people over there that I was from the *L.A. Times* and let it go at that; the only indicators that I was from Colorado were my hotel reservation and my car license plate. You'll note that the card is addressed to me in Aspen, not L.A. . . . it was Gov. Love's official adviser on oil shale, who is also a paid consultant to several oil companies and whom I shall certainly see again after I talk at length with Smith. Wild connections . . . for instance Smith told me on the phone today that Western Oil, which invested some $10 million in oil shale research by the early 1950s, abandoned their research when Union was bought out by Gulf, which is controlled to some large extent by a man named Ludwig who also has a massive interest in the oil tanker (shipping) industry . . . which may or may not account for Gulf/Union's current emphasis on imported oil, instead of research and exploration on the domestic scene.

This is just a small example of what this story will get into. What I see—at a quick and running glance—is that the whole U.S. oil industry is in trouble, but that some companies are in more trouble than others. So that the real action in this thing is not in the conflict between Liberals and Conservatives, or Exploiters and Conservationists—but for the time being it's a fight for survival within the oil industry. Nobody denies that U.S. petroleum reserves are inadequate, but this poses two questions: 1) Where will the U.S. get its crude oil af-

54. New Orleans district attorney Jim Garrison had indicted CIA-connected import–export business owner Clay Shaw for conspiracy in the murder of John F. Kennedy. Shaw would be acquitted in March 1969.
55. Stewart Udall was U.S. secretary of the interior from 1961 to 1969.

ter 1975? and/or 2) Will some other fuel replace petroleum (or begin to replace it) in the near future? Both questions are rife with menace to the oil industry—and when an industry that size feels threatened, people get jerked around. Right? Remember what happened when Jock Whitney's[56] auditors got nervous? Yeah.

I'm telling you all this to let you know that this is going to be a complicated and time-consuming piece . . . but beyond that it has the look of something that might not generate real amusement in Norman Sr. and Buffy's[57] circle of friends. I thought I should warn you about this—as much for my sake as yours, because to do this thing right I'm going to have to put a lot more time into it than I intended to at the start, and I'm going to have to spend either a lot or a little more than that $200 expense allowance. On this type of story I have to learn so much, so fast, that I'm mentally exhausted for days and I can't say anything definite right now in terms of time and expenses—and I don't mean to hassle you with either item because neither one of them is going to worry me if this thing turns into the Fat/Heavy story that it smells like. But I don't see any sense in putting that kind of time, effort and money into it unless I can feel pretty certain that I'm writing for publication (and payment), rather than the censor's hole. In other words, I don't need the $250 guarantee enough to work my ass off on a doomed piece.

Don't take any of this personally. I know *you* want the piece. But how confident are you that the *Times* is going to hang out the oil industry's dirty linen in *WEST?* Like I said, we're not talking about a standard *Ramparts*-type Right vs. Left thing here . . . we're talking about weird Darwinian realities such as Standard of N.J. putting the death-squeeze on Standard of Calif. in order to starve Texaco and, as a left-handed adjunct to it all, using John Galbraith[58] for leverage against Stewart Udall.

You see what we're into? The figure that's being tossed around at the moment is TWO TRILLION barrels. That's a Bureau of Mines calculation of what's potentially available out here, in terms of oil reserves. The oil industry hoots at that figure, but they concede (according to the *WS Journal*) that ". . . 100 billion to 500 billion or more barrels of oil could be *economically* processed from the shale. The latter figure exceeds the world's known petroleum reserves. . . ."

That "latter figure" is also the one that most oil men seemed to take for granted at the Oil Shale Symposium. So, give or take a billion here and there, we're dealing with the biggest potential oil strike in the history of man. The

56. Publisher and former U.S. ambassador to the Court of St. James's John Hay "Jock" Whitney was chairman of the *International Herald Tribune*.

57. *L.A. Times* publisher Norman Chandler, Sr., and his wife, Buffy.

58. Harvard economist John Kenneth Galbraith had argued in his 1967 book, *The New Industrial State,* that giant corporations are not necessarily evil by definition.

biggest so far—the Sarir Field in Libya—is estimated to have reserves of 15 billion, which is three times the size of the East Texas field, the biggest in the U.S.

Jesus . . . I think I hear shots outside; they're shooting my Dobermans. Ludwig has driven his gunboat up the Woody Creek road. I'm beginning to see why you wanted this story. These people make the Hell's Angels seem like a bunch of manacled pansies. The Angels rob a gas station to buy a Smith & Wesson .38 Special from a punk in a tavern . . . but these people buy the whole goddamn Smith & Wesson—or was it Winchester or Western or Olin Mathieson—just to pick up the Mace Gas patent. What you ought to do now, for maximum commercial benefit on this story, is assign somebody like Nick von Hoffman[59] to cover this lunatic research: "Horrible Hunter, formerly of the Frisco Angels, comes to grips with the Big Hammer, in the form of the world's top ten Oil Combines . . . or, Truth in the Shalestones, and let the Devil take the Hindmost."

OK . . . I think you see what I'm getting at here. I'll proceed full bore unless I get some sort of damper words from you. I don't see the *Times* often enough to make my own fine judgements in this area, so I leave it to you—on the huge assumption that you somehow knew what you were doing when you started all this.

Ciao,
Hunter

TO VIRGINIA THOMPSON:

William J. Kennedy, Thompson's literary confidant and barmate since their days together at the San Juan Star, *had just sold his first novel,* The Ink Truck.

May 8, 1968
Woody Creek, CO

Dear Mom . . .

Let's just assume all the usual apologies for lateness, etc., so I can write without going through all the guilty-feeling motions that I'd rather not try to explain right now. The terrible truth is that I very, very rarely write a personal letter these days. By that, I mean the kind of letter that doesn't pertain to something current and unavoidable, questions that *demand* to be answered, money threats, psychic horrors—that sort of thing. I no longer enjoy reading my mail, much less writing it. Every message that comes in here is depressing . . . with extremely rare exceptions, such as last afternoon Bill Kennedy called to say Dial Press had bought his novel. This is the Bill Kennedy from San Juan and Albany, NY. He's one of the best people I know and the novel he sold is a far-

59. Nicholas von Hoffman was a reporter for *The Washington Post.*

expanded version of an unpublished short story I once read; afterwards I was in his living room and told him I thought it was the best thing he'd ever written and that he should push it as far as he could. Which he did . . . so if you see a novel called *The Ink Truck* by Wm. Kennedy on a list next fall, try to buy it. He may have changed the title, but I'll let you know in time to look for the new one.

As for me, I just lost $10,000 when Johnson quit the race. That's one of the contracts I arranged in NY—a quick paperback on LBJ, to appear this summer . . . but two weeks after I signed the contract, he quit, and there went the book. And my income . . . so I agreed to write an article for the *L.A. Times* on Oil Shale, which sounds harmless until you start getting into it, and then it becomes a political and economic atom bomb with ramifications beyond the ken of any normal man. That's what I'm working on right now—trying to make sense of one of the most complicated and politically loaded subjects I've ever encountered. It involves the largest single oil field ever discovered by man—right here in western Colorado, and every oil company in the world is trying to get their hands on it. People who've investigated it in the past have been shot at, threatened, and generally scared off the story. It's the most volatile and high-powered thing I've ever been onto, and my only concern right now is that the *Los Angeles Times* won't print the type of story I'm starting to put together.

So I can't say for certain that you'll ever see the story in print. But until the *Times* pulls me off of it I'll be working on this for the next month or so, at least. I regard this sort of thing as another chapter in my education; at age 50 I'll decide what kind of degree to ask for. At the moment it looks like Mineral Engineering is the best bet; I spent three days in Denver last week at a fiendishly technical conference of oil engineers. Here's a wandering writer who couldn't even pass Algebra at Male High, sitting in on Oil Shale sessions with some of the highest-paid, mathematically-oriented mineral experts in the world. And I have to understand at least enough so that they can't try to talk around me—which they would if they thought I was incapable of dealing with them.

So that's what I'm into right now, and it's totally exhausting. As for other things, I got letters from both Davison and Jim the other day, and the general effect was alarming. Jim wrote to thank me for some small checks and other items I'd sent in lieu of a birthday present . . . and Davison wrote to say that Jim was in serious academic trouble and on the verge of being drafted. I'm not sure how to look at all this; my only flat conviction is that I don't want to see Jim drift into the cannon fodder mill, and especially right now when every life lost in Vietnam is a waste and a mockery of human reason. It's all mechanical now; the talks are getting started and we all know the war's over, in terms of the power struggle, but people will go on being killed right up to the final flag-whistling ceremony. I don't see much point in [him] joining that stupid, tragic list of last-minute casualties, and this is why I've told him he should stay in school at least until the goddamn killing stops, and then he can flunk as spectacularly as he wants to. I don't really think it matters what sort of "record" he compiles at UK, except that he should have enough sense to realize that the alternatives of the moment are far more deadly than the alternatives of six months from now. But of course this is his life, and if he doesn't care enough to understand these things and try to cope with them . . . I know from experience that other people's advice won't make a hair of difference. I don't know Jim well enough, as a person, to try to lay any wisdom on him. Maybe he should come out here for a week or so right after school ends; I could help pay his fare if he couldn't get a car to drive, but I suspect if he wants to come out he'll find a way. I'll help with whatever he suggests.

As for here, things are momentarily good. I have to keep my literary/legal life separate from the daily Woody Creek/Aspen reality . . . which involves a lot of shooting, drinking, talking, and general laziness until everybody else goes to bed and I have to get back to reality and the typewriter and my lawsuits and agents and lawyers and contracts and statistics on Standard N.J. earnings for the past ten years and trying to figure out why they've spent their money on one kind of research instead of another . . . and right now it's 5:10 a.m. and I have to be in Rifle, 120 miles from here, at noon to see a man on this oil shale business, so I'll say goodnight and sign off. Let me know what's happening on that end.

Love,
Hunter

TO CHARLES KURALT, CBS NEWS:

Kuralt had just launched his "On the Road" feature series for CBS News when Thompson began mulling a run for elective office in Pitkin County, Colorado, which was fast filling up with rich weekenders and East Coast exiles—such as disgraced former secretary of defense Robert S. McNamara, whose new condominium in Snowmass Village, a pricey planned community just outside Aspen, had mysteriously burned down a week after he bought it.

May 9, 1968
Woody Creek, CO

Dear Charley . . .

Enclosed is today's issue of the *Aspen Times*. None of it will make any sense to you out of context, but the context, I think, would make a hell of a good TV feature. What's happening in Aspen is a total confrontation between the liberal-Jeffersonian-hermits who more or less colonized the place . . . and the New Breed of planner-developer-builder types as typified by John McBride, who wrote the letter appearing on page 5-C and who also works for the Janss Corp. at Snowmass—the instant city.

At the moment I'm wrapped up in the Oil Shale story, which doesn't have much to do with Aspen at least on the surface, but I've had an article pending with *Harper's* for more than a year, a sort of Aspen Saga, that I'm thinking of re-activating. The story is complicated on paper, but harshly apparent to anyone walking the streets and talking to the actors. It's the sort of thing you'd like, I think—it's the tangible rape of the old dream of "getting away from it all." People who came here 10 years ago to find their own world are now being chased (or bought) out of it by developers from Oakland & LA & Chicago. Yeah, it's the same old story . . . but it's being played out here in very stark and dramatic terms. I think you could define it and lay it out in terms of the camera and words that fit. I could give you enough help to get you started, and I don't figure you'd need any more than that. Actually, you could probably get a pretty quick and accurate word picture of the situation from [Eric] Sevareid. He did a piece last year on Hunter Creek, but that was a long-range abstract sort of thing that would apply to a lot of scenes . . . but since then the Aspen action has come out in the open, with screaming public meetings and court injunctions and physical beatings and a half-mad sheriff who was once a local thug and local architects working for west coast developers who want to build condominiums that will cut off the view of the mountain from the town despite the fact that Aspen's sewage is polluting the river . . . and, jesus, it's too much to try to scratch out in a letter. Ask Sevareid for the general background, but he won't know the current scene because it's just developed. He's a friend of Bob Craig's, who's thinking of running for county commissioner this fall with the idea of getting the rape under control. I told Craig last night that I'm thinking of running for county commissioner myself—to present an alternative as it were, and besides that I think it might be fun. McCarthy got a nice ride out of that alternative thing, and he might even win. I'll be satisfied to make waves, as a candidate or otherwise. I've been running from this plastic shit for years, and now the shitmakers are trying to run me out of Woody Creek and I think it's time to play cornered rat. This is the nut of the story, & also the reason I thought you might like it. Melodramatically yours,

Hunter

TO JIM SILBERMAN, RANDOM HOUSE:

As the epochal 1968 Democratic National Convention drew near, Thompson was eager to secure the best press credentials to cover the scene in Chicago for his prospective book on "The Death of the American Dream."

May 10, 1968
Woody Creek, CO

Dear Jim . . .

I just got the Spring 1968 issue of the *Columbia Journalism Review,* which contains an article ("Find a press seat at the conventions," pg. 24) that gives me every reason to believe that I should get moving on this at once. To wit: I want some sort of press credentials for the Demo convention in Chicago. I covered the '64 GOP thing in SF as part of the *WSJ/Nat. Observer* team, and I know from experience that "press credentials" are largely what you make of them. I was thrown off the floor, for instance, with a valid *Wall St. Journal* floor pass—but when I returned an hour or so later with a stolen Pinkerton badge I was treated like a rich tourist. The same mean freaks who threw me out when I was a journalist welcomed me in the guise of a cop. (I'm still not sure how to evaluate that situation. I got the Pinkerton badge from a mutual friend of [Kentucky Democratic senator] Thruston Morton's son, who (the friend) was hired and fired from the Goldwater[60] palace guard within 24 hours and simply neglected to turn in his badge. But the *WSJ* floor pass, which I came by quite honestly, was virtually useless in terms of realistic access to people on the floor. And not just for me; other *WSJ* staffers had the same sort of troubles . . . and of course there was that scene with John Chancellor [of NBC] being dragged off.)

The point, at any rate, is that I'll be at the convention in connection with the Joint Chiefs project (or the Failure of the Am. Dream, if you prefer), and I'll need at least the facsimile of press credentials to make my way around. The real, honest-injun floor passes are like gold nuggets in press circles, but I think that a letter from you—on your own stationery and in your official capacity—might elicit a Random House floor pass for you or me or anyone else who felt any immediate need for being on the floor. If nothing else, a serious request for a floor pass would probably guarantee a second-level press ticket (which is good for everything on the floor except a reserved seat in the press hole).

But the seat itself is not important except that it commands a ticket that will allow the bearer to pass through the several gates between the public and the action. In other words, a 1-A press ticket at the convention is a pass to the whole action, but even a 4-B press ticket is good in the right hands. The only crucial prerequisite is to have *something*. I think the people who issue these press passes—a semi-sacred oligarchy called "the Standing Committee of Correspondents"—is pretty well aware that a valid press pass, in the hands of a quick-thinking reporter, is not necessarily subject to the restrictions imposed on it by a nervous committee of party press proctors. In other words, I think that any application for a blue-ribbon 1-A press/floor pass will result in some kind of password paper that can be parlayed into a ticket for any necessary purpose. I'm not sure what I'm going to want at this Demo convention, but the one thing I can't do without is an ID card and a valid note for my presence—which is that I'm writing a book for Random House and therefore RH needs a floor-pass.

60. Arizona senator and right-wing 1964 Republican presidential nominee Barry Goldwater had proclaimed that "extremism in the defense of liberty is no vice."

This is true; I could go to Chicago and spend all my time lost in mob scenes unless I have a ticket to the inner circle. I know this is true, on the basis of my experience in 1964. The press ticket is the opener to whatever doors it can breach . . . but without that original press ticket a man looking for answers at a political convention might just as well go to the nearest tavern and watch TV. The opener is the ticket—and that's why I'd be very happy if your secretary could find time to request, in the name of RH, a single press ticket for the convention floor and all other press activities. We might even get it—since it's only a single and the name on the request is Random House—but even if we don't make the elite 1000 I think we'll come off with a functional press ticket.

The first step, of course, is a quite official letter from RH to—I'd guess—the Democratic National Committee, despite the fact that all press requests will end up in the hands of the Standing Committee of Correspondents. But I don't think it would be good form to write them directly, if for no other reason than a deliberate lack of address. They're not looking for mail; it's a power center in the spirit of any Senate Committee . . . and with the same degree of power.

So if you could ask your secretary to apply, through the normal channels, for a Random House press pass at the Demo convention, I think we'll eventually get what I need. According to the *Columbia JRev.*, there are "only about fifty" 1-A floor passes available. But the truth of that figure is lost in the free-substitution ethic that prevails, due to obvious necessity, among the hundreds of press-types at every convention. What I'm trying to avoid here is the necessity of getting in line and begging for the momentary use of somebody else's floor pass. And since I'm relatively certain that RH can root up adequate credentials by means of an executive-type letter, I think that's the easiest way to handle this thing. If *Esquire* can get [junkie novelist] Bill Burroughs accredited, RH shouldn't have any problem with me. Right? Write. And if you have any doubts as to the wisdom of my attending this convention, for christ's sake let me know. I see it as one of the major power struggles of this era, and I want to understand it. So try to get off a note to the Nat. Demo Comm. Tell them that RH has moved to claim its own seat at the Animal Fair.

Thanks . . .
Hunter

. . . ah, shit . . . I just screwed up all my carbons, which happens every time I try to use both sides of a sheet, and that's about once every two years, but Sandy has been screaming at me about "money awareness" these past few days, and this is the goddamn stinking result. I was trying to make a copy for Leon [Friedman] and a carbon for myself.

Anyway, the point of my grumbling about the lack of paperback exposure is that every major book-outlet that's never heard of the H.A. book costs you a nickel for every nickel it costs me. And if Shir-Cliff has sold 650,000 copies at whatever bookmart in Maine he's sending them to, I think it's worth a stab at the national paperback market, or at least five copies to one rack in a major airport. It took me about an hour to search the racks at that huge bookstore in Denver, and after I gave up on finding a copy of *H.A.* I broadened my focus to include *any Ballantine Book*. I worked my way back—all the way back—from the front of the store where people were buying things, to a dingy half-shelf in the rear, about 12 inches from the alley entrance. And there, by Jesus, were six Ballantine Books . . . there was *Flak Over Warsaw,* as I recall somewhat dimly, and *Good Japs Are Dead Japs,* along with four others, all by the same author, [Arizona murderer] Winnie Ruth Judd. So I left that store by the alley entrance. And wrote Shir-Cliff a letter, the sixth in a series . . . and I'm only mentioning this ugly subject to you because I figure you like nickels in large quantity, and that maybe you can prod those people into taking at least a thousand-nickel risk now and then. It might even work . . . right?

Hunter

FROM CAROL HOFFMAN:

Illinois housewife and aspiring author Carol Hoffman so admired Hell's Angels *that she couldn't help but tell its author what she thought of his book.*

May 10, 1968
Tinley Park, Illinois

Mr. Hunter S. Thompson
c/o Random House, Inc.
457 Madison Avenue
New York 22, New York

Dear Mr. Thompson,

First of all, may I compliment you on the excellent job you did in compiling your publication, *Hell's Angels*. I have the book in my personal library and it has been read and re-read for my own enjoyment. Your "associates" still intrigue me.

I am one of the nineteen million bored-to-tears house-wives in this nation! I am married and have three children, two boys, aged 9 years and 6 years. Then I have a charmer of a daughter, twenty months old! I thought I could battle the day to day tedium of my life by writing, so I enrolled in the Fiction Writing Course offered by the Famous Writers' School in Connecticut. Evidently my "creative imagination" has "up and got lost" on me! I was a straight A student in high school and when I received my first two assignments in the mail and found them marked "C," I was bitterly depressed. To me this is as good as failure! I don't accept failure very well! I know your time is very valuable and precious to you, and I also realize that my request is highly irregular for the simple reason that we don't know each other. But for this very reason, I would like to enlist your aid in this project of mine. My utmost intention is to pass this course with flying colors and the flag is at quarter-mast! I am hoping you can give me some general pointers and some moral support. Would you please?

Back to your swingin' Angels!! These fellows sound wild and delirious! I realize there was some danger involved by just being around them, but, speaking for myself and several others I know, I envy you the experience and the fun you must have had with them. You must have had a perpetual ball!! I wouldn't want to wish anyone any bad luck, but I have wondered what the proper, conventional, conforming people in this town would do if your Tiny, Magoo, Terry the Tramp, and Barger were just to cruise down the residential district? Just passing through, so to speak. They would die instant deaths!!!! The people, I mean.

I have only lived here for a year and a half, but I hate this town like rat poison. The Rock Island Railroad transferred my husband here from Des Moines, Iowa. Recently, I made a trip back to my old stomping grounds and I heard through the local grapevine that the Big Gun with the Hell's Angels was in town. There was quite a lengthy story connected with the fellow and his unannounced appearance. But I won't go into that here. Do you know anything that would substantiate such a rumor? Do you ever hear from any of those fellows anymore? Sometimes some firm and lasting friendships develop from experiences like yours.

I know this letter isn't according to Hoyle[61] and that society would frown on my nonconformity. I thought you would like to know that we people do read and yours was the best book I've read in months. Best of luck to you on your future publications.

Hoping to hear from you, I remain,
Sincerely yours,
Mrs. Carol Hoffman

TO STEWART UDALL, U.S. SECRETARY OF THE INTERIOR:

Thompson had read in Newsweek *that Stewart Udall, secretary of the interior through the Kennedy and Johnson administrations, had proposed a government program to hunt down wild horses on federal lands and sell their carcasses for dog food.*

61. Englishman Edmond Hoyle wrote a number of popular eighteenth-century handbooks on the rules of "indoor games."

May 17, 1968
Woody Creek, CO

Stewart Udall
U.S. Dept. of Interior
Washington, D.C.

Dear Mr. Udall:

I thought I'd be calling you this week in connection with a magazine length article on Oil Shale that I'm doing for the *Los Angeles Times.* I've spent the past two weeks dealing with people like J. R. Freeman, John Savage, Russel Cameron, Jim Smith and others, plus numerous phone talks and enough reading to convince me that nothing I might write would be complete until I've talked at some length with you. I'm sure you're aware that you're getting rapped from both sides on this thing . . . and as I see it that's a definite recommendation. Keep in mind that Scott Fitzgerald couldn't spell either. And George Sand[62] had a thing for billygoats . . . so none of us is perfect.

Which brings me to a separate issue, and one that I found myself howling about today with Jim Smith. What in the name of a crippled half-mad jesus are you thinking about with this scheme (according to *Newsweek* 5/13/68) of auctioning off nearly all that herd of mustangs in northern Wyoming for dogfood? If this is the sort of thinking that permeates the Dept. of Interior—as manifested by the sub-human comments of those BLM [Bureau of Land Management] functionaries who worry about the grass these mustangs are eating—then I can't help but wonder if perhaps there is something badly out of focus in the Interior Dept., or at least on that level on which major decisions are supposedly made.

It's a bit of a depressing thing to know that the man who is capable of selling off the last of this country's wild mustangs for dogfood is also the man responsible for coping with the Oil Shale question. I'm sure that connection is as apparent—and as ominous—to you as it is to me. But what I really assume is that *Newsweek* got hold of that story before you did, and that you came up with the obvious solution just as soon as the problem was made known to you. Probably by now you've already decided to move those horses to some other place, right?

Or maybe you own a dogfood factory somewhere on the north edge of Georgia, or . . . well, there's no end of connections in this world, but I guess you know that by now. The link between mustangs and Oil Shale is so weird that it could only be made under these circumstances, and at this accidental time. But as a journalist looking for something to start with—in terms of a point of view on the Oil Shale situation—I can't help but wonder about what sort of man

62. George Sand was the pen name of nineteenth-century French novelist Aurore Dupin Dudevant, who left her husband in favor of liaisons with the likes of poet Alfred de Musset and Polish composer Frédéric Chopin.

would sanction this Final Solution to the Mustang Question. How would that sort of man tend to deal with something as massive and subtle as Oil Shale?

Sincerely,
Hunter S. Thompson

TO ROBERT BONE:

Thompson had gotten to know photojournalist Robert Bone in 1958 when they worked together on upstate New York's Middletown Daily Record *and then at the* San Juan Star. *Bone was now living large in Mallorca.*

May 17, 1968
Woody Creek, CO

Well, Robert, your 5/13 letter was the most cheerful and edifying piece of mail I've had in quite a while. I got back from Denver about 4 a.m. last night, after driving through 5 hours of rain in the valleys and vicious snow/ice in the high country . . . and when I got here there were three pieces of mail: one was from the *L.A. Times,* authorizing $500 (instead of $200) expense money for an article on Oil Shale that I've been doing for a few weeks; another was from my new agent, saying she was appalled at (her carbon of) my letter to the *Times* in which I demanded more expense money, on the weirdest and most bizarre sort of term—(she felt my general attitude would terrify the editor and kill the assignment)—so I just wrote to ask her to ask for an explanation as to how such a letter should have resulted in a 150% boost in expense money and a personal commitment to publish whatever fiendish garbage I finally write. And the nut of my letter was the assurance that I was about to send an article that could not possibly be published in the *L.A. Times*. I said this when they offered me $350 for it, and I said it again when they boosted the price to $500 with $200 expenses; now I'm doing it for $1000 & $500 expenses—and if I'm sure of any one thing in this world, it is that this article I'm writing will never be published in the *Los Angeles Times*. But it's a fantastic subject and I'm learning a lot by bugging right-wing millionaires, which is a hell of a lot of fun for $1500 . . . so what the hell? And so much for all that. It's spring here, and goddamn the snow, but summer will have to come soon and if you can give a fair warning you'll be welcome.

None of which has much to do with my genuinely visceral happiness about your decision to get off to Mallorca and back to the madman's game. But in this case you seem to have some insurance, which is only right in the case of a man who has paid his dues and survived in the total risk league . . . so it's about time you got a few dividends from all that bullshit, and in terms of dividends this job with Fielding sounds like pure gold. Man, $11,000 a year in Spain, with six months of travel and research and a house on Mallorca—I don't see any way you can beat that in this country. The only way to enhance it, I think, would be to write some sort of jangled journalistic log about how it all happened. People like McGarr would buy it in great numbers, because the conventional wisdom these days holds that the sort of life you've been living is no longer possible. Only a lunatic, for instance, would quit an up-mobile job in NY and run off to Brazil for a gig with the Rio Chamber of Commerce . . . and then expect to come back to NY and pick up a job with *Life* . . . and then flee again for a fantasy-style job in/on Mallorca. Christ, you really put the screws to every known theory of how to get by in this world by slowly killing yourself. You've put the lie to all that, and once you get back in the habit of writing for print, you might get a boost out of writing a very understated Bowling Green to NY to Mallorca saga—with huge emphasis on How to Beat the NY Big-Salary-Death-in-Life Syndrome. Shit, you'd sell 50,000 copies in NY alone.

But to hell with all that; it's 4:25 a.m. here and I have to write Stewart Udall to bid my *Hell's Angels* royalties for a herd of wild horses in Montana that are about to be auctioned off for dogfood. I want to top the dogfood bidders and turn the horses loose in some better place—like right behind my house. I have 5 million acres back there. But that's another story for another time, right? I'll let you know what happens.

The question of a Thompson visitation to the Bone castle on Mallorca is already settled—the only question is when, and a good guess at that would be roughly a year from now, when my Joint Chiefs book is due and when, if I ever finish the bastard, I'll probably be willing to give both arms to get out of this country for a mental rest. This is assuming, of course, that the revolution you mention won't rip the country apart in the interim. I think this summer will be a series of horror shows, but I don't see a really revolutionary situation until next year . . . unless maybe Johnson decides to move for a self-draft in Chicago: that could really touch it off. I intend to be there, with a helmet on.

My public works, of late, have been nil. The *N.Y. Times* thing went all to hell when I literally threw it against the wall and let the pieces drift. The *Harper's* piece is hanging, subject to my willingness to leave Woody Creek prior to its publication. My Nixon piece, for *Pageant,* will half-appear in the July issue (or maybe August), but it hardly matters because they cut 15 of my first 20 ms. pages, and then refused to take my name off the shredded remains. I finally gave in and went back to working on my motorcycle. My $10,000 guarantee for a 40,000-word "Fantasy book" on LBJ went down the tube when the bastard ducked out . . . but in some ways that was worth $10,000. Except that now we have Hubert Humphrey. Jesus, keep a room for me over there.

Congratulations on the second womb-child; Sandy's ready for another go in the fall, so I might be up with you on the Kennedy ground-pollution scale. But what the hell again? Keep me posted and see the other side of this page for a further note.

Ciao . . .
HST

TO DAVISON THOMPSON:

Thompson's brother Davison was three years his junior.

May 20, 1968
Woody Creek, CO

Dear D . . .

The delay, this time, is more or less intentional. And pardon the typing, because I can't use my right index finger, which I nearly ripped off two days ago when I wound up and hurled a chunk of wood for Darwin to chase and a jagged piece at the end hooked into my skin and took a piece the size of a dime flying off across the yard. So it's hard to type, and besides that it's about 5:00 a.m. here, so I'm only writing this because I know it's so long overdue and maybe important.

That word "maybe" is of course what we're talking about. The day after your letter arrived, I got one from Jim, thanking me for a small check I'd sent him and talking in general about what he was up to. I mention this only because he wrote his letter about the same time you wrote yours . . . and also because of the contrasting attitudes the two letters conveyed. Yours was easily the more coherent and sensible of the two, and I have to agree with everything you said—including your note about remembering 19 "as a miserable goddamn age." I agree with you 100% on that, but in looking back and trying to recall why I feel that way, all I remember is a year (and more) of bedrock, basic confusion—my first full year out of that Louisville womb and learning far more than my brain could handle in a single year . . . and I'm sure I must have sounded like a fool and a borderline psychotic most of that year, when I talked to people who thought they knew who and where they were at the time . . . but looking back now, I see that if I wasn't Right, at least I wasn't Wrong, and in that context I was forced to learn from my confusion . . . which took awhile, and there's still no proof that what I finally learned was Right, but there's not a hell of a lot of evidence to show that I'm Wrong, either. Which hardly matters—except to say that I'm the last person in the world to give anybody—and especially a brother—a hard time about their "attitude." I agree with you that Jim seems wholly unmotivated right now, but back off for a moment and recall how you felt about going to UK. I remember how I felt; in terms of preference it was 50–50 between UK and volunteering for the draft, which I did on a whim after wrecking Almond Cooke's truck, and when they told me I couldn't be drafted for a month and a half (six weeks, as it were) I went down the hall and joined the AF, where the only hangup was a quick phonecall to Dotson, who vouched for me and made it possible for me to leave 48 hours later. Which sounds fairly horrible, looking back on it . . . but the point is that it seemed pretty reasonable to me at the time, and also that it worked out fairly well because it gave me time to straighten out my own head. And in those terms, I recall age 19 as the year I was most confused and unhappy. That was the year when I thought I should finish my "tour of duty" and go back to some halfass college and get some halfass degree and admit, in fact, that all the people who'd been giving me advice for the past five years were right. But a year later I understood that they were wrong, that they were trying to get me down in the doomsday bag where *they* were, so as to justify their own bad scenes and timid failures . . . and I've never had any reason to believe otherwise.

So I doubt if I'm really the right person to tell Jim that he has some sort of huge obligation to himself and his future and his past, for that matter, to "make his grades" and to "get off probation at UK" and not to "screw up" and all the rest of that bullshit. As far as I'm concerned, his only reason for staying in school is to keep from being drafted, but the situation has changed a bit since we talked at Christmas, and [General Lewis] Hershey's blind stupidity has caught up with him in the form of his decision to draft college grads and first-year grad students instead of high-school grads. This will introduce chaos in all ranks of the army and—along with the Paris/Vietnam talks—return military service to its rightful status as a bad joke. The only problem is that, in the next few months, a lot of draftees are going to be killed and crippled for no reason at all, and that's where Jim has to be careful.

TO ROBERT CRAIG:

Now hunkered down in rustic Woody Creek on land bordering Colorado's vast White River National Forest, Thompson aimed to secure his position at the end of the road.

May 24, 1968
Woody Creek, CO

Robert—

The enclosed letter is one I began just before dawn last night, but it got out of hand and I quit in favor of shooting magpies. The tone of the letter is increasingly weird and outlandish, but since it conveys the spirit of what I was trying to say, I don't see any sense in rewriting it—particularly since I doubt if you'll find time to read it. I will, however, send a copy to George Stranahan, if only because he's rumored to be involved to some extent in the ownership of this property. And if he is, I'd prefer to have him aware of my interest in buying some of it.

You can rest assured that you've made yourself clear as to your lack of eagerness to discuss questions of sale . . . and while I admire your attitude, I'd just as soon avoid the very tangible problems it creates for me. For one, I've been talking with Toby Hess about finishing the basement of the house—a project involving walls, floors, ceilings, etc. and costing several thousand dollars. But I couldn't possibly get into something like this without some kind of assurance that I'll be living here to use the work-rooms I want to create . . . and by "assurance" I mean a lease with an option to renew and/or buy, along with a contingent agreement of some sort regarding financial responsibility for major improvements. You've been entirely reasonable on that score in the past, but the "improvements" I'm thinking of now are too substantial for me to shrug off any prior agreements for payment. No contractor, for instance, is going to come out here and build a $2000 deck around half this huge brown-elephant of a house without knowing exactly who's going to pay for it. The work in the basement will cost at least twice that, so we're talking about fat & ugly bills that I think might disturb you if they came in the mail with no warning.

This is why I keep trying to ask questions about this property; I'm hamstrung in every way, and I'll be damned if I'm going to sit around all summer and let it ride that way. I told you last night in your living room that I could see the "Aspen syndrome" at work in this action, and of course I was right. You assured me I could pick up the survey maps from Scarrow in Glenwood, but it developed that there were/are no survey maps. I asked you at one point about the water rights and you assured me there was no problem, but Morrisey's letter says ". . . you must refuse to warrant title to any water rights. . . ." Meanwhile I'm about to tap the ditch for some irrigation water—on the natural assumption that any land in Woody Creek would have to come with water rights—but after seeing Morrisey's letter I suspect I'll have every landowner from Red Mountain to Basalt on my ass the moment I tap the ditch.

Jesus, the more I write about this thing, the more I come to hate the whole concept of Property Rights. There has to be some reasonable way to deal with them. If you don't want to sell any of these acres—or even if you don't want to sell them to *me*—you could spare us both a lot of trouble by simply saying so. No doubt you could do a lot better by holding the land for five years and then unloading it all to the Levittown crowd. Certainly you can't be blamed for trying to protect yourself in Old Age. Our senior citizens need security, Robert . . . what are pig-farms to the blind, or saw-mills to the deaf? What the old folks want is apple-butter, right? Income. Dollars. Bucks. Take a hint from Billy Sol Estes.[63] Or that freak Gerbaz. Buy a mercury-vapor yard-light on credit, and let inflation pay for it . . . hell, yes. Cultivate a Brazilian sense of humor. Tomorrow, the riots—but today, the mazurka.

Goddamnit, I got sidetracked again. I was talking about a lease and the dim hope of cracking this Aspen syndrome and maybe getting some questions answered. But while we're chipping at the edges of the syndrome I think a malleable lease is the best interim solution. That would be a start, and after running for months in a perfect circle, I'm sort of in the mood for a start—or

63. Billy Sol Estes was at the center of some of the Johnson administration's shadiest financial scandals.

even a finish. I won't expect a reply to any of this because I've gone that route before; but I'll be in touch, and meanwhile, here's the rent. Ciao . . .

Hunter

Robert Craig
Box 1725
Aspen, Colo.

Dear Robert . . .

It was good of you to wave as you passed this afternoon; that plastic bag you ran over when you cut the corner at 65 was your dinner from last night, we were keeping it warm in the sun—in hopes it might tempt you to stop and perhaps point, however vaguely and without committing yourself in any way, to even one corner or line of trees or even a shadow to indicate the limits of this vast property or at least that part of it that doesn't show on the maps your attorney sent me.

As a matter of fact he sent me three maps, all of them decorated with a sort of bastard olde english script and dating, most recently, from the year of Oure Lourde 1917. These are wonderful documents to have and to hold, but I'm sure you understand that they aren't worth a rat's ass to me or anyone else who might be interested in buying some part of this property.

I was particularly pleased with the 1891 map, which seems to prove, beyond any reasonable doubt, that one Frederick Clavet owns the land I'm now living on, and which makes me a trifle nervous about sending you my overdue rent check. It also makes me wonder about Ferdinand Bevy, who seems to own the adjoining land. I trust the "restrictive covenants" you've made with him are a little more stringent than those pertaining to the land in Little Woody, where the enterprising settlers have recently established a pig farm and a commercial sawmill. I think this is wonderful; it's that "creative society" that Butch Clark[64] and [California Republican] Gov. [Ronald] Reagan are talking about. But I don't see much room in it for me, and I'll be goddamned if I want Ferdinand Bevy building a trailer court next to any land I might or might not buy if I could find out where it was and how much it costs.

So that's my problem. And it's compounded, on a daily basis, by the fact that I'm doing a hell of a lot of work on both the house and the grounds—like when you passed today I was finishing that wooden fence that will hopefully discourage these freaks who keep driving in here to ask where they can find the "hunt club" or where to rent a trailer, so I thought I'd close off the entrance—and that's just a small example of the psycho/physical stake I'm building up here. I'm sure you've been made aware of some aspects of this, to wit: the septic tank, the attic insulation, the junk car removal, etc. And next we have the porch, the replacement of some 720 board feet of rotten wood . . . and beyond

64. Ramsey Clark of Texas was U.S. attorney general from 1967 to 1969 and played a key role in civil rights law enforcement.

that the need for some manner of waterproofing or preservative on the house itself, which is degenerating quite visibly after several years of neglect.

There is also the matter of making the bottom half of the house liveable again, after at least two winters (according to Springer's tales) of serving as a sort of giant cesspool. This wretched situation has apparently been cured by the fact of the new septic tank—but it's already flooded once since the tank went in, so I'm still nervous. After nine months of flushing my toilet into my own basement I'm not entirely rational on this point. I kept expecting Juan to come down with typhoid fever, and when that happened I planned to sue you for at least enough money to buy 1000 acres in Montana.

Which brings us back to the original point of all this, which has to do with my frequently-expressed desire to know at least enough about the property I'd like to buy (the small mesa and the Pinion Draw triangle behind the house) to be able to decide whether or not I can afford it . . . and, beyond that, whether or not I can buy enough land in Woody Creek to insulate myself against the rape I think is coming. Whatever restrictions you imposed on the future development of Little Woody would seem to have been drawn up and worded by the purchaser's lawyer if they permit the construction of a commercial saw-mill. Little Woody used to be one of the best little valleys in the world, but right now it's an embryo-horror. I don't see how you can smile at what's happening down there and still talk seriously about "trying to preserve Woody Creek." This question of intent is the one that concerns me most; I'm not about to buy into a giant trailer court, regardless of the profits. When I talk about buying land I'm not thinking in terms of resale value; I'm thinking of a place to live. My income doesn't depend on buying and selling whatever land I can get my hands on to the highest bidder . . . and I'd rather move somewhere else than fall into an orgy like that.

The other side of that coin is the obvious fact that I'm already dug in here, and despite the distance from any literary market I managed to earn some $20,000 last year and unless I get a good money lawyer I'm likely to more than double that this year. One of my problems at the moment, in fact, is how to draw enough money to make a down payment on land in 1968 without being crucified by the tax man. I mention this only to assure you that I'm not talking in wistful, would-be terms when I refer to buying some of this property. Goddamn, if only Hubert[65] were here—I could explain this whole thing in terms of the "finances of joy." I think your man Hubert would know what to do with Woody Creek—sell it all to Butch Clark with a balloon option and a renewable escalator clause to the fifth generation. All water rights to the estate of Martin Bormann, to be held in perpetuity in lieu of gold teeth. Forty pigs and a trailer for every vote, and 200 chickens per year to the cheapest county commissioner. I heard you weren't going to run, by the way . . . so if it looks like another choice between illiterate 10 percenters I'm afraid I'll be forced to offer the vot-

65. Vice President Hubert H. Humphrey would be the Democrats' 1968 presidential nominee.

ers an alternative; my campaign shall consist of a series of lurid improvisations on the theme that "people get the kind of government they deserve." That's a quote from Nelson Eddy,[66] in case you didn't catch it. Or, as [eighteenth-century English writer] Sam Johnson liked to say, "Almost all the absurdity of conduct arises from the imitation of those whom we cannot resemble." And in the words of Alexander Woollcott, "Germany was the cause of Hitler just as much as Chicago is responsible for the *Chicago Tribune*."[67]

That should give you something to think about while you ponder the stark naked reality that the Gerbaz gravel heap is already 1200 feet high, and at 1300 feet it will blot out the afternoon sun. And who, in truth, are the Greedheads?

In any case, I meant to rap off a quick note here, to accompany my rent check, but it seems to have run off the edge. So I think I'll send a copy to Stranahan, along with a photo of the shopping center plans for Trudi's ranch, which seems to be on the market again . . . and several copies of the Woody Creek master plan that Tom Daly helped me draw up; I can't reveal the details except to say that we have a McDonald's golden arch spanning the road above the railroad tracks on the turn to Lenado. And don't worry about your option on that land for a midget golf course on that lot behind Ferris's trailer; Tom wrote it into the plan at Judge Crater's insistence.[68]

Wellllll . . . what else can I say? My rent's paid up, and if you try to evict me out of sheer bile, all I can guarantee is that I'll leave this house in the same shape it was in when I rented it. All the insulation will be in the driveway where HICO left it . . . and, yes, I promise to restore all those pink walls in the bedrooms, and the gravel yard, and the junk cars . . . the Owl Restoration Company has a coast-to-coast reputation, and Woody Creek would be a hell of a place to blow it, right?

TO JIM BELLOWS, *LOS ANGELES TIMES:*

In pitching Oscar Acosta's story on the "brown power" movement to the Los Angeles Times, *Thompson offered smart thoughts of his own on race relations in America.*

May 24, 1968
Woody Creek, CO

Dear Jim . . .

I recently told a friend of mine in LA to give you a ring about the possibility of getting together on a straight/inside etc. "brown power" story. His name is

66. 1930s movie musical star Nelson Eddy died in 1967. It was French writer Joseph de Maistre who said, "Every nation has the government it deserves," in 1811.
67. Critic Alexander Woollcott made the remark at a People's Party rally on January 23, 1943.
68. New York State Supreme Court Justice Joseph Crater disappeared without a trace on August 6, 1930.

Oscar Acosta; he's a Chicano lawyer who's heavily involved in that action and he seems to feel the story gets castrated, somehow, every time the establishment press tries to deal with it. This is why I told him to call you. All I know about "brown power" is what I see now and then in the *Free Press,* and I take their stuff with about three bags of salt to the column. So all I really know about the story is that I'd start with Oscar if I had to get into it. Most people at the core of these color/power movements seem to trade their perspective for their badge, but Oscar has kept his head pretty straight—or at least straight enough to explain the basics of that scene to me on the phone . . . and considering my fear and loathing of the telephone, that's a feat. I can't even deal with Lynn Nesbit on the phone; there is something rude and inhuman about trying to communicate with a piece of black plastic.

Anyway, I told Oscar to give you a ring, on the chance that you might be interested in an intelligent, non-hostile intro to the brown power scene. For my own part I try to avoid any talk of politics and race in my dealings with the pigmented minorities of this country; that sort of talk is a dead-end trip unless you want to convince yourself or sell something . . . but then I'm only a writer. If I were an editor of one of the largest and most influential papers in the country I'd have to consider the implications—however reasonable or otherwise—of the fact that the attitude of the press has become a major factor in the thinking of people who want to tear the country apart. It's a rotten development, I think, but the press has somehow drifted into a mediator's role, and reporters on this scene are more and more forced to think like diplomats in order to get their stories. And by "diplomats" I mean representatives of a foreign govt. Which is why I thought you'd like to talk to Oscar, who understands all this and would like to cut through it.

Sincerely,
Hunter

TO JIM THOMPSON:

At age thirty to his youngest brother's nineteen, Hunter Thompson was a voice of experience for Jim.

May 30, 1968
Woody Creek, CO

Jim . . .

Right after I sealed the enclosed note to you I found your last letter, which I thought I'd lost in the wilds of my desk. Your questions about Tom Dormann and Centre . . . yeah, a lot of colleges have these programs and I've dickered with a few, but the only problem is that once you do "a few" of these gigs, it's like stepping into a beartrap and you can't get out of the next 15 commitments you never made but which have been made for you. The point is that I think I'd enjoy it now and then, but I can't stand the idea of a "speaking tour"—which is what the agencies want from any writer they can sell. I wouldn't mind talking to some people at Centre, but I don't want to haggle about expense money and that sort of thing—so if he's serious, tell him to write my literary agent, Lynn Nesbit, c/o the Marvin Johnson Agcy. 1271 Sixth ave, New York City 20. She protects me from people who want to put me on the road as a traveling freak, and she knows how I feel. Next time I talk to her I'll tell her to make an exception to my normal stance if she hears from anyone who claims to be a friend of my brother. So if Dormann wants to pursue this, it's fine with me.

I got a letter from Mom today that struck me as sort of unnaturally depressing. Gypsy's death, etc. John Ray's[69] death, for unexplained reasons . . . your probation. Yeah. So, with regard to your transferring to any school in Calif, I guess that's out of the question right now. Which is a good thing if you were thinking about the CC Sacramento. Or even SF City. Those are fourth-rate schools, far below UK, and you wouldn't like them at all. San Francisco State is another matter, but any California college or university is financial hell for out-of-staters. They jack up the tuition deliberately, to make room for the ever-increasing tribe of local applicants. I think you're right about getting away from the KY/olde south scene, but you have to be careful about what you trade it in for. Sacramento is no better than Lexington, probably worse. Berkeley or UCLA would be good (John Smith from Louisville is a journalism prof at UCLA and he'll be out here this summer), but if you're on probation at UK your chances of transferring to a better school are pretty slim. I can't tell you in good conscience that your "best bet" is to stay at UK, but at a glance that seems a hell of a lot better than drifting into the army. Remember that deer I shot in Glen Ellen? Remember how it looked after the bullet and the knife? Well that happens to nice all-american boys in Vietnam. Any one of those stinking generals will put you and all your friends in the graveyard or a disabled vets' home, just to take a single hill that won't mean a fucking thing to anybody the day after it's taken. *Avoid that military thing;* that's the best advice I can give you & I know it's not bullshit. This is a tough thing to talk about on paper and I think we'd accomplish a lot more in person. Try to make it out here for a visit. But give a decent warning before you bomb in; I have friends from Calif. here now, and more coming. My temper goes all to hell when the house gets too full. OK . . .

H

TO CAROL HOFFMAN:

Thompson couldn't help but tell Mrs. Hoffman what he thought of her letter.

69. John Ray was Thompson's maternal uncle.

May 31, 1968
Woody Creek, CO

Dear Mrs. Hoffman . . .

You are one of the few people who read my book on the Hell's Angels closely enough to realize that the whole thing was a wonderful rat-fuck and—as you put it—"a perpetual ball." The best part of the action was beating the living shit out of anybody who bugged me. I broke a lot of goddamn faces, just for the hell of it, and usually I had plenty of help because we all stuck together. Terry and Tiny just took off for New York; they stayed here a few days and I gave them your address before they left. They live off the land when they travel, so they need to know places where they can rest and do their thing for a while. They left the coast yesterday after taking me out to the airport. I missed my flight because we got in a fight with some longhair types, but I finally got off. And then that fucking stewardess gave me some shit about my clothes. I punched her around and put some bastard's eye out when he tried to jump in. They busted me in NY and I need money now so I can hire a punk lawyer. Send $500 to me c/o Random House as quick as you can. Terry & Tiny said they'd be here by June 1, but they always get hung up when they travel & if you see them before I do, tell them what happened so they can do something for me. I'm in bad trouble because the editor says I owe them money and won't even give me a goddamn dime. You and Terry and Tiny are the only people I can count on. For christ's sake, do something.

As for that shit-brained writers school, it's a bad hype and a con game and anybody who falls for it deserves whatever happens to them. You must be thick as a goddamn redwood tree to think they'd give you an "A" on the first run. Shit, everybody gets a "C." That way, there's room for improvement, which costs about $500, right? If you give those evil bastards a dime they'll jack you up for the whole thing. You'd be better off sending the money to me. I picked up a fat young boy in Times Square but he's a demanding little bastard & I need a lot of grease for him. This younger generation has gone to the dogs. They're a bunch of communist yellowbellies. Every time I see one I whip on the bastard. I'd like to kick the shit out of somebody right now, for that matter. But my uniform ain't back from the cleaners yet. So I'm naked. Yeah, nothin but crabs between me and whatever I want to hurt. I like it this way. But if you think I'm weird, just wait for Terry and Tiny. They'll show you where it's at, and your friends too, if they want it.

H. "Ratfucker" Thompson

FROM OSCAR ACOSTA:

On June 5, 1968—two months and a day after the assassination of Martin Luther King, Jr.—Senator Robert F. Kennedy was shot in the head in the kitchen of the Ambassador Hotel in Los Angeles on his way to celebrate his victory in California's Democratic presidential primary. He died the next afternoon.

June 6, 1968
Woody Creek, CO

Dear Hunter:

This is a letter in which both the date and the address are significant. Kennedy died today in Los Angeles not far from where I sit. If you saw the event on TV you will recall that the first identification of the suspect was that of a Mexican-American or a Latin-American. The reason being that on that same day the newspapers out here were full of stories related to 13 Mexican-American barrio politicians who had been indicted by the Grand Jury on conspiracy charges, which is a felony, only the previous Friday.

The "conspiracy" related to a prior agreement between these men to disrupt the public schools. You may recall in my last letter, I think sometime in March, I mentioned to you of the high school walkouts, or blowouts, as they are called, that some 10,000 Mexican-American high school students went on strike [over the] inferior educational system. Now it is evident that massive strikes are *not spontaneous* in particular when you are dealing with high school students and serious questions concerning their education. The men in *the groups* that had been talking about it at least since October, 1967, are the people that I mentioned to you that I was working with and have continued to work with, including, *but not limited to,* the militant young chicano group called the Brown Berets of whom you may have read about in *Newsweek;* another group called UMAS, meaning United Mexican American Students, who are a radical group of Mexican-American students in the colleges here in California. Most of the activity centers about the offices of an underground newspaper called *La Raza* edited by Eli Risco, who is a Cuban, and who participated in certain events in Havana prior to Batista's ouster.

Hunter, this letter is rather halting and stilted for two reasons: (1) both my hands are broken and in casts and, if you will recall, I can only write and create on a typewriter; I am not a dictaphone man; (a) because I am chief counsel for the dirty dozen plus 1, or the baker's dozen, as I am referring to the case, I find it difficult to make statements that could be used against my clients. I know you will accuse me of being paranoid, but the fact of the matter is that not only are my telephones bugged but the District Attorney, here in Los Angeles, is out to get me, and it would not surprise me one damn bit were I to be told that an investigator was in fact tailing me. Sounds kind of funny doesn't it? Unfortunately it is true, I haven't written to you about these things primarily because they were small time, that is, local, until this past week-end when the matter got national coverage because of its uniqueness and because it was the last week-end prior to the June primaries here in California. The article I am sending along pretty much tells the story, at least the pertinent facts. The bail was set at $12,500.00 for each of the 13 men. I have to this date gotten the bail reduced to $250.00 for each person with the exception of David Sanchez, Prime Minister of the Brown Berets, whose bail has been set at $1,000.00 because according to the D.A. when they arrested him he attempted to escape. The irony of the matter is that David in fact tried to run out the back door because he had *a date for the senior prom that evening.* He already rented his tuxedo and, he told me after I got him out of jail, that he knew that if the girl were disappointed he'd never be able to make it with her again. They caught him of course along with 4 others, put them in an isolation cell and they immediately went into a hunger strike for three days before I was able to bail them out. I worked on the mass demonstrations and the picketing and the press conferences 20 hours a day for the past six days. I am just about ready to drop dead but it has all been worth it because for the first time the entire southwest is beginning to take notice of what we have been saying for the past year, mainly that the Mexican American is out to get his cut of the apple, *we, too, want a piece of the action.*

An interesting side note to this whole episode is the number of people who have asked to get a share of our apple already. For example: Mrs. McCarthy, the Senator's wife, contributed $8,000.00 to our fund. One of his attorneys appeared in Court Monday morning and approached me and said he had the money for the bail whatever it might be if we wanted it. I turned him down (diplomatically of course) because the people in the barrios were supporting Kennedy, and *although I had no personal interest in either candidate,* I didn't want to in any way offend our people. He still made a water-downed [*sic*] statement of support and did give us the money, so what the hell! Both the Justice Department and the Civil Rights Commission have contacted me and based on my report to them over the telephone they are coming out next week to look into the matter a little more closely. If you can get the tenor of my note, and if by looking at these clippings, you can see that there is a big story here and that there are *only certain people who are privy to the hard facts,* you would be less than the irresponsible hack that you are if you did not at least attempt to follow through on this. Several magazines and newspapers have already approached me for stories. I have turned them down because, as I have indicated above, my hands being in casts I cannot write, and also because I cannot trust them since I do not know them. Even though I am still somewhat pissed at you for that last volley ball game we had in Aspen, I think I would be willing to at least talk with you about an inside story on the whole thing if, but only if, you do not bring [Doberman pinscher] Darwin along with you.

The case is of such importance that I have one of the top lawyers in the Country working for me, namely, A. L. Wirin, of the ACLU, and I have received calls from attorneys in New York, Washington D.C., Texas, San Francisco, all asking to get on the showboat with us; for the first time, unlike the blacks, the militant chicanos have money and publicity on their activities thanks to the foolish political moves of the D.A. [Evelle] Younger and Chief [Thomas] Redding [*sic*] of Los Angeles. I do not yet know what part Mayor [Sam] Yorty had to play in this thing but it is rather evident to any perceptive person that the whole mess, the timing of the Grand Jury indictments, the arrests of the group, was to hurt certain candidates and help other candidates. It is rather significant that Kennedy got the massive number of votes from the Mexican Americans in East Los Angeles, which is to say that the plan, if there was such a plan, backfired! But even if I cannot prove that it was a question of national politics, I am convinced that I will be able to prove that it was politically motivated in so far as the D.A. was concerned, and the continued power of Chief Redding [*sic*] was concerned. On that score there is no question in my mind.

Just one more thing (I don't give a damn if you laugh at me for it), if you call me on this thing on the telephone, whether at my office or at my home, don't expect any direct answers to any specific questions.

And also, I still am planning to go to Aspen and get even with you on that volley ball game, hopefully next month.

Seriously, Hunter, I would like to know very soon if you are interested in this thing, because others are. Although we have some very good writers from within my own group I feel that we are all too directly involved to make any meaningful appraisal of the situation, of the story that needs to be told.

Very truly yours,
Oscar Acosta
Attorney at Law

TO CAROL HOFFMAN:

Thompson's housewife fan from the Midwest had taken to writing him nearly every day.

June 8, 1968
Woody Creek, CO

Dear Mrs. Hoffman . . .

Terry and Tiny got busted for rape in Denver. I'm out of jail and headed for Mexico, where I own a silver mine. Don't send any money; it won't reach me and I don't need it anyway. I appreciate your concern, but your letters are more than I can handle. These are strange and savage times. My condolences to Merle.

Sincerely,
H. S. Thompson

TO MARGARET HARRELL, RANDOM HOUSE:

Thompson looked to his Hell's Angels *copy editor for help dealing with the downside of success.*

June 8, 1968
Woody Creek, CO

Dear M.A. . . .

Somehow the initials seem appropriate, considering this wild heap of garbage I'm sending . . . 867757463544p058$***$@ . . . or which I was in the process of sending 3½ hours ago when I heard a car in the driveway (at 2:30) and now they just left . . . "they" being a guy I barely knew last summer and a girl and a carload of hashish from California—and who showed up here foaming desperate because he'd just heard that the sheriff and federal narco people were waiting for him at his apt. Two hours of wild speculation hiding cars (2) and a little brown bag worth as much as I could make with a best-selling novel. Speed freaks are hard on the nerves—jabbering about heat on the (Sunset) Strip, borrowing shovels to bury the evidence along with $12,000 in small bills. Jesus—summer is coming on again; I can feel the mad vibrations.

Anyway, I want you to mail these two letters for me—from New York—but I thought you'd like to see the background on my letter to Mrs. Hoffman. Notice the dates on her letters; they came like hailstones, one a day, ruining my breakfast. Each one worse than the last, a raving nightmare. I left my final note to her un-sealed, so you can see the end of the saga. At least I hope it's the end . . . and that's why it's crucial that you mail this from NY. I can't allow this woman to find out where I am. So please mail my "off-to-Mexico" note after reading it. The xerox copies are a souvenir for you; they are a stark and terrible example of that secret madness I was talking about in the book. I was talking sort of abstractly when I wrote that stuff, projecting in the sense that I was using a novelist's license for journalism . . . but jesus, it's true. They're out there, and they're real . . . and they're tracking me down. You can't imagine the wild shit that gets forwarded to me via RH. The other letter came in the same mail with one of the Hoffman poems. Show it to Jim, along with my reply suggesting that he contact him (Silberman). Hell, this may be the Great White Southern Dope Novel.

Don't get these things mixed up. All I want you to mail are the two (entirely separate) replies that are already in envelopes. I only left them open so you could read them before mailing. Hang onto the xerox copies and the original Stanford letter. We'll all be involved in a terrible lawsuit if you mail xerox copies of that woman's correspondence back to her. But it struck me as right and necessary that you should see this awful evidence of that syndrome I was talking about. This is really the nut of the whole *Hell's Angels* book . . . jesus, when I read this woman's first letter I thought "No! goddamnit, I can't humor these freaks any longer. . . ." So I wrote what I considered a cruel and final letter. I figured the worst thing I could lay on her was the prospect of a visit by Terry and Tiny, plus a demand for $500.

. . . and you see her reaction. The "rising tide" is worse than I knew; the iceberg is about to flip over and dump all these freaks out of hiding. That stinking arab in Los Angeles:[70] the losers are coming out of their passive cramp; five years from now Sonny Barger will run for president as a moderate. The "new Barger."

Another terrible prospect is that Carol and Shirley will mail me some money and set me up for a mail-fraud bust. She sounds serious about it, and if any money arrives I'll send it to you immediately so you can return it to her with a very rude, severe and wholly impersonal letter . . . saying perhaps that I've been put away somewhere, for my own good, and that any further letters from her will result in the whole file being sent to her husband.

But maybe she'd like that. Her husband must be worse than she is. Where do these people come from? How can they stay alive? Thank god for the American Dream; if it weren't for that I might think these freaks are real. (I have at least fifty letters like that first one; they keep coming, day after day, now that we're into the paperback audience.)

Christ, it's nearly 7:00 & I have to get to bed. Unless I get arrested before noon, I face about six hours of brutal bike-climbing in a few hours. Forcing a motorcycle uphill over logs and snow and rockpiles up to 14,000 feet. For no reason or profit. No sense at all.

Oh yeah . . . Oscar Acosta called yesterday; he asked about you. He's the lawyer for that Brown Beret case in LA. McCarthy gave him $8000 to defray legal costs. And Lee Berry[71] is writing some very good long pieces from Paris for the *Albany Times-Union*. Bill Kennedy sold his novel to Dial and I just finished building a beautiful log fence in Woody Creek. That's the news for now. . . .

H

TO JIM SILBERMAN, RANDOM HOUSE:

Thompson updated his editor on his field research on "The Death of the American Dream."

70. Palestinian Sirhan Bishara Sirhan would be convicted of the June 5, 1968, murder of Senator Robert F. Kennedy in 1969.

71. Lee Berry was a freelance journalist from Albany, New York, who had been introduced to Thompson by their mutual friend William J. Kennedy.

June 9, 1968
Woody Creek, CO

Dear Jim . . .

I'm enclosing a draft of a letter I've been meaning to tone down and rewrite . . . mainly because any rewrite would probably need another "tone job," and that would mean another week on my desk. So read the enclosed for what it is. Selah.

Lynn seems to be handling the foreign rights. I sent her that letter from Penguin that Leon [Friedman] received several weeks ago. Have you sent them anything? I have the impression that *Hell's Angels* bombed terribly in England; somebody sent me *one* tepid review, and that's all I've heard. Except for a constant stream of requests from a freak who calls himself Sir Allan Lane; he keeps sending copies of the paperback edition, with requests that I autograph them for his personal library . . . I signed the first one he sent, but I'll be damned if I'm going to mail any more books to England at $2.50 a crack. Judging from their performance on all fronts, I suspect Penguin's corporate structure was the blueprint for the rape/murder of the British Empire . . . and my concept of "rape" is necessarily conditioned by those cases I treated with in Oakland & points west.

Anyway, Lynn has the Penguin letter, and also a query from a German publisher that Shir-Cliff received last November. At least I assume she has the German query. The wheels of justice, I've discovered, are not the only wheels that grind terrible slow.

. . . And now to the point of this (tonight's) letter. For weeks—nay, months—I've been trying to absorb the fantastic amount of printed matter that fills my box every morning: in addition to three daily papers (the *NY Times,* the *SF Chronicle* & *The Denver Post*) I get about five magazines a day—ranging from *Business Week* to *Open City* to *Human Events* and the *American Rifleman, Time, Newsweek, Life, The Nation, The New Republic* and a regular assortment of flyers for such toys as electric anal stimulators, vibrating plastic penises that "feel like human flesh," and numerous home movies with titles like "Eight Lesbians in a Family-Size Sleeping Bag" . . . yes, that was one I ordered, as I recall, but I have no projector.

Selah, and so much for that. I was trying to say that my mail is driving me mad (I just sent Margaret a mind-boggling sample of the sort of things that come to me, almost daily, via the blithe spirits at the Random House forwarding service. The sequence I sent concerned a crazed housewife in Illinois . . . it's too horrible to explain; you wouldn't believe it unless you read it, anyway. Ask Margaret for that and the other one from the White Southern Dope Fiend . . .). All that keeps me sane is the fact that I can look out my window and see space: sky, mountains, grass, water, horses—and no freaks. If you get a chance you should come out here and see how the non-urban world lives. I'll take you for a ride on my motorcycle.

Anyway, the awful volume of wisdom I'm trying to cope with on this search (or autopsy) inre: the Death of the American Dream has thus far confused me more than it's helped . . . to the extent that I'm losing any hope of a focus, and I think that would be unhealthy. So the idea that came to me tonight took the form of a query letter (a form letter of sorts) to perhaps 30 of the people I might be dealing with in this investigation . . . sort of "Dear Sir, I'm investigating a rumor that somebody killed the American Dream and since the neighbors recently reported screams from your apartment, I thought I'd ask if you might possibly be able to suggest an explanation for these rumors, and perhaps name a few suspects."

I wouldn't presume to *tell* people like George Meany or Tom Kuchel or Doctor Spock or Abe Fortas or Thruston Morton or Cassius Clay or Hugh Hefner[72] or my cattle-ranching neighbors or a dope freak in Malibu . . . that the American Dream is *dead* . . . nor would I want to suggest this to [U.S. commander in Vietnam General William C.] Westmoreland or Roosevelt Watkins. But I think if all these people were forced to confront the *rumor*—which they could then either deny, ignore, explain or confirm—I think I might put the answers and comments together and derive a pretty good notion of where to start looking for the killers. I also think the replies would amount to a good *Esquire*-type article that couldn't do the book any harm if it appeared prior to publication.

So the next steps would appear to be these: 1) For you to send me about 200 sheets of valid RH stationery with about 400 matching second sheets, 2) for you to suggest any and all names who might prove out in terms of suspects or leads to suspects, and 3) for me to draft the query, which I'd assume you'd want to see, since nine-tenths of its effectiveness will derive from the RH letterhead. Let's not kid ourselves about George Meany's reaction to a vaguely unsettling letter about the Death of the American Dream if it comes from an Owl Farm in Woody Creek, Colo. But I think Meany would feel compelled to answer a very formal, cleanly-typed, discreetly worded yet urgently-toned letter on this subject if it came from Random House. Needless to say, we'd have to include a murky hint that failure to reply will be interpreted as lack of interest on this subject, and duly noted when the returns are *published*. Let's make the bastards answer: 1) Is the American Dream still pertinent? 2) If so, how does it apply inre: The War in Vietnam? The U.S. Balance of Payment? Andy Warhol?[73] The Politics of Joy? The editorial policies of *The New York Times*? Ed Sullivan?[74] . . . (the composition of the query would amount to an

72. George Meany was president of the AFL-CIO; Tom Kuchel a U.S. senator from California; Dr. Benjamin Spock the author of *The Common Sense Book of Baby and Child Care;* Abe Fortas a U.S. Supreme Court justice; Cassius Clay the heavyweight boxing champion who would change his name to Muhammad Ali, and Hugh Hefner the publisher of *Playboy* magazine.

73. New York pop artist Andy Warhol was celebrated in the 1960s for his paintings of Campbell's soup cans, silkscreens of Marilyn Monroe, and excruciating "experimental films."

74. Ed Sullivan hosted a popular TV variety show aired by CBS on Sunday nights from 1948 through 1971.

outline of the book . . . and the answers, I think, would provide a tangible framework for my research . . .).

TO NICK RUWE, NIXON PRESIDENTIAL CAMPAIGN:

Nick Ruwe—a midlevel Nixon advance man and associate at the New York law firm of Nixon, Mudge, Rose, Guthrie, Alexander, and Mitchell—had done what he could to gain Thompson access to the candidate and senior campaign staff for his Pageant *article. Ideologies aside, Thompson clearly respected Ruwe's professionalism.*

June 10, 1968
Woody Creek, CO

Nick Ruwe
c/o Nixon Presidential Campaign
Nixon–Mudge
20 Broad St., NYC

Dear Nick,

My long-delayed and oft-scrambled *Pageant* article finally appeared in the July issue, for good or ill . . . (or, as *Pageant* seems to prefer, ". . . either for good or for ill"). If you find time to read it, keep several points in mind: 1) My assignment, very specifically, was to go to N.H. and do a hatchet job on Nixon; my original subject was Billy Graham, but he came down with viral pneumonia last winter, and the editors finally substituted Nixon. So it was simply a question of where to aim me, and your boy won by default . . . 2) I submitted around 45 triple-spaced pages, most of them dealing with backstage, mechanical, seemingly trivial stuff—and 15 of the first 20 of these pages were deleted by the editors; this is sort of like trying to race an 8-cylinder car on 4 sparkplugs . . . and, 3) My central emphasis, once I got to Manchester, was more and more focused on the silent (or at least unpublicized) mechanics of the campaign, rather than the straight "Tricky Dick" article I'd been sent there to write. The comment that interested me most, in the course of that 10-day gig, was something you said one late night as we dealt with the Old Crow jug. . . . I don't feel like rooting through my notebooks to find it, but one phrase I remember distinctly was: ". . . it makes everything else I've done seem pretty dull." The "it," of course, referred to your work as an advance man in a major political campaign. In one of my drafts I took off on this and worked up a long and complicated analogy comparing advance men to horse-trainers and fight managers . . . and I still think it was the most interesting angle I tried to develop, despite the fact that nearly all of it was chopped out for "space reasons." The only example that appeared in print, as I recall, was your explanation of why Nixon stayed at the Holiday Inn, rather than the Wayfarer.

All this came back to me vividly a few moments ago when I read in *Newsweek* that one of [Robert] Kennedy's advance men, Jerry Bruno, looked out at the crowd that had come to see Kennedy's body off at the L.A. airport and said something like, "He would have liked this crowd." I wouldn't have recognized that thinking without the context, in memory, of some of your observations in Manchester. But, given that context, I recognized Bruno at once for an 18-carat gold advance man.

All of which reminds me of another thing you said: that somebody whose name I forget (but I have a *Boston Globe* article by him somewhere in my file) wrote a novel (?) called *The Advance Men* . . . which couldn't be published because none of the subjects would sign a release.

Jesus, that sounds odd, now that I see it in print. Was it a novel? If so, he must have been a piss-poor writer if he needed releases to get the thing published. But then Thomas Wolfe[75] had that sort of trouble, so . . . I'd give it more thought if I considered it relevant, but I don't.

The point is that Bruno's remark revived my interest in the subject of advance men. I recall a story one of Nixon's staffers told about getting accidentally booked into Kennedy's St. Louis suite (or bloc) in 1960, because he had an Irish name and the room-clerk assumed that any sinister-looking east-coast type with an Irish name was with Kennedy. And your story about the [Chamber of Commerce] freak in Nashua who gave you the "you, buster," routine when you were trying to set up that dinner.

And I keep wondering how [Nixon campaign press aide] Henry Hyde got into the act . . . but I guess that gets away from the subject of advance men; I only mention it because I had a beautiful (and deleted) sequence in the article, a fantasy version of Henry's call to *Pageant* . . . but, what the hell. . . .

And back to the point. Which is, in a nut, that I might like to do a quick book on advance men—their relevance, realities, raison d'etre, backgrounds, etc. It's the only critical profession that I know of (or at least the only one that interests me) that almost nobody has ever heard of. Beyond politicians and political reporters, how many people even know that advance men exist?

The other side of that question is the problem of writing and publishing even an article—much less a book—on the subject, without getting involved in a gaggle of lawsuits, arguments, bullshit, etc. Given that probability, my style of research would be pretty useless, and I've never had much use for the Ben Hecht[76] style. That's the TV/showbiz/*Front Page* act . . . but I prefer the sort of "thinking out loud" scene, in fairly congenial circumstances and a long-range mutual interest . . . and on this score I don't think I can be faulted on my per-

75. Thomas Wolfe was the author of *Look Homeward, Angel* and other richly descriptive novels of the 1920s and '30s.

76. Ben Hecht was a newspaper reporter who switched in the 1930s to writing plays and movie scripts characterized by snappy dialogue.

formance in N.H., or even in what I wrote. One of the scenes deleted from my piece was my first encounter with Pat Buchanan (about 30 minutes before I met you), and his very visible and verbal reaction to me was so consistent with what I expected that it took me several days to cool off and realize that my real interest was less in Nixon and more in the mechanics of his (or any presidential) campaign. And my only serious bitch about the article is that it doesn't reflect this interest except by accident. You can't lose 15 of your first 20 pages and still say what you mean; you don't necessarily lose the *sense* of what you mean, but without the details you cripple both the context and the evidence.

And so much for that. I wouldn't want you to misinterpret any of this. If I didn't make it clear in the article, let me say again and now that I went to N.H. with the idea that Richard Nixon was a monster . . . and although I left N.H. with a strange affection for the man, *as a man* . . . I still tremble at the prospect of "President Nixon." He is the unlucky personification of all the root problems that I'm beginning to suspect are going to croak us very shortly. He doesn't realize this, and I think if he did he would want to be something else . . . but he's not, and he can't be. And I wouldn't be writing this sort of thing in a personal letter if I honestly thought it would offend you. Nor would I expect you to agree with me . . . which is more or less beside the point if we're talking about advance men (and I'm not looking for agreement on that score, either).

Jesus . . . this is tricky ground. I just wanted to assure you that I wasn't apologizing for anything I said about Nixon. My interest—and my reason for writing this letter—is beyond any specific candidate in any specific election. I'm interested in *Why Advance Men Are Necessary.* This sounds naive, and especially to you, but in this context your opinions don't matter. You *know* why you're necessary because you've been there, time and time again. And it's as obvious to me as it is to you that a candidate's chances of winning any election are massively influenced by his selection of advance men. I tried to make this point in the article, but I doubt if it came through.

I believe it, and on this point I think you might even admit that you agree. So, I suppose, in closing, that I should pose a tangible question and perhaps a possibility. So: the question—How feasible is the prospect of a *non-fiction* book on advance men? Given your experience with me and my research style, do you think I could get close enough to the reality of the thing to do an honest (short) book or even an article? That's the question. The "possibility" has to do with the fact that I'm momentarily in a position to write a book on almost anything; I assure you I'm not talking pie in the sky. Heh. So let me know what you think—by return mail if possible. And thanks again for the help in New Hampshire. Sincerely,

Hunter S. Thompson

TO OSCAR ACOSTA:

June 17, 1968
Woody Creek, CO

Oscar . . .

Thanks for the letter; I sent it, along with a brief note, to the *NYTimes* magazine, where my name is often cursed. If nothing else, it should result in a call, fairly soon, from a *NYTimes* news staffer, requesting an interview with you. And it might even result in my being sent out there to write something. I frankly doubt it, but if it happens I wouldn't want you to assume that I'd approach it from any point of view except my own—which is now non-existent. Let's keep that in mind, in case it ever becomes necessary to apply it.

How did the talk with [Jim] Bellows go? I'm curious. Call if you can, or send comments. I'm about to hit him with a terrible scandal-laden twist in this Oil Shale thing, and I'd like to know what you thought of him.

And what of [Eugene] McGarr? Whose wife, sister, mother, daughter, friend, etc. is he fucking or chasing these days? Let me know if he shows any signs of getting over that sickness, and I'll write him a decent letter. OK . . . I'll let you know when I hear from the *Times*.

Ciao . . .
Hunter

TO CHARLES KURALT, CBS NEWS:

Kuralt had asked Thompson to write a dust-jacket blurb for his new book about visiting the North Pole, To the Top of the World. *What he got instead was two pages of crazed insults and jokes, which Kuralt understandably failed to appreciate.*

June 20, 1968
Woody Creek, CO

Charley . . .

Maybe I should re-examine my sense of humor . . . did your editor Kroll show you my second, explanatory letter? I don't really blame you for the cavities in my teeth. Christ, I figured they wanted about 2 lines for the jacket, so I sent a wide selection. What do you mean: ". . . the book is doing ok, anyway"?

But what the hell? I've almost given up trying to communicate on any level; my efforts these days are purely physical: building huge fences, digging water ditches, hammering, sawing, growing things, etc. The country seems doomed and I'm not sure yet what to say about it. Or do. The Random House book is a start, but in the meantime I think I might run for County Commissioner this year, if only to gain a momentary forum & hold up a mirror to the town. At the moment there's only one candidate and most people seem satisfied to keep it that way, but rather than see the Olde West drift into Communistic electoral patterns, I think I'd have to make the race myself. The Aspen story is still bubbling, and getting worse. Right now the Fear Trip concerns the several thousand hippies who gathered last week in Boulder to witness the end of the world—but who've been so badly hassled by vigilante groups over there that they announced a move, en masse, to Aspen. This has put the locals in a swivet. The sheriff is running around trying to deputize all the unemployable thugs in town & the county commissioners have scheduled an emergency meeting to consider methods of beating back the tide. This morning, according to bulletins, a vanguard of some 25 hippies was sighted on Independence Pass, trudging downhill toward the town. They were said to be burdened with backpacks & signs saying, "California, Big Sur." The populace is bracing for the worst.

If the above sounds like an exaggeration, I urge you to ponder the enclosed clipping from today's *Aspen Times.* Guido is a Swiss nazi, a local restaurant owner who has a sign in the window of his establishment saying, "No Beatniks Allowed." . . . and he's also the local magistrate (which amounts to the municipal judge) . . . can you imagine the scenes that develop with this sort of freak in a town full of vagrant hippies? Read the letter; it's an application to an asylum.

Anyway, I'll be looking for you in August. I'll be in and out of town, so give a bit of warning when you know your schedule. But I suspect I'll be here around then—in a death-battle with the local nazis and greedheads. I'd like to run for the Senate, but that won't work, so I guess I'll start at the bottom and maybe take a few of them with me on my way out.

Ciao . . .
Hunter

TO JIM SILBERMAN, RANDOM HOUSE:

With the Democratic National Convention nine and a half weeks away, Thompson tried again to make sure he would have the right press credentials to cover the proceedings the way he wanted.

June 20, 1968
Woody Creek, CO

Dear Jim . . .

I have about three letters to you sitting here on my desk, but they're all so goddamn involved that I can't resolve them enough to sign them and send them off. All kinds of wild rambling. I'll do some chopping and send you the bundle in a day or so.

In the meantime, however, I want to assure you that I'm counting on whatever action you've initiated to get me on all the right lists for the Democratic convention in Chicago. I'm not sure what you're doing, but I hope your DC contacts are worthy. I'm planning on going, but it's absolutely crucial that I have the proper credentials. Without them, I might as well watch the show on TV. My experience in SF at the '64 GOP thing convinced me of the value of a "proper pass"—and I suspect the security at Chicago will be so tight that even accredited people will be harassed.

It also occurs to me that a first-hand comparison between the GOP convention and the Demo thing might be interesting in light of what we're after—especially with these settings: the middle of Chicago vs. the beaches of Florida. I see a far-reaching symbolism in the contrast—maybe surface, but maybe not. I think a detailed comparison of the *people* at both conventions might be instructive. Given the candidates and their backgrounds, it seems particularly fitting that Nixon should launch from Miami and Hubert from Chicago. In '64, for instance, neither candidate had any psychic identification with the convention cities—Goldwater in SF? Lyndon in Atlantic City? But this time it meshes. Nixon's Miami is down there in the Old People's Belt, a long way from Whittier,[77] but still the same scene. And Humphrey in Chicago is almost melodramatic—down there in the stockyards, giving drugs to the cows before they get whacked in the head. City of broad shoulders . . . and deeper corruption: "Take this liberal aspirin, dear . . . it's stronger than pain."

What I'm saying is I think I should take in *both* conventions—to find the details in the contrast between Republicans and Democrats in their most shameless public moments, and their chosen backdrops.

If nothing else, we could probably sell this contrast idea as an article—it goes beyond the notion of a specific commentary on a specific thing, so even if all the candidates are murdered between now and convention time, the comparison will still be valid. Neither Miami nor Chicago nor any of the delegates will change, regardless of who gets killed en route.

I suppose—or assume—that your DC contact is equally at home with both Parties, in terms of arranging press accommodations for a Random House author. If not, let me know. We don't have much time, and there's going to be a hell of a press list. The more I think about the idea of comparing the physical reality of these two conventions, the better I like it. And unless I hear from you to the contrary, I'll assume you'll handle the credentials problem in your own style.

I'll send the other stuff as soon as possible, but this credentials aspect is the only rush item on the list.

Thanks,
Hunter

77. Richard Nixon grew up in Whittier, California, a small town thirty miles southeast of Los Angeles.

TO BILL CARDOSO, *THE BOSTON GLOBE:*

Boston Globe *political reporter Bill Cardoso had introduced himself to Thompson on the Nixon press bus in New Hampshire by saying, "Hey, you're the cat who wrote the* Hell's Angels *book." They shared a joint, and a bond was struck.*

June 20, 1968
Woody Creek, CO

Bill . . .

For christ's sake, do me and every other ill-dressed journalist in the world a huge favor, and don't get busted for holding. If a *Boston Globe* reporter goes down for holding on the job, there'll be such a vicious outcry against the "drug-maddened press" that free-lancers like me—who look a bit strange anyway—will be locked up on sight. And besides that, if you ever got busted for holding on the job, you'd be screwed forever in terms of newspaper jobs. You could do almost anything else—punch Nixon in the face while slobberingly drunk at a TV press conference, abuse small children behind bushes in public parks—most editors would giggle at stuff like that . . . but man, once your byline became associated with "dope," you'd be doomed. Beware—for your sake and mine; getting stories without wearing a tie is hard enough already.

Your scene at Laconia sounds a bit like mine at Bass Lake with the Angels—a fear trip, never knowing which direction you'd be hit or busted from. Horrible; I've never been able to read my own book because of those hideous scenes; my memory is still too clear . . . I read a sentence or two and suddenly it's all real again. I like the *Spider* poem ["Collect Telegram from a Mad Dog," October 13, 1965] much better than the book; as a matter of fact I like it better than anything I've written. Did I send you the original? If so, please send it back and I'll send you two copies. At one point I had ten originals, but they're all gone. If you have one, I need it for my secret head.

The *Pageant* thing is the lead article for July, but they cut about half of what I sent, including 15 of the first 20 pages. We had a terrible scene about it—that's why it's a month late and also why I no longer communicate in any way with *Pageant*. They fucked it up so badly that I first asked them to take my name off of it & when they wouldn't do that I sent a long "author's note," but they wouldn't run that either. So I told them to fuck off, and that's the way it ended.

Christ, I wish you'd made the gig as McCarthy's press secy. I'd have immediately joined the press camp. On that end, I'm definitely planning to make the Demo freak-out in Chicago. You should tell the *Globe* that you have special contacts in the underground delegation, which will enable you to get the "rebellious elements" story that no straight reporter can get close to. There's a lot of hell and disruption planned—like blocking the freeway with garbage & that sort of thing. As far as I know, Random House is getting me press credentials, etc., and probably a hotel room—which you're welcome to use if it comes with two beds. I don't know what they're doing for me on that end . . . but you'd be better off doing it through the *Globe* & getting on all the right lists, etc. Otherwise, it's hell; I went through that ticket-sharing scene in San Francisco at the '64 GOP convention, and it wasn't a real winner. I never had the right ticket for where I wanted to be, or if I had the right ticket I didn't have the right ID to match it.

Anyway, I could probably put you in touch with enough of the strange action to justify any pitch you make to the *Globe* on that basis. They can't lose much by sending you—nobody's going to be reading stories out of Concord during that time, anyway, so you'd be potentially more valuable in Chicago than sitting around home. Why not? It's going to be a very weird show, with a lot of good offbeat stories hanging around, even if Hubert H. Humphrey has it fixed from the start. As a matter of fact, the more obvious the fix, the more certain the action. The mean freaks will be quiet as long as McCarthy has a chance, but if he's obviously out of it they'll do everything they can to embarrass Humphrey.

Life here is decent, peaceful and entirely unproductive. I do a lot of physical work, but not much writing. I'm going broke, though, so I have to get back to the words. I see a bad and ugly time coming up, so I guess I'd better write before they lock me up. A Nixon-Humphrey election will set the scene for a total showdown. McCarthy is the last dim hope for a peaceful solution. If I were you I'd get your passport up-dated and ready.

Let me know about Chicago. And don't get busted.

Ciao . . .
Hunter

TO JIM SILBERMAN, RANDOM HOUSE:

July 7, 1968
Woody Creek, CO

Dear Jim . . .

How does it feel to write a letter asking *me* for something? Weird, eh? I guess it's that $5000. Or maybe you're getting mellow in your old age, after all those power struggles. . . .

Anyway, thanks for the letter. I appreciate the interest—and also the new (old) twist. Your notion about "Violence in America" reminds me of something Bernard something-or-other at Ballantine—that fellow who owes me $25,000 and won't answer his phone—anyway, he once mentioned a book on "Violence in America." But that gave way to "The Johnson File," and then he quit and a lot of people were killed . . . and I got so busy clipping articles relating to the death of the American Dream that I couldn't think anymore.

You can't believe the amount of garbage that comes in my mailbox every day. Try *Human Events*[78] for a month or two; it'll send you into the streets with a grease-gun. I had to buy three 14′ shelves, at $1 a board foot, to file all this garbage. Sandy works day and night to file all the clippings I mark in *The New York Times,* the *San Francisco Chronicle* and *The Denver Post*—and I spend all my time speed-reading. My only amusement these days is the wild, atavistic behavior of Howard Hughes. He's the only real freak still on his feet and wailing.[79]

Which is neither here nor there. Your suggested focus on Violence, or Violent People, may be the sky-hook I need to pull me out of this mire of information. Maybe the only way to get at the vitals of the American Dream is to come at it crab-wise . . . focus down close on something specific, then slam the enemy in the balls from some wholly unexpected vantage point.

We're still talking about the same book, and of course we always were . . . but perhaps your notion of narrowing the focus might save my head. Actually, I hadn't realized what a savage, stupid and dissolute nation this is until I began to clip every article that related to the death of the American Dream. The idea of moving to British Columbia has crossed my mind more than once in the past few months.

Other than that, I've been thinking about getting some sort of money statement out of Ballantine—so I can make some kind of agreement about buying this land I'm living on, and get that out of the way—and I've also been wondering if I traded a meal at that restaurant full of rubber plants for $7,500 worth of expense money on the new contract. I say this because of the seven-month time-lag on reimbursement for my NY hotel bill and half my plane fare RT from Aspen. It was, as I recall, $425, plus $150, in that order. Those bills were submitted in January—on Leon's advice—and it's now July. This strikes me as ominous, and makes me very leery of incurring any other out-of-pocket expenses. If that $7,500 "expense money" part of the contract is a joke, I'll be fucked if it's going to cost me any more than it already has. If the joke is on me, I intend to keep it cheap. Selah.

Well . . . pardon that outburst. I meant this to be a friendly letter. I still have to finish off that thing on oil shale. Jesus, what a fantastic subject. It's dull as hell until you realize that these bastards are playing a huge and vicious chess game for literally billions of dollars. I just came back from a chat with a fellow who interrupted one of our earlier talks to take a phone call from "Raddy."

78. *Human Events* is a right-wing social policy journal.

79. In 1968 the U.S. Justice Department's investigation into possible antitrust violations led eccentric billionaire industrialist Howard Hughes to withdraw his offer to buy a fourth gambling casino in Las Vegas.

Admiral Radford,[80] as it were—calling, no doubt, from his semi-private ward in the Old Sailors' Home in Butte.

I get the same sort of feeling in dealing with these mean fuckers as I did with the Angels . . . it's mainline adrenaline, out there on the edge where you can't make the slightest mistake. I've had two sessions with the fellow I talked to today; a few weeks ago he got me off balance when my tape recorder failed and he never let me up . . . but today I wailed on him, no mercy at all, and he blew it completely. It wasn't entirely fair, because I wrote all my questions down last night, and then came to him today after four hours at the motorcycle races . . . the music today was a whipsong, so forgive any echoes that might seem to sing in this letter.

Another subject: the conventions. I can't understand why my press credentials should be subject to the weird, neo-Crumpian politics of East Coast publishing. Why in hell should Random House put the "granting" of convention press credentials on the level of personal favors? I sent you the name of that press committee; all you had to do was send in my name on a Random House letterhead. I can't do it on Owl Farm stationery. What the hell are you thinking about? Those bastards aren't doing me any favor by "allowing" me to see them in action; candidates don't hire press buses because they feel sorry for reporters who would otherwise have to rent cars. And Theodore White's books have made these freaks think twice about brushing off writers. I showed up at Nixon's New Hampshire hq. looking like a refugee from the Final Midnight Mine—with no credentials except my casual word that I was writing something for *Pageant* magazine—and despite my ratbastard garb and cruel comments on the candidate (to his staffers) I was soon granted a private audience and a lengthy, free-wheeling interview that was so obviously an indulgence that it caused a lot of bitching among the other reporters in camp.

And all that for *Pageant*. So why should Random House consider press credentials a favor? Just send a note to the Demo and GOP national committees (at this stage) and tell them what we need—ACCESS, no favors, no free meals, just freedom from harassment. And, as I've said, my experience at the '64 GOP convention in SF (with a *Wall Street Journal* pass) convinced me beyond any shadow of a doubt that CREDENTIALS are necessary, at least for openers. Without a press ticket, you might as well watch TV.

The most obvious hangnail, at this point, has to do with the relevance of my presence at the conventions to a book on The Violent People. I'd prefer to think that I need not try to explain this . . . conventions are the twin orgasms of the American political process, the sperm ceremonies, the conception of the champion and the anti-champion. You can't talk about the NRA or surfers or hotrodders without putting them in the context of the political ceremonies that

80. U.S. Navy admiral Arthur W. Radford, chairman of the Joint Chiefs of Staff from 1953 through 1957, had advocated using massive American force in Vietnam as early as 1954.

eventually inflict the hotrodder mentality on a rice-farmer in the Mekong Delta. Remember those 40′ high mug shots of Lyndon in Atlantic City? He was the Peace Candidate, right?

I guess we should deal with this on the phone, but in the meantime, for christ's sakes disabuse yourself of the idea that a major publisher should have to ask a gang of hyenas for the privilege of watching their candidate in action. Fuck them. Without the press, nobody's candidate would ever get beyond New Hampshire. And I'm all in favor of that; the primaries are a corruption of everything that might be possible in politics.

Well . . . I seem to have gone out of control here, and, as always, it's late. It's always late when I write letters. I just read over what I've said in this one and it occurs to me that it doesn't sound as Friendly Ho-Ho as I meant it to be. That's a language problem. I'm trying to be nice, Jim . . . but it's hard.

Anyway, I'll try to call sometime soon on the Violence focus. Or maybe you should call here. If it's up to me, I'll put it off as long as I can. Life is too pleasant here . . . and that, I suspect, is the hangup. But then you and every other editor would be on the breadline if all writers were happy and in good shape, right? So bear with me; it can't last. I'll be miserable soon, and I'll write you a money-song. Ciao . . .

Hunter

TO LYNN NESBIT:

Thompson's agent, Lynn Nesbit, had proposed an article by him to Esquire *magazine.*

July 15, 1968
Woody Creek, CO

Dear Lynn . . .

Thanks for the *Esq*/NRA possibility. It came just as I was about to resign my NRA membership with a vicious letter. Actually, I just joined and I haven't paid yet, so they've been dunning me. Between the NRA, *Human Events* and the *Conservative Book Club,* I've been taking a real beating in the mails. I thought I'd subscribe to all these things, as part of the AmDream research, but it's driven me to a near-suicidal depression. These swine should be . . . well, ah . . . this may sound funny, but . . . yes . . . I think they should be . . . KILLED!

Anyway, I like the idea of a chat with the NRA. I'm not sure what [*Esquire* managing editor Don] Erickson wants, but one aspect that interests me is what the NRA does with all that money. Dues are $5 a year, and with 900,000 members, that adds up . . . and all you get for your $5 is 12 issues of the *American Rifleman,* one of the dullest and least informative screeds in the history of printing. Members are also offered the opportunity to buy NRA tie-clips and

Zippo lighters at retail-plus. I once bought a set of glasses from them at some brutally inflated price, and the NRA emblem flaked off the first time I put the glasses in hot water.

Maybe a good angle would be something like "Why I Quit the NRA," . . . by A. Gunn Freake. The thrust of the thing could be that the NRA is a hype, that they're using their 900,000 members, rather than representing them. I own about a dozen guns, but as far as I'm concerned the NRA is blowing my gig. That waterhead president (Orth?) doesn't speak for *me*. So, speaking as a badlands gun freak, I have to wonder what they're doing with my $5. I don't read their magazine, I don't have access to "military ammo," I don't get weapons at a discount . . . all I get is a lot of stupid grumbling about maintaining an armed militia, or something like that. They send me form letters that I'm supposed to sign, or rewrite, and forward to my congressman. Fuck them. "My congressman" is a senile bag of pus and he agrees with the NRA, anyway.

*The question is, "Who does the NRA really represent?"

This leads to other twisted questions . . . like, who does Tom Dodd[81] represent? I'm not sure what he's pushing just now, but at one point he was trying to ban all mail-order gun sales. One of the facts of the gun business is that 99.9% of all guns bought by mail are foreign guns. Mail-order guns are bargains, they're cheap. They have to be, or nobody would buy them sight-unseen with payment in advance. American-made guns are available in sporting goods stores, gunshops, drugstores, etc., and always at fair-trade prices. No discounts, no bargains. So the availability of cheap foreign guns cuts into the "buy American" market, and Connecticut is the capital of the U.S. commercial arms industry. The 1967 *Gun Digest* contains a comprehensive "directory of the arms trade." Thirty-six companies are listed under the heading of "GUNS, U.S. made." Eleven of these are in Conn., four are in Mass. (Smith & Wesson, Savage, Iver Johnson and Harrington & Richardson). The other seven (of the top 11) are in Conn. (Winchester, Sturm-Ruger, Remington, Mossberg, Marlin, High Standard and Colt).

The *Digest* has another heading for "GUNS, foreign." Fifty-one companies are listed, and not one is in Conn. The only Mass. entry is Savage, which appears on both lists because the bulk of the guns sold by Savage (as "U.S. made") are made in Europe. Winchester should also have appeared on the "foreign" list; all their rifles, since 1964, have been made in Japan. This has caused them such trouble in the marketplace that my well-used 1960 Winches-

* —& how many of those 900,000 members really support the wild-eyed bullshit that spews out of NRA hq.?

81. Democratic U.S. senator and gun-control advocate Thomas Dodd of Connecticut had been censured by the Senate in 1967 for misuse of funds.

ter rifle is now worth more than I paid for it, new, eight years ago. The new Winchesters won't sell.

Christ, this is beginning to sound like Oil Shale. Why does the president of Rumble Oil agree with John Galbraith? Why does Tom Dodd, the senator for the gunpowder state, want to ban mail-order gun sales? How does the NRA feel about Dodd—who represents Winchester, Remington, Colt, etc.? Or does he? Bangor Punta, a huge cartel, controls Olin Mathiesen, which in turn owns Winchester-Western. Jesus . . . These swine should be killed.

Somewhere in that factual outburst I lost my original point—which was, as I recall, that maybe the NRA is conning its own membership. Who really runs the NRA? What are their salaries? What are they doing for the people who chip in $5 a year?

The answer to that last question, appearing in *Esquire,* might pique the interest of those people who finance the NRA by proxy, and without really giving a damn. The NRA's big stick is its ability to flood the congressional mails with menacing letters, and pound various desks with a sign that says "900,000 Strong." But how strong? Hell, one of those 900,000 is *me*—and as far as I'm concerned the NRA is a corrupt and devious lobby that doesn't even understand my interests, much less represent them.

When I say "me," I'm speaking, very loosely, for A. Gunn Freake—a man who quit the NRA because he decided that it wasn't what it claimed to be, and that its "spokesmen" were either dangerously stupid or consciously sold out—to somebody. There may or may not be a valid argument against nationwide gun registration, or even against guns. I'm not sure and I don't really care, because I don't think those are the issues. But I'll admit it's an interesting argument. My own position is hazy, mainly because I can't make any sense of the "gun control" controversy. It sounds like a Nixon-Humphrey battle. I can't believe, for instance, that Dodd and the NRA are really on opposite sides of the fence. Dodd is so corrupt that he makes Franklin Orth seem like [late Cuban revolutionary leader] Che Guevara; Dodd reminds me of that Dick Tracy character who was always surrounded by a horde of flies. I can believe Ted Kennedy's (D.—Mass.) gun-control speeches, but I can't believe Dodd's. And everything Franklin Orth says reminds me of Roy Cohn's bastard sister, who now runs a white-slave house in Silt, Colorado. I have documents to prove that.

My real point, I guess, is that a frontal attack on the NRA won't make the nut. They're geared for frontal attacks; they wave the flag, sound the rape-warnings and quote the Constitution . . . which makes perfect sense in a nation where (according to the latest Gallup poll) 54% of the population thinks "looters in riots should be shot, rather than dealt with in some other manner."

Given the current national atmosphere, I don't see much sense in mounting another reasoned, liberal and humanistic attack on the NRA. That's playing on their terms. They've spent the past 50 years designing bear-traps for liberal journalists . . . and most of the public evidence suggests that they've done pretty well. They have put Dr. Pavlov's theories[82] to such good and massive use that the membership hears nothing but bells when the NRA is "attacked." So maybe the way to go is *not* to attack them, but to chronicle the efforts of a gun-owning member to find out how the fight is going. Consider the possibilities: A man claiming to be the president of the Woody Creek, Colo. Gun Club goes to Washington to find out how the NRA is doing in this time of anguish and dread possibility for all gun freaks . . . he asks where the battle-lines have formed, and how much the battle will cost . . . and who are the generals?

Well . . . that sounds like a bad joke until you remember that humor first declines and then freezes as it approaches the "Conservative Pole." There is absolutely no humor, for instance, in the Oil Business. I have been dealing, for months, with the walking rich dead. Their nerve-ends are rubber; they don't understand why I smile when they tell me obvious, deliberate lies . . . at first I thought they were hyper-cool, but now I suspect they don't even realize they're lying.

Anyway, the Oil croakers and the NRA footmen were all born under the same rock—by Jay Gould out of Amy Snopes[83]—so if you can convince Erickson to go for a sort of Open (or Simple-Minded/Devious) approach on an NRA piece, I think we could make something of it. I'm not naive enough to think they'd *believe* I was a worried cowhand from Woody Creek (the first thing these right-wing freaks do is check with whomever you claim to be writing for), but I think I might be able to convince them that I, as the owner of 12 weapons worth anywhere from $2500 to $3000 (disregarding the Riot Market, where prices are wildly inflated) . . . that I, a taxpayer (and landowner if Ballantine pays me), am personally concerned with the role of the NRA in the current "gun-law controversy." I want to know if they're getting the job done; and if so, How? And who's getting the juice?

. . . Hold on there, fella! What do you mean by JUICE?

Nothing, nothing at all—that's only a western-slope colloquialism; out there, you know, we're all pretty nervous about water rights—"juice rights," we call them. Yeah . . .

They'd throw me out of the building unless Erickson could assure them that *Esquire* had indeed sent an authentic NRA member to Washington, to check on the hierarchy—the true-hearted president of the Woody Creek Gun Club, where a recent fast-fire shotgun competition featured 2′ × 3′ target-photos of J. Edgar Hoover. The official FBI target is a half-torso silhouette, and the WC group wanted to be as authentic as possible—so the obvious choice for the official FBI target was The Director, himself. That's authenticity. (Photos will be

82. Russian physiologist Ivan Petrovich Pavlov's research on the conditioned reflex showed that dogs salivated at the sound of a bell if it had been rung when they were fed before.
83. Jay Gould was a nineteenth-century American railroad tycoon and financier, Amy Snopes a member of one of novelist William Faulkner's greedier fictional families.

available, pending return of signed releases from participants—not all of whom were happy to have been photographed in the act of firing at J. Edgar.)

All of which brings us back to your question: Could I "get in to talk to people involved in this"? The answer is "Yes," but I can't guarantee what they'll tell me. A *hand-carried* letter from *Esquire* would be a crucial tool, I think. It should be a letter to me, saying that *Esquire* wants an article *from me* on, say, "The Embattled NRA." Orth and his people should have no warning; ideally I'd show up with the letter (wearing my Eddie Bauer trapshooter's dress coat) on a Wednesday, just before lunch—which will put them in a position of having to cope with me very quickly, just as all the secretaries and flunkies are leaving for lunch. With a bit of luck, and the leverage of a letter from *Esquire,* I won't have any trouble compelling some "spokesman" into a 2-hour drinking bout. The sudden appearance of a major publicity opening, just before lunch, will prevent any structured response and deprive them of any employment-agency, desk to chair interview-style advantage. People who left their imaginations in junior high school tend to ramble when they drink—and not all of them blow it. I ran into one fellow on the Oil Shale gig who was surly and sluggish all afternoon of the conference, but after two hours of gut-prodding in the Brown Palace Bar he was counter-punching like a man who'd just remembered what he really enjoyed doing.

Or maybe it just seemed that way to me, as I crested the great hump . . . but I doubt it . . . and in any case I think I'll finish this letter tomorrow. Two acid freaks are scheduled to arrive in a few hours, to build a new deck/porch on the house. They tore the old one off yesterday. And—for an unexpected footnote—I suspect the creation of this porch will end my preoccupation with the physical end of life in the Rockies. I am very conscious of eras, and all I need to finish this one off is a quick action on the either/or purchase of this property . . . which seems, for the moment, at least as important as publishing another book. I suspect, now and then, that I'm off on a bad and atavistic track, but in the hot sun of these Woody Creek afternoons, stone sober and reading the newspapers, watching the TV news, offering a beer to a local reporter who drives out from Aspen to tell me the sheriff says he's going to "get" me because of what I said about the local magistrate, or wailing flat-out on the motorcycle past the District Attorney's horse-barns and going too fast on the gravel road to hear what he's screaming at me . . . yeah, that's life in Woody Creek, and I'm beginning to wonder if there's room enough here for me and all the others who want to Get Out, Off, Away . . . that aging version of the teen-age hippy's dream of The Peaceful Valley, man & nature in harmony . . . right, and Aspen merchants forming vigilante committees to shave the head of any long-haired freak who looks transient and "without visible means of support."

I think I'll offer to trade the Boston University library all my "papers" in exchange for a windowless apartment in the sub-cellar of the library building. That would finish the circle, all the way back to my basement hole on Perry

Street in New York City ten years ago,[84] before I understood that I was living on the verge of the Fourth Reich.

It occurred to me the other night that I should probably concentrate all my current efforts on *The Rum Diary,* because I doubt I'll recognize any part of it if I wait another year. As a hopelessly American writer, I'd be foolish to waste that moment of high drama and terrible understanding, that "high white note,"—as Mr. Fitzgerald heard it, that has to die on the way up, because there's no way it can come down. It's a note that, after a certain point in time and action, you never hear again . . . which is why nearly all good American novels are written by . . . WATERHEADS!

Christ, it's 5:40 a.m. and I just heard the dogs barking so I went outside and, goddamn, there was a huge white truck backing into my driveway with about 100 twenty-foot strips of pure California redwood—a whole truckload of wood that I had to help unload. "You're up early," the man said. "Fuck early," I told him, "I'm still working and what in hell are you doing in my driveway at this hour? I should blow your head off with my special hair-trigger .44 Magnum that I have here on my hip, as you see. . . ." But I let him off when he said the boss told him to be at the sawmill by sun-up. Jesus—Starkweather[85] was right; this poor fool makes $70 a week, he's 50 years old, he works from dawn to dusk six days a week, and he's going to vote for Nixon or maybe even Wallace because he's worried about LAW AND ORDER. Holy shit!

Which reminds me that I told a friend of mine named Lee Berry to contact you. He's in Spain, I think, tracking echoes he can't explain. He's free-lancing and selling nothing except huge, full-page $20 features to the *Albany Times-Union.* Berry won't be worth a penny to you for quite a while, if ever, and I told him most agents really detest broke writers . . . but I gave him your address. No harm in it, eh? I pay for my own paper, and Ballantine owes me five times as much money as I owe Random House. Every time I try to work myself into one of those good old-fashioned adrenaline fits—like I did in the old days, when I actually wrote things—I remember the paperback royalties and I know they're going to fuck me when the Big Split comes. There's no question about this: they're going to do me, for sure. I've been filing my nerve-ends for months, getting braced for it. They say it's coming in August, the Big Grip, when they finally come out of their hole and snarl at me, "Well, now you know—we screwed you to the grill of an Edsel and sold you, as an icon on wheels, to the Arab Commandos. Don't worry, they'll pay you well . . . for your services. . . ."

Of course . . . like all those *Hell's Angels* foreign rights we sold. Jesus, what a ball I had with that money . . . well, why kick that goat again? It blows my

84. Thompson lived in a tiny, black-walled sub-basement apartment on Perry Street in New York's Greenwich Village from April 1958 to January 1959.

85. Charles Starkweather and his fourteen-year-old accomplice, Caril Ann Fugate, murdered eleven people on an eight-day killing spree from Lincoln, Nebraska, to eastern Wyoming in January 1958.

mood, which was pretty good until now. But it tones me up for the coming Rape of August. That's a good opener: "Well, you see, Hunter, the reason we didn't sell even $10 worth of foreign rights—regardless of those query letters—was because Marvin Watson[86] said he was going to close the 4th-class PO's and we knew you lived in Woody Creek—so we figured What the Hell, you'd never get the check anyhow, so . . . we told them to jam it. Besides, we know how you feel about Nazis, Slants, Wops, Frogs, Micks, Spics, Poles and Rubes of every other description . . . We know how you feel: Buy American, Sell American, and keep a stiff upper lip when your sloth and stupidity catch up with you . . . why not?"

Yessir, the countdown is on us. I can feel it. A snow-balling rage that has long since shadowed reason, an iceberg of loose ends—a mountain of floating hair, moving south toward the Sea Lanes. . . .

Hunter

TO JIM SILBERMAN, RANDOM HOUSE:

July 19, 1968
Woody Creek, CO

Dear Jim . . .

Thanks for the $424.62. You're two-up now, so I guess it's my move. I can't bring myself to read my last letter, but I recall the gist of it, and this is the way I've refined that hazy thinking since I wrote . . . to wit:

The massive "American Dream" filing system that I started building on my return from NY is a bummer. The brute weight of it all has paralyzed my head, flooded my drawers and caused me to initiate a vast shelf-building program . . . which is not so crucial as the vicious depression that I've pulled down on myself by using this awful focus. There is absolutely *no humor* in the Death of the American Dream. I can't get out from under it; we are caving in, I'm sure of it, and it's happening so fast that only the daily papers can really keep up. There is *no good news, none.* All these vicious publications I subscribed to on the "RH expense tab" have caused me to chew my fingers down to the main knuckle. *Human Events*, *Business Week,* the *Conservative Book Club* . . . Jesus! I saw these people at the '64 GOP convention in SF and my uncontrollable reaction caused my final split with *The National Observer*. I think the '68 conventions may be the last of their kind . . . the continued existence of the Electoral College will mean the 1972 conventions will be held at the bottom of the sea. You can quote me on that.

Anyway, this AmDream/Violence book needs a much tighter focus than we've given it so far. The open-ended possibility that we all endorsed at the

86. W. Marvin Watson was U.S. postmaster general in 1968.

rubber-tree restaurant in NY was a sort of Definitive Statement of everything that's happening NOW, plus a total background to explain it all.

Contrary to all external evidence, I exist in a steaming funk—relating to this subject—about 20 hours a day. All the bad fantasies that I used in the *Hell's Angels* book have now come true. My mail is evidence of all the rude speculations I made about the fantasies of suburban housewives. Did Margaret show you the file I sent her from the woman in Tinley Park, Illinois? You should look at that file—it's only a few letters, but they add up to one of the most depressing documents ever set in any kind of type. Every time I get one of those things I look at Juan and wonder how I can possibly tell him what to watch out for. The dimensions of what we have fucked up in this country are beyond any coherent explanation. It's beyond any reasonable rage and almost beyond despair—in words, at any rate. But the terrible depth of the cross-referenced reality that I've been building for six months leaves me still unprepared for the sort of shock I received this morning, about dawn, when I called one of my neighbors and said "Your cows have eaten my lettuce, they're shitting on my porch, and I'm going to kill every one of the bastards if you don't get them out of here in 10 minutes."

At that point in my killing rage, I was advised that the laws of Colorado make it mandatory for a landowner (or dweller) to fence his land *against* the entrance of cattle—rather than requiring *the owner of the cattle to fence them in.* In other words, the burden is on the afflicted . . . at which point I said that I really *wanted* the cows in my yard, because it gave me an opportunity to practice random high-speed patterns on my motorcycle—running the cows hither and yon across the landscape, burning off valuable pounds of market meat in the process, and chasing the bastards till they foam at the mouth and fall in their tracks. (The bulls are tricky; they don't always run, and when they charge you have to be very fast and cool with the gear-changes—or they'll crush you.)

Anyway, that's the style—the atavistic reality—that I've been running into in my effort to set up a local fort, if only so I can leave it. As a matter of fact I have come to the point where I think I *should* leave it. I think the trick, right now, is to move to L.A. for at least six months. And to see, first-hand, what sort of hole the freaks are digging for themselves. New York is intolerable and unrepresentative; Chicago is the most representative city in the country, but impossible to live in; which leaves us with L.A., which is still slightly open and possible like Chicago was when a whole generation of American writers abandoned it—for the best of reasons—and despite all the worthy reasons for burning L.A., it is still the main big city to watch, if you want to know what's happening. All the others are salvage-jobs.

Well . . . this is a last effort to rescue this from the "nice but never-mailed letters" file. This is the bundle that haunts my typewriter to the left; to the right is the pile of things that "must be answered." And the whole goddamn pile is a monument to whatever is hanging me up . . . and it must be pretty obvious all around that something is. I'm really not writing much; or, rather, I'm writing a hell of a lot and not submitting much . . . which amounts to the same thing. And it's mainly because there's no humor, no laughter, no redeeming quality of insulated absurdity in the terrible wisdom I've been filing for six months. It's a fucking nightmare, and nothing in my repertoire of snide acrobatics has cut me loose from it. The July 20 issue of *The New Republic* is a fine example of the perils of clipping public documents. Try TRB's 25th anniversary column for a laugh.[87] I have commissioned a bumper sticker that says "Fear and Downhill." I have also commissioned two others, which I won't reveal here. Local issues are so sharp, in terms of what's happening nationally, that I can't avoid them. We're fencing here, on pretty violent terms, and the local power structure is going far out of its way to view me as a colorful wildman from Woody Creek . . . (did I send you that letter, from the *Aspen Times,* where I called the local magistrate a "hate-infected wart on the appendix of humanity"?). Yesterday this human cyst fined a harmless drifter $250 (plus 90 days in jail) on a complaint of "obstructing traffic" in front of a local insurance agency. Four years ago I lived in Woody Creek—so broke that I didn't have a phone or a TV or a radio or any other kind of contact—and so completely without funds that I could only afford to drive into town about once a week for a few commercial beers. The local merchants—these vicious pigs who are forming anti-hippie "vigilante groups" now, with the published blessing of the local judge and magistrate—wouldn't cash a $5 check for me in the spring of 1964 . . . and now these same gutless dollar-animals go out of the way to ignore Me, my general image and my Martin Bormann letters in the local papers—so they can give me credit and reap the benefits of my patronage. These fucking curs, these hyenas, these swine . . . my credit here is unbounded, unlimited, unchallenged. . . .

Well . . . maybe the thing to do right now is to finish off *The Rum Diary* under the sub-title of: "Or—Why I Live in Woody Creek." Which would bring me a bit closer to the things that bug me on a day-to-day basis—a memory voice, talking about how it was in San Juan in 1960 (when you still believed in the Sun), and now—after ten years of NY and Rio and San Francisco and Big Sur and the Rockies and the whole train of staying ahead of tomorrow's *Time* covers . . . trying to get the crucial edge on that hollow, totem-pole system that doesn't even exist anymore . . . but which is still so pervasive, and so awfully weighty, that even its enemies will be better off if it can be brought to its knees slowly, with a touch of the gradual, time-buying politics that will make a little room for a newer, more human structure.

Hunter

FROM OSCAR ACOSTA:

Thompson had sent Acosta an Aspen Times *article quoting him as an opponent of the ski-resort company that already pretty much ran the town.*

87. *New Republic* columnist Richard L. Strout wrote under the pseudonym "TRB" from 1943 into the 1980s.

July 22, 1968
Los Angeles, CA

Hunter,

The only question I have about that article in the *Aspen Times* is—can't you really afford another shirt? You've been wearing that same goddamn shirt now for over a year that I know of; the last time I saw Sandy, my last day in Aspen, she noticed that I had a shirt somewhat similar to that one of yours, only a different color, and she said she was going to get you one; I mean, is this your trade mark now? also, it seems to me you've grown about another inch balder.

The letter from Gerald Walker of *The New York Times:* What would be the reaction, do you think, if I had David Sanchez, Prime Minister of the Brown Berets, send him a very threatening letter; I mean, you know we do have people in New York, and they are not all "boys"; as to his crap about it not being newsworthy, that especially from *The New York Times* is simply a bunch of bullshit; you know as well as I that *The New York Times* creates the news itself. The point of the note that meant more to me was that he seemed to be saying that he did not want to get "you" personally involved in something like this, which is another story in itself, of course.

As to my flamenco dancer . . . it is over with. For reasons that would take me several days to explain . . . in any event, she leaves for Mexico this weekend. Once again, I am sad and lonely, but I am not dead yet.

I guess I simply will not be able to make it to Aspen this summer; I could take one week off, but it will take me a day and a half to drive there, a day and a half to drive back, leaving only four days for all the shit we got to discuss, for all the booze and dope we got to consume, that would require twenty-four hours a day, thus resulting in my returning to L.A. ten times more exhausted than when I left, so I think I better put it off till the fall sometime. In any event, I liked the fall in Aspen best of all; living in that color last fall will be an experience that will stay in my head for the rest of my life.

Hay nos vemos.
Oscar

CHICAGO—SUMMER OF '68:

Thompson's experiences at the chaotic and bloody August 26–29 Democratic National Convention in Chicago were so unsettling that he created the alter ego "Raoul Duke" to tell the story.

August, 1968
Woody Creek, CO

Sometime after midnight on Wednesday I was standing in Grant Park about ten feet in front of the National Guard's bayonet picket fence and talking to some Digger-types from Berkeley. There were three of them, wearing those Milwaukee truck-driver hats with mustaches instead of beards, and their demeanor—their vibes, as it were—made it clear that I was talking to some veteran counter-punchers. They were smelling around for a fight, but they weren't about to start one; they had a whole park to kill time in, but for their own reasons they'd chosen to stand on the front line of the Mob, facing the Guardsmen across ten feet of empty sidewalk. Behind the line of bayonets, Michigan avenue was a crowded no-man's land full of cops, TV cameras and barbed-wire covered jeeps . . . and on the other side of that moat was the Conrad Hilton, its entrance surrounded by a wall of blue police helmets and big sheets of plywood covering the windows of the street-level Haymarket Bar—where, several hours earlier, the plate glass had been shattered by human bodies pushed completely into the bar by the crazed police-charge.

The Berkeley Digger-types were convinced that the earlier action was only a preview of a clash that would probably come before dawn. "The bastards are getting ready to finish us off," said one. I nodded, thinking he was probably right and not even wondering—as I do now—why he included me. I was, after all, a member of the official, total-access press. I had that prized magnetic badge around my neck—the same one that, earlier that day, had earned me a billy-club shot in the stomach when I tried to cross a police line: I'd showed the badge and kept on walking, but one of the cops grabbed my arm. "That's not a press pass," he said. I held it under his face. "What the hell do you think it is?" I asked . . . and I was still looking at the snarl on his face when I felt my stomach punched back against my spine; he used his club like a spear, holding it with both hands and hitting me right above the belt. That was the moment, in Chicago, when I decided to vote for Nixon.

The Berkeley trio had noticed the press tag at once, and asked who I worked for. "Nobody," I said. "I'm just sort of getting the feel of things; I'm writing a book." They were curious, and after a jangled conversation of bluffs, evasions, challenges and general bullshit, I introduced myself and we shook hands. "Thompson," said one of them. "Yeah . . . you're the guy who wrote that book on the Hell's Angels, aren't you?" I nodded. The one closest to me grinned and reached into his jacket, pulling out a messy-looking cigarette. "Here," he said, "have a joint."

He held it out to me, and suddenly, with no warning, I was into one of those definitive instants, a moment of the Great Fork. Here I was in Chicago, in a scene that had all the makings of a total Armageddon, with my adrenaline up so high for so long that I knew I'd collapse when I came down . . . ten feet in front of a row of gleaming bayonets and with plain-clothes cops all around me and cameras popping every few seconds at almost everybody . . . and suddenly this grinning, hairy-faced little bugger from Berkeley offers me a joint. I wonder now, looking back on it, if McGovern would have accepted a joint from McCarthy on the podium at the Amphitheatre . . . which reminds me that I think I read somewhere that McGovern's daughter was arrested for possession of marijuana shortly before the convention (Unruh & Cranston[88]) . . . which hardly matters, because I felt, at that moment, a weird mixture of panic and anticipation. For two days and nights I'd been running around the streets of Chicago, writing longhand notebook wisdom about all the people who were being forced, by the drama of this convention, to take sides in a very basic way . . . ("once again," I had written on Monday night, "we're back to that root-question: Which Side Are You On?"). And now, with this joint in front of my face, it was my turn . . . and I knew, when I saw the thing, that I was going to smoke it; I was going to smoke a goddamned lumpy little marijuana cigarette in front of the National Guard, the Chicago police and all three television networks—with an Associated Press photographer standing a few feet away. By the time I lit the joint I was already so high on adrenaline that I thought I would probably levitate with the first puff. I was sure, as I looked across that sidewalk at all those soldiers staring back at me, that I was about to get busted, bayoneted and crippled

88. California's Democratic Speaker of the Assembly Jesse M. Unruh and U.S. senator Alan Cranston.

forever. As always, I could see the headlines: "Writer Arrested on Marijuana Charges at Grant Park Protest."

Yet the atmosphere in the Grant Park that night was so tense, so emotionally-hyped and flatly convinced that we could all be dead or maimed by morning . . . that it never occurred to me *not* to smoke that joint in a totally public and super-menacing scene where, as the demonstrators had chanted earlier, "The Whole World Is Watching." It seemed, at the time, like a thing that had to be done. I didn't *want* to be busted; I didn't even agree with these people—but if the choice was between them or those across the street, I knew which side I was on, and to refuse that joint would have been—in my own mind—a fatal equivocation. As I lit the thing I realized that I'd lost the protection of the press pass, or at least whatever small immunity it carried in Chicago, if any. That billy-club jolt in the stomach had altered my notions of press-leverage.

With the joint in my hand, glowing in the night as I inhaled, I figured, well, I may as well get as numb as I can. Then, in a moment of fine inspiration, I took a nice lungful and handed the joint to the AP photographer standing next to me. His face turned to putty; I might as well have given him a live hand grenade . . . and then . . . then . . . like a man stepping up on the gallows, he put the thing to his lips and inhaled . . .

. . . and I knew I was home free, or at least I wasn't going to be busted. He'd been standing there very cool and observant waiting for something to happen on the front lines while he stayed on the balls of his feet ready to run when the bayonets came; I could almost feel him over there, a heady presence, vaguely amused at this flagrant felony being committed under the eyes of the National Guard and taking sides, himself, by declining to photograph us . . . it would have been a fine *Chicago Tribune*-style photo: "Drug-Crazed Hippies Defy the Flag" . . . and then, it was *his* turn. When he put the joint to his lips and drew on it very skillfully I knew he had measured the balance of terror and decided that it was safe, under the circumstances, to smoke a joint in public.

I admired the man, and liked him even better than I had the night before when he'd bought me a drink out on Wells street. We had both been caught in a police charge, and instead of running with the mob we had both ducked into a bar, letting the cops sweep on by. Now, 24 hours later, he was sitting on another flash point, smoking a joint—a strange gig for a press photographer. They are a weird breed, estranged in every way from pointy-headed reporters and editorial writers. If reporters are generally liberal in their thinking, photographers are massively conservative. They are the true professionals of journalism: the End, the photo, justifies anything they have to say, do or think in order to get it. Police brutality, to a good press photographer, is nothing more or less than a lucky chance for some action shots. Later, when his prints are drying in the darkroom, he'll defend the same cops he earlier condemned with his lens.

All this was running through my head as the joint came back to me and my sense of humor returned along with my sense of taste and I realized, after three or four tokes, that I was smoking really retrograde shit. "Jesus," I said, "this is awful stuff, where did you get it, Lake Michigan?"

The fellow who'd given it to me laughed and said, "Hell, that's THC. What you're tasting is old Bull Durham.[89] It's chemical grass synthetic stuff. We soaked it in THC and dried it out."

Bull Durham! Synthetic grass! I was tempted to jam the butt of the thing into the little bastard's eye . . . all those terrible charges and I wasn't even smoking grass, but some kind of neo-legal bastardized Bull Durham that tasted like swamp corn.

It was just about then that I got the first rush. THC, DMZ, OJT—the letters didn't matter, I was stoned. Those bayonets suddenly looked nine feet tall and the trees above the park seemed to press down on us; the lights across the street grew brighter, and bluer, and they seemed to track me as I wandered off to see what was happening in the rest of the park.

It didn't take me long to realize that I'd blown my keen-eyed observer thing for that night, and that I should get the hell out of the park while I could still walk. The scene was bad enough with a perfectly straight head; peripheral vision was the key to survival—you had to know what was happening all around you and never get out of

89. THC is the psychoactive compound in marijuana; Bull Durham is a roll-your-own cigarette tobacco.

range of at least one opening to run through when the attack came. Which was no place to be with a fuzzy head . . . I aimed for the stoplight at Balboa street and lurched across to the Hilton bar. A 500 pound cop with blue fangs stopped me at the hotel entrance and demanded to see my non-magnetic hotel press pass. It was all I could manage to find the thing and show it to him, then I aimed myself across the lobby toward the bar, where it suddenly occurred to me—I had promised to meet Duke at midnight.

Now, as closing time neared, the bar was three-deep with last minute drinkers. The desperate scene outside seemed light-years away; only the plywood windows reminded those of us inside that the American Dream was clubbing itself to death just a few feet away.

Duke was sitting with Susan at a table across from the bar. They didn't see me and I stopped for a moment around a corner, standing in a dark spot near a table full of Humphrey delegates with their badges and straw boaters and noisy home-folks chatter . . . waiting for my head to clear; "nobody gets stoned on Bull Durham," I muttered. "What's that?" said one of the men at the Humphrey table. "Bull Durham," I replied . . . and he turned away.

Duke was hunched down on the table, with both hands on his drink and talking very easily. She—Susan—the girl with that electric memory, was sitting next to him, watching his hands as he talked . . . smiling that same vague smile I remembered from . . . what? Five years ago? Yes—almost six now—in San Juan. She looked thinner, not much older, but her eyes were bigger and her cheekbones were sharp . . . a woman's face, no more of that wistful virgin thing. I gave my head a quick snap—an acrobat's trick, they say, to stop the whirling fluids that keep us balanced in those little horseshoes of the inner ear . . . and then I advanced on the table, feeling perfectly balanced.

Duke looked up, and for an instant I thought he didn't recognize me. Then he smiled: "Goddamn," he said. "It's about time." I nodded and sat down in the booth, with words piling up in my head and saying nothing, looking across the table at Susan and smiling, or at least trying to. I felt very obvious—as if everybody in the place was watching me, waiting to hear what I'd say. Susan smiled, "Hello," and I nodded, croaking out an echo, then looking away and calling for a drink. "Some dope fiend from Berkeley just got me stoned," I muttered. "I'll get my head straight in a minute—just ignore me."

She laughed, reaching across the table to touch my wrist—and I jumped, just as the waitress arrived and I ordered a beer. "What kind?" she asked, but I waved her off: "Any goddamn kind, just a beer, a large bottle, terrible thirst . . ."

Duke was watching me with a flat, undecided sort of half-stare; I could see it without looking at him, but when I leaned back and faced him he smiled instantly. "You're a traitor to your class," he said, "sneaking in here to drink with the over-thirty generation."

"I'm thirty," I said. "This is my time, my perfect moment . . ." And I suddenly felt straight; the THC fog was gone, a bottle of beer appeared in front of me and my world came together again. I looked at Susan and smiled. "I saw you at the Fillmore last year," I said. "But when I tried to get backstage they threw me out."

"Oh . . ." her face was confused. "You should have called me, or told them you were . . . or something. . . ." Her eyes flicked up at me, then away, looking down at her drink . . . confused, like me, by five years of living in different worlds. The last time I'd talked to her, in San Juan, she was hysterical at the airport, waiting for the plane that would take her back home to Connecticut for a rest, a hideout, a refuge—away from that nightmare scene of the beach house and the Carnival and Duke, and even me. . . . I felt like touching her, to say hello in a better way than I had—but it seemed like the wrong thing to do. Duke was curling down on the table like a cold wire, sipping his drink without lifting it off the formica. The scene was too weird, too heavy—none of us could handle it, too much had happened, and too far apart.

"Well . . ." Duke shrugged and sat up straight in the booth. "What the hell is wrong with us? Can't we talk like human beings?" He looked at Susan: "Let's do it like an interview, sweetie. You're famous now, and we're just a couple of rude journalists . . . where's your public manner?"

She looked at him, not quite smiling, then turned to me: "Are you as uptight as he is?"

I shrugged, fishing in my pockets for a match. "Yeah," I said.

HST

TO JIM SILBERMAN, RANDOM HOUSE:

Still reeling from Chicago, Thompson submitted his expenses to Random House.

September 3, 1968
Woody Creek, CO

Dear Jim . . .

Enclosed is my expense bill for the Demo Convention Trip . . . and Trip is the word for it. I recall sending you a note of some kind, but I don't remember what I said—except that I wouldn't have missed that nightmare for anything. Hubert is right when he talks about a "new era," but he won't be part of it. The thing that impressed me most about Chicago was not the crazed violence of the cops (even though I got punched in the stomach with a billy club at one point), but the style of the protesters. That scene in Chicago made all the Berkeley protests look like pastoral gambols from another era. On Monday night I saw 3000 lined up behind a barricade of park benches and garbage cans, beating on the cans with clubs and shouting: "Pigs Eat Shit!" . . . at a mass of 400 cops, about 100 yards away, chanting "Kill, Kill, Kill. . . ."

We've come a long way from Sproul Hall and "go limp." No more of that . . . from now on it's going to be hell; those freaks on the barricades stood in clouds of tear-gas and fired spray-cans of oven-cleaner (a lye-acid solution) at the cops . . . they stood and fought, and took incredible beatings. I witnessed at least ten beatings in Chicago that were worse than anything I ever saw the Hell's Angels do; at one point I stood about 20 yards off, while four cops beat a photographer who was rolling around on the sidewalk screaming "Help, Help!" . . . and all I could do was stand there, constantly watching around me to make sure I had running room if they came after me. A half hour later I was talking about what I'd seen in a bar when I suddenly started crying . . . the whole week was that way: fear and tension and super-charged emotions, sore legs from running, no sleep, and a sense of disaster pervading it all.

Anyway, here's my expense tab. I'm going to write about Chicago, and just see what happens. I think I have a central incident to work with, now, and in terms of the book I think I've come out of a fog. Chicago was the reality I've been theorizing about for too long; the evidence exists now, I saw it, I was there . . . and I think I'll have some pages fairly soon. In the meantime, please cope with this expense tab so I can keep functioning; at $664.86, I suspect Chicago is going to be a bargain.

Thanks,
Hunter

EXPENSES . . . HUNTER THOMPSON

DEMOCRATIC NATIONAL CONVENTION, CHICAGO—AUG 25–31, 1968

$168.18. . . . six days at Sheraton-Blackstone Hotel
138.60. . . . RT flight, Denver-Chi-Denver
24.68. . . . Aspen–Denver flight, 8/25 (Vail Airways)
26.25. . . . Denver–Aspen flight, 8/31 (Aspen Airways)
307.15. . . . total daily expenses (seven days), including all meals, cabs, equipment, entertainment (sic) and other items as shown on attached notes

$664.86 . . . TOTAL EXPENSES*

Thanks,
Hunter S. Thompson

*receipts and daily expense notes enc.

TO WARREN HINCKLE, *RAMPARTS:*

A kindred spirit since his first encounter with Thompson early in 1967, Ramparts' *then–executive editor Warren Hinckle would launch the trenchant liberal monthly* Scanlan's *in 1969.*

September 4, 1968
Woody Creek, CO

Dear Warren . . .

Here's the proof. Some people say drugs are more powerful than truth, but I survived all that and got away with the evidence you asked for . . . about what the press people were doing in Chicago, and like I told you before, they were armed. They blew out a whole wall in that hotel I was telling you about; they were all taking that nose-drug—Angina Pectoris[90]—and a lot of other things, too . . . and when they got all high and crazy they'd take turns shooting at this target, and then they took pictures of it and threw them out the hotel windows on the cops. Polaroid pictures, still wet . . . those dirty pigfuckers! I wish I could tell you what else they threw out those windows, but I can't say it in public. All I can tell you for sure is that those dirty, godless, flagless, wrong-souled scumsuckers were shooting at a target that makes me want to puke just to look at it.

They didn't care that nobody else in the hotel got a wink of sleep. Oh no . . . the press never sleeps; not as long as there's something to shoot or fuck or cheat. You think the Hilton lobby smelled bad from those stench-bombs . . . Jesus, you should have smelled those rooms where the press people stayed: drugs, gunpowder, stale urine and fire. They had the target set up against one wall, and they took turns shooting until they all got so excited that

90. Angina pectoris is the paroxysmal chest pain caused by a lack of oxygen to the heart.

they'd begin to bite on each other and break glass and utter strange cries . . . then they'd call room service for more whiskey and drugs and another bellboy to whip.

They treated the help like most people would only treat niggers: they raped the maids and slit the shinbones of the old men. I only stayed because I wanted the evidence and the hippy hookers they kept bringing in . . . oh yes, they had regular orgies when they weren't shooting or taking pictures. And all this went on very close to Humphrey headquarters. I can't use names, of course, but we both know that well-known persons were involved. They got this way all the time, everywhere they go . . . but the decent public never knows; it's kept from them by news managers and slavish hotel owners who don't care what happens on their premises as long as the bill gets paid. Most of these people are connected, one way or another, to the Red Underground. We all know that; the FBI has their records . . . and that's why they act like they do: They don't give a fuck, that's why!

So don't believe anything you read about what happened in Chicago, and remember that the camera, too, can lie—especially in the wrong hands. Goddamn them, they'll spend all night shooting at a likeness of the Director and then take drugs so they can publish newspapers and magazines and talk their deranged and filthy notions into TV tubes.

Well, you asked me for evidence and by god when people question my sources I go all out. What I'm telling you now is something I never told anybody, God Luv Em, and I went to Chicago with a true-jesus determination to give that stinking evil mob every benefit of the doubt. I tried to be as fair as I could with that scum, but when they pulled Old Glory off the Flagpole . . . well, I wanted to choke the yellow opium-eaters. And I knew the Red press had put them up to it, so I had to go underground and see for myself.

Which I did, and now I'm sending you the proof. I'm also in a position to offer you the East Coast franchise for Howard Unruh's Favorite Oven Cleaner . . . a proven product. And massive sales potential. Unruh's Oven Cleaner sells itself: witness the enclosed target . . . the bullet-holes are, after all, just holes . . . but one shot of oven-cleaner virtually destroyed the target.

Judge for yourself.

Yours in fear and loathing,
Howard Unruh

TO LYNN NESBIT:

Thompson's business correspondence, particularly with his agent, was taking on the ever looser and more "gonzo" tone that would distinguish the book he was pitching on the next presidential contest—eventually the brilliant Fear and Loathing: On the Campaign Trail '72.

September 9, 1968
Woody Creek, CO

Dear Lynn . . .

I just found the original of my NRA "outline" letter and, despite the mad overtones, it struck me as a decent piece of rambling. Let me know ASAP on the NRA chances, so I can work it into my outline for the book. I want to get 10 or 12 "scenes" sketched out for Silberman & anyone else who cares (like Penguin?), and then start on them one at a time. I suggested several to Jim (in a letter last nite) and asked for his ideas. The NRA was one; another was the notion of spending a week (the first week in November) in Los Angeles, dealing in a very heavy way with about four pre-selected voters—two from a blue-collar precinct and two from a high-white area. Using a title like "The L.A. Vote," I could try to show why these people voted as they did, who they are, how they live . . . and why they should all be sent to zoo-therapy . . . to prepare for their roles in The Wave of the Future.

Oil Shale was another possibility, but the article you sent to *Esquire* isn't my idea of what I want to say—NOW—about Oil Shale or the oil people. The article, in its present form, is hung [up] in all the loose ends that come with trying to be fair and informative in too little space. I want to really do the bastards, without having to worry about the *LA Times* format . . . so don't send the article to anyone else—assuming that *Esq.* won't deal with it—until I decide how to revise it. As for *Ramparts,* I think Hinckle would rather have a short piece on the problems of publishing an oil shale article than a full-length fog-bank like the one I did. I'll sound him on that and let you know. In the meantime, let's keep the main shot for revisions and possible sale to a rich Nixon/Humphrey–type journal.

Did you, by the way, get any photos in that package from Bellows? Also, did he return a bundle of my first-draft material that I did first as "separate boxes" (his idea), but finally mixed into the main thing. I'm curious about what's being read, seen or pondered in my name. The article was never really finished, despite Bellows' effusive compliments and subsequent croaking. I'll take your word for it that Bellows is "one of the good people." He seemed that way to me, but then so did Hubert Humphrey. My final talk with Bellows was very sad; I'll tell you more about that action if I decide to write something on the subject for Hinckle . . . whom I just sent, by the way, a bullet-riddled photo of Hoover that I found in a Chicago hotel and a psychotic note on the activities of the press people after hours. I doubt very seriously if he has the balls to print it (and maybe that's not the right word)—but if he does I'll let him deal with you. I just wrote him, saying I didn't want my name used in connection with that sickening photo, a copy of which I'm enclosing FYI. They were all over the hallway in that hotel; everybody who saw them wanted to puke, or at least that's what they said. They were mainly press people, so I couldn't believe anything they said. Beyond that, my head was a bit fuzzy from tear gas and a billy-club shot in the stomach . . . so all I can really tell you about this photo is that I picked it up along with all the other press handouts.

Now. . . . a weird and wholly tentative idea for that "open contract" with Ballantine; I've been pondering the long-range view for 1972, the breakdown of current political parties, etc. and I see the Dissident Lineup as sort of like this: The Democratic Anarchists, with no candidate except maybe a symbol like a huge plastic do-nut—and a lot of oven-cleaner to back it up; 2) The Progressive Yahoos, with a program we'll have to wait for—any prediction would necessarily fall short of reality; 3) The Mystic Conservatives (Peace & Power, Drugs on Approved Credit), a sort of Leary-Maddox[91] ticket; 4) The Black Iguana Party, a militant blend of blacks and chicanos, united behind a symbol of sudden death for all human obstacles . . . and . . . and . . . and . . .

Let's deal with this later. The idea, in a nut, is a short fantasy on the 1972 Campaign, assuming the collapse and splintering of the Democratic Party—dealing with the remnants: their programs, candidates, weapons, backgrounds, the convention in Las Vegas, run by Howard Hughes instead of [Chicago mayor Richard] Daley . . . Martin Bormann as chief of security drafted by accident on the 38th ballot, fire and chaos . . . and the Final Solution. That's the nut; shall we lay it on Bernard?

OK for now,
Hunter

TO SELMA SHAPIRO, RANDOM HOUSE:

Since directing Random House's publicity for Hell's Angels, *Shapiro had proven her worth to Thompson as both an informal literary agent and a good friend.*

September 10, 1968
Woody Creek, CO

Dear Selma . . .

Your letters are getting very formal: "I thought often of the Sheraton-Blackstone, etc. . . ." Anyway, you'll be happy to know that I covered that vicious program as an official representative of Random House—so you had a voice on the floor, or at least from the press balcony, when I repeatedly tried to nominate Martin Bormann during the Wednesday nite balloting.

Right. Jim Silberman did the trick, after much arguing, and when I got to Chicago I was treated as brutally as all the other press people—cursed, pushed, chased, punched in the stomach with a billy club, the whole gig. I wore my motorcycle helmet for four straight nights and ran so often and so far that my legs hurt for 3 days after I got home. Those pigfuckers were stupid enough to stage

91. Timothy Leary was a Harvard psychology professor and LSD guru who, it turned out, became an FBI informant in 1974; Lester Maddox had been elected governor of Georgia in 1966 after campaigning on the slogan "Your Home Is Your Castle—Protect It!"

one of their numerous attacks in front of TV cameras, but the really horrible stuff took place in midnight parks, vacant lots in Old Town, doorways on Wells St., and places like that. I was terrified all week; it was the worst scene I've ever been involved in, and that includes the whole Hell's Angels gig.

I'm not sure what I'll write about it, except that whatever I write will be part of the suddenly-active non-fiction book. Right now I'm sorting my notes, reading press comments, and thinking about what it meant—not in the sense of an article on Chicago, but as the death of a whole era that began, for me, one night in 1960 when I was hitchhiking from Seattle to San Francisco and stopped somewhere in Oregon to watch the first Kennedy-Nixon debate in a country bar. A whole generation was driven mad in that interim; I doubt if we'll ever recover.

Maybe Portugal is the answer, and maybe you're right about democracy. I'm getting my passport in order and thinking seriously about quitting if Nixon gets in, and he will. Or maybe I'll stay; we're heading for a horrible showdown of some kind, and I'd hate to miss it.

Back, momentarily, to Chicago: Your mention of Paul Fanning reminds me that I tried to call him while I was there, but he wasn't listed. On Monday night I sat upstairs in Mother Blues and made notes until they suddenly closed the place at 10:30 because of the violence outside in the street. Nobody knew where Fanning was . . . so tell him I tried to look him up. I also tried to locate Studs Terkel for a peaceful drink—but in the end there was no time for peaceful drinks, no time for anything but fear and pills and astonishment and rage and adrenaline.

I'm not sure when I'll get east. Right now I'm trying to hash out a totally-revised book outline for Silberman. For a while I'd almost abandoned the thing, but suddenly I feel like writing 100 pages a day. The novel remains dormant; the summer has been a fore-shortened nightmare of local politics and low finance—vicious dealing and bargaining over land, house, etc. It's been so bad that I think I should probably move to a small apartment in Watts. These dirty bastards are going to take us all down with them, when they go. These rich-Okie dealers and landowners—mean scum.

As for the antlers, yes, they're from a large timber-buck, a Rocky Mountain deer. You can dress them up considerably by taking them to a local taxidermist—who will mount them on a wooden plaque and cover the skull with rich soft leather. What you have is the crude reality. Check the yellow pages for a taxidermist; he'll be happy to transform that head into a trophy as soft and mellow as an old painting. A set of polished horns in wood & leather yes, very nice above your bed.

Well, it's 6:10 a.m. here and I'm going under. My head is much more active than it has been for at least a year. Maybe I'll even write something. Silberman has been very decent of late; I actually feel like I owe him some words . . . and that's a weird feeling, for me.

As for your notion of switching jobs, I naturally oppose it—for purely selfish reasons. Or maybe not "purely." You're one of the very few human beings I met in all that terrible wrangle with the "world of publishing," and if you quit I'd feel like I'd lost a beachhead in a world I have to deal with. But I guess that's purely selfish—except that other people would feel the same way. All us outback freaks need a place to hide in NY, and you'd play hell hiding me in some teacher's lounge in a slum school. That's the sort of thing you could do on a part-time basis, anyway, to see if you really liked it. I'm not sure you would . . . but . . . yeah.

OK for now. I'll probably get to NY this fall & I'll see you then. Ciao—

Hunter

TO ALLARD K. LOWENSTEIN:

One of the sincerest and most courageous left-wing activists of the 1960s, Allard K. Lowenstein had co-organized Mississippi's 1964 "Freedom Summer" protests before turning from civil rights to anti–Vietnam War activities. Rebuffed in his attempts to reserve Chicago's Soldier Field for a rally of his Coalition for an Open Convention, a week before the Democrats assembled Lowenstein declared—correctly, as it turned out—that Chicago was "determined to have a confrontation that can only produce violence and bloodshed."

September 10, 1968
Woody Creek, CO

Dear Mr. Lowenstein:

I trust this is the right address and the same Allard K. I saw in Chicago. If not, well . . . what the hell?

I returned (to Aspen) from Chicago and told everybody to vote for Nixon, as the surest means of seizing the Demo party from the hands of croakers like Daley and [Texas governor John B.] Connally. But now—as I ponder that heinous reality—I suspect I won't be able to bring myself to do that, unless I'm convinced that my Nixon vote is really a contribution to a far, far better thing, as it were. . . . Otherwise, I wouldn't want it on my conscience.

Yet I refuse, under any circumstances, to vote for that sold-out scum-sucking freak who now says he "could have accepted" the minority plank on Vietnam. About ten minutes after that vote I got punched in the stomach by a cop's billy club when I tried to cross the bridge from the Hilton to the band-shell in Grant Park. I showed the swine my super-true-magnetic Stockyards Amphitheatre press pass—courtesy of Random House—and they let me know the score very quickly; I fled to my room at the Blackstone, to pick up my [motorcycle] helmet and running shoes, and emerged just in time to get caught in the

Rommel-style attack[92] on the stalled marchers—the one they pulled off right in front of all the TV lights . . . Wednesday evening on your screen. Selah.

So it occurs to me now—faced with a choice between Nixon & Nada—that we'll all waste our votes, individually, unless we can settle on some way to waste them effectively. Like I went out yesterday and voted for Ken Montfort (the anti-war Senate Candidate in the D-Primary), but I found out today that most of the local peace freaks didn't even vote; they didn't know Montfort's name, much less what he stood for . . . and in terms of the November election they simply won't vote; the few who will can't agree on who or what to vote for.

My own preference is MARTIN BORMANN, whom I tried to nominate from the press balcony, on several occasions, after Alabama and Bull Connor voted for [George] Wallace and Bear Bryant.[93] The Jesuit priest sitting next to me kept me from hurling my binoculars down on [Oklahoma Democratic congressman] Carl Albert . . . and Daley's thugs, sitting all around me, luckily didn't know who Martin Bormann is/was . . . ??

In any case, a vote for Bormann is a vote for nada—unless everybody who agrees with me votes for Martin, too. The point is that we should all get together on some word, name or symbol—it could be almost anything, as long as everybody knows what it means—and then register a huge, coherent Protest Vote for president. The [Eldridge] Cleaver/[Dick] Gregory line won't make it; that's [Jerry] Rubin's gig—"Beat me, you bastards, I'll make it easy for you. . . ."

But I don't need that, and neither do most of the people I've talked to who say they can't vote for either Nixon or Humphrey. They assume—as I do—that some kindred spirit, somewhere on high, will soon unleash The Word, a unity-concept of some kind, a set of simple directions telling how to make yourself heard in November. Whatever word, symbol or slogan that finally emerges doesn't seem to matter. These people need a sign, a pole, a Thing to keep them together. We're dealing, right now, with an incredibly rich talent/influence pool that might—if it doesn't shatter and evaporate by November—be the nut of a whole new thing in 1972.

I'm sure all this is as obvious to you as it is to me, but after a week of assuring people that we'll get the sign in plenty of time to "vote No, together," in November, I thought I'd check with you for some details. You are, after all, one of the few people with enough media-leverage to make The Sign real. It'll have to be something very broad, emotional and vaguely "in." Otherwise, we'll have a scene where dope freaks, Black Panthers and Cambridge cocktail liber-

92. German field marshal Erwin Rommel was known as the "Desert Fox" for his tactics while commanding the Afrika Korps from 1941 to 1943.

93. Birmingham, Alabama, police chief Eugene "Bull" Connor had turned fire hoses on peaceful civil rights demonstrators in the early 1960s with the tacit approval of Governor George C. Wallace; Paul "Bear" Bryant was the revered University of Alabama football coach who still holds the record for wins in the top collegiate division.

als will cancel each other out . . . and we'll all go into a fear-spiral for at least four years and probably eight.

(Looking back on that last graph, I have to wonder if it's possible to bring all these weird elements together under one flag . . . but I also think it's a case of having not much to gain and a hell of a lot to lose. There's not much time; another month of "count on me" quotes from the "leaders" will croak any chance of a working coalition for 1972—or even 1970.)

Do you have any thoughts on this? If so, I'd very much like to hear them—for two reasons, on two different levels: one is personal and obvious, the other is the fact that I'm working on a book that Random House calls "The Death of the American Dream." And I leave you with that . . .

. . . Sincerely,
Hunter S. Thompson

TO U.S. SENATOR ABRAHAM RIBICOFF:

As the whole world was watching the Chicago police club unarmed demonstrators outside the Democratic National Convention, Senator Abraham Ribicoff of Connecticut publicly decried the city's "Gestapo tactics"—to which Mayor Richard Daley responded, on camera through the din, "Fuck you, you Jew son of a bitch. You lousy motherfucker! Go home."

September 22, 1968
Woody Creek, CO

Dear Senator Ribicoff:

I had never given you much thought, as a person or a politician, until that Wednesday night in Chicago when you nominated Sen. McGovern. I was there all week—on press credentials from Random House—and in retrospect your performance stands out as the high point, for me, of that whole nightmarish scene. Everything you did and said that night seemed to rest on a bedrock of decency. It's a very rare thing, in the stinking world of politics, to hear phrases like: "His peaceful soul . . ." and "His wholeness as a man . . ."

I went to Chicago to research part of a book on "The Death of the American Dream," and needless to say my trip was a rotten success. Yet, on the other side of the ledger, I think I'll remember your Wednesday night speech long after I've forgotten the details of the "evidence" I gathered. There was an awesome dignity in your handling of Daley and his thugs, and for a moment that whole evil scene was redeemed—but only for a moment.

I'm enclosing a token contribution to your campaign—the first political contribution I've ever made. I'd send more if I weren't broke . . . and I'd offer to write something for you if I thought you needed a speech-writer, but I don't think you do. I hope to hell you win, because the next four years are going to be a horror show—tempered, perhaps, by the handful of decent men in the

Senate, on the bench, and in whatever other, unforeseen roles or situations that will force a few men to define themselves, for good or ill.

In any case, I think you'll do alright, win or lose. And I feel a little better for knowing you're around. You elevated that convention, for a moment, to a level that made Hubert and all his sold-out dealers look like sewer rats. I'm glad I was there to see it. And, again, the best of luck on all levels.

Sincerely,
Hunter S. Thompson

TO BUD PALMER, GENERAL MANAGER, KREX-TV:

Still incensed by the subpar programming on the only channel he could get in Woody Creek, Thompson once again went after the general manager of KREX-TV.

September 24, 1968
Woody Creek, CO

Dear Mr. Palmer:

Six months ago I watched your tearful commentary on the night of Dr. King's death; it was an impressive performance—and I use that word very deliberately, in light of your influence on the level of KREX-TV's programming since you took over as general manager. Your predecessor, as I recall, retired to work for Richard Nixon; he was an infamous yahoo, recognized all over the western slope for his unenlightened views on almost everything. So it was a hopeful sign—to those of us who can get only one channel on our sets—when the station's management was taken over by an articulate human being who publicly cast himself as a one-time friend of Martin Luther King.

Well . . . with friends like you, Dr. King didn't need enemies. It's you and your swinish, hypocritical ilk who've created and sustained the world that Dr. King was trying to change. You weep great liberal tears in public, but what have you done—regarding KREX-TV programming—that your "old buddy" "Doc King" would have even condoned, much less approved of? It's phonies like you who wander around asking "What's wrong with the younger generation?"

Look in the mirror for a minute, you sold-out penny-pinching freak—you and that other Great Democrat from Chicago, Mayor Daley.

A fellow named Tom Wicker, Washington bureau chief for *The New York Times,* wrote the other day: ". . . the question deserves to be asked: who shaped the society this generation scorns?"

Hubert Humphrey might fit part of that bill, along with people like you and Daley. You weep for Dr. King, yet you manage a TV station that stands as a rancid monument to the worst instincts of the industry. You talk of the need for a better world, yet you treat your TV audience as if they were total waterheads.

Not only have you failed to improve the station since you took over; you've actually made it worse.

To wit: You moved the CBS News back to 4:30 p.m., a time slot most stations use for soap operas for housewives—the only people watching at that time. Has it ever occurred to you that most people work until slightly later than 4:30? Are they supposed to settle for that provincial hash you call the Ten o'Clock News? What prevents you from carrying [Walter] Cronkite at 6:30, as they do almost everywhere else? I noticed you didn't have any qualms about delaying the [Harry] Reasoner–[Mike] Wallace *60 Minutes* show tonight—at the announced time, all I got was *Perry Mason,* which I assume has replaced (on KREX) *Judd, For the Defense.*

This is a goddamned stinking abomination, and a perfect example of the way you've down-graded the programming. *Judd* . . . is one of the best shows on any network, one of the few literate, realistic efforts still made in television . . . and you have the stupid, ignorant audacity to drop it for *Perry Mason,* a piece of cheap hackwork that's been ridiculed in every corner of the legal and TV professions—a bad joke on everybody, and especially the audience. Is it too much to ask of you—to provide even *one hour* a week of something above the level of simian or senile entertainment? Just one hour? Not even in prime time?

I could go on, perhaps, to mention the Jacques Cousteau [oceanography] special that was recently scheduled, but which never appeared—to my knowledge. Or the 20 minute film-advertisements, in prime-time, for Heston tractors. Or the half-hour films on "Vacation Fun in the Great Smoky Mountains." Of Tennessee. Or the *local ads* inserted in those Xerox "Of Black America" specials that were introduced by the Xerox man who said they wouldn't be interrupted by commercials. And running a 2-hour pilot film for some cheap Hawaii cop series—an obvious freebie . . . and no decent movies.

Well . . . I'm sure "Doc King" would be proud of you. You got your hands on a captive audience and fed them the cheapest, meanest kind of swill you could find. You blew the national news, killed the good shows, got rid of the movies and made KREX a *total* wasteland. If a quote from *The NY Times* doesn't register with you, maybe this one will: "By their fruit ye shall know them."

How do you and your station measure up on that scale? If the answer comes hard to you, just give me a ring—or send a message via my local Geritol dealer; I'm sure you know him well.

Sincerely,
Hunter S. Thompson

TO HUGHES RUDD, CBS NEWS:

CBS campaign correspondent Hughes Rudd had stood Thompson up one night during the Democratic National Convention when they had agreed to meet for drinks at a local tavern—but he had the good excuse of having suffered a mild heart attack.

September 25, 1968
Woody Creek, CO

Dear Hughes . . .

Fuck off with your excuses about why you didn't show up at Miller's Pub on Thursday night. So you had a fucking heart attack—so what? Are you some kind of pansy? Hell, you should have had the ambulance take you from the Amphitheatre to the Pub, not the hospital. The next time I plan to meet you anywhere for a drink I'll know what to expect.

Yeah . . . and so much for all that. I just remembered that my humor doesn't always ring bells at CBS, so I won't push it. Needless to say, I'm sorry to hear about the heart action, although in retrospect it strikes me as the most honest and straightforward reaction of that stinking week. It was, in truth, the only way to go you can be proud of yourself.

As for me, I showed up at Miller's around 2:30 and left, very abruptly, around 3:00. I was sitting at the bar, writing feverishly in my notebook so I could drink, later on, with a clear conscience . . . when suddenly I was engaged in conversation by a whale of a man standing next to me—he wanted to know what I was writing and I said I was writing about the Chicago Bears—and that led to a long talk about football, very cordial, open, etc. Then a friend of his roamed up and asked why I was wearing "that funny hat." And that led, by some convoluted route, to the subject of "hippies and dirty scum." Which bugged me—and at one point I shouted, "Yeah? Well I'm one of them, and you're going to see a hell of a lot more of me before you get your fucking pension."

I left shortly after that—to make a short story shorter. I almost left with my head in my hands. They were going to do me, I could see it coming—so I suddenly stood up, left a full drink on the bar, and zapped outside . . . to find a taxi waiting for me. How about that for weird luck?

"To the Pump Room," I said, and we fled. Actually, *Ramparts* had a bunch of rooms in the Ambassador, with a lot of booze and flesh on the tab—so I ended up there. I got back to the Hilton around dawn, just in time for the wild aftermath of the cop raid on McCarthy's hq. People running and screaming in the lobby—bleeding, falling, [veteran CBS correspondent] Blair Clark darting wild-eyed from one scene to another . . . it was the ultimate horror, the final groin-shot that only a beast like Daley would stoop to deliver. It was an LBJ-style trick: no rest for the losers, keep them on the run and if they fall, kick the shit out of them.

So I stayed around all day Friday, mainly sleeping—but for the record I sort of wandered around and viewed the remains, checking the empty suites for echoes, picking up handbills, talking to the wounded, thinking . . . and on Friday night I really went out of my head. I wound up racing around Chicago on a bike, drunk and drugged, burning a week's accumulation of adrenaline. No sleep, a dirty argument with a gaggle of cops in the Hilton coffee shop on Saturday morning . . . and then the plane, four more hours of whiskey in the Denver airport, and finally home around dusk.

It took me two weeks to calm down. I kept bursting into tears at unexpected moments . . . and now I'm trying to write some of it down, but it's hard. Nobody really believes me when I say how terrifying it was, nothing I read compares to what I saw—so I feel like I'm working in a nightmare vacuum, with nothing but my notes to assure me that it really happened. The worst aspect of it all is that "the national press," as it were, (with the lone exception of *Newsweek*) has acted like a gang of abject street urchins, caught in the act. The polls praise Daley and the press hangs its head. What a shitty way to treat the people who actually tried to cover the story. What a rotten bunch of sold-out freaks to work for. Those bastards spend millions of dollars outflanking Daley—and then when they get even a taste of the story, they apologize.

I think you're right about the damage being fatal this time. Nixon's in, I'm out, and the devil take the hindmost. My vote's going for Dick Gregory . . . he's on the ballot here. I think you're in the clear with that advance from RH . . . get the Cortez thing, keep your passport up to date, and dig the free time while you have it. I figure about two years until The Crunch . . . it'll take that long for the would-be vested-interest people to figure out which side they're on . . . and after that it's going to be hell.

In the meantime I have a big house and about 20 acres, all the amenities, more room than I can use, local credit . . . a bike, a horse, 12 guns and, in general, a good place to hide. You'd like it around here . . . give a bit of warning before you come, and if you're serious, hang onto this phone number (303) 925-2250; I've taken great pains to make it unavailable by any public means. If worst comes to worst, however, the keepers of the Woody Creek Store will always finger me . . . or the *Aspen Times*—no man is safe from his friends. And, speaking of that, tell Charley [Kuralt] I just donated one copy of his book (I have two) to the local library—but they rejected it on "literary grounds." And hello to Ann. Ciao . . .

Hunter

TO LAWRENCE TURMAN, 20TH CENTURY FOX:

*Thompson's brutal appraisal of his own first novel—*The Rum Diary, *written in the early 1960s about the escapades of an American reporter for Puerto Rico's daily* San Juan Star*—can't have helped the odds that 20th Century Fox would make the yet-unpublished book into a movie.*

October 3, 1968
Woody Creek, CO

Lawrence Turman
c/o 20th Century Fox
Box 900
Beverly Hills, Calif.

Dear Mr. Turman:

Steve Geller suggested that I send you a note about a novel (*my* novel, titled *The Rum Diary*), which is currently lost in weird limbo. . . . Weird, in that Random House and Ballantine have already bought it; weird in that two years ago I sold it to Pantheon and had the sale croaked by RH . . . and weirder still in that I sold the book on the condition that I'd be allowed to rewrite it, and since then I've never even read it. Mainly because neither RH nor Ballantine seems to give a hoot in hell about novels (or at least mine); they're pushing me on a non-fiction book about "The Death of the American Dream" . . . giving advances, due dates, heavy questions . . . like "Hunter, me boy, when are you going to send us The Wisdom?" I can't escape the notion that I'm about to erupt with some sort of ultimate bullshit; the other day I went into town to rent a chain-saw and the man asked me, "What's going on in this country? What's happening?" And today a potter from New Jersey showed up on my porch and asked, "What does it mean?" I took him inside and made him listen to a SW Voice of America broadcast on Wallace's choice of [Curtis] LeMay as VP . . . then I put on Tom Paxton's album for him—the Vietnam Pot Patrol song, and "1000 Years."[94] And after that he left, mumbling about getting his passport in order.

None of which has anything to do with either my novel *(The Rum Diary)* or my effort, titled *Hell's Angels,* which I'm enclosing for any purpose you might want to put it to. Maybe a wedding present for your daughter. We live in strange times.

In any case, I find myself suddenly jacked up—once again—on the possibilities of fiction. I'm not sure why, except that I'm now trying to make some sort of long-term journalistic sense out of that fascist freak-show that RH sent me to cover in Chicago—The Cauterization of the Duped, The Whipping of the Wounded, Half-Mad in the Streets of Love City, etc. . . . etc. . . .

Which brings me back, in a half-mad sort of way, to my current NY-focused subject: The Death of the American Dream—and the fact that I think I should sit and watch it jell for a while, until Nixon gets in . . . that's the ending I think I need, a fitting climax to the second-saddest story of the last 2000 years.

Which also means I'll be in my own kind of limbo until election day; I want

94. Witty folk singer Tom Paxton's May 1968 album, *Morning Again,* included the song "Talking Vietnam Pot Luck Blues."

to watch it happen, ponder and savor the madness, let it swim around in my vision like a frog in a deadly grease-trap. And in the meantime I thought I might read my *Rum Diary* again, and maybe try to do something extra with it—like selling it to Hollywood for a Million dollars. And also re-writing it, for good or ill.

I haven't seen *Pretty Poison* yet, so I don't know how you handled Steve's book. When I read it I thought, Goddamn, there's a pure weird and steady tone here, a man with a good eye . . . but the ending bothered me, so I wrote Steve and said he'd blown one of the best strange stories I'd read in ten years. I felt the same way about *The Graduate:* it was a third-rate story, stale bullshit in the main, but on film it somehow flowered and grew . . . I recall at least a dozen scenes that I envied, as a writer, and to my mind that's the highest kind of praise. Even the ending of *The Graduate* had élan—a beautiful sort of Walter Mitty[95] hype. It was bullshit, of course: I saw it right after I got back from Chicago, where Walter and his friends got their heads and illusions cracked by a gang of uniformed white-trash swine . . . who were also human, like the rest of us, and just as honest, in their stinking vengeful wrath, as any McCarthy staffer.

All I meant to say, there, was that I was amazed—after seeing *The Graduate*—to realize that not all stories lose in the translation to film, and that in fact, some gain. I guess I saw that first in *The Pawnbroker*[96] (which I'd read, a year or two earlier), but that was such a powerful story that it was a long time, many months, before I could deal with it on a technical, nuts-and-bolts sort of basis.

And to hell with all that rambling. I began this letter as a quick note to ask if you might be interested in reading *The Rum Diary.* I couldn't tell you much about it, except that it's a very inept, very honest tale of very young "vagrant journalists" converging to work on a new english-language paper in the Caribbean. I wrote it about five years ago, and when I start the rewrite I can't help but change it immensely. The first 100 pages are worthless, the characters lack the essential major/minor sort of focus that a good story needs to stay on its feet . . . but, every now and then, as the book reels along, there are scenes that I'd match against anything in *The Graduate,* and maybe even against one or two of the best in *The Pawnbroker.* And there are others that I could never do, on paper, as well as I know they could be on film . . . like there's one with a bunch of young/cynic, hard-traveler types from various U.S. backgrounds, playing touch football with a coconut on a Saturday afternoon beach near San Juan . . . a wistful, underhanded salute to the Great God Football and all those Homecoming Tallahassee/Boulder/Bloomington Saturdays that seem, in retrospect, as a chain of innocent frauds, leading to . . . what? A coconut football game in a world that mocks Homecoming in every way except finally.

95. The sweet, daydreaming would-be hero of a 1942 James Thurber story that was made into the 1947 movie *The Secret Life of Walter Mitty,* starring Danny Kaye.

96. Director Sidney Lumet's 1965 movie of Edward Lewis Wallant's novel starred Rod Steiger as a Jewish pawnbroker in Harlem haunted by his memories of a Nazi prison camp.

Maybe that sounds useless, but I see it as one of the best scenes and comments that anyone could make on the permanent roots of the American Head. But what the hell? Maybe you went to NYU, or some other place where a word like "quarterback" was a bad "Pathology 2x" joke. How many flankers flood a zone? How many receivers mean the passer is left naked? How many dope/drunk drifters will pick up a coconut from some beach in a new and free-style world they can't tolerate? Just last weekend a freak showed up here (coming off a 30 pounds in 3 weeks beat-the-draft diet—which failed), and he said he was too weak to do anything more than sell hash on commission . . . but suddenly there were people throwing a football around in the yard, and within 10 minutes this Bitter-End Fuck America Dope Dealer was out on the grass, pumping like quarterback Roman Gabriel,[97] and grinning like a fool . . . throwing long spirals and catching that weird, off-shaped ball as naturally as he'd light a cigarette.

And fuck all that, too. I got carried away with the possibilities of a scene I haven't rewritten yet—which is already there in the ms., but not properly rendered, as they say. Probably I'm talking to myself, more than you. The freedom of fiction is incredible, compared to journalism. I'm just letting my mind run a bit . . . why not?

Why not, indeed? All I meant to ask was whether you'd like to look at the book before, or after, I do the rewrite? Or—for that matter—if you'd like to see it at all? Because, in all good truth, it's a hopelessly naïve and half-conceived book—as it stands now. I know I can make it better, but I might also make it worse—by killing a lot of valid notes that tend to embarrass me now, in my balding wisdom. My current Random House project is keyed on the death of innocence—the flat opposite of *The Rum Diary*—and I'm not sure if I can do them both, at the same time, without going mad. So if the novel interests you, in terms of film, I think I'd prefer to do that first—to deal with the Beginning, before documenting The End. It seems like the right way to do it.

Well . . . I seem to have carried on, here . . . a bit of good rambling, as it were. But the fucking carpenters are coming in an hour or so to wail in the basement; they are making my writing cave down there, a soundproof room with a big fireplace and redwood walls, a blue floor like a rubber tennis court or an acid freak's golf green . . . to hide from President Nixon, or maybe Wallace . . . and Curtis LeMay, a man whose time has come—and the devil take the hindmost.

Beyond that, and to temper the jangled tone of this letter, I should probably say that I'm going to be working on *The Rum Diary* anyway—if only to save my head from the terrible realities of journalism, at least for awhile. So if you want to see the book in its present, embryo, state—that's fine and easy. If you want to wait and see it finished . . . well, I can't be definite in terms of time, or

97. Los Angeles Rams quarterback Roman Gabriel would be named the National Football League's Most Valuable Player in 1969.

even content (and not even context, for that matter), but I can say for sure that it will be a tighter, more functional story, with a heavy emphasis on plot and absence of bullshit. But, after seeing *The Graduate,* I can't take plots very seriously and I find myself thinking more in terms of scenes, high points, moments . . . and these are the things I might cut, change or fail to develop in my rewrite of *The Rum Diary*, and it worries me.

I wrote a very bad book five years ago, but I wrote some very good things . . . which I might or might not recognize in the course of rewriting a novel to fit the new Random House list. Perhaps I can make it a goddamn bone-connection masterpiece. Or maybe I'll blow it completely. I see it mainly as a salvage job, and they're always tricky—for a lot of reasons, including the market.

And so much, again, for all that. It occurs to me now that I've had a definite boot out of writing this letter, and it also occurs to me that I'm not sure what it says . . . which should concern me very deeply, I guess—in a professional sense—but for some reason it doesn't bother me at all. That's the luxury of writing to total strangers.

. . . Oh christ I hear the carpenters, pushing their ancient VW bus up the gravel driveway; I know they have hammers and power-saws, goddamn them—their noisy smugness, smoking pipes and fancy handmade tool aprons (hair on their faces, mumbling about how it was in New Haven before the world went mad and they quit, drinking wine for lunch and shooting flies out of the air with sawed-off BB-guns), a very weird type . . . at this stage of my chemical frenzy, and with a long day ahead, I think I'll have a bit of sport with them, jangle their heads with some happy talk about LeMay's candidacy, play some old Hitler records. Good fun. And an end to this letter. If the novel interests you, let me know. If not, I'd have blown this night anyway, and probably in some rotten anguished style fit only for burning. So I'll close on that note, and in fair humor . . .

Sincerely,
Hunter S. Thompson

TO DON ERICKSON, *ESQUIRE:*

October 16, 1968
Woody Creek, CO

Don . . .

Lynn Nesbit tells me we have a tentative agreement on a piece on the NRA. I'll call you in a day or so, to hear what you're thinking, but in the meantime I thought I'd sketch out a plot, of sorts. To wit:

I thought I'd go to Washington and ask the boss-shooters exactly what they are doing for us members. There are 900,000 of us out here, chipping in $5 a year—for what? My own suspicion is that the NRA is a harmless swindle, a massive con job, a rich and well-publicized lobby that isn't doing a fucking thing either for or against anybody except the handful of people on the NRA payroll.

Maybe I'm wrong . . . so I thought I'd ask the folks in Washington to put me onto a really successful NRA gun club, preferably in Southern Calif. One of those patriotic groups that gets govt. ammo and other "special advantages." I'd like to drop in on one of the shoot-outs and see for myself why all us gun freaks in Woody Creek are missing out by not hooking up with the NRA. Just the other day, for instance, I blew a huge hole in my living room floor with a 19 gauge shotgun load—a hideous accident caused by a mixture of gunpowder and LSD. The carpenters working in the basement left at once and haven't returned. The Magnum load tore through the hardwood, the sub-flooring, and made hash of the acoustical tile they were installing in the basement. #5 pellets were imbedded in the power-saw table. They said it was like a bomb dropping on them . . . so they left, to go duck-hunting. "That's what you get," they said, "for fucking around with the NRA."

My point, I think, is that the *real gun freaks* dump on the NRA. They'd sooner join an Elks' Club than a formal shooting group. I doubt if Eldridge Cleaver, for instance, was a member of the NRA. But again, maybe I'm wrong—maybe there are benefits I've been missing. If so, I want them. I want to know exactly what the NRA can *do for me*. I want to know what they do with all that money—who gets it, and why.

Well . . . I think you see the drift. I'd like to spend about 3–4 days at the NRA Hq. in Washington, then another 2–3 days at one of their model gun clubs—none of which exists out here in Marlboro country; all the gun freaks I know view the NRA as a tool of the federal govt. This raises several questions . . . which I've already mentioned.

So I think you see where I'm looking. If you have questions of your own, keep them in mind and I'll call in a few days. I'd like to get started on this thing soon.

Ciao . . .
Hunter Thompson

TO DAVISON THOMPSON:

Without saying so directly, Hunter Thompson lamented the Death of the American Dream to his younger brother.

October 16, 1968
Woody Creek, CO

Davison . . .

Your letter arrived a few days ago, was read, sat around for a while, read again, digested . . . but it's still hard to cope with. *All* personal letters are hard for me to cope with these days, increasingly hard . . . because everybody I hear from sounds wretched and screwed up. 1968 seems to have been a really awful year for everybody except maybe Nixon, that evil scheming bastard. My mail is a snowballing nightmare; there is *no* good news. And no hope of any. Nixon is going to win and then implement the Wallace program—like Johnson became Goldwater. [Republican vice president-elect] Agnew is the wave of the future, a stupid shithead, so cheap and useless that he can't understand his own failure. My depression with current politics in this country is so vast that I can't find words to express it.

Your letter, needless to say, didn't change any patterns here. Your sketch of corporate fear and the "terrible twenties" makes me wonder what kind of letters you'll be writing when you're 35. I wonder the same thing about myself, for that matter. And everybody else I know. Maybe it's because we're all around 30 and the game is beginning to look more serious than we realized. The scoreboard looms huge, and nobody seems to be winning. Maybe this year of black politics has showed us a mirror of ourselves—a gang of aging bullshitters and incompetents, like Humphrey & Nixon. That's the best we can cough up, to speak for us. I seriously believe this country deserves everything that's going to happen to it. War, revolution, madness, the whole bag. I'm looking around for another country to live in; it's only a matter of time.

Jim's visit was a pleasant break in my long, downhill funk. He seems oblivious to all the stinking realities, and it's nice to have somebody like that around now and then. But right after he left I took off for Chicago and the convention—and that was pure horror, much worse than it looked on TV. It was a real Hitler scene, the air smelled of fear and desperation. I'm trying to write about it now, as part of my alleged new book, but it's hard to explain except as a final loss of faith in whatever this country was supposed to stand for, all that bullshit in the history books.

Well . . . I hate to write such rotten letters. I wish I could say something cheerful, but I can't find it to say. The other night, for the first time in more than a year, I ate some LSD and relaxed for a while . . . everything was fine until I wandered into the kitchen about mid-morning and found Juan watching Spiro Agnew doing a TV interview. Jesus, what a horror. He's bad enough when you're straight and sober, but on acid he's a babbling, pus-filled nightmare. His eyes are slits and his skull is like a rotten pear—everything he says is a stupid lie. I felt terribly sorry for Juan, growing into a world that can take a man like Agnew seriously.

And so much for all that; I feel sorry for all of us. Your Chagrin Falls culture is amazingly similar to a big chunk of Aspen. About half the town is in hock for their souls to the Ski Corp. and the Tourist Bureau. "Independent" businessmen live in fear of "bad publicity," a "bad winter," "bad people in town," and god only knows what else. And they're all trying to screw each other out of every possible dollar. Never saying it quite like that, of course, but doing it all the same. A gang of cheap whores . . . again, like Humphrey and Nixon. I've about given up in my efforts to buy this house and meadow I call home for the moment; the price went from $30,000 in May to $80,000 in September . . . and I figure I can do a lot better than that in Canada, without having to worry about being put in some kind of detention pen, as a dangerous anarchist heretic. Which I am, and I hope to get worse. If it comes down to a "Which side are you on?" crunch, I think I'll go with the human beings. In clearer terms, I look forward to a split between the Corporate Nazis and the Desperate Freaks, with no middle ground . . . and, as much as I dread that kind of choice, it seems pretty clear and unavoidable. What do you think?

I sent Mom a sour note the other night (I can't seem to write any other kind), but there wasn't much to say. I gather that Jim is going to need some cash around Feb, and I said I could come up with some—although my situation right now is bleak. I have never, for instance, collected a dime on *Hell's Angels* paperback sales, despite sales approaching 500,000. I can't understand why; if I understood these contracts, I think I'd be rich. As it is, however, I can't even get a gasoline credit card. For a free-lance writer, it's always cash on the barrel-head. You people with jobs can at least get a loan. Anyway, let me know when Jim needs a cash transfusion; I've developed a weird talent for producing cash out of nowhere . . . although I'm getting tired of having to do it.

Why don't you call from Kansas City and we can see how a quick visit might work? I expect to be travelling in late Oct and early Nov, but right now I don't know the dates. Do you know if there is a National Rifle Assoc. gun club in your area? If so, I might find an excuse to visit in connection with an article I'm doing. Let me know and hello to Adeliade (sp?). Jesus . . . Addie? I think I'll go to bed.

Ciao . . .
H

TO JANE FLINT:

Although Thompson has always acknowledged that he lent Tom Wolfe some of the audiotapes he had made of the Hell's Angels debauching themselves at Ken Kesey's ranch in La Honda, California—at Wolfe's request, and with the understanding that he would use the material in The Electric Kool-Aid Acid Test—*some fans assumed that Wolfe had lifted sections from* Hell's Angels.

October 18, 1968
Woody Creek, CO

Dear Jane Flint . . .

Thanks for your very detailed evidence inre: Tom Wolfe's "plagiarism" of my La Honda gang bang. I appreciate the instinct that caused you to write me, but I'm not sure what to tell you about the attribution problem. Your weird guess that ". . . maybe you and Wolfe witnessed the same thing at the same time and not the same reaction" borders on the Obscene and even the Half-

Mad. The inference that Kesey staged gang-rapes for journalistic tours—and that Wolfe and I happened to be on the same Gray Line Tour—makes me wonder what sort of crippled reality-show I'm contributing to by writing "journalism." Yours is not the first letter to rumble on this theme, and barring the weird chance of a merciful god it won't be the last. The weird truth that few editors and writers can even imagine is that the "literate public" is far stranger and freakier than the very square world of editors and journalists . . . all of which makes journalism a sort of echo, rather than the Force it seems to be in the context of *Time* and *Newsweek*.

None of which has much to do with Wolfe's swinish plagiarism, which I'm sure was accidental. . . . What he did there, I think, was beef up his narrative with an unpublished revise of my book, meaning to rewrite it for style and tone, but never quite getting around to it. We all do that, I'm afraid, and one of these days—when Wolfe writes something true enough to be worth stealing—I'll feel free to use it more or less as I see fit, and I hope you'll write and nail me when I do it. I'm genuinely amazed to find that anyone reads new books that carefully. I'm neither annoyed nor bored by your observations, and only half-amused.

In any case, I sent Wolfe some tapes relating to that part of my *Hell's Angels* research, and since my account of the gang bang was taken almost directly from my taped account, I'm not surprised that Wolfe's account is very much the same—since it came off the same tape. The only difference, of course, is that I was there and Tom wasn't. Which is only half-important, in terms of true journalism. All journalists improvise on the skeletal truths they drag up—the trick is to do it right and truthfully. Wolfe improvises straighter than most, and besides that he gave me a credit in that part of his narrative that deals with the Angels. This is a standard brand of decency, I think, in the world I have to make a living in . . . which reminds me, for no particular reason, that we all get a little older and less honest every time the sun comes up, which it's about to do here . . . so I'll hang up.

Again, thanks for the letter and the heavy style-eye. I'm forwarding your letter to Tom, for good or ill . . . (yeah, I had to pause, there, to turn some John Fahey[98] records over . . .). Music is the better part of journalism these days, anyway.

Ciao . . .
Hunter Thompson

TO HUGHES RUDD, CBS NEWS:

With Election Day just two and a half weeks off, Thompson was genuinely concerned about his nation's future.

98. Classically trained guitar soloist John Fahey was among those responsible for the 1968 blues revival.

October 18, 1968
Woody Creek, CO

Dear Hughes . . .

I meant to send you my report on "The Press in Chicago—A Study in Degeneracy," but I haven't been able to make a copy. Maybe tomorrow. I'm alarmed at the trend to fearful breast-beating, this nervous deference to freaks of every stripe who write letters to the editor/producer, insisting that all reporters are liars. I got a radio newscast tonight in the car, a report from city hall in NY, where a mob of some 40,000 had gathered to condemn [Mayor John] Lindsay and the President. The newscast (CBS Radio) talked at length about the "fuck the press" atmosphere, but he seemed apologetic about even being alive. If you bastards keep backing up and apologizing to fascist mobs, we're all going to be in a terrible hole. You should send one of your heavies into a mob and have him grab one of these fascist freaks and let him give his own play-by-play of what's going on. That would cure the buggers. [Onetime Democratic front-runner Senator Edmund] Muskie did a variation on that act, and it worked pretty well. Let these pile-driver punks make fools of themselves once or twice, and the others will back off. They're gutless pigs—all mobs are swine; right, left or center. But this "fuck the press" thing is snowballing and the only way to cope with it is to meet it head on. [Edward R.] Murrow did it for everybody last time around, but why create that sort of desperate vacuum again? I wandered into the kitchen the other morning, with a head full of LSD for the first time in a year, to find my son watching [Martin] Agronsky and Rowland Evans goading Agnew on the tube. Jesus, what a horror. They should have destroyed the bastard, instead of just playing with him. Maybe they went to cocktail parties later that day and told how they'd really worked him over . . . but west of the Hudson it didn't come off. *I* dug it, but then I'm a special case out here; as for my neighbors, I'm sure they felt that Agnew had survived an attack by pinko wolves. (Which reminds me that, 2 days later, on Tuesday night, my neighbors got jerked around very severely by the *CBS Playhouse*—the drug scene. I think it was called "The People Next Door." By Wednesday morning the Wallace vote had doubled out here. Jesus, what a bummer that was.)

And so much for all that. My reason for writing was to say that my RH book has become such a weird bugger that you don't have to worry about any conflicts. I've decided to write the first Fictional Documentary Novel. To wit: "Hey Rube! The Memoirs of Raoul Duke . . . or a report on the rape and looting of the American Dream by a gang of Vicious Swine." My friend, Raoul, has agreed to provide details of his secret life. And I'll provide the journalism. Together, we have the artillery to smote the bastards hip and thigh. Smote? Smite? What the hell? It's a mean gig, no matter how you word it. Which reminds me that I expect to be in L.A. for election day; I want to observe some polling places in Hollywood and Watts—more book research. How can I find [*CBS*'s]

Bill Stout? I'd like to mortalize him in print—or maybe just follow him around for part of election day and find out if he's a liar or not. Actually, what I want to do is use "Election Day in Hollywood and Watts" as a peg for a general comment on Southern California and the coccyx of the American dream. I've decided to use this election and its scenes—Chicago, L.A. on election day, the Inauguration, etc., as the loose framework for a book on how it was the year the lights went out. With ten years of quasi-biographical notes, courtesy of Raoul Duke. I mention Stout in L.A. because I think he'll be covering the same general scenes that I'll want to look at . . . and I'm also planning to bear down heavily on the role of the press. I wouldn't want to bug him, but if you think he wouldn't mind a shadow from noon to midnight on election day, let me know and tell me how I can locate him.

On other fronts, I'll be in Washington sometime soon, doing an article on the National Rifle Assoc. I don't know whether I can get to it before election day, or after. Hopefully, before. In which case I plan to get up to NY for some talk with RH and agent, lawyer, dealers, etc. If you'll be around, we can have a drink. I'll send word when I know the dates.

Ciao . . .
Hunter

**the enclosed button is a present for Ann; I got it in the mail today, from *Ramparts,* and rather than give it any thought, I figured I'd pass it along for somebody else to wear—it has a vaguely un-settling quality & might be fun to wear, but not for me. I hate buttons, stickers, labels, the whole bag.

TO VIRGINIA THOMPSON:

Thompson updated his mother on family life in Woody Creek.

October 21, 1968
Woody Creek, CO

Dear Mom—

I have just—less than an hour ago—moved into a new dwelling. I am now the proprietor of a vast ranch, currently listed on the Aspen real estate market at $250,000. My rent is $50 a month, with the situation apparently firm until summer. It is a feudal situation. I have a working stable (with 6 horses), a separate building for my studio, various corrals, jumps & a professional riding ring—a three-level main house with a piano & a big freezer—two fireplaces—two baths—a washer & dryer—and all manner of benefits I haven't discovered yet. It's situated more or less like the other Woody Creek house, but the other one was an Okie shack compared to my current estate. This is really an incredible thing—the lucky result of being in the right place at the right time and having some good friends in Aspen.

I think the thing to do now is have you and Jim come out for Christmas. If you balance the cost of a round-trip ticket (plane or train) against what you'd normally spend on a Christmas at home, the trip won't seem too expensive. I'd offer to pay for the fares, but until some new windfall comes in, I'm dead broke. The $1000 *Esquire* paid for the segment they'll run in the January issue was advanced to me a long time ago—in loans of $100 each—by my agent. Whatever was left went for car repairs, moving expenses and all the expensive details of getting settled in here. The *Esquire* sale postponed publication until mid-January. I hate the delay, but having part of the book in *Esquire* will be a great help to sales. More than ever, I think this book might make money. Which reminds me, of course, that I owe you that $100—and much more. If you get in a tight spot I can borrow the $100 & pay you back when you need it. But if you can wait until publication I think I'll be in much better shape. Either way, let me know. I owe Leah $100, too—and more than that from the past, so I have to balance these things. I also owe Geiger & Clancy,[99] but they're used to me by now.

Anyway, let me know about Christmas. I'll give this letter time to get there, then I'll call. About Nov 1. When I talked to Davison I said I'd be there for Christmas (Lou.), but this ranch was too rare a thing to pass up. Staying here will foul me up in a lot of ways—including my plans with Random House—but I can't pass up this chance to live like a human being for a while. After the Hell's Angels, I think I deserve Woody Creek. For the moment, we're all very happy—Sandy is ecstatic. Juan has 105° temp & Darwin just went through a siege of porcupine quills—in his nose, mouth, eye & throat—many visits to the vet, large bills, etc.—but tonight we're all fine. I am way behind on the work, but now with a headquarters & no immediate money pressures I think the writing will move fast again. *The Rum Diary* was due Aug 1, so I have to rush.

That's it for now. This is the longest letter I've written in two months—& the first in about three weeks. Things have been very hectic here, but I foresee a calm period. Write.

Love
H

tell Jim I can see *elk*—not deer—from my back door. Deer are everywhere, & I can see coyotes outside right now.

TO TOM WOLFE:

Fretful that he may in fact have inadvertently used passages taken too directly from Hell's Angels *in* The Electric Kool-Aid Acid Test, *Wolfe had written Thompson to apologize.*

99. John Clancy was an old lawyer friend Thompson had met at Columbia University.

October 26, 1968
Woody Creek, CO

Dear Dude . . .

You don't owe me any apologies, or even explanations. Not even footnotes. Keep in mind to whom ye speake—a natural word-thief in every way. The weird thing about that gang-bang scene, though, is that we *both* stole it from my tape—which makes me think I should have been a pro football commentator instead of a writer. Maybe I'm wrong, but I think the instant/verbal notes were better and more real than either one of our interpretations. We're both thieves, stealing from Reality—which is like Faulkner's notion of land-ownership (see *The Bear*). Only a mean fool or a twisted ego-freak would try to claim ownership of a scene just because he saw it. Like I said—I'll steal from you when you write a scene I know I can't make any other way.*

So to hell with your deep bows. That was a hell of a good book, and *The Pump House Gang,* which I'm reading now, hits peaks that are even better. Not many, but the good things are better than the best *Acid Test* stuff. So I tend to admire the other book a little more. I don't know about you, but in my own mind I value peaks far more than continuity or sustained effort. Those are for caretakers on the killing-floor. Mr. Fitzgerald spoke in terms of "the high white note," which explains it pretty well—at least as far as I'm concerned. That, in fact, is the theme of the book that Random House is finally forcing me to write. It's due in July & I'm doing my practice runs now, 5 and 10 pages at a time—getting limber.

In the meantime, however, I'll be in NY a/o Dec 5—a Thursday, as I recall—and probably for that weekend. Will you be around? I think it's about time we did a mano-a-mano thing—like having a human drink together. I'll be in Washington from Dec 2 until 5—reachable at the Washington Hotel, I think, or if that fails via Jim Ridgeway, 2920 28th St. NW, Wash. DC.

My king-hell desire, at this point, is to hear one of your lectures on the New Journalism. I really want to know what it is. If all other connections fail, you're invited to lunch with me and Jim Silberman from Random House on Dec 6—call him and say you're coming, at my insistence. See you then, or. . . .

Hunter

*—with footnotes

TO GEORGE KIMBALL:

Journalist George Kimball—who would run, unsuccessfully, for sheriff of Lawrence, Kansas, in 1970—had sent Thompson a galley of his grotesque and depraved new sex novel, which Thompson found so obscenely violent he was appalled to have been asked for a dust-jacket blurb.

November 17, 1968
Woody Creek, CO

George Kimball
c/o Maurice Girodias
Olympia Press Inc.
36 Gramercy Park
New York City 10003

Dear George . . .

Strange twists in this strange and evil world: I just moved my writing hole downstairs to a timeless, lightless dungeon in the basement . . . and in the process of moving I found a letter of yours dated a hell of a long time ago that I'd put in my "answer now" slot . . . but that whole file got lost in the chaos of that stinking little cubicle and—if I hadn't moved—yes, had I not changed desks, as it were, your letter would have withered away, and me under the impression that I'd answered it most cordially and informatively and why can't that fucking Kimball deal with his mail?

Anyway, this book of yours is the foulest, most rotten thing I've ever laid eyes on. It goes so far beyond pornography as to approach a new form of some kind . . . you may be the founder of the Carnal/Axehandle School. Your setting and characters are weirdly similar to the situation in Aspen.

Jesus, I'm too tired and fucked up to carry on here. But I'll be in NY the weekend of Dec 6; maybe we can get together and do about 40 amyls for lunch in the Americana. Call Jim Silberman at Random House and leave word as to how you can be reached.

Ciao,
Hunter Thompson

TO MAURICE GIRODIAS, OLYMPIA PRESS:

Hardly a prude when it comes to erotic literature and good pornography, flat broke as he was Thompson refused Olympia Press's offer of $500 to endorse George Kimball's violent sex book.

November 17, 1968
Woody Creek, CO

Dear Maurice . . .

I was shocked, at first, to think you'd address me on a first-name basis, and especially in the context of a rude solicitation for an endorsement of that hideous drug-nightmare by George Kimball. On the other hand, I was favorably impressed by your offer of $500 for a ten-word plug . . . people have said you were generous, but I didn't believe them until I got your fine and friendly letter.

Unfortunately, I can't under any circumstances endorse that heap of deranged offal that Kimball has coughed up in the shameful guise of art. I'm sure you're aware of Mr. Kimball's background: he has dealt, as it were, with Agents. These people, as you know, are the Enemies of Art. Kimball suffers from more strange diseases than any three people you know; Angina Pectoris is probably the worst and most offensive of these. I doubt very seriously if he wrote that stinking book by himself; it strikes me as the work of a pre-teen visionary of some kind. Frankly I hate the personal connotations in this work; I was there in Chicago, and it wasn't like this at all. You may have seen me on TV: I was in the press gallery with my day-shift people from the Studebaker plant in Gary.

In any case, I'm coming to NY in December to beat the living shit out of Kimball. *Only Skin Deep* is a vicious and intolerable mockery of the whole filth industry; it reminds me of a photograph I recently bought for $50 in the Denver airport . . . it showed a local high-school cheerleader sucking on a garden hose while roaches crawled out of her anus. I think you and Kimball and Daley have gone too far this time: pornography is one thing, but raw obscenity is quite another. Somebody is going to have to answer for this book; if I were you, I'd get the hell out of town.

Sincerely,
Hunter S. Thompson

TO RALPH GINZBURG, *FACT:*

A former staffer at Esquire *and then* Eros, *Thompson's friend Ralph Ginzburg was now an editor at New York's* Fact *magazine.*

November 18, 1968
Woody Creek, CO

Dear Ralph . . .

You're right, somehow, about me and the perverse hibernation syndrome. Ever since I got back from Chicago I've been a ball of fangs, ready to tackle almost anything except this goddamn long-range never-ending book on the American Dream—which I'm coming to NY in a few weeks to discuss, etc. Maybe we can have a beer and ponder any ideas *you* might have. As a writer, I don't see where I have any obligation to deal with the saleable-idea market. That's what editors are for . . . and besides that, I've never had a good article idea in my life. Journalism, to me, is just another drug—a free ride to scenes I'd probably miss if I stayed straight. But I'm neither a chemist nor an editor; all I do is take the pill or the assignment and see what happens. Now and then I get a bad trip, but experience has made me more careful about what I buy . . . so if you have a good pill I'm open; I'll try almost anything that hasn't bitten me in the past.

I'll be in NY on Dec 6–7–8. And maybe Dec 5 & 9, too. Why don't you leave word with Jim Silberman at Random House, so we can at least have a drink. Okay . . .

Hunter S. Thompson

TO THE FEDERAL COMMUNICATIONS COMMISSION:

The failings of KREX-TV had grown so unbearable that Thompson took his complaints over the station manager's head all the way to the FCC.

November 26, 1968
Woody Creek, CO

Federal Communications Comm.
Washington, DC

Gentlemen . . .

I'd like to register a formal complaint against station KREX-TV in Grand Junction, Colorado—and if this isn't the Proper Procedure for filing complaints, then please send me all the proper forms.

I'll assume, however, that a coherent letter is as good a form as any—at least for the moment. And I might also add that I'm complaining on behalf of my four-year-old son. To wit:

For the past two Sundays—Nov 17 and Nov 24—KREX-TV has preempted "Lassie" in favor of full, half-hour advertisements for Black & Decker power tools. This has been done without explanation and despite the fact that KREX-TV has listed "Lassie" in the 5:30 p.m. time slot (in *TV Guide*) on both Sundays. So as far as I'm concerned this is not only a case of the station running paid commercials in prime time—and half-hour, 30 minute commercials at that—but also Fraudulent Advertising. If KREX-TV has sold that time slot to Black & Decker, they should say so in their listings. Please advise me as to what can be done about this.

Thanks,
Hunter S. Thompson

TO LYNN NESBIT:

Thompson's friend Bill Cardoso, who had just been named editor of the Boston Globe Sunday Magazine, *would coin the term "gonzo journalism" in 1970.*

December 16, 1968
Woody Creek, CO

Dear Lynn . . .

Thanx for the Xmas card & tell Richard I may be in touch with him sometime soon. For good or ill.

Inre: The inauguration, I'm definitely going—and if nothing turns up in the way of fat assignments on your end I think I can get $300 from the *Boston Globe Sunday Magazine*. A friend of mine has just become the editor and he is, in truth, a giant real freak . . . the fact that the *Globe* would make him editor of their Sunday mag fills me with a kind of mean karate optimism for the future. Billy Cardoso—remember that name; he'll probably be editor of *Esquire* in two years. The freaks are being sucked into power against their will. Cardoso is the reality of the New Journalism, a generation ahead of Willie Morris & that ilk. I talked to him on the phone today & it was astounding to realize that I could actually *talk to an editor* like talking to a person who knew what I was talking about. My normal reaction to editor-calls is a nervous sense that I'm busting the routine in an Old Folks home.

Anyway, I told Cardoso that I'd like to write him a weird, free-wheeling piece on Nixon's inauguration, but that I couldn't tell him anything definite until I checked with you, to see if anything else was happening on the fat-money front. If we can't find anything fat, I'd just as soon go ahead and do a short piece for the *Globe* for $300 and press credentials out of their Washington Bureau. And maybe some minor expenses. Since I'm going anyway, I might as well enjoy it and drag down some dollars for a $1500 word outburst on The Death of Hope.

I'd naturally prefer a $3000 assignment, and I'm sure you would, too. But if all else fails, let's deal with Cardoso . . . as a matter of fact unless we can get something at twice the price he can pay, I'd prefer to write for him. Let's put the line at $1000; Cardoso's offer beats anything under that—but anything above is a different ballgame. I leave it with you.

Have you tried the Oil Shale thing with *True?*

OK for now; I'm still dingy from all that movement. I finished that trip driving 90 mph from Lansing, Mich. to the airport in Detroit . . . but I think I have a good thing. We'll see.

Ciao,
Hunter

TO THE GENERAL MANAGER, DYNACO, INC.:

December 20, 1968
Woody Creek, CO

General Manager
DYNACO, INC.
3060 Jefferson St.
Philadelphia, PA 19121

Dear Sir:

Over a month ago I sent a one-dollar bill ($1) and a request for the Owner's Manual for the PAS pre-amp, which I recently bought (slightly-used) along with a new Dyna stereo 70-A. You neither acknowledged my letter (containing the dollar-bill), nor sent the book on the PAS, so I'm writing again.

I have several problems with the PAS and the 70-A hook-up, and I need a book on the PAS so I can understand what I'm doing. One, of course, is the standard problem with all Dyna amplifiers—that of putting in a headphone jack. Another is figuring out how to record records on tape with the PAS/70-A set. I had the SCA-35 and had to build a switch into it so I could tape records without putting out a bunch of leads. It seems like you people could install these simple features at the factory . . . unless perhaps you have some institutional bias against headsets and tape recorders.

My other problem concerns the attachment of a center speaker to the 70-A. The book that came with the amp says I have to write the factory to find out how this is done, so this is what I'm doing—without much optimism, since I've already lost a dollar trying to get an owner's manual on the PAS. By all means bill me for another dollar, if necessary. I want that owner's manual at once. There's no goddamn excuse for any reputable company taking a customer's money and ignoring his query.

Sincerely,
Hunter S. Thompson

TO PERIAN AND GLEASON, U.S. SENATE:

Thompson tested his new pseudonym, "Raoul Duke," on two investigators for the U.S. Senate.

December 28, 1968
Woody Creek, CO

Perian and Gleason
Hired Geeks
Juvenile Delinquency Committee [*sic*]
U.S. Senate

Listen you bastards have been lying about this gun control problem, it's worse than you think and I want to warn you right now that if you don't get [Tom] Dodd to pass a total confiscation bill pretty damn quick, a lot of people are going to be killed. I know what I'm talking about mainly because I'm a karate black-belt and I'm about to kill some of these gun freaks that keep writing letters. I'll rip their goddamn heads off and don't think I'm kidding. We have a lot better ways of croaking people in this country than old-fashioned bullshit like guns. I run a karate school out here and my people are so goddamn tough that bullets bounce off their bellies like popcorn balls. These gun nuts are a bunch of softies and if you don't pass a law against them pretty damn quick I'll turn my people loose to enforce the Natural Law. There are more of us than there are of them, don't ever forget that.

In closing, I remain, yours for a violent solution to the gun problem . . .

Raoul Duke

TO WILLIAM J. KENNEDY:

William J. Kennedy—an old and trusted friend since the Puerto Rico days—would win the 1984 Pulitzer Prize for his novel Ironweed.

December 28, 1968
Woody Creek, CO

Dear William . . .

This will not be a good letter. I am going under and I can't say why. Like Mailer, I am writing great sentences and paragraphs, but when I get beyond a page I go all to pieces trying to put too much in too little space.

Anyway, I may be in NY or Boston around the end of January, after attending the Nixon inauguration for reasons of my own. On the other hand, if my money problems don't heal, I'll come back here at once and begin writing anything that pays. If I were you I wouldn't count on getting a fucking penny off your company-store principle. The idea, Dylan said, is to "get you down in the hole that he's in. . . ." Fuck them.

Sandy is pregnant again and can't travel by air, which is only an excuse for cancelling all social movements until I finish something in the form of a book for RH. That should be June or July at the earliest. After that we might get East, and if so we'll definitely sock in on you for a while.

Here's a note for you: the new editor of the *Boston Globe* Sunday mag is a natural freak named Bill Cardoso, who is looking for stuff beyond the New Journalism to "blow New England's mind." He doesn't pay much, but there aren't many editors who'll assign a man to load up on dope in order to cover Nixon's inauguration. He asked me to put him in touch with anybody who's writing weird new stuff of any kind. Check him out if you can; I suspect he's the wave of the editorial future—like [Clifford] Ridley, god bless him, was the wave of the past. I met Cardoso when I was looking at Nixon in N.H. . . . you'll like him.

Glad to hear you liked [Beat poet Allen] Ginsberg. Actually, I made up that quote in my book that goes: "for a guy that ain't straight at all, he's pretty goddamn straight. . . ." Or something like that. He's one of the few honest people I've ever met, for good or ill.

Hello to Dana. I'll call from NY if I make it.

Yours in fear and loathing . . .
Hunter

1969

THE BATTLE OF ASPEN . . . LOCAL POLITICS WITH A VENGEANCE, DEATH TO THE GREED-HEADS . . . FIRST VISIT WITH MESCALITO, DANGEROUS FUN WITH THE BROWN BUFFALO . . . DEATH TRIP TO THE WHITE HOUSE, NIXON *ÜBER ALLES . . .*

The author with nemesis J. Edgar Hoover.
(Photo by David Hiser)

Owl Farm, 1969.
(Photo by Michael Montfort)

Marlboro man, 1969.
(PHOTO COURTESY OF HST ARCHIVES)

Thompson on bear hunt, Montana, 1969.
(PHOTO COURTESY OF HST ARCHIVES)

Owl Farm: Posing for L.L. Bean ad, 1969.
(PHOTO COURTESY OF HST ARCHIVES)

TO OSCAR ACOSTA:

The wild Chicano crusader from East L.A. had sent Thompson his play The Last Laugh of an Indian Gandy Dancer *for a critique, though probably not the one he got—especially after a lecture on the joys of settling down.*

January 3, 1969
Woody Creek, CO

Dear Oscar . . .

OK, I got the play today—haven't read it, of course, due to spending most of the day in bathtub reading that heinous Don Juan book—*A Yaqui Way of Knowledge*. Very weird; that old man really fucked the kid around, eh?

But maybe he *had* something with that Four Enemies bit. You should give that one some thought. Particularly in light of your ugly (self-proclaimed) outlook on the Revolutionary front. What makes you think you're going to catch a stray bullet during some demonstration? Shit, you'll never be that lucky. When it's all over, you'll still be sitting there fasting, waiting for the TV cameras . . . a Yaqui way of publicity. Fuck It; I'm tired of all that bullshit.

If you had any sense, you'd steal some money and buy a ranch on the Western coast of Mexico. Get hold of a good green hillside looking down on the sea and *build* something on it. Make a decent human place where people can come and really feel peace—if only for a few hours, before rushing out again to that stinking TV world. You may well be, as you noted, well on your way to becoming the ". . . middle-aged, loud-mouthed, so-called revolutionary . . ." that you say you deplore. But your concern for your "image" suggests that you like that scene too much—all those microphones and cameras and people asking for statements.

Which is fine . . . but where do you go at midnight, when the last act ends? By doing it that way, you become a freak/pawn in their game. During the five years I worked at jobs, I got fired from every one, without exception . . . and with the single exception of this place I'm in now, I've been evicted from every place I've ever lived. Which proves, of course, that I was right all along . . . and let me tell you why. Shit, my reasons would fill 200 garbage cans. . . .

Well, maybe I'm leaning too far in my own direction here, maybe trying to justify my efforts to build a personal fort where the pigs can't get me except on my own terms . . . but even if I've overdone my thing out here, I'm convinced the instinct is valid . . . like Don Juan's idea of a *sitio*.[1] I think you need at least a claim on a sense of internal order before you can rush out and rip at the world. Who the fuck are you to be preaching about the eternal verities when you can't even manage to find a door to close behind you? What have you built? What have you left behind?

Again, maybe I'm projecting . . . and maybe your play will explain it all. But I don't have much faith in words; people buy them and print them for no reason except that maybe they'll sell. The validity of writing a book (or a play) is about on par with the validity of "making law." Which is no reason for not doing it, but only a fool takes it seriously. Your whole lifestyle (and mine, for that matter) is horrible mute testimony to your reverence for "the law." The men who wrote the Volstead Act[2] thought they were laying God's own truth on us . . . and even the editors of *Time* magazine think they're doing the world a favor; they have their own weird reasons, like The Pope has his, but every one of the fuckers thinks he's doing God's work.

So fuck them all.

And now, two days later, I've finished reading your play—or, more precisely your rewrite of that TV script you sent me about 6 months ago . . . What the fuck makes you think I'd like it any better now than I did then? You think my head is getting soft? That I wouldn't remember it? You'll recall, I hope, that I sent you some comments after reading the first draft, and I find this one essentially the same—although perhaps toned down a bit here and there. But not much. It's still a race/culture exercise, with every character a stereotype—including Jose, the stoic Chicano hero solving the riddle for the rest of society's leftovers. The Eden-Oak bit strikes me, then and now, as a flimsy attempt to wrap your preachings in some kind of neo-dramatic framework . . . but I'm damned if I have any idea why those people were gathered in that auditorium, or what the fuck that man with the Harvard accent was trying to prove.

Maybe I'm thick; you'll have to figure that out for yourself . . . and this may be the finest piece of dramatic writing ever conceived by human hand. I'd like to think so, because I'd like to see you get rich and powerful in the film racket—so you could give me a job here and there. But I doubt if this thing is the ticket. Why don't you try writing about life and reality for a change? Your novel at least had good dialogue—but in this thing you've resorted to the wooden puppet-talk of an old-time morality play. Come down off your fucking cross and look at the world. You've been trying to get yourself crucified for

1. *Sitio* is Spanish for "a space of one's own."

2. The National Prohibition Act, introduced by Representative Andrew J. Volstead of Minnesota and passed by Congress in 1919 over the veto of President Woodrow Wilson, provided for enforcement of the 18th Amendment prohibiting the sale, manufacture, or transport of intoxicating liquors in the United States.

about ten years now, and it's getting so obvious that only your friends are likely to indulge you. I think we could manage it out here for $200 or so, with photos—nail you to a tree above Snowmass, or maybe in Basalt. And for another $100 I could make up a mind-rattling press release and arrange to have it distributed. Why not? You could even arrange to have your biography printed privately. . . .

But that's too easy. They won't even let you starve to death on TV in LA . . . they'll jam a tube down your throat and put you back on the street. That's the real punishment, and frankly I deplore it . . . but why get into that? Writing and politics are all part of the same foul game & I have enough shit on my hands out here without adding your christ-complex to my list.

Yeah . . . and how's that for the naked criticism you asked for? Probably you'd be better off sticking with the lily-livered liberals—because they pay good money for a lot of crap far worse than this thing of yours. The crucial difference is that yours is *obvious;* it's too awkward and serious in a direction they don't want because it's not entertaining. With half the time and effort, you could write a very saleable, harmless thing for TV, and by adopting that viewpoint you wouldn't have to endure this kind of crap from people like me.

Which you asked for . . . right? "I wish you wouldn't hold back," you said. I have it here in print. And so much for that.

As for the acid problem, I don't know what to make of it. All I know is that I wouldn't pay a dime a cap for that acid you gave me in LA. I had the same problem with that big mescaline score I was onto; it turned out to be pure shit. I bought 20 caps for $30, and it was all a bad hype. Since then, however, I've discovered a sporadic supply of excellent mesc. for $3 a cap . . . but if you stumble on anything good in SF I'll happily send you $20 for 20, if that's the price. My stuff is so strong that a full cap means the loss of a night and the next day. I'd like something a bit cheaper and less violent, so consider me good for 20 when you go up to SF—providing you try it and say it's OK.

And that's it for now. I have to get to work. Everybody in the world is shitting on me for not producing, and although I don't see much point in it, I guess I have to write something—if only to pay the rent and taxes. In the meantime, let me know if you can manage to get an address and a phone number. This is the last thing I'll send to 408 Spring.

Ciao . . .
HST

TO THE EDITOR, *ASPEN TIMES:*

As Aspen continued to develop from a quiet mountain town into a swank playground for the rich, famous, and security-conscious, Thompson feared their encroachment down the valley toward Woody Creek.

January 17, 1969
Woody Creek, CO

Herr Editor:

Wonderful . . . yes . . . that's the way I feel . . . back in Aspen . . . Heil, heil! Many times, while traveling, I raised my stein to sing the Aspen anthem . . . "Roll Me Over. . . ." Indeed, we all know that one. They know it in Detroit, and in East St. Louis, too. In East Oakland and Whittier they said I had a certain kind of class . . . and I said, "Why not? I'm from Aspen."

How fine it is to be back! And how wonderful to see that Herr Barnard, the Bürgermeister [Aspen mayor Bugsy Barnard], has finally done my thing . . . and none too soon. If more people realized how many Communists there are in Aspen, and how well-organized they are, we could burn them all out in nine hours. Bring them to me, at the furnace in Lenado. My summer ashes are settled and well-raked; I took the beads and flutes to Spanish Fork, where I traded them for cheap gas. Heil, heil!

I have a list of Reds, and I know where they live. There are exactly 644 known Communists in Aspen. All but 14 have burned their cards since Herr Barnard began his investigation. Of these 14, two are on the police force, one dispenses drugs at Carl's Pharmacy, three run a printing press in the Paragon cellar, one is in the roofing and siding racket at Snowmass, four sell dope while posing as ski instructors, and the other three live in a pumpkin near Ashcroft.

What I say is true. I have a list, which was sent to me from California by Judge Crater.

(Now . . . for the second phase of my memorandum, after a two-week delay. I was called to Washington, yes. . . . For an event of massive importance, a Medical First. . . . Heil! The first chief executive to grow from a dropped pile. I witnessed it all: the dropping, the growth—atavistic reversions and surgical victories—yes, and finally the Big Day, which I attempted to witness, but was driven off the parade route by a hail of garbage. Those *schwein* will pay, and pay dearly. We have ways. . . .)

Ah, but I digress. Indeed, I took a trip, a brief vacation from the cheap unprincipled haggling that passes for news in this soldout valley. The Boss has been told about the dealing here, and his creature, Herr Hickel, has been instructed to study our methods and apply them, on a cost-efficient basis, to the mindless rape of almost everything else.

No other city in the nation can claim to represent both the vanguard and the rearguard of human endeavor. Nowhere else is the tax-structure so advanced and so flexible that the validity of any tax depends on the willingness of elected officials to settle all complaints on a civic-payoff basis. We are on the verge of establishing a really mind-staggering precedent in this area. I think it's wonderful—a tax is valid if the litigant can be bought off cheap, but otherwise—if the geek can hold out long enough—it may be unconstitutional. What better way to spread the Aspen Spirit?

Only one . . . lunatic slurs on the ancient political affiliations of those who challenge local tax law. By the Mayor, no less . . . "Sorry, Bub, we have orders to cut your legs off; Hizzoner says you're a Red." Heil! . . . Meanwhile, the District Attorney is having his neighbor arrested on drug charges, as a final solution to the water-rights problem. And Carl's Pharmacy pays for an ad showing a phalanx of employees giving the Black Power salute. . . . And ski-freaks in Washington talk about a Playboy Club on top of the Hotel Jerome. . . . "Yes, it's a wonderful idea; of course I wouldn't go there anymore, but . . ."

Herr Barnard has told us all this in prophecy. I recall sitting at a gathering at the [Aspen] Institute sometime in the fall—a seminar, of sorts, on the "Future of Aspen," and the Mayor spoke up on the subject of sewage. The sewer system, he said, is approaching its "Hydraulic Limit," which is the point where the sewage starts flowing back to the point of origin—a reversal in the pipes.

Obviously, that Limit has come and gone. We are now awash in our own waste. . . . And humor fails in the long shadow of that reality. Aspen is now Disneyland in the Snow, and to me that has a fine familiar ring: thirty years ago, in my time, we called it the Thousand Year Reich. . . . And we did a lot of building.

TO LYNNE STRUGNELL:

Thompson responded to a bizarre letter from Lynne Strugnell of Villa de la Rosa Aurora, in Belize City, British Honduras. Addressing him as "Dear Hunter," the fan suggested she would beat him up if he objected to her use of "some of your stuff from that groovy book ya wrote on Hell's Angels."

January 33 [sic], 1969
Woody Creek, CO

Dear Miss Strugnell . . .

It's hard for me to cope with the wretched excess of your notion that you might have the prerogative of addressing me, in print, on a first-name basis. I regard it as just another stinking, evil indication of the moral and ethical rot that is driving us all to bad acid.

Beyond that, the magic sound of your address compels me to write and advise you that under no circumstances and in no way in no form or otherwise do you have my permission to reprint my book or any part of it for monetary gain, profit or in any other style except as might elevate me in the public consciousness of Belize City or any contiguous unincorporated part of that area.

Beware . . . I have more lawyers and agents than I could possibly tell you about. Tracking you down in Honduras would be no problem for them; they are a gang of treacherous monsters without mercy even for me, the doomed client. Regarding your own problems, I suggest you go to the Ambassador and confess.

Otherwise . . . thanks for the good letter. I've received a mountain of weird garbage about that book, so a human communication is a welcome thing. As far as I'm concerned, you can do anything you want with the book—or anything short of re-selling it in any way. What do you have in mind? I can't think of any way you could hang me up in Honduras, but I'm sure you could find a few without much effort. My legal problems on that book are still mounting up—no end to them, no hope.

And to hell with all that. The official world is crazier and meaner than we know. I just got back from Nixon's inauguration and my head is still jangled from seeing it. Ah . . . The Horror. Yes . . . President Nixon . . . It's easier to be fair with the Angels than with that freak.

Well . . . good luck with whatever you're doing. Quote me as much as you want, but for christ's sake be careful about selling whatever you're doing. You could complicate both of our lives by getting greedy. Like I say, there's not much you can do in Honduras that would make waves up here.

OK, thanks again for the good words. It's nice to make contact now and then . . . especially from the Villa de la Rosa Aurora. Yeah, that's tough. What the hell is it?

Hunter S. Thompson

*** oh yeah . . . your handwriting indicates that you're
crazy and wound up backwards. Selah.

TO JIM SILBERMAN, RANDOM HOUSE:

For the first time, Thompson reveals why he felt the need to create his alter ego "Raoul Duke."

February 11, 1969
Woody Creek, CO

Dear Jim . . .

[Aspen photographer] Cheri Hiser tells me you didn't see a book in those Haight-Ashbury photos. . . . And, in all truth, I didn't, either. But I hate to see a collection like that just turn yellow in the drawer, particularly since it's the first honest photo-view of the "hippie" scene I've ever laid eyes on. All the other stuff is a reflection of various put-ons—snapshots from the Great Love-In, etc., Yippie press-agent work. But that girl seemed to get into the thing so far that they could look straight at her and never see the camera. . . . Or maybe not the person behind the camera.

Anyway, it suddenly reminds me of all those Hell's Angels photos of mine—all that work and even the stomping, just to get a few wall decorations. I finally got the color stuff back from Ballantine, but I never did see the black & white; the last I heard of it, Chris Cerf[3] had taken it somewhere.

Remember these things when the bell tolls for thee. Tomorrow, for instance, I will mark the 10th anniversary of my discharge from the Air Force by going back to an AF base to do an article on test pilots. I told them I'd be back someday. Ten years ago those pigs made me spend a week painting a latrine, over and over again, 12 hours a day for 6 days—the same four vomit-green walls. And now they tell me they're going to put a driver at my disposal. . . . Yes Sir, whatever you need. . . . Ho, ho. . . .

Yeah. . . . Which means I'm taking off for Los Angeles and Edwards AFB in a few hours. I'll be there (at the Continental Hotel after a few days at the base) until Feb 23 or so. I'll also be drifting around the East LA barrio with my Brown Power man, Oscar Acosta. There's a good article—and even a book—in that action, but Paul Jacobs[4] is the only person who seems to believe it. The Mexican gig, right now, is about five years behind the Black bandwagon. Oscar is the lawyer for the Brown Berets and those people. I once sent his novel to Margaret [Harrell], but she didn't seem to think it measured up. And probably she was right—but Oscar could do a book on the Brown Power business. I won't mention this again until it's time to say "I told you so."

Well, all I meant to write here was a note about those photos. Cheri said she mentioned her astrology book to you, and I guess I should apologize for that. . . . I told her I wouldn't involve myself in that kind of rude hype, and I didn't. But, like Mr. Nixon says, The Business of America Is Business. Or . . . When Nothing Else Works, Try the Stars. . . .

As for progress, all I can say is that I'm learning more than ever. This past year, on paper, has been a total loss and a prelude to bankruptcy. . . . But if I should drop out of the sky in a big jet plane one of these days, you can come to my funeral with a clear conscience. My sporadic jokes about Random House "paying for my education" are really quite serious. You can write it off as a Charitable Enterprise, or an Educational Experiment. I have learned a hell of a lot in the past year. . . . And I might even get a good book out of it.

We'll soon see, I guess. I find myself slipping more and more into the role of my pseudonymonous (?) foil, Raoul Duke, who no longer understands what his journalism is all about. I am still working, for instance, on that goddamned NRA article—which now seems like a nerve center of some kind, touching on every other question or problem that plagues us. The notion of "Gun Control" spreads out, like some kind of malignant ganglia, to almost every story that sounds big right now.

3. Chris Cerf was the son of Random House founder Bennett Cerf, and at the time was an editor at the company.
4. Paul Jacobs was an editor at *Esquire* magazine.

Frightening, eh? And I guess I'd better get back to it, in the few hours I have left. I am sitting in the middle of about 20 stacks of ms. paper, all dealing with guns, crime, murder, madness, fascism, bullshit . . . and Law. Jesus, the freaking goddamn law! The gun problem, for instance, has led me into a detailed grappling with Anthony Lewis' *Gideon's Trumpet*,[5] one of the best things I've read in 10 years. It's a genuine classic.

And so much for that, too. One of these days I'll explain how an allegedly talented writer can produce five pages a day for a solid year and finish with nothing at all. That, too, will be a genuine classic.

Ciao,
Hunter

TO HIRAM ANDERSON, EDWARDS AIR FORCE BASE:

Thompson had agreed to provide the final draft of his Pageant *article on test pilots to his press contact at Edwards Air Force Base for prepublication review.*

February 25, 1969
Woody Creek, CO

Dear Mr. Anderson . . .

Sorry, as usual, to be late checking in. I was late finishing the test pilot article, and consequently I'm late getting this copy to you. But what the hell . . . if I were seriously concerned about time I should have stayed in the Air Force, right? Curtis LeMay[6] would have known how to capitalize on my talents . . . just as he did on his own. Selah.

Anyway, in accordance with our vague agreement, I'm enclosing a copy of the article. I resent it, of course, and if you hadn't been so helpful and considerate I would have found some excuse to skip this exercise . . . but neither you nor anyone else at Edwards gave me any kind of excuse to be vindictive or vengeful in even the smallest way, and if the article itself doesn't make you or the others entirely happy, I'm sorry. It represents a necessarily incomplete distillation of the impressions I got during my visit . . . and in fact I can't see much about it that I'd expect would disturb the kind of hard-nosed, fine-focused pro that test pilots seem to be. I deliberately avoided using technical matter as far as possible, in order to avoid any chance of hassling with an Air Force "truth squad." There are, however, a handful of *possible* errors, and if I've made any factual mistakes I'll appreciate hearing from you at your earliest convenience.

5. *Gideon's Trumpet* was *New York Times* law reporter Anthony Lewis's narrative history of the case that led to the U.S. Supreme Court's 1963 ruling, in *Gideon* v. *Wainwright*, that indigent defendants have a right to legal counsel, if necessary at state expense.
6. Major General Curtis LeMay, head of the U.S. Strategic Air Command from 1948 to 1957 and a hawk on Vietnam since his retirement from the Air Force in 1965, had been American Independent presidential candidate George Wallace's running mate in 1968.

Matters of opinion, as you noted in one of our conversations, are not subject to censorship. In any case, thanks again for the help.

Sincerely,
Hunter S. Thompson

TO JIM SILBERMAN, RANDOM HOUSE:

Researching "The Death of the American Dream" was not cheap.

March 1, 1969
Woody Creek, CO

STATEMENT

Expenses incurred by Hunter S. Thompson in research on Death of American Dream book/project. . . . Six days in Los Angeles 2/14–2/19 '69 *not* including RT airfare from Aspen, car rental in LA or other expenses in connection with article for *Pageant* magazine on Air Force test pilots. . . . All following items pertain to activities in LA proper, *not* the test pilot research expenses, which I billed to *Pageant.*

$191.62	six days Continental Hotel, LA
21.33	books on Calif & LA culture, Pickwick bkshop.
120.00	all other expenses including meals, entertainment, tips, cabs, magazines and papers, etc. (except the following item) computed at $20 per day.
50.00	special "contribution" to Brown Power firebomb fund, as it were—absolutely necessary for access to this very nervous area of activity in east LA ghetto. This is a difficult item to explain on paper. Selah.
$382.95	Total

Thanks,
Hunter S. Thompson

TO JIM SILBERMAN, RANDOM HOUSE:

To Thompson's great relief, Silberman liked his idea of using Raoul Duke's wild escapades as a fictional thread tying together "The Death of the American Dream."

March 17, 1969
Woody Creek, CO

Dear Jim . . .

Thanx for the words. You have focused on my root problem in the new book—combining controlled (and formal) journalism with the jangled reality of my day to day thing. That was my original reason for bringing in Raoul Duke—to let *me* sit back and play reasonable, while *he* freaks out. Or maybe those roles should be reversed . . . ? Or maybe the whole thing should be done in the tone of the Nixon Inaugural piece. That would be more honest, I guess, but it would leave me without a framework, making the book a series of newsy vignettes . . . and that doesn't excite me. Probably the thing to do, for now, is to write a long section with Duke in, just to see how it looks all around . . . and also to get that $5000. And if Duke doesn't work, we can take it from there . . . especially since most of the straight journalism is already written in first-draft form.

Things have gone out of control since I talked to you last. *Playboy* has sent me off to capture the soul and essence of Jean-Claude Killy, the ski freak, and—as usual—what seemed like a quick & easy thing has turned into a complicated monster. My first encounter with Killy, for instance, was at the Chicago Auto Show—in the goddamn Stockyards Amphitheatre, all those ghosts, with Killy and O. J. Simpson selling Chevrolets in the same big room where Carl Albert[7] once peddled Hubert Humphrey . . . christ, what a nightmare.

Anyway, I'll be in New Hampshire tomorrow and most of this week (c/o Bill Rollins, *Skiers' Gazette*, at "The Outlook" in Waterville, or c/o Bill Cardoso at the *Boston Globe Sunday Mag*). Let me know if you think it would be a good thing for me to stop through NY on Friday, on my way back home. If you feel like talking, it's no problem for me to stop in NY . . . so let me know. Friday is sort of open for me; the only question is which hotel (& which city) I'll spend the night in. OK for now . . .

Hunter

TO CAREY McWILLIAMS, *THE NATION:*

March 24, 1969
Woody Creek, CO

Dear Carey . . .

Good to hear from you; it reminds me of a time when I was a writer instead of a dealer. Contrary to your apparent impression, I haven't abandoned *The Nation* for fatter markets . . . I wish to hell it were that simple. In truth, I find myself constantly grappling with senseless, ill-conceived notions for book-chapters and other garbage. . . . Bottomless pits that keep me writing desperately and accomplishing nothing. I have a huge book due in July and another next April, both requiring constant research and travel. I have spent about three weeks at home since Dec 1. As always, I am naked of good article ideas—

7. Democratic U.S. representative Carl Albert of Oklahoma would be elected Speaker of the House in 1971.

despite my constant involvement with good subjects. You can imagine my frustration, I think, when I found myself in Chicago with press credentials from the Demo Nat. Comm. . . . and then no article to write at the end of that incredible week.

My situation at the moment is insane—I have an expense account to go almost anywhere I want, for any good reason, but all I am doing is going into debt to the Diners Club. I just got back from New Hampshire and Boston, and the week before it was the Chicago Auto Show—in that same evil Stockyards Amphitheatre. (There's a possible: Reflections on the Stockyards, Six Months Later, or something like that. I spent two days in that place and was terrified the whole time . . . many ghosts.)

Before it was LA, where my friend Oscar Acosta told me you'd queried him about a piece on the Chicano action there. As a matter of fact I have it here on my desk; he asked me to look it over before he sent it on. . . . And I told him the lead was hopeless. He has a good story down there—combining the Felony-Conspiracy backlash with his own personal challenge (in the courts) of the Grand Jury system. Echoes of the latter surfaced briefly in the Sirhan trial, and about a month ago some LA (I think) Assemblyman introduced a bill in Sacramento, virtually identical to Oscar's brief. His article is a good legal document, but not good journalism. I suspect, now and then, that the best way to tap Oscar's complex and finely articulate grasp of the Chicano situation would be to send somebody to interview him. . . . But not me. I've been privy to too many accidental confidences in that area to be able to write a straight article without losing at least one friend.

At the moment I'm trying to finish a long article on the Nat. Rifle Assoc., allegedly for *Esquire* . . . but I have to leave in a few days for Fort Lauderdale, to check out a book chapter. I hope to avoid this, but if I can't, it might be an article of some kind. Let me know if any of this interests you. Ciao . . .

Hunter

TO JIM SILBERMAN, RANDOM HOUSE:

Japan's Sony Corporation introduced the Beta videocassette in 1969—a development that prompted a Nostradamus-like burst of prescience from Thompson.

March 25, 1969
Woody Creek, CO

Dear Jim . . .

Are you ready for the death of print, books, and magazines? The whole weird future was laid on me tonight by a professor from UCLA Journalism school. The only missing link, he says, is a process for editing video-tape without computers . . . and after that it's a whole new ballgame: No more Hollywood, no more book publishers, no more magazines. . . . I never paid much attention to Marshall McLuhan,[8] if only because he's basically incoherent & needs about five editors. But the forecast I heard tonight is ominously clear, the underground backstairs line from UCLA—and from a man whose checks are signed, as it were, by Max Rafferty and Ronnie Reagan.[9]

The *real* new journalism. He offered to turn me loose with a sound-sync video-tape machine the next time I get to L.A. No bigger than a typewriter, combining the roles of script-writer, director, editor, producer, and . . . yes, even publisher. Tape-cassettes instead of book covers, video-tape receivers instead of magazines or newspapers. Jesus, it boggles the mind. The next time I get to NY I'd like to talk about it; this is a wild new gig. Are you into it? Why not ponder a tape/book experiment? To hell with the undiscovered editing process; that's inevitable, anyway. Why not learn to use the tools before they're perfected? Do you have any screening rooms designed into that new building? Send word. . . .

Hunter

TO THE CHEROKEE INSTITUTE:

Thompson was scrupulous in researching his exposé of the NRA.

April 12, 1969
Box 37
Woody Creek, CO
81656

Cherokee Institute
Box 7243 Dept RM-25
Country Club Station
Kansas City, Mo. 64113

Gentlemen:

Please send at once the following items, as per your ad in the *Rocky Mountain News:*

. . . One (1) Brevettata Tear Gas Pistol, complete with six shells and six blanks . . . one Gun-Unit

. . . Two extra boxes of ten tear gas shells, each box, twenty extra shells in all

. . . One holster

I am enclosing my check for $21 to cover the above items.

Thanks,
Hunter S. Thompson

8. Canadian academic Marshall McLuhan's 1967 book, *The Medium Is the Massage*, presaged a "global village" in which printed books would be replaced by electronic versions.

9. Max Rafferty was California's superintendent of education; former movie actor and future conservative Republican president Ronald Reagan was governor of California from 1967 to 1975.

TO OSCAR ACOSTA:

April 13, 1969
Woody Creek, CO

Oscar . . .

As much as I hate to say this, I'm afraid it's become perfectly clear to me and a lot of other people that you're wasting your time trying to communicate in a language you've never mastered and probably never will . . . especially now, in light of the new information we have on the Mexican I.Q. Factor. Most of the people who know you agree that your best chance lies in moving at once to some border town like Nogales and getting into a small divorce practice or maybe the buying and selling of children . . . anything that won't require you to grapple with the subtleties of composition, which is not your bright suit, as you must know by now.

There is no longer any point in ducking this issue. Sandy cried when she got your last letter; she said it reminded her of the gibberish she used to get from her father, just prior to his fatal brain transplant. That woman in Riverbank should be whipped for the damage she did. I had her checked out and discovered that she's had a serious drug problem for many years & recently caused trouble on a Mohawk Airlines flight between Albany and NYC. It seems she had a large satchel full of transistor radios, all tuned to different stations at top volume and refused to give them up when other passengers became alarmed at the din.

Or was that Thibeau?[10] He sounds in good shape. I knew he'd sooner or later get around to blaming me for his troubles. Moving to NY is pretty drastic and it's never cured anyone else, but what the hell . . . ?

As for your New Lead, I haven't been able to get at it yet. I've been traveling steadily, between bouts with this *Esquire* article, which is now up to 93 finished pages and totally unsaleable—and unfinishable. On top of that, I have a useless *Playboy* piece due in a week, but I haven't begun. I spent 2 wks traveling on it, then hung it up for lost, but due to vicious tax problems I have to at least try to write something for them. After that I plan to quit all articles until the end of summer, concentrating on this stinking book, so I can quit non-fiction altogether and write fantasies. The *Playboy* thing is due Apr 20, and after that I'll try to doctor your thing . . . although you should have told me you'd sent it to [Carey] McWilliams; I had written him a long letter about your whole situation and suddenly you short-circuited the thing. In any case, you're now on his list for LA/Chicano stories, so the best thing to do is wait until he wants something; he rarely buys things he hasn't asked for.

10. Actor Tim Thibeau was a friend of both Thompson's and Acosta's.

If I were you I wouldn't give McGarr any more acid; he's likely to have one of those disastrous delayed reactions and go all to pieces on the freeway some afternoon . . . a racist freak-out, consumed by a sudden overwhelming hatred for all Mexicans and maybe Jews too. His last letter sounded somewhat down; I think he should join the police force and abandon his shameless Irish pretensions. Those potato-grubbing pigs have never been worth a shit for anything. We all know that.

In any case, you're going to have a hard time selling your thing in its present form—which is hobbled by a POV somewhere between legal objectivity and raging bias. I think it should be one or the other, although perhaps the new *Ramparts* might go for the present form, once the lead is re-done. You might drop Peter Collier[11] a note and ask if it interests him; don't send the piece, just describe the situation in a graph or two & see what he says. My name won't do you any good there, since I welshed on a piece for Collier and am in the process now of welshing on a promised book review. Writing has become so difficult for me that it's all I can do to finish a letter.

Aspen is a mudhole these days, wet snow and cold rain, turning to rumors of eviction in the afternoon and followed in the evening by vicious notes from the Diners Club. If I get kicked out of here I think I'll do something drastic, like burn the house and flee to Guatemala.

Well, fuck it . . . I have to get back to work. Good luck in Nogales. . . .

HST

PS . . . are you trying to tell me you think a cop shot a kid at point blank range with a .38 special and not one of five shots went through the body? Were there holes in the seat? Did they change seats? Or was the kid just a real tough spic?

TO JIM SILBERMAN, RANDOM HOUSE:

Desperate for cash, Thompson proposed that Ballantine Books put out a quickie paperback edition of his unpublished decade-old novel, The Rum Diary.

April 15, 1969
Woody Creek, CO

Dear Jim:

Here's a copy of a thing I sent to Shir-Cliff the other day. I talked to him yesterday and then tried to call you (at 4:55PM, your time) but there was no answer. Anyway, I think I've blown an essentially rich and pleasant contract out of the water by firing this notion off in the mails . . . but since I've already done that I figure I might as well bring you into the circle & see what happens.

11. Peter Collier was Thompson's editor at *Ramparts* magazine.

All this really amounts to is a plot to get rid of *The Rum Diary* by publishing it secretly and letting the Ballantine distribution system do the rest. Then, if you feel like putting out a new edition or something like that at some later date, you'll be free to either do so or ignore the thing completely. It just seems to me that we've wasted enough time pretending *The Rum Diary* is a major project, or even that RH intends to publish it. I can see my way clear to put a steady month of work into it, but not the six months it would take to get it up to even the minimum level I'd want for hardcover publication and reviews.

Anyway, read the xerox letter and say what you think. Shir-Cliff said he doesn't give a hoot in hell either way . . . I see definite signs of Nixon's Disease coming over him, a gut despair of some kind . . . or maybe it's just me, maybe he thinks I'm never going to write another book. Actually, I've been writing like a bastard for the past six months. Tomorrow I'm sending *Esquire* 101 pages of an article titled "My Gun Problem . . . and Theirs," with another 20–30 pages to finish it off. This may be the seed of that evil book you bastards have been trying to lure me into doing for two years . . . it's horrifying to think I've done 101 finished pages after only a week of actual experience and interviews. Maybe you should look at the crap and see what it means . . . what it amounts to now, I think—far more than an article—is a heavy chunk of the AD/Hey Rube book. Maybe even a *fifth,* ho-ho, yes . . . and if we can send Raoul Duke out to Lansing, Michigan to see the Pres. of the NRA; put him on a plane with a head full of mescaline . . . well, we might start talking in terms of a *third* . . . eh???

Actually, the thing that sustains me these days is stolen moments of work on a piece of nightmare fiction set in SF, LA and Tijuana. I'll write you a 10-page outline if you promise to sell it to the movies for $250,000. It beats the hell out of anything I've heard of or read in a long time. OK for now . . . back to page 102.

Ciao,
Hunter

TO BERNARD SHIR-CLIFF, BALLANTINE BOOKS:

Thompson had finally received a royalty check for Hell's Angels.

April 17, 1969
Woody Creek, CO

You have great tactical sense, Bernard . . . a check for $15,000 tends to scramble a man's brains when it comes out of nowhere. Needless to say I appreciate it . . . but what really haunts me now is the vision of all that money we might have made if the book had ever reached the mass-market racks. Ah . . . nightmares, nightmares . . .

Anyway, thanx. And, with regard to my recent letter altering various contracts, I urge you to keep in mind that it was only a suggestion, a hazy idea for giving you a book that otherwise won't be published. Leon Friedman[12] called to ask why I was dumping the contract that Lynn had just worked out . . . and I explained that I hadn't meant to dump anything except a dim-looking trip to Fort Lauderdale. Anyway again, I told Leon that I was—and am—amenable to whatever seems best all around. If Silberman wants to sit on *The Rum Diary* for the rest of all our natural lives, well . . . maybe he knows best. And that anti-travel book still looks good to me, regardless of who brings it out. So . . . in closing, I remain, as always, in favor of

Whatever's Right,
Hunter

TO PETER COLLIER, *RAMPARTS:*

*Although he had agreed to review Timothy Leary's two new books—*High Priest *and* The Politics of Ecstasy*—for* Ramparts, *after reading them Thompson reneged out of distrust of the author and distaste for his work.*

April 21, 1969
Woody Creek, CO

Dear Peter . . .

First off (or Early On, as it were), here's $15 for two more years. I assume you'll want to pass it on to the money people. I'd send $100 for a "lifetime" gig if I thought I'd be around for 10 years or so, but given the realities of this vicious age I figure a Lifetime subscription to anything right now is a bad investment.

Actually, the reason I'm sending this to you instead of the addresograph gentlemen is my abiding curiosity as to Warren Hinckle's action these days. The snide backhands laced into your "new-era" statements and fund appeals express the staff position pretty well . . . but it naturally saddens those of us—or at least me—who remember Warren at his high-rolling best . . . and who also remain ignorant of whatever heinous action must have transpired in the last hours. Is he serious about putting out a new magazine? If I had a lot of money I'd be tempted to give him some, if only to watch it burn and hear the screams of the afflicted. Maybe Hinckle was the first victim of the Nixon era—the death of humor and a purge of profligate crazies. In any case, his demise—like [former editor Paul] Krassner's conversion to whatever humorless gig seems to have claimed him—puts another notch in the Great Angst that seems to come on me these days when I wonder if it's worth the effort to go down and clean out my P.O. box. The simple fact of Hinckle sitting there in his office full of bad debts and strange animals[13] lent a sense of possibility to the task of con-

12. Leon Friedman was Thompson's literary lawyer in New York.
13. Hinckle kept a pet monkey and a parrot in his office.

fronting my mail, some slim wild chance that the fiendish daily stack might yield up something with a terrible zang and rattle to it.

Well . . . I seem to be rambling, so fuck all that. I suspect I've said whatever I meant to, anyway. The only other thing on my list at the moment is a note to say something about the goddamn Tim Leary book review I've been promising Susan Lydon[14] for many months. There's no point trying to explain why I haven't sent it in; I've been doing that for so long that I no longer believe anything I say, and not much of what I write . . . and, strange as it may seem, I'm writing a hell of a lot. Probably too much—for the wrong people and the wrong reasons. Everything I start turns into a 100-page screed of some kind. I've made two mean and ugly starts on the Leary thing, but in truth I don't have much stomach for laying another bad shot on the poor bastard. His prose is worse than H. L. Hunt's.[15] Leary is still the same power-freak who tried West Point and the priesthood before he found an opening in the Acid World. He is still hustling the idle rich—at least that's what he was doing in Aspen a few weeks ago—and I guess his hustle still makes the nut, but it's a little sad to see him so completely irrelevant to anyone under fifty. I don't see much point in fucking with Leary except as an excuse to comment on that era he tried to represent. He's nothing but an aging PR man—for himself, and that's a pretty lonely gig these days. Knocking his books won't serve any purpose—unless maybe I'm so far out of touch that I don't realize that a lot of people still take him seriously. If so, well . . . I guess he deserves a mean shot or two.

Otherwise, I have to come over to SF pretty soon to look at whatever's left of Love City; it's a part of this goddamn book I've supposedly been working on for the past year. So maybe the thing to do is use Leary as a touchstone for some comments on that scene. The Haight situation has a particular relevance to me, since that was my last address before coming out here, and the fact of it poses a continuing question in my head—a thing that needs good evidence before I can let it rest. So I'll be over there anyway, and it may work out that I can make good use of a deadline to force a coherent comment out of myself, as a seed for something bigger. I did that with Nixon's inauguration, and the system seems to work. Anyway I'll give you a ring when I get over there, probably in June. Meanwhile, tell Susan L. that, despite all my noble intentions, chances are pretty good that I won't be sending her a straight review of those Leary books. I'll be happy to send them back, or send them to somebody else . . . so tell her to send a line if she thinks that's the best way to go. Either way, I'll give a ring when I get to town. *Ramparts* is the only magazine (except *The Realist*) [whose staff] I've ever enjoyed meeting on a personal basis. Most personal confrontations are disastrous for me. . . . I just had one with *Playboy* that is still

14. Susan Lydon was the book review editor at *Ramparts* magazine.

15. Texas oilman H. L. Hunt self-published a number of ultra-right-wing political tracts in the 1960s.

haunting me, in every way. I think David Pierce (the garbage mayor of Richmond) had the right idea; he is now living on a hashish farm in Nepal, financing his New Life with profits from various hypes and skullduggeries from the old days. . . . I now understand why he panicked when I put you onto that garbage lobby deal.

OK . . . it's getting into dawn here and I have to finish off a 135 page article on the gun lobby—my failed project for this winter. For the summer season I mean to do a thing titled: "Failure," or, "No More Freaks, Good Riddance, and Fuck You All . . ." In closing, I remain, in the necessary spirit of fear and loathing . . .

Hunter S. Thompson

TO DAVISON THOMPSON:

April 25, 1969
Woody Creek, CO

Davison . . .

I assume you have the sweater by now. It's new & fresh from its first drycleaning. I bought it because I liked it, but without knowing how fucking "stylish" it was. At that ski resort in New Hampshire every geek in the place had one, and I had to keep my down parka on the whole time. If I lived anywhere but Aspen I'd wear the thing and like it, but around here it makes me look like somebody who buys from the *Playboy* advertisers guide. Let me know if you feel you can wear it without apologies in Cleveland. I placed an order for another blue sweater, but with a sewn-in Vietcong emblem instead of those goddamn Killy racing stripes.

This new typewriter is difficult to cope with; nothing moves except the ball. I picked it up for Juan, for a $50 IOU. He can't jam it, and I've never seen a better teaching toy. He copies words & learns to spell. I wouldn't be surprised if he could type a simple letter on his own within six months. He handles it better than I do. I'm giving my other machine a rest after just mailing (this morning) that goddamn NRA article I began back in December. It came out to 140 finished pages & I see no hope of getting it published as an article. Maybe a book, but not without a lot more work that I'd rather not get into. But I may have to. As it stands now, I've worked four months for either $1000 or nothing at all. I seriously doubt if any editor will take the time to condense 140 pages down to 35 or so. I'll find out soon enough. Meanwhile the Killy piece was due today, the 25th—and the 5-day extension I got won't help much. I haven't even begun to write, and it will take a miracle to do the thing quickly, since there's not much to write about in the first place. After this, I'm declaring a moratorium on all articles until I can finish a book of some kind. There's one due July 1 for RH, but I won't make that either. All in all, there's not a lot of good news from this end—particularly after borrowing to pay long-overdue taxes, with penalties, charges, interest, etc.

Mom called the other night & talked to Sandy. I wasn't here, but apparently they had a good talk. Sandy said she seemed depressed, but not weird or difficult. There was something about a depressing letter from Jim, but it didn't sound like anything unusual. I've been meaning to send her $150 for my share of that tuition, and I'll get it done tomorrow. I think I have some funds left over from the tax panic. Life continues to become more complicated . . . although Sandy's pregnancy is coming along without problems. The thing is due sometime in July; and then I plan to have myself castrated. (christ, it's 25 of six here and I think the morning radio stations just cut into my night reception from LA and San Francisco, which come in like local stations at night . . . but now it's all static and whistling.) I got up around ten last night, so I suppose I'll be up all day. It was snowing the last time I looked outside; this filthy, muddy spring. . . . Snow, rain, & melting snow drive most people off to Mexico until June, but not me. Maybe next year, after a film sale of some kind. Or something. OK for now. I think Juan's about to get up, which means a taste of Captain Kangaroo & maybe the morning news. I guess I'll be around here until at least June, trying to put a book together. Ciao . . .

TO VIRGINIA THOMPSON:

Thompson wanted to make sure his draft-age brother had the option of staying in college.

April 27, 1969
Owl Farm

Dear Mom . . .

Here's my share of Jim's tuition ($150)—or at least my share, according to Davison. The last I recall, he was going to send half of the necessary $300 . . . so I guess this is the other half. I talked to Jim from Chicago about a month ago and couldn't make heads or tails of what he intended to do about school. . . . But, frankly, I can't see how any honest appraisal of his choice adds up to anything but a potluck of greater or lesser evils. I remember thinking I had a tough way to go at 19, but in fact I had a hell of a lot of options that Jim doesn't have in this goddamn war-maddened world. I'm not sure what I'd do today if my only choice was between staying at UK or getting drafted or going to jail or leaving the country. In all honesty, I think I'd leave the country . . . although I wouldn't want to and I'd feel I was being driven out. But I'd feel like a ghoulish hypocrite if I told anybody these days to grit his teeth and obey orders. Nobody kids themselves anymore about the military building character or anything else worth building. So, if a check now and then can help buy options, I figure it's nothing lost and a chance of something gained. Tell Jim to let me know how his prospects look. As I've said, I rarely *have* money, but I can usually get my hands on some when it's absolutely necessary.

On other fronts, Sandy said she and Juan had a good talk with you last week. I just finished a huge, impossible piece on guns and gun control. And now I have another due yesterday—and that's my rent and spending money, so I have to get on it. Let me know more about how things are going there. I'll be here until July, then probably another burst of traveling—after the baby arrives. Knock-knock. OK for now . . .

Love,
H

TO WILLIAM MURRAY:

Thompson's old friend William Murray, a Princeton graduate now working at The Saturday Evening Post, *had written about the Hell's Angels for his magazine.*

May 7, 1969
Woody Creek, CO

Dear Willie . . .

The Owl Farm is, as everyone knows, my place of residence since 1960. This one happens to be 25 acres and a large house finely situated in a pasture on a dirt road within long mortar's range of Aspen. I am always just a hair ahead of the action. There were those, you'll recall, who scorned my choice of dwelling areas in SF . . . little realizing, etc. So hang tough and wait till you hear about the Kingdom of Endor's scene out here . . . but if you show up out here with a big grin & a legal pad I'll blow your head off.

As for Tom Wolfe, yes, I *gave* him that scene. He called to ask if I had any tapes & of course I sent him the bundle. I learn slowly . . . but I can still smile affectionately at the mirror. Wolfe knows. And he knows that I know. And now, you, too . . . and in time maybe others, as it were. Or maybe not, but why worry? Given the strange and terrible nature of my contract haggling, I'll never be able to write again, anyway. I have now hired a NY literary lawyer, in addition to a new agent . . . and I've blown enough fat assignments to make nine men rich, but sometime soon I might publish something worthwhile. The novel remains in limbo while I spend numerous advances for other books I have no interest in writing. But I sense a crunch coming on. . . . So I may have to perform, if only briefly. I feel entirely on top of things, but the fucking world demands proof, if only to have something to bungle and misinterpret . . . but they pay for that privilege, so . . .

Anyway, regarding your [blues guitarist] BB King piece . . . I assume you understand that I'd never consider paying you a compliment in anything but the most oblique and devious manner. We all have our styles, and that's mine. Just for the record, however, the BB thing was done with a rare, painfully-honest kind of eye . . . not an ounce of fat or bullshit on it.

Jesus, I seem to be slipping.

Anyway, I expect to be out here through the summer, which looks entirely weird and active. I've been traveling all winter, blowing one assignment after another & running up huge bills on my new credit cards. Something will have to come of it very soon—by July 1, in fact, according to my contract. And after that I think I'd like to make a movie. We can ponder this drift on my next visit to your area, which I suspect will be about mid-summer. Sandy is ready to give birth in July, so I'll be here until then. Come on out if you get a chance. I have plenty of room.

Ciao,
Hunter

TO HUGHES RUDD, CBS NEWS:

Angling to get a story about Aspen's overdevelopment on the CBS News, Thompson lay out for Rudd what he saw as an impending showdown between the Freaks and the Cowboys in the rapidly changing resort town.

May 11, 1969
Woody Creek, CO

Dear Hughes . . .

It grieves me to have to inform you that the Kingdom of Endor has been at least temporarily shot down. . . . The Great Aspen Freak Festival is no more, due to heavy local pressure put on the two or three landowners willing to lease land for it. According to the promoters, the thing was derailed at the last possible moment by a flurry of phone calls to record companies by the Aspen Chamber of Commerce, warning of serious physical danger to the musicians. The Chamber people deny this, saying they only called to ask questions . . . and my peripheral interest doesn't allow for running up huge phone bills to establish a minor truth.

Either way, the War is already building (see enc. clip on "Hippie Harassment Suit"). What's lacking now is the focus that the Festival would have provided. The forecast now is for a series of clashes, building to a climax in early August. There is already talk of Vigilante action, to clean out hippie forest camps that have already formed. This happened around Boulder last year: Armed locals on horseback, scouring the canyons and destroying hippie camps (see xerox clip). Anyway, I'll let you know if it builds to anything compact enough for film. The story itself will be around all summer, but it's hard to predict the date of an actual clash. The festival would have been ideal film stuff, but now it's hard to say what to look for—in terms of specific dates. Both Boulder and Aspen have become ritual stopover points on coast-to-coast runs, and the underground word is already out on the freak festival here, so the outlook now is for a vast influx of hairy wildmen, shouting for music and action . . . and gangs of outraged cowboys roaming around with hair-shears. The difference this summer might be a replay of a recent scene at Sun Valley, where a gang of hippies beat a bunch of cowboys very severely. As I've noted on other occasions, non-violence is a dead ethic . . . and god only knows what's going to happen when Nixon brings 100,000 pot-smokers back from Vietnam. I can understand your outrage at the "collegiate gun-toting," but I wonder why it surprises you. We are reaping the whirlwind, and Cornell was only the beginning—like Berkeley in '64. [Mayor Richard] Daley set the style in Chicago; until then, SDS[16] was a peaceful debating society. Hell, even I'm getting harassed by these freaks. Old friends who once condemned my gun collection now call to ask my advice on buying guns. It's getting weird. . . .

Well, so much for all that. Hello to Ann, and tell Kuralt he'd better do his happy stories while he can, because pretty soon there won't be any. We are heading for a firestorm.

Ciao,
Hunter

TO JOHN WILCOCK, *LOS ANGELES FREE PRESS:*

Self-styled "hippie guru" John Wilcock was an editor and columnist at the anti-establishment Los Angeles Free Press, *which reached a weekly circulation of 95,000 in July 1969. Wilcock also published his own counterculture newsletter, to which Thompson subscribed.*

May 13, 1969
Woody Creek, CO

Dear John . . .

I'm sorry to say the Kingdom of Endor has apparently blown its gig inre: The Great Aspen Freak Festival. The available land was withdrawn last week and massive local pressure has scared off the few remaining possibilities. Threats of vigilante action by local rednecks were apparently conveyed to record companies by Aspen merchants who feared a crowd of non-buying hippies would scare off their normal summer trade . . . and under the circumstances, no record company would firmly commit the musicians. The sheriff helped by calling for an emergency appropriation for riot-control weapons.

Actually, the Kingdom of Endor blew it right at the start, by announcing that 100,000 people would come . . . and that scared even the local heads, who

16. Originally a reformist group, Students for a Democratic Society (SDS) had turned revolutionary in 1962 and then splintered apart in 1969, with one faction turning underground into the terrorist Weathermen.

feared it would bring an influx of heat, feds, narks, etc. Unfortunately, the word is already out, so god only knows what kind of a scene we'll have here by the end of July—probably all violence and no music, 50 busts a week and gangs of cowboys shooting at everybody with long hair. I may have to flee.

As it turns out, I was ready to send the piece a few days ago, but decided to hold off when the main promoter told me the Beatles were coming. That seemed a little heavy, so I checked around on the land situation and the thing began falling apart on all fronts. You may want to carry a note of some kind, warning the unwary. From what I hear, the festival rumor is already making the rounds on both coasts and the Denver papers have run a few scare stories—enough to panic the legislature into passing a bill aimed specifically at transient hippies (see enc. xerox clip).

The above is a good example of the bullshit hypocrisy that says "Dissent is fine, as long as it's within the law." Meanwhile, the bastards are busy changing the laws. In this case, last year's legal squatting is this year's $300 fine and 90 days in jail. Fuck them.

Anyway, sorry I couldn't write something on it . . . but I wouldn't want to be responsible for getting a bunch of people out here for a non-existent festival and a summer in jail instead of lying around on a mountaintop full of music. My only suggestion to anybody who still wants to come is Bring a few cans of Mace.

As for me, I think I'll get over to San Francisco and Big Sur, probably around the end of July. Sandy is due to drop a child in mid-July, so I'll be here until then. And of course there's always that goddamn book, due July 1. Jesus! Let me know if you plan to get out this way, or the coast. Ciao . . .

TO BERNARD SHIR-CLIFF, BALLANTINE BOOKS:

May 14, 1969
Woody Creek, CO

Dear Bernard . . .

How in the name of christ can I get a few copies of my book? I've ordered them through bookstores, I've ordered them directly from Ballantine and I have people on both coasts who've promised to send me the first copies they find. This is the third or fourth personal request *to you,* direct pleas. Christ, I'll pay for them. Send me fifty (50) copies and take it out of my royalties. I was right on the verge of apologizing to you for all the slander I've heaped on your sales techniques . . . then I noticed that way more than half of that check you sent was from hardcover royalties. Where in the name of creeping jesus have you buried those 550,000 copies you told me you had printed? If I ran that company I'd see your ass on welfare within 24 hours.

Meanwhile, I'm sitting here staring at about 400 pages of disconnected bullshit that may or may not boil into a book . . . and a letter from Silberman saying he's willing to relinquish *The Rum Diary* if the rewrite is as embarrassingly bad as the original. You publishing freaks are as evil as the pro football owners—and that gang of cynical swine should be fed into whirling blades.

Jesus! What a stinking day! I feel like whipping on a cop. Please send me those 50 books.

Hunter

TO JIM SILBERMAN, RANDOM HOUSE:

Grappling with how to get The Rum Diary *published, Thompson reflected on the beauty of F. Scott Fitzgerald's* The Great Gatsby, *his investment in Yellowknife Bear Mines Ltd., and the difficulties of writing for* Playboy *and* Esquire.

May 15, 1969
Woody Creek, CO

Dear Jim . . .

I sent your 5/6 letter on to Lynn & told her I wouldn't write any deal-shattering letters until I heard from her . . . but in looking at your letter again I see a thing out of focus, and in the interest of general honesty and keeping things straight I thought I'd try to correct it. I refer, of course, to the inference that I'm going to correct a few typos in the *Rum Diary* manuscript and then ship it off to market. I wish I could do that, but I know it's impossible. I can sit here and *say* I'm going to change a few lines, drop a few graphs and then fire it off . . . but I know better. So if you're basing whatever you're doing on the assumption that I'm not going to put any work into the rewrite, it seems only fair to warn you. . . .

The idea of giving it to Bernie was mine—inspired by the need to get the book out of limbo and early burial, for good or ill. My intention, for now, is to rewrite it mainly as a tight, visual narrative, with a minimum of philosophical bullshit—and hope to sell it as a film script. Actually, I see it as a way of loosening up a lot of old muscles, in order to get back into fiction-writing—or narrative-writing. The fact that a *ms.* exists is good enough excuse for using it for experimental purposes: having a cheap fling at blatantly visual writing, in line with that future-theory I sent you a month or so back—the concept of using the writer's eye as a camera lens, instead of Henry James' infamous window.

Speaking of that, I was reading *The Great Gatsby* again the other night, looking for a quote . . . and it struck me, in light of all this heavy [Ernest] Hemingway publicity going around, that *Gatsby* is better than any three of Hemingway's books lumped together . . . and I wonder what that means, except that re-reading *Gatsby* makes me wonder why I bother with nonfiction . . . but now I think of George Orwell's *Down and Out in Paris & London* . . . well, fuck . . . it's late and I've spent the day on the phone, hopefully settling my long-knotted efforts to buy this land-fort. It seems to be set now—a great breakthrough today, freeing my head for concentration on other things. It is no small trick out here in this land-grab, price-spiral frenzy to seize a $90,000 nut for $10,000. The ability to write a $10,000 personal check seems to be worth at least $100,000 in these weird times. In the grip of euphoria after settling the land deal, I finished the day by buying into the Arctic Circle oil strike—200 shares of Yellowknife Bear Mines Ltd. I think it's about time I participated in the economy, if only for educational purposes. If things keep breaking right I expect to set up the first Videotape Publishing House—coiled plastic books with miniature, battery-pack viewers—selling for $3.49 each. Maybe I'll hire you on, if things get lean on your end. Let me know.

As for writing—yeah, that antique bullshit—I've been trying to find time to edit my 2nd carbon of the 140 page monster I just sent off to *Esquire*—that NRA/Gun Lobby thing. Lynn suggested I send you a copy, and I will, but not until I finish this garbage piece for *Playboy* on Jean-Claude Killy. It has degenerated from quick money-job into a surly, back-handed commentary on the role of Public Relations in American Life. I think I have finally figured out what is knotting up everything I try to write these days—somewhere a lot longer ago than I like to admit, I suspect I began taking myself seriously. I think that accounts for the treacherous compulsion to lace everything I write with heavy, Greco-Roman wisdom . . . and that's the humor I want to burn out by means of this *Rum Diary* rewrite. With all the unbearably serious action almost everywhere these days, it seems like the nadir of twisted gall for a stockholder in the Yellowknife Bear Mines Ltd.—or even a writer—to take himself seriously, except in terms of survival.

OK for now. I hope you can handle all this wisdom—or at least the instinct that prompted it. All I meant to say, when I started, was that I wouldn't want you to be painfully surprised if *The Rum Diary* turns out to be one of the great weird-narratives of our time—the first of a trilogy, including "Bullfight" and "Burial at Sea." Yours for the gilding of all our lilies . . .

HST

TO DAVE FOGEL:

Dave Fogel had invited Thompson to speak at a gun control symposium in Maryland.

May 19, 1969
Woody Creek, CO

Dave . . .

Thank christ I won't be able to make your conference in Maryland . . . although frankly I'd like to do it, and in fact I'll try to at least stop in if I'm anywhere nearby. You might, in the meantime, try to interest that guy I mention in my last jangled letter from Washington—Carl Perian, chief investigator for the Senate JuvDelinq. Subcommittee (c/o Tom Dodd). He's a weird bugger—arrogant and narrow-minded in the classic Liberal tradition—but he could probably do you some good in terms of future publicity. Personally, I have to wonder about anybody who can get money from the current administration—particularly for anything except bombs and guns. How did you manage it? The whole notion of "good works" strikes me, for now, as a waste of energy. I am gearing down, mentally, physically and all other ways, for a very serious gig—maybe terminal.

Everybody I know on the activist circuit is buying guns. When the bastards start using shotguns to defend a vacant lot, we are not far from the Big Hammer. It may be that events will empty the prisons in ways you never plotted . . . I hope not, but I'm damned if I see any light at the end of this stinking tunnel. Anyway, stop by for a peaceful visit while there's still time.

Ciao . . .
Hunter

TO THOMAS H. O'CONNOR, IRVING LUNDBORG & CO.:

Even if he had *gone "establishment" enough to be building a stock portfolio, Thompson drew the line at investing in communications monopoly American Telephone & Telegraph, and he let his broker know it.*

Tom O'Connor
Irving Lundborg & Co.
San Francisco, CA

May 19, 1969
Woody Creek, CO

Tom . . .

I was expecting a call of some sort tonight—for no particular reason—but, failing that, I thought I should take to the writing machine to advise you that the idea of owning stock in ATT is so wholly and basically repugnant to me that I can't possibly live with it. I don't care if it's guaranteed to double in six months—or even triple. I want no part in it.

Why don't you take the ATT chunk of the $5000 and put it into Smith & Wesson, or whatever specific division it is of Bangor Punta that deals heavily in riot-control equipment—Mace and that sort of thing. Ideally, I'd like to buy S&W/Bangor Punta stock now, then spend all summer driving it up, then sell in the fall. Firearms are getting to be like diamonds—and ATT is a clunker's gig, for sure, so let's get right into the action. Dump the ATT stuff & buy Bangor Punta—or Smith & Wesson if you can narrow it down that far. I can live with British Petroleum and Yellowknife Bear Mines, but I'll be goddamned if I want to look in my mirror each morning and see an ATT shareholder. OK for now . . .

Hunter

TO THE DISABLED AMERICAN VETERANS ASSOCIATION:

Thompson crafted a thoughtful anti–Vietnam War response to a fundraising appeal from the Disabled American Veterans Association.

May 19, 1969
Woody Creek, CO

Disabled American Veterans
Cincinnati, Ohio 45214

Gentlemen . . .

I am returning your stamped envelopes. My son ran off with the small green license tags you sent. . . . But I doubt if they would be much use to you anyway. The stamped envelopes are legal tender, however, and maybe you can use them for something else.

My first impulse was to send you a check . . . but I caught myself on some vagrant memory of having read somewhere that the DAV fully supports the War in Vietnam . . . which, if true, strikes me as a stupid, ignorant and half-mad stance that no American citizen in his right mind could possibly endorse, even tacitly, by sending a contribution. The senseless butchery in Vietnam is too awful for any words—from me or anyone else. And the only thing more awful and senseless than the butchery is the twisted reality of an organization like the DAV supporting the war.

If I'm wrong on this point, please inform me at once—with a copy of some pertinent DAV statement or position paper—and I'll send you a check for $50 . . . along with a very sincere apology. But if I'm right, I suggest you abandon this vicious, demented hypocrisy and look for honest work. Sincerely,

Hunter S. Thompson
Box 37 . . . Woody Creek
Colorado 81656

TO VIRGINIA THOMPSON:

Thompson's mother had written to tell him that she was selling the house he grew up in.

May 23, 1969
Woody Creek, CO

Dear Mom . . .

It's 4:30 Saturday morning here, and I'm just getting to work—far behind on everything, stone broke again, and coming to hate the sight of a typewriter. Your news about the house is good, I guess, but I naturally view it with mixed feelings. There is definite irony—for me, at least—in the fact that I got your letter the morning after I spent hours on the midnight phone, settling a very complicated deal to buy this place. Since I have no income of record, no property, no credit, no job history, no education and no advancement prospects—it takes a considerable amount of fine haggling to get hold of a $77,000 property in the midst of a spiraling land market. I think I've sent pictures of this house, which is part of the deal—along with the smaller, next-door house that Noonan is living in, and about 25 acres with a spectacular view and another fine house-site. You'll have to get out here and see the whole thing, once it's settled. I assume it's set, but I won't be sure until around mid-July—about the same time Sandy is due.

Anyway, it is weird to get your news of the house-sale just as I'd bought one for myself. Under the circumstances, $18,000 seems low—but that's only by comparison with this fiendishly inflated land market around Aspen, which is totally out of control. Quarter-acre lots in town sell easily for $15,000 and up, and raw pastureland five miles from the nearest road goes for $3000 an acre. It would take me several hours to explain how I fell into this deal. I have to take some pictures of the whole area soon, for survey and contract purposes, and I'll send you some prints. If the deal goes through, my life will be considerably less pressured, since I've been living for the past year with the knowledge that it was only a matter of time before the whole place would be sold out from under me.

Hopefully, I'll be able to get back to Louisville sometime this summer, for a farewell visit with the house. Let me know more specifically when you plan to move, and where. The next few months are going to be a nightmare of complicated action, with a book due July 1 (impossible), a baby due July 15 and the house sale to watch over—along with a necessary research trip to the Coast for several weeks, and god only knows what else. My Doberman bitch is expecting pups in a week or so, the cat is ready to drop kittens, and . . . well, why go on? Let me know more about the house situation when you can, and tell Jim we'll be expecting him for a visit when he gets fired. OK for now . . .

Love,
H

TO SELMA SHAPIRO, RANDOM HOUSE:

Publicist Selma Shapiro was Thompson's biggest booster at Random House, always telling the higher-ups that he had more talent—if less discipline—than Norman Mailer or Tom Wolfe.

May 25, 1969
Woody Creek, CO

Dear Selma . . .

I just found the letter you wrote just before you left. I'm not sure what prompted me to root through my stack of unanswered mail to find it. Once a letter gets into that stack, it invariably disappears. The only ones I seem to answer are the ones I deal with at once . . . and since you were leaving, there was hardly any sense in replying at that point, when I got it.

Needless to say, the letter was vaguely embarrassing. Anything decent or human makes me nervous; I am much more at home with people I can abuse or play games with. Maybe that's what you meant by my "WASP attitudes." . . . (break) . . . I just had to rush outside with a shotgun to drive off a vicious tomcat who comes around every night to attack my pregnant female, but the bastard got away again. I guess this is a good example of my WASP attitudes. Well, what the hell? It used to worry me that I was really an evil redneck, but now I sort of like it . . . and with summer coming on, I may find time to exercise some of my ancient, brutal skills. The action in Berkeley is only the beginning, I think. Someday very soon, freaks are going to shoot back, and I'm not sure what's going to happen after that. I've been amazed, in the course of my wanderings this winter, to find how many people are seriously preparing for a street-war—and most of them want it. All they need is an excuse to start shooting, just enough chaos to guarantee they won't get caught. The more I learn about this country, the more I think I should live somewhere else. I don't mind the idea of armed revolution as much as I fear the aftermath. I'd be locked up, regardless of who won. . . .

Well . . . fuck all that; it's a depressing thing to write about except for money, and right now that's exactly what I should be doing. I have a silly, useless article for *Playboy* due about 6 weeks ago, and I want to get rid of it and get to that book. I am much further along than I seem to be, in terms of actual ms. pages, but not nearly far enough. The hangup is articles—although most of them fit the book research. Too well, I think. It's no longer possible for me to write a short, concise article. The thing on the National Rifle Association for *Esquire* eventually came to 140 pages, after many cuts. I sent it on to Erickson, but god only knows what he'll do with it. I think he was expecting about 35 pages. The space and freedom of book-writing has completely spoiled me for articles. I'd much rather write 300 pages than 30—but it's hard to spurn a quick shot at $2000 for some meaningless piece of tripe for *Playboy* . . . although I have somehow managed to get hung up in that one too.

Actually, my main efforts for the past year have been in the area of seizing a land fortress in Woody Creek, and I think that's finally happened. If you recall my compulsive rage at a publishing contract that seemed to cheat me out of $5000, consider the shape of my head after finally arranging a formula that would make it possible for me to buy a $100,000 piece of land (with two houses) for $77,000 . . . with only $4000 to my name at the moment & no real prospects for more, and no hope of bank financing. That last royalty check provided me with the illusion of vast wealth, so I was able to parlay a meagre nut into a brief but effective display of MONEY POWER . . . yes, heavy dealing. You'd be amazed at the reaction you can stir up by wandering around a boom-town like Aspen, spreading the word that you're looking for a way to get rid of $10,000 *instantly,* waving a checkbook around, buying $2 drinks instead of beer . . . jesus, I had stockbrokers calling me from San Francisco, people with all manner of fantastic land and mining deals, dope dealers looking for a partner, gun runners from L.A. . . . and the end result was a mountain of instant-leverage to force this land thing through . . . and that's all I really wanted in the first place. You'll have to come out and see it next winter; arrange a publicity conference or something like that, tell them I've broken my spleen and can't travel, so you have to come out here and confer.

Yeah . . . I know, I'll have to write a dingbat huge-selling book to make it all work. So I guess I'll have to bear down. It's hard to take that whole gig seriously these days, particularly when I can't think of anything else I have to do or prove. My only serious game at the moment is this notion of writing a fictional documentary and refusing to admit it's fictional . . . but that's a different kind of subject, and first I have to get this goddamn *Playboy* thing done. It's 4:00 a.m. now and the 6:00 news is coming up, then the sun . . . and it's getting so I hate to go to bed on these bright green mornings. The other day I was heading for the bedroom when I saw the tree-merchant out in the yard, so I loaded up on enough pills to carry me through the day and did a tree-planting act, with much beer and music . . . but now I owe for the trees, and a lot of other things, and the people who thought I was rich two weeks ago are due for a shock. In the meantime, though, I think I have the land-fort settled, and that's as important as a book or any other breakthrough. I am tired of being driven around like a mangy dog; after 10 years of being evicted from every place I've lived in—without exception—the prospect of a personal fort has become an obsession, and now that I have it settled I may be able to focus on some newer and heavier main project.

Jesus, I have just 2 more hours until the news, so I'll have to quit this rambling. Looking at your letter again, I see Frederick Exley's name;[17] I'm reading his book now. There is something very good and right about it, hard to define. He's not a "good writer" in any classic sense, and most of what he says makes me feel I'd prefer to avoid him . . . but the book is still good. Very weird. I suppose it's the truth-level, a demented kind of honesty. . . . As for *Portnoy's Complaint,* I can't get up the interest to deal with it. Philip Roth has never interested me as a writer; maybe he's different in person. But I'll read the book and say something to prove I got through it. Or maybe not. I recall feeling the same way about Styron's book,[18] but I finally abandoned it—despite my 10-year

17. Frederick Exley's 1968 novel, *A Fan's Notes*, tells the story of a man—also named Frederick Exley—who wrecks much of his life via failings from excessive drinking to his obsession with University of Southern California and New York Giants football star Frank Gifford.

18. William Styron won the 1968 Pulitzer Prize for Fiction for his novel *The Confessions of Nat Turner*, a fictionalized account of the 1831 Virginia slave rebellion led by the real-life Turner, who was executed for his actions.

booster's campaign for *Lie Down in Darkness,* which I still think is one of the best books in English. But maybe that's just my WASP thing . . . although I think Malamud[19] is as good or better than anybody I can think of right now. I've never paid much attention to the Black/Jew/WASP problem; it strikes me as a waste of time and energy. My prejudice is pretty general, far too broad and sweeping for any racial limitations. It's clear to me—and has been since the age of 10 or so—that most people are bastards, thieves and yes—even pigfuckers. There are not many good people in this world, and in terms of racial action I like Dick Gregory's notion: "This isn't a matter of black and white—it's a matter of right and wrong."[20]

OK . . . and so much for all that. I'm enclosing a matchbook cover from a restaurant that comes to me on the highest recommendation, a neighbor of mine who owns the Paragon (french restaurant in Aspen) which enjoys the high praise of that [Craig] Claiborne fellow from *The NY Times.* Anyway, Bruce LeFavour says the King Wu is the best Chinese restaurant he's ever been in—and Bruce is a certified gourmet, a graduate from some famous chef's school in Paris and does all the cooking for the Paragon. If you can make it out here for a conference of some kind, I'll buy you a dinner there. I won't ski with you, but what the hell . . . you can't have everything.

Probably I'll get to NY sometime this summer. I have a hell of a lot to do, mainly on both coasts, and I have to be here in July when Sandy is due to hatch a second mutant Thompson. The cat and my Doberman bitch are also ready to hatch . . . every female in the area is pregnant. I feel like Johnny Appleseed—dogs, cats, children, trees, grass, huge wooden structures, pottery, metal sculptures; I have a euphoric sense of building a dynasty of some kind. So maybe I should grow a beard, along with all the rest. We'll see . . . and in the meantime, tack this King Wu ad someplace where you won't lose it, and when I get to NY we can go down there and try it. See you then. . . .

Love,
Hunter

TO JIM SILBERMAN, RANDOM HOUSE:

Thompson submitted an inventory of all the periodicals he was reading in his daily pursuit of the Death of the American Dream.

19. In 1967 Bernard Malamud won both the Pulitzer Prize and the National Book Award for his novel *The Fixer*, about a poor Jewish handyman in early twentieth-century Russia who is arrested for a crime he did not commit.

20. Dick Gregory was a prominent African-American civil rights activist and comedian.

May 25, 1969
Woody Creek, CO

Dear Jim . . .

Here is a relatively complete list of the various newspapers and magazines I've subscribed to in the course of my far-flung research on the Death of the American Dream. Some are obviously more relevant than others, and the list includes a few I'd obviously get anyway, but none that can't be reasonably linked to the subject-matter—and your title.

The most pertinent objection, as I see it, is that no human being could read all this bullshit and still have time to write a long book. Accordingly, I am letting a lot of the subscriptions lapse—things like *Business Week* and . . . jesus, I guess that's it . . . and in scanning the list I notice a few that Sandy left off: the *American Rifleman, La Raza, New Left Notes, Rolling Stone* (the paper, not the book), *Washington Monthly, The Nation* . . . goddamn, it boggles the brain.

Anyway, please send the funds. My secret land purchase and other long-term investments have left me naked of cash. That $5000 for the first third of the book looks better and fatter every day. The moment I finish this rotten *Playboy* article, I'll bear down on it. I've written a complete outline of the book, but I think I'll wait a while before sending it along. The fiction aspect is so prominent that I want to be sure it's going to work before committing myself. OK for now . . . and thanks:

Hunter

Magazine/Newspaper	Date Subscribed	Cost
New York Times	4/8/68	$22.60
Newsweek	4/18/68	2.97
Foreign Affairs	4/21/68	8.00
American Scholar	4/21/68	5.00
Time	4/23/68	2.40
Conservative Book Club	4/25/68	4.81
Business Week	4/25/68	10.00
Transaction	4/25/68	6.00
Columbia Journalism Review	4/25/68	6.00
National Observer (Newsbooks)	4/28/68	4.45
Ramparts	6/2/68	12.50
New Republic	6/18/68	10.00
San Francisco Chronicle	6/24/68	12.00
Current	6/24/68	2.00
Time	7/24/68	3.97
Life	7/24/68	2.97
San Francisco Chronicle	9/24/68	12.00

Psychology Today	10/17/68	6.00
Mayday	11/2/68	7.50
John Wilcock's Newsletter	11/30/68	6.00
New York Times	12/2/68	21.50
Life	12/2/68	3.98
Esquire	12/2/68	15.00
Playboy	12/2/68	8.00
Columbia Journalism Review	12/2/68	6.00
I. F. Stone's Weekly	12/25/68	11.95
Chicago Journalism Review	12/16/68	5.00
Atlantic Monthly	1/8/69	4.25
Evergreen Review	1/18/69	9.00
Rolling Stone Book	3/12/69	9.00
San Francisco Chronicle	3/25/69	12.00
SDS Literature	3/27/69	10.00

TO THOMAS H. O'CONNOR, IRVING LUNDBORG & CO.:

Only a few months after buying stocks, Thompson was ready to get out of the bearish market.

June 8, 1969
Woody Creek, CO

Tom O'Connor
Irving Lundborg & Co.
San Francisco

Dear Tom . . .

I'm returning this goddamn thing you sent me the other day; it doesn't tell me anything except that my losses are confirmed by computer. I saw [Robert] Craig yesterday and cursed him savagely for advising me to fuck around with the stock market in the first place. I should have known better than to buy into anything that goddamn bonehead Nixon was running.

Tell me—is there any likelihood that this stinking downhill slide will reverse itself anytime soon? By "soon," I mean within the next six months. If not, I think I'll quit while I'm still solvent . . . and by quit I mean SELL, boom, fuck it. If the health of the market depends in any way on Nixon ending the war, then the market is going to be a sinkhole for the next two years and I want no part of it. As for particulars, all I know for sure is that Bangor Punta has lost one point in three weeks, while ATT and Brit. Pet [British Petroleum] have lost about three points each. And I'd rather not know about Yellowknife right now; I suspect the quotation would drive me up the wall.

Unless you know something I don't, let's quit. I have to assume, of course, that you do know something I don't—since you're a stockbroker and I'm not.

But my problem—as I noted earlier—is that I can't afford to wait for Nixon and his 19th century money-wizards to come to grips with reality. He apparently wants to beat all his opponents to death, and in that case I think things like Bangor Punta are the only kind of stocks to own. . . .

Well, to hell with all this. I see no point in haggling about it. Frankly, I see no light at the end of the tunnel . . . and unless you do, let's sell or switch, or at least do something. I have the feeling right now that I'm on a long downhill run, and I don't like it. Let me know soonest. . . .

Thanks,
Hunter S. Thompson

TO CHARLES KURALT, CBS NEWS:

Kuralt's "On the Road" segments for CBS were a bit too upbeat and down-home for Thompson's taste.

June 9, 1969
Woody Creek, CO

Charley . . .

I think it's about time you got off your Nero act and get down in the mire with the rest of us. Primarily, I think you should launch a personal vendetta against Justice William O. Douglas; that evil old bugger is so crooked that he has to screw his pants on every morning. I'm counting on you to bury him.

Where are you? You should get through Aspen for the summer freak festival. I wrote Hughes [Rudd] about it, but the news angle faded when the moment of confrontation faded into infinity.

Maybe you should come out here for Jack Benny's concert.[21] Yeah . . . I'm serious. He's doing a straight classical concert for the Aspen Music Associates . . . the old, respectable folks. Jack Benny. Can anyone doubt that Nixon is running things?

Fear and loathing. You should get that bastard Douglas before he can do any further harm. The dirty old geek is worse than B. Baker and Walter Jenkins combined.[22] Forswear those ancient clocks and nickelodeons. . . . Dig the mud! And send word. . . .

Ciao . . .
Hunter

TO OSCAR ACOSTA:

Thompson shares his first bad LSD experience with Acosta.

21. Comedian Jack Benny was seventy-five years old in 1969.
22. LBJ's close personal aides Bobby Baker and Walter Jenkins had been hauled up on financial and morals charges, respectively.

June 9, 1969
Woody Creek, CO

O . . .

Well, I finally came down to it—a really ugly acid trip. I took one of those blue buggers of yours on top of a full mescaline pill after about 30 sleepless hours at Phil Clark's annual Daisy Duck party with 6 hours of beer and straight vodka in cups . . . and I finished the day in a paranoid frenzy, driving Tim Thibeau off the property with a loaded .44 Mag. My main horror, all afternoon, was a firm conviction that I was locked in a clutch of junkies, real needle freaks . . . and even now I suspect maybe I was right. That's the trouble with acid: you can never be sure you're hallucinating. Anyway . . . I'm giving it up for the duration. Either way, it's too heavy.

Otherwise, not much action here. The Killy piece is still not finished, a terrible mess on my desk. Thibeau is here for the summer with a carpenter's license from Chicago; John Pond just arrived with a woman from Brazil. . . . No optimism in either camp.

Esquire sent a conditional acceptance on the Gun-piece, but it still has to pass the final test with Harold Hayes.[23] I'd put the chances at 50–50. Don Erickson, the Managing Editor, spent about a week cutting it down to 50 pages . . . the trouble is I don't know which 50. We'll see. How are you faring with *The Nation*? On balance, I see a mean heavy summer coming up—and pure hell in the fall. Send word. Ciao . . .

HST

TO WILLIAM J. KENNEDY:

Thompson sent a quick catch-up note to novelist William Kennedy in Albany.

June 9, 1969
Woody Creek, CO

Dear Fatback . . .

I just found a letter from Lee Berry that I thought I'd answered months ago . . . and it says he'll be moving on "by March." In other words, I have no idea where he is. Do you know, via the paper? Is he still sending the stuff? Any word? Addresses? If so, tell me.

No word from you since the last drug-aborted visit. I assume you're too embarrassed to face it. But what the hell? You're getting old and crazy . . . why not face up to it? Send a line. I gave that ski sweater I was wearing to my brother in suburban Cleveland . . . and I think the pants went into the padding for my new Doberman box, with eight new tenants. My price is $250, but for you I might go $199.

23. Harold Hayes, formerly of the New York *Herald Tribune*, was editor of *Esquire* magazine.

I just got word from *Esquire* that, instead of hurling my 3-month-late 140 page gun article out the window, Don Erickson fought it down to 50 pages that he now intends to submit to Hayes, the final eye. I'm amazed; chances are up to 50–50 on that news, and I guess I'll know in a week or so. It seems like a bad, stupid joke to go through all that for $1000 . . . but I'm getting a little tired of writing articles that everybody praises and nobody prints. "Tired" ain't really the word. I think "dead" is more like it. Now all I have to do is finish that stupid fucking thing for *Playboy*—that ski piece. Yeah, that too—hung up . . .

What word on the novel? What date? Be sure to send a copy to Selma Shapiro at Random House; I told her you would. Have you read *A Fan's Notes* by Exley? Try it.

I have a plot for August—involving travel on your part—but I don't dare mention it now. We'll see how things work in the meantime. And also in the meantime, send a word. . . .

HST

—and Berry's new address

FROM WILLIAM J. KENNEDY:

Kennedy's novel Legs *had just been purchased by Dial Press.*

June 21, 1969
Averill Park, NY

Hunter:

Berry's address for a very, very few days is c/o US Consulate, Visitors Mail, 2 Avenue Gabriel, Paris, France, and then he will be coming home. I don't know whether a letter you write after reading this will reach him. I'm writing him today and I'll tell him you were interested and maybe he'll send you a new address. He covered the Cannes film festival, then came back to Paris, then planned to go to London for a week, then to Paris again and home; so he told the editor here. I have had no recent word.

My news is that I sold another novel, in April. Dial bought it for 4½ Gs, payable in 4 installments. Book is a fictionalized version of the life of Legs Diamond, the gangster. He was killed in Albany. A most unconventional approach to the material, however, which you'll see in due time. Definitely not another gangster story. Meantime this week I got the galleys on *The Ink Truck*, which as far as I know is still scheduled for September publication. *Esquire* dicked around with a fragment of *The Ink Truck* for a month or so and almost bought it. Your friend Erikson (sp?) went ape for it, so said my agent. Rust Hills dug it and pushed for it, but Hayes ultimately said it was too much (40 manuscript pages) for the value (an unknown writer). So it moved along elsewhere. I got an apologetic note from Hills, hoping I won't hold it against *Esquire* when I've got more fiction to peddle. Robie McCauley at *Playboy* couldn't spot anything to excerpt in it, but he thinks I'm a most original cat. All this praise gets me nothing without a publication. I'm pessimistic about marketing any fragments before publication, but we keep trying.

Re: August. Our kids are going to Puerto Rico to spend some time with their grandmother. Probably leaving second last week in July. We're tentatively thinking about going down in August to retrieve them and have some Fun In Sun, also get Num in Rum. I've assumed that you were still interested in this trek. If you are, then it is time we began coordinating travel schedules, itineraries and length of stay, etc. I'm flexible on the dates, but August is definitely the best month. Send your plans soon.

2nd novel, by the way, was sold on basis of 150 preliminary pages which are already dead. I've done nothing but read and do research ever since the sale. By August I may be started on the writing again.

Haven't read *Fan's Notes* by Allen [*sic*] Exley but will try to find it. Am locked in on the prohibition era, Borges[24] and mysticism. Which reminds me that I wrote Allen Ginsberg[25] and told him you were by and that we almost made the scene at his place. He regretted we didn't; said he wondered where your head was at these days.

Any sounds from McGarrsville? Best to Sandy.

Mr. Kennedy

TO DAVE ALLEN, KREX-TV:

As a dedicated night owl and news junkie, Thompson relied on his sole TV channel's 6 A.M. Mountain Time broadcast of the CBS Morning News *from New York to catch up on the rest of the world before going to bed. Besides, his friend Hughes Rudd had just become a regular contributor to the program.*

July 3, 1969
Owl Farm
Woody Creek, CO

Dave Allen
Program Director
KREX-TV
Grand Junction, CO

Dear Mr. Allen . . .

I was shocked and outraged yesterday morning to find that KREX-TV had dropped the *CBS Morning News*—and replaced it with nothing, absolutely nothing. I find this hard to believe. What could possibly possess a man to drop the best news show on television and replace it with NOTHING? Beyond that,

24. Argentine fiction writer Jorge Luis Borges.
25. Beat poet Allen Ginsberg had coined the 1960s term "flower power."

I'm sure you realize that cutting a one-hour news show in the morning amounts to cutting the station's news coverage almost in half . . . and to people like me who can't take time in mid-afternoon to watch the [6 P.M. Eastern] Cronkite news (and who live beyond the reach of any TV cable service), it eliminates national news altogether. And I say this with full knowledge that KREX does indeed have a 10:00 p.m. "news" show . . . which is sort of like a record company offering "The Songs of Joan Baez, by Winnie Ruth Judd."

Speaking of *Judd, for the Defense,* I notice you've finally put him back on the schedule—along with Johnny Cash[26]—and for those two reasons I'll spare you the kind of letter I might otherwise have written. You may recall my comments when you dropped *Judd*—which has since won an Emmy[27] and also been cancelled. But what the hell? Last year's *Judd* is better than anything on your current schedule, and I'm grateful. The Cash show is a merciful balance to that monstrous waterhead-zoo called *Hee-Haw.* Christ, that should embarrass even KREX, and I say that with my head still reeling from that hour-long commercial you ran the other night: The "Miss Wool" contest—an obvious fraud on the viewer.

In any case, I strongly urge you to re-fill the 6–7 a.m. slot with Joe Benti's CBS news. It *can't* be that expensive, and I know I'm not the only person who misses it. Sooner or later the KREX management will have to learn that a station becomes competitive by running good programs, not cheap ones. Meanwhile, I will of course file a formal complaint with the FCC, as I have twice before in the past—if the *CBS Morning News* fails to re-appear within a week or so. It seems to me that chopping the station's news content by half amounts to cynical mockery of the whole "public interest" concept. I hope you'll consider this aspect.

Thanks . . .
Hunter S. Thompson

TO JOE BENTI, CBS NEWS:

Joseph Benti anchored the CBS Morning News *from early 1966 through August 1970.*

July 4, 1969
Woody Creek, CO

Dear Mr. Benti . . .

I'm enclosing a letter (copy of) that I just sent to the geek who controls the only TV station I can get on my set. If there's any way CBS can influence the

26. Like others in tiny rural markets, KREX-TV was "shared" by the major networks, allowing the station to air both the *CBS Morning News* and ABC's prime-time programs *Judd, for the Defense* (about a flashy, liberal-leaning lawyer) and the country music/variety *Johnny Cash Show.*
27. *Judd, for the Defense* star Carl Betz won the 1969 Emmy Award for outstanding continued performance by a lead actor in a TV drama series.

fucker to pick up your morning news show again, I assure you that I won't be alone on this end of the tube. TV is a goddamn nightmare out here anyway (see copy of 9/68 letter for context; [former station manager Bud] Palmer has since quit & fled the area), and the loss of the only first-class news show on the air is a serious, hurtful thing. If there's any way you might help to revive the show on KREX, working from your end, I'd certainly appreciate it . . . although I can't imagine how you could lean on some yahoo dingbat who figures all the news is a Red plot anyhow.

Unfortunately, these same yahoos are going to have to open their own heads pretty quickly, or some of them are going to start shooting at us . . . certainly me, maybe you; "us" is a risky term these days. Anyway, your show is one of the best things on TV; the difference between your action and Cronkite's is as obvious as the difference between Studs Terkel and Eric Hoffer[28] . . . and that was a fine series you did with Terkel; he's one of the best people around.

Actually, the only thing wrong with your show is the vicious, sloppy presence of that pigfucker, Hughes Rudd. Christ, what a bummer! Can't something be done to get that filthy acid freak off the air? I know the bastard and I can testify, flat-out, to the absolute basic foulness of the man. . . . I've tried to convince his wife to come out here and live with me, but he has some fiendish hold over her. I suspect he has something on Frank Stanton, owner of CBS, too. You owe it to yourself to get the goods on that swinish pervert.

OK for now. Do what you can to reinstate your show out here . . . and I'll hassle the pigs from this end.

Thanx,
Hunter S. Thompson

FROM TOM WOLFE:

Wolfe had seen a photograph of Thompson in an unlikely magazine.

July 5, 1969

Dear Hunter,

As you may know, I never DID make it to Aspen—in fact, never got a foot out of New York, as seems to be usual with me in the summertime. A freaking unfinished magazine article (& a weird movie) stymied me. A real mis-cue on my part, I guess—especially since I just picked up a magazine that singled you out, in full color, as one of the major tourist attractions of the Rockies (or was it your chopped BSA?)

Yours,
Tom

28. Studs Terkel was an author and columnist for the *Chicago Tribune*, Eric Hoffer a San Francisco–based socialist writer.

TO TOM WOLFE:

July 10, 1969
Woody Creek, CO

Dear Tom . . .

Sorry you missed the "action" out here. It weren't much—a gang of dilettantes, haggling over details, for an audience of nazis. It's beyond me to see how you can function on that circuit, unless it pays a hell of a lot . . . and even then, I wonder.

Anyway, what magazine were you talking about inre: that photo of me and the bike? It puzzles me; the only photographer who's been out here in a long while came from SOVFOTO and swore he wouldn't sell anything within the continental limits of the U.S. What magazine? What issue? Could you instruct your secretary to send me the details: I have my own reasons. . . .

The bike, by the way, is a Bultaco—a lightweight Spanish bugger, built for dirt-riding instead of freeways. My BSA was three times the size of the one I have now; wholly impractical for mountain riding . . . but more and more, in the shank of these long summer nights, I miss the big one. Or maybe it's just that I've been a long way from the edge for too long; getting flabby and slow. We'll see, I guess—the book was due July 1.

Ciao . . .
Hunter

TO DAVE ALLEN, KREX-TV:

Upon receiving Thompson's complaint about the CBS Morning News *being taken off the air, an annoyed Allen wrote back, taking issue with his foul language and rude asides. It was not the type of reply Thompson was expecting.*

July 10, 1969
Woody Creek, CO

Dave Allen
Assistant General Manager
KREX-TV
Grand Junction, CO

Dear Mr. Allen . . .

Thanks for your letter of July 7. I was particularly struck by the fact that you "take exception to the profanities utilized in (my) letter" . . . and to that I can only say Fuck Off.

I take exception to 99% of the cheap goddamn garbage you put on the air. Your scheduling is a monument to everything rotten in America . . . and you have the gall to sit there and call my July 3 letter "profane." You ignorant freak; from now on I'll address you on your own level.

You're a fine example of the kind of waterhead who has crippled the whole television medium. If you think my letter was profane, you should take a look at the Real World sometime—the world you tried to censor when you cut CBS News.

But it's still out there, old sport, and it's closing in. Did you really think you could duck out of reality by fleeing Pennsylvania? Why don't you send *Gunsmoke*'s Marshal Dillon out to arrest me for my profanity?

Sincerely,
Hunter S. Thompson

TO JIM SILBERMAN, RANDOM HOUSE:

Frustrated that Playboy *had killed his Jean-Claude Killy piece as too wild to publish, Thompson forwarded the article to his Random House editor, along with his latest invoice for expenses incurred in tracking "The Death of the American Dream."*

July 10, 1969
Woody Creek, CO

Dear Jim . . .

Here is an unedited copy of my *Playboy* article on Jean-Claude Killy. It'll never run, so I thought I'd send this version along to see if you see any salvageable parts for the book. As I said, the only aspect that looms large—to me—is that accidental return to the Amphitheatre, beginning around pg. 40 and running to pg. 50 or so.

I urge you to read this section, since it comes very close to what I see as the backbone of the book . . . and for that reason it might be a fine ending. Or maybe the Nixon Inaugural should be the ending . . . and this Killy/Stockyards thing should come as a mid-book epitaph to the Chicago/Convention section, which is now in the process of shaping itself.

Anyway, read at least the section from pg. 40 to 50 . . . and the rest of the piece if you have time. It is now in the doom-shute at *Playboy.* The initial vote, I've learned, was 2–1 *for* it, but the negative vote came from Jim Goode, the article's editor, who deplored my scurvy comments on Chevy and that crowd . . . all of which were quite deliberate and even edited down considerably from my original version, which was intolerably vicious, even by my standards. They shoved me into a world that I've spent 10 years getting away from, and all it proved to me was that I was right back in 1958, when *Time* fired me, and in 1959 when I was fired from the Middletown (NY) *Daily Record* for sending a plate of lasagna back to the kitchen of a restaurant owned by a local advertiser—which led to a massive scene in the publisher's office, demands for apologies, etc., and thence to the dole at the NYState Unemployment Office.

I have not sought employment since that time, and on balance it's been a good 10 years . . . the same 10 yrs that I mean to use as spiritual background for the whole book, for good or ill. I suspect that parts of this Killy thing—particularly the beginning and the end—are pertinent enough to use in some way, but I'm not sure how they will work chronologically. Maybe you can see a pattern. In any case, I'll be sending a large and vaguely disorganized bundle in a few days. Meanwhile, hang onto this Killy piece and fit it in, if possible, wherever you see fit. As for the NRA/Gun thing, *Esquire* has yet to render a final judgement. Erickson apparently spent many hours chopping it down to a length suitable for presentation to H. Hayes . . . and a decision of some sort should be public in a day or so. Lynn will probably know before I do.

Frankly, I'm appalled at the time and space I wasted on all that dead/theory garbage . . . which amounts to saying that I agree with the style and tone of your comments. The Killy piece suffers from the same kind of affliction—a maddening compulsion to do all my thinking in print. I'm as aware of this problem as you are, but it continues to plague me, and cripple my articles, which would certainly be a hell of a lot more saleable if I could keep the focus on people, words and action—rather than the internal dialogues of HST. Hopefully, I can keep this in mind during the construction of the book . . . and if I seem to be slipping, for christ's sake remind me. On other fronts, thanx for the action inre: my various newspaper/magazine subscriptions (the check). I'm not sure how much I really learned from that heap . . . and I wonder how much time I wasted by reading all that bullshit. Maybe my next book should be a commentary on American Journalism. One of the things that struck me most—in my reading of three daily papers—was the vastly different worlds portrayed in the *NYTimes, Denver Post* and the *SFChronicle.* Neither *Time* nor *Newsweek* comes close to "capsuling" the vast, mad sprawl that appears in *any one* of the three—much less all of them. And TV news is a different world entirely. Even on CBS, Joe Benti's morning news portrays a different world than Cronkite and Sevareid show in the evenings: CBS's resident philosopher at dawn is Studs Terkel, and at night it's Eric Hoffer . . . two worlds, like Joan Baez and Winnie Ruth Judd, Ramsey Clark and J. Edgar Hoover, Mark Rudd and General Hershey[29] . . . with nothing in common except ignorance.

And so much for that. There are, to be sure, several levels of ignorance in this world . . . just as Faulkner was fond of noting the various levels of cowardice.[30] Selah . . .

My only other question at this time concerns funds. You didn't answer my query about the chance of my using some part of my expense budget to simply sit here and write. At the moment I have $2,121 in pressing bills to cope with,

29. Folksinger Joan Baez; trunk murderess Winnie Ruth Judd; former U.S. attorney general Ramsey Clark; FBI director J. Edgar Hoover; Columbia University senior and SDS chapter head Mark Rudd; and U.S. Army general Lewis Hershey, who in 1965 had tried to initiate "punitive reclassification" into the draft for antiwar protesters with deferments who had been arrested.

30. In his Nobel Prize for Literature acceptance speech in Stockholm on December 10, 1950, William Faulkner claimed that "the basest of all things is to be afraid."

in addition to Sandy on the verge of giving birth at any moment . . . and since I've spent only half my expense budget I feel it's only reasonable to apply some portion of it here and now, where it's needed, instead of casting around for ways to use it up on travel. Accordingly, I'm enclosing a bill (statement??) for $1500, which I hope you'll see fit to pay. Let me know on this . . . and if I don't hear from you soon, I'll call.

Sincerely,
Hunter

***

July 10, 1969

STATEMENT

Misc. expenses incurred by Hunter S. Thompson in the process of coping with reality on a day-to-day basis while working on the "Death of the American Dream." The author deems these expenses far more pertinent, at this point, than any he might otherwise be forced to incur by means of ill-advised travel at a time when the progress of the book manuscript can best be served by work at the typewriter—rather than running up bills on airlines and other exotic money-suckers, such as hotels, car rentals, etc.

The author is much aware, on the other hand, of the need for proper accounting language and standard procedures of a sort. Accordingly, let the record show that this "statement" is in fact a Travel Voucher: to wit . . .

$25 . . . . . per day, for 60 (sixty) days of travel and related motivation to that end
the creation of a final manuscript for the A/D book.
$1500 . . . . . total

Thanks,
Hunter S. Thompson

TO L. A. GORMAN, L.L. BEAN:

Thompson maintained a regular correspondence with the customer service staff of Maine-based outdoor outfitter L.L. Bean.

July 15, 1969
Woody Creek, CO

Dear Mr. Gorman . . .

Thanx for your letter. My general complaint about the "new" Bean style is too general to document without massive effort . . . but for two outstanding examples let me cite the green duck "lounger" and the (formerly) sheepskin gun case. The Lounger is a piece of cheap crap by any standards: I have two of them, mainly due to my wife's lapses in judgement. The green canvas is so flimsy that my first one is now torn to shreds after one summer's use—and the local canvas-artist offers to repair it for a figure of $14.00, which is just about what the thing costs. Needless to say, I've abandoned the thing; it now serves as a shade-object for my eight Doberman pups . . . and also, I might add, as a very bad advertisement for Bean products.

The gun case example doesn't affect me personally, since I bought mine (the real sheepskin model) before you down-graded to green canvas—at roughly the same price. A friend of mine just bought one of your new models, and when he brought it out to the house recently I was shocked . . . and of course he reacted badly to the comparison. The "new" Bean gun case looks like a 99 cent Jap model, while my older, sheepskin case is an obvious quality item.

Anyway, that should do for starters. I hope you can reverse this (apparent) trend.

Yours in hazy faith . . .
Hunter S. Thompson

FROM TOM WOLFE:

Astronaut Neil Armstrong, commander of the U.S. Apollo 11 mission, had taken a man's first small step on the moon on July 20, 1969. Most Americans agreed it was a "giant leap for mankind."

July 21, 1969

Dear Hunter,

It all comes back to me out of the mists. . . . The picture of you was in the *USIA*[31] magazine that appears in the Soviet Union—or else it was in the Soviet slick magazine that appears here. I'll tell you who can unravel this mystery: Ted Streshinsky, Box 674, Berkeley, Calif. He is a photographer, and I'm pretty sure it was he who showed that magazine to me. Ted took the pictures that went with the original article I did on the Merry Pranksters.

I gather you're near the completion of your book—or can at least THINK about same. I wish I were as far along. I've got to get serious and quit jumping for every available copout, such as lectures. Lecturing is easy, lucrative and a nice ego melon & prosciutto, but I guess it is essentially a form of the world-wide Grand Jackoff.

Salutes and Bows,
Tom

31. The United States Information Agency is a branch of the Department of State.

TO TOM WOLFE:

Thompson leaves unsaid that days earlier, after a number of miscarriages, his wife, Sandy, had delivered a stillborn baby.

July 25, 1969
Woody Creek, CO

Dear Tom . . .

Thanx for the lead; I'll write Streshinsky and find out which one of those Red swine crossed me. Which hardly matters, really . . . because it was all a hype anyway.

Your comments on "getting serious" and "copouts" added gas to what I'm beginning to see as my funeral pyre . . . a long string of articles, all bounced, reflecting a general rage at almost everything. My reflection in every newspaper shows me a festering sociopath, flirting with freakout psychosis . . . grinding my teeth at every newscast, every headline. I find myself watching the horizon and hoping to see flames . . . meanwhile dealing steadily in guns, nothing big, just everybody wanting them and asking where, how and what kind to buy. It's a mean crazy atmosphere for writing books—or even one. Dynamite seems a lot quicker.

Anyway, good luck with whatever you're working on. Mine will be either very good or a total disaster, depending on how I use the tension that keeps building here. OK for now . . .

Hunter

TO JIM FLUG c/o U.S. SENATOR EDWARD M. KENNEDY:

On July 18, 1969, Massachusetts senator Edward M. Kennedy had driven away from a cookout on tiny Chappaquiddick Island and off a bridge soon after, drowning his passenger, twenty-eight-year-old campaign aide Mary Jo Kopechne. Kennedy took nine hours to report the incident to the police, and later pled guilty to leaving the scene of a fatal accident. On July 25 he was given a two-month suspended sentence.

July 27, 1969
Woody Creek, CO

Jim Flug
c/o Ted Kennedy
Senate Office Building
Washington, D.C.

Dear Jim . . .

The crush of recent events compels me to send a note, offering my services on a wholly professional basis. Your man very obviously needs writers; that Hyannisport show was a bummer—not even its friends could defend it.

I'm sitting here pondering *Esquire*'s cut version of my 140-page NRA/Gun Control article, wondering why I ever agreed to do the thing in the first place. I *may* be able to live with the version they think they want . . . but maybe not; it may have to be a book-research thing and not an article at all. We'll see . . .

Anyway, no matter how I handle this article thing, I can't possibly blow it as badly as Ted Kennedy just blew his beach-orgy act. Like I say, he needs writers—and as it happens I can see my way clear to offer my services no sooner than the late spring of 1970. Previous commitments will keep me away from politics until then—or at least off the breaking stories.

So, for good or ill, you can feel free to bid for my services anytime after Xmas. They will, of course, come high—given the treacherous realities of a seller's market. That Hyannisport statement sounded like it was written by and for Melvin Laird.[32] All it said to me was "Four More Years of Nixon."

We can do without that, I think. And by '76 Teddy will be a sort of pre-aged Kefauver[33] figure; while I, and a lot of people like me, will be permanent expatriates from the U.S. political scene. For good or ill . . . but in the meantime, for christ's sake tell your man to get himself a competent driver the next time he feels the need for a little head. OK for now . . .

Sincerely,
Hunter S. Thompson

TO WILLIAM J. KENNEDY:

July 29, 1969
Woody Creek, CO

Well . . . I said I'd write, but I'm damned if I have any stomach for it. Everything that could possibly go wrong here has gone—except for the total failure and rejection of "the book." And that has to be next. Particularly since I can't seem to write it. I envy your enthusiasm, the San Juan trip . . . it all seems Right. Like maybe there really is a Good Troll King, with his one good eye focused constantly on the Great Scoreboard, keeping track. . . .

Hopefully this is just a passing funk. But it's been a hell of a long one, more like rot than fever

(now, four days later . . .)

In the wake of riots and violence connected with the CBS-TV feature, done by my friend Hughes Rudd. Watch for it soonest. Fantastic local upheavals, broken nose for the cameraman, etc. . . . scurvy threats at me: old friends

32. Melvin R. Laird served as U.S. secretary of defense during President Nixon's first term.

33. Liberal Democrat Estes Kefauver of Tennessee led the U.S. Senate's 1951 investigation into organized crime.

blaming me for not "getting them interviewed," others claiming I "staged" a fight for the cameras—a real nightmare story, reminiscent of that Shirley Jackson thing, or *The Visit.*[34]

Anyway, I need a lot of sleep. [Paul] Semonin threatens to arrive tomorrow. I have two more months to write the wretched "book." Have a good time in the surf. Ciao . . .

HST

TO DON ERICKSON, *ESQUIRE:*

Thompson had received a detailed memo regarding his NRA piece for Esquire *magazine.*

August 4, 1969
Woody Creek, CO

Dear Don . . .

I'm still pondering the NRA piece—actually just got back to it after . . . well, no point in details.

Anyway, I see your point about the failed, fussy ending. That's an extension of *My* gun problem, which I never really solved, in print or otherwise. I'll get that done. I'm assuming, by the way, that I can cut and chop this xerox copy of yours; if not, call at once. I'll be a day or so sketching the new order—so call quick if you want to preserve this copy.

[*Esquire* editor Robert] Sherrill's memo is something else again. I think the man has spent too much time in P. J. Clarke's. He may have a point or two, but in the main he sounds like somebody from the Greenwich Tweed/Sport and Ralley Club—the owner of a Morgan, two Singers and a Stutz—trying to explain away the Southern California Hotrod Cult. He is talking about a gun-world that I knew for 20 years in Kentucky—and still know when I go back there, despite the twisted reality of a gun-culture flourishing in a land where gun-freaks have killed all the game except a few coons and rabbits. There are still a few deer, I guess, but . . . well, that ain't the point, is it?

Sherrill's rude assumption that I "buy only handguns" clashes badly with his notion of me slaughtering deer and draping their "pitiful, beautiful heads" on my "shithouse wall." When in fact I gave up hunting about three years ago, despite (or maybe because of) the deer and elk who (which?) graze in my backyard about six months out of the year. If I wanted to shoot the buggers, however, I sure as hell wouldn't do it with a handgun; I have four excellent rifles for that sort of thing, along with four shotguns that I use for 90% of my shooting these

34. Shirley Jackson's chilling 1948 short story about small-town brutality, *The Lottery*, and German director Bernhard Wicki's 1964 movie of Friedrich Dürrenmatt's play *The Visit*, about a woman who returns to her European hometown to offer a fabulous reward for the murder of the first man who seduced her.

days—most of it at clay pigeons. Beyond that, Sherrill's idea of the .44 Magnum is straight out of Dick Tracy; compared to the Luger he seems to revere, the S&W .44 Magnum is a goddamned esthetic marvel. It is at least 100% more accurate, about 300% as efficient, and as a piece of machinery it compares to the Luger like a Jaguar XKE compares to the basic Volkswagen. Sherrill's disdain for the M16 ("a gun that sprays bullets like a water hose") ignores the fact that the original Luger was designed to hold a 29-shot drum clip (like a sub-machinegun) and came with a cheap, heavy-wire shoulder stock—for street-fighting purposes, like the M-1 carbine, the M16, or a semi-automatic water hose.

But to hell with all that, too. I use letters, now and then, as drafts for later things—test-runs, of a sort—and I suspect that's what I'm doing now. My essential point is that Sherrill's views amount to some kind of archaic counterpoint to everything I meant and still mean to say. I can probably incorporate them in some way—as an echo, perhaps, to some wistful woodsmen whose daddies could blow a fly off a pig's back at 500 yards . . . which is nice to know, but it doesn't have a fucking thing to do with skyrocketing gun sales in 1969.

That was the point I tried to make with my little tale about the day my P-38 arrived. All my other guns were bought for Sherrill's reasons—but seconds after I lifted that piece of cheap shit out of the box I knew I'd bought into a new scene.

Maybe I should explain this better in the piece—along with a few other things. Needless to say, I saw no point in keeping the shards of that D.C. hotel-bar scene as a lead . . . so I'll start at the bottom of pg. 3, with the arrival of the P-38 the day after Kennedy died.

That's easy enough—and a better, cleaner ending won't be any problem . . . but I'm not optimistic about incorporating that atavistic bullshit of Sherrill's. Maybe he should come out of his martini-shelter and write his views in the form of a box—exposing me in BF [boldface] print as a vicious asshole, a demented werewolf of some kind, loping naked across these high mesas on sunny afternoons, fouling the air with my rank breath, clutching a .44 Magnum and with only one thought in my head—to slay these stinking beasts, fetch up a feast for the maggots, make the world safe for green-headed flies.

Indeed. And in fact why not a main feature on the Gun Madness, as it were? Let Woodson D. Scott dredge up a nice, ghost-written piece on how it feels to be the new president of the NRA? Get somebody like that wiggy bastard, Carl Perian, to speak for the other side . . . or maybe Tydings,[35] with his fine sense of prose; he is up next year, and listing badly in the wake of Chappaquiddick. Perian would be better: the truth is not in him; he's so crooked he has to screw his pants on in the morning . . . but he talks well, and his No.1 assistant is Gene Gleason, the old *World-Telegram* crime-buster (a fact I saw no reason to mention in the text, for a variety of reasons . . .).

35. Democrat Joseph Tydings was a U.S. senator from Maryland.

Anyway, it's a nice idea—a fatback feature on the American Gun problem. This piece of mine could be the wild card in an otherwise traditionally-stacked deck. That photo I sent you earlier of some freak shooting at a J. E. Hoover target would make an eye-catching cover . . . and if that's too tame, well, I'll check around for something heavier.

Meanwhile, I want to get this thing out of my head and failing hair. So, unless I hear from you in the next few days—like before Aug 11—I'll send you my new version, based more or less on the notions we've (now) talked about. Maybe I can work the "Sherrill section" in by way of dismissing it . . . or maybe not. If the rewrite fails, let's raincheck the whole business until I write this Gun Section into The Book, now titled "The Whipsong." Or, "The Reluctant Education of" . . . yes . . . Me. I see no way to avoid taking responsibility for it, so it will have to bear my name.

What I'm getting at here is that I'd rather not sweat through a series of rewrites of an article that will definitely be part of a book, anyway. So if what I send you soonest doesn't work, I urge you to wait around for a look at the final draft. It might be fun—or maybe a terrible disaster. We'll see. . . .

Meanwhile, you might want to wrap some rose-colored glass around your eyes and scan a long piece on Jean-Claude Killy (more or less) that I just sent to Lynn. It's a vicious thing, with a short but violent history—a tale I leave to Lynn.

So, for now . . . thanks for the good effort that went into condensing the NRA piece. I even appreciated Sherrill's memo, for good or ill. It's at least something to grapple with, and a man with my kind of problem is nearly always plagued by grapplehunger . . . like a beast with itching teeth, whatever's hard will serve. Even petrified wisdom.

OK for now. Keep the faith, whatever it is . . . and be sure to let me know if you find yourself on the bellygun market.

Beware,
Hunter S. Thompson

TO ELIZABETH RAY:

Thompson's maternal aunt, Elizabeth "Lee" Ray, had always been particularly fond of her wayward nephew Hunter.

August 8, 1969
Woody Creek, CO

Dear Aunt Lee . . .

Thanks for the birthday present and the nice note to Sandy—which won't be answered, since I've told her to forget any references or replies to that situation. She appreciated your note, but under the circumstances I think she'll be better off forgetting about the whole thing. Thanks for your kind thoughts—and, as always, for the cheque.

Things are worse than normal here: too many visitors and too little work. Just a few minutes ago, at 4:40 a.m., two musicians from Los Angeles wandered in, wanting to hear their latest record on my hi-fi set. We listened for a while with the earphones, made a few collective criticisms to be sent back to the producer in Hollywood, then they wandered off with one of my extra mattresses. At the moment they are bedding down next door, I think, in the guest house on this property I'm trying to buy.

Otherwise, life here continues chaotic. My book was due in July, but I'm not even half-finished. I keep saying I'll get back to Louisville for a quick visit, but I can't find time to get away from here. From now until Christmas, I mean to work exclusively on the book—a crash program, as it were. It has to be done.

Love . . . .
Hunter

FROM OSCAR ACOSTA:

Acosta had sent Thompson yet another of his literary efforts between legal cases and bizarre outbursts, this time a screenplay. Acosta got back the usual harsh honesty.

August 15, 1969
Los Angeles, CA

Hunter:

I am temporarily staying in an apartment in Hollywood, and looking for a house in East L.A. So, my permanent address will be—until I'm fired or quit—the office on this bullshit letterhead.

So my movie script is racist? Why, cause the "hero" happens to be a Mexican? Do you assume that whenever a guy writes about persons other than anglos that he's racist? In fact, the story is about the Garden of Eden, the creation, etc. . . . The end of the world as seen through the eyes of a Chicano living in 1969. . . . And, as every good Baptist knows, there weren't very many of us in Eden. I've worked on the cosmology, the philosophy, the characters, the blah-blah, for over two months, and all I get from a guilt-ridden, candied-ass, anglo hack is that it's racist . . . or is it that your [sic] pissed cause Harold Trader gets it in the end? That it? You want to be the hero? . . . Anyway, an agent's got it now, wants me to start working on the script, but I've been at it seven days per for the past two months so I don't know when I'll get to it.

The letters I'm sending between [Sirhan attorney] Cooper and me are, I think, very funny. What I don't have, is a copy of the newspaper article, five inch headlines, saying COOPER INDICTED . . . for theft of a grand jury brief on a different case . . . I didn't know until that day, the day before my last letter to him, why he was being so uptight. Any decent reporter and certainly the Feds would love to have copies of these letters . . . same issue: misuse of a brief related to a Grand Jury Indictment. You think I should?

ZETA

TO JIM SILBERMAN, RANDOM HOUSE:

Lacking a focus for his book, a dejected Thompson works out his frustrations with his Random House editor.

August 30, 1969
Woody Creek, CO

Dear Jim . . .

It's 5:45 a.m. Labor Day here and I'm just finishing a book section telling how me and Raoul Duke delivered a new Pontiac from the Bronx to Seattle in 1960 and then became politicalized while hitch-hiking down to San Francisco. Like everything else I've written for "the book," it makes no sense at all in terms of continuity or focus. I still have no idea what I'm supposed to be writing about—in terms of titles, chapters, jacket blurbs and that sort of thing. I see a lot of connections in my head that I can't make on paper, and consequently I have no real image of what I'm doing. That "American Dream" notion becomes increasingly meaningless—mainly because it fits everything I write, and most of what I read. You might as well have told me to write a book about Truth and Wisdom. The slower I come to the necessity of linking Nixon, Chicago & the NRA, the more I wonder why—and *if*—anybody should waste their time reading this kind of bullshit. It seems useless and contrived, particularly since neither you nor Shir-Cliff have ever hinted at what you think I'm writing about . . . beyond that American Dream bullshit, and I think we should stop hiding behind that, particularly if anybody expects to get a book out of this nightmare. Faulkner had it right when he talked about seeing "the world in a grain of sand"—which is the absolute opposite of what I seem to be doing. I don't even have a beach to write about, much less that crucial "grain."

OK for now. Let me know on the money items, and particularly if you have any ideas about this book I'm writing. At the moment it amounts to about 400 pages of useless swill. My need for a focus is beyond critical; it borders on paralysis and desperation. I am running off in every direction, writing fiction one night and straight journalism the next. No doubt there is light at the end of the tunnel—but which one of these fucking tunnels are we dealing with? Send word. . . .

HST

TO S. LEVY, DELL DISTRIBUTING CO.:

At last, the tables were turned: Thompson had been asked to provide a credit reference for his paperback publishing company.

September 6, 1969
Woody Creek, CO

S. Levy
Credit Dept.
Dell Distributing Co.
750 Third Ave NYC 10017

Dear Mr. Levy:

I am, of course, quite flattered to receive your "second request" for information inre: my Credit Experience vis-à-vis Ballantine Books Inc. Perhaps by now you have received my answer to your "first request." My tardiness was due to the considerable time and effort expended in compiling the information you requested.

All I can do now, on this second run, is to amplify and re-emphasize the gist of my initial comments, to wit: The risks of extending a credit line to Ballantine Books involve far more than certain financial loss; it is a question of your physical and mental well-being—indeed, your survival. Once you commence dealing with junkies and deranged thieves you are forced to deal on *their terms* . . . which are savage in every way. Do you realize what goes on at Ballantine? . . . What sort of people work in that place? Didn't you read about poor Silberman at Random House, who had to have his leg amputated? And that's only one case.

Take my word for it: You do not want to get involved in a vicious underworld of drugs and violence. Trying to collect a debt from Ballantine is like trying to steal a chunk of meat from a pack of wolverines. They will come right in your yard and take it over if you let them. And the next day they'll be right on your porch barefoot, weighing one hundred and thirty pounds. But if you say to them, "Hold on, wait just a minute," they'll know they're dealing with someone who'll stand up. Your only hope, at this point, is to get up on your hind legs and screech at them, "No! No!" Then, before they retaliate, you'll quickly hire some thugs to go over to 101 Fifth avenue and beat the living shit out of somebody—maybe three or four people, whatever you decide.

Let me know how it turns out—and also if you need credit information on anyone else.

Sincerely . . .
Hunter S. Thompson

TO OSCAR ACOSTA:

Thompson had been working on his own initiative on an article about the Atomic Energy Commission's nuclear weapons tests in the western United States.

September 24, 1969
Woody Creek, CO

Oscar . . .

I am sitting here working on a long article on the AEC and the oil companies and these fucking death bombs they are setting off in Colo, Nev, etc. . . . and I don't have the vaguest fucking idea where to send it. Look around you and see what has happened, in the past few years, to the handful of national magazines that used to print mean shit about the fatbellies. This fucking polarization has made it impossible to sell anything except hired bullshit or savage propaganda. I write the same way I always did, but for the past two years my stuff has been either brutally edited or rejected, outright, as the work of a crazed extremist. Once-"radical" editors have been deposed, bought off or emasculated. Go to any magazine rack and see how many articles you want to read. Nobody is confident enough, these days, to attack anything except cripples—The Mafia, junk dealers, black hoods, etc. . . . all the people without real public leverage. I had no problem when I talked about the Hell's Angels, but it's a different thing to hit on GM[36] and the Oil Industry. At least in magazines; books are still a bit looser, but I'm not sure how much. Hopefully, I'll find out soon.

In short, I don't even know where to send my own stuff, much less yours. I have no decent contacts, my agent is a computer and most NY editors think I'm crazy. I don't know about McWilliams; maybe I'll send this current thing to him, and find out.

I dug your thing in *Con Safos,* but knowing you made it different for me. As for general criticism, I'm not about to start knocking the work of people who figure I'm a *gaubaucho* (sp?)[37] pig to begin with. It's like me telling musicians what I think about their work and/or their bands—even when they ask. It's always a fucking nightmare, "Now waitaminnit, what the fuck do you know about music. . . . Whatdoyou mean, Noisy bullshit? You think you know more than our producer?"

None of that for now. I'd sooner write a long critique of Black Panther poetry than step into the quicksand you're offering. What you have to understand is that good writing isn't necessarily saleable, and a lot of people get rich writ-

36. General Motors Corporation.
37. *Gabacho* is Spanish for "Frenchman" or "Frenchified Spaniard."

ing awful bullshit. Editors are nearly always dim assholes and the American press, in general, is a pile of hired shit. You think you have trouble relating to McGarr . . . well he's a fucking soul-brother, compared to the others. Remember Jim Bellows? He's considered a secret radical/freak by the NY axis. And McWilliams is seen as a goddamn screaming Red.

Frankly, I don't think writing is where it's at these days. Neither the fatbellies nor the crazies believe anything they read anyway, and most of the others are too stoned to even talk, much less read. This book I'm supposed to have been working on for 2 years strikes me as the most monstrous waste of time I've ever got bogged down in. Even if I manage to finish the goddamn thing, I can't see any reason why anybody should read it, even for free. The only thing I've enjoyed writing in the past year is the enclosed clip on Aspen politics; it has stirred up a neo-streetfighting scene. The final wild irony is that John Wendt is going to have to defend the lawsuits; he's the *News'* lawyer & he begged them not to print it. Not for legal reasons, which are hazy, but because of the social nightmares involved.

I think it's about time I began to wail seriously on these people. I am going crazy out here; life is too easy and I'm getting nothing done. Hopefully I can settle this land deal by early 1970, then flee and rent the house for enough to make the payments. I am into the final stages of that deal, but unfortunately I no longer have the down payment—a flat 10K. So I'm into a bullshit juggling act, playing for time and hoping I can hit for 10 sometime soon, on something. It would be a bitch to come so close to nailing down 2 houses and 25 acres—and then blow it at the wire.

Looking at your 8/27 letter again, I don't see all those questions you mentioned this afternoon . . . except that broad question about *Con Safos*. It's not *your* egos I'm worried about, but all the mean bullshit that erupts every time I express *mine*. I can't even get along with SDS these days, much less the Brown Berets. All that really interests me, for now, is getting hold of somebody who can make me an expert in the use of dynamite. Or anything better. Maybe when we get down there you can put me in touch with somebody who's into that action. Meanwhile, let's postpone this haggling until I get to LA, which should be around 10/15 or so . . . depending on what happens in Chicago. I'll let you know.

HST

TO JOE BENTI, CBS NEWS:

Having won his latest bout with KREX-TV, Thompson had his CBS Morning News *back—and immediately turned on anchor Joseph Benti for the program's growing "soft news" focus and for its failure to air Hughes Rudd's story on the troubles building in Aspen.*

October 2, 1969
Woody Creek, CO

Joe Benti
CBS News
524 W. 57th
NYC 10019

Dear Mr. Benti . . .

I thought you'd like to know that KREX-TV in Grand Junction, Colo. is again carrying the *Morning News*—at 6:00 a.m., about 70 minutes from now . . . and, according to the station manager, they are carrying it just for me. Nobody else watches it, he says. Only me. And I'm 120 miles away, no hope for the advertisers (local) . . . and of course that makes for a fine, tightly-knit news show: no commercials at all. If you did anything on your end to compel this concession, consider this a note of thanks. If not, well . . . You're welcome.

Which is not really the point. I thought I should register a formal complaint regarding the back-stairs politics that erupted in the wake of Hughes Rudd's Aspen story last summer. The technical merits of the piece strike me as powerfully secondary to the fact that the word in Aspen, as it were, has it that friendly connections between CBS and the Aspen Institute got the story killed. The calls to Salant[38]—from Bob Craig, Wm. Stevenson[39] & his creature Merrill Ford at the Institute—are not only a matter of record, but a matter of heavy speculation in local taverns. The initial reaction (locally) was anger at CBS for coming here to film the problem in the first place, but after a month or so the reaction changed to contempt for a national network without the balls to even back up one of its cameramen who had his nose smashed by a local drunk. And it burns the shit out of me, personally, to know that one of the most thoroughly honest men working for any network (Rudd) should have his action edited and buried by a gang of fatbacks whose only claim to distinction is that they still get Christmas cards from Mayor Daley.

Aspen is full of walking corpses who keep telling each other, "I was for Stevenson, but Joe McCarthy scared me to death."[40] Their cemetery is the Institute, with a board of directors including McNamara, Reuther, Justice Brennan and ex-cabinet (Navy) guru Paul Nitze (sp?), majority stockholder in the

38. Richard Salant was president of CBS News.
39. Thompson's former landlord Robert Craig, who once made *Life* magazine's list of America's 100 Most Promising Young Men, was executive director of the Aspen Institute, a posh think tank best known for its pricey "executive seminars," from 1953 to 1963; former Oberlin College president and U.S. ambassador to the Philippines, William E. Stevenson was the Aspen Institute's president from 1967 to 1969.
40. Adlai Stevenson was the Democratic presidential nominee in 1952 and 1956, Joe McCarthy the notorious red-baiting Wisconsin senator.

Aspen Ski Corporation. It's a goddamned evil shame that a gang of aging bunglers like this should have enough leverage—via Salant—to kill any story that CBS News wants to air. Stanton[41] was out here in June, a featured speaker at the annual Design Conference, and he made a fool of himself by delivering a gaggle of hoary platitudes that not even Dwight McDonald could stomach.

Which is more or less extraneous, except as a context/indicator for CBS's credulity-rating in Aspen. Later in the summer Dan Schorr was here and offered a comment or so, in private, regarding the size and specific gravity of the corporate balls. (Naturally, he was full of praise for everything CBS stood and still stands for; and so was Rudd, in the rude course of his own visit. These gentlemen are nothing if not loyal, which is understandable. . . .)

But I don't have any particular loyalty to CBS, so I might as well say that this whole matter of the CBS/Aspen gig—against the continuing background of the CBS/Chicago '68 coverage—leaves me completely convinced that Nicholas Johnson[42] is right . . . that you people are in fact a gang of cowardly, self-censoring swine; and that CBS finally found its own level with the purchase of the NY Yankees.

I watched Nicholas Johnson chew the fat, as it were, with Wallace and Herman[43] and that waterhead from *Time* . . . and as far as I was concerned it was one of TV's finest moments in 1969. Maybe Wallace thinks he won, but he probably thinks he won that round with Daniel Cohn-Bendit,[44] too—on *60 Minutes,* a while back. Wallace is yapping at the heels of that lecherous old geek, [Eric] Sevareid, while romance with Eric Hoffer is so cheap and ugly as to mock any rational comment.

Well, to hell with all that; I just came back downstairs after watching your show. Your coverage of the Conspiracy trial is a cheap cop-out. Why don't you run one of those [Studs] Terkel-style interviews with Mike Royko?[45] Never in hell, eh?

In closing, I suppose that common decency compels me to offer my condolences. You are sitting there with an incredible magic journalism tool in your hands, but you can't even gear it up to compete with *Time* magazine.

And fuck this action; I have better things to do.

Sincerely,
Hunter S. Thompson

41. Frank Stanton was president of CBS, Inc.

42. Nicholas Johnson headed the Federal Communications Commission.

43. Mike Wallace was a CBS News correspondent; George Herman hosted the network's Sunday morning public affairs talk show *Face the Nation.*

44. Daniel Cohn-Bendit led the massive May 1968 student protests that closed France's University of the Sorbonne and then paralyzed Paris and other French cities when millions of workers joined in the demonstrations.

45. Mike Royko was a popular columnist for the *Chicago Sun-Times.*

TO BERNARD SHIR-CLIFF, BALLANTINE BOOKS:

Shir-Cliff had sent Thompson the premiere issue of counterculture cartoonist R. Crumb's Comix *magazine.*

October 5, 1969
Woody Creek, CO

Dear Bernard . . .

Thanks for the *Comix.* I've seen [R.] Crumb's stuff before and always (or usually) get a boot out of it—but it's hard to believe many people are going to pay $2.95 for it. Maybe a buck. . . .

Which is your business, and possibly you're right. The book is too large for easy shop-lifting, but—like the sex magazines—it's a natural for stand-up reading at the magazine rack; particularly if the alternative is paying 3 bucks to take it home.

So . . . I hope you're right, but I can't see the thing as a big seller. A lot of it is very sharp satire—sharper than most book-writing these dreary days, and it wouldn't surprise me a hell of a lot if we all looked back in 10 years to say, Yes—R. Crumb was the [Henry] Ford of a new art form. Good luck.

Meanwhile, I am flipping around like a shark out of water, organizing a freak-uprising in the wake of that article I sent you. Given the current polarization, we have no choice but to go for a takeover bid—motorcycle racer for mayor, freaks for the council, etc. The election is less than a month off and right now we're down about 2–1, but with massive possibilities in the unregistered freak vote. I have spent the past three days posing as either Ken O'Donnell or Larry O'Brien, or both—with a touch of Lenny Bruce on the side.[46] One of our new posters says: "Register Freaks, Not Guns." Another: "Vote the Straight Nazi Ticket; Profit *Über Alles.*"

Silberman's book (christ, the very mention of it fills me with an urge to go immediately to bed and sleep for 15 hours) . . . anyway, I've developed such an inordinate fear and loathing for the whole subject (the American Dream) that I no longer have any sense of doing anything meaningful. All work on the book seems like a mockery of myself & reality, a dutiful charade that can't be avoided, due to contracts, but which in truth is pure bullshit. I have written Silberman to say that I no longer understand what I'm supposed to be writing, and in fact I never have. I've told Lynn the same thing . . . but I keep getting beautifully-typed letters saying "Dear Hunter, keep up the good work on the book,

46. Kenneth O'Donnell had been JFK's appointments secretary and occasional hatchet man; Lawrence O'Brien, the Kennedy administration's chief of congressional liaison, was now chairman of the Democratic National Committee; controversial nightclub comedian Lenny Bruce had died in 1966.

your progress is wonderful and we all await the final wisdom." It's like calling the FCC to complain about TV programming; no hope of communication.

Frankly, I'm not sure what I'm doing. I may have a book in all this irrelevant bullshit I've written, but even if I do I'm not sure it's worth publishing. My problem—once again—is that I've forgotten what it's all about. I have no title, no subject, no focus . . . all I really have is a sense of despair so massive that my nerves are rotting out with the weight of it. I have a feeling of having been sent up on the mountain to write something I never understood—and that I can't come down to reality again until I write the fucker. And bring it with me. For perusal and strange comment by people who live in some kind of rotten, pressurized bee-hive on the East Coast.

Money is the only new factor in my thinking these days. For the first time in maybe two years I can see the total final end of my income . . . as a matter of fact I saw it about a month ago. Which reminds me: Did I accumulate any *HA* funds through August '69? I'm in dire need of money; keep that in mind.

And my long-smoldering concern about Silberman's book has finally transmogrified into a far more serious worry about my own gig as a writer. I'm beginning to wonder if I'll ever see my stuff in print again; I guess that's why I was so pleased with the Aspen article, which netted me $50—the first real writing-money I've *earned* in two years, not counting royalties.

(Jesus, I just rushed upstairs to answer the phone, thinking it was somebody with a crisis about the Aspen election . . . and found Joe Benti from CBS on the wire (and a news producer named Lewis), insisting on giving me all the details to refute my claim that CBS censored a recent Aspen feature, after backstairs pressure from such as McNamara, Reuther and that evil crowd. Eric Sevareid is a good buddy of some of the people who were slurred; ditto Stanton and R. Salant. So I've been arguing with Benti for the past hour, and now I have to get out a two-page mind-bender on local politics—threatening the freaks with mass nut-cutting if they fail to register and vote to protect their own interests—indeed, their very balls. So . . .)

Yes, I'll quit while I still have time. I have to carry off a demagogic outburst in about two hours, and I'm tired . . . but not for the right reasons. I much prefer the kind of fatigue that comes after a burst of good writing—good published writing. Maybe we can work something out; I'm getting scared. Ciao . . .

Hunter

TO HUGHES RUDD, CBS NEWS:

Rudd had been robbed and beaten near New York's Central Park and had written Thompson a graphic account.

November 15, 1969
Woody Creek, CO

Dear Hughes . . .

Jesus, what next? Heart attacks, muggings . . . maybe you should consider buying a chinchilla ranch in northern New Mexico. I got a note from [Bill] Stout[47] today, saying he'd missed me in L.A., and giving the news of your street-fighting action. If it's any condolence, I nearly got killed in NY one summer night down on St. Luke's place in the Village . . . and a month later I was back on the streets with a big hunting knife, looking for the rogues. Broken ribs hurt like hell for a while, and a broken nose makes for difficult breathing, but they pass. I just saw an old friend in L.A. who has a bleeding ulcer and can't drink . . . now there's real trouble. So if I were you I wouldn't worry about a few cracked bones.

Rather than carry on here, let me say that I'll be in NY for lunch on Dec 6 (shuttling up from Washington) and will probably stay the weekend. I have to get straight with Random House. What are the chances of getting together with Charles [Kuralt] for a peaceful nonviolent drink Dec 6 or 7? I'll call from Washington earlier that week. Meanwhile, for christ's sake, lie low.

Ciao . . .
Hunter

TO OSCAR ACOSTA:

The Thompsons seem to have misbehaved during their October 1969 visit to California.

November 15, 1969
Woody Creek, CO

Dear O . . .

Thanx for the call. I was out at the time, dealing heavily—and arriving at a nut of $150 for 100. I have samples, but haven't tried them yet. All references and indications are good. I'll be sure in a few days. Your deal of 50 for $125 doesn't make it. The (big) dealer price in Aspen is 50 cents a hit. That's 50 cents each. I just missed a deal of 100 for $75. So somebody down there is screwing you pretty badly—since *cost* is about 25 cents each, or less. Anything over $2 each is like selling joints on the street for a buck apiece. And even at $2, it's like buying a used car off a lot in Pasadena for the advertised price.

Anyway, let me know quick if you want some of this lot I'm about to go for. I can't afford the full 100 unless I have help with the nut. I realize that I owe

47. Bill Stout was a *CBS News* correspondent.

you some dope, but right now I'm truthfully broke—and the stock market has destroyed my cushion. All I can make on my own is 50, and I'll send you a few of those por nada—but if you want 10 or 20 you'll have to let me know quick, and send cash. Murphy says he's coming out this weekend, so I figure to spin off 10 or 20 there . . . so if both of you want in, I'll go for the full 100—at $150. If I don't hear from you by Sunday I'll figure you're not interested.

On other fronts, I think I owe you a general apology for my sub-human behavior during my visit. I feel, in retrospect, a bad echo of McGarr on a humping trip. Even Sandy admits that we both went a bit beyond the pale on all fronts—from running up bills to drugs, to laying bad trips on other people. Particularly you. I'm sorry about the times that I seemed crazed, impatient or inhospitable . . . but for reasons of the flesh I have to say that I'd probably do it again, so be warned. You got caught in the tides of a sort of honeymoon, 10 years delayed.

On balance, however, it was an excellent visit. Maybe the SF trip was ill-advised—or maybe it was only bad acid. If I had to do it over again I think I'd stay in L.A. But thanks again—mightily—for the use of the car. I think Sandy wrote Socorro,[48] but since most of the action was my fault, I'll add a word or so for me. Particularly about the acid . . . although as a partial excuse, I hope she understands that it's impossible to enjoy acid in the company of somebody who visibly disapproves of it. That's a bad trip both ways.

On that score, I'm enclosing (on the navel of the beast) one of your very excellent blues. I did one the other night and ran amok for about 6 hours . . . and, now, on second thought, I think I won't send it unless you ask for it. I don't want to jangle Socorro any worse than I have already. But take my word for it: Good acid still works. One tiny tab of that blue shit put me right around the bend. And also be warned that much of the street acid these days contains Strychnine (sp?), which gives you a nice buzz along the spinal column before it sends you vomiting to the emergency ward. Be careful what you buy—particularly from the kind of dealer who doesn't mind charging "a friend" top street-corner prices for mes.

OK for now. I have to get back to ugly work for an hour or so before dawn. With Murphy en route, I can't count on much work or sleep this weekend.

That Cuba trip sounds interesting, but I think I'd feel obligated, if I went, to cut cane like all the others. You're probably right in saying I could avoid it, but avoiding it would put me in a position I'd just as soon avoid. You know—the gringo journalist thinks he's better than we are, etc. . . . And right now I really have to sock in here and finish a book, for good or ill.

Send word when anything breaks. I'll be here.

Ciao . . .
H

48. Socorro was Oscar Acosta's wife.

TO JIM SILBERMAN, RANDOM HOUSE:

At last, Thompson began to hone in on a peg for his book on "The Death of the American Dream": anti-establishment grassroots politics as modern democracy in action.

November 19, 1969
Woody Creek, CO

Dear Jim . . .

I may have finally found that Grain of Sand I mentioned in earlier letters. For the first time in nearly two years, I see a gimmick for tying all my wasted bullshit together in a book—titled "Joe Edwards for Mayor."

This harks back to that clipping I sent you (my screed from the *Aspen Illustrated News*) . . . and the fact that it caused massive upheavals and polarization in the town. It also caused me to run my own candidate for mayor—and after a crazed and unnatural campaign that kept me awake for three weeks straight, we lost the election by one vote. Out of 1200 or so. We scared the living shit out of the Aspen Power Structure (the Ski Corp, Atlantic-Richfield and the Institute, with a board of directors including Paul Nitze, Robert McNamara, Walter Reuther, Justice Brennan and more fat Washington names than would fit on this page) . . . beginning in mid-Oct. with a 29-year-old candidate, a local head and bike-racer known as the "hippy lawyer," we mounted a campaign that made the Old Uglies seem like Norman Rockwell cartoons. The aging liberals refused to support us; they went with a silly old Republican shop-keeper lady who was compared, in *Time,* to Lindsay[49] . . . so we had to fall back on whatever clout we could muster in the name of Freak Power.

Incredibly, we won the actual vote by 6—then lost the absentee-ballot count by 7 . . . and even now our tying vote is wandering around somewhere in Guatemala, unreachable by phone or cable. We got one vote from Nepal, two from Mexico, and numerous others from both coasts. On balance, it was the goddamnedest political scene I've ever heard about, much less been involved in. When we began this thing I said it would be my last effort in terms of the existing political context. For my own satisfaction, I wanted to give "the system" one more chance—so I could honestly say, when the time of the firebombs came, that I'd gone as far as I could in that other game, and found it wanting.

So it came as a bit of a shock to find that a handful of bearded freaks—with *no political experience* and only three weeks to do everything from scratch—could come within one vote of taking over a town like Aspen. One more week

49. A moderate, even progressive, Republican, New York City mayor John V. Lindsay was touted as a coalition-builder and his 1968 presidential bid supported even by his state's Liberal Party.

would have made us easy victors. And now, in the general euphoria that still lingers, we are already forming a sort of government in exile—preparing, next year, to seize one of the three County Commissioners' posts and . . . yes . . . even the Sheriff's office. One of our gimmicks to get the freaks registered was a promise that, if Joe Edwards won the Mayor's race, then I would run for Sheriff. Edwards' loss leaves me technically free of any obligation to make that race, but the success of the Edwards campaign has politicized hundreds of dropouts who are hungry, now, for another head-on clash with the Fatbacks. There is not much question in my mind that, two years from now, we will totally control this town . . . and by that time, too, we will have the formula ready for export. Any comparison between Lindsay and Joe Edwards makes Lindsay seem to the Right of Spiro Agnew. We had one or two Lindsay-type candidates available here, but we settled on Edwards because our gossip said he was the only one who could muster the Freak Vote—the under-30 heads and erstwhile apolitical hippie types who, like me, wouldn't cross the street to vote for Lindsay. The NY vote was a triumph of a New Coalition, but the Aspen vote signaled the appearance of a whole *new electorate.*

So . . . that's my new gimmick. I've been sitting around here (and also in Los Angeles for the past two weeks) trying to work it into the dull and dated garbage that you still call, I guess, The Death of the American Dream. I think I can use all the Nixon stuff, plus the doomed *Esquire* Guns article, plus the *Playboy* JC Killy piece and also the LA stuff and even the Oil Shale research. Maybe not all of it, but enough to show the Aspen campaign in a national context. The joke in all this is that I suddenly see a bedrock validity in the American Dream; the Joe Edwards campaign was a straight exercise in Jeffersonian Democracy. In a sense, it was an echo of the '68 McCarthy campaign, but the difference lay in our ability to politicalize people who never knew or cared about the difference between Gene and Joe. We organized a mock election at the high school and won with 75% of the vote. The editor of the high school paper is now part of our half-underground Government in Exile.

All of what I say here is necessarily less than the whole truth, but I trust you see what I'm getting at. The possibility of a book titled "Joe Edwards for Mayor" gives me that tight-focused chunk of absolute reality that even the craziest, weirdest kind of journalism needs to hold it together. What The Book has lacked, all along, is a reason for writing it. But now, in the wake of this virgin political experience, I think I have that reason. On Sunday night I have to make a speech of sorts at a private high school (or prep school as it were) about 40 miles from here . . . and I'm going to tell them that, contrary to recent experience, that we can in fact beat the Fatbacks on their home court. Incredible as it seems, existing law is actually on our side. (We found that out when the Mayor tried to challenge our freaks at the polls; the DA and the city attorney refused to intervene, so we had to give a crash-course in election-laws to a dozen or so bearded poll-watchers . . . we armed them with tape-recorders and xerox copies of law book pages, which caused chaos at the polls and beat the challengers down to whimpering jelly. . . .)

In a nut, what we proved here is that Freak Power is no joke; this is our country, too, and we can goddamn well control it if we learn to use the tools. And it's fun; the Edwards campaign was a wilder trip, for me, than any acid I've ever eaten. . . . I stayed awake for three and four days at a time, incredibly high on the notion of taking over the world. And we weren't fucking with sheepherders; the new mayor (by one vote) is either the State GOP secy. of some sort, or a GOP national committeewoman, or maybe both. One of her main supporters was Leon Uris.[50] We also had the current administration savagely against us—along with the *Aspen Times,* a bastion of Humphrey-style liberalism. Beyond that, we had a wholly unknown candidate. I had never spoken to Edwards until I called him one Saturday night and said, "OK, you're it." Edwards himself was only a symbol of the power we suspected was there—mainly in the street-freaks and boomers, the night-people and the dope-culture. But when the deal went down, we had some of the heaviest establishment names in town on our side—in print, and making radio spots. Our whole campaign was a death-rattle for local business, the profit ethic and "common sense." We promised to cut the tourist area in half, bar autos from the downtown streets, terminate the approaching 4-lane highway 10 miles from town, tax developers out of existence (or at least out of Aspen), force the cops to say "sir" to hair-freaks and hippies, and generally croak the Boom that has made Aspen a retail gold-mine for the past 20 years.

And we came within one vote of doing it. Which leads me to believe that we may have a story here—if only because it has changed my whole notion of what's possible in America. On a purely personal basis, I'm prepared to give the system one more chance—mainly because I honestly believe we can win this war. We can take the machinery of reality away from the Fatbacks; they are too far gone in slow-witted corruption to deal with a serious challenge.

Hunter

TO RON DORFMAN, *CHICAGO JOURNALISM REVIEW:*

The editor of the new Chicago Journalism Review, *launched in the wake of some questionable coverage of the 1968 Democratic National Convention, had asked Thompson to write an essay for the magazine on the symbiotic relationship between the press and publicity-seekers like the Hell's Angels.*

50. Leon Uris was the author of historical novels including 1959's best-selling fiction book, *Exodus,* published in 1958.

November 19, 1969
Woody Creek, CO

Dear Ron Dorfman . . .

You asked for some words on "how the news media and folks like the Hell's Angels feed on each other," but . . . I have a feeling I did that once, in a book called *Hell's Angels*. The Angels were an obvious "story": they were physical, tangible, weird, loud, menacing . . . and so hostile, so strange and threatening, that few reporters ever tried to confront them as human beings. There was, after all, no need to. The Angels were a "good story," even from a distance. They loved publicity, but only when they dictated the style and content; covering the Angels was like trying to make sense of an Eisenhower press conference—it was easier, and funnier, in the long run, to simply write it the way it looked and sounded. Both Ike and the Hell's Angels managed to soft-con the press for quite a few years. Finally, in 1959, people like [James] Reston and [Harrison] Salisbury on the *NY Times* began writing the rude truth about Eisenhower. Salisbury's coverage of Ike's aborted trip to Japan—when threatened demonstrations caused him to terminate his mission in Okinawa—was a new kind of journalism for the '50s. And mine on the Angels, I suppose, was part of what is called the "New Journalism" of the '60s.

But the whole concept of a "new journalism" is bogus—unless we admit that honesty in a journalist is something new. The old, Hearst-style journalists had a privileged relationship with power—and they paid for that privilege by keeping a lot of warts and chancres off the public record. This tradition is still strong—especially with big-city newspapers, TV news departments and national newsmagazines. The first issue of the *Chicago Journalism Review* cites a few good examples of this, i.e. 1) One Step Forward, Two Steps Back, and 2) Giving Readers the Business.

So the "new journalism" is nothing more than a repudiation of the whole concept of privileged communication between newsmen and their sources. The Hell's Angels were outraged when I called them "losers." They were, and still are—yet I only knew this because they took me into their confidence. In the same way, none but a handful of trusted aides would have known that Hubert Humphrey "planted a wet kiss on the TV screen" the night of his nomination—if he hadn't allowed a few reporters into his suite while he watched the balloting. Nixon learned this lesson in 1960 and '62. This year he treated the press like a bunch of scorpions, playing "influential" reporters off against each other and awarding private interviews like gold stars for good behavior. I spent 10 days following him around in New Hampshire and by the time I was finally granted an audience I felt almost lucky. This feeling passed very quickly, however, and now—on the basis of what I wrote—I have no illusions about getting a job as a White House correspondent. For the same reasons, I'll have a jaundiced view of any correspondent who seems "close to Nixon."

The first issue of the *CJReview* cited this same problem in another context: "Are the Media Provoking Violence?" The article concluded: "Right now—whether editorial writers like it or not—violence is paying off in publicity as well as political response."

Well, I guess that's true to some extent—but I don't think it calls for a "new Policy," as the article suggested. I was in Chicago for that week of the Democratic Convention; I had press credentials for the Amphitheatre, a room at the Blackstone and a motorcycle helmet for the streets . . . and none of the incredible violence I saw was provoked by the media. The violence was an integral part of that scene; it had been building for years, all over the country, and Chicago was only an outlet. A CBS newsman who'd covered the April 27 peace march in Chicago said the local police were just as brutal then as they were on Wednesday night in front of the Hilton. It's been my experience, in fact, that the presence of cameras and TV lights usually forestalls violence. This was certainly true in the Bay Area, where I covered most of the anti-war demonstrations and "free speech" action from 1964 to '67. Police violence was always muted by the presence of the media . . . and if the "antis" were provoked in any way, it was usually to verbal excess. The whole purpose of a demonstration, after all, is to score points for The Cause—to convince the great mass of neutral witnesses that the protest is Right.

A prime intention of any left/radical demonstration is to provoke the minions of the establishment (the police) to violence, and thus expose the "brutality" and "hypocrisy" of an establishment that claims to stand for "peace and democracy." On these terms, the reaction of the Chicago police was a great victory for the demonstrators. They made their point.

Admittedly, the news media played a major role. Scenes of violence and police brutality were photographed, written about, and shown on TV screens from coast to coast. And why not? It happened; there was nothing twisted or untrue in the TV coverage. Mayor Daley's refusal to allow the networks to broadcast live from the streets forced them to work with film, and gave me the luxury of first being part of a scene and then watching the same thing later on a screen somewhere. In retrospect, some of the worst scenes I witnessed in person were never filmed. None of the really vicious beatings I saw occurred in front of the Hilton . . . that Wednesday night scene was only the tip of the iceberg.

Can anyone honestly say that Chicago would have been non-violent if the news media had ignored everything except the official program at the Amphitheatre? Can all those murders in Alabama[51] be traced to excessive news coverage? Did the news media provoke the Detroit race riot in 1943?

There is all manner of violence going on in this country every night of every week, and only a small percentage of it shows up on TV screens. Check the po-

51. A number of Freedom Riders and other civil rights activists had been murdered in Alabama beginning in 1961.

lice blotter in any big city newspaper; it's a horror show. Probably there were fewer serious injuries during the whole week of the Democratic Convention than on any Saturday night in metropolitan Chicago. While working on the Hell's Angels book I spent a lot of time in the new-slums of East Oakland, and I still tremble at the casual acceptance of violence that prevailed in that world. The kind of violence the news media are accused of provoking is usually the showbiz variety; the TV scenes from Chicago featured police charges and quick billy-club action. . . . I didn't see any films of ten-minute beatings with teeth being kicked out or four-on-one groin stompings.

Should the news media deal with this kind of violence? I think so. A middle-class voyeur who gets his kicks from watching [TV-show characters] Mannix or Marshal Dillon punch people around should be given the chance to watch a *real* beating—a terrified man, like himself, screaming and crying for help with blood in his eyes and not able to breathe.

Right . . . a bit of that on TV, or detailed descriptions in print, would drain a lot of the charm from our fantasy-violence. Or maybe not; this is an old notion when you consider that traffic offenders have been forced to watch gory-accident films for years, in almost every state—and it hasn't made much difference. More than 50,000 people will die this year on the highways.

It also begs the question about "media provoking violence" in situations that are essentially political. I spent election day and the rest of that week in Los Angeles, where an old friend of mine is deeply involved in the Chicano/Mexican Brown Power movement. He wanted me to write about it—and even though I didn't want to, I tried to interest two national "serious" magazines and they turned it down. One of these, the *NY Times Sunday Mag*, had called me the day after a bunch of Black Panthers walked into the California state capitol carrying guns, and asked me to rush out to the coast to do a story—on the Black Panthers. But, a year later, the same editor wasn't interested in a story on the still-peaceful Brown Berets in Los Angeles—from me or anyone else.

My friend, a lawyer working full-time in the Chicano movement, was first depressed and then bitter . . . he couldn't understand why the Black Panthers were such a hot story and the Chicanos weren't. I could explain the editors' lack of interest very simply and cynically: "Your people have to kill somebody," I said. "You need a good riot, with a lot of burning." Which was true, I'm afraid. A Mexican riot in east Los Angeles—on the scale of Watts—would very definitely get a lot of nationwide coverage. And it may happen. "It's coming," my friend told me. "That's the last thing we want, but if that's what it takes we'll do it. We have a lot of people who think we should have done it a long time ago." The next day he brought one of those people up to my hotel room—a stocky, flinty-eyed little Mexican who smoked a lot of grass and talked very casually about having blown up a building a few weeks earlier. "Dynamite's easy to get," he said. "At first we were scared like hell, but once we got started it was fun. We blew that place all apart."

I was interested, amused and generally sympathetic—but I still didn't want to do an article on the Brown Power thing. The Chicanos couldn't understand my attitude: they would give me all the help I needed, they said. I would have the "inside word," the real truth; I'd be privy to all their action. And there was the hook, the other end of the Hearst ethic. I was being offered a privileged relationship with Brown Power—but what would they say when I wrote about marijuana and dynamite and petty in-fighting, power-struggles within The Movement, stupid statements that would make them sound like a gang of teenage freaks if they ever appeared in print?

The Hell's Angels had presented the same kind of problem—the assumption that my privileged communication carried the obligation of not writing anything "bad" about them. They never understood that I saw myself as a journalist, not a special pleader. They seemed to feel I should lie for them in print like their lawyers lied for them in court.

My leverage, with the Angels, was the fact that I was writing a book, a one-shot thing over which they had no control because when I finished the book I'd also be finished with the Angels. They understood this, and seemed to accept it. I laughed off all suggestions that I "join the club," if only because by joining I'd have compromised myself as surely as if they'd hired me as a public relations man. My gig would have been blown just as badly as if I'd written any articles about them before I finished the book.

The November 18 issue of *The Nation* carries an article by Kenneth Gross, a reporter for the *NY Post,* on the difficulties of covering the recent New York City teachers strike. "In the beginning," he says, "Ocean Hill appeared to be available to journalism, but as the story grew, as the attention focused with more intensity, we became locked in. Eventually, physically locked in. . . . The cops were on one side, and since they stood with us, it was superficially concluded, we must be on that side, too. . . . Reporters who managed to establish a rapport with the governing board or the community also faced a test. They were not able to perform as journalists, but were expected to become agents. It was natural. The united Federation of Teachers behaved in exactly the same way, but the intimidation at Ocean Hill was thought to be greater. A group of white reporters were sitting in the office of the unit administrator when a group of black toughs appeared. They studied everyone's press card and jotted down our names and affiliations. 'We're going to be watching what you write,' one of the kids said. 'You'd better not come back here if we don't like it.' "

Hunter S. Thompson

TO WARREN HINCKLE, *SCANLAN'S MONTHLY:*

Unlike Playboy, *Warren Hinckle's bold new* Scanlan's Monthly *eagerly accepted Thompson's no-holds-barred first-person take on the Jean-Claude Killy phenomenon.*

December 6, 1969
Woody Creek, CO

Dear Warren . . .

Here's the Killy piece. I have a clean copy around here somewhere—right here in this goddamn room, for that matter—but I've been looking for the bastard for two days and nights and I can't find it.

Meanwhile, this half-ass copy should be enough for you to make some kind of initial judgement. I've had so many different comments on it that I've lost track. Some people dig it for the word-action; others hate it for the style and tone. The editors of *Playboy* really despised it: Their edit/memos ranged from "This is a good *Esquire* piece" to "Thompson's ugly, stupid arrogance is an insult to everything we stand for" and "This is our last adventure with H. Thompson; from now on we'll read his prose in book-form, or not at all. . . ."

David Butler, the editor who assigned the piece—despite my assurance that it would never see print (in *Playboy*)—confirmed my ho-ho phone assumption that I am now on *Playboy*'s blacklist. Butler's own comment was, "I don't really like the piece, but that's not the point—which is that N. Mailer shouldn't be the only writer who can get away with saying what he really thinks. . . ."

Butler's a decent sort and I don't want to blow his gig any worse than I already have. He told me, for instance, that [Hugh] Hefner has been trying for 5 years to get Chevrolet to advertise in "the book." I knew, from the start, that the whole thing was a terrible bummer. On my first night in Chicago I was drinking with one of the Chevy PR people when he was suddenly joined by his old friend, Vince Tajiri, *Playboy*'s picture editor, who had dropped by the hotel to invite Killy's PR team over to "Hef's House" for a swimming party . . . which didn't include me. No room in the pool for a writer assigned by Tajiri's magazine to write a long profile on the person they really wanted on the scene that night—for photos—J.-C. Killy, who didn't show up.

So all I missed, as it turned out, was a few hours in the company of a gang of assholes. But the point is that nobody knew, when they told me that my services wouldn't be needed for the rest of the night, that Killy wasn't going to grace the scene they were setting up. Tajiri didn't know me from a dog in the manger, but he knew I was working on assignment from *Playboy* . . . yet the cocksucker told me to get lost when he wanted to use my subject for a night of orgy/promo pix . . . and he did it in the presence of Killy's main PR hooker, which queered my act for good.

Looking for parallels, well . . . let's say that 2 years ago [*Ramparts* editor Peter] Collier assigned me to write a profile on Eric Hoffer, who didn't particularly dig it, but who went along with the act until one night in a bar we ran into Stermer,[52] who said, "Say Eric, let's you and me bug off to some real action, and dump this bum. . . ."

Anyway, I trust you see what I mean. I've done a lot of weird shit in 10 years of free-lancing, running a lot of heavy gauntlets with no real credentials and only the grease of human decency to get me through (like conning Sonny Liston,[53] Ted Sorensen and the President of Peru into long exclusive interviews when I wasn't even working for anybody) . . . but never, under any circumstances, have I been shit on so totally as I was in the course of this *Playboy*/Killy thing. That whole goddamn magazine is a conspiracy of anemic masturbators . . . scurvy fist-fuckers to the last man. Like a gang of wild whores or the inmates of some terrible peg house, the editors of *Playboy* roam the world by telephone, trying to get everybody down in the same bad hole where they are.

Yeah . . . and to hell with all that. I have a bundle of letter-carbons, discussing the horrors of working for those jackals. Maybe that would put a bit of wild hair on the piece. I don't see any chance of getting Butler to yield up those confidential memos; he read them to me, on the phone, as a personal favor—or maybe for reasons of his own. Anyway, I insisted on knowing *why* they wouldn't print it. One memo, for instance, said: "Publication of this article would certainly cause Head Ski to drop us permanently from their ad schedule, and cost us any chance we might have with Chevrolet . . . etc." Oddly enough, there was one ranking editor who wanted to publish the thing. Butler wouldn't tell me who he was & I wasn't really that curious, but in fairness I should say that there was *one*. . . .

Which hardly matters, for now. Read the thing and do what you will. Naturally I'd prefer to see the thing done whole, but it's obvious even to me that it's cuttable. I knew, all along, that it wasn't going to run, so I didn't worry about length, redundancies, or constant focus. There are obvious chunks that can be dropped with no real loss to the Main Theme, as it were. . . .

I think I've noted (or marked) some of the cuttable chunks on the margin—although some of the most obvious chops contain some of the things I like best . . . like the whole link with the Stockyards and August '68 . . . or the optional lead—marked with letters "A" through "M," instead of numbers. The A–M section might fit anywhere, or nowhere. . . . Why don't you read the whole thing and see what you think, then we can haggle, if necessary.

Unfortunately, the last 26 pages had to be xeroxed off this goddamn orange paper, which for some reason defies xeroxing. If you want to run the thing, maybe you can make your own copy and return *all* of these orange pages to me, as soon as possible—in case I can't locate my other copy. For the moment, you have the only copy of pages A through M and 1–77.

52. Dugald Stermer was the art director at *Ramparts* magazine.
53. Sonny Liston was heavyweight boxing champion from 1962 to 1964.

Another potential hang-up is that *Skiers' Gazette,* a trade tabloid, is talking about serializing the whole thing, as is, for $200 a chunk . . . and although that sounds unlikely, it's a definite possibility because the editor of *SG* is a left-bent dope freak who hates skiing and skiers. They've run some really foul, insulting shit, so this Killy thing might be right up their tube.

I don't see any problem with conflict of interest on this score, but let me know if I'm wrong. In any case, there's no point in haggling until you've read the piece . . . so do that first, and then we can fuck with details. (My apologies for the dim xerox of pages 78–101, but it was either that or nothing. . . .)

On other fronts . . . MaryAnn mentioned a 2000 word shot on the recent Aspen election. I hope to get that done in a day or so. Right now I'm trying to work it into this stinking book that I have to deliver to Random House in order to pay many debts and get free of what has come to be a fuckawful nightmare. The election was a bummer; we came within 6 votes (out of 1200) of taking over the town, and in the process we scared the shit out of all the Fatbacks who've been running this town since 1945. I'm enclosing a screed I did for one of the local papers (owned by the same lad who owns the *Skiers' Gazette*) . . . and which caused massive howling and ugliness when it appeared. It was my first appearance in local print & the reaction was extremely savage. The fuckers accused me of "negativism" . . . "it's easy to criticize, etc. . . ." Right. Everybody talks about the weather, but . . .

So I called Joe Edwards one Saturday at midnight & said "My man, you don't know me and I don't know you, but three weeks from now you're going to be the Mayor of Aspen." In less than 10 days we registered about 300 street-loonies who never even thought about voting. . . . Freak Power was the theme, and it worked. We beat the buggers stupid. The day before the election the Mayor went on the radio and said that within 24 hours he was going to have at least 150 hair-freaks in jail for perjury and false swearing . . . and beyond that, they'd have the living shit kicked out of them if they showed up at the polls. We tried to have the mayor arrested for "intimidating voters," but the bastard hires & fires all the cops, including the chief . . . and when I called the DA he said he couldn't get involved . . . we would have to do our own "policing."

Which we did, with numerous bearded poll-watchers and full complement of auxiliaries just outside the 100-foot limit. Even our sympathizers complained about the hair-cordon all around the polling place. But it worked; we disqualified all but two voter-challenges, whip-lashing the poll-judges with all the fine points of Colorado election law. . . .

And so much for all that, too. This is not my night for coherence. Since losing the election we have declared total war on the Fatbacks—on two levels: Like, tonight I spent about five hours on the phone, gathering evidence to bust the County Attorney. There are three Wards in the city; the county is a Fourth Ward . . . and we are Ward Five. On the public level we are dealing now with the City Atty—mainly to keep sharp—and gearing down for next year's election when the Sheriff comes up, along with one of the 3 Cty Commissioners. Ward 5's candidate for the CC slot is a man with a beard down to his sternum . . . and our man for Sheriff is . . . well, shucks . . . I hate to sound uppity, but I may as well admit that it's me. Right: Sheriff Thompson . . .

Which is only a rumor, but the mere possibility has made a lot of people physically sick. Three weeks before the Mayoral election Joe Edwards didn't even know he was running, and Freak Power was a bad hippie joke. But now, in the wake of that 6-vote loss, we are clearly capable of almost anything; we are sitting on the largest Bloc Vote in the county . . . and even the pig-people realize it. I tell you this politics gig is a wild and heavy trip; I got about as high on that election, for 21 straight days, as I've ever been on acid . . . and I can see, now, why people get addicted to this thing. Like Mailer & his hopeless dream of the White House . . . or, failing that, Gracie Mansion[54] . . . Super-Freak Goes to the Supermart.

So the password in Aspen these days is BEWARE. Ward 5 is gearing down for a serious Takeover Bid . . . and meanwhile, on that other level, we're into a fire and dynamite trip. Make the fatbacks understand how vulnerable they are—not only at the polls, but every hour of every wretched day. Agnew can't help them out here. The fat is in the Fire. . . .

& OK for now; it's dawn & I'm tired. One of these days I'll send Random House a 100 lb. bag of my letters . . . or maybe a half-mad wolverine in a cardboard cage. Why not?

Indeed . . .
Hunter

TO DON ERICKSON, *ESQUIRE:*

Thompson made a last-minute attempt to get his NRA article published.

December 9, 1969
Woody Creek, CO

Dear Don . . .

Astounding to hear from you. I sort of assumed the gun piece had died on the vine—or the cutting-room floor, as it were. I'm a trifle paranoid about the politics end of this writing business; I can't handle it. At almost the same time that I was fuming out here with Sherrill's memo I was putting the finishing touches on a piece that ultimately got me black-balled with *Playboy.* They asked for a profile of J.-C. Killy and cursed me savagely for the thing I gave

54. Norman Mailer had pledged to use the money from his 1969 Pulitzer Prize for Nonfiction for his book *The Armies of the Night* as "the first contribution" to his campaign for the Democratic nomination in New York City's mayoral race.

them. That episode, along with the Gun Piece hassle, left me wondering if it was possible for me to communicate any longer with anyone east of the Rockies.

I still wonder, for that matter . . . but if you're still interested in the gun piece, I'll send a new version. Since my last effort I went hunting for the first time in four years and—with the help of a little mescaline—got locked into a trauma that found me spending 48 hours alone in the badlands, chasing antelope by day and scribbling crazily all night in the back of my Volvo wagon, by Coleman-lantern light . . . wondering what the fuck I was doing out there.

On top of that a man came out the other day and tried to sell me a machine-gun. He wanted $200 so he could pay a speed-freak to break a man's arm in town. I couldn't afford the gun, but it was wonderful fun to shoot. Which reminds me of the enc. clip from the current *Rolling Stone;* things are even worse than I said in the original article; every dope-freak I've talked to in the past year is on a violence trip. Maybe Woodstock[55] is the wave of the future, but I doubt it. Haight St. was peaceful when I lived there, but that was 3 yrs ago.

Actually, I haven't written anything in about 2 months, due to a sudden, total involvement in local politics. We launched a Takeover Bid that came within 6 votes of installing a 29-yr-old bike-racer as Mayor of Aspen. I promised to run for Sheriff if he won, and I may still do it. Freak Power is out in the open here. One man, one vote . . . Beware the rising tide.

OK for now. I'll get back on the piece and send a new version ASAP.

Ciao . . .
Hunter

TO STEVE GELLER:

After the loss of the Aspen mayoral election and Sandy's painful miscarriage, the Thompsons went to Los Angeles for a two-week vacation of sorts.

December 10, 1969
Woody Creek, CO

Dear Steve . . .

Your letter was here when I got back from LA. After the Aspen election I was so wound up that I had to get out of town for a while, so I sent my son to Florida, seized my wife and fled to the Continental Hotel for about 2 weeks. She was still in a slump after losing the last kid, and I was lingering along in a killing rage after losing the Aspen mayor's race by 6 votes . . . so we decided to sacrifice the Diners Club card for 2 crazed weeks in Hollywood, face to face with the drug culture in a huge rented Pontiac, Chicano dealers and Brown Power freaks lurking around the roof-top hotel pool at noon—mescaline poli-

55. More than 400,000 mostly young music fans had assembled August 15–17, 1969, at Max Yasgur's farm in Bethel, New York, for the notably peaceful Woodstock Music and Art Fair, featuring Jimi Hendrix, the Jefferson Airplane, the Who, and other major rock acts.

tics far up in the smog, 12 floors higher than the Strip . . . looking down on all that wild crap, buying honeydew melons at the Farmers Market and hurling the rinds off the balcony at passing cars . . . a very debilitating trip in all, and I'm sorry I missed you.

It never occurred to me, of course, that you were actually living nearby. In my mind you exist as a small & wiry bugger, lurking intensely on a midnight street-corner beside some shoe-factory in Troy—making notes, notes, notes—compiling some awful indictment that nobody understands.

Jesus, I guess that sounds bad, but I don't mean it that way. If somebody asked me tonight whose book (new) I most looked forward to reading sometime soon, I think I'd say yours. As I told Shir-Cliff—and you, too, I think—I dug *Pit Bull* on a level that I don't spend much time on these days. Hard to explain, but it's there. Try another one of Bernard's offerings called *Nog*, or the one from a different house titled *A Fan's Notes*. A man called Exley wrote the latter . . . no reason to like it, except that it's nice to read something straight, now and then.

Anyway, I certainly would have called if I'd had any idea you were there. Your money/writing schedule makes me tired, just looking at it. I spent a whole day while I was there out at UCLA, experimenting with video-tape scenes in the J-dept. I'm fascinated by the notion of being able to make your own film & then play it back instantly on the tube. Dennis Murphy (*The Sergeant*) & I went out there and worked out on the machine long enough to see the future . . . which is not bound-books, as I see it. If Nixon fails in his efforts to destroy the economy, I think we're into a decade of wild experiments—mainly with film; that whole medium seems on the verge of falling into the hands of people who can use it.

All of which reminds me that I'm many months overdue with that wonderful Random House offering called "The Death of the American Dream." I hate to spend 3 yrs writing a pile of worthless shit, but that's what I'm into—a sophomore jinx on all fronts. I've done everything I can to put it off, but now—stone broke again—I don't see any way out. Just write the fucker and clear the decks . . . take the beating and play counter-puncher. Fuck them. I hope your agent is better than mine; who is it? This is really a stinking way to have to make a living. I got into politics recently and ran amok with energy I haven't been able to tap in years. We made a takeover bid here, and came within 6 votes of doing it. I think maybe Hollywood is the last place in America where a writer can still ignore Agnew in good conscience; he'll never matter there, either way. I spent most of election day '68 at an outdoor pub on the Strip, called Alfies—with time off, now and then, to visit various polling places around the city—and my central memory about Hollywood on that day is that nobody either knew or gave a fuck about anything . . . like "Nixon who?"

So maybe I half-understand your mention of "missing New Haven terribly." Or maybe not. My focus here has come down—quite unexpectedly—to the hard and vicious realities of how my world works . . . like I spent most of today gathering evidence inre: Conflict of Interest in the County Attorney's Office. This filthy bastard has spent 20 years beating us all like a set of silly gongs. He has run this county like a private fief, and made himself a millionaire in the process. His brother represents LBJ's oil interest, two counties away—which now comes down to how many nuclear blasts the oil companies need to fuck us all.

Anyway, that's my scene for the moment, I'm trying to finish off that pile of crap for RH, and meanwhile going hard & fast about 20 hrs a day with reality. These greedy screws are selling the very earth I live on, and—for good or ill—I think the time has come to say "No More."

The time has also come to get off this letter-writing gig, grind out a few words for money. So I guess I'll do that. As for the "Handwriting" you mentioned, look back on what I've said for what I see—the only hope, for now, is to get down on the killing floor with those evil fucks, and beat them in public. Agnew is the final flower of the "Fuck it" syndrome. Right . . . Let Adolf do it. That's where we're headed, and when they have the War Crimes trials for this era, I don't want to have to say I wasn't involved.

Which brings me back to your line about the crabs and "*real* bullshit." That's a beautiful line and maybe I'll use it sometime (with proper credit, of course), but don't let your eagerness to get it off (later) make you blind to the weird & volatile realities of the scene you're waiting to comment on (later). Remember Hubert Humphrey; he sold his ass for a tomorrow he'll never see—not even in his memoirs. And so much for all that.

Hunter

TO BERNARD SHIR-CLIFF, BALLANTINE BOOKS:

December 12, 1969
Woody Creek, CO

Dear Bernard . . .

It strikes me as possible and even probable that the passing of a year has yielded up a few royalty-dollars inre: the *Hell's Angels* sales. I certainly hope so—because I need funds in a very definite way. And not for Xmas presents, either.

So if my account shows anything on the fat side, I hope and pray you'll send a cheque at once. Selah.

On other fronts, I'm still laboring with that foul bummer of a book about the American Dream, or some such bullshit. It is the bane of my fucking existence, and has been for longer than I care to remember. Just recently I had to take a few months off to run a political campaign, which resulted in such an incredible outburst of energy (on my part) that I suddenly understood what a terrible hole I bargained myself into, with regard to that pigfucking book.

Actually, I have about 400 pages stacked here beside me, and it's all bullshit. There are so many things worth dealing with that I can't understand how I trapped myself on a shit-kicker. In this era of assholes, all I want to do is smite them hip and thigh. That Aspen/politics article I sent you led to a mayoral campaign that ripped this town asunder. We ran a 29-year-old bike racer for mayor and lost by six votes. There was no end to the madness and crazed action; I didn't sleep for three weeks. We took on the Aspen Ski Corp.—with directors like [Robert] McNamara and Paul Nitze and a whole gaggle of power freaks—and beat them stupid with flying squads of bearded hustlers and street people. Freak Power was the theme, & in three weeks' time we organized a flat-out takeover bid that came within 6 votes (out of 1200) of seizing control of the town.

And so much for all that. The only hope for this evil book I'm trying to rake together is that I might be able to work the Aspen campaign into it. That would lend it a hint of the energy that I haven't been able to find for it up to now.

Anyway, please take a look at my account and see if there's any cash on hand. And if there is, please send it along. Contrary to NY rumors, I'm not dead or drug-stupored. My only problem, of late, has been a creeping suspicion that I've forgotten how to speak whatever language is currently in use east of the Rockies. I no longer have any faith in my ability to communicate with you folks back there in Cocktailville.

All I want to do, right now, is get this fucking millstone of a book off my neck and get on to things that matter. You can help by sending along a check for whatever royalties I have coming. Thanks . . .

Hunter

TO HUGHES RUDD, CBS NEWS:

Thompson wrote Rudd about his escapades in Los Angeles with Sandy and his confidence in the rising "Freak Power" prospects in the coming election.

December 13, 1969
Woody Creek, CO

Dear Hughes . . .

Christ, it seems incredible that I still haven't answered your letter of 10/1. Time has gotten wholly out of hand here, beyond my control . . . and the more I think about your comments on my general life-style here, the more I tend to agree. One of these bright mornings I'm going to wake up and find that 10 years have gone by, and that I haven't done a fucking thing. So the program now is to get this stinking book done, for good or ill—and at the same time try to make some arrangement for buying this house—then rent the house for enough to make mortgage payments and bug off, for a while, to somewhere else. I can't say where. Maybe even land a job of some kind, just to get myself re-oriented in the Real World. At the moment I would far rather be working on a film of some kind, instead of this rotten journalism . . . but there's no hope of ducking this thing without getting myself totally blacklisted. So I guess I'll be here all winter. After that, I can't say. . . . On other fronts, Sandy & I just got back from a 10-day freakout in LA, dedicated to the total destruction of my credit, by means of running up huge, unpayable bills on the Diners Club card. We ran completely amok & accomplished nothing, but we had a wonderful time. One of my central memories recalls an evening of mescaline and a load of honeydew melons I bought at the Farmers Market. Then, with a room full of rum and music and freaks, we had a melon-eating orgy on the (hotel) balcony overlooking the Strip, and afterwards hurled the rinds down on passing cars. There was also a vast amount of high-speed driving on the freeways, mainly late at night in a million-horsepower Pontiac, full of mescaline. In all, it was a wretched and debilitating scene . . . and soon they'll want me to pay for it.

And again to other fronts: I got a decent long letter from Joe Benti—after also receiving a nerve-rattling early morning phone call from him and the producer (Lewis, I think)—all concerning your Aspen piece, Nazis in high places, network censorship and all that bullshit. The Aspen hassle was clearly getting out of hand, so I told him I'd never mention it again unless he did—which seems fair. It also seems that you people have enough to cope with at the moment: with Agnew on one flank & Nicholas Johnson on the other, that battle seems out of my hands.

You'll be happy to know, however, that my latest effort on the home front resulted in the total political destruction of the Mayor and the city council. We launched a serious takeover bid and came within 6 votes of electing a 29-year-old dope-smoking bike-racer as Mayor of Aspen. The old guard candidate, the current mayor's creature, was whipped to jelly. A silly old bitch won; she was backed by people like Leon Uris & that real estate geek who rented the house to you—along with Dunaway & the *Times,*[56] the Contractors Assn and the whole cocktail set, plus a heavy chunk of the failed liberal establishment who said they dug our program but couldn't tolerate our people. On election day we staffed all three polling places—one of which was Guido's—with teams of heavily bearded poll-watchers. The mayor had threatened to sic goons on our freaks if they showed up to vote & the police chief refused to guarantee access, so we organized our own goons, armed with tape recorders and reams of legal documents, among other things—and beat them stupid on all counts. We actually won the "love" vote by five, but we lost the absentee ballots by eleven—primarily because of skullduggery in City Hall. I ran the campaign for all practical purposes, and now I have hundreds of new enemies. It feels wonderful. . . .

56. Bil Dunaway was publisher of the *Aspen Times*.

Anyway, that was what caused me to flip out for LA. The campaign kept me awake for three weeks & I thought I was going down there for a rest, but it didn't work. So I slept for about 2 weeks when I got back here, and now, in the press of sudden poverty, I have to get back to work.

Which reminds me that it's late—and letters don't pay. One of the things that emerged from the mayoral campaign was a fine sense of a rising tide. We registered about 300 loonies in the city and now we have another rich lode in the county. So the next project is to bust the County Attorney, the kingpin Cty Commissioner and the Sheriff. Next autumn should be a hummer out here. Total confrontation.

I'm beginning to think that Agnew doesn't realize what he's up against. The *real* Silent Majority is the Rising Tide. If a serious freak ran for President in 1972—and if he could muster enough money & talent to get himself launched—I think he could come very close to winning . . . but this is a long and twisted subject, and like I have said I have to do some money writing.

So, for now, well . . . Merry Xmas & all that crap. Sandy talks constantly of both you and Ann. Keep in mind that we have a decent guest-room and say hello to Benti when you see him—and Kuralt, that swine. Christmas is a rotten hype & all we can do is ride it out. Say hello to Ann for me, and send word. . . .

Ciao,
Hunter

—also Hello to John, wherever he is . . .

TO THE EDITOR, *ASPEN NEWS* AND *ASPEN TIMES:*

Signing himself "Adolph," Thompson sent his local newspaper an anti–Vietnam War satire worthy of Jonathan Swift's "Modest Proposal" to end hunger in 1729 London by feeding the orphans to the poor.

December 14, 1969
Woody Creek, CO

Dear Editor,

My reason for writing this letter is unfortunate, but I can no longer live in Aspen without doing something about the absence of feeling about the war in Vietnam. I am not the only one who feels this way.

Accordingly, I want to explain our action before we do it, because I realize a lot of people won't understand. On Xmas eve we are going to burn a dog with napalm (or jellied gasoline made to the formula of napalm) on a street where many people will see it. If possible, we will burn several dogs, depending on how many we find on that day. We will burn these dogs wherever we can have the most public impact.

Anybody who hates the idea of burning dogs with napalm should remember that the American army is burning human beings with napalm every day in

Vietnam. If you think it is wrong to burn a dog in Aspen, what do you think about burning people in Asia?

We think this will make the point, once people see what napalm does. It hurts humans much worse than it hurts dogs. And if anybody doubts this, they can volunteer to take the place of whatever dogs we have when the time comes. Anybody who wants to try it should be standing in front of the Mountain Shop about four o'clock on Xmas eve, and he should be wearing a sign that says, "Napalm Dog." If this happens, we will put the jellied gasoline on the person, instead of an animal. Frankly, I'd rather burn a human warmonger than a dog, but I doubt if any of these will show up.

Sincerely,
"Adolph"
(for obvious reasons I can't state my real name)

TO JOHN WILCOCK, *LOS ANGELES FREE PRESS:*

This essay-length missive to the editor of the Los Angeles Free Press *explained "Freak Power" and outlined the political strategy Thompson would use the next year in his campaign for sheriff of Pitkin County.*

December 17, 1969
Woody Creek, CO

Dear John . . .

Your query about me writing something for the Xmas issue came at a weird time: I had just finished a wild election campaign here, and with a day's rest I took off for LA and a 2-week freakout to clear my head. So by the time I got back here I hadn't slept for six straight weeks (except for naps here and there) and I needed about 2 weeks of sleep to get my head together. So I obviously can't get you anything for the Xmas Issue, unless it's running unconscionably late—like [Paul] Krassner's 10th anniversary issue of *The Realist.*

The best I can do is lay off a quick rambling first draft on some subject that I hope to come up with by the time I get to the next paragraph of this letter. At the moment I can't think of a fucking thing to tell you except that I'm always in the market for fine mescaline. I know you don't fool with dope, but maybe some of your enemies do—and if you run into any of them in the next month or so, I hope you'll pass this message along.

Other than that, I suppose you might be interested in the LA hotel situation. As you know, I've always favored the Continental, where you visited me in the course of that wretched publicity tour for Random House. I've been back there several times since then, and the place gets weirder and weirder. This recent visit may turn out to be my last, if only because I paid for the whole thing with a credit card that will soon be taken away from me. There was also a heavy mescaline factor, which led to crazed behavior in the room and around the roof-top pool. We spent one evening hurling honeydew melon rinds off the 10th floor balcony & down to the Strip below. It took a long time for them to reach the street, and when they did they exploded with a heavy smacking sound. I got these melons at the Farmers Market one afternoon, for no particular reason except that I knew they would taste good. But when I returned to the room it was full of freaks and loud music; there were candles burning and strange posters taped to the wall . . . and before long we ran amok. Fortunately we had the sense to hurl the garbage at a sharp angle, so that when pigs began sweeping the hotel, they began far enough away from our area so that we had time to move out very leisurely.

None of which really matters. I just wanted to let you know that the Continental is still a decent place to stay—although [real estate mogul and former singer] Gene Autry has sold it to the Hyatt House chain and the prices are up about 50%. But they can't shake the freak-image: The hallways still rumble with the sound of rock bands rehearsing, the elevators are still full of Halloween people and the late-night balconies are still a fine sideshow. At one point, on this last visit, I looked down and saw a man in jockey underwear climbing across the front of the hotel like a white chimp, crawling from balcony to balcony in a very confident way, as if he knew exactly where he was going and had been there many times before. Maybe it was the manager, investigating routine complaints . . . whoever it was seemed very agile; he was moving about eight floors up from the street, with nothing below except space and sure death if he fell.

On other fronts, I suppose I might mention the recent Aspen election. We made a serious attempt to elect a 29-year-old bike-racing head as mayor . . . and after a savage, fire-sucking campaign we lost by only six (6) votes, out of 1200. Actually, we lost by one (1) vote, but five of our absentee ballots didn't get here in time—primarily because they were mailed (to places like Mexico and Nepal and Guatemala) five days before the election.

Yeah . . . this is probably worth talking about for a moment. Because we came very close to winning control of the town, and by coming so close I think we may have learned—and proved—some things that might be helpful in other places. Frankly, when we decided to run a serious candidate I didn't think we had a chance in hell . . . and, besides, I've been telling myself for two years to forswear, at all costs, any personal involvement in local politics. My life-style is not entirely suited to lengthy power-struggles with any small-town establishment. One of the most obvious facts of our campaign was that every cop in town would be fired, at once, if we won . . . the Chief being no exception. Beyond that, I promised to run for Sheriff next year—against the incumbent—if Joe Edwards actually won the Mayor's race this year.

So the fatbacks were looking at a double-barreled nightmare every time they saw an Edwards poster, or a hair-freak wearing one of our "pocket-posters"—a red hand with two fingers raised in a Victory (not "peace") symbol. We almost used the clenched red fist, but at the last moment we decided that it would be too heavy for a lot of the people we would have to keep on our side if we wanted to win.

There, in a nut, is the problem. We were out-numbered, so our only hope of victory lay in convincing a hell of a lot of people that we normally never see or talk to that we were, in fact, RIGHT. We began with a hastily-organized effort, about six people, to work the streets and the bars, as quietly as possible, persuading heads to *register.* This was the hardest part of the gig, because it had to be done weeks ahead of the actual campaign—before Edwards announced and before we could begin whipping the fatbacks with anything public. The idea was to first mobilize our hidden vote—Freak Power—and then, using that as a power base, go after the small but very vocal "liberal vote." I was convinced that we could win by putting these two blocs together . . . and as it turned out I was right: That combination would have won by at least 100 votes out of 1200—but it never occurred to me that most of the local "liberals" would back off at the last moment, leaving us with what amounted, in the end, to an "under-30 vote" and a hundred or so defectors from the old, failed-liberal camp who said, "Fuck it, let's run flat out this time . . ."

Their help was invaluable. They not only voted for Edwards, but they came out front in newspaper ads and went on the air (the local radio station) and said exactly *why* they were going to do it. Beyond that, their money contributions paid for more than half our campaign; the rest came from small contributions and the sale of our pocket posters . . . and when it was all over, we came out a few dollars ahead, despite our total failure to concern ourselves with finances while the campaign was happening. I spent about half my time at the radio station (there was no TV), dragging people in to tape Edwards endorsements—dragging Edwards in to make policy statements—and making sure the next day's schedule would carry a heavy load of our ads. Nobody ever worried about the cost, and in the end we paid every penny of the bill—despite the rotten cop-out of the radio station's owner, who finally endorsed our opponent in the main local paper, which he also owns.

Early on, our opponent—a 55-year-old lady shopkeeper—grabbed the crucial noon-hour time-slot for a paid and heavily-slanted "question and answer session." There was nothing we could do about losing that chunk of prime time . . . but we neutralized it by getting a local, Murry Roman style rapper to do a brutal take-off on the (L.A.) Ralph Williams Ford commercials, selling Aspen, instead of used cars . . . and running it immediately after the old lady's Q&A sessions, with a background of Herbie Mann's "Battle Hymn of the Republic." It was a wild, inspired piece of work—a masterpiece of audio/political zappery, and I dug it so much that I made myself a tape. If they run contests for that sort of thing, this one would be a sure winner. On the station logs it appears as "Bill Greed commercial," and in retrospect it seems like the clearest of all our statements.

Not even our supporters liked it. The satire, they said, was too heavy, too rude and angry to make any voting points with the so-called "neutral types" we knew we had to convince, in order to win. Even Joe Edwards, our candidate, was afraid of it. After the first day, the opening flute notes of that Battle Hymn on the radio caused heads to snap around and all conversation to stop . . . while everybody listened to Bill Greed's crazed and venal sales pitch—an awful, artful mockery of every effort that had ever been made, then and now, to "sell Aspen!"

Which gets us back to the whole point of the campaign: The argument that a gang of big-city greedheads are selling this place out from under the people who came here to live in quiet, noncommercial peace, like decent human beings—and to escape the urban horrors that plagued them in L.A., the Bay Area, Chicago and New York. Most of us are living here because we like the idea of being able to walk out our front doors and smile at what we see. On my own front porch I have a palm tree growing in a blue toilet bowl . . . and on occasion I like to wander outside, stark naked, and fire my .44 Magnum at various iron gongs I've mounted on the nearby hillside. I like to load up on mescaline and turn my amplifier up to 110 decibels for a taste of "White Rabbit"[57] while the sun comes up on the snow-peaks along the Continental Divide. And when I drive into town, still hung on those peaks, I like the idea of calling for a Tuborg in a place where the bartender says, "Wow, man! You need an anchor rope . . . do you have any more of that shit?"

Which is not entirely the point. The world is full of places where a man can run wild on drugs and loud music and fire-power—but not for long. I lived a block above Haight street for two years, but by the end of '66 the whole neighborhood had become a cop-magnet and a bad sideshow. Between the narks and the psychedelic hustlers, there was not much room to live.

What happened in the Haight echoed earlier scenes in North Beach and The Village, among others . . . and it proved, once again, the basic futility of seizing turf you can't control. The pattern never varies: a low-rent area suddenly blooms new and loose and human—and then fashionable, which attracts the press and the cops at about the same time. Cop problems attract more publicity, which then attracts fad-salesmen and hustlers—which means money, and that attracts junkies and jack-rollers. Their bad action causes more publicity and—for some perverse reason—an influx of bored upward-mobile types who dig the menace of "white ghetto" life and whose expense-account tastes drive local rents and street-prices up and out of reach of the original settlers . . . who are forced, once again, to move on.

One of the most hopeful developments of the failed Haight/Ashbury scene was the exodus to rural communes. Most of the communes failed—for reasons that everybody can see now, in retrospect (like that scene in *Easy Rider,* where

57. The Jefferson Airplane song "White Rabbit" featured soaring vocals by Grace Slick.

all those poor freaks were trying to grow their crops in dry sand)—but the few that succeeded, like the Hog Farm in New Mexico, kept a whole generation of heads believing that the future lay somewhere outside the cities—where one good scene after another had been first settled, then publicized, then busted. The pattern had become almost a ritual.

Which gets back to Aspen, where hundreds of H/A refugees tried to settle in the wake of that ill-fated "summer of love" in 1967. That summer was a wild and incredible freak show here, but when winter came the crest of that wave broke and drifted on the shoals of local problems such as jobs, housing and deep snow on the roads to shacks that had, a few months earlier, been easily accessible. Many of the West Coast refugees moved on, but several hundred stayed; they hired on as carpenters, waiters, bartenders, dish-washers . . . and a year later they were part of the permanent population. By mid-'69 they occupied most of Aspen's so-called "low-cost housing"—first the tiny mid-town apartment hovels, then out-lying shacks, and finally the trailer courts.

So, by the autumn of '69, it was obvious—to anybody who had any dealings with the dope/young/freak culture—that a serious voter-registration effort might yield up a formidable power-base for a new kind of candidate. Aspen's last mayoral election, in 1967, had been decided on a plurality of some 50 votes, out of a total of 650. This time, we knew, the total would—or could—be more than 1000 . . . and, given the kaleidoscope realities of a three-way race, we thought a Freak Power candidate might have a good chance of winning.

Which was true—except that I assured Joe Edwards, in the course of persuading him to run, that he would certainly have the support of our never-tested "underground vote," but also of the older "liberal" bloc, which agreed with us on nearly every issue. Edwards was the perfect coalition candidate: He was a 29-year-old head and bike-racer, whose only known success in a year of law practice had been a far-out, wild-eyed suit against the city for "harassment of hippies." Beyond that, he was on the platform committee of a newly formed liberal-action group called the Citizens for Community Action—which seemed to guarantee their support. Both Edwards and the CCA were pro-hippie, anti-development and generally opposed, on all fronts, to the plastic money-fuckers who've been selling every chunk and parcel of this valley they've been able to get their hands on for the past ten years.

A series of CCA meetings had distilled the issues—and a small but very articulate voting base—for a genuine, grass-roots revolt. The program, in a nut, was to drive the real estate goons completely out of the valley: to prevent the State Highway Dept. from bringing a 4-lane highway into town and in fact to ban all auto traffic from every downtown street. Turn them all into grassy malls, where everybody—even freaks—can do whatever's right. The cops would become trash collectors and maintenance men for a fleet of municipal bicycles, for anybody to use. No more huge, space-killing apartment buildings to block the view, from any downtown street, of anybody who might want to look up and see the mountains. No more land-rapes, no more busts for "flute-playing" or "blocking the sidewalk" . . . fuck the tourists, dead-end the highway, zone the greedheads out of existence, and in general create a town where people can live like human beings, instead of slaves to some bogus sense of Progress that is driving us all mad.

Obviously, we had a heavy program . . . and in retrospect I have to wonder how in hell we came within six votes of winning the whole gig. One of our problems, on election day, was that all of our poll-watchers were bearded. Even our liberal sympathizers objected to the image we were presenting to "the public." But in fact we had no choice: The lame-duck mayor had spent half the previous day on the radio, screeching threats of prison terms and gang-beatings for any hair-freak who dared to show up at the polls. I tried to have him arrested for "intimidating voters"; his broadcasts were a clear violation of the law—but the D.A. told me to get fucked. "You'll have to police the election yourselves," he said—and so we did. But the only people willing to be Edwards poll-watchers tended to be weird-looking.

The Mayor was running his own candidate, the local magistrate, and by the final week of the campaign he knew he was in bad trouble. It was obvious, by then, that Joe Edwards—the Left candidate—had built such a tidal wave of momentum that the Right was already croaked . . . and that the only question, on election day, was how far the freak tide would carry. The fatbacks' only hope, in the end, was the old lady/shopkeeper whose platform consisted of an endorsement by the local Contractors' Association and her claim that all she really wanted was to "be the town's den-mother."

She was the "middle-road candidate," the androgynous Ike-figure of all our nightmares . . . and although she won only one of the three wards, she won that one (a new, Orange County style sub-division) so heavily that her Agnewville vote finally cancelled our wins in the other two wards. The final tally wasn't in until after midnight, and by then our headquarters was a madhouse of bad mescaline freakouts and loonies screaming for dynamite. I had the presence of mind to remain un-armed—which proved wise, because by the end of election night I was in a killing rage.

We had run the whole campaign with a power-nut of about six people, and when the final count came in, each one of us knew at least three people who hadn't bothered to vote or who'd mocked our efforts to persuade them to register. "Politics is bullshit," they said. "You fuckers are kidding yourselves with this Joe Edwards bit . . . you don't have a chance." By dawn of the next morning we had the voting lists together and it was easy to see why we lost: Almost thirty of the town's most infamous heads had either failed or refused to vote. Some were too stoned to make it to the polls, others had left town, temporarily, without making the five-minute effort to sign up for an absentee ballot . . . a few had forgotten, they said, to register . . . and another dozen or 80 had simply opted out, insisting that it wasn't worth the effort.

So the new Mayor of Aspen is a giddy old lady who would feel honored to go down on Agnew. Looking back on the election, there are two ways to see it: 1) That we were lucky to mobilize enough heads, on a one-shot basis, to come within six votes (or one) of winning anything . . . or 2) That our last-minute rush to make Freak Power a voting reality came close to a weird and "impossible" victory . . . and that the Edwards campaign forged a power base and a new voice in this county that, in future elections, the fatbacks can't ignore.

In the uproar surrounding the mayor's race, nobody noticed that we managed to elect two heads to the City Council. Those two, along with the two liberals elected, gives us a probable 4–2 majority on the Council—which is crucial on issues like Hippie-Purges, Dope Crackdowns, Pork Barrel expenditures and that kind of crap. There is no question that now—for the first time—local laws are going to be enforced on a fair and equal basis. No more hair-hassles, or busts for blocking the sidewalk . . . and it's weird, in retrospect, to see that it took only two years to turn that whole scene around.

The next step looks like one of the heaviest—getting rid of the Sheriff. He's up for re-election in November of 1970, not many months away . . . and if the Joe Edwards campaign was any indicator, we have the votes to elect almost anybody with a valid claim to sanity. At the moment I seem to be the only serious challenge-candidate—and that's a horror, because I'm not really looking for work these days, and particularly not as the Main Pig. My supporters assure me, however, that I'm likely to be sucked into office by means of a spontaneous draft, so I am already hard at work compiling a list of qualified deputies to carry the load. My own responsibility, as I see it, will be mainly philosophical.

Christ . . . I seem to be running on. All I meant to say was that we made a serious Power Bid here, and almost won. I mention it because the formula we used could work in a lot of other places, particularly in any town or small community with a recent influx of heads & urban refugees. The formula, as such, sounds simple, but making it work can be a goddamn nightmare—unless, of course, you start with a clear majority. Otherwise, you have to work off of a minority power base and somehow persuade a lot of straight/alien types that you're *Right*.

The first step is getting your own people to register, without frightening the potential opposition into some kind of backlash panic. This is tricky, because it has to be done quietly. At the same time, you need a candidate freaky enough to convince even hard-core dropouts that voting might be worth their effort . . . but not so freaky that his name or the very sight of him will cause shock-tremors in the straight community. And finally, he needs a program—on the surface, at least—that makes excellent sense. It can be weird and radical, but not cheap and crazy. In Aspen, for instance, Joe Edwards was able to advocate and successfully defend the idea of laying grass-sod on all the city streets and banishing autos to parking lots on the outskirts of town . . . but his campaign would have been doomed from the start if he'd talked about legalizing marijuana, a far less radical notion than tearing up the streets. We did everything possible, in fact, to avoid the "hippie issue," because Edwards' bias was so well known that any discussion could only have hurt. There was no point, we felt, in backing ourselves into that kind of treacherous corner—it would have made the campaign a suicidal joke—like Tim Leary's bid for the governorship of California. There is a massive difference between self-promotion and self-preservation. I've never had much taste for Leary's trip, and electoral politics is such a foul and rotten game that only a fool would play it except to win and move on to something better.

Which reminds me that I have to get back to writing for money, so I can put together enough to get out of the country on short notice—which seems likely if my sheriff's campaign results in anything but total victory. Probably you recall what happened to that fellow Yablonski, who tried to unseat the president of the Mine Workers union. He and his family were murdered in their home within a month after the election.[58]

And so much for that. My whole point, in the beginning, was to say that we proved out here—against a powerful, wealthy and relatively sophisticated opposition—that Freak Power can work. It would take me more space than I have here to explain the details and various circumstantial problems, but if anybody's curious, tell them to write me and I'll try to line it out. The crucial point is that it can be done without a numerical majority and without any crippling compromise. Some places would obviously be easier than others, depending on the opposition, issues and the nature of the local economy. Like Butte, Montana might be a little tough, since it's run by the Anaconda Copper Co. And Youngstown, Ohio, would be nasty, for different reasons that amount to the same thing. But I can think of several places that look easy—although they probably wouldn't be if I named them. I can't think of anything more likely to unify a town than a rumor saying it's been marked for TAKEOVER by the International Freak Conspiracy.

On this note, I see where Bill Graham, the Fillmore man,[59] has decided to make a movie about a bunch of heads taking over a town in Colorado . . . if the film ever appears it will make things viciously difficult for anybody who wants to try it for real. It would be like trying to organize a motorcycle club in a small town where *The Wild One* has just played at the local theatre.

58. Former United Mine Workers president W. A. "Tony" Boyle was convicted of responsibility for the December 31, 1969, murders of rival UMW leader Joseph Yablonski and his wife and daughter.

59. Music promoter Bill Graham owned the Fillmore Auditorium in San Francisco and the Fillmore East in New York.

But what the hell? When Agnew becomes president we won't have to worry about elections—except as film fantasies and weird scenes from the past—so there's no real point in bitching about a greedhead like Graham sabotaging a scene he'll never need. But on the off-chance that we'll still be able to vote a year from now, he could do us rural refugee types a favor by not terrifying the natives with a film that will cause us all to be driven back to the cities like tribes of lepers.

Well, shit . . . this is way too long and not half as coherent as it might be, but I don't have time for a rewrite so you'll have to cope with it, for good or ill. Right now I have to get back to my project; I've developed a process for deriving a powerful hallucinogen from potatoes. The patent is pending, so I can't discuss it until at least next year. Selah.

I hope the paper goes well. Here's $5 for my renewal. I forgot to send it earlier, when I got the notice. My life has become very chaotic; this pastoral existence has made my brain soft. Once I get this potato business under control, I plan to move to Watts and join the police force.

Ciao,
Hunter

FROM OSCAR ACOSTA:

Acosta's antics continued to take their toll on his legal career.

X-mas eve, 1969

Hunter,

Slightly uptight cause in an hour or two I might be in jail; maybe because I was fired yesterday; maybe because I finished the play after nine months on the fucking thing; maybe because I took two bennies to keep me going.

It is the second job I've been fired from in the past two years and both times for the same reason: my fanaticism, my radicalism, my nationalism. What gripes me is the dirty pool. . . . I'm something of a damn good lawyer. I use the law, within its own confines (they know nothing of my extracurricular activities). Possibly, I may make new law . . . a thing that happens to one lawyer out of a million. I speak freely and directly. It is for this that they move against me . . . how can I not advocate the overthrow of the government? Without seeming too paranoid, too egotistical, I know it was not simply the incompetent Board of Directors that did it. . . . It was men from Reagan's staff and men from the Ford Foundation. . . . As absurd as it sounds, I actually have Senators ([Alan] Cranston and [Edward] Roybal) and Congressmen (Burton and Brown) and Assemblymen (Brown and [Jesse] Unruh), etc., who have, of late, been responding to my requests. I have never given them a damn thing, never once even hinted that I would . . . and yet they respond. Which means that they are aware of me. At least.

What do I do with this near power? Where do I go from here? It would be absolutely impossible for me to run for elective office . . . I haven't paid taxes in five years . . . I've advocated victory for the Viet Cong, etc. . . . and, of course, I'm a well known acid freak.

The last thing I want to do is be a middle-aged, loud mouthed so-called revolutionary. It's got to be the real thing for me. The last thing I want to do is die from some stray bullet during a "civil-rights" demonstration. Jesus, that would really spoil it for me . . . to say nothing of my image.

I'm sending you the play. I think it's finished. I'll go over it one more time before I submit it. I'd really appreciate it if you could give me your opinion, advice, or what have you. . . . As you know, I've really put myself out for this one. Except for the novel of 1960, I haven't spent this much time on anything. Myself, I like it. It may even be a good play. I wish you wouldn't hold back. The criticism you gave me of my long, short story was very helpful, technically, but more importantly, it gave me the extra boost I needed to start writing again. . . . All I get from the workshop and those lily-livered liberals are things like: Wow! Great, man! It really works! . . . What the fuck can I do with that?

The remaining acid from that batch we consumed . . . it worked as well as any other I've tried. I took it with six persons, once, and with four others, once . . . it worked for all. So, your theory was wrong. It's something to think about, wouldn't you say?—which reminds me: did you buy the mesc? I can get either for a buck a cap in S.F., wholesale. Next month I'll be going up, so if you're interested, let me know.

I'll be leaving the office by the first of February . . . call me collect any time.

I repeat: tell me what you think of the play.

Z

TO HUGHES RUDD, CBS NEWS:

Rudd had run up quite a tab during a recent visit to Woody Creek.

December 28, 1969
Woody Creek, CO

Dear Hughes . . .

I'm enclosing an itemized account of your expenses in the course of the Aspen gig. As you see, it takes care of the bulk of your $21,000 outstanding . . . and all I ask is an even split when the nut comes in. Shit, I'll take a third—or even less. Why not settle for $2500 and call it square? It took me a long time and a lot of research to put this thing together.

As for Spade Cooley, you deserve whatever happens to you on that one. Hell, even I knew—far out in Woody Creek—that Spade had cashed in. Next time, use Mitch Greenhill's name;[60] he's good for 10 more years, at least.

60. Spade Cooley and Mitch Greenhill were folk musicians.

For christ's sake don't tell Benti I said he "admitted that CBS had yielded to pressure" in the course of our phone call. He didn't. In fact both he & Lewis insisted, at great length, that nobody from Stanton on down would dare to touch a fucking second of their news time. And I said that I fully understood this & felt overcome with shame for my rude notions of pressure from somewhere UP. Shit, I know better than that—even while your friend Craig is sitting out here telling me how he and "several others" killed the piece in the "best interests" of Aspen. Which gave me a good chuckle until I realized that the thing had, in fact, been killed.

Anyway, I don't want to get into that again. I got a good letter from Benti—written from his home in the grip of a hashish frenzy—and if I could find the thing I'd try to answer it in kind. Which reminds me that on Xmas day I *gave away* about two ounces of hashish, never dreaming it was worth $75 per. Now, stone broke again, I tend to question my sanity. Actually, I question it daily, and for many more reasons than my tendency to dispense drugs like Florence Dooley.[61]

Christmas was the same old annual nightmare out here, and NYr's will be worse. I am locked into an orgy of betting on football games & constant haggling with the bookie. I am considering having his arms broken for $100 each, but right now I can't pay the hit man—not until the bookie pays me. So you see the problem. They're closing in on me, I think. Agnew was right . . .

Ciao,
Hunter

***

ITEMIZED EXPENSES . . . out of pocket & otherwise, incurred by Hughes Rudd during work and research on doomed Aspen/Hippie piece—August '69

$1,769 . . . . . Misc. food and drink for H. S. Thompson during 10 days of probing into local mores, habits, kinks & philos. bkgnd. of same
1,000 . . . . . @ $100 per day to H. S. Thompson for protection from local thugs, authorities, etc.
190 . . . . . S&W .44 Magnum revolver
88 . . . . . ammunition for same
4,650 . . . . . drugs and drink for sub-advisors and special consultants (LSD, mescaline, hashish, beer, wine, marijuana, Old Nightrider whiskey, black rum and Jimson Weed . . .)
1,120 . . . . . car rental and repairs after riot
987 . . . . . damage to camera during riot

61. University of Georgia football coach Vince Dooley was a regular Florence Nightingale in some respects.

220	surgical fees, inre: Cameraman attacked during riot
600	rental fee, glass dwelling with sun exposure
9,362	mental anguish and possible brain damage—H. Rudd & family—due to savage harassment, abuse and attack by local merchants & influence peddlers . . . also for Soul Challenge and other spiritual crisis, lack of sleep for prolonged periods and general nerve-rot.
$20,986	Total expenses for Rudd Aspen encounter

1970

THOMPSON FOR SHERIFF . . . THE FREAK ALSO RISES . . . WILD VICTORY IN HORSE COUNTRY, DISASTER AT THE AMERICA'S CUP . . . NIXON'S MASSACRE AT KENT STATE, THE NIGHTMARE OF RALPH STEADMAN . . . JUST HOW WEIRD CAN YOU STAND IT, BROTHER, BEFORE YOUR LOVE WILL CRACK? . . .

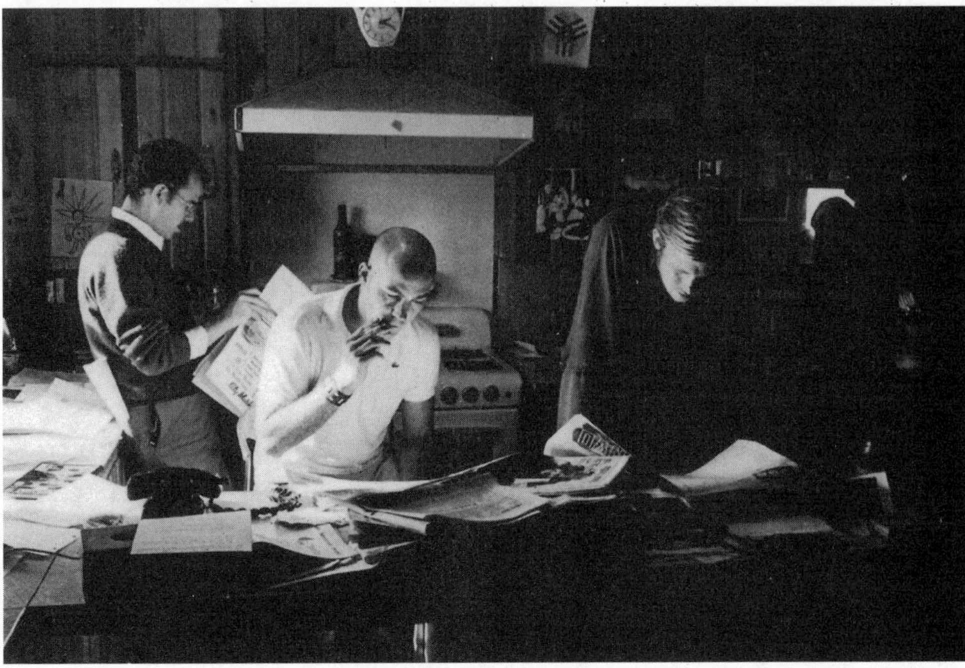

In kitchen at Owl Farm during sheriff's campaign.
Left to right: Bill Kennedy, HST, Ed Bastian.
(PHOTO BY DAVID HISER)

Voting, 1970. With Sandy, Bill Noonan (Freak Power candidate for county coroner), HST. (Under Colorado law, the coroner is the only official with the power to arrest the sheriff.)
(PHOTO BY BOB KRUEGER)

"Beat them to death with their own rules": with Oscar Acosta at Freak Power headquarters.
(PHOTO BY BOB KRUEGER)

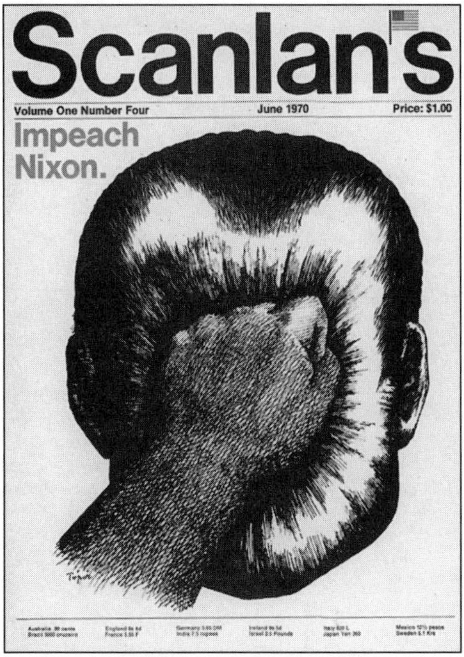

Cover of Scanlan's, *June 1970.*

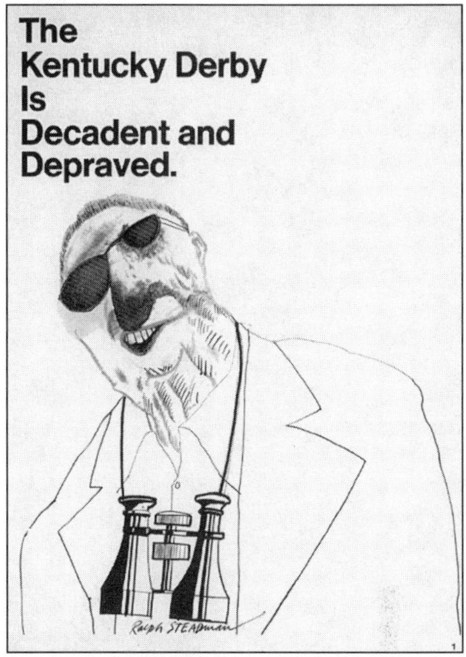

Scanlan's, *1970.*
(Drawing by Ralph Steadman)

Wallposter #5.
(Poster by Tom Benton)

Warren Hinckle.
(Photo by Ralph Steadman)

TO SELMA SHAPIRO, RANDOM HOUSE:

Going through her files at Random House, Hell's Angels *publicist Selma Shapiro came across a photograph Thompson had sent of himself—naked—taken in Haight-Ashbury. She one-upped the joke by sending it back.*

January 1, 1970
Woody Creek, CO

Dear Selma . . .

Words fail me at this time. What can a man say to a person who returns a stark-naked photo of himself? Probably next week the publicity manager for *Today* will send back my Phi Delt pin . . . and I'll find that special locket I gave Jay Allen[1] on sale in some dingy East L.A. pawnshop.

Well . . . life is ugly. We do what we can, but the scales tell the story every time. Fear and loathing is everywhere. The swine have come home to roost.

In the meantime, I trust you are still selling well. And that life in NY still rattles around on those peaks that those of us in the outback will never know. OK for now. I'll send word when I finish wrapping my new product.

Ciao . . .
HST

TO STEVE GELLER:

Still hoping to get The Rum Diary *made into a movie, Thompson updated a Hollywood friend about his venture into local politics.*

January 8, 1970
Woody Creek, CO

Dear Steve . . .

You got it all wrong. It wasn't *me* who ran for mayor. I was the guru, the main hustler, the hype-monger. I called the fellow one Saturday night and said, "Yes, you *must* make the race . . ." and after that I didn't talk to him for another

1. Jay Presson Allen had adapted Muriel Spark's 1961 novel, *The Prime of Miss Jean Brodie,* for the stage in 1966.

two weeks, or a few days before the election. And I'd never talked to him before that. By that time he'd seen his name on posters all over town and heard his program lined out with a flute background on the local radio and huge full-page ads in the paper saying what he was going to cure and croak if elected . . . and finally he began to take it all seriously: at a crucial public meeting, just as it looked like we were losing momentum, he suddenly emerged from his funk and ate the other candidate alive. It was like the first Kennedy-Nixon debate . . . and with another two days we'd have won handily. Actually, it was the heinous copout of the local liberals that beat us.

But fuck all that. It's history now, and I'm not sure what to do with it. Right now I'm using it as the lead-in for a book on . . . well . . . who can say? But I thought you should know that I didn't run for mayor. My gig is saying and writing all the shit that a candidate can't say, for fear of alienating huge blocs of voters. And this was done—except for six votes. Now, looking back and ahead at the same time, I'm not sure what to make of it. Possibly, we laid the groundwork for a total takeover out here. Or maybe we just kicked up a one-shot stir that will never work again. I'll know by the end of next summer, when two more crucial elections come up—Cty. Commissioner & Sheriff. By winning those two, we could snap the spine of the Establishment. The mayor's race was largely symbolic, but these next two involve real power.

I'm not sure I want to get that far into it, since victory would almost definitely mean staying here another year, at least, to make sure our new world is properly wired. At the moment, I'm more inclined to finish this goddamn book for Random House & then move out fast to somewhere else, for a year & maybe more. I'd like to keep the house here & rent it out for enough to make payments, then flee to a good beach. Maybe Mexico, or maybe even Malibu. I'm not sure where, but I'll definitely be moving before the next snow (or next winter). Probably it will all depend on what I can do with this stinking book; it's another one of these personal journalism nightmares, and thus doomed in terms of a film sale . . . and all I really want is to get it out of the way and start on something totally new. But I've eaten their advances, so now I have to puke up a book . . . and although it bugs the shit out of me, I guess I have to do it.

Yeah, and I've said all that before. Which reminds me, speaking of film sales and that action, that I think the last thing I told [20th Century Fox's Lawrence] Turman (on the strength of your intro, as it were) was that I'd send him my novel, *The Rum Diary,* whenever I had it rewritten to my satisfaction. But that now appears to be a hopeless pipe dream, so if you run into him anywhere along the line, tell him he can have the original ms. pretty cheap. The sale might be complicated, due to the fact that Random House may or may not own the book. I know they have a binding option on it. Ballantine wants to publish it, but they're bound by the RH option and my sad insistence that I'm sooner or later going to rewrite it. The result is a dead stalemate. My own feeling about the book is that it's a good story (in terms of having a beginning &

an end, etc.) and it has a few very high points . . . but as a novel, it sucks. There is too much overwritten silliness; and in a weird way it reminds me of *Easy Rider.*[2] I'm not sure what a "Gentile film" is, in your words, but to me that film was badly un-conceived. I recall being shocked by the violent ending—not because of the violence, but because I couldn't quite believe the fuckers would end it that way, in a total cop-out. I felt the same way one night in Las Vegas at the second [Sonny] Liston–[Floyd] Patterson fight, which I covered for *The National Observer.* The shock of that fluke victory made Liston seem far larger than he really was—until [Cassius] Clay got hold of him, and that one didn't really surprise me.

Anyway, if Turman is looking around for long-shots at the moment, tell him to ring me up. My cash position is grave & last week I agreed to trade my motorcycle for a piece of weird metal sculpture . . . so I guess I'm on the down side of a bear market on all fronts.

As for getting out there again, I'm not sure when or how. I financed that last trip on my Diners Club card, which will shortly be seized by the rightful owner; they have already begun to threaten me. Besides, I'd probably scare the shit out of you if we met anywhere except here. I tend to freak out when I go on the road. On that last trip I'd planned to stay at Bob Gover's[3] house in Malibu, but by the time I finally got there I was so crazed on mescaline that he hid from me. I find most writers to be painfully delicate on their home courts . . . and I'm the same way. So maybe we can get together some night in the Pump Room or the Staten Island ferry. The only writer/person I can deal with in Hollywood is Dennis Murphy, whose wife fears my deranged influence. He derives from the ancient, pre-Esalen, Big Sur culture that will surely survive in history as one of the finer places to have lived in the 1960s. He's writing something for CBS or something like that; say hello if you run into him on the cocktail circuit.

And that's about it for now—seeing 3 pages in the till—I have to wonder at another night gone down the tube. What makes a man write letters, night after night, instead of profitable manuscript pages?

Right now I have to get back to my option—which means writing something that will give me an honest choice between savage head-on political action and another few years of backed-off writer's perspective. If I get into bomb-throwing, and that sort of thing, I'd prefer to do it as a matter of conscious choice, instead of necessity. And on that score, I think the fat is in the fire. Indeed . . .

Hunter

2. Dennis Hopper's groundbreaking 1969 movie, *Easy Rider,* cowritten with Terry Southern and costar Peter Fonda, told the counterculture tale of two bikers in search of "the real America."

3. Bob Gover, author of *One Hundred Dollar Misunderstanding,* was now trying to make a movie about what he believed was America's impending revolution.

TO DENNIS MURPHY:

Dennis Murphy—author of the 1958 novel The Sergeant *and grandson of the founder of the Big Sur steam baths that spawned California's Esalen Institute—was now a successful Hollywood screenwriter, and as such presumably flush with cash.*

January 8, 1970
Woody Creek, CO

Dear Dennis . . .

Let's get on with this Colonel Wong fast food business. I need the franchise to go along with my drive-in theatre. My option expires on June 1, at which time I need $10,000 cash and 80K more in the bag. At the moment I have nothing.

My best advice to you is get out of that fucking group. If you spent more time in the company of human beings you wouldn't need those bell-bottom crutches. Frankly, I think you should get out of Hollywood. The proper route, I think, is to convert the Big Sur house into a sort of mysterious high-powered action-farm for drugs, politics, and general sporting prowess. Build trap-shooting houses on the cliff and floating gong-targets out there in the kelp. Put a Dow-Jones ticker in the kitchen and 12 private phone lines, along with AP & UPI in the living room. Grow many peyote cactus on the hillsides, alongside the world's most savage moto-cross course. A man from Tassajara was here for Xmas, proposing strange alliances; we could work those in, along with heavy dealing in firearms and bogus passports. A printing press would be necessary. Also a first-class chemical lab. But we could work these things out with little effort. Let me know. Ciao . . .

HST

FROM OSCAR ACOSTA:

Acosta had been wounded by Thompson's hard criticisms of not only his writing, but his behavior in general.

January 11, 1970
Los Angeles, CA

Hunter,

. . . Your most consistent criticism has been directed at my use of the mass media. You've not substantively objected to the tactic or the goal—for the simple reason that you don't know what they are—but merely to my appearing on t.v. and making public statements to the press.

This seems very strange coming as it does from a former newspaper man and present magazine writer. A writer who's written a book, who has gone on publicity stints on t.v., radio, etc. A local citizen who writes letters to the editor, organizes a campaign for a mayoralty race. And who shows no signs of doing anything differently in the immediate future.

I'll be the first to admit that the whole thing started as part of another "trip." By some fortuitous circumstance, I woke up in the middle of an emerging struggle for recognition by a large group of persons who had previously been ignored. For three months I sat back and observed their total lack of competence in dealing with the press and with the power structures. If you'll recall, the level of communication consisted of articles appearing in *La Raza* . . . cuss and more cuss. An inarticulate rage, a blind fury.

They asked me to be one of the spokesmen.

In 1966–67, when I first started working as a lawyer, I was hounded to death by these same type of groups asking me to speak for them. Perhaps you don't know, but the cause of my anxiety which led to Aspen was this very demand. For nine months I went to a psychiatrist, took his numerous pills, slept *twelve* hours a day, all because I could not respond to the demands of . . . that's right, my people.

My answer was the Big Drop, and I got as far as Aspen.

In many ways, the people in Aspen, the total community of The Ski, offers the best this society can afford. You have money, beauty, smallness and privacy. There is art, culture, intelligentsia and the usual meanness. I found I could drink, smoke, drop acid and play the clown along with the best of them.

But after six months of unconcern with the world outside that Ski Resort, I could no longer tolerate the isolation which is a form of pure egotism.

. . . So, I found myself in L.A., a lawyer, a would-be writer, an articulate man, having gone into the world of drugs, mixed with the comfortable anglo, and still I had no credibility, no power and no appeal to broads. . . . In a word, If I Could Not Make It In This Anglo Society, How In The Fuck Was The Average Poor Person Going To Make It???

But I didn't want to be or become simply another politician on the make. Out of self-interest they pander to the system they allegedly despise. I have insisted that I be allowed to develop my own style, speak my own words and live my own life. To this end I dress as I please, speak as I please and advocate the use of drugs as I please . . . for which I have been permanently excluded from employment with the L.A. County government, the Federal Legal Services Programs, and, most recently, from the Mexican American Legal Defense Fund. Last year, before I started here, I asked for employment with all the liberal-to-radical legal organizations . . . Zero. These rejections I take as a mark of honor, for I know of no other lawyer who has been so black-balled for speaking his piece.

I cannot seriously believe that you really believe that I either enjoy the public appearances or that I have become a pawn in their own game. . . . Once every month I take acid. I question myself, under acid, about the value of my situation in East L.A. Several times I've left with the idea of not returning until I was absolutely convinced of its value. . . . I'm still here.

. . . For me to drop out this time would be the last cop-out for me. Were I to turn my back on this challenge without giving it my best of college tries would lead to suicide. . . . In a sense, I have no choice. I must make every effort to become a leader of men. The time will come when I can go sit on an island, sipping suds, dropping acid, chasing after broads and comfortably writing my memoirs and other such pleasantries.

No man can become a leader without a base of support. My natural base is with the Mexican American. I cannot hope to "reach" them without the use of the mass media. And the mass media only caters to "newsworthy events," as you should know. Reporters simply will not take down my words, my ideas, without some "event" around which they can "tell a story." And so I stage an event, be it picket, sit-in, walk-out, three day fast . . . or what have you.

The score to date: Some of my writings are being used in college courses. At least a hundred Chicanos are in law schools under some scholarship or another, because they want to "be like me." Literally, thousands of Mexican people feel a bit more secure because they have "their lawyer" to defend them. Hundreds of men and women are no longer afraid to get up and speak to anglo administrators, having seen me—a lawyer!—rap at and bad mouth them publicly. There is without doubt an awakening, a questioning, a MOVEMENT in the Chicano communities throughout the country; both the *N.Y. Times, The Nation* (once again) and other persons who are not as easily fooled as some have asked for material. The *L.A. Times* is considering my writing a weekly collumn [*sic*]. I'm teaching at UCLA Law School, the first Chicano teaching at law school in the country. To some extent, Fidel Castro is taking us seriously. To some extent, the leaders in Mexico are beginning to take notice of us. I have many, many men and women whom I can trust, whom I can turn to if the going really gets bad. If I really wanted to, there are many broads who would gladly pull down their pants for me. . . . I am writing more and better shit than I was before East L.A.

And you want me to build a retreat!

You dumb motherfucker, I'm trying to build a society, a country, a land where we can live in peace without having to pay taxes to and be jailed by those petty, little men. . . . Do you think my vision is so limited? Do you think I merely want a broken down barrio? And do you seriously believe that a ranch, however big, would satisfy me? So I buy a ranch in Mexico and a few hundred persons can flake out or work on it. What in God's name makes you think that that government would leave us alone? Haven't you heard what happened to [Timothy] Leary? Or to all those other socialist reformers who got their little communes going? Shit, look at Drop City. In fact, look closer to home, look at Owl Farm. Can you freely plant grass? Can you really keep the cops off your property? Don't you still have to pay taxes in support of a government that is bent on destruction of the human race?

I've told you before, your sanctuary is nothing more than a temporary prison. Your dissatisfaction with the world around you has, unfortunately, led to more drugs and more rage. If you were not before, you are now simply an anarchist, the lowest form of politics. It is easy, simplistic and totally without value to merely curse the darkness . . . in fact, you remind me of the hippie and the militant. The former wants to be let alone and the latter, to destroy, so he can be alone. Your desire to "build a personal fort" is, at best, infantile.

Your involvement in the campaign was the first thing you'd done since I've known you for which I had some respect—I know nothing of your writing, having only read that one unfinished article for *Esquire* and *Hell's Angels* you had already done. It seemed to me that at last you were coming out of your shell. The letters to the editor, including the article about Aspen, I consider only a "trip."

And that is what has bothered the shit out of me for the past two years. On the one hand I have felt that of all the people I have known, you were the closest to being a man, my equal. But still you were my opposite in terms of ACTION, without which no person can be a man. At first I ascribed the different life styles to different cultures, different predicaments. But as I came to see the reality of the world-wide conspiracy of destruction, then I realized that it was the good guys against the bad guys, and not merely the racial/ethnic minorities against the white imperialists. All of which meant that the struggle was just as much yours as it was mine . . . But still you sit on your ass and look forward to football on t.v.

Finally: If I had really wanted to, I could have written a thing for t.v. some time ago. I have not because I am what I am. I'm going to try to write what I want. If I can't, then fuck them. I *did not* write the play as propaganda. If it's no good, it fails not because of my ideological beliefs, but merely because I am not yet a good dramatist. My attempt was merely an attempt to describe the rage which acid has produced within me in the land called Elsinore: Mankind Is Doomed. Period.

Enclosed you'll find the final draft of *Perla Is a Pig,* which theme, in my opinion, is not much different from the play. Merely a different style.

Z

TO WILLIAM J. KENNEDY:

Kennedy had sent Thompson a copy of his first novel, The Ink Truck, *published in September 1969 by Dial Press.*

January 12, 1970
Woody Creek, CO

Goddamn, I was certain I'd written you—but then my desk is full of things I was "certain" had already been dealt with or solved . . . and the awful truth is that I can't seem to get anything really done. It's beginning to look like a serious problem. My income has fallen to nothing and my daily realities are more and more chaotic. I write a vast number of pages every night, but they add up to nothing. Very depressing.

Your Dec 22 letter was full of weird news . . . although not really, I guess, since nothing is really weird anymore. The Agnew wind is on us for real, I think, and this year's horrors will seem like cotton-candy by 1971. The cocksuckers are going to want to settle a lot of old scores—not so much with individuals as with a whole presumptuous lifestyle that calls them ugly. And of course they are; they are a gang of old fucks who will leave a lot of scars on this world before they go.

And so much for that. Your bad fuckaround at the *T-U* [*Albany Times-Union*] sounds nasty but entirely predictable, in light of what I just said. We dumped on Nixon's people for 10 years, and now they're going to dump on us. Fire this one, evict that one, jack up the interest rates, fill the jails—teach the scum a lesson. You may have the answer, in the form of academic sanctuary, but I think they'll start closing that one down, too. And even if they don't, I'll never make it in that league, so I don't give it much thought. Frankly, I look forward to a grim and mind-smashing downhill slide on all fronts.

Right now, next to my typewriter, is a letter from Random House, wanting to know if I'm still alive . . . and implying very strongly that I might be closer to dead than I think, if I don't send them a manuscript very soon. This stinking book just sits here in the form of a huge pile of junk paper. It makes no sense at all. I have no interest in getting it published, except for money—and that's what it's come to now. I am stone broke again, owing 2 publishers something like $17 grand, and with most people under the impression that I died from drugs at least two years ago. My interest in books is so close to nonexistent that I wonder if I'll ever write another one. The temptation is to say I'd rather write a film, but the ugly truth is that I don't feel like writing anything at all. I don't feel particularly lazy—just hopelessly cut off from the kind of people who read things. Or edit them. Or publish them. I don't even want to talk to those people, much less work with them.

But my options are somewhat limited, I guess, so in spite of this stinking angst I suppose I'll have to play that game again—give the jackals another word-toy, to keep their machine going. The only decent thing that's happened to me on the writing front in two years arrived in the mail today—a letter from Warren Hinckle, former editor of *Ramparts*, saying they'd bought my Jean-Claude Killy article for his new magazine, *Scanlan's Monthly*. The first issue is due in March, and I assume it will be something like the old, fire-sucking *Ramparts*. If their taste for my Killy article is any indication, I'd say it will be a boomer. For one thing, the piece ran 110 ms. pages—for which they paid $1500, or better than *Esquire*. For another, the piece in print will be prefaced by a letter, from me, detailing my troubles with *Playboy*—calling the editors a gang of scurvy fist-fuckers and saying a whole lot of ugly things about the back-stairs action that led them to first assign the piece, pay all my expenses for three months, and then reject it with incredible venom. I figure they don't deserve the luxury of black-listing me in private—they should come right out and say it all in public, and that's what the article is all about.

Other than that, I can't tell you anything helpful about the magazine. Hinckle has weird and violent tastes. Maybe your agent can find out something. Mine is useless.

As for *The Ink Truck*, I assume it shared the fate of most novels. Sandy read it and didn't like it at all for about the first half, then decided she liked it. Both she and Peggy Clifford[4] seem to feel you work too hard to write like a writer . . . and on the basis of your 12/22 letter, I can't really argue with them. For whatever that's worth . . . and since I know I do the same thing, well . . . what can I say? Except that maybe it's best to write like something else. Actually, I think I understand the complaint, but the only instance I can cite right off is my distaste for your word "Bolly"—which they dropped, I see, from the title. It reminded me, as I said, of [Beatle] John Lennon's book, *In His Own Write*—which I thought was a piece of silly shit . . . and so much for all that, too. I haven't read *The IT,* but like I said, I won't admit it when I do, so why talk about it?

No word from Lee [Berry] or [Eugene] McGarr. No word of any importance from anywhere, on any subject, for any reason. Even the *Observer* has cut me off, so I didn't read Greene's review. He's OK—nothing at all like Ridley & a weird bird to be working for the *N.O.* Frankly, I think we're all fucked. Journalism is a hype and fiction is worse than bridge. Probably Agnew is right . . . and I leave you with all that. Ciao.

HST

TO JIM SILBERMAN, RANDOM HOUSE:

As the deadline loomed for his book on "The Death of the American Dream," Thompson tried to buy some time from his editor with a detailed outline of what would develop into his best-known work, 1972's Fear and Loathing in Las Vegas.

4. *Aspen Times* columnist Peggy Clifford owned a local bookstore.

January 13, 1970
Woody Creek, CO

Dear Jim . . .

Your 1/9 letter came as something of a relief. I'd been expecting it for months—like a demand note on a long overdue mortgage.

First off, let me assure you that I'm well aware that we're into another year . . . another decade. As you so artfully phrased it. Second, I massively agree with your notion that "It would be splendid to be publishing (me) once again. . . ."

I wish I could explain the delay. It bothers me to the point of stupid, self-destructive rages in my own house—which is not really *my* house and probably never will be, due to total mismanagement of all my funds and efforts to secure a land-fortress. In a nut, my total inability to deal with the small success of the H.A. book has resulted—after three years of a useless, half-amusing rural fuckaround—in just about nothing except three wasted years. I came out here hoping to live in lazy peace with the locals, but finally—and inevitably, I think—that dream of "the Peaceful Valley" went from nervous truce to nasty public warfare. Last fall I found myself running a "freak power" rebellion that came within six votes of taking over the town . . . and the valley, for that matter. So now a lot of those people who called me a friend in those days when I was still trying to live the Peaceful Valley myth now call me a communist dope-fiend motherfucker. No more of that waving from my porch at friendly cattle-driving neighbors; I finished that one night a long time ago when the subject of Vietnam came up in a friendly rancher's kitchen. I didn't realize it then—but now, in edgy retrospect—I see how the whole problem began with a harmless mention of Vietnam.

Not that it wouldn't have begun over something else. Hell, almost anything in these ugly pigeon-holed years. When I lived here in 1963 the cowboys dug me; for a few months in the winter of that year I shot deer for $5 a head for a cowboy who sold the carcasses in town for $10. He would take the orders in town, then drive out to pick me up; he drove and I shot . . . and we had a good thing for a while, but one day he decided to show me how to shoot with my .44 Magnum; six shots later his face was bleeding in six places from the terrible recoil, and that sort of ruined our relationship. Now, in the wake of this new polarization, he is one of many locals who tell each other—in the course of their steady tavern-talk—that the valley would be a lot better off if somebody broke both my legs and dragged me back to Haight street behind a pickup truck. This kind of talk came out of the recent local elections, which I think I mentioned to you in a letter about that time. Or maybe I sent you that clipping from the *Aspen News*. That started the war; the election formalized it—and now we are all stuck with it. At least until next autumn, when our new and probably over-confident power-base is already geared to the idea that I'm going to run for sheriff. Our wild campaign mobilized a local, freak/young electorate that had never seen itself . . . until we lost the mayor's race by six votes. Now, after coming so close, the buggers are convinced that next time, with a little planning, we can beat the fatbacks like old gongs. I may, in fact, run for sheriff, but only as a smokescreen for some less obvious Freak Power candidate for the County Commissioner's office. There are all kinds of weird possibilities . . . particularly since I see this kind of power-struggle as one of the big stories of the 1970s. All we had to do, in Aspen, was persuade the freaks to *register;* the actual voting was fore-ordained. And our midnight registration campaign jumped the number of voters from 670 in 1968, to 1600 in 1969. In other words, we dragged the drop-outs back in—at least long enough to vote, and we found enough of them to almost overturn a very sophisticated local establishment. The freaks and young heads they've been trying to "run out of town" for the past two years came back to haunt them on election day. We sent teams of bearded poll-watchers to all three wards—all of them armed with tape recorders and xeroxed copies of all pertinent laws. And, despite illegal threats of violence and prison terms from the mayor, the cops and the D.A., we managed to run our people through a gauntlet that scared the hell out of them . . . and after 12 hours of crazed action our tally was 522. The Establishment candidate—a 55-year-old lady shopkeeper and former GOP committeewoman for Colo.—had only 517. Then they counted the absentee ballots, and the final tally was 533 to 527, against us. It was a long and brutal night.

Anyway . . . that's the situation that I'm trying to use, at this point, to start the narrative of what you call the AMERICAN DREAM book. I am still hung on the idea of running a narrative through it, rather than letting it go as a series of dis-jointed commentaries on scenes that may or may not hang together. But I've had a lot of trouble with the notion of mixing up a fictional narrative with a series of straight journalistic scenes. I'm convinced it *can* work, and I've done it before, but the problem now is that I'm so self-conscious about the mixture that I can't let it work. The fiction part strikes me as bullshit and the journalism seems dated and useless. In the H.A. book I paraphrased a lot of dialogue without giving it a second thought—but now that I'm doing it consciously I give every line so many second thoughts that paralysis has become my work-pattern. It's embarrassing to think that I can't compete, in book form, with cop-outs like *Medium Cool*[5] and *Easy Rider* . . . but the compulsion to write something better and more real than those things has left me with what amounts to nothing at all—except a bundle of weird article-carbons. It's heartening to hear you say that you have a chunk of the manuscript—but as

5. *Medium Cool* was director/writer Haskell Wexler's innovative 1969 movie about a TV cameraman who stays detached from the events he's covering, including the 1968 Democratic National Convention in Chicago.

much as I'd like to get that $5000 that comes with sending in a proper third, I can't honestly say that you have anything more than a heap of useless bullshit.

(Aside—I just got a note from Warren Hinckle saying he's scheduled my doomed *Playboy* piece on Jean-Claude Killy—or "flackism in America," as you said it—for the first issue of his new magazine called *Scanlan's Monthly.* He sounds happy with the notion of running the whole 110 page article, along with some correspondence with *Playboy* . . . and since he sent me a check for $1500 I guess I'm happy too. God only knows what kind of magazine he has in mind, but if he can drum up anything like the old, high-flying *Ramparts,* I know I look forward to reading it. As an editor, Hinckle is one of the few crazed originals to emerge from the jangled chaos of what we now have to sift through and define or explain somehow as "the 1960s.")

And that's really what I'm trying to write about. As it sits now—in this heap of terrible garbage on my desk—the AD ms. begins in Aspen, on election night in 1969, with a quick recap of Joe Edwards' mayoral campaign and me sitting on the floor in headquarters, completely burned out after three weeks of sleepless work, wondering what kind of madness had caused me to be there. What kind of bullshit, delusions or common ego-disease had cast me in this weird role—as a mescaline-addled campaign manager for a 29-year-old Texas lawyer & dope-smoking bike freak in a Rocky Mountain ski resort? I gave it a lot of thought that night—while we waited for the ward-tallies—and finally I traced it back to that night in September, 1960, when I quit my expatriate-hitchhiker's role long enough to climb down from a freeway in Oregon and watch the first Kennedy-Nixon debate on TV in a tiny village near Salem. That was when I first understood that the world of Ike and Nixon was vulnerable . . . and that Nixon, along with all the rotting bullshit he stood for, might conceivably be beaten. I was 21 then, and it had never occurred to me that politics in America had anything to do with human beings. It was Nixon's game—a world of old hacks and legalized thievery, a never-ending drone of bad speeches and worse instincts. My central ambition, in the fall of 1960, was to somehow get enough money to get out of this country for as long as possible—to Europe, Mexico, Australia, it didn't matter. Just get out, flee, abandon this crippled, half-sunk ship that A. Lincoln had once called "The last, best hope of earth."

In October of 1960 that phrase suddenly made sense to me. I'm not sure why. It wasn't Kennedy. He was unimpressive. His magic was in the challenge & the wild chance that he might even pull it off. With Nixon as the only alternative, Kennedy was beautiful—whatever he was. It didn't matter. The most important thing about Kennedy, to me and millions of others, was that his name wasn't Nixon. Far more than [Adlai] Stevenson, he hinted at the chance for a new world—a whole new scale of priorities, from the top down. Looking at Kennedy on the stump, it was possible to conceive of a day when a man younger than 70 might enter the White House as a welcome visitor, on his own terms.

That was a weird notion in those days. After eight years of Ike, it was hard to imagine anyone except a retired board chairman or a senile ex-general having any influence in Government. They *were* the government—a gang of rich, mean-spirited old fucks who made democracy work by beating us all stupid with a series of billion-dollar hypes they called Defense Contracts, Special Subsidies, and "emergency tax breaks" for anybody with the grease to hire a Congressman.

Yeah . . . and why worry this thing any longer, particularly in a letter? My point is (or should be) that since 1960 I've gone through so many personal brain-changes—in so many special places and rare scenes—that I still don't know exactly what brought me, in the fall of '69, to that election-nite headquarters in a room above the Elks Club in Aspen, Colo. . . . brooding about the fate of a candidate I barely knew & whose name hardly mattered.

(Time out for an hour to read the galleys of the Killy article; my wife just came back from the P.O.—with a huge envelope about 20″ × 30″. The pages are incredibly heavy, with a protective tissue sheet between each one (or two). . . . Hinckle doesn't fuck around; but where will I find an envelope big enough to fit this thing when I have to send it back? . . . Aside from that, the swine have lopped off the whole end of my original ms.—about 25 pages of high-white prose that I thought was the best part. Goddamn the tasteless pigs. This magazine action is about on par with writing copy for FoMoCo pamphlets. Not even your friends can make room. . . .)

Which is as good a reason as any, I guess, for writing books—they may be the only word-form left where a writer has even a slim hope of getting something published the way he really wrote it. I've been writing for a living for 11 years, and never—not once, not even with my poem in *Spider* magazine—have I ever had anything published straight. The H.A. book was the closest I ever came . . . and that's sad when you recall all the terrible senseless haggling we went through.

And so much for all that. I see I've wasted another night by writing "letters." It seems to be that with all that fine talent you command, you could come up with some working idea about how to put all this deranged garbage into a saleable package. Five pages a night for three years mounts up to a really massive lump . . . we could call it "The Uncensored Ravings of HST—a P.O. Censor's View of the 1960s." Or—"Fear and Loathing in the '60s—from the files of Hunter S. Thompson."

I leave you to ponder it. And meanwhile I'll look back and see what I've said here, if anything. Many words & no focus; that's my epitaph for the past three years.

And, speaking of history, I trust you noticed the unspeakably savage public re-birth of the Hell's Angels. Did you read the coverage in *Rolling Stone*? That scene at the Altamont rock festival shames my worst fantasies; the sharks finally came home to roost.[6] There is no doubt in my mind that Shir-Cliff seized that opportunity to send all remaining PB copies of my book to a warehouse in the Mato Grosso. . . .

Odd . . . but lines like that don't seem so funny anymore. One of the problems with owing people money is that it undermines most of what you say about them—for good or ill. This crippled debtor status leaves me robbed of all that righteous anger that I had so much fun with for so long.

Which drags us back, I guess, to the question of "the book." And all I can say about it, for sure, is that I want to get it written and DONE . . . finished, gone, off my neck and somewhere way behind me. I loathe the fucking memory of that day when I told you I'd "go out and write about The Death of the American Dream." I had no idea what you meant then, and I still don't. I remember telling you this on those steps outside your office . . . and in several letters since then. I don't remember exactly when my hazy angst turned to desperation, but at this point even a word like "desperation" seems stale.

That's a nasty word and maybe it's the wrong one for this—because I guess if I really felt desperate I'd have sent you a bundle of pages by now . . . even bad pages. But I keep telling myself that if I juggle my research a bit longer, it will all fall into place—a magic framework, or formula, to make sense of this swill. I have it all here: two rooms full of notes and memos—but all I can do is juggle it. I spend most of my waking hours in a black rage at almost everything, but every time I sit down to write about it, I end up with 10 pages of finely-phrased bullshit that I never seem to mesh with what I wrote the night before, or the night after. I don't want to make it sound any worse than it is . . . but I'm beginning to think the situation is really pretty bad. The angst has become malignant; I feel it growing in me, choking the energy, causing me to flail around like some kind of dingbat. There is a weird, helpless kind of rage in not understanding how I can write so many pages and still not get anything written.

Your suggestion about making "bookends" of "reports on those extremes" sounds convenient, but I can't see how it could work without dropping the whole idea of a narrative, linking the scenes. Maybe we don't really need that, but without it I see the book as a jumble, a lazy copout that won't say much of anything except as a limp advertisement for what it could and should have been. I'm coming around to the idea that I'd be better off writing a bomb than nothing at all . . . but I haven't come so far that I'm ready to write a thing that even *I* think is bad. The problem harks back to *The Rum Diary*—which I've always wanted to publish, but I'm beginning to wonder now if I might not have killed the book entirely by brooding and haggling over it for so long. About three times a year I have a dream about what might have happened if

6. Hell's Angels hired to provide security at a free Rolling Stones concert at the Altamont Speedway near Livermore, California, on December 6, 1969, had gone berserk and murdered a young African-American fan.

Pantheon had managed to publish *The Rum Diary* before you got a hold of *Hell's Angels.* That lost option haunts me in some kind of left-handed way. If nothing else, it might have saved me from getting locked into this nightmare assignment of explaining the Death of the American Dream.

Christ, I shudder every time I see that term in print. I should have taken Shir-Cliff's advice and done a book on surfers. Hell—anything at all would have been better than this millstone: Cops, Winos, Scumfeeders . . . anything with a focus, a subject, some reason for writing about it, a handle . . . or even just a fucking excuse. As it is, I feel like some kind of pompous old asshole writing his memoirs. I feel about 90 years old. Why in the name of stinking jesus should I be stuck with this kind of book? Maybe later, when my legs go. Fuck the American Dream. It was always a lie & whoever still believes it deserves whatever they get—and they will. Bet on it. There is a terrible wave building up, and by my calculations the deal will go down in the winter of '74–75. When [James] Baldwin wrote *The Fire Next Time* he was talking about 10% of the population—but this time we're looking at 50%. If Nixon makes it to '76 he'll have to be carried out of the White House on a strait-jacketed stretcher . . . and Agnew will be dragged out by his heels.

Yes . . . I seem to be getting a bit wiggy, so maybe I'd better close off. I wish I could end with some kind of happy reassurance about The Book. Maybe—with a touch of inordinate luck—I can find a narrative opening sometime soon and break out of this terrible bind.

Thompson ravings . . . cont.

Jesus, looking back at that heap of mad swill (pages 1–6), I have to wonder if perhaps I haven't gone mad. Read it and let me know how it sounds on that end.

Meanwhile, I thought I'd try to outline the situation as briefly and cogently as possible. Keep in mind that the following is done off the top of my head—sort of howling at the moon. But it might be easier to do it this way, than to keep on rambling in straight letter form. So . . . to wit:

THE PROBLEM: My book is long overdue. The material exists, the research is done (with one possible exception)—but no book exists.

WHY? (The reasons listed below are not necessarily in order of relative importance . . . but maybe)

1) The title, main concept, is so broad and pretentious that I no longer feel able to cope with it. Actually I never did. What I said that night in the Four Seasons was that "Anything I write is going to be about the death of the American Dream"—in the same sense that the H.A. book was "about" the death of the AD. But that's not the same as going out and writing a book with *that* as the working title. I wouldn't read a book with a title like that & I see no reason why anybody should read one from me. It sounds like something from Publish or Perish league. I've been saying this in letters—to you, Lynn, Bernie,

etc.—for more than a year, but nobody has ever answered them. (See specifically my letter to you dated 8/30/69.) But, once again, let me hark back to Faulkner's concept of "seeing the world in a grain of sand." The job of a writer, it seems to me, is to focus very finely on a thing, a place, a person, act, phenomenon . . . and then, when the focus is right, to *understand,* and then *render* the subject of that focus in such a way that it suddenly appears in context—the reader's context, regardless of who the reader happens to be, or where. Thus, you focus on some scurvy freak in Oakland who calls himself a "Hell's Angel" & write about him in such a way that any dingbat stockbroker in Cleveland can *see himself* somehow in the image of that scurvy freak. Some people have to be forced to relate; others only need an excuse . . . (shit, that last line sounds like it came from somebody who might write a book called "The Death of the American Dream." Strike it . . .). The point is that a good book is about people, not theories . . . and my problem is that I don't have any real people in these situations I'm writing about, nothing to hook a reader and drag him into the scenes. (Except possibly myself, in the sense of my own involvement—but let's save that possibility for later.)

2)—and this may really be #1—but it's hard for me to say or even know, for certain, just how worried I really am about producing a "bomb"—a bad "second book"—and by "bad" I mean rotten reviews (or none), wretched sales and a general all-round bummer. I'd be kidding myself if I said this wasn't a serious factor—although probably I'd be far less concerned about it if I were convinced that I had (have) a really good book in the works. This never bothered me in terms of the HA book, because when I began the thing it never occurred to me that I was getting into a "serious book." I saw it as a quick & easy way to get $6000—by rapping off a hairy commercial shocker on a subject that didn't particularly interest me, but which seemed very saleable. It was only after several months of research that I began to take the book seriously—and then, as I recall, I went into a deep funk and couldn't write a word for many months. And I never would have got the bastard written at all if I hadn't been deathly afraid of seeing the contract cancelled the day after the deadline. Now, looking back on what eventually came of it, I find myself brooding over the fact that only a bare handful of all those favorable reviews seemed to recognize the book I thought I'd written. So there is no rational reason for my concern with reviews. I know what kind of people write book reviews—I used to do it myself—but . . . well, fuck that. . . . The nut of the problem is that even though I dismiss nearly everything written about the HA book as silly, unctuous bullshit, I know that it all made a difference—in the sales figures, if nowhere else. And the sales figures, I know, determined what kind of advance I got for the AD book . . . so I have to consider the notion that a Bomb this time around might make the third book even more of a problem. I wouldn't mind a Bomb if I thought I could get out from under it without screwing myself for the next five years . . . but it scares the hell out of me to think that this unholy pressure to produce a second book might destroy whatever small leverage I have. At the moment I see four possibilities: a) I could write a good book (one that I like) that won't sell; b) or a bad book that sells . . . and I could live with either one of these, but the real nightmare is c), that I might write a *bad* book that won't sell. I intend to do everything possible to avoid that. The fourth option d), is the odd wild chance that I might write a *good book that sells.* This is what I'd like to do, and the only thing I'm dead sure of right now is that—to make it both ways—I'm going to figure out some way to avoid coming down to this typewriter every night with the stinking idea that I'm going to tell the world about the Death of the American Dream. If I can't shake that, we may as well call the whole thing off. It's a terrible bummer & it won't work. I knew it—and said it—all along, but everybody seemed to think I was kidding. But now, after two years of being hung up on that nightmare, I have to assume that it's obvious on all fronts that I've screwed myself to the floor and I'm losing my fucking mind. It's jangled me to the point where I can't even write articles, because every time I try one I tell myself "This will of course be part of The Book"—so I end up writing 100 page screeds that nobody will print, and the horrible fact is that I never even knew what book they were supposed to be a part of. The whole thing is a disastrous myth & I have to get out from under it before I get so twisted that I have to go back to daily sports writing. Shit, anything would be better than this awful scene.

So . . . let's try to finish this; I've been working on it for nearly 10 days and that should tell you more about why you don't have a book ms. than anything I say here. The two main problems (see 1) and 2), above . . .) are so much a part of each other that they seem like a knot. To wit: It seems crucially important that my second book be either good or successful—not necessarily both, but at least one of those—and, after two years of false starts and generally wasted effort, I still can't see any way to write a book worth reading unless I can rid myself of the notion that I'm stuck with the task of explaining "the Death of the American Dream." I just can't get serious about writing a bad, dull book that I honestly feel is going to be a bummer in every way.

Which brings me to the final category: *POSSIBLE SOLUTIONS*

1) We could settle, very quickly, on a new working title—although I think it's a little late for this as a real solution. It might have worked a year ago, when I first suggested it, but at this stage of my desperation the mental grooves are too deep—and too obviously dead-ended—to be cured or altered by anything as superficial as a few changed words.

2) Nonetheless, the title has to go . . . and that raises the question of a new focus. Why am I writing this book? What is it about? People ask me and I can't say. So if you want to help, as you say, there is the question and the problem all at once. I don't have a title *in my own mind.* Yours is unacceptable and I long ago rejected it as an explanation of what I'm supposed to be doing.

Here are some possibilities:

A) I'm writing a series of long articles that may or may not illustrate a theme. Most of these incidents take place in 1968–1969 & center on domestic political situations—which a lot of other people have written about. I can do them with (or, from) a special POV, but is this enough? Thus, your notion of "bookends" begs the question. It could give the book an *appearance* of a beginning and an end—but what's really in the middle? Even so, this is a viable option; I don't like it & I'm not sure anybody else will, but rather than suffer any longer with the notion of writing a "final wisdom book," I may be better off just whacking out a Thompson version of *The Pump House Gang*.[7]

B) I could focus almost entirely on the fictional narrative aspect of the book & downgrade the journalism to the level of background—using scenes like Chicago and Nixon's Inauguration as a framework for the trials and tribulations of my protagonist, Raoul Duke. This is the approach I like best, but it's also the one that's least realized at this point. I haven't been able, so far, to make Duke a human being; he hasn't come to life—not even for me. So the narrative still looks like a phoney gimmick to string a bunch of articles together. Another problem with this approach is that the American Dream millstone keeps intruding & it strikes a false note. It addles the dialogue and forces me to keep backing off and pontificating. (Which recalls for some reason that Fitzgerald wanted to call his book about Gatsby "The Death of the Red White and Blue." FYI)

C) This one is tricky; it's the idea of emphasizing *my own involvement* with these various scenes to the extent that I become the protagonist—somewhat in the style of Frederick Exley's *A Fan's Notes*. The problem here is one of perspective and control: My ego comes through very heavy, even when I try to write the straightest kind of journalism . . . and I'm not sure what might happen if I deliberately set out to write what amounts to a (limited) autobiography. The Killy/*Playboy* piece is a good example of this tack—as opposed to the far straighter and less personal approach that I tried to use in the *Esquire* gun piece. Somewhere between these two, in terms of style and tone, is the Nixon Inaugural article for *The Boston Globe*—although that one is almost pure impressionistic journalism, larded here and there with a few old cudgels and HST bias points. And—in a far different vein—we have that Los Angeles mescaline trip, which is almost intolerably impressionistic. I like all these chunks for different reasons, but I'm not at all sure they can work as a *whole book*. Maybe if we put them together the whole will somehow be more than the sum of its parts. But the nightmare is that the parts may seem so wretchedly disjointed as to contradict each other and make no sense at all.

The problem with this (C) possibility is that all these seemingly contradictory stances make fine sense to me—for good or ill—but I realize that people like you and Lynn and Don Erickson and the editors of *Playboy* can't make any

7. Tom Wolfe's *The Pump House Gang* was published in 1968.

sense of them at all. And that's not a judgement—just a flat recognition that we live in different worlds . . . which harks back, I see, to my original notion that my real job is to write a sort of literary common denominator. Which brings us right back around to the main question: THE FRAMEWORK . . . . . ????? Assuming the basic material is already half-formed & that most of the research is done, the missing link is more a packaging concept than anything else. That sounds simple, but it's not—at least not to me. Maybe I shouldn't even be thinking about it; and I probably wouldn't be if this were my first book . . . but in this situation I tend to over-write, over-research, over-worry, and, obviously, to under-produce. I suspect the writing would go pretty fast if I could see from "A" to some point around "P" or "Q" . . . but as it is, I can't see far beyond "C" or maybe "D." God knows, it's too much to ask to be able to see all the way from "A" to "Z," but . . .

Well, let me try, once again, to capsule the options:

1) There's the *Pump House Gang* approach; the main advantage here is that it looks like the easiest and fastest way to "produce" a book and get on to something better. More than half of this one is already written in more or less final draft. The rest wouldn't be much of a problem—and the final result wouldn't be much of a success, either. It would be more of an advertisement (and that recalls *Advertisements for Myself*[8]) than a coherent piece of work.

2) There's the Raoul Duke approach, which is essentially a very contemporary novel with straight, factual journalism as a background. I don't know any precedents to cite for this one . . . which is probably why I like it best. If it works it could be a very heavy, major book. But if it fails—like it has so far—the results could be anything from a published bomb and a personal disaster, to—even worse—many more months of crazed and fearful haggling between me and RH, trying to prevent a bomb/disaster by working the ms. to death. And that would drive us both crazy. One of the problems here is that you have no ms. sample of this approach. Maybe I should do a final draft of some chunk & let you see it before we settle on anything definite.

3) The other option is a sort of *Fan's Notes* approach—using straight newsreel scenes instead of private traumas for a narrative. This approach would fall somewhere between *Pump House* and *Advertisements for Myself.* And in a sense it might possibly be done by simply dropping the fictional protagonist and basing the narrative simply on my own involvement—although not to the extent of a Mailer-style bit. That's too much even for me. (But more personal involvement than *Pump House,* for instance, in that the story would be first person instead of third.) Here we have a problem with the fictional aspect, à la Exley, in that my backgrounds involve well-known or at least sensitive people. The Raoul Duke gimmick in #2 (above) gives me far more leeway to improvise on reality, without distorting it, than I'd have without Duke. He can play the

8. Norman Mailer's 1959 book, *Advertisements for Myself.*

lead role in scenes I couldn't even use otherwise, because in the context of non-fiction I couldn't "prove" them. Duke is only semi-fictional, but just hazy enough so I can let him say and do things that wouldn't work in first person. Like smoking a joint on Nixon's press bus; I can't say who actually did this because he's now a ranking editor on a major metro daily. It tells a lot about Nixon and the press corps that when I warned him (the press head) about the odor, he said, "Shit, this crowd is so square they don't even smell it—I've been doing it for weeks." And he was right. One alternative, of course, is for me to say that *I* covered Nixon with a joint in my mouth—but since I didn't, I'd rather not bias my observations that heavily; and besides, the irony of the story is that they expected *me* to be smoking grass, but it would never have occurred to them to suspect this other lad.

Anyway, that's a good example of my problem. Duke gives me a lot of options on the journalism front, but he also presents a hell of a problem with the narrative. Once I bring him in, I have to keep him there, even when I don't need him. And I have to make him real. The original idea was to use Duke, like Gatsby, to illustrate that Death of the American Dream theme—but that's a horror when you start with the theme and work back to the character. It *may* work the other way, but I can't be sure until I see the character . . . and so far his symbolic value keeps queering his reality. On the other hand, his value as a sort of "cover" & safety valve solves many of the problems I have with the straight journalistic approach. I can insist that everything he says and does is true, but I can also refuse to identify him for obvious legal reasons.

So the root problem appears to be how to handle the fact/fiction balance. Maybe there should be no fiction at all . . . but I can't get very enthusiastic about coming out with a handful of articles about stale scenes. And—re-thinking #3 (above) I don't see how I can get away with much fiction & still use the situations I've researched. A first-person account, with the author as protagonist, would have to be pretty straight . . . so the only real difference between #1 and #3 is one of emphasis. Any continuity in #1 would lie in the style & POV—a series of articles with only the claim of a theme to tie them together. And #3, without any fictional aids, would only differ in that the individual sections (articles) would be lashed together in a grid of super-charged rhetoric that would make the book more essay than journalism. The difference between *Pump House* and *Advertisements for Myself.*

***

And that's about it for now. Before I tack on a final graf or so, I want to go back and read over what I've said . . . but even if none of it makes sense I hope there's no doubt in your mind that I'm almost desperate to untangle this book and get it done. I don't want you thinking I'm sitting out here with a head full of dope, grinning at the sunsets or spending my time on skis. I skied *once* last winter, and not at all so far this year. The problem is not lack of time at the typewriter—but this goddamn wild juggling of unworkable solutions to what might be a simple problem if I could back off far enough to get it in focus. That's where you can help—by considering the options from your end and hopefully coming up with something more specific than How Nice It Would Be if I could tell the world about the Death of the American Dream. I genuinely want to get this book written, and it's beginning to look like I'm stuck on a problem I don't understand. If you can see it more clearly than I can, for christ's sake, say so.

After reading over the first 17 pages of this monster, I don't see much point in trying to edit or revise it. You asked what the problem is—and I think this letter is a pretty good answer. Not that I haven't said it all before—see my letter of Aug 30, 1969—but this time, since you asked, we may be a little closer to coming to grips with it. I hope you can come up with an idea or two for untangling the bastard. If this book can be made to work it could be a real boomer . . . and maybe that's the problem; maybe I should get rid of this notion about writing on stone tablets and start thinking in terms of perishable print.

But even if that *is* the problem, I'm so locked into the stone tablets that I don't know how to back off without plunging myself into despair. Hell, you're an editor and you're paid to solve this kind of nightmare puzzle. I'll expect a finely-reasoned answer very soon. Meanwhile, I'll try to finish off a Duke/fiction section—even a very short one—so you can put that in your comparison shopping bag.

Thanks . . .
Hunter

TO WARREN HINCKLE, *SCANLAN'S MONTHLY:*

Feeling vindicated since the start-up Scanlan's Monthly *had offered to pay him well for the Jean-Claude Killy piece* Playboy *had killed, Thompson objected when Hinckle tried to cut the last ten pages.*

January 20, 1970
Woody Creek, CO

Dear Warren . . .

Here's the galley-package—and a new version of the original ending that I hope you'll use. To me, the original ending was the nut of the article; it was the only part of the piece where I sat back and took a serious, non-violent look at what I'd seen and been through. There are parts of the piece, as it stands now, that make me sound like a pompous, vindictive freak . . . and that's OK; I can live with it . . . but at the same time it seems a bit rotten to cut the only part of the piece that partially redeems me. When I did the original version there were only two sections I really liked: One was the flashback to the '68 Demo convention & the other was the ending.

You cut both of them (also the Boston airport lead) . . . and although I realize we're dealing with space problems, etc., it seems only fair to restore at least this brutally shortened version of the ending. I've cut the original ten doomed pages down to 2½ or around 800 words. That doesn't seem like a hell of a lot to fit in somewhere. It seems a little on the cheap/mean side to go after people with a meat axe without explaining WHY—or at least trying to. As it stands now, in your edited version, I come off as some kind of vicious, petulant drunk who slinks off at the end, muttering garbled slurs to himself.

And this would be OK, too—if I'd really ended the piece on that note. But I didn't. I tried, in the end, to make some kind of sense out of all that wild garbage I'd been through . . . and to chop it off leaves me standing there at the end with a bloody axe in my hand and no apparent reason for the heinous crime I laid on those shitheads. Hell, I may be crazy as a fucking loon, but it seems only fair to let me testify.

Beyond that—and also to spread the onus to your end—it seems to me that my new, revised ending gives the piece a sort of ethical context that elevates it above the level on which it now seems to exist—that being a wild-eyed, ho-ho axe-job on almost everything in sight. I'm not sure what kind of magazine you're getting out, but if you're looking for any kind of literate audience I think this Killy piece will go down a lot easier if they find some kind of rational light at the end of the tunnel. There is also the fact that, if anyone who reads it calls me a mean, half-bright asshole for writing what I did, I'll naturally say that "Hinckle cut all the sense out of it."

On the other hand, if you run this new 2½ pg. ending, I'll take all the blame myself. On the whole, the editing job was excellent—particularly since you were dealing with 110 pages—but cutting the whole ending was a trifle heavy, I think. Why run amok at the end?

I trust you see the point—and to make things easier, in terms of space, I've marked up a few possible cuts on (galley) pages No. 6, 10, 13, 14, and 15. I'll trade these chunks—or almost anything else, for that matter—for the 2½ pages I'm enclosing with this letter. We've labored this far with the fucker, so let's finish it off right. Thanks.

On other fronts, why haven't I received any promo stuff for *Scanlan's*? You're the last person in the world I'd expect to launch a new magazine by word of mouth. Do you plan to solicit subscriptions? Do you understand the nightmare of trying to sell magazines off the newsstands? I'm on every goddamn mailing list in the world, but so far I've received nothing about *Scanlan's Monthly.* Where is your head? If I were you I'd send out notices promising a freshly cut human ear to every charter subscriber . . . then announce to the *NYTimes* that you've hired an army of speed freaks to go out and get the ears. That will get people thinking . . . and a massive mail response, too. You should burst on the publishing world like a wolverine with a head full of Sandoz acid.

OK for all that. As for that awful Moon-shot scandal, I'm sure you realize that Arco, Idaho is now buried under 3 feet of snow.[9] They would track me down and chop me up like hamburger if I tried to lurk around for investigative purposes. We should wait till the snow melts—for photos, as well as sleuthing. Meanwhile, I have a desk full of awful revelations. I'll sift them and send word. But for christ's sake use my new version of the original Killy ending.

Thanks again,
Hunter

TO TOM O'CONNOR, IRVING LUNDBORG & CO.:

Thompson's stock investments had not been doing well.

January 20, 1970
Woody Creek, CO

Tom . . .

The more I think about it, the more I become enraged at the idea of your taking a leisurely ski vacation in Aspen while the "investments" you made for me were going down the tube. Your casual stupidity leaves me in a bad hole. [Robert] Craig wouldn't tell me where you were staying over Christmas & I was too distracted to hunt you down . . . but next time I hear you're in town I'll damn sure make the effort. I think we should discuss the idea that a broker's responsibility begins and ends with his commission. What you need, I suspect, is a stiff dose of calcium in your diet . . . and we can talk about that, too.

Sincerely,
Hunter

TO OSCAR ACOSTA:

Taken aback by Acosta's last emotional missive, Thompson denounced his friend as a "Mexican dunce with the morals of a goat."

January 20, 1970
Woody Creek, CO

Dear Oscar . . .

Your letter came on the same day that a friend who just made his first LP asked me what I thought about it. I told him (he insisted that I give an honest opinion) and he immediately freaked out and cursed me with all his heart. It's the oldest goddamn story in the world. And I'm through with it. I don't ask

9. Some conspiracy theorists insisted that the July 20, 1969, Apollo 11 moon landing had actually been a staged government hoax.

people what they think of my act—or my writing, for that matter—and my life is a lot easier, I think, for not going around asking for criticism. Even from good friends. (Yeah—I recall asking you to read that Gun article, but not with the idea of arguing with you if you said it was a heap of shit. My idea was that maybe you'd see some obvious flaw or contradiction that I'd missed from being too close to it . . . and as I recall you hit one or two things that helped.) Anyway, the next thing you send me I'm going to praise to the fucking skies—no matter what it is or says or isn't. Maybe you should send your stuff to [Tim] Thibeau.

As for my criticism of your "use of the mass media," it seems to me that I was talking about your over-indulgence, not your "use." That Xmas eve gig struck me as a fine idea and well done; it even got a big play in *The Denver Post.* But to follow it up, almost instantly, with a melodramatic "fast" struck me then—and still does—as very bad strategy. Maybe I'm wrong; maybe you got fantastic coverage out of it—I don't know. But from my own POV, the Xmas eve thing looked like a legitimate story and the fast looked like a too-obvious PR shuck. A good reporter doesn't mind being used, particularly if he's basically sympathetic—but you have to keep in mind that nearly all journalists hold PR men in serious contempt. They cherish the illusion of their "objectivity" and they snarl at the notion that anybody can "use" them. Which is bullshit, of course, but it's one of those Golden Rules they teach in journalism schools and it hangs on. Like the bullshit about Blind Justice they teach in law schools.

Anyway, I can't go into long arguments about law and journalism right now. I have a lot of crap to get done and I'm way behind—and seriously broke, to boot. Most of your letter seemed written for The Ages, as it were . . . and although I agreed with most of what you said, I don't see much point in haggling about it. Nothing you can say is going to change my opinion of that screenplay you sent. There's nothing wrong with writing propaganda, but you have to be pretty damn good at it before you can get away with calling it something else. And despite your disclaimers, *Perla Is a Pig* is a very different kind of writing from that screenplay. *PIP* is a good story about real people; that other thing is hung up on racial & cultural symbols.

And so much for that. Random House is on my ass very seriously for not sending them a book ms., and I have to get at it. In closing, let me suggest that you look back at your carbon of that letter (to me) and ponder graf #2 on pg. 1 . . . the insane implication that my deliberate refusal to render advice caused you to take 150 acid trips and destroy your mind. Just read it over and ask yourself how it sounds.

And before you start writing a "collumn" for the *LA Times,* you should at least learn how to spell column. (See what kind of things journalists notice?) Cheap shit . . . but that's the way they think.

Other last-gasp notes: Most of what you said about my scene out here is true . . . and the mindless isolation worries me to the point where I plan to get out of here before next winter. But I want to try to get this house nailed down first—because I want to have a place where I can live like a human being when I get tired of all the screaming bullshit that comes with trying to change a nation of vicious assholes. That's what I meant by saying you should get hold of a hillside somewhere—not as a solution, but a potential refuge from solutions. You already seem half-mad from running around the streets with a head full of acid, with no address & getting constantly fired . . . but those are all details; the real problem is that none of it seems to be doing your head any good. You've got yourself so wired up with that Jesus-complex that you cause more problems than you cure. . . . (Well, that's a bit heavy and I don't mean it to be ugly—but that Jesus thing is very acute in your case; your letter reeks of it.) And shit, maybe you *are* Jesus . . . and now, looking back at your letter, I see no point in trying to argue with you. (Now I see your final pronouncement about "Mankind is Doomed. Period." Which is true—and all the more reason for trying to save at least a small chunk, instead of insisting on the destruction of the whole thing because they won't give you credit for saving it all.) But I learned a long time ago that you can't reason with preachers, so fuck it.

I got a very depressed note from McGarr today. Why don't you check on him—without your soapbox. He's a good person & you don't need acid to talk to him. You have to realize that you come on very strong with most people & most of them don't need it. They have their own problems. The only exception I can think of offhand is me. I don't have any problems. OK . . . Hello to Socorro . . . and, as always, send mescaline. Ciao . . .

Hunter

Enc. 2 caps mesc.

TO BILL CARDOSO, *THE BOSTON GLOBE:*

Scanlan's *looked promising enough that Thompson suggested to talented friends that they write for it, too.*

January 29, 1970
Woody Creek, CO

Dear Bill . . .

You really ought to get out of that fucking Boston & into someplace where culture is happening. I've been brooding over my copy of [Frederick Exley's] *A Fan's Notes* for more than a year—pushing it at the bookstore and that kind of shit. It's a terrible fucking book—breaks every conceivable rule, etc.—for some reason it's one of the best things I've read in years.

You should try your own kind of weird writing on *Scanlan's Monthly.* They would dig an anonymous piece (or at least unsigned) by a big-time journalist who went to Israel and spent all his time with Mandy Rice-Davies and a bunch of dope-crazed Arabs. If you could do the whole piece in the same style of your

2 grafs in the letter, it would be a zinger. I could probably sell them on the idea if you want to do it. They're running a weird show down there in NY—a madhouse of some kind, with edit rooms in a converted ballroom above a pub near Times Sq. I called them last Sunday at midnight & the office was full of people, all twisted. God only knows what kind of magazine it will be. I hate to say it, but there was talk of cutting the Boston airport lead off the Killy piece; I'm fighting all cuts, but with a 110 pg. article my position is untenable. The first issue should be out around March 1.

I was kidding about writing a column—or maybe I wasn't. If I can't get this book done I'll be out on the street looking for work. Your letter gives me the fear—maybe I'll really get to work. Hopefully I can get onto a schedule of working six days a week and totally amok on mescaline every Sunday. For the past month or so that's been my act: Loading up on Sat nite, locking the doors, building a huge fire & turning up the amplifier—wiring headphones to the bed with strange lamps burning and humping myself to a frazzle. Try mescaline—I recommend it highly. Or have I already said that?

A friend of Lee Berry's showed up today, looking for a cheap house. I killed him with a double-strand spear gun & the dogs cleaned his bones almost instantly. Berry is OK; he's in NY now. Try him again sometime—after he gets rid of that Italian hair-do. OK for now; I have to get back to work. Hello to Susan . . .

Ciao,
Hunter

TO VIRGINIA THOMPSON:

Thompson reflected on his youngest brother's difficulties finding meaningful employment in Kentucky.

January 29, 1970
Woody Creek, CO

Dear Mom . . .

Sorry to be so late getting back. Bruce Innes & his band have been here for 2 weeks & the chaos has been worse than usual. I'm also into a money bind—not gut-serious, but constant mounting pressure to "produce" a new book, and it keeps me in a sort of muted rage at all times.

Jim's situation sounds grim, although not a hell of a lot worse than mine at age 20 . . . remember that letter I wrote you when I got fired from the *Middletown Daily Record* right after I bought the Jaguar? But maybe Jim's scene is different—if only because he doesn't seem to have any idea what he'd even *like* to do, much less what he *can* do. At that point I at least considered myself a writer. The situation with his friends sounds bad, but maybe he's just growing away from them a lot faster than I grew away from mine. By age 25 I no longer had anything to say to my old friends in Louisville; maybe Jim is just making the break a bit earlier. But actually I don't know him or his friends well enough to even guess what the problem is.

It sounds OK if he wants to come out here in May. Probably June 1 would be better, or maybe not—depending on the weather. It's hard to have anyone here when it's cold outside, because we can't get away from each other & the snow makes the house a sort of fort & refuge. In the spring, once the sun gets a grip, there's always plenty of work to do outside & our world expands about 500%. I wouldn't want to commit myself for any length of time, since it's entirely possible that it might get on my nerves. But he could come out for a week or so and maybe longer if it worked out. There's a DIM possibility that I might be able to get him a job of some kind, but again that depends on what he feels like doing. And what he *can* do. What is his address in Lexington? I haven't sent Davison anything either, but I have a pair of boots for him—and I'll get them off sometime soon. Anyway, send Jim's address. And if you talk to him, say I wrote and mentioned having him out for a week or so in the spring—when there'll be plenty of work to do.

Otherwise, things sound pretty good there. I hope drink isn't a problem—and I don't get the impression that it is. Unless there's something serious I don't understand about Jim's situation, it doesn't sound like anything to panic over. We'll see. Maybe I'll be able to see it more clearly after a week of having him out here. Meanwhile, I have to get back to work on this stinking book.

Love,
H

TO EUGENE W. McGARR:

Close since their drinking days in New York when both were copyboys at Time *magazine, Thompson and McGarr had begun to drift apart after the Bronx native moved to Los Angeles.*

January 29, 1970
Woody Creek, CO

Dear Gene . . .

(I don't recall ever having used that formal opening, but the tone of your letter leaves me no choice . . .) Anyway, it sounded sort of grimly honest—not exactly the kind of thing I'm accustomed to get from you. At least not in the mail. Right???

I'm sorry my visit was such a bummer and in retrospect I understand what you mean. One of the reasons, I think, was that it was mainly Sandy's trip. I had no reason at all for staging a $2000 freakout that I can't possibly pay for (since I couldn't justify the trip to Random House, they won't pay for a cent of it)—but Sandy has been so generally depressed since that child-death thing that it seemed necessary to get her away to some weird and different scene. And it seems to have worked just enough to keep things level here. It was sort of a long-delayed mescaline honeymoon—an orgiastic Trip that got her back in my world for a while. She was beginning to feel seriously left out, I think, and blowing a Diners Club card is an easy way to stay sane—if that's all it takes.

Oscar cursed me too—for the same kind of reason, I guess. But what the hell? I behaved irresponsibly and perhaps inhumanely, but at least I spent my goat hours very pleasantly with my wife, and she dug it, so I have to say it wasn't a bad trip from my own point of view. The child-death thing had gotten to her in a way that had me worried; she was getting very freaky about a lot of things, very depressed and not happy with life in general.

But so much for all that. I had no idea that you were any more anxious to "make contact" with me than you were a year earlier, or the year before that. Or . . . etc. Now, reading your letter, I feel like a giddy asshole . . . or maybe not, because all you had to do was suggest that Sandy stay with Eleanor while we zapped off to one of the beach towns for a day of beer and babbling. You can't expect to drop into a dope freak's hotel room at the cocktail hour and get locked into serious talk. I had a vague feeling that you weren't particularly happy with life, but I wasn't about to grab you by the elbow and demand an explanation. That's not my style . . .

. . . whatever else *might* be, and I really can't say. I've always communicated with most of the people I call friends on two very distinct levels: One a sort of verbal fuckaround and the other . . . well . . . whatever the term is, you're right in saying we haven't been working that channel for a while. I don't know why. I figured your mind had fused completely to your groin. Now, looking back, I think I understand you a little better than I used to. It's an interesting subject and we should ponder it sometime—the notion of fucking as an outlet for frustrated energy. I'm sure a lot of people have written about it, but I haven't read their works, so it still interests me. Personally, I find frenzied humping an excellent substitute for hard writing. My humping action seems to decline in perfect inverse ratio to the number of pages I write each night. But maybe I'm just weird.

It's also a fact that almost everybody I know—or used to know—seems hopelessly fucked up right now. Sending you that old *Time* mag. piece was no house-cleaning accident; I spent hours looking through trunks for the fucker. For my own reasons. I'm sitting out here in a deep and wretched funk, trying to write a book I don't like and which makes no sense to me—but which I have to finish very soon or find myself screwed to the floor & back on the streets looking for a sportswriting job. It scares the shit out of me; the pressure is much worse than it was with the first book—which set me up for a guaranteed failure this time around. The only way I can beat it is by writing a goddamn brain-ripping beast of a book, but so far I haven't figured out how to do that. And my brain gets a little knottier every 24 hours.

Anyway, I figured you might like to know you aren't the only person floundering around. Kennedy's last letter was unspeakably depressing; Semonin is so weird that he won't even talk to me; Oscar is going mad because nobody will crucify him; [John] Clancy calls at awful hours and howls about failed dreams; [Jo] Hudson is doing the best metal sculpture in the country & he can't make a dime; Dennis Murphy had to be taken to a health farm . . . and I'm sitting out here in the goddamn snow, trying to explain it all and not too far, on some nights, from thinking seriously about suicide.

Living in LA is probably a lot worse than living here. I don't expect any real human contact in Aspen or WC, so I'm not haunted by the lack of it. Living down there would drive me wild, I think: The smell of money and action is all around—particularly for you. NY was that way for me for 10 years. I walked past the Random House building, knowing I could write all kinds of wonderful profitable shit for them, and also knowing I couldn't get past the dimwit old receptionist in the lobby, no matter what I said. Then, for a year or so, I roamed around the building like I owned it—bringing in snakes and drugs, drinking heavily while using the long-distance phones, disrupting people who had all sorts of work to do . . . well, why go on? I blundered into a scene that no amount of plotting would ever have got me into.

But fuck all that. I may still put it out, and in the meantime there's no sense hassling you with it. Shit, you've done the same kind of act . . . and now you're brooding around your house in Topanga Canyon . . . and confused. You didn't say why, but that's not hard to figure either. I wish to fuck I could lay off some kind of healing wisdom—for either one of us. We have come a long way from those Sunday nights at Time Inc. when everything seemed possible—probably inevitable. There was plenty of time then. Maybe the nut of the problem now is a new sense of Time. To me, anyway, it is suddenly conceivable that I might start falling apart at any moment, and blow the whole thing . . . for the first time in my life I can see over the hump. Time is suddenly a terrible factor. Like I said, it wasn't any accident that you got that 10 year old *Time* clip in the mail. After I located it and read it about 18 times I thought, Now who should I send this to?

Actually, I don't feel *corrupted*—but more like a fool. Maybe you should ponder that. I don't know. But I don't get the feeling that you've spent much time in the past few years doing things you really want to do—or even any one thing you can really get high on. Maybe you should try that. Make a film you can really get into, instead of somebody else's commercial. I recall how I felt after two years of writing for *The National Observer*—they gave me just enough leeway to keep me from going mad, but after I finally quit (or got fired) I realized I'd been going mad all along. And all I had to do for money was write a $100 article about some gang of shitheads called Hell's Angels. I did it for a month's rent and nothing else . . . but then I got into it and the situation began developing, and I got more into it . . . and eventually I paid about three years' rent & was given an opportunity to make an ass of myself on national TV.

So even the answers make no sense. By writing a money-making book & even digging it for a while, I managed to get myself into serious debt to the IRS, the Diners Club and a rich landlord from Michigan. And also to two publishers. At the moment I need about $37,000 to get even, and I see no hope at all. And no time either. Fuck them.

Anyway, try to shake your paranoia long enough to realize that I'm still human enough to want to spend some time pondering things with you. I might seem a bit rusty, because I don't spend much time on that level . . . but, shit, I'll give it a whirl. Let me know if you have any good ideas about how to work it.

Ciao,
Hunter

TO MITCH GREENHILL:

Thompson, a lifelong fan of American folk music, had known songwriter Mitch Greenhill—whose father was Joan Baez's agent—since 1960 in Big Sur.

January 30, 1970
Woody Creek, CO

Dear Mitch . . .

God only knows where you are, so I'll send one copy of this to the old Mi-Wuk village address, and another c/o the record Co. . . . Anyway, I got the Eric Von Schmidt[10] album & liked it. He seems like one of the few originals still floating around. The other day a friend of mine in Aspen who writes children's books told me Eric V.S. was going to illustrate it, and I said it couldn't be the same person, but it is. Very weird . . . Particularly that Florida gig. Next time I go down there I'd like to stop by and see him. Florida is one of my favorite places to drive, particularly at night—on the beach or in the outback, very fast. Sandy's mother is in Deland, near Daytona. Is V.S. anywhere around there?

The *Brains/Sky* album is a hell of a lot better, I think, than his first one, which I've had for a while. That "Wood Man" is a boomer—the best thing on the record. If I get a chance I'll try to plug it somewhere. Meanwhile, thanks for sending it along. I dig it & I'll get it played locally, anyway . . . which won't help much, but it won't hurt either. Right now I'm having a sort of weird go-round with Bruce Innes. Remember the little Canadian who had his guitar up at the house in Big Sur that night? He's playing in Aspen with a new group (The Original Caste—a god-awful name) at the Red Onion for something like 3 grand a week. That's a possibility for you; a terrible fucking audience, but good money. Maybe you could put something together with Rosalie.[11] Right now

10. Renowned early-1960s folk–blues singer Eric Von Schmidt left music for a career in graphic arts after recording his second album in 1965, returning with a third release in 1969.
11. Folksinger Rosalie Sorrels.

there's a Bluegrass group called the Joplin Forte alternating with Bruce. If you're onto a booking agent, you might have him call Werner Kuster, one of the owners. Let me know if you're interested; I can't do you much good with Kuster—he's a nazi & he hates me—but I can get stuff played on the radio station & that might convince him you're real . . . or at least saleable.

Bruce is into a strange gig. Have you heard a single called "One Tin Soldier"? That's his. And now they have an album coming out, but it's fucked by horrible arrangements—all kinds of horns and strings and organs in the background. TA (Talent Assoc.) is doing it—mainly as a vehicle, I think, for a gaggle of second-rate songs by Dennis Lambert and Brian Potter, the producers. Bruce has two really first-class songs on it—"Country Song" and "Sweet Chicago Blues"—but they're screwed by the hyped-up Fifth Dimension style arrangements. They wanted me to write some bullshit for the liner notes, but I said I couldn't tolerate all that background noise. Even so, those 2 songs I mentioned are two of the best I've heard in a long time. "Sweet Chicago" is a sure hit, but the producer hates it because it's too heavy. It's a Lightfoot[12] style thing about Mayor Daley. CBS did a thing on Aspen's hippie war last year and picked up that song for a sort of theme—but the news moguls killed the whole bit. If I can manage it, I'll send you a tape—good chance for a single right now—with the Chicago trial going on.

Meanwhile, life in the snowbelt humps along. We had a savage election and almost won control of the town . . . lost by six votes. The next step, they say, is that I'm going to run for sheriff this fall . . . and I might, if only to scare the living shit out of the fatbacks. We could win, maybe, by importing about 500 heads during the summer and keeping them around until election day—or even qualifying them for absentee ballots. I'm going to check with the SDS whips in Denver & Boulder about putting something really vicious together—a flat-out takeover bid, beating the sheriff and the county commissioner all at once. The combined vote for the mayor's race was less than 1500, so it wouldn't take many new voters to seize control of the whole county. If we get something going I'll let you know; we'd probably need a music festival or two, for morale purposes.

OK for all that. Oddly enough, I was trying to get control of my desk last night & I found an old letter from you—talking mainly about the Detroit Lions. I guess I was two years early; next year they'll mop up in the Central. Take my word for it. Probably you've been around the bay long enough, by now, to fall into the hideous shadow of the 49ers. Those fuckers . . . but I see hope for them next year. One of their problems seems to be that the coach hates niggers. What kind of asshole would keep Clifton McNeil on the bench all year?

Anyway, I may see you before then. I have one more chunk of research to do on this stinking book for Random House, and it involves a trip to SF. Where

12. Gordon Lightfoot was a popular Canadian folksinger.

are you living? Send word. Rosalie Sorrels was here briefly in the fall & seemed in good shape—not rich, but still excessively human. [Michael] Solheim has gone over to the cocktail set—hopelessly pussy-whipped; he drinks Alexanders now, and wears pink bellbottom shirts . . . constantly hustling business among local Republicans. An awful spectacle.

As for me, I plan to take whatever small profits I get off this new book and set up a mescaline factory in Woody Creek. Hopefully I can make enough on sales to pay the rent and keep myself in a blazing stupor for the rest of my days. I bought a set of $100 earphones with red lights that flash at 95 decibels. I've worn out two copies of [Herbie Mann's] *Memphis Underground* & burned 2 cords of pinion wood this winter . . . get naked & gobble mescaline by a huge fire & the whole house vibrating with sound. Try it sometime; it's fun.

Ciao—

Hunter
& Hello to Louise

TO PAUL KRASSNER, *THE REALIST:*

Yippie cofounder Paul Krassner didn't bite on the "10-pg. screed" Thompson mentions he wrote in an L.A. hotel room after trying mescaline. The lyrical tale would be published as "First Visit with Mescalito" in Thompson's 1990 collection Songs of the Doomed.

February 10, 1970
Woody Creek, CO

Krassner . . .

You treacherous cocksucker; where is my copy of the 10th Anniversary Issue? I've been waiting for it for two years . . . or almost . . . maybe 17 months, but why haggle? Is it out? Was I excluded? If so, I'll have my lawyer rip your lungs out with his bare hands. You owe me that issue; I paid for it, and I consider it a sacred obligation. Somebody told me the other day that you were dead, that you were riding down Sixth ave (down? Maybe it was Seventh?) in a cab when your head swelled up like a penny balloon and exploded . . . too much acid, they said . . . no blood at all in the brain-remnants. You should have taken my advice and abandoned all drugs while there was still time. . . .

It's too late now; you might as well double up and go hard all the way to the end. But meanwhile, I want that 10th Aniv. Issue. If copy is the problem I can probably send you something; the selection on my desk ranges from Painfully Straight to Intolerably Weird. At a glance I see a 10-pg. screed that I wrote on a stolen IBM Selectric in a room at the Continental Hotel in LA while in the grip of a heavy dose of mescaline that I ate without realizing what it was . . . a very strange morning, which included a plane trip to Denver. Anyway, let me know what's happening about that issue. . . .

Thanks,
Hunter S. Thompson

FROM OSCAR ACOSTA:

February 10, 1970
Los Angeles, CA

Hunter:

In the first place, I doubt that I sent the play for your criticism of my lifestyle; in the second instance, you did not in any way criticize the play—character, plot, suspense, story, did-it-work—but rather rapped on what I'm doing . . . which was the reason for my response. We've hardly talked about the play.

I hadn't written until now cause I wanted to wait until it no longer mattered, and also I was catering to your whim of "let's not haggle" which is your usual cop-out to any serious dispute with me. Having got down to it, I find I must continue the response to your last letter where you, again, indulged yourself.

I don't "go around asking for criticism" as you suggest; many moons ago I decided that I, me, and only me, knew more about myself and my writing than any one else. The novel I wrote convinced me of that. After several good writers—Mark Harris, Van Tilburg Clark—and editors of the five largest publishing houses in the USA told me I was good, etc., and yet not one seriously thought of getting the thing published, I then decided never to be a "professional" writer . . . which means a guy that has to print in order to eat. I never showed anyone my junk until I met you, and since then—except for [Margaret] Harrell—I've not shown it to anyone for *"criticism"* except for you and a poet friend of mine in S.F.

The fact of the matter is that I like what I write, generally, and I know that very few persons whom I respect will be as wild about the shit as I am. . . . You are the perfect example. You think you know about the issue of race in this country, which has led you to conclude that it is not really an issue at all, and so when you read a play that deals with the issue of race as seen in the context of survival of the *human* race, you consider the theme irrelevant and simplistically brand it racist. Quite a neat trick if you can pull it off.

For a campaign manager who couldn't get several hundred votes for his candidate, you really presume too much when you object to the "use" of the media, couching the criticism in old Alpha, Beta, Gamma, rah-rah, bull-shit.

You assume that the publicity around the fast—etc.—was for the purpose of spreading the good news to the Anglo public! Coming on the heels of the St. Basil's Bust scene, you felt it too cheap, trite, p.r.-ish.

Any organizer worth his salt would tell you (1) All efforts of publicity are directed at communicating to the people you're trying to organize . . . which in this instance is the Chicano. (2) All demonstrations, etc., are a means of finding some basically non-violent work to get them (the Chicano) involved. (3) When the press has massacred you (as it did on the St. Basil's Bust) and given you an image you do not want, you must then immediately find some gimmick to counter it. (Which is what I did here . . . McIntyre had branded us as violent revolutionaries, etc., which he could hardly do after we had a very Christian fast.)

. . . And you're right about this stuff not doing my head any good. I know of no other way to get the things I want for myself and for others. If it was only me, and you'll never believe this, I'd go drop out again, only this time in a warm climate, tropics preferably. I'd drink my ass off and maybe write a line or two. But here I am and likely to remain so because there simply ain't no other place for me to go. I've made a plunge into a world of ideas and feelings that are simply unescapable. Words like ego-trip and Christ-complex are not only meaningless in this context, but infuriatingly trite. I would hope that the one thing the acid did for me was to make me realize that EGO is a wonderful thing, so long as you don't get carried away with it, laugh at yourself now and again, yet remain constant in your belief that you *are* Super Spic, Heo Cholo, Zeta, Brown Buffalo and occasionally Oscar Acosta, esq. then having believed that, there is simply no reason for a *Christ* complex. In fact, I am superior to Christ, and I say that as seriously as you say that you've found your *sitio* . . . which only leaves the salvation bit.

I am not now, nor have I ever been a missionary. I ain't here to save nobody. That is Christianwhore piss. The White man's way of helping people. Live in the barrio because I am of the barrio, and all the fucking propaganda about revolutionaries fighting for the people, the community, etc., happens to be true in my case . . . in a word, I'm fighting for myself who is totally identified with the community of the poor.

And when I read this stuff and the past letters, listen to my old tapes, listen to myself talking with guys under acid, booze, and all evil forms of dope, I realize just how far down the road I've gone on my eternity trip . . . but don't you think for one minute I don't laugh at the written for eternity, as it were, just as much as you did when you wrote it.

Which still raises the ultimate question I've been asking for the past three years . . . Is it still a trip, or have I arrived at my destination?

. . . God damn it, Thompson get off my back and say something decent for a change! Which, I think, is where I came in.

orale,
Z

TO WARREN HINCKLE, *SCANLAN'S MONTHLY:*

Thompson's Jean-Claude Killy piece was finally published in Scanlan's Monthly.

March 2, 1970
Woody Creek, CO

Dear Warren . . .

Thanx for the copy of *Scanlan's.* I gave out both subscription cards & I don't have the magazine now so I can't subscribe formally . . . but if you'll put me on the list and tell your nark to send a bill, I'll pay it. Probably you have some excellent reason for not trying to sell the fucker via mail promotion, but I'm damned if I can see it. . . .

Editorially, the first issue looked good and up to par . . . but Graphically, it was a fucking horror show. It looks like it was put together by a compositor's apprentice with a head full of Seconal. If I were you I'd put out an all-points bulletin for [Dugald] Stermer; he has his work cut out for him. . . .

On lesser fronts, I want to impose a condition on anything I may or may not sell you in the future—to wit: That any "cartoon/illustration" by Jim Nutt will not be allowed within 15 pages on either side of my byline. His Killy drawing not only wasted two pages, but it separated (my) letter from the article & rendered the letter useless. And beyond that I found my name at the bottom of Nutt's cartoon.

None of which is really serious (to me, anyway—because, after all I'm only a writer . . . but if I were an editor I'd make some heavy serious changes in the graphics for issue #2 . . .). And thanx for the good editing on the Killy piece; I very much appreciate your indulgence inre: the parts I wanted in.

At the moment I'm all wound up with the first issue of the *Aspen Wallposter.* Tomorrow is publication day & although it's on a far smaller scale than *Scanlan's,* the tension is still pretty heavy. We decided to let the old paper die & go with a completely new form of experimental graphic/journalism. I'll send you a copy when it hits the streets. And if the *Wallposter* name rings a bell . . . well, I'll never deny it. The concept is the same, but the design & graphics are (as far as I know) completely new.

OK for now. Let me know about the Oil Shale thing. At the moment I'm working on a fast obituary for Terry the Tramp[13]—who committed suicide in the wake of Altamont, according to a note I just got from Jann Wenner. Very shitty . . . for a lot of reasons.

Ciao,
Hunter

13. Terry the Tramp was one of the Hell's Angels featured in Thompson's 1967 book about the biker gang.

TO VIRGINIA THOMPSON:

Thompson updated his mother about his Aspen Wallposters *and difficulties at home.*

March 7, 1970
Woody Creek, CO

Dear Mom . . .

Here's a quick note in the midst of chaos, to bring you up to date. I'm enclosing a copy of Issue #1 of my first publishing effort; it's an entirely new journalistic form, and it may work. We're already into #2. It's a left-handed effort, but fun—and the only publication that will print my stuff without cutting it.

Speaking of that, I assume you noticed the Press Section (p. 42) of this week's *Time* (March 9). Their story about the birth of *Scanlan's Monthly* quotes a somewhat unlikely line from my article (in *Scanlan's*) on Jean-Claude Killy, the french skier. It's the same piece I did for *Playboy*—the one they refused to print. Probably *Scanlan's* is available in Louisville. Also, for the files, I got a fairly old booklet (1968, I think) from the USIA [United States Information Agency], called "Americans & the Arts," which for some reason has a photo of me in the Aspen section. I can't send a copy—or copy the photo, because it's in color. My copy came from U.S.I.A., 1776 Pa. Ave, Wash. D.C. 20547—Wesley Pederson, editor.

That's about it for the good news. On other fronts, Sandy is even now (at this moment) suffering through another miscarriage. Only 2 months along, this time. Very depressing. And, as always, there's the money crunch—compounded by my problems with this goddamn book that won't work. I'd like to quit it, but I can't because I owe them so much money. At the same time, it keeps me from working seriously on anything else. So sooner or later I'll stumble through it and get on to better things.

I got a good letter from Davison the other day, the first in a long while. But no reply to my letter to Jim. I asked him out for a visit in the spring. We'll see what happens. Davison didn't seem to know any more about his 4-F thing than you do.

OK for now. I have to get some work done before dawn.

Love,
H

TO OSCAR ACOSTA:

Thompson's fine eye for graphic design showed in his Freak Power campaign's innovative two-sided Aspen Wallposters, *which presented smart political writing as art suitable for hanging.*

March 9, 1970
Woody Creek, CO

Dear Oscar:

Your last letter was wonderful; I agree with everything you said—even the racist swill. As for M-1 firing pins, I think I have a heavy gun dealer in Denver, but I've put off any action with him until I can come up with some cash . . . and right now I'm still stone broke. I'll let you know when I find out anything . . . but in the meantime I wouldn't worry about buying them anywhere; M-1's are totally legal & you can surely get a better price in Calif. (see enc. ad for a start).

I'm enclosing Issue #1 of a thing that—as far as I know—is a completely new concept in journalism. We sell the *poster* for a buck & the edit stuff is free . . . and we sold 500 of the fuckers in the first three days; gave away about 200 & we're now rolling Issue #2, with an arty-erotic cover-poster and a strange bag of insult/wisdom on the back. We'll hump the thing as long as it works, or until it stops being fun. We may add pages & sell subscriptions & ads . . . but maybe not. Anyway, it has a lot of possibilities—here & elsewhere—because it requires no real overhead, office, salaries, & that bullshit. One of the main hangups is the dingbat printer, a useless fucker who can barely spell his own name. But we can solve that. Lawsuits are another problem, but I've spread the rumor that we have heavy financial backing (from the east) & welcome lawsuits as a form of advertising. This County Atty. mentioned in #1 is known to be the heaviest & meanest lawyer between Denver and Salt Lake . . . which ain't much, but his firm handles big oil and water rights cases, for people like LBJ's brother & various oil companies. He was the biggest target I could find . . . and meanwhile [Joe] Edwards is preparing a lawsuit against him on conflict of interest grounds, which if nothing else will force him to quit as Cty. Atty., in order to defend his ore interests. Summer here is going to be weird & active. I plan to run a strong race for Sheriff & drive the fuckers wild. The Edwards campaign left us with virtual veto-power over any liberal/Demo candidates in the coming County elections. Freak Power is now an accepted reality; we can't win on our own, but the lib/Demos can't win if we run a third candidate—which we will. At the moment we're holding out for Edwards to run for the main County Comm. spot, which—if we can win—will snap the spine of the local political establishment, take out their biggest wheel (J. Baxter—Bugsy's med. partner).

So, despite your drug-gibberish, my various power trips are going well here. How about you? I didn't get a lot of confident vibrations off that issue of *La Raza* you sent. Once again—and fuck your objections—I think you should get off that "How Long O Lord?" binge & narrow down to some kind of specific issue where you can take the *offensive*. One of these days you'll realize that the fuckers you're up against don't care if you live or die; they'd just as soon deport you, or—failing that—kill you. So the only way to deal with them is to scare them; find a weak link & focus on that, instead of fighting the whole chain.

Well . . . I'll get off that. No point in sending you up the walls again. How was that mescaline? You didn't say. And what about that $1 a cap stuff you were going to pick up in SF? What is McGarr into? Another sex trip? I couldn't tell from your letter, but it didn't sound like you got your heads together. From the tone of his last letter to me, he's got to get into something heavy pretty fast. Why don't you try applying his talents to something like arms-buying? He'd do well at that kind of dealing; give him a percentage of whatever's available, & turn him loose. One of the main things I've learned out here is that there are all kinds of very able people wandering around with no place to use their energy. They want to get *into* something. On this *Wallposter* thing I needed somebody to *sell* the fucker, to actually hustle it in the stores & on the streets . . . so I turned the whole sales/circulation gig over to a dropout painting contractor from Laguna Beach, a head I barely knew & who seemed so fucked up that [Sheriff] Whitmire was threatening to bust him as a dangerous public nuisance. He offered to help distribute the posters, but we needed more than just help, so I offered him a third of whatever we made, above costs, and the bastard has been on the streets ever since, selling about 100 a day. He's organized a hellishly effective gang of street vendors, lined up the airport & the car rental agencies—even the gift shop at the fucking Holiday Inn, which I savagely raped in my article. Tomorrow I'm going to walk into the *Aspen Times* & pay the printing fee with 285 one dollar bills. And we'll have about $200 clear. Mainly because of this bastard's energy.

The same thing happened during the Edwards campaign. People I'd never seen or heard of appeared & insisted on getting into it . . . while more than half the people we'd counted on blew their roles completely. The only trouble is that I'm not sure how to duplicate that trick; I'm not sure what really drew those people. Looking back, it's easy to say we obviously had a wave building for us—but, shit, the wave wasn't even visible *to me* until less than a week before the election. So, in honest retrospect, I have to think that all we did was create a very loose structure for a lot of un-focused energy trips. Very weird . . . and I'm still pondering it. All I know is that anybody who can figure out a way to put other people's un-used energy to work has a hell of a tool in his hands. No doubt you have a huge energy reserve down there—far more than here, even per capita—so you might consider this notice.

Which is only a suggestion, and I mention it only because I'm just learning about it. Politics, I think, is far more than Politics. It may be the ultimate high . . . and maybe adrenaline is the real super-drug. I read Aldous Huxley's *Doors of Perception* and saw his comment about mescaline and adrenaline having essentially the same chemical base . . . which makes perfect sense.

And so much for all that. I have to go upstairs and call the hospital. Sandy is in there again with another miscarriage—a real nightmare version, this time, since it puts me head on with the abortion laws. She's only two months pregnant, but the pain is so bad she can't stand up . . . and the pigs say they can't do a therapeutic abortion. All they do is keep her drugged up on codeine and wait for God to work His Will. The D&C operation is as simple as pulling a tooth, but they won't do it . . . and this is Colorado, which recently passed a "liberalized" abortion law. Man, I'm coming to really hate that word "liberal."

Speaking of hospitals, how did that cell-hanging case come out? You might try writing something about that; your description was vicious (the autopsy). A new writing market is *Scanlan's Monthly*—editor, Warren Hinckle, 451 Pacific, SF 94133. The first issue is out; see the March 9 issue of *Time* (press section). *Scanlan's* bought my piece on JC Killy, the one I did for *Playboy,* but which they wouldn't print. Hinckle is the ex-*Ramparts* editor. You might stop by and see him the next time you're in SF; tell him what you're into & see what interests him. He's a fiendish boozer, but not much on dope.

As for your Christ complex, I'll leave it alone for now. But convey my condolences to Socorro. Sandy still feels bad about your accusation that she didn't insist on bringing Socorro along on that wretched SF trip—even though I keep telling her that she had nothing to do with it. That was *our* decision, as I recall—based entirely & quite reasonably on *our* experience with eating acid in the company of people (or even one person) who hates acid. The only flaw in our formula was that rotten goddamn acid you had. If we'd had good drugs, Socorro would have hated every minute of the trip—and maybe she would have anyway. (The Diners Club, incidentally, is about to seize my card; I owe them something like $1200 from that trip, & I have no hope of paying—which doesn't bother me much, because the day I got back here I applied for a Carte Blanche card—using Diners as a reference—and it came about a month ago, just about the time Diners started getting ugly. Fuck them.)

And that's about it for now. Say hello to Socorro—and particularly from Sandy—and lay some heinous racial insult on Benny, from me. You might also keep in mind that my Sheriff's campaign will make the "new politics" look like something out of [President Warren G.] Harding's high school notebooks. It might be worth your while to come out and watch. Hell . . . come anytime.

Ciao, Hunter

TO D. PORTER BIBB:

David Porter Bibb III had been a friend of Thompson's since high school, when both were members of the Athenaeum Literary Association.

March 14, 1970
Woody Creek, CO

D. Porter, etc. . . .

For the past few months I've been picking up weird vibrations indicating your return to the land of the living—or maybe just the land of the visible, which isn't necessarily the same thing. I refer, specifically, to Altamont—

strange quotes from one "Porter Bibb, spokesman for the Maysles Bros. . . ."; the mysterious voice.

That's a strange place for you to turn up. I thought you'd gone totally down the tube—into corporate fuckarounds with that silly hat of yours, the one you wore when I last saw you. At that point you were looking for "18 thou & low visibility. . . ." Selah.

What now? Send a line between deals. I am, of course, in contact with people who would like to twist your head off. And mine, too, for that matter. It gives me a wild rare boot to know that after all this time—and all that I wrote—that people are actually shocked to find the Angels whacking hippies at a rock festival. The sharks finally came home to roost; and the only wonder is that it didn't happen sooner. But fuck that. . . .

Send a line & affirm your gig, whatever it is. Or come out and hang around Aspen. It's weird here; I'm running for Sheriff.

Hunter

TO JANN WENNER, *ROLLING STONE:*

In November 1967, twenty-one-year-old New Yorker Jann Wenner launched Rolling Stone, *a hip rock-music tabloid that quickly developed into a glossy, ad-fat pop-culture magazine. When Thompson met the shrewd young publisher in San Francisco in late 1969, Wenner immediately commissioned him to write an article on the Freak Power movement in the Rockies.*

April, 1970
Woody Creek, CO

Jann . . .

Here's a bundle of artifacts that I thought I'd send ahead, so you'll have something to use for fillers if the photos don't measure up . . . which is likely, considering the batch I collected today. Your friend Jackie is sick—or maybe she's just avoiding me—but so far I've drawn a vague blank on that end. I'll run her down today & see what happens.

My own (local) photographer came up with a pile of shit, by my lights . . . but I'm enclosing his whole bundle in another package later today, & I think he has three or four useable shots in the batch.

Working with photographers always drives me fucking crazy—mainly because I always end up feeling responsible for whatever they can't or won't do. In this case I ran into a bog of lethargy. Maybe somebody's spreading the word that you only pay $1 a hit for fotos . . . I don't know, & I hate to hassle with those non-linear bastards.

Anyway, I've tossed in a few fotos from my *Wallposter* futures file, along with this rude collection of *Wallposters* & campaign art. The little felt pocket-poster was our "button" last year. And one of the main differences between the

'69 and '70 campaigns is that we have dropped the peace/victory sign, in favor of the fist. (See Krueger foto showing "Aspen Racing Assn." T-shirts at local track). Mama Ned Vare's logo will be a red fist with a small "6" inside—to remind the laggards that last year we lost by only 6 votes. Vare is running the big race for County Commissioner and there are several decent shots of him coming in Krueger's box.

My own logo will be the rotten Owl (see above), and I'm enclosing a sketch of my campaign poster that you can easily create for reproduction if you need some art to break up the text—and if the photos don't grab you any heavier than they do me. You might also use that "Today's Pig Is Tomorrow's Bacon" thing out of *WP* at the end of the sheriff article. And maybe some other bullshit from various *Wallposters.* (That word "Anon" on the front of #1, by the way, means "Soon . . . Again . . . Forthwith." We meant it as a warning to the fatbacks, meaning we were getting ready to fuck with them again, using [Joe] Edwards or any other name.)

Anyway, call me if any of this shit puzzles you. I'm sending it mainly as back-up material. OK for now . . .

Hunter

TO JANN WENNER, *ROLLING STONE:*

Thompson and Wenner were striking the first of many deals to come: an agreement that Rolling Stone *would run mail-order forms offering* Aspen Wallposters *at discount rates to the magazine's readers.*

April 23, 1970
Woody Creek, CO

Dear Jann . . .

OK . . . but first let me explain the X-factors in both the Sheriff's campaign and the 25 cent *Wallposters.*

First: I saw that photo/caption in the last issue about the lad who was running for sheriff of Virginia City—and although it sounds fine, that scene is a long way from ours. This one is getting very grim (already into dynamite—see enc.) and our real opposition goes by names like 1st National City Bank of NY, "First Boston," and the Aspen Ski Corp.—with directors like Rbt. McNamara, Paul Nitze & other Washington heavies. What we've been trying to do—since we lost last November's mayoral race by six (6) votes—is seize control of what the opposition regards as a working gold mine. And it is. The idea that a 29-year-old bike-racer head almost became the Mayor of Aspen last fall has put the fatbacks in a state of wild fear; at the moment they're trying to pass a new City Charter that would disenfranchise most of "our" voters & also bar most of "our" candidates from running for office. So—to destroy this New Charter—we have to mount a serious campaign almost instantly. The charter election (Yes, or No) is in June. And if we can beat them on that, I think we can generate a fucking landslide in November—not only in the Sheriff's race, but also in the crucial County Commissioner's contest—and also for the ballot proposition to change the name of Aspen, officially, to Fat City. This would wreck the bastards, and give us working control of the whole county.

Anyway, I trust you see the problem—both in timing and magnitude. My sheriff's gig is just a small part of the overall plot, which amounts to a sort of Freak Power takeover bid. It began last Nov. and won't end until Nov. '70. So maybe you should ponder the timing of any article; for my own purposes, I'd rather do it sometime this summer, like August, when we're well underway. Or I can wait until after it's over . . . although chances are that I'll be somewhere in Chuck Alverson's territory by that time, if I lose.[14] If I make a serious run at the sheriff's thing, I'll either win or have to move out. That's the tradition here—and it'll be especially true in my case. Last summer was heavy with violence, and this one looks nine times worse. Last year the dynamite action didn't even start until mid-July, but this year it's already heavy in April . . . and last fall's near-miss election has given the local freaks a huge shot of confidence for whatever lies ahead.

So . . . on the "Sheriff's Campaign" article, I'm inclined to look at it as part of a far larger thing. If Freak Power can win in Aspen, it can win in a lot of other places . . . and in that context I'd just as soon do the article fairly soon, maybe in time for August publication, so that what we've learned here might be put to use somewhere else, before November. The important thing here is not whether I win or not—and I hope to hell I don't—but the mechanics of seizing political power in an area with a potentially-powerful freak population. (As a passing note, there, I suppose I should say that if I *do* win, I'll serve out the term—although not without the help of a carefully-selected posse and a very special crew of deputies, most of whom are already chosen and working to register my constituents.) We found, last fall, that registration is the key to freak power.

And so much for all that. I can do the piece sooner, or later; I'd prefer sooner, but what the hell? We're into it anyway, and by autumn a hell of a lot of people are going to be leaving this town: The only question is Who they're going to be.

***

As for the *Wallposter* . . . Yeah, why don't you go ahead and say we'll sell *individual issues* for 25 cents each, but only to people who mention *Rolling Stone* when they write. The painful truth is that it will cost us forty-five (45) cents to do this, but we may glean enough subscriptions to break even. That 45 cent figure is based on printing costs averaging—for the first 3 issues—between 21 cents and 29 cents per poster; plus 13 cents for each mailing tube, plus 7 cents for each

14. Thompson's friend Chuck Alverson, a *Wall Street Journal* reporter, had given him police documents about the Hell's Angels to use in his book.

stamp. But we've given it some thought, and decided to go ahead and spring for whatever happens. The only condition is that we'll cut off the supply whenever we run out of back issues—which probably won't happen, since we can always run off another 1000 or so, when we run low. This is the only advantage in dealing with Aspen's only printer; the disadvantages are obvious—although we beat a lot of them on #3, by refusing to let the printer do the layout, copy-editing, etc.

Well . . . . . . 3 days later now, & I've just talked to Warren Hinckle about doing a piece on the Kentucky Derby for *Scanlan's*. I'm leaving in a few hours for Louisville, so I want to get this off quick—so here's the word on the *Wallposter.*

25 cents each for "sample copies" to anyone writing on the basis of whatever they read in *RS* . . . this will cost us money, & we'll cut it off whenever it starts looking like a serious loss . . . but in the meantime, along with the 25 cent each offer, we'll also sell cut-rate subscriptions (to *RS* readers) for $10 each—for 12 issues. Our normal rate, for tube-mailed posters, is $25 for 12—and believe it or not we have about 100 takers, on the basis of two issues. Without pushing it; we didn't want subscriptions—for obvious reasons, mainly the work involved, and that's why we said $25 for 12. But now, since we're into subscriptions anyway, I figure we may as well get all we can . . . particularly since a 12-issue subscription, including all back issues, would naturally end around November of 1970, a date that happens to coincide with our local political climax. In other words, at this point we're not willing to guarantee anything *beyond* 12 issues. Because, like I said earlier, if I run for sheriff and lose, I'll be gone from here by Xmas.

Right now the political balance looks about 40/60 against us—but that's without the crazed brilliance that we'll naturally bring to any serious effort we decide to make. So I figure the real balance, right now, is roughly 50/50—which means, if we don't make any serious mistakes, we'll probably control the town & the county by November of 1970. This includes the Sheriff's race, the (more important) County Commissioner's race, and also the referendum to change the name of the town to "Fat City."

So there is a definite ominous weight to the notion of *Wallposter* #13—which will announce either our victory, or our wretched defeat. Or maybe, if the timing works out, we can make #13 our "election issue." That would be fitting—no matter who wins.

Meanwhile, we are being sued by the County Attorney, who claims that *Wallposter* #1 forced him to quit his job. He wants more money than the Meat Possum Press Ltd. can ever earn, so fuck him—we welcome his action. In *WP* #4 we intend to go for his throat & goad him on to further frenzies. The town is empty now; #3 ain't selling at all, but after this lull—when the summer session begins—we will get on the fuckers for real, with #4. And then bear down even further with #5, 6, 7, etc.—up to 12 (or 13), at which point we'll re-assess our leverage here, and do whatever's right.

So that's it for now; I'm off to the Derby. Let me know *when* you'd like the Sheriff article—and write the Random Notes *Wallposter* note however you see fit; we'll honor it. OK . . .

Hunter

TO WARREN HINCKLE, *SCANLAN'S MONTHLY:*

Thompson was leaving for Louisville the next day to cover the Kentucky Derby for Scanlan's. *His first choice for illustrator was* The Denver Post's *Pat Oliphant, who had won the 1967 Pulitzer Prize for Editorial Cartooning, but Oliphant couldn't make the trip—luckily for Ralph Steadman and the future of Gonzo journalism.*

April 28, 1970
Woody Creek, CO

Dear Warren . . .

Inre: the KyDerby piece—I just talked to Pat Oliphant & found him darkly unhappy at having his unlisted veil pierced at 2:15 a.m. I didn't tell him, but he was dealing with a veteran of midnight calls to James Reston[15] (collect) from phone booths in places like Arco, Idaho—wild queries from the far interior, demanding to know why the Soviet Army chorus wasn't allowed to perform in the U.S. One Sat. night I tracked Reston all the way from Times Sq. to his weekend hideout in Leesburg, Va. And I got an answer that I should have taped—wild screeching in the night. Very rude, I felt. But the call was not in vain.

Anyway, Oliphant said he probably couldn't go to the Derby, but he'd like to do some drawings & would call you tomorrow (Wed, 4/29). At that point I called a friend in SF, a good photog named Bob Chamberlain, formerly of Aspen, but I couldn't reach him either. By then it was too late to call eastward, so I postponed queries to Danny Lyon at Magnum and a fine young photog in Chicago—Rob Guralnick, who once worked with me on a word/pic feature on Nixon's Inauguration for *The Boston Globe*. Lyon, Chamberlain and Guralnick all have the same kind of camera-eye, & from an editor's POV I don't see much difference between the 3. From *my* POV, I'd prefer drawings by Oliphant—or maybe Searle.[16] But shit, by the time you get this we'll have settled all that anyway . . . so no point in hassling it any further for now. I'll be talking to you in a few hours.

So . . . as far as I'm concerned, I'm off tomorrow for Louisville. The first step, as I see it, will be to rush up to the horse-breeding country around Lex-

15. *New York Times* columnist and Washington bureau chief James "Scotty" Reston was a close friend of many of the Democratic politicians he covered.
16. British illustrator and cartoonist Ronald Searle was known for his satirical cartoons in *Punch* and *The New Yorker* as well as his grim drawings of his experiences in a World War II Japanese POW camp.

ington (80 miles), if there's time . . . or, if not, get out to the track and hang around the stables for a day or so, then hunker down in the awful social whirl. The story, as I see it, is mainly in the vicious-drunk Southern bourbon horseshit mentality that surrounds the Derby than in the Derby itself. And—as a human product of that culture/mentality—I think I can see it pretty clear.

My first stop in Louisville will be at my mother's apt., or Mrs. Virginia Thompson at the Louisville Free Public Library. You can reach me through her, although I may or may not be staying there—depending on whether my brothers are there with their families. And if all else fails—assuming you want to reach me for some (or any) reason—try calling me c/o Jim Pope at the Louisville *Courier-Journal & Times*. I'll check with him tomorrow about press credentials, etc.

Otherwise, I'll figure on getting you at least 5000 words, or somewhere between 5000 and 10,000, by Thursday of next week—May 7. I'll try for Wed, or maybe even Tuesday if I stay in Louisville to write the thing, instead of rushing back here. Probably I'll do that . . . and also probably call you on Monday to see how we stand on time & space.

As for expenses, I can't say for now what they'll run, but between RT plane ticket, car rental and clubhouse (Derby) ticket/expenses, I can't see less than $500. That's assuming I can stay at my mother's apt—which I think I can. Otherwise, we might have nasty rental problems, because Derby Day in Louisville is like Xmas in Aspen, Carnival in Rio, or a motel-frenzy at the Indianapolis 500. But I have enough friends in Louisville so I'm not worried about finding emergency space for myself and whatever artist/photog we decide to send along.

The $1500 fee-money looks good from here—and so does the article. I think we've stumbled on a good genetic accident. If you see any problems, call me in Louisville at the (above) number or call Sandy here and have her track me down.

OK for now. If I can keep it in mind I'll be after you tomorrow for the names, etc. of *Berkeley Barb*[17] distributors—who might also distribute the *Aspen Wallposter*. I'm enclosing a copy of #3—which posed such space problems that we had to drop about half the copy, including our *list* of advertisers and also our non-advertisers, along with local subscription rates, many special awards and other standing heads; and also a handful of local news items, which included the genealogy-statement featuring you and the Chicago *Ramparts* Wallposter. But don't worry—we'll get it in next time.

Yeah . . . & I'm serious about running a Hinckle mug shot with the genealogy-statement, so if you have one around for general PR purposes, send it along. But for christ's sake don't send anything slick or straight; we need photos that will make people puke and howl for their lawyers. With only one page, you have to bear down.

17. The *Berkeley Barb*, a left-wing political weekly, reached its peak circulation of 85,000 in July 1969.

And that's it for now. I have to get some sleep before rushing off to confront my festered childhood. God's mercy on us all.

Sincerely,
Hunter S. Thompson

TO PAT OLIPHANT, *THE DENVER POST:*

April 29/30, 1970
Woody Creek, CO

Dear Pat . . .

Your call a few moments ago caught me on the way to bed, hoping to get around 3 hrs sleep before zapping off in the great white sky to Louisville for the annual horse shit & bourbon orgy. Sorry you couldn't make it. As I told Hinckle, I can't think of anyone who could do that kind of scene as well as you could—even Searle or Magnum photographers; so probably what I'll do now is locate a kid (photog) in Chicago who worked with me on a Nixon-Inaugural piece—he had a fine strange eye.

Anyway, I won't be getting to bed today—blowing off for Ky. in a few hours, but if I get hung at the Denver airport I'll give a call and maybe we can have a drink. Otherwise, I'll try to catch you on the way back next Wednesday (May 6)—and maybe we can figure out a fine American folk-scene we can do together. Maybe the Indianapolis 500, or a Labor Day picnic in Detroit. Whatever's right . . .

Meanwhile, I'm enclosing copies of the first 3 issues of the *Aspen Wallposter*—a total experiment in the un-worked fields of the newest New Journalism. Sometime this summer we may try to pressure you into doing a cover for us—on the order of Mauldin's[18] covers for the *Chicago Journalism Review.* But I'll talk to you before then . . . & if I miss you in Denver, come on over to Woody Creek for a few crazed days. Anytime . . . just give a ring far enough ahead to be sure I'm here, which is almost all of the time. We have a huge house with plenty of space for anything you want to bring: kids, dogs, bikes, guns, whatever . . . even wives.

As for the *Wallposters,* I can't apologize for all the wretched mistakes . . . but if you read the copies in order (1, 2, 3) you'll see that we're beating them; mainly by firing all the printer's "experts." Fuck them; they should be put in welfare camps—for the congenitally incompetent.

OK for now. I have to get upstairs and call Hinckle. And get my plane ticket—and call my poor mother to warn her that I'm coming back, once

18. Bill Mauldin won Pulitzer Prizes for Editorial Cartooning in 1945 for his World War II drawings for United Feature Syndicate and in 1959 for his political cartoons in the *St. Louis Post-Dispatch*.

again, to whip the shit out of everything I was raised and brought up to hold dear. Selah.

TO BILL CARDOSO, *THE BOSTON GLOBE:*

At the last minute, Scanlan's Monthly *assigned British illustrator Ralph Steadman—known for his work in* The Times *of London and England's political satire magazine* Private Eye*—to accompany Thompson to the Kentucky Derby. Steadman's savage, dead-on drawings would define the Gonzo look.*

May 15, 1970
Woody Creek, CO

Billy . . .

Your letter was waiting for me last week when I got back from Louisville. Very weird. I went there to write a strange piece on the spectacle for *Scanlan's Monthly* . . . and the whole scene nearly killed me, along with the British illustrator on his first trip to the U.S. See *Scanlan's* #4 (June, I think) for details. It's a shitty article, a classic of irresponsible journalism—but to get it done at all I had to be locked in a NY hotel room for 3 days with copyboys collecting each sheet out of the typewriter, as I wrote it, whipping it off on the telecopier to San Francisco where the printer was standing by on overtime. Horrible way to write anything.

Anyway, you should have given a ring or hung around long enough to get into the Derby action with us. I was there about 7 days, then up to NY for the final writing. Horrible, horrible. . . . Maybe you can zap out here and do a story on New Journalism and Newer Politics in Aspen. I am running for sheriff in the fall; we're about to take over the town. OK for now; let me know if you or Susan can find us any outlets. Thanx. . . .

Hunter

TO WARREN HINCKLE, *SCANLAN'S MONTHLY:*

Thompson and his new British cohort put themselves in quite a mint-julep haze through Derby week in Louisville; the result was the brilliantly written and illustrated article "The Kentucky Derby Is Decadent and Depraved," which appeared in the June 1970 issue of Scanlan's. *The bylines read: "Written under duress by Hunter S. Thompson" and "Sketched with eyebrow pencil and lipstick by Ralph Steadman."*

May 15, 1970
Woody Creek, CO

Dear Warren . . .

Well, what the fuck can a human being say after a scene like that last one? I just read over the Derby article for the first time and it strikes me as a monument to whatever kind of limbo exists between humor and tragedy. I wish there'd been time to do it better—or room to run all that bullshit about Louisville's super/Agnew society. Goddard[19] & I cut about 4000 words on Sunday night, dropping most of the socio-philosophical flashbacks and weird memory jogs in favor of the straight chronological narrative . . . and in retrospect I think that was the only way to go.

With another week I might have honed it down to a finer, meatier edge . . . but in fact we were lucky to get anything at all. Returning to the scenes of my youth was not, all in all, an exceptionally wise idea. After 4 days without sleep—due to all-night, soul-ripping doom & disaster talk—I arrived in NY in a state of crazed angst, far gone in a pill-stupor and barely able to think, much less write. Goddard's ominous patience was all that kept me functioning. He's a first-class head to have on your side in that kind of crunch and I'm sorry to hear he's leaving. God only knows what will happen to the NY end of your action without his calming influence. On the several occasions when I nearly ran amok—particularly when I lost my wallet (with all cash & credit cards) in a tavern mob watching the Knicks-Lakers game on TV—Goddard's steady head was the only anchor in town. Once again—he's good, and I hate to see him go.

Which is neither here nor there, for now; particularly in light of the heinous imbroglio I made myself a party to last weekend. I was never sure what was happening, or why, in terms of timing, but early on I had the feeling that I should have gone to SF instead of NY, to do the writing. The Royalton was fine, but I'd have been a hell of a lot happier—and probably more functional—if I'd been in a position to know what was going on.

But what the hell? We're over that hump now—for good or ill—and my only consolation, in reading the article, is that I helped Steadman get his drawings. He's good; probably better than anybody working in this country—but they didn't like him in Louisville. And not at the *NY Times,* either; the *Times* offered him a job, but turned down all his extant drawings of Nixon, etc. . . .

As for *Scanlan's* general action . . . well, what little I saw of the NY scene leaves me slightly worried. Something is badly lacking in the focus, the main thrust—and $10,000 ads in the *NY Times* only emphasize what's missing. Which is none of my business, really—and most definitely out of place after putting you through all that jangled action last week—but under normal sleep-cured conditions & a fairly straight head I'd like to see *Scanlan's* work. Maybe it is, but the vibes I got in NY were somewhat mixed—and the only cure I can see is impossibly drastic.

The fucker *should* work. It's one of the best ideas in the history of journalism. But thus far the focus is missing—or maybe it just seems that way to me; perhaps something missing in my own focus. And I won't argue that, but . . .

19. Donald Goddard was managing editor of *Scanlan's Monthly.*

well, I suspect there's a heavy difference between *Scanlan's* problems, and mine.

But maybe not, and fuck the whole business anyway. I have enough problems with this goddamn one-page *Wallposter* and my slow-boiling sheriff's campaign. Fear & Loathing in the Outback. Fuck them; we will beat them like gongs. Not many months left in this era; not even a year, as I see it, and maybe less. Maybe it's already gone.

Which hardly matters, for now. All I really meant to do here, when I started, was to say that I wish I could have written a better Derby piece . . . and also to advise you to send my cheque to Lynn Nesbit at the International Famous Agency, 1301 Avenue of the Americas, NYC 10019. My advisors have warned me that agents get 10% of *everything*—fair, foul, or otherwise.

Why not? And if ever, in small moments, I might chance to feel a hair guilty for not coughing up a super-organized soul-piece . . . all I have to do is summon up the memory of Sidney[20] booming off, at dusk, to Gallaghers and then to The Garden, hunkered down in the soft back seat of that grey Cadillac with his evil chauffeur and bodyguard. Christ, I asked that surly middleweight fucker if there was any ice in the bucket (in Sidney Zion's office) and he looked at me like it was all he could do to restrain himself from ripping out my floating rib and eating it. I was tempted to Mace the bastard, but instead I backed off and went downstairs to have a Scotch with poor Steadman. Indeed. And, in closing I remain,

Yours for Peace in our
Time . . .
Hunter

TO JIM SILBERMAN, RANDOM HOUSE:

May 17, 1970
Woody Creek, CO

Dear Jim . . .

By now you should certainly have received your copies of the *Wallposter;* I sent them at you from three different angles, hoping that at least one batch would get thru. So I'll proceed on the assumption that you have some notion of what I'm talking about in terms of the Aspen political scene.

Which is suddenly far more complicated—in my own mind & in light of our talk in the Waldorf—than it was just a few weeks ago. The complications arise from the addition of a new and perhaps ulterior motive to my local political action. I've only been back here a few days, but even in that short time I've run

20. Sidney Zion was listed on the *Scanlan's* masthead as Hinckle's coeditor.

sharply afoul of the mixed/motive problem . . . and I have, of course, dealt with it just as sharply; with all the harsh decisiveness of a man not quite sure of his motives.

Rather than bore you with the details, let's focus on the two main problems—which are really only one: Nobody—not even my friends & henchmen—really believes I'm going to run for Sheriff. We've all agreed, thus far, that it's a wonderful fear-joke to keep the greedheads off balance, but I'm not sure what kind of terrible shock-tremors it might send through our "organization" when they realize I'm serious.

It will drive the old liberals into a catatonic funk, and perhaps derail our County Commissioner campaign entirely—because the idea of my running for Sheriff is so incredibly outrageous that it won't go down easily with some of our pragmatic young radicals. But the fatbacks are setting it up for me: A careful spy/monitoring of the Demo & GOP caucuses this week shows that the only two candidates in Nov. are likely to be the incumbent Sheriff and the ex–Chief of Police. And I think I can deal with a 3-way race—forcing the other two dingbats to cannibalize each other's power base.

We'll see. When the fuckers realize I'm serious it will drive them wild. Even my closest allies will hate the idea. It's a lot further down the road than they ever thought I'd try to take them—and they'll do everything possible to keep me from doing it.

But fuck all that. It has to be done. Not because I want to be Sheriff, but because that seems like the best and most dramatic way to destroy the local power structure: Make them understand that Agnew is right, that their worst and most awful fears are about to be confirmed—like a Nigger Mayor in Mississippi, and in fact I'd probably try to get an endorsement from Charles Evers, who strikes me as one of the better human beings walking around these days.[21]

And so much for all that. I'll try to keep abreast of events with a daily diary of sorts—in the interest of history—but in the meantime my hand is being forced, to some extent, by events such as these:

1) I have tentatively agreed with Jann Wenner, editor of *Rolling Stone,* to write a long piece for the *RS* July issue on "Freak Power in Aspen," using my sheriff's campaign as a focus for all the rest. This will tip my hand a little earlier than I'd prefer to have it tipped, and even if I can put the piece off until August it will still put me out on the public hustings too early . . . although I might be able, through artful rhetoric, to dull the shock of my candidacy by means of strange humor and confusion. Ideally, I'd prefer to jump into the race at the very last moment, capping a tidal wave of rumor and speculation that

21. Charles Evers, along with Fannie Lou Hamer and Hodding Carter III, had led the formation of the Mississippi Freedom Democratic Party, which challenged the state's regular slate of racist delegates to the 1964 Democratic National Convention.

will sweep me into office before my opponents have time to recover from the shock.

2) And this one isn't crucial right now, although it may be as soon as it happens: I've told Hughes Rudd at CBS about the chance of my running for sheriff, & he's already planning to do a news/film thing on it . . . and once that happens it will blow the thing wide open. Hughes was out here last summer, and did a piece (which CBS killed) that got his cameraman beaten and his whole crew seized . . . but I think I told you about it. In any case, I suspect he'll come back for his second shot like Attila the Hun on a vengeance trip . . . and once his thing hits the airwaves it will polarize the town completely.

3) But what the hell? #3 is a minor thing; it's tied up with that left-over *Esquire* article on "Gun Control" that I did last year and which Erickson sent back for a rewrite that I never gave them. But now, as it happens, I think I can work a completely new version of that piece into the first section of the Freak Power ms. Because, by a piece of weird luck, I took a weekend out of last fall's Mayoral campaign to go north and spend a few days on a fine, mescaline flavored antelope hunt—deliberately bugging the wardens and other hunters by driving into their midst with a huge red Peace symbol on my car and behaving in a most unorthodox manner for the duration of the hunt (which I attended by means of a special permit, gained in a lottery of the most limited & esoteric nature; only the cream of the crop could even have qualified for that hunt, and when dawn came up on the great Kill-Day I was able to mingle, as it were, with Colorado's special hunting elite. A gang of cheap pigs who were not at all charmed by my style . . .

But that hardly matters, for now. We did well up there; many antelope steaks, and more bent minds than we could righteously handle. Which seems maybe frivolous, but in some small way it made the point that we're also trying to make here in Aspen: That the Rising Tide is a far bigger thing than any ephemeral argument about Peace or Drugs or Hair. We are going to deal with the buggers, head-on & on their own turf, as it were—and beat them. Because they're not smart enough—and besides that, they're Wrong. And I think they know it. Their desperation shows in the madness that caused the killings [of four unarmed antiwar demonstrators] at Kent State—and in the political bottom-feeding that made Agnew vice president.

So it seems only right & reasonable to push the fuckers until they go completely crazy.

Hunter

TO LYNN NESBIT:

The Kentucky Derby story came out so well Thompson told his agent to try to sell it in Hollywood.

May 21, 1970
Woody Creek, CO

Dear Lynn . . .

Here's a ragged copy of the KyDerby piece I did for *Scanlan's.* No clean copy exists—due to circumstances beyond my control at the time. I was locked in that stinking hotel room with a head full of pills & no sleep for 6 days, working at top speed & messengers grabbing each page out of the typewriter just as soon as I finished it. No carbon, no rewrite, no time to even look back on what I'd written earlier.

But what the hell? My main concern now is to get paid for the rotten ordeal. *Because I have no money.* And by my count Hinckle owes me (or *us,* as it were) a total of $1977.27. This would cure most of my really urgent problems—like rent, phone, food bills, etc. I can't imagine Hinckle refusing to pay the tab, so unless you foresee real problems you might consider just sending me a cheque as soon as possible. Like maybe today. Or yesterday. In any case, please let me know on this score. Thanx. . . .

And meanwhile, here's an odd notion that stuck in my head after Carol—far gone in a fit of levity during our phone talk—mentioned something about selling this Derby ordeal as a film of some sort. Which strikes me now as a notion of exceptional merit. No question about it at all: What we have here is a classic of the narrative art—The strange and heart-warming story of a wild-haired English artist and a crazed expatriate Southern journalist hurled into the maw of the heinous Kentucky Derby spectacle. Indeed. Their hopes, their fears, and their final dissolution—against this awful background. I see it as a combination of *Dr. Strangelove* and *Gone With the Wind.*[22] And on that basis I urge you to sell it at once. . . .

The narrative framework is all here, in the article. And much of the rest exists in chunks of background color, social comment and tangent fantasies that had to be cut from the final (*Scanlan's*) version. A film treatment would be no problem, and we could do all the camera work at next year's Derby—if the buggers will let me in. But of course I have wigs for that kind of rude action. . . .

Anyway, I think it's a fine idea. But of course you'll have to read the bare bones ms. (enc.) to see what I mean. No doubt the final (film) product will gross about $30 million—particularly in the midst of a Depression movie-boom. Let me know what you think, and how the offer stacks up. Meanwhile, I'll be waiting—in a maelstrom of debt & anguish—for a check for the *Scanlan's* article. I realize you have certain logistics problems, but with that massive

22. Director Stanley Kubrick's brilliant 1964 movie, *Dr. Strangelove or: How I Learned to Stop Worrying and Love the Bomb,* and director Victor Fleming's classic 1939 epic film adaptation of Margaret Mitchell's Civil War novel, *Gone With the Wind.*

organization at your command I have every faith in your ability to find somebody to cope with this thing.

Thanks,
Hunter

TO JUAN DE ONIS, *THE NEW YORK TIMES:*

Thompson and fellow reporter Juan De Onis had spent a good bit of time together at the Press Club in Rio de Janeiro when both worked in Brazil in 1962–63.

May 21, 1970
Woody Creek, CO

Dear Juan . . .

Sitting here in the foul dawn light of my burning bush & hearing the radio belch out a sound that I finally recognize as "Bossa Nova" . . . with the sun coming up over Woody Creek & Aspen it occurs to me that I've drifted a long, long way from that time when my worst worry in the world was being cut off the tab at Mr. Money or missing out on the invite-list to a Leonel Brizola[23] press conference.

And the reason I mention all that now is the odd notion that you might be able to steer me onto a place where life is still that simple: Maybe Angola, or the south of Chile? Who is the *Times'* stringer in Sardinia?

At the moment I am locked into local politics—to the extent that I am, quite logically, the Alternative Candidate for Sheriff of Pitkin County, Colorado . . . and also the half-publisher of a *Wallposter* that may or may not be the leading edge for a whole new kind of journalism. For good or ill, I have become the Carmine DeSapio[24] of Aspen—using that awful image more for the fact of my day/night Rio-style shades than for any implied corruption. . . .

In fact I've found that booming into politics with a Great White Hammer makes it almost impossible to deal gracefully with Corruption. The cocksuckers don't even want to know my price . . . and in truth I suspect they're counting on Agnew and the McCarran Act[25] to finish me off before I finish them.

23. Leonel Brizola was the arch-leftist, anti-American brother-in-law of Brazilian president Joao Belchoir Marques Goulart, who was overthrown in a 1964 military coup after his economic policies sent the country's inflation rate soaring.

24. Carmine DeSapio was boss in the 1950s of the Society of Tammany, a corrupt but generally effective fraternal organization–cum–political machine that had controlled the New York state Democratic Party since the middle of the nineteenth century. Ironically, DeSapio himself brought about Tammany's downfall—and his own—by reforming its autocratic system in favor of direct elections of local party officials by the rank and file.

25. The McCarran Internal Security Act, passed by the U.S. Congress in 1950 over the veto of President Harry S Truman, drastically curtailed the legal rights of Americans accused of being communists.

And they may be right . . . my stomach for protracted conflict is not quite as strong as it used to be, and I'm beginning to wonder just how strong it really was in the first place. The fucking years flip by like pages off a cheap calendar, and sometimes it's hard to understand how all this savage death-screaming can really amount to much.

Particularly when I think of Joao Goulart & his wife & all those fine ideas he had—& all the time we spent trying to get next to him just long enough for a real quote. But that was in another country, right? And things are different now. Do you have an address for J. Goulart today? I think I'd like to send him a letter.

Or Lou Stein?[26] Weird memories in these morning hours. Let me know if you hear of any salaried post where a man can live on the beach and wear a white Palm Beach suit to work now & then in some warm, hump-happy outpost where the booze is still cheap and the new is still nice and Black & White like it was, for sure, back there in the good old days. Indeed . . .

Sincerely,
Hunter S. Thompson

TO THOMAS E. ROSETTI, NEW YORK POLICE DEPARTMENT:

Thompson had lost his wallet in a Third Avenue bar while in New York to finish his Kentucky Derby article for Scanlan's.

May 23, 1970
Woody Creek, CO

Thomas E. Rosetti
Property Clerk
Police Dept.
City of New York
New York 13, NY

Dear Mr. Rosetti:

Thanks very much for your notice of May 20 (File No. 70M19236). I trust this refers to my wallet, which I reported "Lost or Stolen" in a phone call from the Royalton Hotel to the desk officer at the (NYC) 18th Precinct at approximately 3:30 a.m. on Sunday, May 10. The wallet actually disappeared a few hours earlier that evening, while I was trying to watch the Knicks-Lakers game on TV in a bar on Third Ave. That's when I noticed it, anyway. But I don't suppose those details matter much at this stage.

So here is the description you asked for. The wallet is small, black leather with a card holder & a money clip, about the size of a pack of king-size ciga-

26. Lou Stein was a mutual friend of Thompson and De Onis when all three worked as Latin America correspondents based in Brazil.

rettes. It contains—or contained when it disappeared—between $15 to $25 in cash & an American Express card #69 043 670 898 and a Carte Blanche card, Number unknown, but containing my signature. There was a Colorado driver's license with my photo on it, a Blue Cross card, Overseas Richfield (Sinclair) credit card and, if I remember correctly, a second Colo driver's license *not* containing my photo. There were also some business cards (*National Observer*) and several other items including a PBA press badge & a stockholder's card from Irving Lundborg & Co. in San Francisco. And my auto registrations: For a '64 Volvo wagon and a '57 Chevy sedan.

That should do it, I think. And if you can put yourself in my position for a moment, I'm sure you'll understand how much I appreciate getting your notice. Getting out of NY & back to Colorado with no ID & no credit cards was a real bastard of a trip. Please send the wallet COD by the quickest & safest method—and if you have a moment I'd appreciate a word about how you found it. Thanks again for your efforts.

Sincerely,
Hunter S. Thompson

TO DON GODDARD, *SCANLAN'S MONTHLY*:

Scanlan's *managing editor Donald Goddard had announced he was leaving the magazine after only four issues.*

May 27, 1970
Woody Creek, CO

Dear Don . . .

Thanx for the note. I checked with the Bank of Aspen & they said it's OK for you to keep the lighter. You'll also be happy to hear that I got a note from the NYPolice dept., saying they'd busted a junkie with my wallet in his possession. The remains will be sent to me, they say, upon proper identification—of whatever the freak didn't consume in his short-lived frenzy.

Well . . . so be it. That was one of the worst trips of my life, anyway, so what the hell?

My Sheriff's campaign has gone to the back burner—temporarily—due to heavy pressures on me to run against Wayne Aspinal for his 11-term seat in Congress. Hell, why not? Run the old buggers to earth & rip out their bowels. This may be the year of the Rising Tide—and I'd hate to miss it.

Either way, my next five or six months look like a strung-out replay of my last five or six days in NY. I limped back home & slept for about a week, then leaped out of bed like a cougar & began hounding the postmaster for money/cheques from *Scanlan's*. The expense cheque arrived a few days ago, & I spent most of it on a clutch of transplant Bristlecone Pines for the front yard. Since that junkie stole my American Express card & ran up frightful bills in strange places like Louisville, Ky., I don't have to worry about paying those things off. Thank god for that.

On the other hand, Warren hasn't sent me any copies of the magazine, so I can't be sure my Derby piece even got printed. This would cause me certain difficulties in local financial circles, and to avoid this kind of problem I have set the International Famous Agency on Sidney [Zion], with instructions to snap his femurs if he hesitates for even a moment in the matter of fee-payment. I can't look back on that effort with anything but shame & horror, but under the circumstances, I insist on full payment.

Which is neither here nor there, for now. I suppose you're off for London & a new life selling tacos. God only knows how *Scanlan's* NY office will hold together now. I was quite depressed by the deranged & un-focused chaos of the place—& I told Warren that I saw your departure as a very ugly & ominous event. I hope he can pull that goddamn monster together very soon, but in truth I don't see much hope. I keep having visions of Sidney being borne off toward "the Garden" in that grey Cadillac with that evil-looking bodyguard at the wheel. Awful . . . awful . . .

Anyway, thanks again for the very human help that kept me from running totally amok during that hideous scene—and it seems even more hideous now, because I never managed to write that thing the way I wanted to . . . so the whole effort begins to look, in retrospect, like a horrible joke of some kind. Maybe Ralph's drawings will pull the thing out. I hope so, because the writing is lame bullshit.

Dealing with Ralph made the whole rotten trip worthwhile for me, in some kind of odd sense. I liked the bastard immensely, and his awkward sensitivity made me see, once again, some of the rot in this country that I've been living with for so long that I could only see it, now, through somebody else's fresh eye.

In all, it was not a bad trip. Although it was a hell of a lot more than I bargained for, in too many ways. But again, what the hell? I wish you whatever luck you need back in the olde country, and when I flee across the water—probably this fall—I'll make an effort to track you down & buy you a Guinness under better conditions than we had in NY. Send me an address when you get one. And in the meantime I'll be after Ralph to draw us a cover for the *Aspen Wallposter.* Maybe he'd like a job in Washington. Hell, every new Congressman should have a personal artist on his staff.

OK for now. I have to get back to my politics. Ciao . . .

Hunter

TO HUGHES RUDD, CBS NEWS:

Deep into his campaign for sheriff, Thompson pondered running for the U.S. Congress.

May 27, 1970
Woody Creek, CO

Dear Hughes . . .

The madness is on us for real, I think. Between now & November the deal will go down on all fronts. Let me give you a taste of how weird things really are: Tonight, in the midst of plotting my campaign for Sheriff, I got a call from my local political nerve-center with the word that I should abandon the Sheriff's campaign and tackle Wayne Aspinal for Congress. And it's not such a bad idea in these twisted times—although in truth I'd prefer to be Sheriff. But in the course of the next 2 wks I'll be checking with the Colo. Vote-power people, & we'll see how it looks. Frankly, I'd prefer the Senate—but 2 yrs in the lower house might hone my instincts a bit for '72. Selah.

The harsh truth of the matter, as I see it, is that the local liberals have suddenly understood that I'm serious about running for Sheriff—& that I'll probably win. So I told them I'd seriously consider running against Aspinal, too—without withdrawing from the Sheriff's race. This will send a lot of people back to the law-books, but Colorado law is so weird that my chances of running for both offices at the same time are about 50–50. And I see no reason why I shouldn't whipsaw the buggers if the law allows it.

Meanwhile, you could do me a tremendous favor by putting your research dept. to work on what will surely be a simple problem from a vantage-point in NY, but which looks like a bastard for me. To wit: I want to know the name (& current address, if possible) of the man who quit the Justice Dept. and became the Chief Cop at Woodstock. He is credited, in underground circles, with keeping that scene under control—and I think I could use his wisdom out here, inre: the Sheriff's campaign. I also plan to check with Charles Evers for a quote about how it feels to be a Nigger Mayor in Mississippi. He (Evers) is the only politician in the nation I can really identify with right now. . . .

On other fronts, I called you about 2 wks ago—just before taking off to "cover" the Kentucky Derby for *Scanlan's Monthly.* But they said you were out of the country. And for all I know you might be long gone, by now, to some O. Henry[27] kind of post in Panama City. I hope not—because if even half of the horrors now shaping up here actually come true, I'll need some human coverage. The idea of challenging Aspinal in a Farm/Ranch district is so awful that I hate to even think about it—and I wouldn't, under normal circumstances, but with the way things are going I suspect this may be the last election we'll have in this county for a while. And I'd hate to think I let the chance go by. Probably the wisest course would be to seize the Sheriff's ring here, for now, then put my act together for a Congress challenge in '72. But I sense a frenzy building—

27. O. Henry was the pseudonym of renowned short-story writer William Sydney Porter, who began spinning tales noted for their surprise endings while he was imprisoned in Ohio for embezzlement.

a Rising Tide, as it were, and if this looks like the time to sweep the Old Fuckers out of the saddle, well . . . why wait? But the chances of *anyone* beating Aspinal in Western Colorado are about on par with Charles Evers' chances of beating Stennis in Mississippi.[28]

In any case, it would make a weird book; and in the midst of a quick & brutal swing through NY last week I had a few ales at the Waldorf bar with Jim Silberman, and he seemed to feel that I should focus my long-delayed book on *my own* political scene, rather than keep on suffering with the useless, abstract bullshit that has hung me up for the past two years.

But I guess, in the end—with a depression coming on—I could get by a bit easier on a Congressman's $42.5K nut than I could on the Sheriff's $8000. And with the stakes that much higher, combined with the sight of Aspinal's soft underbelly, well . . . at least it's worth checking out.

Meanwhile, however, I hope you can check that Woodstock (ex–Justice Dept.) cop for me. I'd like to talk with the man & get some working ideas—just in case I can't beat Aspinal & have to settle for Sheriff. OK for now . . . and thanx:

Hunter

TO PAT OLIPHANT, *THE DENVER POST*:

May 27, 1970
Woody Creek, CO

Dear Pat . . .

Just thought you'd like to know the Kentucky Derby action was a nightmare of such massive & horrible proportions that even now, at a safe distance, I find myself loath to even think about it. But the "story" got done—at fantastic cost to *Scanlan's*—and the English illustrator they sent, Ralph Steadman, was absolutely first-class. If you haven't seen his stuff you definitely should (*Private Eye,* London *Times,* etc.)—he's better than almost anybody currently working in the U.S. In fact there's nothing like his style over here. His work makes people like Searle & Levine[29] seem like old eunuchs. The *NY Times* offered him a job, but wouldn't use any of his work. A fine fellow. We spent 5 days in Louisville and barely escaped with our psychic lives. Sorry you couldn't make it, but in retrospect I'd ask you again. That was definitely your kind of scene. And that kind of graphic journalism is a completely un-tapped vein in Amerika. All we need is somebody to pay for it. Yeah . . .

28. Democrat John Stennis of Mississippi was elected to the U.S. Senate in 1947 and kept the seat until 1989. As Armed Services Committee chairman, he backed U.S. involvement in Vietnam but called for limits on the president's powers to commit troops.

29. Illustrator David Levine was known for his pen-and-ink caricatures in *The New York Review of Books*.

Anyway, I'll be over there around June 4–5–6, to put our next issue of the *Aspen Wallposter* together at the new print shop in Boulder. We've doubled our size, tripled our costs, taken on ads, and decided to go full bore against the grain in this time of despair & recession. I think we are about to clear the decks in this crippled, death-haunted country, and for precisely that reason I'm having a hard time deciding whether to run for Sheriff of Aspen (which I think I can win fairly easily) or kicking out all the jams and running for Aspinal's seat in Congress.

So when I get over to Denver next weekend I think I should talk to a few people like Craig Barnes[30] & Gebhart & Maytag—just to see how they're thinking. And I'd definitely like to have a beer with you, if you have a loose hour or so. So if you get a weird Emergency call from the Owl Farm, don't worry. It's only me. It took about 2 hours to get your phone number last time, and now I've lost it—but what the hell? See you when I get over there.

Hunter

TO MIKE MOORE, *SKIERS' GAZETTE:*

Skiers' Gazette*'s Mike Moore helped Thompson put together advertisements for the* Aspen Wallposters.

May 30, 1970
Woody Creek, CO

Dear Mike . . .

Tom's in the hospital & this fuckawful notion of putting an ad together has driven me wild. I tried seriously for a while—witness the enclosed sheep foto with attached excerpts—but that looks like shit so I thought I'd just send it along with the word to do whatever you think is right. All this sales/advertising bullshit that goes along with being a "publisher" is driving me crazy. One of the few really fine things about being a writer is that you put your product in a fucking envelope & send it off and maybe the check comes back & sometime later you may or may not read the swill. But by then it hardly matters. Fuck them. We're a nation of pigs & we get what we deserve—*Hee-Haw,* Salems & Wide Track Pontiacs.

I was thinking about doing a page or so of copy for the *Wallposter* ads, but probably you should just run this letter instead—with whatever layout fits.

So why should anybody send us $25 to get 12 issues of the *Aspen Wallposter* in 12 fine mailing tubes? Well . . . because that's what it costs us, more or less, to make the bastard exist. We—Tom Benton and I—are using the thing

30. Craig Barnes was a member of the board of directors of the Colorado chapter of the liberal lobbying group Common Cause.

about half & half for political/journalism purposes. If we can sell enough copies to make the *Wallposter* pay for itself we can give enough away to create some kind of working unity on Aspen's political front. This Valley is full of people who came here for reasons other than to turn the whole place back into a nazi-thinking condominium-complex & make it a safe & saleable resort for the Texas Cavaliers & the Atlanta Ski Club. There is a hell of a huge difference between skiing as a sport—or even as a lifestyle—and skiing as an industry, a boom-time fad like golf or bowling. Or beating up Peace Freaks on your lunch hour.

But fuck skiing. All it is, in Aspen, is a swollen sugar-tit for a gang of aging nazis who are not the local establishment. The *Wallposter* is the voice of Aspen's counter-culture—the people who last fall came within six (6) votes of electing a 29-year-old bike racing head/lawyer as Mayor (The '69 Joe Edwards campaign). And before 1970 is out they may—or may not—seize control of the town & the whole valley, or at least enough control to short-circuit the greedheads & land-rapers who've descended on the place like a plague of water rats. The conflict has already degenerated into dynamitings, street-violence and a sense of almost constant political crisis that never lets up, not even in the off-seasons. On one side are the cops and the Mayor and the County Commissioners, along with local realtors and corporate land developers from Chicago & LA & Texas—and even NY & Boston. These people see Aspen as a *resort,* and they want to *sell* it. And they *are.* Indeed—for the past 20 years they've been selling harder than New Orleans street-pimps.

The other side is a weird mix of locals, liberals, freaks, dropouts, ranchers, heads, geeks & other less commercially oriented types who see Aspen as a place to live—not to sell—a refuge, of sorts, from the same kind of rotten urban madness that these scum-sucking developers are trying to sell here in Aspen. The town is already faced with horrors like smog, parking-problems & sewage in the drinking water. The Aspen Ski Corp. has threatened to put a limit on lift-tickets—raising the specter of $100 a day ski-tourists standing in the lift-lines from dawn until noon, then being turned away "because of the quota."

The summer looks more and more like Coney Island. A Holiday Inn is already here—right next to the route of the new 4-lane highway in town—and there's also a Minnie Pearl Chicken Palace going up, just across the street from Stein Erickson's ski shop. Selah.

That's about it. I see I've already run too long. And in truth I'd prefer to run *Wallposter* excerpts for ad purposes—instead of this watery bullshit that reads, in retrospect, like a cheap imitation of even the most left-handed gibberish in any of the three *Wallposter* issues we've done so far. Probably I should describe them, but right now I'm not up to it. Today, after all, is Memorial Day (dawn is just coming up) and Sheriff [Earl] Whitmire has told the city fathers that he & nine others are going to be killed before the clock strikes midnight—by a gang of motorcycle huns from Ely, Nevada, a drug-crazed swarm of Hell's Angels types called the Savage Explorers. Whitmire—my opponent in the fall election—says they're going to blow up the courthouse, the bank & Guido's restaurant, then kill all the local police & their civic soul-brothers. And after that, rape the Priest's daughter . . .

Wonderful. Who could ask for a better show on this fine American Holiday? I think I'll load up on mescaline & drive into town for the action—lock into a ringside seat by a window in the Jerome Hotel tavern and watch the annual police riot. Like last July 4—curfews, posses, jeeps full of drunken cowboys with shotguns, local realtors & sheepherders wearing Notre Dame football jackets ganging up on young longhairs, huge dynamite blasts on Little Nell & handgrenades in the Woodlander bar . . .

Why not? Get it on while there's still time. Because when I'm sheriff of this county we're not going to stand for this nonsense. No more of these atavistic spectacles. Memorial Day will be a different scene next year: My deputies will be supervising the planting of sugar cane in all the high pastures above Hunter Creek, Owl Creek, Woody Creek, & all those lush acres now held by Aspen-Wildcat. Then a record fall harvest—by teams of trained Weathermen. The contract is fixed. History will prove me out, or at least absolve me.

And the *Aspen Wallposter* will provide a very fine and vivid historical record of the events between now and then. Indeed. Today's Pig is Tomorrow's Bacon. (Or maybe today's—so let's end this wretched advertisement and get into town for the Butchery.)

OK for now. And don't forget, folks—*Wallposter* #4 is due on June 10: A massive, double-size issue, jam-packed with obscenity, treachery, dementia and horrible news of every description—all of it true, which makes it even worse. In closing, I remain yours for Creative Law Enforcement . . .

Hunter S. Thompson

TO RALPH STEADMAN:

"The Kentucky Derby Is Decadent and Depraved" launched a remarkable correspondence as well as a brilliant collaboration over three decades and beyond.

June 2, 1970
Woody Creek, CO

Dear Ralph . . .

You filthy twisted pervert I'll beat your ass like a gong for that drawing you did of me. You bastard . . . stay out of Kentucky from now on. And Colorado too. . . . Fuck you!

And so much for that. I just saw the June *Scanlan's*. The article is useless, except for the flashes of style & tone it captures—but I suspect you & I are the only ones who can really appreciate it. The drawings were fine, although I think they fucked up the layout—as usual—quite badly. They also cut about one-third of the article, in addition to the 4000 or so words that Don & I cut in NY. In all, a bad show, & I'm sorry it wasn't better. Maybe next time. I'd like nothing better than to work with you on one of these strange binges again, & to that end I'll tell my agent to bill us as a package—for good or ill. Nothing binding, but certainly a notion worth trying. The only saving grace of that Derby scene was having you around to keep me on my rails. What are you up to now? How did NY pan out? What next?

In a week or so I'll send you some photos of our main LBJ-style antagonist in the fall election. Also my opponents for sheriff. With fotos and some text, maybe you can rush up some drawings for the *Aspen Wallposter.* In fact we'd use either one of those Nixon drawings right now—if not as a cover, then as a big inside drawing. Issue #4, now going to press, is double-size & folded—4 pgs, in other words; a cover, a back & 2 inside pages. We need good art. Pat Oliphant from *The Denver Post* has said he'll do a cover for us. I'll see him this weekend in Denver, at a formation-meeting for the Radical Journalists Union, or some such. He said he was looking for you in London that same weekend when you were in Louisville with me. Strange Irony—since he was the first artist I called to work with me on the story. He said you were one of the few artists in England he wanted to meet. . . .

OK for now. I'll send you the fotos & other data for the drawings I mentioned—but in the meantime, send us anything you can't sell. Or for that matter, anything you feel would be a good sort of interior advertisement for you inre: the U.S. press. We're constantly sending *Wallposters* to editors in NY, SF, LA, etc. So a heavy weird drawing in the *Wallposter* might get you a good assignment somewhere. Or maybe not. I can't say for sure. Why not get *Private Eye* or the *Times* to send you over here to cover my Sheriff's campaign—a Steadman-eye view of small town politics in the American Rockies? In fact that sounds good enough to send to my agent. If you haven't picked up anybody to represent you, let me know & I'll see if Lynn Nesbit from IFA wants to handle your act. She's about as good as they come, I'm told. She has Tom Wolfe & that sort of thing. Even me. So let me know—on all fronts.

Ciao,
Hunter

TO HERB CAEN, *SAN FRANCISCO CHRONICLE:*

The San Francisco Chronicle's *venerable Herb Caen had coined the term "beatnik" in his column of April 2, 1958.*

June 19, 1970
Woody Creek, CO

Dear Herb . . .

Here's a sample of what, as far as I know, is a totally new form of journalism. At least in terms of graphics—and in terms of content, too, if you consider that we've decided to completely ignore all libel statutes and beat the bastards like gongs at every turn. The Meat Possum Press is judgement-proof—and exists, in fact, as a vehicle for new forms of local political action—including my campaign for Sheriff this fall. I expect to be elected without much trouble. On a platform of "Creative Law Enforcement." (And as a matter of fact if you have an address for Sgt. Sunshine—Richard Burgess, I think—I'd like to check & see if he has any ideas.) Otherwise, I hope to get some wisdom from Wes Pomeroy, the main cop at Woodstock—and others of the same ilk.

But in truth the *Wallposter* is more fun than politics. But in a fairly serious vein I think the #4 *Wallposter* is a completely new form of journalism. Numbers 1, 2 & 3 were derivative, in a sense—from all kinds of sources, but most recently & specifically from the "*Ramparts* Wallposter" that Hinckle & his crew put out at the '68 Demo Convention in Chicago. So Warren is really "the Father of the Modern *Wallposter.*" Selah.

And so much for credits—for whatever they're worth in these rotten times. No point in explaining the details of this queer experiment; a quick scan of the first four issues, in order, will show you how we've coped with the problems. Or failed to cope with them. After #3 we were banished from Aspen's only job printing shop—which is owned by the *Aspen Times,* oddly enough—and we moved our printing-action to Boulder, where the union-shop prices were so high that we had to sell ads to make the nut. And if you look very closely at the top of *WP* #4, on the cover, you'll see how the printers (or the pressmen) sabotaged us inre: the "Impeach Nixon" line above the target. At first they refused to print it, but the union business agent in Denver said they had to—because it was legal—so they went back and censored us, in their own subtle way, at the last moment. The owner of the printing house said he was sorry, & explained that the pressmen thought "Impeach" meant "Assassinate," & they botched it because they felt it was wrong and "unpatriotic." Which says quite a bit, I think, about Freedom of the Press in middle amerika . . . and organized Labor, too. Particularly since all it said was "Impeach Nixon."

Anyway, I thought I'd send this along—for good or ill. To prove, if nothing else, that journalism is still at least half-alive in the great American Outback. For four issues, anyway. I can't guarantee #5—not even if we have to print in San Francisco. Which may happen. Maybe at the *Chronicle* plant, eh? Check it out & let me know.

Thanks . . .
Hunter S. Thompson

TO GEORGE MADSEN, *ASPEN TIMES:*

Local radio deejay and Aspen Times *reporter George Madsen had sent Thompson a letter riddled with spelling errors questioning how he earned a living and implying that he must be selling drugs.*

June 23, 1970
Woody Creek, CO

Dear George . . .

Gee willikers, you sure are curious. Do you really "wonter" (sic) where I get my "bread"? Well, George, I wonter too, sometimes . . . and maybe we can talk about it one of these days on your Ratio Progrim (sic). You bring your questions & I'll bring mine, and we can hold hands while we hash things out. You interest me, George. I wonter about your mind . . . and I'd particularly like to ask you about what you do with that photo of "Jilly" that you say you "keep hidden until after the kids go to bed." God damn, George, I bet you're just a king-hell bundle of fun after midnight.

Maybe I couldn't tell you too much on the ratio . . . but I could sure as hell teach you how to spell "establishement" (sic). People tell me I have a talent for teaching old hacks and shitkickers how to spell . . . but I doubt if I could be much help to you on the subject of how I make my "bread." Because that's a world you'll never know, George . . . never in hell. I could show you a mirror; or some samples of your own fine prose . . . or maybe some Jimson Weed. I get the feeling that maybe your head's a little tense. Perhaps we could do up some acid and get heavy on your Ratio Progrm (sic). Thank about it, George, and let me know.

Sincerely,
Hunter

TO JIM SILBERMAN, RANDOM HOUSE:

Thompson revealed to his book editor that his campaign for sheriff was really just a means to an end of the "Death of the American Dream" concept.

July 6, 1970
Woody Creek, CO

Dear Jim . . .

Things are proceeding as planned—or almost: We now have *two* Freak Power candidates for County Commissioner this fall, instead of one. This is posing some very harsh strategy problems, strikingly reminiscent of the national Demos' dilemma (sp?) with, say, McGovern & Ted Kennedy. Our McGovern (city councilman Ned Vare—see enc.) can't win . . . and our Kennedy, a sure winner, is swearing he won't run. My own notion, for now, is to force/coax/compel our Kennedy into the CC race—and then, without consulting him, run my Sheriff's campaign so far to the Crazy Left of him that he will look like a fine moderate by comparison. (The only problem here is that some people think I might *win* by going Left/Crazy—that in fact it will take that kind of campaign to mobilize the young/drug/fun-hog vote, which is clearly the biggest bloc—by at least 2–1.)

So, rather than try to run a two-track, dual-level effort—with me catching the left/crazier and our Kennedy-type holding the liberals—we may decide, by autumn, to run the whole thing on straight freak-power, leaving the liberals to suck wind. Our decision on this will be fateful, and indeed at some point I might be faced with a serious insurrection inre: my Sheriff's campaign—which the local liberals still refuse to take seriously. But when they understand that I really intend to run, they're going to freak out . . . and at that point we'll all have to decide just how valuable they are. (And in fact they're already useless, *to me,* but I hate to think that I might—by running some kind of bull-headed & egotistical Freak Power campaign for sheriff—destroy our chances of electing the Kennedy-type in the CC race.)

We'll see. This worries me—particularly since the final chunk of my book depends on my running for sheriff. It would make me feel a bit shitty to get rich off the shattered remains of our action here . . . and the only solution, as I see it, is to run a Sheriff's campaign so wild & weird as to guarantee my defeat—in 1970—but which will seem, in 1975, like a fine and reasonable effort. In retrospect. This will be difficult, but I think I can manage it.

In the meantime, I plan to write the first third of the book around last fall's Joe Edwards campaign, laying the groundwork and background for the Savage Campaign of '70. And I assume, of course, that upon receipt of this portion (one third) of the book, you will instantly send me $5000. I am putting it together right now, in fact, in the skeleton form of an article for *Rolling Stone.* Carey McWilliams has asked for a piece on the Sheriff's campaign, but I hesitate to say I'll do it for him, in light of the book action. What do you think? Send word. . . .

Thanx,
Hunter

TO RALPH STEADMAN:

Steadman had agreed to draw President Nixon for the next Aspen Wallposter.

July 6, 1970
Woody Creek, CO

Dear Ralph . . .

Indeed. Send the Nixon drawings as soon as possible, *airmail.* All you have to do is submit them to what we in the colonies call a *copy camera* (the *Times* probably has a dozen of them on the premises) and send us 8 × 10 *copies.* That way, you never have to let the originals out of your hands. (But if you've already sent the others, don't worry—we'll have them copied and return them unharmed.) In any case, we want the Nixon art for #5, which is now in the works—so make haste!!!

While I think of it, Pat Oliphant—*The Denver Post*'s political cartoonist—says hello. He's coming up with his family this weekend for a stay, & to do some Aspen drawings for us. Maybe I told you . . . ??? . . . but he was the first artist I called when I got the idea about doing the Derby piece. But he couldn't handle it because he had to go to a cartoonists' convention in *London.* And when he got back he lamented the fact that he hadn't met *you.* He wasn't sure where you were . . . until I told him about the Derby & he saw the drawings. Very weird. . . . He's very big over here (Pulitzer Prize, etc.) & says you're the best in England, that Scarfe[31] stole all he knows from you, etc. . . . But I straightened him out & told him what you were really like.

As for *Scanlan's,* Warren has been mumbling something about sending me to Australia to do a piece about the kangaroo slaughter . . . & I said OK, but I wanted you along to do the art. If you push the Alaska tangent from your end, we can probably work up a dual assignment out of it somewhere. I also suggested a series of Thompson-Steadman visits to "sacred American institutions"—like the Super Bowl, Labor Day in Detroit, Mardi Gras, etc. . . . we'll see what happens.

Inre: the other (local antagonist) drawings, I'm still looking for a clutch of decent photos to send you. It's imperative that your drawings *resemble* the monster we are going up against. We intend to make heavy use of your drawing—not only as a *Wallposter* cover, but also for street-art. I'll send details when I get the right photos. Very soon . . .

Your thing with the *Times* sounds fine. Are they letting you run loose and vicious? Heath[32] seems like perfect fodder. I think you are heading for a sort of Nixon-era over there. Good luck . . .

I'm also enclosing *Wallposter* #4, which lists you as chief of the London bureau. We have plenty of extras, so if you know anybody who runs a bookstore, let me know and I'll send you some *Wallposters* for sale in London.

And . . . as a closing note, you'll get a boot out of knowing that I'm trying to sell our Derby nightmare as a screenplay. No luck, so far, but I've just started trying. I'll keep you posted.

Ciao . . .
Hunter

P.S. Jim, my youngest brother, is living out here with me now & says hello. He's the one you *didn't* draw. . . .

31. British artist Gerald Scarfe was known for his magazine illustrations, particularly of his friends the Beatles, such as his sketchy portrait of the band for the cover of the September 22, 1967, issue of *Time* magazine.

32. Conservative Party leader Edward Heath became prime minister of Great Britain in 1970. He brought Britain into the Common Market and instituted austerity measures against inflation. He was turned out of office in 1974.

TO LARRY O'BRIEN, DEMOCRATIC NATIONAL COMMITTEE:

Back in 1964 Thompson had written to Lawrence O'Brien, then a White House aide to President Lyndon Johnson, asking to be considered for the governorship of American Samoa—and to his surprise had received a serious and courteous reply. Shortly after the 1968 election, O'Brien had been named chairman of the Democratic National Committee.

July 7, 1970
Woody Creek, CO

Dear Larry O'Brien . . .

Your last letter—rejecting my application for the Governorship of American Samoa—still cuts to the quick when I read it. And I'd forgotten all about you, except for that one foul blow, until I saw you tonight on TV—in what has to stand as one of the most wretched & ineffectual uses of free network time in the history of television.

You came off worse than Nixon, and that's not easy. All it did—for me and all of my friends who watched—was confirm our sad conviction that the Democratic Party is doomed to extinction. I say this as an experienced politician. Last fall I was campaign manager for a 29-year-old Freak Power candidate for Mayor of Aspen. Beginning on October 1, we mounted a whirlwind registration campaign (2 wks before our candidate decided to run), and we lost the election—to a state GOP committeewoman—by only six votes. We did this despite active opposition from the incumbent (Democratic) mayor, the one-owner local media-cartel & all local Demo functionaries. Now, looking forward to November '70, we're entirely confident of beating both the GOP & the Democrats in the crucial County Commissioner race.

In this context, and against this very active background, your presentation tonight of the "Democrats' Case" against Nixon seems almost as lame and irrelevant as the Humphrey-style bullshit we get from the *local* Democrats, whose once-dominant influence has withered so badly since 1964 that they are now out-numbered 4–1 by Independents & 2–1 by Republicans.

Meanwhile, we have no trouble getting new voters to register—as Independents—and to vote for the kind of candidates who once might have run as Democrats. If I were you I would ponder this kind of development, particularly in light of the upcoming 18-year-old vote. How many students can George Meany[33] deliver?

But what the hell? It's a waste of time, I think, to be writing this kind of letter . . . and in fact I began it as a sort of joke, harking back to those days when

33. George Meany was president of the American Federation of Labor–Congress of Industrial Organizations (AFL-CIO) from 1955 to 1979.

you still had enough humor in you to cope with my application for the Governorship of American Samoa in the same spirit that led me to write it. And it seemed terribly sad, tonight, to watch you sitting there like a tired old ward-heeler, presiding over film-clips of JFK.

I can't even wish you good luck, because I honestly believe that the best thing that can happen to the Democratic Party is for the whole goddamn thing to simply disappear. As a gang of impotent relics, you people are blocking the road. There is a hell of a lot of energy waiting to be unleashed on the Nixon mob, but men like you & Humphrey are never going to tap it. So why don't you get the hell out of the way & let us get on with the job?

Sincerely,
Hunter S. Thompson

TO *THE POLICE CHIEF:*

The Police Chief *was a monthly magazine for cops.*

July 8, 1970
Woody Creek, CO

The Police Chief
1319 18th St. N.W.
Washington, D.C.

Gentlemen:

I would like to subscribe to *The Police Chief.* Please send me the annual rates at once, or—if possible—start my subscription immediately and bill me. Time is a factor, since I am currently running for the office of County Sheriff, and friends have told me that *The Police Chief* magazine might be a great help to me while campaigning.

Thank you,
Hunter S. Thompson
Chief Magistrate
Box 37
Woody Creek, Colo.
81656

TO NICHOLAS VON HOFFMAN, *THE WASHINGTON POST:*

Left-leaning Washington Post *Style section writer Nicholas von Hoffman had claimed in an article for the* New American Review *that after the* Post *ran his particularly harsh column decrying the April 30, 1970, U.S.–South Vietnamese invasion of Cambodia, the Nixon administration had tried to co-opt him by soliciting his views at an "impromptu" meeting—set up by White House press secretary Ronald Ziegler with the president's domestic policy adviser, John Ehrlichman, who, von Hoffman wrote, ended their conversation by telling him: "We're counting on leaders like yourself to keep things calm."*

July 9, 1970
Woody Creek, CO

Dear Nicholas von Hoffman . . .

In the wake of tonight's Board Meeting, with the other members gone wild outside on fire and strange drugs, it is not an easy thing for me to sit down here & inform you by mail that tonite you were voted . . . yes . . . get ready . . . the New Chief of the *Aspen Wallposter*'s Washington Bureau. The salary is $96,000 per annum—payable when the Meat Possum Press Ltd. (our parent organization) goes public & net stock sales reach $500,000. In the meantime, we have a man who will co-sign your loans free of charge, for almost any amount.

The duties of the Washington Bureau Chief are commensurate with the salary. Your only task—once your appointment is confirmed—will be to pass on occasional rumors & libels too heinous for publication anywhere else. The *Wallposter* is judgement-proof, and we intend to keep it that way. I'm enclosing #4, the most recent issue, and any others I can find. As you see, by the masthead, we are rapidly expanding our staff. Tonight we fired both the LA & SF bureau chiefs—& we had good reasons. "T. M. Goddard" is the pseudonym of a San Francisco lawyer gone mad on cocaine; and Oscar Acosta, our man in LA, has not been rational since he was defeated, last month, in his campaign for the office of Sheriff. Warren Hinckle has agreed to re-organize the ruins of our SF hq., and Dennis Hopper will take over LA. The NY bureau chief will be fired tomorrow. Indeed, he was due for the axe tonight, but the meeting went out of control before we could cope with that matter. Two of the directors went down to the river-bridge with a case of dynamite, and Pat Oliphant—who signed on today as Illustrator in Residence—has gone up on the mesa to shoot bats with a .410. And his wife, they say, has gone after him with a handful of horse tranquilizers.

In any case, I want to welcome you to the team & finish this letter so I can get some sleep. We lead active lives out here in the West; our office operates 25 hours a day & you can rest assured that our facilities will be made available to you whenever you check in. Our next issue will be going to press in a week or so, and unless we hear from you at once your appointment will be realized on the masthead. As for filing, my only query for now concerns Ray Price, Nixon's speechwriter. Is he still there? Is he alive? The last time I saw him he was losing badly at liar's dice with Pat Buchanan . . . and I worry about him.

In closing, allow me to congratulate you once again on your appointment to the far-flung *Wallposter* staff. Your salary will begin piling up the moment we hear from you.

Sincerely,
Hunter S. Thompson
Editorial Director
Aspen Wallposter

TO CARRIE PETERSON, WJZ-TV13:

The free Rolling Stones concert that drew 300,000 to California's Altamont Speedway on December 6, 1969, had turned deadly when a group of Hell's Angels hired to provide security for the band went berserk and beat a young black fan to death, allegedly for brushing against one of their motorcycles.

July 14, 1970
Woody Creek, CO

Carrie Peterson
Contact WJZ-TV13
Television Hill
Baltimore, MD 21211

Dear Miss Peterson . . .

Thanks for your letter & your interest in my Hell's Angels book. Random House was correct in saying that I am "presently not appearing to discuss (the) book"—mainly because I've had nothing to do with the Angels since I finished writing about them, and I think it would sound a bit silly for me to get propped up on TV and try to sound wise and/or hip on a subject I'm no longer qualified to talk about.

As for East Coast bike-gang "experts," I don't know any of them either. Several years ago I talked briefly to some people from a gang called the "Pagans," from the Washington/Baltimore area . . . and they were very interested in picking up hints on how to act like Hell's Angels. But I couldn't help them much, and still can't. As a matter of fact I became very tired of being cast in the role of a PR man for the Angels, and that's why I stopped talking about them—in public or anywhere else.

Since Altamont, however (Dec '69), I've found myself defending what I wrote from time to time—on the grounds that what I wrote in '66/'67 was a blueprint for what happened in '69—and that aspect of the book is the only one that interests me now. What I said then was that the Hell's Angels and all their ilk were the vanguard of an Agnew-style constituency—a new breed of Brownshirts, as it were—and now, three years later, I believe that far more strongly than I did when I wrote it. Both the Weathermen and the Hard-Hats are blood-cousins to the Angels . . . and if you feel like talking about *this* aspect of the book on TV, I wouldn't mind having a shot at it.

I get to NY now & then, and occasionally to Washington, but at the moment I'm locked in here trying to finish a new book for RH. Beyond that, I'll be running for sheriff of Aspen in the fall . . . and right now I'm trying to put my campaign platform together. (Which suddenly reminds me that one of my platform consultants lives in Falls Church, Va., so perhaps a trip east might work out. . . .) Anyway, I have no idea what's involved. We'd all be better off if you contacted my agent, Lynn Nesbit, at the International Famous Agency (jesus, that sounds awful—but those fuckers are agents for the Grateful Dead, too . . .).

From my own POV, I'd just as soon come east and rave on TV almost anytime between now & Sept—if only because I could justify the trip for various other reasons. But September and October will be busy months here, and after that I won't be doing any traveling until maybe late November—depending on the outcome of the local election.

So what the hell? If any of this interests you, check with Lynn & let me know. If not, good luck with whoever you can dig up.

Sincerely,
Hunter S. Thompson

TO RALPH STEADMAN:

Warren Hinckle had given the go-ahead for a Thompson-Steadman Report in Scanlan's Monthly *debunking America's most venerable institutions.*

July 18, 1970
Woody Creek, CO

Dear Ralph . . .

Prepare yourself; I suspect we have struck a very weird & maybe-rich vein . . . but instead of laboring over details I'll just enc. a copy (see below) of a suggestion I sent about 2 wks ago to Warren Hinckle . . . to wit:

". . . I thought I'd pass on a suggestion that one of my enemies laid on me today: "Why don't you just travel around the country and shit on *everything*?" he shouted. "Just go from New York to California and write your venomous bullshit about everything that people respect!" Which sounds like a nice idea—a series of Ky. Derby–style articles (with Steadman) on things like the Super Bowl, Times Sq. on New Year's eve, Mardi Gras, the Masters (golf) Tournament, the America's Cup, Christmas Day with the Chicago Police, Grand National Rodeo in Denver . . . rape them all, quite systematically and then we could sell it as a book: "Amerikan Dreams. . . ." Ah yes, I can hear them weeping already . . . where will the fuckers show up next? Where indeed? Ponder it, & send word. . . ."

That (exactly as reproduced above) is what I sent to Warren—& yesterday he called from NY, saying "Yes, let's try it." He suggested that we call it "The Thompson-Steadman Report" and bill it right from the start as a long and awful series (or maybe he said Steadman-Thompson . . . heh . . . I can't quite recall). In any case, he told me to *call* you at once & get started in London, but I couldn't figure out what exactly I would say . . . and I think it behooves us, at this point, not to waste any more of *Scanlan's* money than we have to.

Because I think this Rape-Series is a king-bitch dog-fucker of an idea. We could go almost anywhere & turn out a series of articles so weird & frightful as to stagger every mind in journalism. "As we buckled down for the approach to New Orleans I snorted the last of our cocaine. Steadman, far gone on acid, had locked himself in the men's room somewhere over St. Louis & the head stewardess was frantic. I knew I would need psychic strength & energy when we landed—to meet the press limousine & get on with our heinous work. . . ."

Can you grasp the lunatic possibilities of such an assignment? Pure madness . . . on a scale hitherto unknown . . . we could travel with courtesans & bearers, rushing from one scene to another in a frenzy of drugs & drink. Indeed . . .

The only problem is that I told Warren I'd decide on two definite scenes for us to deal with between Aug 1 and Sept 30. It's obviously going to cost a fantastic amount of money to bring you over here and keep you living well for long periods of time—so our trick is to settle on two "things" to rape in the space of 5 or 6 weeks. . . .

(pause 40 minutes for call to London)

Well, so much for saving money. Good to talk to you again. Dawn is breaking here & I guess you're looking at noon. Very strange to jump all that way with a small black instrument. . . . Anyway, that Labor Day picnic in Detroit idea sounds better & better, particularly if we can focus it on "What happened to the American Labor Movement?" Almost like the Derby gig, except with a different breed of decadence. Fantastic art possibilities, but a bit more difficult on the writing end—needs research, old quotes, dead dreams, etc. But as a feature I think it looks strong. And very timely, in terms of U.S. politics.

So the next step is yours—select a good scene over there, either England or Ireland, that we can handle in August, or even in late September if necessary. We can work the travel either way: I could come over there in Aug. and work on the first article, then we could come back here for the second (& maybe a third) . . . or else you could come over here first for Labor Day in Detroit & maybe one other, then we could zip back to England for a third piece.

But logistically—in terms of my work schedule & my sheriff's campaign & also for maintaining Warren's interest—I think we'd fare better by doing the *first* piece over there, then getting back here by Labor Day. I'll check with Warren tomorrow & let you know how he reacts. But in the meantime it's important that you come up with some weird project that we can do over there. If you get a good idea, just send it by cable *to me,* c/o Warren at *Scanlan's* in NY; that way, it'll get to both of us, quick & cheap.

OK for now. And, again, it was good talking to you. Let's focus very hard & nicely on this thing—like Zen masters, or NY pawnbrokers. I can have my agent arrange the finances for both of us, if that suits you. Or we can work it out separately—or any other way. I really don't give a fuck. It looks like excellent fun, & with things going as they are, I suspect we'll be needing some of that.

Ciao
Hunter

Another possibility on this end is the America's Cup yachting races (in Long Island Sound) in late Sept., beginning Sept. 15. That would give us Labor Day in early Sept., then the sailboat thing (near N.Y.) in the same month. Let me know how it strikes you.

H

TO WARREN HINCKLE, *SCANLAN'S MONTHLY:*

July 20, 1970
Woody Creek, CO

Dear Warren:

I talked to Ralph (Steadman) the other night & he dug the idea of a Rape-Series on Amerikan Institutions. He said, however, that he was pretty well tied up over there during August, but he planned to be free in Sept. & found the selection fairly thin. Most of my favorites, unfortunately, seem to fall in mid-winter—The Super Bowl, the Orange Bowl Pageant in Miami, Mardi Gras, New Year's in Times Sq., Xmas day with the Chicago Police commissioner, etc. . . .

But after a day or so of thinking, I see two that look good in Sept. One is the UAW [United Automobile Workers] Labor Day picnic in Detroit, or "The Fat Remains of the American Labor Movement, circa 1970." We could use the picnic as a focus & bkgnd for a fairly heavy article on what's happened to Labor in this country. This could be handled, I think, mainly with interviews and descriptions—along with a few fine quotes from Gompers & the Wobblies.[34] And meanwhile, Steadman could be drawing the swine—not only at the picnic, but maybe a few faces from DRUM & that crowd, to get a nice contrast.

The other Sept idea is the America's Cup yachting races, beginning Sept 15 on Long Island Sound, I think, or at least somewhere in that area. That one looks a bit like the KY Derby thing—an orgy of decadence that we'd more or

34. Samuel Gompers (1850–1924) founded and in 1886 became the first president of the American Federation of Labor; the Wobblies were members of the radical socialist Industrial Workers of the World (IWW) union, which sought not better labor conditions but a workers' revolution.

less have to feel out while it was happening. No doubt we'd need heavy press credentials, well ahead, to get anywhere near the nexus of this one. We could also use a good connection in the Newport yachting crowd. I used to have one or two, but I'd hate to have to count on them now. Maybe Roy Cohn[35] knows somebody. . . .

Anyway . . . that's it for openers: Labor Day in Detroit, and the America's Cup in Newport. There are others. I'm building a nice list . . . and, yes, here's another: Right after I talked to you the other day I mentioned your notion of a Thompson-Steadman Report series & its general tenor to a local wizard . . . and he said, "Christ, the first thing you should do is give that poor bastard a chance to get back at you for that terrible shit you laid on him at the Derby. This time you should go over to England & get trapped in *his* territory & let him get even with you. . . ."

Which struck me as a fine idea, and only fair, on its merits. I told Ralph to check around & see what kind of weird scene he could come up with—perhaps in late August. Maybe something like the English Derby, or whatever they get excited about over there. Maybe stage a gang-rape in Westminster Abbey. Whatever's right.

So that's about it for the moment. Let's see what Ralph comes up with on his end, but in the meantime we have those other two over here. Or any others that might come to mind . . .

Ciao,
Hunter

TO THE GENERAL ORDNANCE EQUIPMENT COMPANY:

Thompson was eagerly preparing himself for sheriff's work.

July 28, 1970

Gen. Ordnance Equip. Comp.
P.O. Box 11211
Freeport Road
Pittsburgh, PA

Gentlemen:

Please send me all details on your CHEMICAL MACE MK-V non-lethal weapon. In my present position as Chief Magistrate of this small hamlet we could only afford two or three, depending on the cost—which is also why we don't have any official stationery or letterhead. But as I am now a candidate for the office of County Sheriff I soon expect to have a much larger budget at my

35. Roy M. Cohn, chief assistant to Joseph McCarthy during the Wisconsin senator's communist witch hunt in 1953–54, had become a controversial corporate lawyer. Cohn would be disbarred in 1986.

disposal. In the meantime I want to learn as much about the technical aspects of the new urban-style police work as I can.

So my question for now is, What is the unit price for one MK-V weapon and enough reloads to test it properly? Maybe a half dozen?

Also, please send details on discounts for bulk orders, both weapons and reloads. Thank you.

Hunter S. Thompson
Chief Magistrate
Box 37
Woody Creek, CO 81656

TO W. S. DARLEY & CO:

July 28, 1970

W. S. Darley & Co.
2000 Anson Drive
Melrose Park, Ill.

Gentlemen:

Please send me your latest Police Supplies catalog, as advertised in the June, 1970 issue of *The Police Chief*. I apologize for not writing on my "official letterhead," as specified, but if you ever saw this small hamlet of which I am Chief Magistrate you would doubtless understand why I have no official stationery.

Frankly, my business is breeding Dobermans, and until recently I saw no point in concerning myself or my neighbors with the business of Police Supplies. But I am now a candidate for the office of County Sheriff in a very close race, and to some extent my chances of winning depend on knowing what I'm talking about when it comes to technical things. For this reason, I thought I should get a copy of the Darley catalog, so I can talk in terms of costs and effectiveness and that sort of thing.

Your cooperation is appreciated. Thank You.

Hunter S. Thompson
Chief Magistrate
Box 37
Woody Creek, CO 81656

TO MITCH GREENHILL:

July 28, 1970
Woody Creek, CO

Dear Mitch . . .

Chances are decent for a gig out here in late August or Sept. Two places definitely looking for acts, and perhaps others. Hard to say right now. But one place is owned by an ex–Detroit Lion end & tomorrow I'll take your "Instant Replay" down for him to hear.

The other definite thing is run by a friend who just staged a ragged sort of folk festival that sold out both nights. He asked me about Rosalie Sorrels because he met her once. I mentioned you & said you now had a vicious group. He seemed interested . . . but he got nervous when I asked about money. Not much available on that end, I think, but maybe if you signed up for the next folk fest. He could sell you to that place where Bruce Innes was making $3000 a week last yr. You couldn't get that for starters, but $1500 would be bottom, I think . . . and once you got here we could put you to work doing political rallies. I'm running for sheriff, anchoring a Freak Power slate.

The main question would be your availability—and how much cash you'd want. I don't see much trouble lining up a gig that would pay all travel expenses, etc. . . . and if you feel like giving it a whirl I'll turn the whole thing over to Mike Solheim[36] & let him play promoter, handle all details, etc.

Let me know how you're fixed for action in Sept–Oct. or even late Aug. Also check with Rosalie if she's around. Maybe we can get [Eric] Von Schmidt up at the same time.

In a nut, what's fairly certain is a gig that would cover all your expenses . . . but a guaranteed money-maker is something else. Do you have a tape of the group? I have stuff of yours & Rosalie's. Give it some thought & send a group-tape if you feel like taking a chance on it. Otherwise, we can probably get you like $30 a night solo anytime you want to come out. But with a bit of planning we can do a lot better. Send word. . . .

Hunter

TO WARREN HINCKLE, *SCANLAN'S MONTHLY:*

Hinckle had commissioned Thompson to review The Police Chief *magazine for* Scanlan's.

July 28, 1970
Woody Creek, CO

Dear Warren . . .

Here's the *Police Chief* thing—far longer & more twisted, of course, than our original concept. About halfway thru the bugger I suddenly realized that I was onto a very rich vein. Maybe it dawned on me when I suddenly looked over the top of my typewriter & saw a book titled *The Weapons Culture.* Then

36. Local housepainter Michael Solheim, one of the three original members of Aspen's Freak Power Party, became Thompson's campaign manager.

I looked to my left & saw a whole shelf of books about Weapons, Crime, Violence, Guns, Killing, Rape . . . jesus, the whole room is full of them.

Anyway, what occurred to me was a regular feature on Weaponry—in the style of Dr. Hippocrates. The nation is full of potential bomb-throwers & snipers who know *nothing* about the technical aspects of their chosen Trades. I think we should *help* these people, and I can think of no better way than to capitalize on my new-found conduits into the official Police Establishment. We can drive the fuckers crazy by discussing the pros & cons of all their newest weapons—small but important things like the fact that Army Surplus gas masks are no good against the new "improved CS." And addresses of companies which *make* the new masks, so that freaks can rip them off.

Given the rude temper of these times, I daresay this is a stroke of fucking genius. We can create, with Raoul Duke, a virtual clearing-house for information on all forms of violence. Answer all questions, dispense strange advice of all sorts . . . and meanwhile keep a fine tap on *The Police Chief* & other cop books, in order to expose everything they come up with. Also things like "How to Seize a Floating Rib, How to Choke a Vicious Dog" . . . & other small items like "Why Slash Tires When It's Easier to Cut Off the Inner Tube Stems."

No doubt the FBI would visit you very soon after the first column appeared, so you'd have to protect my identity if at all possible. In fact I decided to use my well-worn pseudonym, Raoul Duke, so as not to blow my cover with *The Police Chief* & all the various agencies, supply houses, etc. that I've written to, asking for information & weapons. If I signed this piece or any other with my right name, they would soon have me blacklisted in every corner of the Police Establishment. But now, since I've already established myself with *The Police Chief,* I suspect the rest will be easy. We could actually order police weapons and *test them,* then publish the results. We could buy a fucking pepper fog machine & test it in Golden Gate Park at a Shriners' Picnic. Jesus, the possibilities are massive & totally open-ended. Every freak in the nation would buy the magazine to keep posted on the newest weaponry . . . how to neutralize it, steal it, use it, etc. I see a vast market for this kind of information, and I see no reason why we can't dispense it quite legally.

Ponder this idea—a regular monthly Weapons feature by Raoul Duke—and let me know. I am already into that scene very heavily, as an adjunct to my Sheriff's campaign, so the first wave is already on order. As the Chief Magistrate of Woody Creek, my legal credentials are unimpeachable. I am also a member of the PBA, the NRA[37] & the Aspen Racing Association. These are important. . . .

Meanwhile, FYI, I'm enclosing my only three copies of *The Police Chief*—for excerpting. You'll note that I quoted mainly from the June issue, which

37. The Patrolmen's Benevolent Association and the National Rifle Association, respectively.

seems like the heaviest—note the cover, and also the ads. But I must have these back. I tried not to cut or mark them, so you could reproduce anything that looks ripe.

You'll also notice, on pg. 39 of the June issue, an Advance Registration form for the 77th annual Police Chief conference in Atlantic City, Oct 3–8 . . . and I suspect I'd be eligible to attend this function as a righteous member . . . and I also see that they list a registration space for *guests*. See pg. 40. Perhaps Steadman might like to come along & we could check into the Parlor Suite at the Traymore (hq). This looks like a winner—a fine load of material for Raoul Duke, in addition to a straight chunk of the Thompson/Steadman Report. We could slip Duke straight into Enemy headquarters, then use his column to report anything heinous for use under my own real byline.

Let me know about this. It looks like a winner to me—particularly since it follows hard on the heels (as it were) of the America's Cup races just a few hundred miles north. I've lined up a 50-foot yacht for that one, I think, but I won't be sure until next week. The candidate for County Surveyor is going to NY in a few days to check it out. The boat belongs to an ex–Aspen ski instructor & freak/drifter; he charters it in the Caribbean in the winter, and in Connecticut in the summer. This weekend he's taking out John Lindsay & party . . . and I think he'd get a boot out of particpating in *Scanlan's* America's Cup coverage. We could seize the boat for expenses, then rent out space to selected members of the Freak Press—sail right into the midst of the Newport fleet, flying the red & black flags of anarchy & revolution, launching mace canisters off the bowsprit & hire the Grateful Dead to perform on the foredeck. Old Newport hands would break down & start vomiting at the sight of this fiendish vessel full of crazies. Paint a huge red fist on the balloon jib & a motorcycle hanging in the dingy rack. It would be a rotten outrage, but if we called it the *Scanlan's* Press Boat I suspect it might prove out to be a good investment. Or at least a very weird trip . . .

So consider these things: 1) A regular weapons feature by Raoul Duke, 2) Reservations for Steadman/Thompson at *The Police Chief*'s convention, and 3) Covering the America's Cup from *Scanlan's* Press Boat, complete with the Grateful Dead. (I can confirm the boat by Aug 1, if necessary. The races are around Sept 15–20.)

OK for now,
Hunter

TO U.S. SENATOR WALTER F. MONDALE:

Minnesota Democrat Walter F. Mondale had succeeded his mentor, Hubert H. Humphrey, in the U.S. Senate. In 1976 he would do so again as the first Dem-

ocratic vice president since Humphrey, and again in 1984 as his party's presidential nominee—unsuccessfully, again just like Humphrey. The difference was in Mondale's sincerity and refusal to go along to get along in Washington.

July 31, 1970

Senator Walter F. Mondale
Senate Office Building
Washington, D.C.

Dear Sen. Mondale . . .

At some point in your hearings on the Migrant Labor nightmare, you said something I'd like to use in a book I'm currently working on for Random House. I heard it on TV & expected to read it somewhere in the press, but nobody seemed to pick it up. To the best of my memory, what you said runs something like this: "The capacity of this nation to inflict pain & suffering on those without power is virtually unlimited."

Would you be kind enough to send your own correct version of that quote? I'd rather not have to quote you on the basis of a quick & left-handed memory.

Thanks,
Hunter S. Thompson
Box 37
Woody Creek, CO
81656

P.S.—Your *Face the Nation* appearance last Sunday was one of the most encouraging political developments I've seen in a very long time. You came across very straight—despite the cheap, half-brainless context. And I know that's not easy. If you decide to run for President or anything else, let me know if I can help. —HST

TO PAUL KRASSNER, *THE REALIST:*

Krassner had asked Thompson to write a pre-election piece on his campaign for sheriff of Pitkin County.

August 12, 1970
Woody Creek, CO

Dear Paul . . .

Yeah, your letter got thru & found me in the middle of writing almost exactly the piece you asked for—but I've already agreed to give it to *Rolling Stone.* Wenner asked about a month ago.

What I *can* do for *The Realist,* however, is a piece *looking back* on the election, saying a lot of things that I'm having to be coy about in this *Rolling Stone* gig. Like there's a lot of strategy that I have to skirt because lining it out right now could hurt our takeover bid. My sheriff's campaign is only one part of the overall plot—and I have to keep it under control, in public, so as not to fuck the rest of the action.

Think about a piece in November, rather than now, & let me know. Also consider the possibility of coming out here sometime in September to speak at one of my rallies. At the moment I'm looking around for a name band to anchor a list of "speakers." Do you know any? There wouldn't be much money involved, but I think we could cover all expenses . . . and there's also the added attraction of getting in on a *winning* campaign for a change. My chances, at the moment, are booked about 40/60, & I haven't even begun to whip on the bastards.

In preparation for the campaign I have shaved my head right down to a bright bald dome. Very strange & menacing. I have also joined the International Association of Police Chiefs & plan to attend their conference Oct 3 in Atlantic City. Hinckle has first shot at this story, but if he doesn't want it maybe we can work something out. I'm also trying to persuade him (Warren) to hire a *Scanlan's* press boat for the America's Cup races—to enhance the coverage. I want to hire the Grateful Dead to play on the foredeck & sail right into the Newport flotilla with a gang of drug-crazies on board. But so far I can't get this act confirmed. If it works I'll be in NY for the races & maybe I can get you on board.

OK for now. Send word on all fronts. Thanx . . .

Hunter

**George Kimball just left today, after a vicious three-day strategy conference. He's running for Sheriff of Lawrence, Kansas, but with no hope of winning. This is a strange phenomenon—Albert in Berkeley, Oscar Acosta in LA (he got 110,000 votes), Kimball in Kansas & me in Aspen—with no prior collusion.[38] Very odd. . . .

ASPEN TIMES CAMPAIGN ADVERTISEMENT:

Thompson lay out a stark campaign platform in this paid advertisement in the October 8, 1970, Aspen Times.

38. Among the Freak Power Party's 1970 candidates, George Kimball won the Lawrence, Kansas, Democratic primary contest for sheriff running unopposed, but was trounced in the general election; Stewart Albert lost his bid for sheriff of Berkeley, California, but did get 65,000 votes; and Oscar Acosta tallied 110,000 out of some 2,000,000 votes cast in the race for L.A. County sheriff.

October 8, 1970
Woody Creek, CO

ONLY SERIOUS PEOPLE CAN LAUGH
F. FELLINI

TO WHOM IT MAY CONCERN:

Contrary to widespread rumors and a plague of wishful thinking, I am very serious about my candidacy for the office of sheriff in the coming November election. Anybody who thinks I'm kidding is a fool—739 new registrations since the September primary is no joke in a county with a total vote of less than 3000, so the time has come, it seems, to dispense with evil humor and come to grips with the strange possibility that the next sheriff of this county might very well be a foul-mouthed outlaw journalist with some very rude notions about lifestyles, law enforcement and political reality in America.

Why not? This is a weird twist in my life, but despite the natural horror of seeing myself as the main pig, I think it has to be done. Or at least tried. We have come too far to back off now; the experiment that began last year with the Joe Edwards campaign is coming together, and this time Aspen is ready for it—not only for a new kind of sheriff, but for a whole new style in government, the kind of thing Thomas Jefferson had in mind when he talked about "democracy." We have not done too well on that concept over the years—not in Aspen or anywhere else—and the proof of our failure is the wreckage of Jefferson's dream that haunts us on every side, from coast to coast, on the TV news and in a thousand daily newspapers. We have blown it—that fantastic possibility that Abe Lincoln called "the last, best hope of earth."

This is the nightmare that our politicians have forced on us, even in Aspen. This valley is no longer a refuge or a hideout from reality. For years that was true; Aspen was the best of both worlds—an outpost of urban "culture" buried deep in the rural Rockies. It was a very saleable property, as they say in show business, and for 20 years the selling-orgy boomed fat and heavy.

And now we are reaping the whirlwind—big-city problems too malignant for small-town solutions, Chicago-style traffic in a town without stoplights, Oakland-style drug busts continually bungled by simple cowboy cops who see nothing wrong with kicking handcuffed prisoners in the ribs while the sheriff stands by watching, seeing nothing wrong with it either. While the ranchers howl about zoning, New York stockbrokers and art hustlers sell the valley out from under them. The county attorney has his own iron mine and his own industrial slum at the mouth of the valley. The county commissioners are crude, dimwit lackeys for every big-city dealer who wants a piece of the action. These rapists should be dealt with just as harshly as any other criminal. This is 1970—not 1870. The powers of the sheriff's office can be focused in this direction. Why not?

Hunter S. Thompson

ASPEN TIMES CAMPAIGN ADVERTISEMENT:

Thompson's second paid advertisement appeared in the Aspen Times *on October 22, 1970, next to a photo of the Freak Power candidate glaring at smug-faced incumbent Sheriff Earl Whitmire.*

October 22, 1970
Woody Creek, CO

"THE EARTH BELONGS TO THE LIVING . . . NOT TO THE DEAD"
THOMAS JEFFERSON, IN A LETTER TO JOHN W. EPPES, JUNE 24, 1813

The Random House Dictionary of the English Language defines "Freak" as ". . . any abnormal product or curiously unusual object . . . a person or animal on exhibition as an example of some strange deviation from nature; monster. . . ." Indeed. A very heavy image. And the same dictionary defines "power" as . . . "the ability to do or act; capability of doing or accomplishing something." So in the context of semantics or straight word logic, the phrase "Freak Power" is a sloppy contradiction of its own terms. How, after all, could a group of deviates and monsters be capable of acting together to accomplish something? They would be helpless and impotent, almost by definition, a noisy hellbroth of quirks and demented energy far beyond any channel or focus. Yet, despite the obvious irony of the phrase "Freak Power," NBC, the *Los Angeles Times'* finest traveling police reporter and maybe a few people in Aspen have apparently taken it at face value. And shuddered somewhere in between glee and horror at the thought that some mob of buggering, drug-crazed geeks might be ready to seize the county courthouse and put all the burghers on trial for their lives.

In truth, that phrase was a crude, but super-effective piece of political theatre—which worked too well, so now is the time to bury it and move on to the serious action: the task of returning local government to the people who live in this valley, instead of the greedheads—and their local agents—who only want to invest here.

Which raises a point about Freak Power that I'd like to make before we close the coffin. For some reason that has to embarrass me as a writer I failed to make it clear that I use the word "freak" in a positive, sympathetic sense. In the ominous, ugly-splintered context of what is happening in 1970 Amerika a lot of people are beginning to understand that to be a freak is an honorable way to go.

This is the real point: that we are not really freaks at all—not in the literal sense—but the twisted realities of the world we are trying to live in have somehow combined to make us feel like freaks. We argue, we protest, we petition—but nothing changes.

So now, with the rest of the nation erupting in a firestorm of bombings and political killings, a handful of "freaks" are running a final, perhaps atavistic experiment with the idea of forcing change by voting . . . and if that has to be called Freak Power, well . . . whatever's right.

H.S.T.
Hunter S. Thompson
for Sheriff
Committee
Rev. Thomas Benton,
Spiritual Director

TO JIM SILBERMAN, RANDOM HOUSE:

Everything had gone as planned: Thompson lost the election, but gained plenty of material for his stalled "Death of the American Dream" book.

November 23, 1970
Woody Creek, CO

Dear Jim . . .

Well . . . I thought I might as well answer your letter of Nov. 3—election day as it were—and confirm the tragic rumor concerning my loss. The margin was roughly 1500 to 1065. The GOP candidate got about 150 votes—after the party abandoned him massively, by means of a huge telephone campaign on election eve, and avoided that crucial three-way vote split that we were counting on. In the other (County Commissioner) race, the Democrats abandoned *their* candidate and swung massively to the GOP incumbent, producing the same kind of final tally. Against us.

On election night our Jerome Hotel headquarters was a scene out of some other world. Every freak in Christendom was there, it seemed, including those from *Life, Harper's, LOOK* and a film crew from London—along with the camera crew from Woodstock and a bona fide Swami from India. It was a fantastic scene and naturally we all loaded up heavily on mescaline & tequila . . . to ward off the chill. I'm enclosing 3 photos: one, the classic Hoover & Friend shot, and two others from election night . . . the "thumbs down" shot came at the moment of the axe, when the down-county trailer-court precincts reported in . . . and the other, with all the cameras, was taken during my "final statement," which was made in a total mescaline frenzy and I remember nothing of what I said except: "This is my last press conference. You won't have Hunter Thompson to kick around anymore, you motherfuckers. . . ." The whole thing is on film & appeared the other night on British Indep. TV. The Woodstock crew is still haggling over who owns the rights to the two weeks of film they shot. They're trying to sell it as a film titled *Stoned on Politics*. I got a copy of their sales pitch from a producer (?) they approached; they don't seem to want me involved in the film in any way . . . which will almost certainly lead to bad trouble.

But what the hell? At the moment I'm concerned with other things. Like how to cope with this "Final Notice Before Seizure" that came today from the IRS. They want $2200 by midnight on Saturday, Nov. 28. After that, they say, they'll come out here and seize everything I own. Tonight I called Warren Hinckle and demanded at least some part of the $5290 *Scanlan's* owes me . . . and he was of course sympathetic, explaining that everything would be OK in a few days when the current issue of *Scanlan's* comes across the border from Quebec in a fleet of black trucks. In other words, my ability to pay the IRS depends on Hinckle's ability to smuggle 100,000 sabotage-bomb manuals past U.S. Customs in huge trucks. I've seen that issue; I helped them put it together in SF & as a matter of fact I have two articles in it (one is the lead piece), and I know Nixon won't want it let loose in the U.S. One of the worst items it contains, in fact, is a two page ad for the *Aspen Wallposter,* half of which is a full page color photo of Nixon with blood drooling out of his mouth, a *Wallposter* cover that we couldn't get printed anywhere in Colorado. Horrible, horrible . . .

Anyway, I assume you see where I'm at. The Repression has come down on us full-bore here; the Fatbacks are trying to Mop Up while they're ahead . . . sensing a mandate, perhaps, or maybe just trying to croak us completely before May, when the Mayor and entire City Council will be up for election again. And that will be a very heavy election . . . because the one wild fact that got lost in the overall results of this past election is that *we won the city of Aspen.* The *county* vote destroyed us by such a huge margin that it offset our victory in town. (In my own precinct, for instance, I lost by 300 to 90.) But there is no escaping the harsh truth that all four city precincts voted for a Sheriff's candidate who insisted, throughout the campaign, on his right to keep on eating mescaline after he was elected. I refused to compromise on this issue—or any other, for that matter—and still got a 40/60 split on the vote. *The entire vote;* not just the Freak Power segment. In other words, I got a bigger percentage of the vote in Pitkin County, which is hugely Republican and where Freaks make up roughly 30% of the electorate, than Jim Buckley did in NY State.[39]

Contrast this to the showings of the Peace & Freedom candidates in California, the Raza Unida in Colorado or even the liberals in New York . . . and then ponder the implications. I'm still not sure what they mean myself, but another odd factor to add in might be the up-coming 18-year-old vote and the fact that I won the straw vote at the local high school by something like ten to one. In other words, I'd have won easily—even admitting that I smoked grass and ate mescaline whenever I felt like it—if the 18-, 19-, and 20-year-olds had been eligible to vote.

This harks back, I think, to our conversation in the Waldorf bar last May, and your notion that I was (am) somewhere far out on the leading edge of the National Reality. Maybe this country is almost ready for Freak Power on the highest levels of national politics. Maybe a presidential candidate in 1972 could actually *gain* votes by admitting that he smokes marijuana and laughing about it on network TV. That's essentially what I did. In fact I dismissed marijuana as a low-level "stupor-drug" and said I preferred "more active" things—such as mescaline, and occasionally, Acid.

We were all astounded by the (lack of) reaction to this kind of talk—from a candidate for Sheriff, no less. I have a tape of a public exchange between me and an ex-SS officer (a valid Nazi) about mescaline, and he ends up saying, "Well . . . I have to admire your honesty, it's incredible. . . ." And I think the fucker voted for me. If nothing else, I turned him around in public—with about 100 people gathered in a room to hear me talk—so totally that our exchange produced at least 10 votes out of that hostile crowd, and maybe 50.

39. James Buckley was the Republican candidate for the U.S. Senate from New York.

This was the most outlandish aspect of the campaign—the fact that we could actually overcome the multi-onus of a candidate who was not only insanely ugly, stone bald, and advocating "Freak Power" with casual references to "pigfuckers" and "shitheads" and "greedy scum" . . . but who also admitted to committing felonies as a way of life and whose massively-distributed campaign posters featured a double-thumbed red fist clutching a peyote button.

This is something to talk about . . . and I'm doing it right now for *Rolling Stone*. We have another huge "Freak Power" feature coming up in about two weeks. It was due today, in fact, but Wenner agreed to postpone it until I could sort the whole thing out . . . and he also mentioned that it was going to run as a major piece, with many photos, rather than a brief news-item-type follow-up to the original piece. Probably around mid-December . . . for good or ill.

So . . . we come to the question of THE BOOK. Indeed. And the only real question, right now, is whether this Aspen politics gig should be the framework for the whole thing, or perhaps just a couple of chapters in a long rambling gig about politics in America. What occurred to me the other night is that somehow this Aspen political freakout—particularly my own brutal involvement—might be the same kind of accidental framework for a book that my Hell's Angels involvement provided. Maybe "The Battle of Aspen" might be a working title for a book that would actually delve into politics far beyond Aspen . . . all the way back to New Hampshire in early '68, Chicago, election day in LA and all the other things. Because all that really led to the scene that just happened here. Without Chicago I would never have run for Sheriff—or even launched the Joe Edwards campaign. So it all makes a very definite kind of progressive sense—at least in my own mind, and hopefully in print.

So . . . what do you think? If you want to go with "The Battle of Aspen," that decision will amount to far more than just a working title. It will amount to that definitive framework that we've lacked ever since you shackled me with that nebulous "American Dream" bullshit. Which has hamstrung me ever since.

What I have in mind—if the B/A idea works—is an opening chapter based very heavily on the Oct 1, '70 *Rolling Stone* piece.[40] In other words, the book would open almost exactly like that article opens . . . then with a flashback to Chicago and perhaps the NRA gun-control piece . . . then into the Sheriff's campaign and another flashback to Nixon & McCarthy in New Hampshire (also Kennedy) and others, including the foul ghost of Humphrey . . . and LBJ . . . then as a sort of screeching climax, the final third of the book would be a detailed account of this past election, the framework for which you'll be able to see very soon in *Rolling Stone*. We could also use the (*Scanlan's*) Jean-Claude Killy piece in there, on the strength of its connections to Ski/Aspen and

40. Thompson's article "The Battle of Aspen," about his 1970 Freak Power campaign for sheriff of Pitkin County, ran in *Rolling Stone* #67.

the Chicago Stockyards Amphitheatre and other, less tangible connections that might be even more pertinent, in the end, than the others.

If this idea grabs you, let me know at once. Probably we should talk about it on the phone—maybe at some length. Because once I get started on that "Battle of Aspen" framework, there will be no turning back.

My advisors, in fact, are already gearing up (down?) for the Presidential campaign in '72. They seem to think that I could beat Nixon handily with the same kind of campaign we ran here—now that we know the ropes, and which mistakes to avoid. Naturally, I refuse to run—unless they offer me the Democratic nomination and about 100 million dollars to blow on a brutal, mind-bending campaign that would stagger the National Consciousness. (You would have been stunned, by the way, at my public performances—with a fleet of mikes and cameras & even huge glaring lights in my face; at first I couldn't believe it myself . . . but after the first few scenes I found myself actually digging it; very strange, maybe a sort of Hitler instinct . . . but there is something very wild in being able to look out at a huge crowd and actually communicate with it. . . .)

Which is neither here nor there. For now, what I need from you is a definite opinion inre: "The Battle of Aspen." Should we do it that way? Will it make us all rich? Will you send me $5000 when I send you a third of *that* book? Have I made myself clear in terms of what it will/might/could be? Do you have any other, *better* ideas? Alternative frameworks? Titles? Vagaries? Dead-end fuckarounds?

Until I hear from you I'll be down here in the War Room (that's what we named it during the campaign) hashing out the new *Rolling Stone* piece. But meanwhile I think we should deal very quickly with this Battle of Aspen idea—because if you like it, it's already happening . . . and if you think it won't work, well, I think you'd better come up with a real ballbuster of an alternative. Because we're way, way overdue . . . and I'm getting hungry.

OK for now. Call when you get this digested. Ciao . . .

Hunter

TO CAREY McWILLIAMS, *THE NATION:*

The Nation *had run an editorial supporting Aspen's Freak Power Uprising.*

November 23, 1970
Woody Creek, CO

Dear Carey . . .

Thanks for the letters and especially the editorial in the recent issue. You may have a point. We actually won the city (Aspen proper), and only lost the whole county by about 60/40 . . . which is a hell of a lot better than any Freak/Left/Weird/Radical/New/Young/Etc. candidates did in most parts of the country. Consider P&F in Calif., Raza Unida in Colo. or even the liberals in NY. What neither the *Times* nor *The National Observer* said, incidentally, is that we ran straight at the bastards with an out-front Mescaline platform. My drug tastes were discussed quite openly, not only in the newspaper but also in mass public forums . . . and through it all I refused to say I'd stop eating mescaline if I got elected. Marijuana got lost in that scramble; we completely jumped over it—to the extent that I probably could have won if I'd compromised to the extent of forswearing mescaline if they'd let me keep smoking grass. But we refused to compromise at all, on *any* issue . . . and we still won the city. Which is weird . . . and certainly worth thinking about. The question now is whether to go even further in the May '71 City elections (Mayor & Council), or whether to back off a bit and try to consolidate local strength with some kind of sure-fire, non-frightening slate that won't scare out such a brutal negative vote. They were totally terrified this time; people came out in wheelchairs & on stretchers to vote *against me.* Not *for* anybody or anything else; just *against* the Freaks.

Anyway, as far as doing a piece for you is concerned, I think I can probably do something fairly short and focusing on one aspect of the campaign, rather than the overall thing—because I'm doing that for *Rolling Stone,* as a sort of follow-up on the Battle of Aspen. Jann Wenner asked me for it about midway in the campaign . . . and since he also offered to pay about twice what he paid for the last one I really didn't have to grapple with the idea very long before getting down to it.

I just got off the phone with Warren Hinckle in SF—a last-ditch midnight effort to salvage some of the funds they owe me for things I did for *Scanlan's* before the crunch. Today I got "Final Notice Before Seizure" from the IRS, telling me I have to raise $2200 before midnight on Saturday or they're coming out here to attach everything I own. I'm also about to lose my American Express card—which was very hard to get—and which will make my free-lance life very difficult in the future if I lose the bastard.

So you see the problem. As always, I'd like to write a good long piece for you, but I always seem to be in the position of a wild boar in a running battle with a pack of hounds & I never seem to have time to do the kind of things I want to do. Beyond that, I'm trying to learn to play the flute because it strikes me that most of today's real literature pops up in music instead of in fiction or even personal journalism. For instance at the moment my writing room is full of "New Speedway Boogie" by the Grateful Dead. It says more than anything I've read in five years.

But what the hell? I'll send you a campaign poster . . . and plan on getting you a piece (say 2500 words) in 2/3 weeks. I have a hell of a lot to write. All at once. I think the time has come to Do It. OK for now.

Ciao . . .
Hunter

TO JIM SILBERMAN, RANDOM HOUSE:

Tom Wolfe had sent a note of encouragement to Thompson, who was still being pursued by the IRS.

November 25, 1970
Woody Creek, CO

Dear Jim . . .

Here's an addendum to my last, long letter . . . and maybe something you'll want to keep in your file. Tom Wolfe's new book came today (*Radical Chic & Mau-Mauing the Flak Catchers*) and on the title page was a hand-written note, to wit:

> "Dear Hunter, I present this book in homage after reading the two funniest stories of all time—J.C. Killy and The Derby—(*Scanlan's*). You are The Boss! Not the sheriff, maybe, but you are The Boss!"
>
> Tom Wolfe, Nov 16, 1970

For whatever it's worth. If nothing else, it makes me feel good. Particularly right now in the shadow of the Tax Man. The IRS mogul in Denver was extremely surly when Joe Edwards called him yesterday . . . saying my case had already been assigned to a "field agent" who would be "calling on (me) shortly." So we are now in the process of stripping the house of all money-valuable items: guns, amplifiers, motorcycle, sculpture, etc. And both typewriters (this one belongs to the new Community School, in town).

Anyway, I trust you see why I'm very much interested, right now, in getting The Book concept settled . . . so I can seize that opening $5000. Your cooperation will be greatly appreciated.

Sincerely,
The Boss

TO TOM WOLFE:

Wolfe's fourth book, Radical Chic & Mau-Mauing the Flak Catchers, *satirized the cynical self-interest of activists and do-gooders on both sides of America's racial divide.*

November 25, 1970
Woody Creek, CO

Dear Tom . . .

Your new book came today & I read the whole first section before Sandy mentioned that you'd written something up front. She read it as something like, "You are one of the boys . . ." but I deciphered your arcane script and dug it immensely—despite the massive lack of evidence to support your idea. At the moment I think you're running way out front, and not just because you've sent more books to the press. With the possible and perhaps fading exception of [Ken] Kesey, you're about the only writer around that I figure I can learn from. Very quick into *Radical Chic* I suddenly understood that one of the main strengths of your weird, super-detailed style is a definite dramatic tension that comes with the idea that something very brutal and final might happen to the subject on the very next page, or maybe the next paragraph. You convey a kind of doomsday confidence in your evidence that almost precludes the necessity for summing it up . . . a sort of mercifully suspended judgement that amounts, in the end, to a horrifying indictment . . . maybe Guilt by Detailed Suggestions is the right phrase. Whatever . . . it works. I found myself hungering for the Axe to fall. . . .

Or maybe I'm just projecting some of my political wisdom, gleaned from the last campaign. We used the same technique—given that one of our opponents was a moral junkie and the other a twice-convicted felon illegally running for office. We managed to taint them savagely by floating rumors that we then refused to discuss in public, thereby implying that we were "Above That Sort of Thing." It worked very nicely . . . although not quite nicely enough.

Indeed. We lost. And you missed a hell of a good story. I thought about calling you early on, but my position seemed to preclude that kind of out-front hustling. As it was, I was heavily damned for "the publicity," even though I spent about half the campaign trying to avoid it because I could see it was killing us. Now I understand that Agnew was Right about the press. They are a gang of cheap swine—even the ones who try to help and be friendly. What the campaign needed—in retrospect—was somebody with a kind of super Third Ear (or Eye); somebody who could sense, somehow, what was happening and Why.

But nobody like that showed up . . . and now it's left for me to write the Epitaph for Freak Power. At the moment I'm doing a follow-up for *Rolling Stone,* and given my current financial circumstances I suspect I'll also try to whip something up for Random House. The Tax Man is after me in a very serious way, demanding 2 grand by midnight on Saturday or we go to war. Seizure proceedings. Those cocksuckers. I called Warren Hinckle the other night to get the 5 grand *Scanlan's* owes me and he said my payment hangs on a shipment of some 100,000 copies of the long-delayed "next issue" getting across the border from Canada this weekend. In other words, if the whole shipment is seized at customs—which it certainly will be—then *Scanlan's* is doomed and croaked. And I think that's a foregone conclusion. That gang of Pigs on the NY end: Zion, [Bob] Arum, Roy Cohn, etc., should be hung by their fucking heels & beaten with wire whips.

But fuck all that. It's making me crazy. I shall, of course, prevail. But it's wearing me down. I dig the battles, but I don't have much stomach for The War. The shitheads keep on breeding, multiplying. You croak one & two more slither out to replace it—like getting rid of Johnson and gaining Nixon/Agnew. Jesus, what next? Where will it end? I think maybe Kesey is right.

Ciao,
Hunter

TO WILLIAM J. KENNEDY:

Kennedy had sent Thompson his own account of the night he had spent standing guard outside Thompson's campaign headquarters.

December 5, 1970
Woody Creek, CO

Bill . . .

I just read your piece again & it seems a lot better than it did before . . . although at that point I probably wouldn't have liked anything I read, no matter what the fuck it said. But I still don't like the lead; it takes a long time to overcome. Actually, that word "Kibbitzer" might be what puts me off. I've always deplored your penchant for those rotten, cute little words—like "bolly," etc. But we've talked about that, so to hell with it.

My own piece—for *Rolling Stone*—is still laboring along. I missed the first deadline & it's beginning to look like I might miss the second—which would get it out about the middle of January, with yours, and for that reason I'm going over yours again to match up loose details . . . like the temperature outside on that savage Wednesday nite when you did guard duty. You had 18 and my first draft said 12, so I guess I'll go with 18, since I really didn't check at the time. (There was another mistake, I think: You quoted that "SDS" note as saying "This will only be used *on* Hunter Thompson if he is elected sheriff." The tape says "This will only be used *if* HT is elected. . . ." A definite difference.) There was another one where you quoted me saying, "My blood ran cold. . . ." Which of course I'd never say . . . but what the hell?

Anyway, here are two photos I thought you'd like. We have about 7 million to sift through, but these are dupes so I thought I'd send them along—to Dana.[41]

I assume you got straight with *Harper's* & that the thing will be in the Feb issue. Let me know if I'm wrong, because I'll want to get some extra copies & Aspen only gets about six, in all.

41. Dana was William Kennedy's wife.

Meanwhile, in addition to the *RS* piece, I seem to be drifting toward using this Aspen political scene as the basic framework for "the book." Silberman seems to dig it, and right now I'm inclined to write just about anything he'll give me quick money for. The taxman is after me for real: "Final Notice Before Seizure" & that sort of thing, which is grim. I wonder if this has any connection to Bromley's[42] employment with a division of the IRS? Paranoia? After *that* election?

OK for now. Send word. . . .

H

TO SIDNEY ZION, *SCANLAN'S MONTHLY:*

Sidney E. Zion was coeditor of Scanlan's Monthly *and apparently in charge of its editorial budget. Thompson thus attached an invoice of his fees and expenses for the three articles he had done for the magazine.*

December 8, 1970
Woody Creek, CO

Dear Sidney . . .

After several weeks of extensive and increasingly anguished phone conversations with Warren (Hinckle) and (atty.) John Clancy in San Francisco—and (atty.) Leon Friedman in New York, I was advised tonight by Leon that the reason I have not received a sizeable cheque from *Scanlan's* is that my bill (statement, money demand, etc.) was never received by you in the New York office. And that once you received my bill there would of course be no problem at all in effecting prompt payment . . . to me . . . in order that I might transfer these monies, at once, to American Express and the Internal Revenue Service.

As Leon has probably told you, and as Clancy has certainly told Warren, the American Express computer has red-lined my number to the tune of $1,035.30 (all incurred in the course of that disastrous month on the road for *Scanlan's*) . . . and the IRS has sent me a "Final Warning Before Seizure," which means their next step is to come out here and sell everything I own at a public auction. These developments have naturally disturbed me—coming, as they did, hard on the heels of my tragic loss at the polls.

But what the hell . . . eh? No point in boring you with the details of these rotten, stinking, fiendish fucking nightmares that I somehow got myself into. The point right now is to get out of them . . . and to that end I'm enclosing a

42. Bromley was a biker who showed up at Freak Power campaign headquarters in Aspen and volunteered his services as Thompson's bodyguard as well as to procure any explosives the candidate might want. He turned out to have been hired by incumbent sheriff Earl Whitmire for reasons that remain unclear.

bill/statement I sent Warren about a month ago. That one was the end result of a settlement worked out between him and Clancy, and I assumed it had been passed on to the NY office for payment.

I realize, of course, that your normal procedures have been even further addled, of late, by elements of fascist insanity relating to printers, unions, customs, Mounties and that sort of thing . . . and I understood, Sidney, I sympathized . . . despite the soaking sweats that occasionally seized me when I recalled that conversation at Sardi's about . . . what was it? Something about establishing nerve damage? Brain damage? Goddamn . . . I have it on the tip of my tongue . . . but again, what the hell?

In any case, the enclosed statement is necessarily a summary of all the items I've tried to pull together since that heinous trip—the original purpose of which was to put off the Taxman and lay in at least a minimal cash reserve to cover my campaign expenses. What happened, however, was a total disaster on all fronts—including the loss of what small cash reserves I had at the time I took off for SF & Portland (that's the $559.80 item). I should have listened to Steadman, who'd been warned by one of your guilt-plagued operatives to do nothing at all until he got money ahead. Consequently, when we had to charter a bi-plane out of Newport to avoid arrest at dawn, I had to put Steadman's fare on my AmExp card & also give him enough cash to get into town from La Guardia. That whole twisted scene at Newport was so rotten, so bad, so crazy and unreal from start to finish that even now I hate to think what it actually cost me . . . overall.

. . . I ask you, Sidney, where will it end? Who can you trust these days? Even in publishing?

And so much for all that—just a touch of the natural wigginess, to clear my head for a final statement. Which naturally concerns money . . . and I need that money at once. Any delays might prove disastrous. The Taxman has already assigned his "field agent" to my case, and the first thing he'll try to seize is my car . . . and that will cause me real problems. Which I'd much prefer to avoid, and even a partial payment from your end would get me off that hook and make my life human again. I have every reason to believe, in fact, that a quick shot of $2500 or so would stymie the buggers completely . . . and then we could haggle about the rest. Because all I want right now is to get these swine off my back . . . and since you owe me enough money to get that done (absolutely no question about your owing at least *that* much), well . . . that seems like the thing to do right now. At least that's the way it seems to be.

So let me know something at once. It's imperative. Yes . . . speed is of the essense. Essence? Essense? Whatever . . . after all these words, I trust you get the point . . . & spelling be damned.

Thanks,
Hunter

TO JOHN LOMBARDI, *ROLLING STONE:*

John Lombardi, the Rolling Stone *editor assigned to Thompson's Freak Power campaign article, unwittingly prompted "Raoul Duke" to put together his list of the ten best albums of the 1960s.*

December 11, 1970
Woody Creek, CO

Dear John . . .

The Aspen photo packet will be delayed a day, so I can skulk around town & find whatever photog calls himself "Trout Fishing in America."[43] He's the one who got the shot of the guy voting on the stretcher—which I have—but I want to find the person who actually got the photo. Otherwise, I'm sending about 25 shots—maybe even 30, depending on the final mix—so Kingsbury[44] can fuck around with a layout all the way from zero to super-heavy. If the selection I send seems a bit rife with shots of HST . . . well, I worked with the two main campaign photogs in an effort to show the *chronology* of the action, as we all saw it . . . so a lot of the photos inevitably show my skull from many angles. But what the fuck? All I ask is that you *return* any and all fotos you don't use. The caption-list contains a few comments inre: my own favorites, but these merely reflect my own taste . . . and I know Kingsbury has his own, so to hell with all that too. Whatever's right . . . .

On other fronts, I enjoyed our long talk the other night . . . and after I hung up I realized that was the first human conversation I'd had with anybody since the election . . . since the advent of the Deep Funk that came down almost instantly afterward, not because we lost so much as the Taxman & the Bill Collectors & the *Scanlan's* fuckaround & the local shitheads running wild with their victory leverage and mainly, I think, the final rotten understanding that America is really Amerika . . . for different and deeper, more final reasons than the Panthers ever figured. Those poor bastards are just brushing the nerve-ends right now; they have no idea what's going to come down on them when they really start scaring the Right People. There'll be a nigger hanging on every telephone pole . . . along with a lot of Blacks, too.

This is what my half-born piece is about. If I can get a tentative lead together—and maybe the shape of an ending—I'll send them along with the photos, FYI . . . and if you need an excuse to keep the thing timely, keep in mind that Phil Hill is due to "take office" in Lawrence (Kan.) on Jan 11. But he won't. Those fuckers will abolish every JP office in the state, rather than let a

43. The narrator of Richard Brautigan's nonlinear 1967 novel, *Trout Fishing in America,* uses that title phrase as various character names as well as to describe places and moods, usually as metaphors for innocence under threat of being lost.

44. Robert Kingsbury was Jann Wenner's brother-in-law and *Rolling Stone*'s first full-time art director.

certified freak into office. And that's the whole story, as I see it. The cocksuckers are into a Rule or Ruin gig, and the only kind of Voting they'll tolerate is the same kind Marshall Ky[45] says he's for in Vietnam. Only as long as it's a means to the Right End. . . .

Right? right . . . which gets back to that gun control article I mentioned, and the main problem aside from the length was that I changed my whole mind on the subject somewhere around midstream, and since then not much has happened to bring me back around . . . except that now it's 24 hours later & I've spent the last few hours talking with an *Esquire* writer/photog team who flew in to do (part of) a feature on "the politics of costume" . . . or maybe "the costume of politics" . . . or some such flaky bullshit. But it hardly matters what they want. I learned my lesson about the press during the campaign . . . so tomorrow I'm going to set up my own photo for the fuckers: The New Posse, posed & armed to the teeth on the courthouse steps—as a heinous mockery of that shot *RS* used in the pre-election story. No more of this free-form press-relations fuckaround; from now on it's the iron fist.

Also . . . I checked on the Nitty Gritty Dirt Band & found they left town—replaced by ex-Monkee Mike Nesmith with something called The First National Band—which is just as well, because I don't have much stomach for studio-born road-shows. But I resent your assumption that Music is Not My Bag (or whatever you said) . . . because I've been arguing for the past few years that music is the New Literature, that Dylan is the 1960s' answer to Hemingway, and that the main voice of the '70s will be on records & videotape instead of books.

But by "music" I don't mean the Nitty Gritty Dirt Band. If the Grateful Dead came to town, I'd beat my way in with a fucking tire iron, if necessary. I think *Workingman's Dead* is the heaviest thing since *Highway 61* and "Mr. Tambourine Man" (with the possible exception of the Stones' last two albums . . . and the definite exception of Herbie Mann's *Memphis Underground,* which may be the best album ever cut by anybody). And that might make a good feature: some kind of poll on the Best Albums of the '60s . . . or, "Where it was at in the Rock Age." Because the '60s are going to go down like a repeat, somehow, of the 1920s; the parallels are too gross for even historians to ignore.

45. Nguyen Cao Ky was prime minister of South Vietnam from 1965 to 1967 and then its figurehead vice president until 1971, when he was eased out of power by Nguyen Van Thieu and fled to California, where he opened a liquor store in 1975.

So, for whatever it's worth—to either one of us, for that matter—here's the list from Raoul Duke:[46]

1) *Memphis Underground* ("Battle Hymn of the Republic") H. Mann
2) "Mr. Tambourine Man" (*Bringing It All Back Home*) Zimmerman
3) *Highway 61* . . . Zimmerman
4) *Workingman's Dead* . . . Warlocks et al.
5) *Let It Bleed*
6) Buffalo Springfield first album
7) *Surrealistic Pillow*
8) Roland Kirk . . . (various albums)
9) *Sketches of Spain* . . . M. Davis
10) Sandy Bull . . . #2

Jesus, what a hassle to even think quickly about a list like that. Even now I can think of 10 more I might have added . . . but what the fuck, it's only a rude idea. But a good one, I think, and particularly for *RS*. The implications of the final list would vibrate far beyond the actual music . . . it would be a very heavy fucking document. You may want to give it some thought. . . .

OK for now. I have all the fotos together & I'm sending them along with brief captions, so we can get this thing started.

Ciao . . .
Hunter

TO ELIZABETH RAY:

December 30, 1970
Woody Creek, CO

Dear Aunt Lee . . .

Thanx as always for the Christmas check; this year it went into the campaign-debt fund. We ran up massive bills almost everywhere . . . and they all came due when we lost. But I guess that's an old story with losing candidates.

Anyway, here are two campaign pieces that may or may not explain what it was all about. (The *Aspen Wallposter* is our monthly publication—Tom Benton does the art & I do the writing.) The net result of this last incredible cam-

46. The complete specifics of Raoul Duke's list of the ten best record albums of the 1960s are as follows: 1) Herbie Mann's 1969 *Memphis Underground*; 2) Bob Dylan's March 1965 *Bringing It All Back Home;* 3) Dylan's August 1965 *Highway 61 Revisited;* 4) the Grateful Dead's June 1970 *Workingman's Dead;* 5) the Rolling Stones' December 1969 *Let It Bleed;* 6) Buffalo Springfield's January 1967 *Buffalo Springfield;* 7) Jefferson Airplane's February 1967 *Surrealistic Pillow;* 8) jazz innovator Roland Kirk's albums in general; 9) jazz great Miles Davis's 1959 *Sketches of Spain;* and 10) multi-instrumental overdubbing virtuoso Sandy Bull's July 1965 *Inventions (for Guitar, Banjo, OUD, Fender Bass Guitar, Electric Guitar)*.

paign seems to be that I'm now plunged heavily into national politics—but on some very odd level that doesn't seem to fit with anybody's idea of Left or Right or Center or anything else. And that's just about the way it should be, I think, but it's a very hard stance to explain . . . and it always has been. The *New York Times* article comes as close as anything written during the campaign to explaining what it was all about.

If nothing else, I certainly learned a hell of a lot . . . I'm working on a book about the campaign. Hopefully, it will be finished in a few months. And I'll send you one of the first copies . . . for good or ill. Thanks again for the check. Love . . .

Hunter

1971

FEAR & LOATHING IN LAS VEGAS . . . QUEER NIGHTS IN THE CIRCUS-CIRCUS, DRAG-RACING ON THE STRIP . . . BROWN POWER IN EAST L.A., TOM WOLFE FLEES TO ITALY . . . INVASION OF THE JESUS FREAKS, A GENERATION RUN AMOK . . . SHREWD ADVICE FROM THE SPORTS DESK . . .

The famous roadside test in Monterey during the Rolling Stone *Big Sur Conference in 1971. Thompson passed the test by catching his sunglasses behind his back when they fell off his head during questioning.* (Photo by Annie Leibovitz)

Hunter S.Thompson
author of Hell's Angels
Fear and Loathing in Las Vegas
A Savage Journey to the Heart of the American Dream
Illustrations by Ralph Steadman

(Drawing by Ralph Steadman)

Hunter Thompson with Oscar Zeta Acosta, Caesars Palace, Las Vegas, 1971. (Photo courtesy of Cashman Photo Enterprises, Inc.)

Rolling Stone *staff, Big Sur Conference, 1971. Left to right: Tim Ferris, Andrew Bailey, Grover Lewis, Paul Scanlon, Bob Kingsbury, Jann Wenner, Jon Landau, HST, Brian Cookman, Jerry Hopkins, Tim Cahill, Bob Greenfield, Joe Eszterhas. Front row: Tim Crouse, Charles Perry, Ben Fong-Torres, David Felton.*
(PHOTO BY ANNIE LEIBOVITZ)

Hunter Thompson in Las Vegas, 1971.
(PHOTO COURTESY OF HST ARCHIVES)

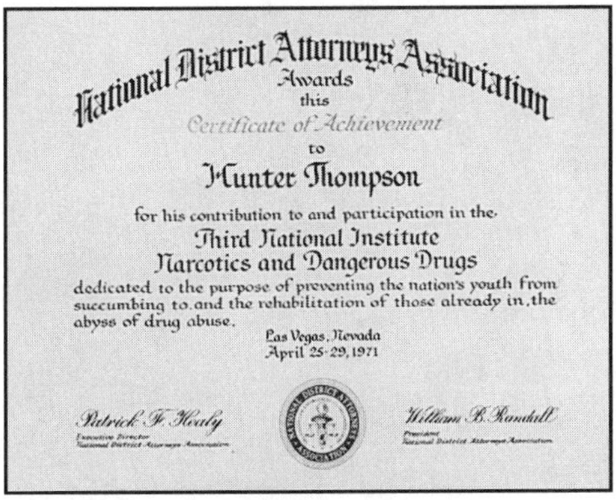

Official certificate from the District Attorneys' Drug Conference.
(PHOTO COURTESY OF HST ARCHIVES)

FROM WILLIAM J. KENNEDY, *LOOK:*

Thompson's friend William Kennedy had a new job.

January 25, 1971

Hunter:

Some you win, some you lose.

I've been named book critic for *LOOK* magazine. My first column will appear in the March 23rd issue, on sale March 9th. This assumes that they print what I write. Signed a contract last week after only about a month's worth of waiting. They knew my work from about a year ago, things I did for the *Observer* and the *T-U [Albany Times-Union]*. I won't get rich but I won't want for much for a while either. Out of the blue, really. I hadn't given a thought to it until they called me up and asked me to be a candidate for the job.

I talked to Selma Shapiro and she hooted mightily: "From Albany to *LOOOOOOOK!!!!!* I don't be-LIEVE it!!!"

So much for Selma's faith.

I'm writing Peggy [Clifford] tonight also and will send her a copy of the article as soon as I can find one. I am in the usual chaos, topped by some unusual frenzy. I get about 12 books a day. My predecessor says some days you get 60. Stop by with your wheelbarrow when you're in the area.

All right for now. Will you make sure to send me your *Stone* piece? I don't get near a newsstand. I'm subscribing to it but I'm afraid I won't get it in time to see your work.

Got a call from Dick Elman[1] the other night. He's got a 600-page novel coming out about a professor who murders his wife. He's getting restless with his agent who thinks the book is too strong. Don't understand. Elman also divorcing. Denne Petitclerc's[2] novel on LeMans coming out around May, I think.

Yes, yes, yes.
Kennedy

1. Liberal writer Richard Elman had reviewed Thompson's *Hell's Angels* for *The New Republic.*
2. Kennedy's good friend Denne Petitclerc was a former reporter for the *San Francisco Chronicle.*

TO ROBERT LIPSYTE, *THE NEW YORK TIMES:*

Thompson pitched the sports angle on the rape-of-Aspen story to an editor friend at The New York Times.

January 27, 1971
Woody Creek, CO

Dear Bob . . .

It just occurred to me that we're sitting on a really wonderful sport-story out here, but for some reason the hired ski-press can't seem to get into it. What's happening to Aspen is that it's faced, very suddenly, with the same kind of socio-political reality that's stomping down the aisles of every other sport from boxing to pro-football . . . or at least trying to. Anyway, the town is committing financial suicide, rather than cope with all these terrible new afflictions that have suddenly rushed in from the Outside World. The merchants have chosen to hunker down in a brain-swamp of Nazi/Agnew platitudes . . . and their lunatic stance is all that keeps local politics interesting. The Ski Patrol, for instance, just voted to unionize under the Teamsters, and now there's talk of a savage strike, complete with picket lines on the ski lifts & imported thugs pounding strikebreakers, etc., etc. . . . and all this with another (Mayor & city council) election coming up in May . . . and tonight I attended Aspen's first John Birch Society rally, at the new Holiday Inn. The Fatbacks are gearing down for Waterloo, a last stand . . . and like I said, it looks like a king-hell Sport Story. FYI . . .

Hunter

TO WILLIAM J. KENNEDY, *LOOK:*

January 30, 1971
Woody Creek, CO

Dear William . . .

Your note inre: *LOOK* was the best news I've had in fuck knows how long. I didn't realize those fuckers even reviewed books, but if Selma's into that action I know it must be *important.* Indeed, you'll probably blow up to about 300 pounds of free booze by mid '71 . . . you'd better be watching yourself; this is a very ominous watershed for us all, and since I'll probably never have an opening to say it again, I might as well belch it out now. . . . Yes . . . You have just Been Bought? Sold Out? Bought IN? What is it . . . ? I'm no longer sure.

Are you?

I think that's a righteous question. And I'll start reading *LOOK* to find out some hints at the answer. But in a nut I see this as a really terrifying development all around. The deal continues to Go Down. For us all. And where, they ask, *were you* when the Great Ace fell?

Where indeed? Denne Petitclerc turned up in my driveway last night, leaning nervously on his horn & yelling that last year he made 250,000 dollars & the Taxman took it all & where could he rent a peaceful cabin in Aspen? What could I make of a scene like that? What could *you* make of it? What will the Taxman say next week when he comes for his crucial One Grand—according to the schedule [Thompson's tax adviser] Shellman rigged up—and I tell him I can't be bothered with that kind of cheap left-handed shit because all my 250K per yr. buddies are embarrassed to be seen in a house that is known to be haunted these days by the Taxman?

Horrible, horrible . . .

Anyway, it's a weird but absolute truth that about 30 minutes before I got your letter inre: *LOOK* I was standing in the shower & for some reason thinking about *The Rum Diary,* which led to a side-shot on your action & found myself wondering why my life was so bound up in the failed dreams of crazy Irishmen (Clancy, Hinckle, you . . .) and I came out of the shower sort of slumped & ill-humored and grumbling at Sandy . . . & then she gave me your letter, which I opened with a baleful sort of snarl . . . and I tell you by christ it was the first honest ray of light I've seen since Election Day. If you were anywhere around I'd smack you on the fucking ear and drink off the rest of your whiskey. With a crazy burst of laughing & nasty raps on whatever gang of assholes stumbled into that kind of hopeless mistake . . .

Yeah . . . good show. For good or ill. The terrible irony, of course, is that it should have happened at least 10 years ago. Why do the bastards always learn so late? And so long after the crucial eviction-or-else rent was due? You should make it your business to focus on the High Things that are happening *Now*—which is risky, because it involves a constant kind of out-front value judgement act that nobody else on the Publishing/PR Grog scene can possibly understand. Their gig is "Whatever's Safe" . . . and that leaves a lot of room for "Whatever's Right." Consider it . . . and Good Luck. OK . . .

Hunter

TO SELMA SHAPIRO, RANDOM HOUSE:

January 30, 1971
Woody Creek, CO

Dear Selma . . .

Bill Kennedy just sent me a note containing a nasty quote from you about hicks sneaking into the Big City. I always suspected you of living behind a rude, commercial eye . . . and the raw, naked & supremely focused ambition that drives you was never more clear than when you turned your back on all your best aesthetic instincts and stripped that naked bird/shooting/California shotgun photo of me off your wall and sent it back for revisions. That was a callous, rotten act—and it plunged me into a savage, mindless sort of drug frenzy that lasted for maybe two years.

In any case, I'm enclosing the latest issue of the *Wallposter*—including my most recent Personal public-release style photograph. This one is a real fucking *Winner,* and when I tell Silberman that it has to be the jacket foto for the next ugly book, I don't want any tasteless shit from *your* department. I have *all the graphics* well organized . . . and beyond that I've lined out a fantastic Hired Pig campaign that will bend them all stupid. All that's left, of course, is *The Book*—which I must get back to, for now. It's stone gibberish, but what the hell? These goddamn kids will buy anything, won't they?

Best commercial wishes,
Hunter

TO JANN WENNER, *ROLLING STONE:*

Thompson was toying with committing to write a regular column for Rolling Stone.

January 30, 1971
Woody Creek, CO

Dear Jann . . .

This comes in the midst of a certain amount of work/priority/message chaos—some of which resulted from those fucking telegrams of yours that got here three days late. Jesus, you should know by now—don't ever fuck with Western Union (I got your first one in the midst of writing a proposal for various acts geared to the 1, 2, 3 notions you outlined in your last letter . . . but when I figured you'd be here in a matter of hours I said, Well, fuck this, we'll wait & talk about it . . . then I called Rock[3] & he said No, maybe Wednesday . . . or maybe now, but in any event I'll gear the fuckers back up and send them off ASAP). And Rock, in the meantime, will get the brunt of the Wild Boar message . . . yes, we *need* that heard.

Anyway, the nut of what's left hanging here is some idea of consolidating *what we have* on Aspen, along with some hazy ideas on LA/Chicanos vs. Vietnam (with lengthy notes & samples) . . . along with a very definitely double-edged idea about the notion of doing a regular sort of column for *Rolling Stone*—which is always a good idea, in abstract, but I remember I agreed to it once for *Ramparts,* [and] the idea of filling one page a month was never quite hashed out between [editor Peter] Collier & myself—much less that wiggy bastard Hinckle. But it *was* a good idea; I never denied that—although it was hard to lock into for $150 or $200 a month. Because what happens to anybody who

3. San Francisco financier and MJB Coffee Chairman Arthur Rock was *Rolling Stone*'s landlord and a member of the board of directors of Wenner's Straight Arrow Publishers, Inc.

gets into any kind of forced/regular writing is that he's bound to make a useless fool of himself now & then . . . and it's hard to set a price on that kind of reality.

But to hell with that for now; at best it's just a vague notion—maybe born of my continuing frustration at always having to dump about nine-tenths of everything worth writing about, the inevitable free-lancer's compulsion to always fire your *best shot* . . . which kills all of the fast raps & left jabs en route to all those classic Kayos.

Right . . . but let's not forget that the KO's are where the main survival/nerves live, and we all have to scrape those evil fuckers once in a while, if only to pay the rent. Or maybe the real word is "dues." Which I suspect maybe you might have a hard time understanding. No fault of your own—or anyone else's, for that matter . . . just some accident of history, and maybe the main thing you lost with Lombardi[4] was his gut understanding of that concept. Which lent a definite *depth,* or dimension, to most of what he did or got into. But what the hell . . . ?

Excelsior! Right?

I'll get this jangled package to you as soon as I get it all straight . . . & meanwhile I'll eat some snails with Rock & bug him a bit about all the scenes that he *should,* of course, be In To. Right! Wild Boar & Wolverines. But *discretion* is the word, eh? And why not? We're all discreet when we see the need. Even me . . . And that's about it for now.

OK . . .
Hunter

TO U.S. SENATOR WALTER F. MONDALE:

Minnesota senator and future vice president Walter F. Mondale—one of the few Washington politicians Thompson respected—had taken less than a month to reply to his July 31, 1970, letter.

February 1, 1971
Woody Creek, CO

Dear Senator Mondale:

Sorry to be so late with a reply to your letter of August 24, '70 . . . but my correspondence & indeed my whole lifestyle were plunged into limbo last autumn when I became involved in one of the most savage & unnatural campaigns of modern times. I refer, of course, to my "Freak Power" bid to unseat the incumbent sheriff of Aspen, Colorado. Which failed—by a roughly 40/60% split when the local Democrats & Republicans combined in a last-minute coalition to beat us.

4. Former associate editor John Lombardi, who left for *Esquire* in the summer of 1970, had been instrumental in bringing Thompson on board at *Rolling Stone.*

There's not much point in explaining this tragedy, but for your general amusement or whatever, I'm enclosing a *New York Times* clip for some background. And also one of our *Wallposters* . . . and if I can find one, a copy of a thing I did for *Rolling Stone*. I'm not sure what any of this might explain to you, but my general idea in sending it along is that we might possibly have stumbled on something very important out here. Aspen is a solidly GOP town by registration, but in 1970 all four city precincts voted solidly for a "Freak Power" ticket—which is not quite as bad as it sounds (see *Rolling Stone*), but bad enough to generate a landslide against us in the two rural/suburb/trailer-court precincts; and that was what beat us. . . .

And that's about it for now . . . except maybe to urge you to *think* about the weird implications of this Aspen/Freak Power thing. On the surface it seems entirely local, but stripped of those menacing fright-words the Aspen campaign boiled down very simply to the notion of running a completely honest political campaign—saying exactly what we thought & what we planned to do. My platform was a bit heavy & towards the end we were forced to tone down the *language*—but *not* the *realities*, and in the final analysis it hardly mattered whether we planned to "tear up the streets" or merely "ban autos from the city-center & turn the streets into malls." The real issue was Power . . . and Who was going to have it. This was clearly understood on both sides, and as a result we turned out an incredible number of voters, more than anyone thought was possible.

What I'm getting at here is the fact that we managed to tap a huge bloc vote that nobody even suspected was alive in this town. These were the people—nearly all under 25—who understood that our "freak power" slogan was not an insult but a compliment. This was a difficult thing for the local ACLU-type "liberals" to understand; they didn't like being appealed to as "freaks."

But what the hell? They speak a dead language, anyway . . . and the whole point of this election was to Win on our Own Terms, with *no compromise*. And this, I think, was the key to the massive vote we turned out, both *for* and *against* us. The town was plunged into total hysteria for more than a month—and in the end, the opposition (the GOP & the Democrats) turned out every possible vote; they brought people on stretchers down from the hospital, they wheeled in 90-year-old vegetables, *they did everything possible* and still lost all the city precincts.

Which wasn't enough to win a *County* election for us . . . but I'm convinced that what we proved here will sooner or later be crucial in national politics. This is especially true, I think, in light of the fantastic national (& even international) press coverage we got. (This was a serious problem for us, as it turned out—we simply couldn't handle the bastards; especially the 8-man film crew from London with their light-banks & color-cameras that followed us *everywhere* for the final two weeks of the campaign.)

But there's no point rambling on about all this at the moment—although it occurred to me that the *concept* might interest you. Or maybe it might interest [George] McGovern—whose only conceivable chance seems to be a successful appeal to precisely the same vote we managed to tap here in Aspen. ([Edmund] Muskie has already blown it & [Edward] Kennedy . . . well . . . that's hazy, for now, but the haze won't matter if McGovern can somehow manage to tap the national equivalent of Freak Power. . . .)

Which is interesting—right? And all I meant to do here was answer your letter of 8/24. Which I seem to have done, for good or ill. So . . . all I can say for now is Hang On. You seem to be doing OK, & it's nice to know that there's at least one straight voice in that twisted arena.

Sincerely,
Hunter S. Thompson

TO SIDNEY ZION, *SCANLAN'S MONTHLY:*

Thompson would make good on his threat "that the name Sidney Zion is going to stink for a long, long time" by dragging it through the mud and worse in Fear and Loathing in Las Vegas.

February 5, 1971
Woody Creek, CO

Dear Sidney . . .

You worthless lying bastard. I just talked to the IRS man in Grand Junction (Colo.) and he read me a letter from some goddamn lawyer of yours (to the IRS), saying *Scanlan's* didn't owe me any money at all and that you refused to honor the $3400-plus Assignment to me of funds owed *Scanlan's* from Select Magazines Inc.

The truth, of course, is that *Scanlan's does* owe me money & that the figure actually represents a *compromise* arranged after long haggling with Warren Hinckle—who signed the document (Assignment) in his capacity as Vice-President and Editor of *Scanlan's Monthly.* This debt was affirmed by Warren, in good faith, and it strikes me as absolutely incredible that *you* should have anything whatsoever to say about it. In fact I'm astounded to find *you* speaking for *Scanlan's* in any way at all—especially to a writer. You never showed anything but total contempt and disinterest in writers up until now . . . but now that American Express has seized my credit card for *Scanlan's*-incurred debts and the IRS is threatening to seize my personal belongings & put them up for public auction . . . now you have the stupid, greedy gall to say the magazine doesn't owe me any money.

What the fuck would *you* know about *Scanlan's* dealings with writers, financial or otherwise? The only interest you ever showed in the magazine, as I recall, was that useless, atavistic series on "dirty kitchens" that was a constant embarrassment to everybody connected with the magazine. Beyond *that,* it never occurred to me that you had any interest or connection with the editorial side. As far as I or the other writers were concerned, Hinckle was the *editor* & you were some kind of two-legged nightmare to be avoided at all costs. Which was easy, because not many of the writers spent time in Sardi's or Gallaghers.

My only clear memory of you in the office was the time you roared in & began yelling at Don Goddard (then the Managing Editor) about some useless trivia when he & I were trying to put a long-overdue lead article together for the June issue. That was my Kentucky Derby piece, which Hinckle was waiting for at the printer's in San Francisco. And then, while Goddard tore his hair, you tried to get me to accompany you to Gallaghers "for a drink." Later, after you'd gone off in a sulk, I asked Goddard if that was your normal behavior at deadline time, and he said it was usually much worse—so bad, in fact, that he could hardly wait to flee *Scanlan's* employ just as soon as that issue was out. I later heard he was "fired," but the truth is that he was *driven out* by your constant tirades and total lack of concern for the editorial side of the magazine.

But to hell with all that. I only mention it to show why I'm shocked to find that *you* now claim to know what *Scanlan's* may or may not owe me. You never knew *anything,* Sidney. You were *humored.* You were a fucking drag on everybody . . . and now you want to act like an *editor.* Bullshit! You wanted to hold up publication of the "Guerrilla Warfare" issue last September, in order to establish damages in some lawsuit you were planning at that time. I heard you suggest that to Hinckle in Sardi's, and I recall being shocked at the notion that your only interest in publication had to do with winning or losing a lawsuit. Once again, the editorial side of the magazine meant *nothing* to you.

As Harvey Cohen[5] said to you one night in Elaine's: "You're a *pig,* Sidney. *You* are the enemy!"

So now you're proving it, with me. To deny that *Scanlan's* owes me any money is such a goddamn rotten lie that I'm surprised even *you* would try to carry it off. You've caused me a tremendous amount of trouble: 1) First the loss of my American Express card, which as you know is a crucial loss for a freelance writer (especially for $1100 or so—or about half of the *expenses Scanlan's* owes me), and 2) This crisis with the IRS, a debt I'd planned to pay off with *the rest* of the money *Scanlan's* owes me.

These are not small items, Sidney, and you can goddamn well be sure you haven't heard the last of them. Hinckle has at least tried to square that debt, but you—you lying bastard—have just told me to fuck off. As far as I'm concerned you should drag your treacherous ass off to some cheap gig selling used cars in Hoboken, which is where you belong. In ten years of dealing with all

5. Harvey Cohen was a staff editor at *Scanlan's.*

kinds of editors I can safely say I've never met a scumsucker like you. You're a disgrace to the goddamn business and the only good thing likely to come of this rotten disaster is that the name Sidney Zion is going to stink for a long, long time.

Sincerely,
Hunter S. Thompson

cc: Lynn Nesbit
Warren Hinckle
IRS
& others

TO JANN WENNER, *ROLLING STONE:*

Thompson had been working on an article commissioned by Warren Hinckle on the police murder of Chicano L.A. Times *writer Ruben Salazar when the bottom fell out at* Scanlan's Monthly.

February 8, 1971
Woody Creek, CO

Dear Jann . . .

Too many loose ends for tying in one letter—so here are Two, for the moment.

1) Xerox bill for that Aspen stuff (at your request) and also bill for two phone calls to Oscar Acosta inre: LA/Chicano piece. Total—$20.85. Thanx . . .

2) Large item is a half-edited galley of that Salazar LA/Chicano/murder piece I did for *Scanlan's* but which got lost somewhere between layout & press-time 4 months later. Understandably, no doubt. I guess. Maybe because it was written while the coroner's jury was still out . . . but it's in now, & the verdict supports my thesis about 85%. Which is weird. It was sort of a hung coroner's jury.

Anyway, I've been talking to Acosta off & on for the past few days & he's told me a hell of a lot about what's going on down there (savage polarization, revolution in the revolution, etc. . . .) but the sum total of what he's told me sounds more like a novel than an article. It sounds like a perfect nightmare of a story—even for somebody with long-time blood/drug/madness ties to the radical Chicano vortex. Despite my near-total access to the craziest & meanest corners of that East LA militant scene, I still can't find that special happy *peg* to keep the story moving in the context of *any* given narrative situation. The *whole* story is too open, too sprawling & contradictory to fit in the "article" framework . . .

. . . which is why I'm enclosing this Salazar piece. Because it offers a natural framework & a good narrative. And besides that it embodies a hell of a lot of painful research & detail that would take about two weeks to duplicate. This could provide the *nut* of a new, up-dated piece on the same scene—beginning *now*, flashing back to the Salazar murder for a focal point & narrative, then finishing with post-Salazar developments up to now again.

So . . . consider it. And let me know ASAP. I just (today) got over a terrible crisis-hump with the IRS by coming up with an instant Grand at the last moment, about 2 hrs before the seizure deadline. The fuckers were poised to tow my car off, impound my bike, seize my turntable & amp—the whole gig. And they were serious—which I didn't really believe until this morning at about 9:00 a.m.

Anyway, the pressure is off for the first time since the election. I now have two more months until the next & final ($1300) deadline. But right now 2 months seems like a lifetime—considering that they *must* leave me alone for that long. And that's time enough, I think.

So . . . given a choice between Vietnam & LA, I still prefer Vietnam. That's one of the best stories of the past five years, a natural setup . . . while the Chicano thing is a natural bummer & in fact I wouldn't consider it except for the existence of this Salazar thing, which would give me a running start.

***

The political scene out here remains grim. It's beginning to look like we not only peaked but shattered in that last election. Rather than go into detail on that, right now, I'll enclose a chunk of rambling stuff that I've had around for a few days, ready to send but without any real reason to. Except that now some of the stuff I've marked with red bracket-lines (see left border) might fit into any "Aspen letter" you plan to run.

Jesus . . . these crippled attempts to put "the Aspen story" together are driving me deeper & deeper into permanent freakiness. But for whatever it's worth, here's more. I'll eventually get it together for the book, but what the hell? I don't see much point in editing this stuff; just use what you want & fuck the rest.

As for Rock [a major investor in *Rolling Stone*], I definitely think he should be arrested. The fucker is floating around like some kind of un-programmed energy-bomb, adrift in the sea-lanes of a reality he can't seem to mesh with. And I suspect he's capable of raising serious hell if he ever gets focused. Maybe we should run him for Mayor of Aspen this spring. What Arthur needs is some Responsibility, something to settle him down & get him anchored. It makes me nervous to know that people like that are running around loose, with all that static lightning stored up in them. . . .

. . . hell, maybe we should run him for President in '72, on a national Freak Power ticket. Wait until the Convention & then launch him out of nowhere with a special 2 million *Rolling Stone* press run & thousands of hysterical half-naked groupies swarming into the floor of the convention . . . chanting "Rock!" "Rock!" "Rock!"

Christ, it can't miss. I'll plant the seed next time he comes out. He's sure to go for it. Why not?

Indeed, why not? . . . Anyway, let me know on the Chicano gig. Right now I need some sleep; to curb this manic euphoria that comes with shucking the Taxman for a while. OK for now . . .

HST

TO MAX PALEVSKY:

Three years after Rolling Stone *premiered, Jann Wenner's fledgling empire verged on financial collapse. Thanks to some gutsy dealmaking that would look even shrewder later, his company was bailed out of near-bankruptcy on January 8, 1971—Wenner's twenty-fifth birthday—by the arrival of a $200,000 check from high-living self-made computer mogul and cutting-edge wannabe Max Palevsky, who insured his investment by severely tightening Straight Arrow Publishers, Inc.'s business operations.*

February 8, 1971
Woody Creek, CO

Dear Max . . .

Enclosed are two specimens of what purports to be the finest Chicano mescaline—straight from East L.A. I haven't analyzed it yet, but the source has always been reliable in the past. I understand that your interest in these matters is entirely rooted in the same socio/political/research that I naturally share—since we're both In Journalism, as it were, and also into Politics. Which makes us both political scientists, and on that basis I feel it's entirely fitting that I make this evidence available to a fellow scientist. Selah.

And so much for all that. It's entirely possible that I'll be in LA sometime soon. Jann is muttering about a piece on the Chicano/Pig war in East L.A. & I'll check with him in a day or so to find out. If I get down there maybe we can get together for a beer, or a beaker or two of tequila. In the meantime I suggest you speak to that dingbat who calls himself "Arthur Rock." I suspect he's looking for trouble out here in the peaceful Rockies . . . and by god if there's one thing we won't tolerate out here it's a dingbat looking for trouble.

OK for now. Sincerely . . .
Hunter S. Thompson

TO JANN WENNER, *ROLLING STONE:*

"Strange Rumblings in Aztlan"—Thompson's investigative piece on the August 29, 1970, murder of journalist Ruben Salazar by a Los Angeles County

sheriff's deputy—appeared in the April 29, 1971, issue of Rolling Stone. *Thompson left open whether Salazar "couldn't possibly have been the victim of a conscious, high-level cop conspiracy to get rid of him by staging an 'accidental death.' The incredible tale of half-mad stupidity and dangerous incompetence on every level of the law enforcement establishment was perhaps the most valuable thing to come out of the inquest."*

February 10, 1971
Woody Creek, CO

Dear Jann . . .

Christ, I just read that Salazar piece from start to finish—for the first time—and discovered a terrible jumbling in the lead. I don't know who edited the thing; I just turned it in on my way from SF to Newport for the America's Cup story, but my version ran chronologically from the time I heard about Salazar's death in Portland, Ore & then on to LA, meeting Oscar at the airport, etc. & then into the investigation.

In this version, something drastic happened to that chronology. It doesn't make any real sense until around Galley #3. Which is neither here nor there, for now, but it bothers me to see how scrambled it reads up front. Also, my section breakers are missing: verbatim quotes from the Calif. Penal Code, Sec. 187, the legal definition of "murder."

Anyway, it don't matter none . . . but it bugs me just the same. (Oh, yeah, there are some photos—in rough sequence—of the murder action. I got the originals from Joe Razo at La Raza & I assume he still has them; I returned the photos to him after Hinckle used them for the *Scanlan's* layout. . . .) Selah.

Which reminds me; you mentioned Clancy had called about selling *Scanlan's* to *RS*—which strikes me as an interesting *idea,* in the abstract, & that's all it was, as I recall, when Clancy first mentioned the idea of talking to Palevsky a month or so ago . . . but even now it strikes me as a fetching sort of idea. What comes to mind, right off, is some kind of 1970s version of a Time/Life empire; two entirely different publications locked into the same nexus . . . *real* freak power . . . but keep in mind that I'm talking just about the concept, the *general idea;* beyond that, I think I'll pass for now . . . but if you want to talk about it, hell, give a ring. I'm always good for talk about empire-building.

And so much for all that. I began this letter about 40 hours ago, but most of the time since then I've spent ram-rodding this goddamn effort to change the election date. *The troops are not into it.* And I guess that's part of the story, too. Like I said, the question now is not so much whether we *can* put our act back together again—but whether it's worth the effort. In the *long* run . . . or even the short, for that matter. If Aspen had a best-seller list, the United Farm Catalog would be #1 right now. An alarming number of our people are ready to abandon ship, rather than face another futile shutdown. Which leaves me in the awkward role of playing Keeper of the Flame—or maybe just "main hustler" instead of Main Pig.

Anyway, that's why I'm late finishing this letter. And the main point, as I recall, was to get you a quick outline of the upcoming Aspen piece . . . so here's that: very much off the top of my head & subject to massive change, but fairly reliable in terms of length, thrust, theme, etc. . . .

To wit: Well . . . this was supposed to be the *outline,* but I began & kept going 5–6 pages with a quick-opening scene with me & Vare[6] hunkered down in this cabin & debating the wisdom of making another full-scale assault on the fatbacks in May . . . and this led to the same kind of speculation I mentioned on the phone the other day: The future of freak power (?) in Aspen or anywhere else . . . and whether or not we might all be better off not wasting our time with this bullshit & bugging off for somewhere else. Which led, of course, to the question of *where.* And after a long & torturous talk we got back to the notion that in fact we had no choice but to hang on here . . . because if we're going to have to stand & fight *somewhere* (& I think that's painfully obvious, whether we like it or not) we both saw the heavy advantage of working in a scene where we already have a proven power base . . . a town that last November voted not only for Vare (for County Commissioner) but also for a sheriff whose only compromise on the "drug question" was to say he would not eat mescaline *on duty.*

Given a bit of rest & perspective, this has the appearance of a very heavy reality . . . and all the more so when you lump it with the fact that the local Democrats & Republicans only beat us by collapsing into a last-minute desperation coalition (with each party agreeing to sacrifice a main candidate) that avoided the three-way vote split we were counting on. Which was crucial, and which we probably would have had if I hadn't written the bastards a perfect blueprint for beating us with that Battle of Aspen article in *RS.* . . .

Anyway, my new lead takes off from a private conversation between me & Vare about whether this battle is worth fighting any longer (which gets into the "Is the *country* fucked, too?" argument) and also our reluctant plans for coping with what looks like an almost certain Mayor/Council election in May. So the *dialogue* of the lead involves both our loss last November & our private argument about whether to try again—in Aspen or anywhere else. I'm totally convinced that this argument has far-reaching *national* ramifications . . . because it's beginning to look like the '60s gave birth to a whole generation that now has no place to go—or at least no *obvious* place, and in truth not even a real direction. I was living 2 blocks above Haight Street in the spring of '66 & I remember that sense of a whole new world taking root—but in retrospect

6. Freak Power candidate Ned Vare had narrowly lost the race for Pitkin County commissioner in November 1970.

that era seems more like a speed-laced acid trip than anything real, and since then not much has worked out. The movement to rural communes went limp pretty quick . . . although now I suspect we might be heading for a really massive "flee the cities" movement. Not to communes or anything formal—just *out,* a serious panic trip in *any* direction.

Maybe even Aspen—which gets back to the theme. We tried to run the opening wedge for a New Boondocks program . . . but we blew it. So I guess the next section should deal with *why* & *how* we blew it: Our mistakes in strategy, direction, organizing, internal squabbling, etc. . . . All the stuff that combined to get us stomped at the polls. (And despite all the *points* we made & the chance of a new direction we *may* have created, I guess A. Rock has a point when he says "the first business of a politician is to get elected.") Which is true, I guess—but it sidesteps the question of *why?* And it also misses the whole point of the Aspen campaign—which was that we ran the public line between the necessity for winning and the weird possibility of *winning on our terms.*

That was the only thing that made the Aspen campaign worth the effort. Hell, any shithead can *win.* Look at Nixon. To him, the end justifies any means. But our idea was that maybe the means could *be* the end . . . The Concept *is* the solution. If the idea had been to simply unseat a stupid backwoods sheriff, I sure as hell wouldn't have shaved my head & flooded the town with posters showing a double-thumbed red fist clutching a peyote button.

But . . . so much for all that. The fact is that we ran what the *NY Times* called "the most bizarre political campaign on the American scene today" and, despite all our mistakes, disasters & panic-trips, we wound up winning the city of Aspen and only losing the county by a 45/55 or so split—against the *combined* muscle of both major parties. In other words, on Nov 4, 1970, "Freak Power" was the largest & most powerful *single* political voice (or tangible vote-bloc identity) in Aspen & in fact the whole county . . . and I think this is worth pondering.

Anyway, the piece should move from the opening Vare/Thompson conversation inre: Freak Power here & elsewhere . . . to the May election & brief prospects . . . to the Big Question (fight or flee) & a brief discussion of that (in the context of the '60s) . . . and then back to the Nov. election and a detailed account of our mistakes . . . along with heavy emphasis on the fact that we won the city & only lost the redneck county because of a last-minute GOP/Demo trade-off.

So in essence that leaves me with all kinds of options, once I get the lead done. And the ending, I guess, should focus on the "what next?" question. In Aspen & elsewhere. Or: "An Epitaph (?) for Freak Power." Something like that. Or, Where do we go from here?

OK for now. . .
Hunter

TO LYNN NESBIT:

As usual, no matter how hilariously jangled an account he sent to his agent, Thompson couldn't hide the fact that he was on top of every one of his projects.

February 22, 1971
Woody Creek, CO

Dear Lynn . . .

I need advice at once. My priorities are becoming badly scrambled. The other night I found myself roaming around my house in a crowd & wondering who might be good for the price of a pack of cigarettes while Billy Hitchcock's[7] girlfriend is cooking up a pot of peyote tea on my stove and Jann Wenner is on the telephone screaming at Gates Lear Jet in Denver trying to charter a plane to LA at once because he (Wenner) can't communicate with Bob Rafelson who's too stoned to remember where he left (or put, or sent) *his* Lear Jet that he just flew in on . . . and all this is happening in the kitchen while Arthur Rock is having some kind of public crisis in the living room wondering out loud whether to put a million dollars behind McGovern along with his partner Max Palevsky who seems to own not only Xerox but *Rolling Stone* & just about everything else in the fucking world except enough mescaline to get thru the nite on . . . and the instant Wenner gets off the phone it rings & here's Clancy & Hinckle both crazy drunk at the Plaza trying to sell *Scanlan's* to Rock for a massive tax loss and Rock is so stoned he thinks it's [New York Mayor John] Lindsay calling him for money to fight Muskie & McGovern . . . and somebody says, "No, it's Max demanding drugs" and meanwhile Clancy is shouting "It's all over, your money is doomed." And all I can curse him for is being drunk & Irish or maybe Jewish, or at least a lawyer . . . and suddenly people are yelling "Hang up! Hang up on that bastard!" Which Clancy hears & goes crazy with rage because he thinks they know *he's* calling . . . but actually nobody knows *who's* calling, or cares, but they want to call a doctor because Rafelson has freaked in the kitchen & fallen on top of a huge sleeping Doberman, which has bitten him & drawn blood . . . and Rock is screaming "I knew these goddamn dogs would turn on us sooner or later!" And my wife is crying because somebody poured the peyote tea into the chicken curry . . . and the minute I hang up on Clancy, Wenner yanks me aside & says "Look at this"—which is a list of inoculations I have to get before leaving for Saigon on June 1, and it occurs to me that I might as well start right then by shooting up with that fine chicken curry tea . . . but at that point I'm still trying to be rea-

7. Multimillionaire and LSD enthusiast William Hitchcock had turned over his Millbrook, New York, estate to Timothy Leary, whose drug experiments Hitchcock considered a holy quest.

sonable, although Noonan the mad Coroner[8] is slobbering over Rafelson's wound and suddenly the phone rings again & this time it's Oscar Acosta in East LA, screaming that the Pigs have surrounded his house & are about to finish him off with mustard gas . . . and just then the door opens & some freak rushes in yelling, "We need a thousand dollars at once for the lawsuit." Which is a lawsuit to tie up the Aspen city govt. for the next two years, guaranteed chaos & civic/fiscal collapse . . . and just then I remember that I haven't paid the electric bill & the lights might go off any minute & I don't have any kerosene & now all three Dobermans have gone wild on the smell of blood & the noise is so bad that I have to hang up on Oscar & leave him to his fate and . . .

. . . Well, why go on? That scene is pure fiction, of course. It could never have happened. Especially in writing. And to that end I suspect you should bury the first page of this letter. All I meant to convey, when I started, was a sense of stone-mad helplessness in a scene so weird that it's hard to understand how the *host* to all that craziness could be too broke to buy a pack of cigarettes. So let's chalk it off to fiction, for now, and focus down on a few facts. To wit:

Wenner wants me to become a "Contributing Editor" of *Rolling Stone.* Which seems fine to me, but I'm not sure what it means in terms of money, obligations, time, problems, advantages, etc. I deliberately avoided talking specifics with him, until I could find out what an arrangement like this would mean in terms of contracts & that sort of thing. For instance, my first assignment would be to spend six months in Vietnam, covering the U.S. retreat in a series of articles that would eventually become a *Rolling Stone* book. I said Fine, because it's a story I'd very much like to work on . . . but I hesitated to commit myself to a book until I talked to you (although I asked John Sack[9] about it & he said "no problem").

Anyway, that's just one loose end. Another is a piece that I originally did for *Scanlan's* called "The Murder of Ruben Salazar" (the Chicano journalist killed in LA—by the cops) that Wenner now wants to buy for *Rolling Stone,* along with a week's worth of up-dating that it definitely needs. We didn't mention any price on this . . . although what Hinckle had agreed on was $1200 to me and $300 to Acosta for the legwork (the piece was bought, edited, set in type & sent to the *original* printer, but by the time the goddamn thing got printed finally in Montreal Hinckle had dropped both the Salazar piece & another by Min Yee in favor of his (Hinckle's) introduction. Which is neither here nor there; I only mention it to give you some background).

Which leads me to another problem, of sorts. At some point in the midst of the election madness I agreed to do an "aftermath" piece for *Rolling Stone*—which I never really did, although about six weeks ago I sent John Lombardi

8. Louisville native Billy Noonan, a friend of Thompson's brother Davison, had been the Freak Power candidate for Pitkin County coroner in 1970.

9. John Sack was a contributing editor at *Esquire.*

about 200 photos & 140 pages of first-draft text that I was essentially writing for the Random House book. The text began with my *Scanlan's*-commissioned coverage of the America's Cup yacht races last September & then jumped to Aspen & the madness of the Sheriff's race. I wrote it that way because—as I told Silberman—I intended to open the book with a quick America's Cup scene and then run through a series of flashbacks (50,000 or so words) leading up to the 1970 freak power election. In other words, my idea was to write a long rambling article that would eventually become the *first* and *last* chapters of the American Dream/Battle of Aspen book. This came to mind perhaps because the same kind of setup worked out very nicely, by accident, for the Hell's Angels book. In that case, *Playboy* commissioned a Hell's Angels article that they eventually rejected—but in retrospect the rejected *Playboy* article was transferred almost word for word into Chapters One and (Final—I forget that number) of the book.

So that's what I decided to do on this too. And the only problem is that Wenner wants to buy *both* segments *as articles.* In other words, he wants the America's Cup piece (no price mentioned) and also the "Freak Power Election" piece (which I thought had been rejected in embryo by Lombardi just before he moved to *Esquire,* but which Wenner now wants to resurrect—for $1000, a price that Wenner tells me you muscled out of Lombardi). And I use that word "muscled" in a friendly sense; the only point being that Wenner feels that $1000 is the price already agreed on for the #2 Aspen piece. And that's fine with me—unless it happens to get in the way of a serial-sale for the book. Which is not impossible if I sell it in tandem with that America's Cup/opening chapter scene . . . in other words (& I explained this to Jann) I'm not sure how Silberman would feel if I told him I'd already sold the first & last chapters of the book as *Rolling Stone* articles. I recall his reaction to my insistence on selling the *entire* Hell's Angels book to *Esquire* for $1000, and I'd just as soon not be made to feel that stupid again. (I'm particularly sensitive on this score after hearing that Dave Meggyesy, my #2 bodyguard during the campaign, just sold his football book to *LOOK* for $12/14K. That figure *didn't* come from Dave; & maybe it's only a rumor. . . .) But in any case I think you can probably see, by now, the roots of the general money/politics hassle behind this thing . . . and I offer my profound apologies for making it seem so complicated.

But I'm afraid it is. (Recall pg. 1, above.) But for now let's try to keep it as simple as possible . . . and to that end, here's the schedule:

a) I've already agreed to deliver the "Freak Power" piece to Jann in SF on March 15. The agreement is that the draft I deliver at that time will be app. 100 pages long & "at least 75% finished." March 16 will be spent in SF, working verbally on the Aspen piece—deciding how to finish it off. March 17 will also be spent in SF, deciding what we need to complete the Salazar/Chicano piece. Then, on March 17, I will go to LA & spend 3 to 5 days gathering whatever bullshit I need to update & flesh out the Chicano piece.

After that I will fly back to SF & finish off both articles (Aspen & LA Chicano). . . . (Jesus, what the fuck have I *agreed* to? This is the first time I've lined this gig out on paper—& even now, on the upswing, it looks like the Final Speed Trip.)

b) and so much for that. By March 25, at the latest, I should have two very large features finished for *RS*. This ignores, however, the America's Cup sequence that Jann wants to buy as a separate article but which I've already written, very roughly, into the first draft of my Freak Power piece that is also the final chapter of Silberman's book. In other words, on March 15 I'm going to be standing around Wenner's office in SF with about a third of Silberman's book in my hands—in rough draft, of course—but even then with ½ of that third already sold for $1000 and Chapter One not yet sold but very much on the block at that time because there's going to be no way to ignore it or even dodge the issue once I show my draft to Wenner. He's already said that he wants both ends of the thing—which is fine, except I'm not sure what that leaves us to sell for serial rights. If anything.

So consider that. On March 15 I'll be standing in SF with three articles in my hands, as it were: 1) Salazar/Chicanos, 2) Aspen election, and 3) America's Cup, which is also the lead into Aspen-election. #1 is the piece originally commissioned by *Scanlan's* (but not paid for—not even the expenses, which contributed largely to the loss of my American Express card). Anyway, this one is not only written but already set in type (final galleys) and all that's left is to write a new lead, a new ending and a fee.

#2 is already committed for the $1000 fee that I assume you agreed on with Lombardi—although in the last phone-talk I had with him we both assumed that the Aspen piece was croaked (for *RS*) and the last thing I recall telling him was "Yeah, I definitely want to go to Vietnam, but I can't agree to anything until you've talked to Lynn." And that was the last I heard: from you, Lombardi or Wenner—until Wenner called a month or so later & said he not only wanted the Aspen & Chicano pieces, but he also wanted me to go to Vietnam for six months. Which is the next problem to cope with, but before we get into that let me finish off the list (above) by harking back to #3, the America's Cup thing that Wenner wants to buy but which is also the Opening chapter to Silberman's book. And #3 is the only one of these not already committed, at least verbally, to *Rolling Stone* . . . and I say this on the assumption that you somehow sold them that Aspen piece for more than they originally agreed to pay for it & also when both Lombardi & I had already decided to junk it.

Which leaves us—for good or ill—with the Ominous Vietnam Caper and the Contributing Editor Gig still un-resolved. (Which also leaves me—not incidentally—with about two months to finish Silberman's book, before jumping off to Saigon. . . .)

Ideally, my departure for Saigon should be delayed until I finish that book for Random House (much of which is already written in rough form) and then I can flip off for Saigon as a *salaried,* Contributing Editor of *Rolling Stone*—for six months or as long as it takes me to get either killed or dis-accredited by the Army press office. In the "contributing editor" context, Jann spoke of "a salary, a draw & expenses." But I have no idea what this means—although I assume it's the same kind of gig Sack has with *Esquire* or Frady has with *Harper's.*[10] Or maybe not. I was once appointed "Aspen bureau chief" for *Ramparts,* at $150 a month with no duties at all. I was supposed to write a column, as I recall, but the cheques never came & the columns never got written & looking back I suppose all that was for the best. Although maybe not; who knows?

(Also, before I forget, Jann expressed interest in publishing a *photo book* titled "Freak Power in the Rockies," composed of photos taken during (mainly) this last campaign, but also many others to give the thing dimension . . . but he said "Of course we'll need *your* text." Which is cool. Shit, I'll write anything. But it might prove awkward if that "text" for the photo book also turns out to be the final chapter of Silberman's book, which is already sold & published as a *RS* article, etc. etc. etc. . . . but I felt I should mention that, *too,* despite the complications.)

So . . . what we have here is a terrible hellbroth of loose ends that might—despite all odds and probabilities—fit into a sort of accidental package focused mainly (hell, *entirely* . . .) on *Rolling Stone.* Which is fine. All things considered & naturally for my own reasons I can't think of any publication in the country I'd rather get into than *RS* (only a *relative* judgement A-Z, on *publications*—nothing else) . . . and that includes a lot of logos I'll only allude to, quite gracefully, without listing their names because the list probably wouldn't make much sense to you & maybe to me either, once I give it some thought . . . but what the hell? As long as New York exists I suppose we're all slaves to it, in some awful unnatural sense, and after reading (tonight) the current issues of both the *National Lampoon* & the *NY Review of Books*—& also after watching [Tom] Wolfe & Buckley[11] on TV last week—I have to wonder if maybe Goldwater might have been right when he said New York should be cut loose & floated out to sea . . . and then I remember that evil treacherous pig Sidney Zion (a lawyer) & then I wander upstairs & turn on my TV set for the morning CBS news & I see that demented old hag [Israeli prime minister Golda Meir] who looks so much like LBJ that I freak at the sight of her . . . & it occurs to me that maybe Arafat[12] has a point, after all. Yes, the Jews should be driven into the Sea—along with the Irish & the Spics & the Okies & the Niggers & all the rest.

Indeed. We are *all* pigs. And I can tell you from bad experience that that's a nasty truth to live with . . . but that's another, longer story & no point getting

10. Marshall Frady was a contributing editor at *Harper's.*
11. William F. Buckley, Jr., hosted the TV talk show *Firing Line* on PBS.
12. Yasser Arafat became chairman of the Palestine Liberation Organization in 1969.

into it now. Except that it leaves me vaguely baffled at the continuing contradiction of my decent relationship with Jim Silberman (a definite point here is that I think the R.H. book should still be first priority, right?) who I'm sure is a rotten bastard, on some level, but so far I haven't been able to place it. What is it about Silberman? It's impossible to be comfortable with a man whose essential foulness remains hidden. That dirty bastard!

Wow! None of that, eh? If I learned nothing else from that last election, I was battered to a painful understanding that my sense of humor lacks range & easy mesh quotient. Which made a nasty difference in the last election: Like, when I said I planned to "put the (incumbent) sheriff on trial for his life" when I won . . . well, a lot of people really *believed* that. Which was hard to explain in the crunch, & which also hardly matters here. . . .

I seem to be drifting . . . but after all these goddamn pages, why not? I think most of the serious points are made, and despite any gibberish I might get into now, in closing, everything I said about those numerous negotiation gigs with *Rolling Stone* is absolutely serious. Beyond that, the March 15 deadline ignores the definite likelihood that I'll be talking to Jann on the phone between now & then—about all kinds of small things & details, but since I've already agreed to sell him all these goddamn articles & to go to Vietnam & also to become a Contributing Editor *in principle*—which I can't really explain except that I've said Yes to all these things without mentioning money except for the $1000 shot for the Aspen piece—well, it looks from this end like you might, as they say, "have your work cut out for you."

If nothing else, we're talking about the sale of a few articles for a grand or so each . . . but beyond that we're talking about a long term relationship that could (& should, I think) involve a decent amount of money—not only in terms of article fees but also book rights & other money options that would naturally come with any contractual association with an aggressive & ambitious little bugger like Wenner & a "magazine" that's obviously looking to expand in every conceivable direction. In this sense, it's a bit different from the same sort of gig with, say, *Esquire*—because *Esquire* is more or less static, for good or ill, while *RS* is very definitely kinetic, also for good or ill.

Maybe there's no basic difference in signing on as a contributing editor for either one. But the point is that I don't know. I have no point of reference, and I suspect I'll need one soon. Tomorrow I'll make a serious effort to locate Sack down in Georgia—not only to find out what *Esquire* gives him for first refusal rights on everything he does, but also to find out about expenses, etc. in Vietnam. In the meantime, I'm counting on you to make sense of all this gibberish and come up with some kind of arrangement that will allow me to become not only rich & famous, but also safe from the Taxman. My feeling, for now, is that I have nothing to lose by hiring on with *Rolling Stone* . . . but what I need to know is what it's worth, in terms of straight dollars—particularly when it has to be laid out on 3 levels (salary, draw & expenses) & also considering book rights, options & other future expenses.

OK. Maybe the best thing to do, once you've digested this letter, might be a phone talk . . . very soon, right? Indeed . . .

FROM TOM WOLFE:

February 25, 1971
Le Grande Hotel
Rome, Italy

Dear Hunter,

I've been in Italy on a LECTURE TOUR, which has been pretty funny stuff. My audiences look at me as if I were a new Oldsmobile, nothing more and nothing less. I tell them about you and the ANGELS from time to time, and they seem to think you're crazy. That's just the point, I tell them. No writer in Italy would think of such an excursion, because it would be UNPROFESSORIAL—that's the going frame of mind among writers here, journalists included.

My new JOURNALISM book I expect to wrap up, finally, in March. I have a section of the ANGELS slated, but I am tempted to use one of your superb *Scanlan's* pieces (too uproarious for words, man).

Followed your SHERIFF fight with great relish. . . . You accomplished more by NOT winning, just coming close, I think.

Keep 'em flying!
Tom Wolfe

TO JANN WENNER, *ROLLING STONE:*

Bitter from his dealings with Sidney Zion, Thompson tossed around the idea of writing a scorching exposé on the now bankrupt Scanlan's Monthly.

February 28, 1971
Woody Creek, CO

Jann . . .

Here's a real hummer for you: "Farewell to *Scanlan's.*" Give it some thought—forced visits with Hinckle & Zion, along with word-photos of earlier, happier visits in the old days. Before the money ran out.

Yeah . . . and this is a *mean* trip, for sure. And in truth I'm not sure I'm mean enough to do it—but it *is* an idea. And the truth is that while *Scanlan's* had money, it *was* a good idea. Hinckle was the only editor in America you could call at 3:00 a.m. with a sorry idea & feel generally confident that by the time you hung up you'd have a $1500 story in your craw, plus massive expenses & whatever else you needed to get the thing done . . . but it was hard to know, even then, if the thing would ever see print; because the final gamut was yet to be run. Indeed . . . there was Sidney Zion, the Money Man, who spent his days in Sardi's & his nights in Gallaghers & Elaine's, Holding Forth . . . then reeling back to the office to fuck over the editorial people . . . the writers (like me) and the artists (like Ralph Steadman) & even the staff editors like Harvey Cohen & that poor straight British bastard Don Goddard . . . and god knows how many others.

Anyway, it's a terrible vicious idea. But it still burns the shit out of me that those pigs bought their own public stock at 5 cents on the dollar & now that they're going bankrupt they're going to pay off their creditors & stockholders (including themselves) at *8 cents.* So even in bankruptcy the editors come out ahead . . . right? Or maybe wrong? I haven't investigated this well enough to be sure, but the figures are clear enough. So here we have the great muckraking journalism experiment as a stinking rip-off: everybody gets fucked except the (2) people who bought their stock at 5 cents on the dollar.

Anyway, this is a shot we should probably give some thought to . . . because even though the bastards deserve it & also that a story like this would clear the decks of a whole legion of bad shuck-hustlers . . . yeah, even then, there is still the question of how a final shot like this would serve the Greater Good. And I think that's the question we should weigh. Frankly, I'm inclined to do it—or at least to pursue the initial interviews & scare the mortal shit out of both of those bastards—but in the final analysis I think it's a thing we should talk about quietly. (An example that occurs to me is the Toronto Peace Festival thing—which burned Brower & that crowd,[13] but which established a larger truth that in the end was worth the effort.) It was *right* to fuck Brower . . . & as far as I'm concerned it's not only right but necessary to fuck Zion. But I wonder about Hinckle. Although the piece could be done in a way that would spare him, more or less . . . but, well . . . give it some thought & we'll talk it over when I get there on March 15.

Ciao . . .
Hunter

TO TOM WOLFE:

Thompson may have had a point: Wolfe's white suits and jet-setting probably wouldn't *have gone over well with Ella Reeve "Mother" Bloor, the radical pro-temperance suffragette who cofounded the U.S. Communist Party in 1919.*

13. Environmental activist David Ross Brower, executive director of the Sierra Club from 1952 to 1969, cofounded Friends of the Earth in 1969.

March 3, 1971
Woody Creek, CO

Dear Tom . . .

You worthless scumsucking bastard. I just got your letter of Feb 25 from Le Grande Hotel in Roma, you swine! Here you are running around fucking Italy in that filthy white suit at a thousand bucks a day laying all kinds of stone gibberish & honky bullshit on those poor wops who can't tell the difference . . . while I'm out here in the middle of these goddamn frozen mountains in a death-battle with the taxman & nursing cheap wine while my dogs go hungry & my cars explode and a legion of nazi lawyers makes my life a goddamn Wobbly nightmare. . . .

You decadent pig. Where the fuck do you get the nerve to go around telling those wops that *I'm* crazy? You worthless cocksucker. *My* Italian tour is already arranged for next spring & I'm going to do the whole goddamn trip wearing a bright red field marshal's uniform & accompanied by six speed-freak bodyguards bristling with Mace bombs & when I start talking about American writers & the name Tom Wolfe comes up, by god, you're going to wish you were born a fucking iguana!

OK for that, you thieving pile of albino warts. You better settle your goddamn affairs because your deal is about to go *down.* "Unprofessorial," indeed! You scurvy wop! I'll have your goddamn femurs ground into bone splinters if you ever mention my name again in connection with that horrible "new journalism" shuck you're promoting.

Ah, this *greed,* this *malignancy!* Where will it end? What filthy weight in your soul has made you sink so low? Doctor Bloor was right! Hyenas are taking over the world! Oh Jesus!!! What else can I say? Except to warn you, once again, that the hammer of justice looms, and your filthy white suit will become a flaming shroud!

Sincerely,
Hunter

TO VIRGINIA THOMPSON:

March 3, 1971
Woody Creek, CO

Dear Mom . . .

As always, the same old reasons for not writing. Your last letter came at a time when I had to borrow $1000 at midnight on Sunday—to keep the Taxman from towing my car away at dawn on Monday. *Scanlan's* went bankrupt owing me $5260—which plunged me into serious trouble with the IRS & also caused American Express to seize my card & take me to court. So, ever since the election I've spent most of my waking hours screaming at lawyers in SF, LA & NY (& also at IRS men in Denver & Aspen) . . . but all to no avail. In the end I got no money out of *Scanlan's* & neither the IRS nor AmExp altered their forced-payment schedules. So at the moment I owe the IRS another (& final) $1300 on April 7, and I owe AmExp about $1200 yesterday.

Anyway . . . to hell with all that. I'm getting that end of things under control, more or less, by hiring on as a roving editor of sorts for *Rolling Stone* in San Francisco. This means that most of what I write for the next few months (or longer, if the deal works out) will appear in *Rolling Stone*—which Jim gets, as I recall. My problem now is to get on an even keel again from that disaster with *Scanlan's*.

Meanwhile, I find myself infamous & stone broke. Aspen is full of journalists demanding to interview me. Today it was James Reston Jr. from the *NY Times* . . . and the May issue of *Esquire* will apparently include me in some kind of horrible photo-spread (in gibberish . . .). There is also talk—among West Coast political-financiers—of my running for the U.S. Senate from Colorado in '72. Which is fine, but meanwhile I'm about 4 months behind on the rent & the Taxman is even talking about auctioning off my Dobermans. Horrible, horrible . . . but what the hell?

Enclosed are some weird memos of the campaign that you might like. Bill Noonan's full-pg. newspaper ad in the *Aspen Times* (in his losing race for Coroner) just won the state Press Assn. Award for the best ad of 1970. I'd send a copy if I had one, but by now they're all collector's items. Inre: your letter of 2/1 . . . Yes, I'd definitely like to have the London Fog coat & the white pants. My wardrobe is like that of some Yukon trapper. Send them at once, and thanks.

At the moment I'm trying to finish a huge Aspen-election aftermath article for *Rolling Stone*. I have to take it over there on Mar 15, then immediately go to LA to finish off a piece on the Mexican-American vs. police scene down there. At the same time, I have to come up with a film-script to show some producer in LA and also decide how I can finish the Random House book in time to go to Vietnam for *Rolling Stone*.

In other words, everything is coming to a head at once. As usual. The RH book is so long overdue that it has to be done by this summer . . . so the options for autumn are either making a film or going to Vietnam for a few months. All this will have to be decided by the end of March . . . but right now it's all very hazy.

I've had no word from Davison or Jim since our phone-talk. Did Jim ever get that belt we sent? I didn't want to punch the hole in it because I wasn't sure what size he wears, but the idea was that he should get the hole punched.

How are things going there, in general? Better than here, I hope. Sandy is a volunteer teacher at the new experimental school, headed by Sylvia Ashton-Warner. Constant problems on that end . . . in addition to a constant crisis-atmosphere in local politics. I seem to spend most of my time during the day playing political boss, and I'm getting goddamn tired of it. Hopefully, we'll be able to lease this house next winter & live somewhere else. Maybe Saigon or Hong Kong. Right now it doesn't make much difference.

OK. That's about it from here. Send word from that end.

Love,
H

TO TOM WOLFE:

On assignment to cover Nevada's Mint 400 motorcycle race for Sports Illustrated, *Thompson had spent most of the past six weeks enduring and writing* Fear and Loathing in Las Vegas, *his groundbreaking Gonzo chronicle of "a savage journey to the heart of the American dream." Wolfe would pronounce the resulting book "a scorching, epochal sensation."*

April 20, 1971
Woody Creek, CO

Tom . . .

Here's the final version (of Part One) of that Raoul Duke in Las Vegas thing. Jann said he gave you an earlier, now obsolete version—although in some ways I like the early shot better, because it moves faster. I've found that it's almost impossible to sustain that kind of speedy madness for 10,000 words. I'm still working on Part Two, but it's not working out so well. This is the kind of thing that has to be done in a straight run, I think, and all in one place. The first draft of Part One, for instance, was written by hand on Mint Hotel stationery during an all-night drunk/drug frenzy while I waited for dawn to come up so I could flee without paying. I typed the section you have in a motel in Pasadena, but changed hardly anything from the original crazed draft. Then I left it alone for about 10 days while I worked on that Chicano thing . . . and when I tried to get back on top of it, out here, I found my mind locking up every time I tried to write.

This happens every time I leave the scene of a piece—physically and mentally—before actually writing it. So in terms of Gonzo Journalism (pure), Part One is the only chunk that qualifies—although even the final version is slightly bastardized. What I was trying to get at in this was [the] mind-warp/photo technique of instant journalism: One draft, written on the spot at top speed and basically un-revised, edited, chopped, larded, etc. for publication. Ideally, I'd like to walk away from a scene and mail my notebook to the editor, who will then carry it, un-touched, to the printer.

But I think that will take a while to hash out.

Anyway, you can do whatever you want to with this. I just wanted you to see that Raoul Duke is pushing the frontiers of "new journalism" a lot further than anything you'll find in *Hell's Angels*. I think the main thing is to find some sort of academic-type justification for the Photo/Mind-Warp approach. Otherwise, the grey little cocksuckers who run things will keep drawing that line between Journalism and Fiction.

But fuck them. It's *their* problem, anyway. I told some creep from *Sports Illustrated* that I had this weird account of the thing they sent me out to cover, but they didn't even want to look at it. Just send us a 500 word text block, they said . . . because we need something, after all, to explain these incredible bills you ran up. So I'll send them their caption after I finish the main gig, which should be today or tomorrow.

Sorry we didn't have more time to talk in SF. Maybe you can arrange for me to come to NY & address the Columbia journalism faculty. Otherwise, I'll be locked in out here all summer, finishing that gibberish for Random House. Let me know if you feel like coming out for a few days. Plenty of room here.

OK . . .
Hunter

enc. "Fear & Loathing in Las Vegas," by Raoul Duke (for *Rolling Stone*).

TO TOM VANDERSCHMIDT, *SPORTS ILLUSTRATED:*

Tom Vanderschmidt had "aggressively rejected" the fifteen-thousand-word masterwork Thompson submitted in place of the fifteen-hundred-word motorcycle-race coverage asked for and expected by subeditor Pat Ryan, who would go on to become editor of People *magazine.*

April 22, 1971
Woody Creek, CO

Tom . . .

Sooner or later you'll see what your call (to me) set in motion—a fantastic mushroom. Tomorrow I'm going back to Las Vegas for another bout with the swine. Very heavy duty.

Meanwhile, tell whoever Pat Ryan is that I'm right on the verge of sending her those 500 words she wants. I offered her the true Gonzo interpretation, but she insisted on a small mess of pottage. People like that should be sent back to answering flip-buzzers.

Anyway, your instinct was right. The Lord works in wondrous ways. Your call was the key to a massive freak-out. The result is still up in the air, and still climbing. When you see the final fireball, remember that it was all your fault.

Okay, and thanks again for calling.

Sincerely,
Hunter

TO LYNN NESBIT:

Thompson spelled out his thoughts on the final direction of Fear and Loathing in Las Vegas, *his Vietnam project, and his presidential aspirations.*

April 23, 1971
Woody Creek, CO

Dear Lynn . . .

Here's the $20 I owe you from the Polo Lounge. Actually, I'm just trying out this stationery I stole, and since I couldn't think of anybody else to write . . . well shucks . . .

Anyway, I called Silberman today and sold him a book for a massive price. It's called "Fear & Loathing in Las Vegas, by Raoul Duke—Doctor of Journalism" . . . or something along those lines. The first half is already done: 15,000 words of mean gibberish that is already sold to *RS*. The second half will be done when—and if—I survive the National District Attorneys' Conference on Narcotics & Dangerous Drugs, which begins Monday April 26 in Las Vegas. I plan to attend—accompanied, of course, by My Attorney. Mr. Acosta will meet me there with the tools of our hellish trade.

If you want to chat about this—and I think we probably should—you can call me at the Hotel Flamingo until Thursday, when I'll probably stop thru San Francisco to edit the original Vegas Piece and put my initials on the final draft of the *Rolling Stone*/Random House Merger.

The book idea is based on my notion that the original 15,000 words that *Sports Illustrated* rejected—plus another long narrative based on the Drug Conference—equals two articles for *RS* and one short book for Random House. Silberman offered me 100K for it; maybe you can ease him up to 110 or so.

In any case, I sent him the first 41 pages of the final draft. He should have them by Monday—at which time he plans to announce his decision to send me $33,333 for openers. He'll probably deny this when you call, but it's true. Take my word for it.

In any case, the Vietnam book arrangement seems settled. You'll have to work out some arrangement whereby the "joint" aspect of publishing [it] is between *RS* & RH. I don't want anybody fucking around with the author's share.

OK for now. Jann, by the way, has no idea that I'm doing this "Phase Two" of the Vegas thing. Silberman agreed to underwrite all expenses on the old "American Dream" account—so all I owe *RS* is first refusal rights. Which hardly matters, because nobody else is likely to publish it anyway. (Silberman suggested the *Police Gazette;* do you have any good contacts there?)

In any case, I think it's safe to assume *RS* will publish the Drug Conference thing, as a follow-up to the Mint 400 nightmare. I spoke at some length tonight with Dave Felton, de facto asst. editor of *RS,* but he doesn't have the money authority to make $2000 assignments to lunatics. And Jann is still in England. So as far as *RS* is concerned, I'm going to Las Vegas this time for Random House—and if we get a good *RS*-type article out of it, they'll be happy to look it over.

Very complicated, eh? But I think I have it all under control—as always. The program for the next four months looks like this:

a) Go to Las Vegas on 4/25 & do another 15,000 words on the DAs' drug conference . . . then sell this to *RS* for $2000 or whatever you can get.

b) Take the same piece—in addition to the first Las Vegas article—and sell them both to Random House for a quick short book, for autumn publication.

c) Finish the Aspen article for *RS*, collect another $2000, then send a copy of that article to Silberman—as the final chunk of bulk copy for the "American Dream/Battle of Aspen" book.

d) Collect $5000 from Random House for the "first third" of the AD/BA book, then spend June and July whipping that book into some kind of recognizable shape—with the help of some workhouse editor that Jim said he'd assign to the task.

e) Around Aug 1, collect another $5000 from RH—with the ms. almost finished—and prepare to leave for Vietnam for *RS*.

f) Leave o/a Sept 1 & begin writing articles for *RS* and also for joint *RS*/RH book. Finish final editing of AD/BA book in my Bangkok villa, collect another $5000, and continue writing articles until Jan or Feb, 1972.

g) In the Spring of '72, return to this country and run for President on the Freak Power ticket—a Man on a Weird Horse.

OK for now. Let me know if any of this leaves you un-settled. Also let me know if you know anybody who'd like to rent my Aspen villa next winter. John Sack had first option, but he decided it wasn't elegant enough. How can I explain that to my friends?

Yours in Fear & Loathing,
Hunter

TO JANN WENNER, *ROLLING STONE:*

Back from his trip to Las Vegas with Oscar Acosta, Thompson was broke, trying to iron out the details of his upcoming trip to Vietnam, and all the while steadily shaping his classic Fear and Loathing in Las Vegas.

May 7, 1971
Woody Creek, CO

Dear Jann . . .

Thanx for the various xerox things (payments list to Lynn, Saigon letter, etc.). . . . I sent a note to that fellow Garstang (see enc. Copy), and I definitely want to talk to him before I go. Be nice to him if he calls or comes by . . . and consider that "Saigon Notes" idea. Also, it might be good to trade subscriptions with the *Vietnam Guardian* . . . that could provide a good check-in point when I get there. If nothing else, the astrology charts are extremely weird in the context of Vietnam/combat. Maybe worth reprinting as a tail to Saigon notes. (There's also the idea that anybody who subscribes to *RS* from Vietnam will probably be a long-time subscriber—for reasons too complex for exploration here; just take my word for it—us vets know how it is.)

On other (money) fronts, it seems beyond any question that you owe me a few hundred bucks . . . which I need, right now, so I can send off a check to L.L. Bean for some special Saigon action-clothes. At the moment I have $92 in the bank, and the Bean check is $96—so I haven't sent it, and I won't until I get some funds.

Anyway, according to your list, you still owe me $500 on the Salazar fee. This assumes, also, that $520.85 has already been paid against my Salazar/Vegas expenses . . . which according to Sandy's figures amount to $922.04. (No, I already sent a bill for that $20.85—phone calls item—so the remaining unpaid expenses come to $422.04.) This, plus the $500 more for Salazar, means you owe me $922.04. Nine hundred & twenty-two dollars and four cents.

That should bring us up, in time, to the Second Las Vegas gig (not counting expenses, which will be split between *RS* & Random House—with *Spts. Illust.* absorbing a chunk of the expenses like hotel & room service, etc., from the first Las Vegas trip . . . but I haven't sent them *anything* yet. I just keep playing "One Toke Over the Line . . ." And "Let It Bleed."[14] As a matter of fact right now I'm trying to put them together with some of my super/secret/weird/voice tapes from Vegas II (Two) . . . driving around the countryside with my attorney, asking for the American Dream. We got some very strange replies: ". . . burned down by junkies" . . . "got electrocuted while taking a shower in the car" . . . "The American Dream? In *this* town?"

Anyway—and by all means correct me at once if I'm wrong—once you pay me for that outstanding $922.04, we'll be even (except for your share of expenses on Vegas II) up to now. In other words, the $922.04 should cover all fees, expenses & retainers to date, including Salazar & Vegas I—which still has 1000 or so words to come; not necessarily to finish it, but to tie up some loose ends and launch us into Vegas II.

Has Alan [Rinzler] talked to Silberman inre: book/possibility arrangements on that? I'm working on the assumption that we're talking about a 30,000 word shot in two (and possibly three) sections. I say *three* because the night before I left, this last time, I *found* the American Dream, and it might be necessary to go back and drill some wisdom out of the freak who put it together.

But that won't be necessary until the first two parts are finished and ready. Then we can see if we need that wrap-up. I think we will, but why haggle about that now?

14. Rock songs by (Mike) Brewer and (Tom) Shipley and the Rolling Stones, respectively.

***

I assume you got my clip inre: the Aspen elections. Total disaster for our side. Arthur Rock's candidates survived, but just barely. For the past two days [Tom] Benton's gallery has been full of people we've never seen before—all of them wanting to know who should be hit first. I think we're into a long, nasty summer here. The next election is a year and a half away, and in the meantime we're stone fucked. If Aspen is a political preview of the national scene in '72, god's mercy on us all. We're back into a total underground scene here—which is fun, now & then, but a bummer for the long haul.

Anyway, we'll see. Come on out when you get time. I'm concentrating on setting up this "Vortex" thing in this valley . . . which means that between now & Sept. I have to find a buyer for this big mesa just west of me. Maybe you should send Max out here to look it over. He could build a huge stone tower in the middle of 100 or so acres, then fence the thing off and establish a grazing preserve for wolverines & wild boar all around him (and when he wasn't around, the tower could be used for "Rolling Stone Scholars in Residence." Whose only extra-cranial duty would be to feed the boar and exercise the wolverine(s)).

OK for now. Send the
cheque. Thanx,
Hunter

TO MAX PALEVSKY:

In 1961, Palevsky and five fellow technicians left their jobs in L.A.'s nascent small-computer industry to form Scientific Data Systems with their own $80,000 and another $1 million from Wall Street investors. Eight years later, electronics giant Xerox Corporation bought the company for $94 million, making Palevsky good potential neighbor material for Thompson.

May 7, 1971
Woody Creek, CO

My Dear Doctor Palevsky:

In the interest of Science, I feel I should warn you that those seeds you exhibited on the occasion of my last visit are of excellent non-commercial quality. Extremely mild and happy, perhaps the best I've ever seen for mating purposes. You should be extremely proud of that crop: the mildness and consistency are without parallel in my experience. Selah.

On other fronts, I ran into a friend of yours at the Aspen Airport the other day: One James Smith, an oil-dealer of sorts. He spoke well of your house in the desert: it seems he snorted up a hooker of laudanum out there with Tom

Braden,[15] then came to grips with God. But you know how these oil-men exaggerate. . . .

In any case, I just sent a note to Jann about a lot of things—including an embryo-stage land-use experiment we're trying to put together out here in this valley about 10 miles out of Aspen. The main man is George Stranahan, whose relationship with Champion Spark Plugs is much the same as yours to Xerox. He's about your age, but far more suave & intelligent . . . currently serving out his final year as a physics prof. at Mich. State.

Anyway, after spending several million to buy up this entire valley, which backs into 5 million acres of the White River National Forest, he's now pondering some very weird ways of dealing with the land—the main idea being to effectively "retire" the land, take it permanently off the local real estate market, by selling a handful of large chunks to people with no interest in re-sale or sub-dividing.

These people would be selected with an eye to some sort of cranial unity. George is already dealing, for instance, with the Rev. James Reston—which appalls me; I figure if I have to live next door to an editor, I much prefer Jann to Reston. Why go to all this trouble to create a St. Petersburg in the Rockies?

But that's only the Big Sur/Pebble Beach aspect of the thing. The other side involves long-term leases, for little or no money, to a small community of genuine freaks who'd be willing to build their own city on a huge 800 acre mesa that would otherwise become a stone-rotten subdivision.

Well . . . I see the hopelessness of trying to explain this thing in a short note. And I can't really speak for George, either, so all I can say for sure is that there's a very large mesa right next to me for sale at a definitely sub-market price to the right person for the right reasons. If this concept interests you at all, let me know. It's a weird trip, but it needs a lot of talk to say what it actually is. OK for now . . .

Ciao,
Hunter

TO JIM SILBERMAN, RANDOM HOUSE:

Thompson braced his book editor for the imminent expense bills from Las Vegas, which he acknowledged might seem "unreasonable," but were "all in the interest of Journalistic Science."

May 9, 1971
Woody Creek, CO

Dear Jim:

Here's a copy of the *finished* parts of "Fear & Loathing in Las Vegas." For ID purposes, this is "Vegas 1." And, depending on how #2 turns out, there may

15. Tom Braden wrote a liberal political column for the *Washington Star.*

have to be a brief "Vegas 3." Maybe not. The necessity for a #3 would only come after a few hours on the phone with the owner of the Circus-Circus. If he's the stone-Alger[16] freak that he almost has to be, on the evidence, then I think it would be worthwhile to go down there and observe him at close range. Maybe get some insight into how his gig was done, along with some inside wisdom on the financial/leverage ethic of Las Vegas.

Only a genuine freak could have created the Circus-Circus. Which is where I finally found the American Dream . . . not an easy thing to explain in a few words, as I think I mentioned earlier. This last trip got into far heavier and more serious things than we have in this (Vegas 1) section, enc. What began as a joke and a casual rip-off somehow developed into a serious quest that incredibly yielded up the Main Fruit. I'm fairly certain about what I finally discovered down there, but whether the combined narrative of Vegas 1 & 2 will support that kind of massive conclusion is something we can only guess at right now.

In any case, what you have (enc.) is Vegas 1, about 90% finished. We need one bridge scene between parts 2 & 3, then a short wrap-up to Part Three. This involves maybe 2000 or so words—at which point *Rolling Stone* will pay me the final $500 and Vegas 1 will be theirs—to publish as is, or perhaps to hold and wait for Vegas 2 & maybe 3. But, unless you've made some arrangement with Alan Rinzler, *RS* is not financially involved in anything beyond Vegas 1.

I had thought, until tonight, that they were into the whole project on the basis of that $500 they sent in reply to my desperate telegram from the Flamingo (yes—that one . . .), but as it turns out, that was my June retainer, not expense money, so as it stands now—after talking to Jann Wenner a few hours ago—*RS* seems to have paid $1500 (out of $2K) for Vegas 1, but so far I've paid all my own expenses for this thing (except for an original cash nut of $300 from *Spts. Illustrated*—and the Mint Hotel bill, which I never saw, for a variety of ugly reasons) . . . but in any event, I have a fairly hefty Carte Blanche bill on my hands, for Vegas 1, as well as Vegas 2, which is in fact quite crucial. This means you'll be getting a bill for something just under a Grand in the very near future—to be applied, I trust, against the American Dream expense account, which to my knowledge is still capable of absorbing this amount. (Yeah, don't say it—I know we're nearing the end; in more ways than one, etc.)

Which is neither here nor there, for the moment. No doubt some of these expenses are "unreasonable." Like renting a white Cadillac convertible and then soaking the bastard with the hard-crusted, sun-baked scum of 100 grapefruits and 2 dozen coconuts and 26 pounds of catsup and french fry residue—along with a layer or so of vomit and a goodly number of bad dings, dents, and scrapes that were covered, thank christ, by an extra $2 a day for total insur-

16. Mid-nineteenth century American author Horatio Alger wrote more than one hundred boys' books featuring heroes who rise from rags to riches through hard work and virtuous living.

ance. The car was not a happy-looking machine when I turned it in . . . but they just gritted their teeth and took it. (This is/was the Insurance side of the American Dream—the terrifying underbelly of Actuarial Tables.)

Anyway, the point is that you can't send a man out in a fucking Pinto or a VW to seek out the American Dream in Las Vegas. You want to be able to come roaring into the Circus-Circus in a huge Coupe de Ville and *know* the insanity of watching people jump and run and salute and all that crap . . . which is crazy, of course, but the insane truth is that the difference between $15 a day for a Mustang and $20 a day for a white Cadillac convertible is *massive* in LA or Las Vegas. That extra $5 is a ticket to Their World—that and constantly giving dollar bills to "boys" for quick unctuous service. (Which comes hard when the driver of the Cadillac is a huge gross drunken Chicano wearing a yellow fishnet T-shirt with a long hunting knife & a bottle of rum in his hand; but even that kind of culture shock disappears with a $2 tip, instead of just $1.)

Incredible. And I guess I'm just sort of talking off the top of my head about this—maybe laboring a bit to justify the "unreasonable" side of the expense tab. But of course this is not a *reasonable* story. This is a tale of gross excess on many levels. And those details are hard to fake. There is no way to understand the public reaction to the sight of a Freak smashing a coconut with a hammer on the hood of a white Cadillac in a Safeway parking lot unless you actually do it . . . and I tell you it's *tense*. They don't like it at all. It rips their nerve-ends in a very extreme way.

Like ordering two servings of "Crab Louey" in the Flamingo, then sending it back, uneaten, but covered with broken light-bulb glass. With cigarettes put out in the sauce, and the crabmeat floating in spilled gin . . . with maybe a condom full of Coca-Cola on the tray.

This is horrible. I admit it, and naturally I regret ever having participated in such a spectacle. But it was all in the interest of Journalistic Science. Or maybe Behavioral Science. I've always been heavy into Science, on all fronts.

And so much for all that. What we have to do now is figure out what we have here. Vegas 1 is just an article for *RS*—a 15,000 word drug frenzy. But if Vegas 2 turns out to be another 15 or 20,000 words, then we're talking about a book-length project—and a book. Which is a different thing from just an article. So maybe you should ponder Vegas 1 and tell me what you think.

The DAs' conference wasn't as grisly as I expected. Those dumb fuckers know nothing at all about the realities of the drug culture. The keynote speaker said—and I quote—"We *must* come to terms with the drug culture in this country." And from that point on, the whole conference bogged down in 1959-style gibberish. The whole thing was so dank & atavistic that I had no trouble dividing my time between the Vegas drug underworld and the National DAs' drug conference—leaving The Dunes in the white Cadillac to look for mescaline while the others were eating dinner, then coming back at night to watch films, with the others, about the mind-bending horrors of people given over to drugs. It's a very strange feeling to walk into a room full of 1000 cops with a head full of mescaline and listen to them telling each other about the terrors of the "drug problem." (Many strange details and anecdotes on this theme, but no point getting into them here.)

What I'm going to do now is try for a quick finish/run on Vegas 2—although at the moment I'm not sure if I'm writing a long article or a short book, or maybe both. I'll send a copy of this letter to Lynn (and also to Jann), so perhaps we can put that concept together and figure out just what the hell I'm writing . . . because I don't see much point in writing a 35,000 word magazine article that will probably involve all manner of savage editing/cutting hassles, and particularly not in light of all the other time-pressed bullshit I have to do, unless we're looking pretty realistically at a *book*. It would be a disaster, I think, to allow this thing—which is essentially a speed-writing project—to get bogged down in one of those open-ended, un-framed "American Dream"-type nightmares, where I just keep writing and writing and writing without any real idea what I'm writing *to*. What kind of *hole,* I mean. I keep saying this, and I'm past worrying about whether it's a terrible failure on my part, as a "writer," but the awful pragmatic truth is that unless I see the Hole I have to fill—along with a definite honest deadline—I'm never going to finish *anything*. You simply can't expect a profligate freak to write on a banker's schedule; that's a difficult mix to maintain except at sporadic adrenaline peaks—that special rage that comes with the specter of some real or imagined rip-off. Indeed . . . yes . . . let sleeping dogs lie, eh? (Lie? Ly? Lay? Fuck sleeping dogs. . . .)

Yeah . . . this has gone on long enough. All I meant to say, in the beginning, was that I need some idea of a *framework* for this thing. Vegas 1 came very quick & easy—maybe six or seven actual writing days—but that was because I knew what sort of hole I was writing to.

Which is no longer the case. At the moment I don't know if I'm writing a book or an article, and that makes a hell of a difference when it comes to leaving things in or out. At this point, however, I don't see any possible way this thing can get off at less than 30,000 words. We already have 15K, and 10K more in first draft, so we're already flirting with a book-length project almost by accident. The question now is whether to push it all the way—writing to a 40,000 word hole and thinking in terms of book-money, or trying to chop the whole thing into the framework of a $2000 article and get on to other things. Either way. Although naturally I'd prefer to go the book route. But I don't want to think in those terms unless it's realistic. So let me know ASAP. This thing has to be done quickly or not at all . . . and the Fat is in the Fire. Selah.

Meanwhile, it's dawn here & I have to go down the road & steal a bale of hay to make a nest for my Doberman bitch who's about to have a litter. Maybe you'd like a few pure-bred champion vicious Dobermans to leave around the office at night. To rip the lungs out of all those writers who keep trying to break in and alter the small print of their contracts. Let me know about this . . . and tell Selma I'll send her drug-order just as soon as I can rake it together. OK for now . . .

Ciao,
Hunter

TO GEORGE KIMBALL:

Kimball—a writer for the underground press—had run for sheriff of Lawrence, Kansas, on the Freak Power ticket in 1970.

May 9, 1971
Woody Creek, CO

George . . .

I've just been talking to Jann Wenner *(Rolling Stone)* about you—suggesting that he get you into writing some articles, in addition to that record-review gig. My motives were mixed, of course. Aside from your undeniable mastery of the medium, I want Wenner to have the experience of dealing with somebody more demonstrably crazy than I am—so that he'll understand that I am, in context, a very responsible person.

This seems to have escaped him, up to now. We just had a bad argument over my expense account—like who was going to pay for the rental of a white Cadillac convertible & a gross of coconuts in Las Vegas. I suspect I lost . . . but what the hell?

I'm getting used to that. We just had the mortal shit stomped out of us in last week's city elections. How are things going in Lawrence? In Aspen, it's back to the Underground. We've completely blown our public leverage here. At the moment I'm Aspen's answer to [African-American civil rights activist H.] Rap Brown—feeling lucky to be on the streets.

I assume you saw that cheap bullshit in *Esquire*. Lucian [Truscott] said you were coming out here to join your hat in the picture. Benton is holding the hat for ransom—$100, he says; he took it back right after the photo. That was a bad trip, with nasty repercussions here. I got blamed for making us all seem like giddy chimps. Including myself.

But what the fuck? Come on out when you get time. We're having a "Death of Freak Power" spectacle on July 4—a vicious parade, with brawls, bombs, etc. A guaranteed bummer. Send word.

Love,
Hunter

TO DAVID FELTON, *ROLLING STONE:*

Former L.A. Times *writer David Felton became* Rolling Stone's *Los Angeles editor in early 1970, moving to the San Francisco headquarters as associate ed-*

itor a year later. Known as "The Stonecutter" for his glacial pace and brilliant work, Felton was assigned to edit "Fear and Loathing in Las Vegas" for the magazine—which included handling Thompson's expense accounts.

May 9, 1971
Woody Creek, CO

David . . .

You scurvy pigfucker. I was just about to send you some mescaline when I talked to Jann & found out that all my daily expenses on the Salazar/Vegas stories were disallowed—for reasons of gross excess & irresponsible outlay. That $500 you sent wasn't for my expenses at all; it was my fucking *June retainer,* which means I was spending my own money all that time.

Yes—for all those coconuts, for that hammer, all those lightbulbs, the White Whale . . . You treacherous pig.

So here's the deal on the mescaline: The first two pellets will cost you $211 each (that's the $422 in daily expenses that got disallowed)—and the other 98 will be free.

No wonder my attorney bought that Gerber Mini-Magnum in order to cut your throat. Shit, I paid for that thing, too.

You devious pervert. $211 is cheap for the likes of you. Don't blame me when you get castrated leaving the building one of these nights. Rumormongers of your stripe shouldn't be allowed to procreate, anyway.

I'll expect your cashier's check for $422 within ten (10) days; after that—when I've toted up my Vegas 2 expenses—the price will rise sharply. Up to something like $298 each.

You dirty Catholic bastard. I had you pegged from the start. If I were you I'd get my ass back to Azusa, or wherever that rotten place was that I got trapped in.

Sincerely,
Dr. Gonzo

TO OSCAR ACOSTA:

Thompson was still haggling with Silberman and Wenner over expense tabs for the Vegas trips.

May 13, 1971
Woody Creek, CO

Oscar . . .

Strange dealings here. I'd been putting off sending you that knife because I wasn't sure it should go to the office address—or *any address*—and meanwhile waiting around for a $422 "general expenses" check from *RS* on the *first* Las Vegas trip—and also telling Dave Felton that he was about to be castrated by drug-crazed Chicanos some night when he left the building . . . when all of a sudden the phone rang about 2 nites ago and there was Wenner, enraged at the "totally wasteful" nature of my expense account (due to angry prodding, he said, from the Business Mgr.)—and saying that all my "per diem" expenses would "have to be absorbed in the fee."

This means that *RS* refuses to pay a dollar toward anything but "basic" expenses for either Las Vegas trip—which leaves me $422 in the hole after Salazar & the Mint 400, even including the $300 from *Spts. Illust.,* etc. And god only knows how deep in the red after this last trip—although I think I can get $500 out of Random House; Silberman says he never got that telegram, and that he would certainly have sent the money if word had reached him.

All of which leaves me more or less up in the air—not only inre: expenses, but also in terms of where to move with Part 2 of the Vegas piece. Which is heavily complicated, but not to you. I wanted them to send you a check for RT plane fare from SF to Vegas to SF, which I think is fair, but at the moment I'm not even sure they're going to pay for the White Whale. My Carte Blanche tab is $527, and none of the Vegas DA conference bills are in yet . . . so the next gig is up to Random House. By my count, we did about a Grand in Three days, and I suspect my chance of payment on that depends entirely on what Silberman thinks of the "Vegas 1" sections I sent him (the stuff you read in the Flamingo). If he sees it as a moneymaker—in some form—he'll pay; otherwise, I'm into Carte Blanche for another lost card & a lawsuit.

I suspect it will turn out OK, but I won't know for a week or two. Meanwhile, let me know if you still want that knife, and if the office address is right for mailing. Also call and tell me what's happening with the various tensions, threats, etc. And if you have one of those UCLA student union reprints of the Salazar article, I'd sure as hell like to see one.

On other fronts, it's 8:30 a.m. here and Benjy has just hatched a surprisingly small crop of four rat-size Dobermans—two males & two females. In two months they'll be the size of big cats, and if you're serious about wanting one, you'd better let me know. If I get the whole pile of expense money from Random House, I'll give you one for nothing at all. Otherwise, you'll have to pay for the ear and tail cutting & shots, which comes to around $75. But since I have only 3 to sell or give, you should let me know at once. I plan to keep a female, for breeding purposes.

(I called Socorro's number the other night after you called—after Ed Bastian[17] called to find you—but there was no answer.) I'll let you know how this Expenses-hassle turns out. The World Is Full of Pigs. But keep this to yourself.

Ciao . . .
HST

17. Ed Bastian is Thompson's neighbor in Woody Creek.

TO JIM SILBERMAN, RANDOM HOUSE:

May 24, 1971
Woody Creek, CO

Dear Jim . . .

Here's the rest of Vegas I—with the exception of 1000 or so words on the Mint 400 itself that will fit between the end of "Insert A" and the beginning of "Part 3." *Rolling Stone* isn't interested in this, but *Sports Illustrated* insists that I write "at least a few hundred words" to justify the trip. So I will—and then we can include that in the story, too.

Anyway, I just talked to Wenner & he says he wants to hold Vegas I (which he's already paid for & claims to like immensely) until I send in the complete text of Vegas II—and then run them back-to-back in consecutive issues, with illustrations by Ralph Steadman. (I've insisted on Steadman, because he's the only illustrator I know of who understands the Gonzo journalism concept; he has lived thru it twice, and he'll catch the style & tone of this Vegas thing instantly.)

All of which leads me to believe Jann (& Alan) are probably thinking in terms of a book in addition to the two long articles. Nothing was said about this tonight, and I didn't ask—but I doubt if they'd go to all the hassle & expense of getting Steadman to illustrate the thing unless they had something more than a 2-part article in mind.

Which is fine, I think—although I'm not sure how we'll work out this odd triangular thing that seems to have cropped up. They've already paid for Vegas I (but not the expenses); Wenner bought that on the basis of the first seven pages in rough draft . . . but Vegas II, the DAs' conference, was a Random House job as far as I'm concerned (particularly as the $500 they sent me was my June retainer, instead of expenses) . . . and it was only tonight that Jann definitely committed *RS* to buying the thing.

I trust all this is clear. The only two questions still hazy in *my* mind are: 1) Who's going to pay that $1000-plus expense tab & save my Carte Blanche card . . . and 2) Will "The Vegas Diaries of Raoul Duke" become a book? Or merely a 40,000 word article?

What do you think? I trust your judgement implicitly as long as I agree with it. So let me know what it is.

Ciao,
Hunter

PS—I'm definitely in a *writing* mood these days; the angst has come to a head—let's not blow it this time.

TO D. JACKSON, AMERICAN EXPRESS:

American Express had the gall to cancel Thompson's card for nonpayment of his substantial Las Vegas bills.

June 1, 1971
Woody Creek, CO

Dear Mr. Jackson . . .

Of course you were "unable to reach (me) by phone." And you're going to play hell reaching me any other way, either. You bastards refused to talk to me when I called; you refused to talk to my attorney . . . and now you think I'm going to answer your goddamn silly telegram. At my own expense . . .

My position is extremely simple. But every time I've tried to call there and explain it, I've been routed off to some goddamn elevator boy. After three expensive efforts, I got tired of talking to people who could barely speak english—much less understand what I was saying. How would you feel if you kept calling my house for prolonged conversations with my seven-year-old son? He deals with any calls I don't feel like taking. . . .

In any case, my point has always been that I would very much like to get back on an even keel with American Express. I made frequent use of my card, as your records will show. They will also show that I paid my bills quite regularly . . . until *Scanlan's* magazine went bankrupt without reimbursing me for my (credit card) expenses on a 6-week, coast-to-coast assignment.

This happened at a time when I was running for Sheriff of this county—so naturally in the chaos of a political campaign I made no attempt to deal with routine things; and by the time I got around to dealing with things like credit card bills, I found that my American Express card had been cancelled.

This was not the sort of precipitate action that was likely to coax up prompt payment . . . so I naturally put your bill at the bottom of my list. Where it remains. Why in hell should I hurry to pay your bill when you've already put me on a list full of criminals? Every establishment in this county that accepts American Express credit cards has my name on a list of people who should be arrested if they show an AmExp card. What kind of stinking treatment is that?

You swine put me on a list of criminals, then you refused to talk to me when I called. All I wanted to do was explain why I hadn't paid the bill as promptly as in the past . . . and that I wanted to get the thing settled without problems . . . but I kept getting switched back and forth from one goddamn extension to another, talking to various elevator boys who kept screaming "Pay now or else!" at me . . . and meanwhile all this subhuman gibberish went on my phone bill.

So I finally figured, "To hell with that Nazi Computer." I don't *need* my AmExp card. I have others. And I pay those bills. Why the hell should I worry about some gang of flunkies who keep yelling at me from New York? There was no way to speak with anybody in authority in that organization. I tried; my attorney tried . . . and finally we just let it ride.

My position today is the same as it was when this stupid trouble began. I'll pay the bill if my card is reinstated. Probably I'll pay it anyway, but by the time you squeeze that 1000 or so dollars out of me in the courts you'll be deep in the red on this Account. As long as I remain on that list of criminals, you're going to have to deal with me as you would any other criminal . . . and with the slightest hint of any defamation of character I'll cross-file on you. My attempts to deal with you "people"—to pay this bill—are a matter of record. I made every conceivable attempt to be reasonable with you people—and in every case you treated me like a criminal pig!

So from now on you can deal with my attorney: Joseph Edwards, Atty. at Law, Wheeler Opera House; Aspen, Colorado. He'll be back from vacation in a week or so, and when he returns I'll instruct him to deal with you in the proper fashion.

In the meantime—or at any future date—I remain open to any reasonable settlement of this ugly nightmare. And by "reasonable," I mean some settlement that will leapfrog your elevator boys and get us back on that normal human level on which I can pay my bills and continue using my AmExp card.

Do not fold, spindle or mutilate this letter.

Sincerely,
Hunter S. Thompson

Note: Direct all further correspondence on this matter to my attorney (see above).

TO JANN WENNER, *ROLLING STONE:*

In what "began as a quick note to wrap up loose ends," Thompson asked Wenner to at least lend him the money to cover the sizable expenses he had accrued while in Las Vegas.

June 1, 1971
Woody Creek, CO

Jann . . .

I just ordered a handful of Congressional reports & other wisdom on "Drugs in Vietnam" from Ted Kennedy's Legislative wizard, Jim Flug—another Aspen Alps type. Hopefully, he'll send me a huge carton of bullshit full of quotes & obscure wisdom, which will definitely come in handy later on. In any case, he's a fairly heavy bugger & I figure I can count on him to supply me with anything potentially damaging to the Administration—now or later.

Also . . . could you address the enclosed letter to Sandy Bull[18] in NY? Thanx. Any address that will get to him. It's nothing heavy; just a note saying I'm waiting for his record, "as a summer antidote to all that 3rd-rate shit Jann peddles." I figured he might work a little harder with that kind of poke. . . .

18. Multi-instrumental, overdub, and improvisational virtuoso Sandy Bull would release his last album, *Demolition Derby*, in 1972.

Maybe I could review the fucker when it comes out. I think he's one of the main talents around. Most of the people I see in the Record Review section these days should feel privileged to carry Sandy's equipment around. I can see where you might feel a bit self-conscious about pushing him, but for the same twisted reasons you have to consider that you might have *buried* him in your basement. That kind of charity can be fatal. You don't want to put the bastard in a hole where anything *RS* does on him looks like a house-hype.

But fuck all that. All I meant to do, when I started this, was to wrap up a few loose ends . . . to wit:

1) forwarding this letter to Sandy

2) the possibility of buying four (4) AR-3's [speakers] at some kind of reduced price—2 for me, 2 for Benton. Possible? Price?

3) also, any chance of a discount on one of those new Dyna amps—like the one you have in the office? Or maybe an AR amp, along with the speakers. Whatever's right . . .

(I'm also looking for a list of "*RS* Notes" now—including all the above & also the following. . . .)

4) One copy of *The Anarchist Cookbook*[19]—currently unavailable here . . . (Lyle Stuart, publisher) . . . Possible?

5) The strange intelligence that *RS* has suddenly appeared for sale in two very unlikely places in Aspen—City Market (a chain supermarket) & Carl's Pharmacy, a mini-chain run by one of the worst assholes west of St. Louis . . . which hardly matters; the point is that your new distributor is apparently *good.* Neither one of these new outlets in Aspen would *touch RS* on their own—so apparently the state-level feeder is giving it to them, and it seems to be selling. I can't be sure, because I don't dare even enter either one of those places.

Which is excellent, overall, but Benton was somewhat stunned to find his exclusive dealership shot all to hell. I told him it was God's Will, and besides that it paid my rent—if not my expenses.

Shit, I see that maybe the time has come to end this letter . . . no more random points from my accumulation of "*RS* notes." I'll get that xerox about the man who yanked his eyeballs out to you as soon as I can persuade Sandy to take it into the xerox place. Right now she's impossible to talk to: my Carte Blanche bill for both Vegas trips is $1,289.45—and they don't take partial payments; I learned this the hard way.

Anyway . . . I recall that there was some question in your mind when we talked the other night about whether I had already drawn my June retainer. And I said that I thought I had. But this was only because you had already told me I had—although naturally it never occurred to me that I was asking for my June retainer, in advance, when I sent that telegram from Vegas for the $500. I

19. *The Anarchist Cookbook,* written by William Powell and published in 1971, provided instructions for making Molotov cocktails and other low-level terrorist devices.

thought I was asking for *expense money*—and when it arrived, with no explanation, I figured that's what it was. So that's how I spent it . . . and when I told Acosta about the "Expenses/Denied" disaster, he chuckled and said, "Oh, so what we spent out there was *your salary?*"

"Yeah," I said. "That's what we did."

Ah . . . fuck this. I think the thing to do is for you to *lend* me the $1K-plus to pay off Carte Blanche. That way we can worry later about who should righteously pay the tab. Fuck. Maybe *I* should. I'll never deny the thing was excessive. But I don't recall spending anything, out there, that didn't strike me as being *necessary at the time.* But this is a hard thing to argue or defend; it drags us into the realm of the preternatural. . . .

All I really care about, frankly, is not losing my last & only credit card—which is the only thing that enabled me to do that whole Vegas thing in the first place. That card is important to me. I *must* have it. And I will. That $500 you just sent will pay off the first leg—but if I do that it will leave me owing the Woody Creek store so much that Sandy refuses to go in there to argue anymore, which means I won't get my mail. The WC Store (& P.O.) is effectively off-limits to me . . . I take my watch off when I go into the place, once a month, of necessity . . . because I know from long experience that even in brief, unexpected scuffles you almost always knock your watch off . . . and it's a bummer to have to go back and ask for it. Which is why I switched to Timex . . . but now that I have this goddamn rotten Accutron I'd hate to lose it in a flurry of stupid violence.

Actually none of this is serious right now. It's all bullshit. The solution, I think, is for me to send Carte Blanche a personal check for $512, or whatever, today, and worry about the other shit later. If *RS* can lend me enough to pay them off, that's fine—and this notion of a loan is only contingent on Silberman's decision to *not* pay the expenses on Vegas I.

There is, of course, no reason why he should. At this point I have no idea what he plans to *do* with Vegas I. It came on him out of the blue. And for that matter, I guess it came on *you* that way, too. So in truth you aren't *obligated* to pay those expenses, either.

But none of this will matter to Carte Blanche. All they want is a check, which I'll send them today. We can work out the details later. First we'll see what Silberman says . . . and then we can think in terms of a loan as a solution of last resort . . . the crucial thing is not to lose this card. That's all I really give a fuck about.

Meanwhile . . . let me emphasize that under no circumstances should I ever again be given my monthly retainer in advance. Sandy's reaction to my intelligence that I had accidentally spent my June retainer in Las Vegas—without realizing it—was something like what you might expect from Janie if you came home one night and said you'd just sent all your available cash for next month to Tim Leary in Algeria, so she would have to make do. . . .

One other note: I got the bundle of Salazar/issue copies . . . but they arrived a week or so late, along with my Airmail copy of the current issue, because of that goddamn insane address that must be posted somewhere in the mailroom. I'm enclosing it. What does it take to get the bastard changed? You can be sure I'll have it done next time I come over—but why should a simple thing like getting somebody's address straight require drastic measures?

The obvious problem (see enc. Label) is that sending something to both Aspen and to Woody Creek is the scaled-down equivalent of sending something to both San Francisco and Oakland. The Owl Farm is a Woody Creek address—*not* Aspen. The WC Zip Code is 81656.

The Aspen zip code is 81611. These hamwit geeks go crazy when they get something addressed to *two different postal areas.* Everything gets to me eventually, but for fuck's sake let's get my address right. It's:

Dr. Hunter S. Thompson
Owl Farm
Woody Creek, CO 81656

I have another address in Aspen, which is actually the *Wallposter* box. This is K-3, but I only use this one for dope & other things that can be properly addressed to the *Wallposter. This address should be stricken from all* RS *records;* it is not listed in my name & the box is checked infrequently. And rarely by me. For various reasons . . .

Anyway . . . jesus . . . I've interrupted this letter so many goddamn times—having 4 two-week-old Dobermans in the house is not easy . . . christ, I keep forgetting what I was bitching about.

Probably the point about that $500 expense thing got ahead of the others . . . but don't worry about it. Like I said, I know my Vegas expenses were excessive by any normal standards. But the terrible excessive truth is that they *were* genuine out of pocket expenses.

(I just checked my bill-stub again and the valid Carte Blanche figure is $1089.45—or $200 *less* than the figure I had on pg. 3, above. $492.26 is the corrected, final adjusted figure for Vegas I . . . and $597.19 for Vegas II. . . .)

This is horrible; I admit it—but it's also for two people, two car rentals, two separate trips, etc. . . .

Which is neither here nor there at the moment. As I said, let's wait & see what RH does with the lunatic bill I sent them. If they pay it, I'm home free (with Carte Blanche, at least) . . . although we still have the specter of that $500 June retainer somehow dribbling thru my fingers. (Actually, $70 of that was for a good portable radio—which I had to get because the one I bought at the Chicago convention was finally & inevitably ripped off.)

Which doesn't matter either. I think I'm going crazy. It's 10:33 in the morning & this is the longest letter I've ever written. It began as a quick note to wrap up loose ends.

Don't let the money thing hassle you—unless you have $500 or so extra lying around. I don't want to be the asshole who stomps across the editorial budget, demanding more than anybody else for things like white Cadillac convertibles. But on the other hand I'm fucking well tired of losing credit cards so that editors can pay their bar tabs. If the money's there, I honestly think you should pick up the tab for Vegas I—despite the obvious fact that the whole thing got bogged down in terrible excesses & bad misunderstandings about what various monies were for (like that $200 I drew in SF, for instance, I really thought was for SF expenses . . .).

Anyway, fuck it. If the money's not there—or if it's any kind of real problem—I'd be a fucking idiot to keep yelling about it. So I won't mention it again unless I need some kind of emergency loan to pay off Carte Blanche—and I won't mention that unless it's *necessary.*

OK for now. My brain is drifting back to politics. It should be drifting to bed, but for some reason I think I'll stay up and go looking for elk on the bike. I did another one of those airborne over-the-hump & crash in the water gigs last evening . . . but this time I didn't stall; I just hung on and came boring out, drenched with mud & gasping for breath . . . and it was a wild high feeling to go screaming off across the meadow instead of lying there on the bank.

Maybe there's a lesson in this. Never let off. Keep it screwed on—for good or ill.

Ciao . . .
H

TO JIM FLUG c/o U.S. SENATOR EDWARD M. KENNEDY:

Now a salaried "national correspondent," Thompson had official Rolling Stone *letterhead suitable for making requests of Senator Ted Kennedy's legislative aide.*

June 1, 1971
Woody Creek, CO

Jim Flug
c/o Sen. Ted Kennedy
U.S. Senate Office Building
Washington, D. C.

Dear Jim . . .

It feels weird for me to be writing on any kind of corporate or institutional stationery—but this one doesn't really bother me. I still live here in Woody Creek, and my "editorial" involvement consists of periodic trips to the coast, primarily to deal with projects like the (enc.) Salazar gig. I'm listed as a "contributing editor," but that doesn't really explain it—and at this point I doubt if any real explanation is necessary.

What I have to do for the summer is finish off a book for Random House, then leave for Saigon in September—to cover "The Retreat & Total Dissolution of the U.S. Army." My current arrangement is to spend six months there, then to get back here for the '72 campaign. So in the unlikely circumstance that you might want to rent a big house about 12 miles out of Aspen next winter, let me know. . . .

In the meantime, I wonder if you could get me a copy of that "Drug Report" that AP says was "prepared for the House Foreign Affairs Committee, by Rep. Robert Steele, R—Conn." I'd also like to have another document mentioned in the same AP story (5/27/71—*D. Post*), to wit: "An earlier report from the House Armed Services Committee also described corruption in the drug trade among South Vietnamese officials, but stopped short of indicating how heroin gets into Vietnam. . . ."

Could you possibly get me copies of these two reports? No author or Congressman is mentioned, by AP, as a primary source for the Armed Services Committee Report. Steele is named as the "principal author" for the FgnAff Comm. Rpt (House), and there is also mention of a "Morgan F. Murphy, D—Ill." He worked with Steele. . . .

What I'm trying to do is arm myself totally for a heavy six-month gig in Vietnam—two articles a month for *Rolling Stone,* then putting all the articles into an instant book in time for the Nov '72 election. I suspect we'll be running something heavy out here about that. How about you?

Yeah, I know that one's loaded. But I'm naturally curious. Keep me in mind if you want to do something Serious. Camelot[20] won't make it this time around. This time it's going to be heavy . . . and that's it for now. Send word.

Thanx—
Hunter S. Thompson

TO JIM SILBERMAN, RANDOM HOUSE:

In 1970 Thompson investigated the tragic death of journalist Ruben Salazar, a writer for the Los Angeles Times *and leader in the East L.A. Chicano community. Thompson's provocative article was dropped by* Scanlan's *but later published by* Rolling Stone.

June 2, 1971
Woody Creek, CO

Dear Jim . . .

Here's a copy of my Ruben Salazar article (*RS* 4/29) for your personal files—just in case nobody sent you one. It's a long fucker: 19,200 words, and it should probably be read straight through.

20. Camelot, the city the Knights of the Round Table called home in the legend of England's King Arthur, was the term used to describe the idealization of President John F. Kennedy's administration.

One of the interesting technical aspects of this one is that it's *two first drafts*, both written at high deadline speed, but almost six months elapsed between the writing of the center section (done for *Scanlan's*) and the color/culture update that was done for *Rolling Stone* to bracket the actual Salazar story. But an odd mixture of circumstances made them both first drafts—the *Scanlan's* section was actually written by hand, about half of it done on TWA's "redeye express" from SF to NY one night in September of '70.

But that evil fuck, Sidney Zion, didn't like it. So it was croaked . . . for a while, anyway.

Anyway, I felt it was the kind of thing I *should* get into print—for a lot of weird reasons that got tied up, somehow, with personal friendships and the paying of personal dues and that sort of gibberish. But in the end it was done, and for all its flaws I like it. When those scurvy pigfuckers shoot me, I hope some biased geek from somewhere like Woody Creek does the same thing for me—flaws and all. The way I saw it, Ruben Salazar was a journalist, not a Chicano—and I personally believe they shot him intentionally, but I couldn't prove that (all of my research and interviews were done *before* the inquest—before the cops would talk to the press—and the only reason I resurrected the story was that the result of the inquest incredibly confirmed the story I'd put together in the first days after the murder . . .).

Anyway, I think you should read it. Particularly right now, since we don't have much time to put all this American Dream bullshit together. In that context, I think Salazar's last utterance is a very special thing: "That's impossible; we're not doing anything." Then he stood up and caught a tear-gas bomb in his temple.

And by any "normal" standards, he *wasn't* doing anything. But Restrepo,[21] who was with him, said Salazar had been talking all day about . . . but shit, now that I write this for the first time, I see again that I'm sure Restrepo couldn't possibly understand, for sure, the kind of thing he claims to have understood in Salazar. (I recently had to intervene with the KMEX-TV management to keep Restrepo's job . . . a wild threatening letter to Danny Villanueva.[22] . . .)

Which hardly matters, for now. I was savagely pilloried in print by the heavy street militants—but oddly enough the editors of the Chicano paper at UCLA came to my defense & reprinted 30,000 or so copies of this article in *La Gente*. It began on the front page & consumed almost the entire issue . . . and yesterday I picked up *The Denver Post* & saw my name mentioned by a Chicano columnist as the only *gabacho* journalist who wasn't like the others. . . .

None of . . . wait . . . yes, here's another Chicano matter. Oscar Acosta, the

21. Guillermo Restrepo was a twenty-eight-year-old reporter and newscaster for East L.A.'s KMEX-TV when the station's news director, Chicano journalist Ruben Salazar, was murdered by a sheriff's deputy on August 29, 1970.

22. Danny Villanueva, a former kicker for the Los Angeles Rams, was general manager of KMEX-TV, a bilingual, Mexican-American station.

Chicano Lawyer, is currently writing his memoirs. They are being published by *Con Safos,* a Chicano quarterly, and he's half-mad to get them published in book form. I have the first installment, in the current issue of *Con Safos,* but since it mentions me I'd prefer to wait and send you the next installment, which I assume will not bring me into it . . . anyway, it's called "Memoirs of a Brown Buffalo" and the theme is that "everybody's trying to kill the buffalo." This is how Oscar sees himself, and it would take too long here for me to explain the validity of what he's saying. Right after the *RS* article came out, for instance, six of these heavy militant street crazies showed up at his apt. and said it was time for him to go out to the desert and die—they had guns, and they were ready to do him because he "said too much" to the gringo writer (me) . . . so now he's up in Berkeley for the summer, writing his book and lecturing one hour a day in the Chicano Studies program.

It might be a good book to publish. Oscar is definitely a writer. I sent his first novel to Margaret [Harrell] a few years ago . . . & she said it needed work . . . which was true . . . but with a little help from a good editor this new thing he's writing might be very good. Certainly worth looking at—if only because it's an intensely personal statement from a main figure in the mushrooming Chicano/Aztlan movement.[23] Let me know if you'd like to look at it. . . .

***

The other thing I'm enclosing is a Memo (22 pgs.) I just sent to Bert Schneider at BBS—regarding a film based on *The Rum Diary.* The chances of this working out are much higher than anything associated with a standard commercial relationship—for reasons I see no point in explaining now. It's a personal thing, a quirk of fate. I explained it to Lynn. But let's wait & see what happens. My private guess is that we'll get a film out of it . . . but?????

OK for now. Send immediate word inre: Vegas. And also I *must* have that expense check for the Vegas trip. Time is important. Crucial. I am dancing on the edge here. Send word. . . .

Thanx,
Hunter

TO BERT SCHNEIDER, BBS PRODUCTIONS:

Thompson wrote Bert Schneider in great detail about the logistics of making The Rum Diary *into a movie.*

23. Aztlan is the part of the nineteenth-century Mexican nation that was occupied by the U.S. government and broken into Texas, New Mexico, Arizona, and the southern half of California. As Thompson wrote in his April 29, 1971, *Rolling Stone* article on the murder of Ruben Salazar, "The word 'Chicano' was forged as a necessary identity for the people of Aztlan—neither Mexicans nor Americans, but a conquered Indian/Mestizo nation sold out like slaves by its leaders and treated like indentured servants by its conquerors."

June 2, 1971
Woody Creek, CO

Dear Bert . . .

Barbara just got back from the 88th leg of her odyssey and told me you people were feeling overdue about getting some kind of working chunk of *The Rum Diary* from me . . . which made me wild & nervous, because Michael didn't make this deadline entirely clear to me before he took off for Guatemala.

Consequently, I'm enclosing a few bits of things I've been working on—not in the sense of sending you anything official, but mainly to assure you that I am indeed grappling with the fucker . . . along with a lot of other things, at least one of which might also turn into a good film (see enc. Sample of "Fear & Loathing in Las Vegas". . .).

Anyway, my problem on *The Rum Diary* is not in the grappling—which is easy & fun, for the most part—but mainly in the fact of my own ignorance about what we need, on paper, before we can start talking seriously about a film. I told Michael I'd "write five scenes," but that was before I got into it and realized that I'll probably be writing 10 pages for every two minutes on film . . . which means a minimum of 450 pages of fairly tight script/dialogue and that's a bastard of a thing to just dash off and stick in the mail, on the odd chance that somebody at BBS might take a liking to it and perhaps send a cheque for the rewrite. . . .

I started off doing a few scenes (see enclosed yellow pages), but it was instantly apparent that I couldn't just sit down & rip them off, out of context. That one shot about the airplane hassle, en route to San Juan, where the protagonist asks the old man to sit on his hand, is a scene in itself—visually—but on paper it needs a lot of explanation. Our protagonist, C. Barn, is in an extremely crazed, wired, state of mind—this can be established by about 33 seconds worth of facial expressions on film, but in print it's a bastard to explain *quick*. How fucked up would *you* have to be to ask your PanAm seat-mate to sit on your hand?

Anyway . . . what I've done (enc.) is wrap up the few brief shots I've done here—in addition to the 370 page novel that Random House bought a few years ago, on the basis of my assurance that I was right on the verge of rewriting it—and for now I thought I'd just send them along, for good or ill, and on the general assumption that they'll probably weigh more than nothing at all.

Perhaps the central problem in these dealings is that Michael is reluctant—for reasons you'll probably understand as well or better than me—to confront you with anything but a king-hell 12-star boomer. It's the classic story of the Coach's Son Trying to Make Good . . . but of course being merely "good" is not enough on that trip; you have to be *super.* Like Pete Maravich[24] . . . or whatever his name is.

24. Louisiana State star guard Pete Maravich set the NCAA basketball single-season scoring record of 44.5 points per game in 1970.

Which is neither here nor there in my case. I labor under the equally heavy onus of having no other source of income except my 10-year gig as a free-lance writer. *Rolling Stone* is currently paying me $500 a month as a "contributing editor," but that adds up to $6000 a year—against my annual *minimum* needs of something just under $15K. And this will probably go up to $20K or so when I take on the additional burden of paying off these two houses and the 100 acres that go with them; the payments will start falling due in a month or so.

This should explain, more or less, why I can't righteously lock in and spend the next three months on a 450-page screenplay for people I barely know, and with no prior understanding of any kind. Rafelson is hopelessly crazy; that's clear. He's a refugee from the Lionel Olay[25] syndrome—the Big Sur doomed elegance/secret/hero trip—and although I admire that POV immensely, I have to remember that Lionel wound up paying his rent with street-acid. And he died of an aneurysm. . . .

What all this is leading up to, I think, is a fairly critical question . . . to wit: What do we need before we can start talking seriously about putting *The Rum Diary* together on film? There is no doubt in my mind—and Michael agrees, I think—that we have a super-visual story to work with. The novel, itself, is a massively flawed masterpiece, but even on that level it is full of very *physical* behavior. The San Juan drink/drug/madness underground, as a backdrop to the American Dream destroying one of its main worshipers. On a purely visual level, we have mass violence in The Palms, street-brawls in old San Juan, idyllic carnality on stone-white beaches, a terrifying cock-fight scene far out in the central mountains . . . we have casinos, skin-diving, politics, fear, idealism, violence, madness, lust, flesh, brutality & twisted behavior. . . .

Shit, it's almost an AIP film[26] up front. The setting and the basic story-line make the "American Dream" overtly seem like pure gravy—except that the American Dream gibberish is all that makes the film worth doing.

That's more or less what I'm looking at here: The long chance of a film vs. the guaranteed (financial) success of several journalism projects. Frankly, I'd much prefer to stomp heavily into film—like a lot of other people, I guess, and the only difference between mine & a lot of other people's stories, right now, is that I can actually make a living as a journalist/writer/etc. . . .

This may end when the Las Vegas saga appears, because I doubt if 1971 America is ready for Gonzo Journalism . . . but that's not a problem here. That one is coming out anyway, for good or ill, and I'll deal with the reaction as it erupts. . . .

What concerns us, right now, is some kind of valid format for proceeding with this *Rum Diary* thing. Obviously, you need enough to convince *you* that

25. Lionel Olay, a freelance journalist and screenwriter Thompson befriended in Big Sur in 1960, had died of a stroke in November 1966.

26. American International Pictures (AIP), an independent production company founded in 1955, put out a slew of profitable low-budget horror movies by director Roger Corman throughout the 1960s and '70s.

it's a good film. I'm already sure of this, and I think Michael is too—although he doesn't want to confront you with it until it's already a guaranteed screamer. For instance he doesn't want to submit the script until it's refined and heavy enough to convince Orson Welles[27] to play the part of Stone. . . .

Which is fine. But like I said, I'm not independently wealthy—and it's my story, so before we get into a 450 page script, I think we should at least consider some terms or possibilities inre: the financial possibilities. Perhaps just the normal, step-by-step shit, or maybe something different . . . although not quite so different that I have to write the whole goddamn thing before we talk about what it might or might not be worth.

My summer (of '71) is extremely heavy with long-overdue projects. I have a long book, unconscionably overdue, for Random House, that has to be finished before I can take off for Saigon in September and spend 6 months covering "the Retreat & Disintegration of the U.S. Army" for *Rolling Stone.* This may or may not work out, but for now it's scheduled. And also this summer—in addition to the Random House book—I have to finish this short saga on Las Vegas that also looks like a book.

And so much for that. I only mention these things to line out the problems that might or might not interfere with my getting full-bore into the *Rum Diary* project—until we can figure out what it might be worth, all around. If only to assign it a place in the general priority-schedule. If the fucker was worth a million dollars to me, for instance, I'd definitely be tempted to clear the decks and hump it along with a focus bordering on total craziness. . . . But if it's basically a friendly "On Spec" project, well . . . I'd still like to do it, but the bulk of my energies would have to go into projects for paying my way in this rotten world. Once again, for good or ill . . . Shit . . . I was almost ready to start apologizing for what might seem like a greedy/grasping trip, here . . . but it suddenly occurred to me that you fuckers are zooming around in Lear Jets & that sort of thing. Which is *right,* of course, but I get the feeling these days that maybe I should have a Lear Jet, too.

Why not?

Indeed. And that's the main reason I'm sending this letter—with this hazy chunk of samples—instead of a final-carved, super-refined 450 word script. Not that I wouldn't *want* to, but I simply don't have a loose & lazy summer at my disposal. And beyond that, if some evil amoral waterhead like Rafelson can fly around this doomed nation in a Lear Jet, I think it's only fitting that I have an elegant Jet Commander at my disposal. . . .

What should happen at this point, I think, is that you should read over the enclosed gibberish and see if it strikes any sparks. The 22-page Memo is full of

27. Orson Welles, the renowned actor, writer, producer, and director of such classic movies as 1941's *Citizen Kane,* received an honorary Academy Award in 1971 "for superlative artistry and versatility in the creation of motion pictures."

references to the 370 page novel manuscript, but I think there's enough in it to let you see where the story is aiming. And the yellow pages—a rough draft of what I think should be the opening scene—is only included to give you some idea about *how* it might be done. The next step, as I see it, would be to write some interpretation.

What I need is some kind of definite framework to work with. I could send the *novel* ms., but I would only do that with the warning that it's nearly 10 years old . . . and in truth I think the only value it has, now, is that it's full of the kind of odd details and valid, on-scene mental/emotional shots that will make the film true. You can't fake the sense of terror, for instance, that comes with being stomped in a palm grove—for no legal reason—by a Clutch gaggle of Puerto Rican cops . . . or the crazy midnight vibrations of a San Juan jail. This stuff is already in the novel, and it would be hard to get again. Very hard. And definitely painful for whoever had to get it.

Anyway, the novel *exists*, if anybody wants to read it. But the story Mike & I have talked about is quite a bit different from the tale that's told in the novel. Maybe a good thing for you to do, at this point, is to read thru all this crap and then talk to Mike . . . and then maybe the three of us should get together and hash the thing out. Because if the possibility of turning this thing into a film lies with what I can put on paper *before* we talk about it . . . well . . . I doubt if we'll get started anytime soon.

The problem is not in *putting* it on paper, but the *time* factor: It will take me at least two months of steady work to write the film properly, and a lot of that writing would have to be done more or less on location in Puerto Rico. Because obviously these scenes are going to have to change a bit, visually, to fit what the camera will see. And that's fine. Except that I haven't *been* to San Juan in a few years, and I know it's changed drastically. So any valid script would have to be written on the scene as it exists today.

One good thing, for instance, is that the *San Juan Star* actually exists. It was just bought (from Cowles [Communications]) by the Newhouse chain, I think. . . . Cowles bought it from the lunatic who began it around 1960 . . . and we have the original Managing Editor (now the Book Editor of *LOOK*)[28] to work with us on newsroom details and that sort of thing. In terms of shooting, the physical problems wouldn't be any worse than a set in California.

As far as I'm concerned, we're about 70% home when we start. The rudiments of the story-line already exist *on paper*, in the form of the novel. The only completely new factor is the character of the protagonist—which Mike & I have already solved, more or less to our own satisfaction, but which will inevitably change as the story takes shape on film.

I'm absolutely convinced it should be done. And if I were independently wealthy, I'd go ahead & do it on my own.

28. William J. Kennedy.

But I'm not. I have no money at all. None. So what we do with this thing now depends mainly on BBS. The next logical step would be (or at least *seem* to be) for you & I and Mike to go over to the patio in the Beverly Hills Hotel and talk heavily & crazily for three straight days . . . or, if that hotel makes you nervous, we can go out to the Carioca in East LA and hassle it there.

Whatever's right. As far as I'm concerned we have the fucker about two-thirds under control. All we have to do now is settle the filthy realities. Which should definitely be done *soon* . . . Because of my own priority problem (see above) and the definite possibility that if we get this thing going seriously, I might have to re-schedule a few of my own realities.

Excelsior . . .
Hunter S. Thompson

TO JANN WENNER, *ROLLING STONE:*

Rolling Stone *had won 1970's prestigious National Magazine Award for Specialized Journalism for its coverage of the Altamont debacle and for David Felton's June 25, 1970, piece on Charles Manson (cowritten with British music journalist David Dalton). The Columbia University judges lauded the magazine for "challenging the shared values of its readers."*

June, 1971
Woody Creek, CO

Jann . . .

Right after I hung up last night I realized you said the award was for "unstapled" journalism—but the word I got was unstable. Which made me wonder why you seemed so pleased. Or maybe I just felt guilty—one of those Freudian misunderstandings. Since I was working on the Las Vegas piece at the time, it figured. "Unstable," indeed! Those swine. Next year we should demand a Gonzo category—or maybe *RS* should give it. Of course. "The First Annual *Rolling Stone* Award for the Year's Finest Example of Pure Gonzo Journalism." First Prize: a gallon of raw ether. Second: a Pepper-Fogger, donated by the ELA Sheriff's Dept. Third: A free trip to the 1972 Mint 400 in Las Vegas to anybody with the balls to go out there and apply for *Rolling Stone* press credentials.

And so much for that. I'll talk to Silberman & see what he says. He told me once that he "trusts my instincts." But he was probably lying. Anyway, I'll want 20% off the top of any merger I can effect . . . or a giant-size A/C bullet suitcase, whichever proves out to be the greater value.

As for juggling contracts inre: the American Dream/Battle of Aspen book, I think it would be a mistake all around for me (or you) to propose that right now. Silberman has treated me with an almost preternatural decency thus far, and I don't want to screw him until he gives me a good excuse. (Yeah . . .

"screw" is the wrong word, I know—but I think that's how he'd see it.) And I doubt if it would help your relationship with him, either.

The best way to deal with it, I think, is to see if we can work out some mutually pleasant agreement inre: the Vietnam book. And if that works, maybe we could use it as a sort of pattern. . . . I think a *RS*/RH hookup would be a good thing, especially for *RS*. The trick is to convince Silberman that it would be good for RH. Maybe you and Alan can figure that one out.

If so, let me know & I'll try to help. Silberman still owes me a huge favor for the murder of my snake on Random House turf.

OK for now. The Vegas piece should be all in by the time you get this. My only fear is that that fucking idiot Felton will ruin it, like he did the Salazar piece.

Ciao,
Hunter

TO JANN WENNER, *ROLLING STONE:*

June, 1971
Woody Creek, CO

Jann,

Sorry we didn't have more time to talk last nite—but come out again & give me some warning. (*Not* via Western Union.)

Anyway, I think we're putting together a very unlikely & potentially powerful Karass out here—& considering the people involved, the initial stages are bound to be difficult. Especially when we all get stoned, early on. Selah . . .

Which is really just a standard occupational hazard these days (strange irony, though, that your social/computer date should have ended up with Bob Rafelson—maybe you should examine that).

Meanwhile, I think we managed to touch most of the main bases—perhaps in spite of ourselves—& after a few hours of idle thought, I can't see how that "contributing editor" gig could be anything but a good shot. (In that context, you have to recall my prior associations & consequent trauma. . . .) I'll check with Lynn & Silberman for possible hang-ups & then get back to you . . . but in general I like the idea & in my own mind, it's a thing I'd like to do. It seems to fit that idea of a Karass—which is a concept I think we should push—maybe even as a newer & more sophisticated version of Freak Power. Because—in *my* mind, at least—they're 2 verbal means to the same end.

But the power of a word like *Karass* lies mainly in *not* pushing it. There's a massive political potential in that concept—if we handle it right & gently . . . & with the idea that it might provide a decisive rally-concept for 1972 Presidential Politics.

It seems to me that McCloskey's[29] trip is actually the first shot in what suddenly looks like a real fight for survival. That cheap bastard *must* be beaten in '72—& to do that I think we have to get him on *the defensive* at once, & *keep* him there . . . in other words, to shape the challenge & make sure he sees it coming, so he *has* to focus on re-election, instead of War with China. . . .

Which is what he'd prefer to do anyway. He's a stone politics-junkie, a total campaigner. Which means he'll have to be stomped on his own turf, on his own terms . . . which makes him a natural set-up for the time (& Nixon) honored Green Bay Packers strategy of breaking the enemy by "running at his strength" instead of his weakness—thus knocking him off balance at the start.

It's straight [Packers coach] Vince Lombardi wisdom, but Nixon has learned it so well that he'd never recognize it coming at him from us—from any kind of Freak Power, druggy/radical ethos—because nowhere in his own mind or in the minds of the people he hires (Pat Buchanan, Ray Price, etc.) to think *strategically* for him is there any room for the idea that some ragtag coalition of dopey liberals & freaks could possibly understand the brutal simplicity (& political application) of Lombardi's "run at their strength" ethic. When I had my historic "pro football debate" with Nixon in N.H. in early '68, I got the powerful impression that Vince Lombardi was the only man in America that he viscerally respected. Lombardi was a *winner,* with a deceptively simple strategy: "Run first at their strength—Beat them there & the rest is simple."

Which works—in politics as well as pro football. In '68 Nixon beat HH *not* by emphasizing their differences—like Goldwater challenging Johnson in '64—but by smiling overtime to pick up wavering *Humphrey votes*—and especially on the issue that a brand-new un-encumbered *Republican* president would *be able (politically) to end the war* in Vietnam—while (Pres.) Humphrey would be too locked into the LBJ trip & thus unable to make any radical changes in the National War Policy.

In other words, Nixon confronted the Democrats *not* with a *different* program for Vietnam, but with the mystic necessity of clearing the decks & installing a whole new (Republican) machinery—an administration *completely free,* he said, of that web of doomed obligations that would inevitably hamstring a (Demo) Castle-keep like Hubert Humphrey.

Which proved to be absolute bullshit—which hardly matters now, because the point we want to see & focus on here is that Nixon beat Humphrey on what should & could have been Hubert's strongest argument—to end the war in Vietnam at once, because LBJ fucked up. Nixon's bargaining strength—according to the perpetually lame & grasping wisdom of people like *NY Times* guru James Reston—was that *any* GOP president could afford to *admit* that

29. Republican congressman Pete McCloskey of California would threaten to introduce an impeachment resolution against President Nixon in the U.S. House of Representatives in June 1973.

the U.S. was wrong in Vietnam—while no Democratic regime could possibly run the risk of repudiating 10 years of Demo (LBJ-JFK) strategy.

Thus Nixon pre-empted what could have been Humphrey's main argument. It was a straight Lombardi-style "game plan," & it worked. Nixon actually won the election by claiming that *only he* could end the war.

TO JIM SILBERMAN, RANDOM HOUSE:

It's even more remarkable that—by his own admission—Thompson wasn't *on drugs while working on* Fear and Loathing in Las Vegas.

June 15, 1971
Woody Creek, CO

Dear Jim . . .

Thanks immensely for the check. It came, unfortunately, in the same mail with a notice from Carte Blanche that I was Cut Off. I've cursed Wenner for making this nightmare possible by his penny-wise, pound-foolish fiscal concepts, but for now I'm into fighting with the goddamn computer. What your check does, however, is give me the leverage to *bargain* with the swine; I can at least offer to send them a check immediately, provided I'm reinstated. (This didn't work with American Express; once that computer nixed me, I stayed nixed.)

Anyway, we'll see on this one. But in any case I definitely appreciate the check. The only thing that vaguely alarmed me about your letter was your statement, to wit: "You know it was absolutely clear to me reading Las Vegas I that you were not on drugs. . . ." This is true, but what alarms me is that Vegas I was a very conscious attempt to *simulate* drug freakout—which is always difficult, but in reading it over I still find it depressingly close to the truth I was trying to re-create. To this end—and right after your letter came—I ate a bunch of mescaline and went to a violent, super-jangled car race last weekend with Lucian Truscott from *The Village Voice,* and I was relieved to find that we—along with about 10 other people—experienced the same kind of bemused confusion with the reality we had to deal with that Raoul Duke & his attorney had to cope with in Vegas. We were completely involved with what was happening—but our involvement was not so much on a different level as from a different POV [point of view] than the people in the grandstand around us. A man behind us was more excited; a man in front of us was alarmed at the behavior of a truck-load of freaks who seemed more scrambled than we were—but our overall approach to the race and the scene was consistently Strange, in the same sense that I tried to make that Vegas thing consistently strange.

But to hell with all this. What depresses me is your statement that it was "absolutely clear" to you that Raoul Duke & his attorney "were not on drugs." Because my conception of that piece was to write a thing that would tell what it was like to do a magazine assignment with a head full of weird drugs. I didn't really *make up* anything—but I did, at times, bring situations & feelings I remember from other scenes to the reality at hand. I might even claim, for that matter, that this was done by consciously tripping the fabled "LSD Recall and/or Flashback Mechanism."

But this is a difficult subject, & there's no point in trying to come to grips with it here. What I'm talking about, in essence, is the mechanical Reality of Gonzo Journalism . . . or Total Subjectivity, as opposed to the bogus demands of Objectivity.

But fuck all that, for now. All I ask is that you keep your opinions on my drug-diet for that weekend to yourself. As I noted, the nature (& specifics) of the piece has already fooled the editors of *Rolling Stone.* They're absolutely convinced, on the basis of what they've read, that I spent my expense money on drugs and went out to Las Vegas for a ranking freakout. Probably we should leave it this way; it makes it all the more astounding, that I could emerge from that heinous experience with a story. So let's just keep our personal conclusions to ourselves. . . .

***

Inre: Vegas as the end of the American Dream book, I definitely disagree. Lynn has already urged this on me, and I told her that—although I share her (and your) sense of urgency about "Getting the Book Done," I'd hate to wrap it up with a stone-crazy "drug orgy" that might impeach the essentially serious tone of the book as a whole. I can't see coming off a thing about Aspen politics (or the Murder of Ruben Salazar) and sliding into a freakout in Las Vegas that was originally conceived in such madness that I didn't even want to sign it with my own name.

I might be wrong on this—and I told Lynn that I'd probably "defer to Silberman's judgment on this," which is true, but I want you to keep in mind that I'd just as soon not be dismissed as a Drug Addled clown . . . and I'm afraid that might be the effect of ending the AD book with the Vegas thing.

My notion of a proper ending remains the Aspen/Sheriff thing—which is more or less written, and I should definitely send you a copy, so we'll at least know what we're haggling about.

The main problem with everything, right now, is that it all has to be done immediately . . . which in the terms of my own history is probably instructive, but despite all that I'm still a bit leery of making a Public Fool of myself, just to get a book out. There is always the chance, of course, that *I am a fool,* but I'd prefer to make some asshole like Peter J. Prescott[30] figure that out for himself, rather than give him the kind of Drug Handle that the Vegas thing would offer.

I don't see any real point in trying to pass the Vegas thing off as the work of "Raoul Duke," either. But I get the feeling that "my image," as it were, might

30. Peter J. Prescott was a well-known literary critic.

not suffer so drastically if that one appeared separately as something like "The Vegas Diaries of R. Duke." I like to think that I can still draw the line between savage humor and brute-serious journalism . . . but maybe not; and I suspect that when the final truth is known, if ever, there will be no real difference at all. Frankly, I've never seen one, myself.

In the meantime, I'm enclosing an accidental classic of a photo that was taken by one of those wandering bar-room photographers in Caesars Palace on one of those nights during the Drug Convention. On the left is Raoul Duke, and on the right is "my attorney." (His real name is Oscar Acosta—the Chicano lawyer—but I've promised not to publish his name in connection with this foto, without his permission. This is not the kind of story that would help him politically in East L.A.)

Publication of the foto, itself, is no problem—and I suspect that the use of his name won't be any problem, either, once the time comes. The key consideration is How the Story is treated: If we're both to be made out as Fools, then the caption should be "Raoul Duke & Attorney in Caesars Palace."

But this is something we can worry about much later. The important thing, right now, is to finish Vegas II and also the Aspen piece. After that, we can see how it all fits. But—from my own point of view—I think Vegas I & II should be separate entities. You shouldn't worry about RH control over this, in light of the fact that you've paid the major part of the expenses for Vegas.

For that matter, you should put aside all worries or concerns or even paranoid delusions about any of this material somehow slipping out of your grasp. As far as I'm concerned—and I've explained this to Wenner—you've endured a lot of half-mad bullshit from me during the past two years, and as far as I'm concerned you have first call on any material that you think should go into this long-overdue book. My only concern, inre: Vegas, is that I don't want to confuse payment of a legitimate debt with the permanent destruction of my credibility as a writer.

But I assume you understand this, so until we come to some serious disagreement you can assume I think you're doing the right thing. I'm not going to start piecing off things to *Rolling Stone* or anybody else without warning you far in advance—and not even then until we've had a human talk.

Which seems vaguely like make-work, right now. At this point, I'm not even sure *RS* has agreed to pay my *expenses* in Vietnam, so that Sept 1 departure date is hardly definite. My only serious concern, at this point, is to get this goddamn evil AmDream book out. Vegas is secondary, and Vietnam is third. (My idea that Vietnam might be included in the AD book was clearly useless; it emerged from a panic notion that the War might be over by October—and this seems hopeless now.)

On the other hand—thinking realistically—I get the impression from Wenner that he's dead serious about getting me to Vietnam, so any momentary haggling about "expenses" will probably be settled pretty quick.

Next week, in fact. He & his wife are coming out here for a week or so, and on the basis of his last visit out here I have to assume the talk will run fast & heavy. So if there's anything in this letter that addles or disturbs your thinking, you should get your reply off at once. Or call. My experience with Jann is that when he starts calling me every 24 hours—which has been the case during my solitary funk this week—that he is definitely into something. And if that's the case, I'd prefer to be absolutely firm with you before I start making extraneous agreements.

To that end, I'll try to xerox & mail a copy of my half-finished version of the Aspen/Sheriff thing tomorrow. Selah. . . .

Another upcoming thing, next week, is a summit-conference on Vortex. That's the name I've given to this valley; my friend & landlord, George Stranahan, has bought the whole thing, and now we're trying to figure out what to do with it. Mike Murphy is coming out from Esalen, along with Wenner. What we want to do is come up with a completely new concept of land use &/or occupancy—something that transcends the old notion of "ownership." Do you know anybody who's into this? Or any pertinent books? If so, you should tell me at once. We have a rare situation here—a whole valley (including a small sawmill town) that the owner wants to use for some kind of genuinely revolutionary supra-ownership experiment . . . and I find myself in the weird position of being the Contact Man. We plan to incorporate the place immediately, then get on with the business of Destroying the Concept of Land/Ownership in Perpetuity.

Not communes. That concept strikes me as hopelessly naïve—or at least naïve to me, given over, as I am, to my mania for privacy. And the handful of others now involved seem to feel the same way. So this leaves us with a weird hellish problem: How to codify privacy and at the same time croak the notion of fence-lines.

I suppose this can't make much sense to you there in The Pit . . . but the point, as I see it, is to establish some viable alternative to The Pit. When the world narrows down to the point where I can leave my house in Woody Creek & be in LA in 2 hrs, or NY in 4 hrs (not counting time-zone differences) . . . there is no longer any sense in this lifestyle. The Techno/Demographic realities of 1971 are in total conflict with the idea that any amount of money can buy absolute domain over any physical territory. This is becoming clear around Aspen, if not in NY.

But this is a different story, and I'll get to it later—when we get something working. Meanwhile, I'll send the Aspen thing & also Vegas II. And on your end, let's confront the mechanics of getting a good book together by September 1. OK for now . . .

Hunter

TO JANN WENNER, *ROLLING STONE:*

Thompson's ongoing agonies over expense accounts and contract negotiations serve as a cautionary tale for freelance writers.

June 15, 1971
Woody Creek, CO

Dear Jann . . .

I'm sending today, under sep. cover, an accidental classic of a photo to go with the Vegas thing. As I noted in the margin, Acosta's name should not be mentioned without his permission. He's not opposed to the use of the photo, but as of now he's concerned about seeing his name etched permanently in the caption. I understand this, and agreed that he would only be identified as "my attorney."

My own caption-ID is *personally* immaterial to me. The Raoul Duke byline, however, might now be entirely viable if Random House decides to use Vegas II in the American Dream book—by HST. This is an option that Silberman bought—very cheap, I think—when he paid the Expense tab for both Vegas pieces (less $500 that was paid out in cash & remains un-reimbursed). What he paid was the Carte Blanche bill, but not in time to beat the computer that took my card. The swine cut me off last week—no warning at all, just a massive cut-off & a vicious letter from the Harbour Detective Agency, saying I should cut my card in half & send it back. I refused, of course, but that doesn't alter the fact that my number is now on the "to be arrested at once" list that circulates among CB dealers.

The fact that I blame you for this is probably unjust in the long run—but of course there was never any real question of "the long run." All I wanted to do was pay off my card, and talk about Fiscal Responsibility later.

Which is neither here nor there, for now. The deed is done. I am now naked of credit. And this ugly fact is going to put a bad crimp in my working-style for a long time to come. Selah . . .

***

As for Vegas, it's coming along very slowly. Silberman thinks it should go in the AmDream book, but I disagree. By picking up my expenses, however, he bought the right to decide. As I noted in previous letters—both to you and Silberman—he had no contractual obligation to pay the whole nut. I'm impressed, however, by the shrewdness he showed in buying effective control of two books for $102.10. If you want to get seriously into the publishing business you might do well to watch Silberman's left hand—never mind his right—and see how he deals with the rudiments. What we are into now is a situation where Silberman has the right of First Refusal on Vegas II, in terms of book rights. If he wants Vegas II for the AD book, it's his—leaving *RS* (Straight Arrow) with nothing but First Serial rights on Vegas I.

Like I say, I disagree with this. The Vegas stuff is too twisted, I think, to anchor a serious book. But what will probably happen, now, is that I'll have to persuade Silberman of that and then trade him "The Battle of Aspen—An Epitaph for Freak Power?" for the entirety of Vegas. And this dealing will be subject in a lot of ways to The Schedule—my planned departure for Saigon on Sept 1.

So we'll have at least this to ponder when you get here. Sandy says you called Sunday & then today. I was far into madness on Sunday—Lucian Truscott showed up with a huge bag of mescaline—and today I was too cosmically pissed off to talk about anything. Especially money—which you seem to have indicated would be the subject under discussion. I had a terrible scene with the dentist earlier today: One of the side-horrors of Vegas II was that I bit down on something that cracked three of my teeth—a problem I was unaware of until I went in a few days ago for my routine 6-month cleaning.

I've also been locked into this Vortex (new concept of land use & ownership) thing for the past few days. We can't figure out what to *do* with this fucking valley, and this impotence is driving me nuts. Maybe you have some ideas . . . ??? Mike Murphy (Esalen) is coming out in a week or so & I plan to prod him for ideas. When exactly do you plan to be here?

Shit, I'll call him tomorrow. I'm vaguely concerned, among other things, about that "Jesus Freak memo" from the Sports Desk . . . if there's any possibility that it might be published, I want to talk about it first. (Meanwhile, I've prepared Sports Desk Memo #2—On the subject of "Drug Lyrics in Rock Music.") The very nature of this format makes the writing a bit heavy. #1 began as a joke—and perhaps it ended that way. I can't be sure. Whenever I belch out my bias that strongly, it takes on an element of craziness . . . and I want to be careful of this. In the past two weeks I've received copies of two different books that used "selections" from *Hell's Angels,* and in both cases I was shocked at what happens to my stuff when it's printed out of context. All it takes is a few cuts on the Humor to make the rest seem like the ravings of a dangerous lunatic.

Anyway, we can deal with these things when you get here. It's possible that [Bill] Noonan will be gone, and if he is you can stay in his house—which would probably be preferable, from your end, to using the guest room here. Which is definitely available—complete with White Sound. But I'll talk to you tomorrow, before you get this, and get a fix on your travel dates.

OK for now . . .
HST

TO TOM WICKER, *THE NEW YORK TIMES:*

New York Times *Washington bureau chief Tom Wicker was a soft-spoken North Carolina liberal known for his eloquent opposition to the Vietnam War and other injustices. He would write in his 1978 book* On Press *that "the true freedom of the press is to decide for itself what to publish and when to publish it."*

June 18, 1971
Woody Creek, CO

Dear Mr. Wicker . . .

I just finished your piece on "The Greening of the Press" in the May/June *Columbia J-Review*—perhaps the best or at least the most consistently-committed thing of yours I've ever read. Your out-front public education has been one of the minor-spectacles on the press scene during the past few years.

Nothing snide or nasty about that; it's definitely meant as a compliment. Most people with your kind of leverage seem to hunker down & start snarling when their natural preconceptions go down the tube . . . but you seemed to have learned from it, which would seem to be such a natural thing that it shouldn't need a compliment. But I think it does.

Which is neither here nor there—at least not in the context of your *CJR* piece. The thing made a perfect, ominous kind of sense from beginning to end . . . and from my own POV as a long-time special pleader, I was particularly jerked up by your conclusion, the last 3 grafs:

"The novel, the good novel, has always been the best journalism." And ". . . we must create the kind of conditions in which they (all those good writers) can do their best work."

Which raises the point—and the reason I write this letter—that, despite the visceral wisdom of the point you make, I get the feeling that what is actually happening is exactly in the opposite direction of what you advocate: that what we see today is a savagely collapsing market for the kind of journalism you seem to value. And so do I; and a hell of a lot of others. . . .

But the truth—which your Columbia speech never even hinted at—is that the market, and therefore the possibilities, for the kind of writing you're talking about has shriveled drastically in the past year. I never really gave a fuck for *Harper's,* but at least it was an opening, a possibility. . . .

Or maybe not . . . a quick spin on my own bitch here might be that *Harper's* was really a waste of my time & money & paper. Just a stylish sinecure for a handful of writers who couldn't find elbow room or whatever at the *Times.* Or Mailer's private bazooka . . . but to hell with all that; it's not that important. *Harper's* at least *passed* for the kind of journalistic format that you and all the others—including me—say is necessary.

On another level, I recently covered a motorcycle/dune-buggy orgy in Las Vegas with the *Life* bureau chief from LA, and he said that both *Life* and *LOOK* were in terminal trouble . . . and I said that was a fucking shame, but that if he wanted to take about a 90% cut in pay, we might create a position for him as *Rolling Stone* bureau chief in Miami.

He smiled. It was a bad joke. He could no more work for *RS* than you could write editorials for the NY *Daily News*. But the point, once again, went far beyond the real or rumored vulnerability of any one or two magazines: Once again, it was Main Doors closing, possibilities shut off. . . .

To this end, I'm enclosing a thing I recently did for *RS*—not because I think it's especially valuable in itself, but it seems to me to be the *kind* of thing that almost certainly couldn't be published anywhere else in American journalism. As it happens, this was a first-draft deadline special, and it has a few nasty holes in it—but even if it were absolutely perfect, journalistically, I doubt if I could have sold it or even given it away to any other publication with any sort of readership or circulation. Not even the *LA Times*—Salazar's own newspaper—would have touched a thing like this; not even after the inquest confirmed the Chicano militants' charges on almost every point except the charge of First-Degree Murder.

Well . . . no real point pursuing this. And whatever *Rolling Stone* might or might not publish is equally beside the point. Because it's hardly the sort of major, national journalistic voice that you seemed to be talking about. *RS* could do everything right, and still be useless. Its readership is not only relatively small, but also relatively bent. . . .

The real horror, to me, lies in the fact that there is absolutely no vehicle in American journalism for the kind of "sensitive" and "intellectual" and essentially moral/merciless reporting that we all understand is necessary—not only for the survival of good journalism in this country, but also for the dying idea that you can walk up to a newsstand (or a mag-rack in Missoula) and find something that will tell you what's really happening . . . or at least what a certain group of editors honestly believe is happening, based on whatever mix of truth & facts & madness they've managed to rip out of the mire.

What is happening all around us (or at least around me—and I travel a lot) is a sort of tandem nightmare in which there are fewer and fewer *examples* of the kind of journalism you say is necessary . . . and meanwhile more and more people are using that scarcity as an excuse or maybe even a good reason to turn their backs (or heads) on journalism entirely. The people I deal with most often—for good or ill—simply don't relate to newspapers & magazines. They might scan a daily paper for something specific—something they're looking for—but the idea of reading the daily paper for "news" or general information, as I do, simply doesn't occur to them. A lot of them *read* the paper, but it's more for amusement than wisdom.

***

Tom Wicker/*NY Times*

Dear Mr. Wicker . . .

This thing has been lying around on my desk for a while & chances are pretty good, right now, that I'll never finish it—not as a letter, an essay or whatever sort of rambling screed it was turning into.

There is also the fact of the *Times'* recent dealings with the boys in Fat City. My reaction to that is pure admiration & even envy. That's one of those things I would like to have been a part of.

Which is neither here nor there, in terms of the point I was leaning into, with this half-finished (enc) letter. The *Times,* for all its space & valor, will never be enough of a market—by itself—for the kind of journalism you talked about in the *CJR* piece (see attached). The point I set out to make was that while we all see the desperate need for that kind of journalism, the market realities are shrinking drastically. Realistically, the overall trend is *away* from the kind of journalism you argue for.

My reason for enclosing this lengthy clip of mine from *Rolling Stone* is somewhat hazy to me now—except that it seems to illustrate, for good or ill, the kind of article that there is virtually no market for today. It doesn't even fit comfortably in *RS.* Which is all the more reason for saluting whatever misguided, bad-budget instinct caused me to publish the thing.

Which changes nothing. The problem of a shrinking market for good journalism is still with us, and it appears to be getting worse. (If you know something that would lead you to argue with this idea, for christ's sake let me know at once. Not that I'm looking for work, myself; I have plenty for now—but if I'm wrong about what strikes me as an almost terminally critical trend I'd like to know about it.)

OK for now. This thing got out of hand. It began as a letter—not to argue with you, but to agree and then point out that all your speeches on the need for Better Journalism are useless gibberish in the face of a diminishing demand for Better Journalism. This was my point & my question.

Ciao . . .
Hunter S. Thompson

TO SIDNEY ZION:

Sometimes Raoul Duke had to step in where Hunter S. Thompson knew better than to tread.

June 18, 1971
Woody Creek, CO

Sidney Zion
c/o Sardi's
234 W. 44th St.
New York City 10036

Dear Sidney:

It would sure be wonderful to see you right now, Sidney. You rotten Quisling pigfucker.

But I get to New York now & then, and of course we'll run into each other one of these days . . . we'll have a real scumbag of fun when that happens, eh?

Keep me in mind, Sid. I wouldn't want to go so far as to say "The Arabs were right." But I was. You cheap pig bastard.

In closing, I remain: Yours for ole times' sake . . .

. . . your buddy,
Raoul Duke

TO JANN WENNER, *ROLLING STONE:*

Thompson offered Wenner some etiquette tips in anticipation of his upcoming visit to Woody Creek.

June 19, 1971
Woody Creek, CO

Jann . . .

Inre: Housing & our talk this afternoon:

First, my guestroom has been a standing offer for quite a while; no question about that. If I seem at all hesitant or vaguely reluctant about it, the reason is that other good friend visitors in the past—mainly left-radical types—have reacted unnaturally to its "cell-like" nature. And I've become a bit sensitive about this. I don't like having to *defend* my hospitality after the first night.

I *like* that room, myself—but maybe that's because it's a bit like the War Room. The trouble, I think, is that I failed to seal off the 18″ × 10″ window near the ceiling—leaving this one ray of morning light to remind occupants that something is drastically wrong with their quarters. But the place is fine at night, which is the only time I tend to use it, myself.

In the meantime, however, I'll take care of that window. No point ruining an otherwise comfortable tomb.

And for that matter, I have plenty of room on the porch or in the yard for anybody who's heavy into midnight winds and harsh sunlight. And porch beds, too. . . .

***

I just wanted to get that one thing straight. It's a fine room, with the best bed in the house, but it lacks one thing . . . and I'd rather not hear any more about it. I've taken a lot of demented bullshit about my guest room, so I thought I'd warn you. . . .

***

As for Bill Noonan, he plans to leave for Alberta on July 5 or so—for 2 weeks. His house will be open—kitchen, bedroom, living room, etc.—and when I asked him about you staying there today he said, "fine," but in the interest of generally human reasons I think it would be better if you sent him a note, yourself, and asked him about it personally. He would feel a lot better about it, that way. This would only be a formality; he's already said Okay to you staying there . . . he's such an exceptionally decent fucker that if you showed up & needed a place to stay he'd insist on giving you his bedroom while he slept in the car . . . and it's exactly for this reason that I think it would be better if you sent him a note and just asked if you could use his place while he was away. This would also spare me the onus of seeming to use his place as a guest-house—which I do, now and then, but only with mutual friends—and he'd appreciate a note or a phone call to accent that mutuality. The point, of course, is that *he'd* rather offer you his house than have *me* offer it.

I know it's a simple thing, but us folks out here in Vortex are simple people—and we don't like to step on each other until it's necessary. Selah.

***

So on the general front, you should just plan on coming anytime it feels right. Aim here & plan on socking in for as long as it feels comfortable. The cell is yours as long as you want it. And if you want to move across the yard to Billy's place, that's fine too. Whatever's right. I know that when I get out on the road with Sandy I like to get weird and fuck a lot, which occasionally causes problems in close quarters.

But that's up to you. For all I care you can fuck all night on the living room couch. Rafelson will be here the whole month with his videotape, which he claims to use only for unspeakable sex scenes. He's rented a house in town; that was mandatory—I can't have a lunatic hanging around, waiting for me to act lewd. The fucker is seriously crazy; he may be a problem.

Anyway, the housing thing is fixed. You'll have the run of the Owl Farm—both the Owl House & the Iguana House. And who could ask for more? (Rafelson, for instance, couldn't get Iguana House for less than $1000 a week.)

***

Another thing: Yes, I want those two AR 3x speakers (or if they have a newer, improved model of the 3a, get that). And the way to pay for it, I think, is to take like one speaker ($167) out of the next retainer, then the second speaker out of the retainer after that. I'd also like to get two *Bose* speakers, in addition to the ARs. They should cost about the same.

And of course I'll need a first-class amplifier to drive these fuckers. The Dyna is probably adequate, but since we're dealing on this level I think I'd prefer the Heathkit ARW-15. This is the factory-wired top-of-the-line Heathkit—including both the Amp & the FM Tuner: Why not? After I talked to you today I played *Sticky Fingers*[31] a few times, and there were instants when both the high & low ends blew out on me. I think the combination of two AR-3s, two Bose and a Heathkit ARW-15 would just about clear the decks of any technical problems on the listening end. My Dual 1019 remains adequate for a turntable, so if you can handle this other stuff—and take it out of my retainer at something like or less than $175 a month—I think that's exactly the way to go.

What makes this arrangement feasible is that Random House will owe me $5000 when I give them "the first third" of the AD book—that third, at least, is inevitable. In terms of sheer volume, it will have to be there with the submission of either Vegas II or the Aspen/Sheriff gig. Either way . . . I foresee a $5000 windfall in the next month or so.

On other fronts, I recall some suggestion that I "didn't like" the past few issues. We got side-tracked on this, and I never got back around to saying that it wasn't that I "didn't like" them. (I chalk that off to Felton's penchant for inflammatory, Hearst-style journalism. . . .) No . . . what I said to David was that the past few issues seemed to be singularly lacking in anything savage (i.e. Heavy, Weird, Mean, etc.). But then I recalled that guy Esterhaus (?) [Joe Eszterhas's] thing on Kent State, which was absolutely first-rate. That final thing about the phone call (anonymous) saying his daughter was a whore & got what she deserved was so foul & insane that it could only be understood by somebody who has dealt personally with the kind of people you have to deal with in order to run for Sheriff of Aspen on the Mescaline ticket & still get 1000 votes. This is what I told Max [Palevsky] & he refused to believe—that you have to personally confront these rotten bastards, on their own turf, before you can understand how genuinely & terminally sick this country is.

We are fucked—or Doomed, as it were—and when I asked you about that financial-analysis thing today, it was only a natural adjunct to all the other evidence. And this is all the more reason, I think, to seriously consider this Vortex thing—as a hedge against total disaster, if nothing else.

What may be coming is the worst 5 (or 10) years since the Reconstruction—a National Nervous Breakdown, with nothing sacred, no holds barred & god's mercy on all those left out in the open.

There's no particular reason why I should lay this on you—and certainly no reason why you should take it seriously—but these are the basic vibes & in-

31. The Rolling Stones' album *Sticky Fingers* came out in March 1971.

formation I'm getting, and despite your wretched performance on my Carte Blanche crisis I feel obliged to pass them on. It probably gets back to that old thing about hanging Together or Separately . . . or maybe, in some looser & less articulate context, a word like "karma" will do. . . .

What the fuck? We'll have plenty of time to talk about this. You should blow off for Aspen with total confidence that your reservations are the best that any *human* in the Western World could hope for. You have the whole Owl Farm & all its weird facets at your disposal . . . and this is a very rare thing (ask Lucian Truscott—he just spent 3 nights sleeping in his VW with his girlfriend because he failed to make reservations).

OK for now. Keep that Vortex gig in mind—any precedents, ideas, prior-type experiments, etc.—like *Canyon.* I suspect this thing might be a bit more important, in the long run, than seems to be at the moment.

Ciao . . .
Hunter

TO JIM SILBERMAN, RANDOM HOUSE:

Thompson proposed a solution to the impasse he felt he had reached on his American Dream book.

June 27, 1971
Woody Creek, CO

Dear Jim . . .

Here's a notion that's occurred to me off & on for a while, inre: the AD book. But under the current time/circumstances, I think we should get these ideas out front & *deal* with them, to wit:

After several hours of shuffling (and/or "organizing") two years of AD material, it occurs to me that the shit is so hopelessly inconsistent—in the context of time, tone & focus—that perhaps our only serious hope of getting it all together in book form by Sept 1, '71, might be the (Mailer) *Advertisements for Myself* format, i.e. lacing all this bullshit together chronologically, as best we can, then having me write transition intro(s) to each section. This would get around the grim possibility of having to rewrite the whole trip . . . but it also raises the notion of trying to lump a bunch of articles together & turning the lump into "a book" by means of some fast/heavy update transitions. Under the circumstances, I suspect I could live with this idea. How about you?

The alternative is a brutally-serious, time-sucking re-write of *all* these articles—which might or might not turn out to be worth the time and effort. My personal analysis, for now, is that the further opportunities of the moment (the Saigon book, the definite possibility of a film based on *The Rum Diary,* and also the Vegas "book") make me wonder how long it's going to make sense—financially or any other way, for *either one of us*—to keep me tied up with this goddamn American Dream bullshit. We might consider the massive possibilities of getting it out of the way and moving on to better things. It *is* a millstone; it prevents me from focusing seriously on anything else—while at the same time tying me to a project that I've never understood or had any real faith in.

So why not just lash this fucker together—using Aspen as a focal point & proper climax—and set me free to deal with the world of the 1970s? The '60s are over; and I think I can lay that era to rest with a long, rambling (final third of the book) article on the Aspen/Sheriff gig. With this format, we could *begin,* more or less, with the "Battle of Aspen" piece that I did for *Rolling Stone* last October, then flash back to things like New Hampshire '68, Chicago, Election Day in Hollywood & the Nixon Inaugural . . . and use all these as a sort of kaleidoscope background for the Aspen/Sheriff finale.

That would leave me with only one-third of the book to write (in first draft)—and not even that much, really, because I have about 15,000 words on the Aspen/Sheriff thing already done.

This would also leave us free to do Vegas One & Two as a book, instead of forcing it into the AD book.

So ponder this & let me know what you think at once. Our time is running out. Thanx . . .

Hunter

* St. Arrow *bought* Oscar's memoirs.

TO MARK PENZER, *TRUE:*

Gonzo journalism was a hard sell at first.

June 30, 1971
Woody Creek, CO

Dear Mr. Penzer:

Lucian Truscott suggested I send you a note inre: writing something for *True,* but at the time—a few weeks ago—I had nothing even halfway for sale. Then I suddenly got a piece back from *Sports Illustrated* (a freakish thing of about 3500 words), with a note saying that since they'd only asked for a 250 word caption, they felt no obligation to pay me that same dollar-a-word rate for an article that might make 99% of their readership stupid with rage and sick social feelings.

The piece has to do with the 3 or 4 days I spent "covering" the "Fabulous Mint 400" (bike & buggy) desert races in Las Vegas. A friend of mine at *SI* sent me out there as a sort of lark, with no real assignment except to come back with a caption to justify expenses . . . but for reasons of my own I wrote a much longer & dirtier thing than they wanted. (I write excellent captions, but it struck me that a scene like that deserved a bit more. . . .)

SI disagreed. Maybe because they didn't like references to people being "beaten stupid" and "sucking ether to get twisted." They stuck by their original concept, insisting that what I'd sent them was an over-written caption instead of an article . . . and now they want to buy the whole piece & chop it up for captions.

Which is okay, I guess, but after talking with Lucian when he was out here doing his trout-fishing gig, I thought I might send the thing along to you—on the off/odd chance that the piece, as written, might fit more in the *True* format than into *SI*'s caption-mold. Beyond that, and beyond the simple money factor, I hate to give those doomed corporate castratos a good, first-place piece & watch them cut it up for captions. I understand perfectly why they can't use it as an article: It's too rude & weird—but I hate to just shrug it off like a pound of used meat-writing that didn't fit *SI*'s bridge-club format & so had to be butchered down like offal.

Anyway, my agent—Lynn Nesbit—has a copy of the thing at IFA in the Time-Life bldg. Or I can send you one from here. Except that would take longer, and you'd wind up having to deal with Lynn anyway, if the thing interests you . . . and if it does, we should keep in mind that I'd just as soon add a few heavier & nastier grafs (to the version Lynn has), in order to burn off the smog that came down on me when I tried to write something "suitable" for *SI*.

The only real problem, right now, is that I have to know something *quick*. *SI* just sent me a bunch of forms to fill out, in order to satisfy the Taxman before they can send me any money—and unless I have something better to do with the piece, I might as well just let them have it for captions.

I would, however, prefer to sell it as an *article*. And at this stage of the hassle, I don't really give a fuck what kind of money I get for it—within reason, of course, and Lynn would have to be the final judge of that. If you want to take a look at the thing, however, you should call her & say you got a note from me that said money was/is secondary to getting the thing published as an article.

Under different circumstances I might have been able to send you something better, but this thing just boiled up by accident & I figured Why Not? As a total literary entity, "the incredible Mint 400" could use a few stiff shots of something or other before I'd want it to go into the archives—but in retrospect I guess I've felt that way about everything I've ever sent off.

What we need to do now is first find out quick if the piece interests you at all—either Lynn's version, or mine, which would take a bit longer. After that, we can figure out how to deal with the fucker.

All I need at the moment is an immediate reply of some kind. Probably the phone would be best—late afternoon, your time. Or call anytime at all & leave a message with whoever might happen to answer the phone here during morning hours. I never know who might answer when I'm asleep, but the rule is that they have to take all messages word for word . . . and it tends to work out, for good or ill.

Unless I hear something from you ASAP, as it were, I'll assume that I might as well go ahead and let *SI* chop the thing up for captions. Let's say I won't do anything with the bugger until July 9. That gives you a week to brood on the idea, get the piece from Lynn, and call if it interests you.

OK for now, and thanx . . .

Hunter S. Thompson

TO JIM SILBERMAN, RANDOM HOUSE:

Silberman had asked Thompson whether Fear and Loathing in Las Vegas *was journalism or fiction.*

June, 1971
Woody Creek, CO

Dear Jim . . .

Under normal circumstances it should never be necessary for a writer to explain *how* his work should be read. In theory, all literature & even journalism should be taken on its own intrinsic merits—above & beyond (or even *below*) the confusing contexts of whatever reality surrounded the act of writing. This was the keystone of the New Criticism, a now-discredited "school" of elitist/academic criticism that flourished in the 1950s and largely accounted for the massive loss of interest in all forms of "fiction" writing by the end of the 1960s—or at least all forms of "fiction" except what some managed to peddle as "new journalism."

This is a term that Tom Wolfe has been trying to explain, on the lecture-stump, for more than five years . . . and the reason he's never been able to properly define "the new journalism" is that it never actually existed, except maybe in the minds of people with a vested personal interest in the "old journalism"—editors, professors and book reviewers who refused to understand that some of the best of the country's young writers no longer recognized "the line" between fiction and journalism.

Where the senile strictures of the New Criticism made traditional "fiction" irrelevant, the hopeless stagnancy of traditional journalism—the Hearst/Hecht mentality—made it impossible for anybody who took himself seriously as a Writer to work for a newspaper or even a magazine. In 1960 the pinnacle of journalism was an editor's slot at Time Inc., and the pinnacle of fiction was selling tone poems about the bird-baths of your doomed youth to *The New Yorker.*

The choice was pretty grim. You could either "get involved in reality" and be a rewrite hack for *Time,* or you could hunker down with your intensely private memories and be a star on the cocktail/fiction circuit. But, either way, you were fucked—particularly if you were 20 years old and inclined to take the real world seriously. There was simply no room, no way to make a living, in that twilight of the Eisenhower Era, for anybody who might want to bring a writer's fine eye & perspective to the mundane "realities" of journalism.

Probably the first big breakthrough on this front was Jack Kerouac's *On the Road*—a long rambling piece of personal journalism that the publisher (Viking) called "fiction" because if they'd said it was "journalism" no Literary Critic would touch it. Not even the book editors for *Time* and *The New York Times*. And if *they* ignored it, the book would die on the vine.

As it was, *On the Road* had sold less than 20,000 copies in hardcover at the peak of its infamy . . . and it was only after Allen Ginsberg's *Howl* got busted for Obscenity and the trial was covered by *Life* that Kerouac became notorious as "the spokesman for the Beat Generation." And, with that, the mass media had a profitable excuse to recognize what they called "a whole new style of writing."

But the only thing new about it was the sudden official sanction for novelists and poets to focus on the world we were all living in. Lawrence Ferlinghetti's savage description of a testimonial dinner for "good ole Ike" was written in the form of a poem,[32] but it was really not a hell of a lot different from Harrison Salisbury's articles, on the front page of *The New York Times,* about Eisenhower's aborted "good will trip" to Japan in 1960. It was clear that both Ferlinghetti and Salisbury were calling the President of the United States a jibbering, ignorant old fool, surrounded at all times by thieves and flunkies and self-serving advisors who were either hit-men for the Captains of Commerce or in some cases the Captains, themselves—like Defense Secretary Charles Wilson, president of General Motors, or Treasury Secretary Robert B. Anderson, one of America's most powerful oil barons.

The "Beat" writers were a main force in the national uprising of 1960 that resulted in the shocking defeat of Richard Nixon, the incumbent vice president, by a relatively unknown senator named John F. Kennedy. The same people who instinctively identified with the mad angst of *Howl* and the high speed underground rebellion of *On the Road* also understood—personally, if not politically—the importance of beating Nixon. Because it was clear, even then, that he represented what Robert Kennedy, in early 1968, called "the dark side of the American character." Both Kennedys understood this—which was easier for them than for most of the rest of us, because in the protracted combat of a political campaign you are forced to *know* your opponent—because every move you make, every word you say (even privately, because any sign of weakness or pessimism in a candidate might demoralize everybody around him) . . . your whole lifestyle is geared, hyper-critically, to *dealing* with the enemy, which means you get to know him pretty well. Perhaps not personally, because even in scenes like Debates and Personal Confrontations the campaign machinery intrudes and overwhelms . . . in the same sense that the frenzied

32. Beat poet Lawrence Ferlinghetti, founder of San Francisco's renowned City Lights bookstore, published "Tentative Description of a Dinner Given To Promote the Impeachment of President Eisenhower" in 1958.

public machinery surrounding a Heavyweight Championship Bout makes it just about impossible for anybody involved in it to act human. At least not on a public level. The roles are not created for the actors, no more. And mystery is always in vogue.

TO JIM SILBERMAN, RANDOM HOUSE:

In one day, Thompson sent Silberman three detailed missives—on "The Battle of Aspen," "Fear and Loathing in Las Vegas," and "The Death of the American Dream"—as he struggled to combine the themes into a worthwhile book.

July 12, 1971
Woody Creek, CO

Dear Jim . . .

I see two very distinct & different ways to go with the AD book:

1) To do it as a series of chronological scenes, using *Advertisements for Myself* type bridges to jump from "Nixon in New Hampshire" to "Chicago" to "Gun Control" & then "The Battles of Aspen."

This would pretty obviously amount to a line-up of old articles, laced together by freshly-written bridges. This notion worked pretty well for [Norman] Mailer; at least in retrospect—I don't know how it sold. But under the circumstances I think we might be better off going with . . .

2) Which would start with the Battle of Aspen piece (almost verbatim out of *Rolling Stone*), then flash back to New Hampshire, etc. . . . and then finish with my still unfinished Aspen/Sheriff piece that's titled "The Politics of Armageddon."

In other words, to use the two Aspen pieces as the framework, with the other stuff as background. That way, we could call it "The Battle of Aspen" & give the structure a unity that I think it would lack if we did it as a chronological series, with bridges.

The problem with #2 is mainly *time*. It would take a lot of rewriting to work New Hampshire, for instance, into "The Battle of Aspen."

Unless maybe we *completely reversed* the *Advertisements for Myself* idea and *used the dated articles as bridges*. In other words, the nut of the book would be two separate accounts of Aspen elections with things like the Nixon Inaugural laced into the narrative in italics. This would require some skillful editing, but if we could do it right I think it would make a better book.

The narrative would begin & end in Aspen—structured around the '69 and '70 elections (two separate stories), but the real story, on a different level, would be in the scenes (like New Hampshire & Chicago, etc.) that drove me so far into activist politics that I found myself actually running for sheriff.

Chronologically, this would make for numerous digressions & a fairly scrambled time sequence, but I think we could keep this under control by editing the thing so that it moved, overall, from the first stirrings of political rebellion here in Sept '69 . . . to the terrible doomed frenzy of our Freak Power campaign here in Sept/Oct/Nov of '70. And then, as a sort of epitaph, The Aftermath . . . when they mopped us up in the Spring of '71.

In this way, it would be the story of a genuinely indigenous political rebellion—so starkly contemporary that I could run for sheriff on the Mescaline Ticket & still get 45% of the vote—with the moral of the story being that if you challenge the bastards on that level you had damn well better win; because if you lose, you're fucked.

What this would amount to is "The Political Education of Hunter S. Thompson (or Raoul Duke)"—how a classic example of the late-'60s dropout culture (one of the original, 1964–65, settlers of the Haight-Ashbury, SF, Acid-Rock world) finally drifted so far into activist politics that he finally found himself riding the crest of an energy wave that he never knew existed.

The nut of the story, I think, is the weird truth that I began that Aspen/Sheriff campaign as a joke & a smokescreen . . . only to find, once it got rolling, that I had accidentally touched one of those long-lost nerve-ends in the American Dream, a concept that appealed very intensely to a hell of a lot of people. Far more than I ever thought possible.

The "Battle of Aspen" piece in *Rolling Stone* drew a fantastic amount of mail from all over the country & indeed all over the world. I still have a huge pile of letters on the floor behind me, that I've never answered . . . none of them are especially profound, but the thread that ties them all together is a sense of excitement at the idea that "freaks" are finally beginning to take political power into their own hands.

This is something we demonstrated pretty heavily in that last election, even though we lost—and it's also a thing that could have a heavy bearing on the '72 and even '76 elections. I keep pounding on this theme with everybody I talk to.

Mike Murphy, the president of Esalen Institute, was just out here for a week & I've finally convinced him—after ten years of mean argument—that even Esalen *must* get into politics. Jann Wenner, *RStone,* is here now for a week, and he's agreed to work with Murphy to set up a Politics of Armageddon conference at Esalen in September—with the ultimate idea being to mobilize the new 18–21 vote, along with millions of now-stagnant votes of the 1960s' Dropout Culture . . . in order to drastically change the whole power-balance of electoral politics in 1972. Ideally, the Esalen conference would result in a radically different (but not necessarily "radical" in the old political sense) platform—a document that would represent the interests of the 40 or 50 million potential voters who won't go to the polls at all, unless we can jerk them out of the mire with some kind of heavy/wild trip like the Freak Power campaign in Aspen.

I think '76 might be too late for this kind of uprising. Four more years of Nixon's mob will make the Presidency not worth winning. It will be like winning a civil damages lawsuit against a man who long since went bankrupt.

In any case, it will be imperative to make a strong run at the bastards in '72, in order to muster the energy/action for '76. We learned that in Aspen. You have to convince the long-term drop-outs that their votes are critical. We did that in '69—which accounted for our incredible 45% showing in '70.

***

Anyway, I trust you see the drift of my thinking—which is also why I prefer AD/book option #2. I suspect the Battle of Aspen might blossom into a savagely *relevant* book, while a collection of old HST articles—even with beautifully written bridges—would probably get lost in the shuffle.

I *know* I'm right on this score. There *are* more of us than there are of them. We can *beat* the bastards, but only if we can shake off the old-liberal death-wish that has haunted every liberal-type "loyal opposition" candidate since Adlai Stevenson. Except the Kennedys, and of course they were killed.

They threatened that in Aspen, too—death & dynamite if I won, & even if I refused to drop out of the race—but we ran it straight back at them: We brought in vicious political bikers from Madison, black belt karate politicos from Denver, a pro-football drop-out like Dave Meggyesy from SF . . . along with a mind-boggling media presence from almost everywhere.

And all this worked. We (almost) beat the bastards at their own rotten, mafia-style game, in addition to stomping them totally on the ideological level. We *forced* a coalition of the two political parties; we forced each party to sacrifice one of their two main candidates—and even then they could only muster a 55% nut.

***

Well, no point in this long ramble about politics. You asked for my "table of contents," and I guess the only real answer is the same question I've been hurling back at you for three years: What the fuck is this book *about?* A table of contents for *what?*

What we've done, thus far, is amass a bundle of articles that don't add up to much unless we can lash them together. We have the New Hampshire [article, "Presenting: The Richard Nixon Doll," July 1968] (about half of which appeared in *Pageant*); we have the Nixon Inaugural piece from *The Boston Globe;* we have that 150 page odyssey on the Gun Control question that was done for *Esquire;* we have the Killy/Chicago piece that appeared, minus most of the Chicago section, in *Scanlan's* after *Playboy* bounced it. We have that Test Pilots thing that was chopped up for *Pageant* ["Those Daring Young Men in Their Flying Machines," September 1969], and also "Election Day in LA" that was done at the same time & never published anywhere.

There is also the "Murder of Ruben Salazar" and a first-draft of that "America's Cup" piece that I was doing for *Scanlan's* when the crash came . . . along with the American Legion Convention in Portland, which mixed with the Sky River Rock Festival. . . .

And also the Kentucky Derby piece.

But the main one, I think, is the Battle of Aspen, in conjunction with the followup piece that is still not finished. That strikes me as the only one of the lot that will be just as ripe in the spring of '72 as it was in the fall of '70. The other stuff is important, I think, but I suspect it was more important to me, personally, than it will be to the book. If I hadn't gone to Chicago, for instance, I would never have launched the "Joe Edwards for Mayor" campaign that led me to run for sheriff.

What we lack, at this point, is the saga of the Aspen/Sheriff campaign . . . but most of this is written; not entirely put together, but virtually all of it done in first draft. About 20,000 words already done, in addition to the 10 or 15 thousand in the *Rolling Stone* piece.

That gives us a working nut of about 40,000 words—even before we start thinking about which sections to use out of the collected articles. The Nixon Inaugural piece, for instance, is short enough to run verbatim as a kind of section-breaker—while the Gun Control thing and even the Killy/Chicago piece are both too long to run except if we chop out the pertinent excerpts.

The overall idea, then, is to frame the book as the story of two political campaigns in Aspen . . . and then somehow fit in all the stories that led (me) up and into these campaigns . . . with the lesson being that the Two-Party system is the lie that is choking America . . . and the articles you have, in carbon & clips, are the story of those scenes & events that created the two-part, Aspen Elections narrative.

I hope this is clear. The trick will be in devising a format to fit the articles & old carbons into the 2-section Aspen-based narrative.

I see no real problem in this, except time. The real problem, as always, is getting you to tell me something except what a wonderful goddamn amusing writer I am. This shit about the American Dream has gone on long enough. Since we signed that original contract I have *lived* the fucking thing more intensely than anybody I can think of. I have gone to the mat with the bastards for two years in a row. And I think we learned (even proved) enough here to begin exporting it. This is what I'm working on now with the Esalen conference—and it's also what I'd like to write a book about while I'm still wired.

So for fuck's sake let's *do it*. If you don't like this notion, let's *argue* about it. My research is *finished*. What I want to do now is write a *book*.

I'm enclosing a very loose & tentative outline, based on the idea described above: Two main sections, two Aspen elections—interspersed with background chunks from '68 thru '70. In other words—reversing the Mailer *Ad/Myself* structure—the main narrative will be in the first person, cut here & there by third-person or maybe even retrospective first-person accounts of scenes that explain why, and how, I came to do the foul things I did.

By this formula, I might run about 41 pages of straight chronological narrative about the "Edwards for Mayor" campaign in '69, then flash back to 5 or 10 italicized pages on New Hampshire in '68 . . . then 33 more pages of the

Aspen '69 narrative . . . then cut to 13 pages on the Chicago convention . . . then more on Aspen, slashed to the Nixon inaugural . . . then back to the climax & finish of the Edwards for Mayor campaign. A six-vote loss.

End Section One.

Section Two, in the same format, would be framed by the Aspen/Sheriff campaign—incorporating flashbacks to things like the Kentucky Derby, Election Day in LA, Gun Control & America's Cup—along with a sense of epitaph (with details) for rock festivals and Haight Street.

A quick outline for this format is attached, but it won't make much sense to anybody who hasn't read this letter. What *you* should probably do is read "The Battle of Aspen" again and see if you can understand the politics frenzy I got into—beginning with New Hampshire & Chicago, then snowballing crazily after the '69 Aspen campaign.

***

If you can understand this, you owe me $5000 *at once*—because at least one third of the book is already written and sitting there in your hands (see enc. Outline). As a matter of fact I suspect that delivery of that $5000 (for the first third) might be exactly what we both need to force this monster thru to the finish. It would certainly give *you* more incentive to focus on the fucker—and the proven assurance that the final two-thirds would net me another $10K would cause *me* to clear the decks & gear down even to the extent of moving out to a motel to get the bastard finished.

Right now, for instance, I have Wenner & his wife staying next door—ostensibly on vacation, but at noon tomorrow (4 hrs from now) Jann is going to be over here demanding to see the climax scene from Part Two of "Fear & Loathing in Vegas." (It won't exist, of course, because I've spent the past 4 hours on this letter.) But I think I've finally crystallized my own vision of the AD book. I think we should title it "The Battle of Aspen" & move, full-bore, from there. I'll send my vitally important comments on the Las Vegas book in a separate envelope, which I'll write immediately & mail along with this one.

Meanwhile, I'm spending my off-hours playing volleyball and snorting cocaine with Bob Rafelson. His initial reaction to the *Rum Diary* film project was, "Yes, let's do it right *now.*" But of course that's impossible, and he's starting a film of his own in September. So I think the thing to do is get off to Saigon, then come back for the '72 campaign and *then* do *The Rum Diary.* That will give me the time & incentive to rewrite the novel in tight visual/narrative form.

And also by then I should have:

1) The AD/Battle of Aspen book in print

2) hopefully, the short Vegas book in print

3) and also a Vietnam book going to press

I'm also on the verge of settling this land-purchase project—with no money down: an accomplishment that will cause me to rank, sooner or later, with the handful of Great Financial Wizards.

Anyway, that's how things stand at the moment. By my lights, I've given you enough, with this bundle, to begin talking seriously about sending me that $5000 check for the First Third. If not, I think you owe me a serious, working alternative . . . because in terms of the book as I see it now, you have the first third.

The Vegas book is a separate thing, as I see it (see tandem letter).

So ponder all this and let me know at once. I am ready to wrap the fucker up ASAP, but I'll need something more than mere fuzzy encouragement from you before I can tighten down the screws and blitz everything else to get this thing finished.

OK for now,
Hunter

TO JIM SILBERMAN, RANDOM HOUSE:

Thompson included a separate letter on the Vegas project.

July 12, 1971
Woody Creek, CO

Jim . . .

I'm not sure which of these envelopes you'll open first, but I thought I should separate this memo on the Vegas project from the long letter and AD/Battle of Aspen outline.

It seems absolutely clear to me that I'm writing *two different* books—particularly if you can agree with me that the AD book should go as The Battle of Aspen. I can't see any way to mix a 40,000 word Vegas/drug-nightmare into that, without destroying the AD book & my reputation along with it.

Wenner will be over (he's sleeping not about 100 yards away) in four hours to do the final editing on Vegas One. That's 20,000 words, completely finished & ready to send to the printer as of tonight. I think I've persuaded Jann to get Ralph Steadman (the British artist who worked with me on the KyDerby piece) to do the art for Vegas. I don't know how you could work this out in terms of money with *RS*/Straight Arrow, but it seems to me that—having paid the bulk of my expenses on both Vegas pieces—you have at least a first option on what now looks, irrevocably, to me, like a 40,000 to 50,000 word book called either "Fear & Loathing in Vegas," by H . . S . . T . . or "The Vegas Diaries of Raoul Duke" by Hunter S. Thompson.

Vegas Two is already 10,000 finished words, and it looks like an easy 30,000 before I can wind the bugger up. Jann has already decided to run it in two consecutive parts—presumably with Steadman's art, and I see no point or hope in trying to fit the Vegas thing into AD/Aspen.

Beyond that, since you already have 20,000 finished words of a 50,000 word book, I don't see any real problem with *Rolling Stone;* as I see it, they blew any control they might have had over the book rights by refusing to pay my expenses. I can still *sell* it to them, of course, but only if you reject it for RH.

I think you'd be crazy to do that. Line for line, the writing in Vegas is a high-speed minor classic—and beyond that, it's the definitive epitaph statement for the Benevolent Drug Era of the '60s. We are heading for a far more vicious time. We are already there, in fact, but it won't become generally obvious for a year or so. Wenner & I have spent the past two nights, all night, hashing out meanings and trends and directions—and for the immediate future it's all crazy/*down,* no matter how you look at it.

The only hope is a drastic political uprising—the kind of thing that would shock Birch Bayh & McGovern,[33] and curdle whatever blood Teddy Kennedy has left.

Meanwhile, I am running full speed to finish Vegas Two. I assume you have *all* of Vegas One . . . and I hope you won't push whatever prerogative you might have to include Vegas in the AD/Aspen book. . . .

Unless you can convince me that I'm absolutely and finally wrong in the way I see the two books now . . . which is that Vegas and Aspen are two different stories. By putting them together, I think the style & tone of Vegas would fatally cripple any impact that the AD/Aspen book might have—and I think it *might* have quite a bit.

But not if the author is apparently whacked on ether & acid 25 hours a day.

On the other hand, I would kill the whole mad style of Vegas by trying to make it fit the AD/Aspen format.

Which leaves me in the position of having submitted a book to you—and expecting a reply in that context. If you're worried about contractual hassles with *Rolling Stone,* forget it. Jann's not going to hang me up on a book-contract, and neither will Alan [Rinzler]. They *like* you . . . which is weird, or maybe that's just what they tell me.

Anyway, I'm willing to admit a touch of pushiness here, but even so, I'm sure you'll take it in stride and give me a quick definitive word on two things:

1) I figure you have "the first third" of the AD/Aspen book in hand, which means you owe me $5000 or at least a detailed explanation of why you don't . . . and;

2) I figure a submission of 20,000 finished words entitles me to some kind of tangible reaction from you inre: The Vegas book.

When you deal with both of these items I figure we'll be well on the road to fame & fortune—and I intend to become increasingly savage on both fronts,

33. Birch Bayh was a Democratic senator from Indiana; George McGovern was the Democratic senator from South Dakota who would be the party's 1972 presidential nominee.

if only for the sake of creating the kind of tension that will force me to get something finished and published. I have the first halves of two books sitting here on my desk, and it's driving me crazy to sit here and stare at the fuckers.

Send word at once. Call. Come out for a visit. Do something. Anything. Help!

Sincerely,
Hunter

TO EUGENE W. McGARR:

Thompson belatedly updated his old friend.

July 28, 1971
Woody Creek, CO

McGarr . . .

Inexcusable failure on my part. Totally inexcusable. Except in your case. You seem to have all the time in the world.

Anyway, I called you almost instantly after I got the phone message, but the phone rang dead. Maybe that was during your trip to SF . . . and then I began failing; not only with you, but with everybody.

My mother sent me a bunch of postage stamps for my birthday, with a properly hurt & neglected message.

But I don't know what to tell her. What can I say? About my act? My life? My world & wherever it's going? Who knows? About nine-tenths of the time I feel like an obvious fool—but the rest of the time I *know* I'm a saint & a hero. I seem to be in a state of conflict at all times—most of it wasted energy.

Fucking [Paul] *Semonin* came to town last night. Staying at a house down the road. I haven't seen the bastard in three years—haven't even heard from him, or even *about* him. But I know he's down there . . . & it's 9 a.m. now, which means I probably won't sleep, so I guess I'll see him soon.

Just stare at the fucker. What else? I have no idea what to say. And I'm not sure it matters. Horrible to think that the arrival of Semonin should boil down to just another hassle—just something else to cope with.

But it's true. For a while I thought I was drifting off & turning weird . . . then I read over some of the stuff I wrote (even 10 years ago, like *The Rum Diary*) and I see that I'm still on dead center, for good or ill. I don't seem to have learned much.

Clancy continues to plague me—but now that he's legitimized his madness, it no longer seems quite as interesting. Maybe it's the Belli[34] syndrome. For a

34. Prominent California attorney Melvin Belli represented numerous celebrity clients and appeared as an evil alien on an episode of NBC's *Star Trek* in 1968.

while I thought he was focused on a serious political freakout for '72—a concept which occupies more & more of my time these days—but it turned out that he was looking for shuck/profits & another Pat Paulsen.[35]

[Tim] Thibeau was just here & told me about some heinous scene where the two of you went up to his airee (sp?) [aerie] and got the word about going out in the rowboat . . . which pretty well explains the kind of cheap gibberish he seems to be into now. Nine out of every ten sentences that pass his lips contain the phrase: "ripoff." Tonight he is in Chicago, attending an organizing meeting for the "Fred Harris for President" campaign. All the Radicals are there. Clancy went with Warren Hinckle. The radical delegation from SF.

As for me . . . well, I'm the Sports Editor of *Rolling Stone*. How's that for progress?

Around Oct 1, the plan is that I'll move to Washington DC and write a political column for *RS*—until Nov '72, at which time I'll do something very active & definitive.

Meanwhile, I'm trying to finish two books at once. Oscar can tell you as much about them as I can. He's crazy as a fucking loon, but for some reason I can handle Oscar's kind of craziness—as opposed to Clancy's. Oscar just sold his memoirs to the book division of *Rolling Stone*. The bastard had better deliver.

Which reminds me that I owe *RS* 20,000 words a/o yesterday. The second half of "Fear & Loathing in Vegas," by Raoul Duke. Watch for it around October—first in the magazine & then in book form.

The other book is the political monster that I've owed Random House for 3 years . . . and for now it looks like the title will be "The Battle of Aspen" . . . using the framework of the two elections here to reflect on the past four years of national politics and other action.

Shit . . . I see that I'm writing a very *informative* letter. A far cry from yours of 6/24, which I found tonight in my "Deal With Immediately" pile. I find that if I don't do something immediately, it never gets done.

Hopefully, I'll get over to SF around the end of Sept, before moving out to Washington . . . and maybe you can get up there for a calm beer or two at that time. It occurs to me that the past few times I've seen you, I was essentially a spectator for your sex problems . . . or frenzies, as it were.

I think I mentioned this to you once or twice before—just about the time I got terminally tired of it. Oscar reports, however, that you still have a touch of Dork Fever—inre: that recent trip to SF. Maybe you didn't spend enough time in locker rooms as a child; almost everybody has genitals, Gene. The coach wasn't lying. We *all* fuck; we're *all* beasts . . . and I'm honestly not try-

35. Comedian Pat Paulsen mounted a mock campaign for president in 1968.

ing to be nasty, here, but it's puzzled me for quite a few years now that you seem to have felt that fucking was the highest & only worthwhile thing a man could get into.

Shit . . . that's a cheap shot & I'm sorry for it. I *know* better, but it *is* a valid impression. Maybe if I can lash together the kind of stone-mad political uprising I have in mind for next year, we can put you to work on other orifices. The schedule is heavy & I'm already far behind. Too far. I'm beginning to get The Fear.

OK for now. Call or send word . . . and maybe I'll see you in SF in about 6 weeks. Meanwhile, I guess Semonin says hello. I'll find out, for sure, in about 10 minutes. Ciao . . .

H

TO LYNN NESBIT:

It was always so hard to find good help.

August 12, 1971
Woody Creek, CO

Dear Lynn . . .

You'd better watch your drinking, or whatever. Your call earlier tonight put me so off-balance that I couldn't eat breakfast when I hung up. Normally I refuse to even answer the phone at that stage of my day, because my head doesn't usually get functioning until about 3 hrs. after my body wakes up, but this time I sort of grabbed the thing automatically, thinking it was probably some kind of . . .

. . . but to hell with all that. Congratulations on your second revolutionary birth. And also to Richard [her husband]; along with a warning that I mean to stomp him into terminal poverty this autumn on the point-spreads. Tell him I'm already prepared to lay $100 at 5–1 that the 49ers will be in the Super Bowl . . . and only a lunatic would turn down a bet like that.

Indeed . . . and now to business:

I'll assume there's no doubt in anybody's mind that we're now talking about *two books:* Vegas, and the Battle of Aspen. Vegas is about two thirds finished at the moment. I'll send both you & Jim a copy of the first 50 pages of Vegas 2 that I just shipped off to *RS.* That should give Silberman about 35,000 finished words, and that's sure as hell enough for some serious contract talk . . . which is, of course, *your* gig.

The Ballantine hang-up is a definite problem. I hate to give them Vegas as a substitute for *The Rum Diary,* because—if I remember the origins of the two-book contract correctly—*The RD* was sort of thrown in for nothing. And Vegas seems like too good a thing to use for a contract breaker. I could rip off a ms. for that purpose in three days. For years I've wanted to write the Final Pornographic Novel, with an opening something like this:

"I kicked the fucking door off its hinges. The girl backed into a corner, trying to cover herself with the curtain. I could see she was going to scream, so I bashed her against the stove. She fell. I sat on her naked chest and pulled her front teeth with my Chinese bolt-cutting pliers. Then I grabbed her by the hair and forced my throbbing, uncircumcised member into her mouth . . . etc. etc."

Yeah, one of those. I figure that kind of opening would make Ian Ballantine cry[36]—and god only knows what it would do to his wife. I owe that bastard something for sending me a check for $21.20 when I pleaded for a $1000 advance to pay off the taxman. (He finally sent me the grand last week, but not until Ballantine's share was safe in the company vault.)

Anyway, if faced with the specter of having to use Vegas as a contract breaker, I'd prefer to send in a tentative draft of *The Rum Diary,* rewritten as above. I don't think I'd have to submit more than 10 pages, to get us off the hook. You could explain that my numerous experiments with LSD have changed not only my writing style but my whole personality—and that I'll never again be the same.

I figure Ballantine is worthless anyway. They blew the *Hell's Angels* pb. distribution shamefully.

I'd feel a lot happier if we could make an arrangement of some kind with Shir-Cliff at Pocket Books. I'm not sure how *good* he is, for money-making, but I like his instincts. And he's also a good person to drink with when I come to NY.

None of which matters a hell of a lot, I guess—except to emphasize that I think we can work out a cheaper way to dump that Ballantine contract than giving them Vegas.

Another angle on that, which I couldn't mention on the phone today because Bert Schneider's de facto protégé was standing in the kitchen with my wife, is that—based on idle talk during Rafelson's few coherent moments during his stay here—I got the necessarily vague impression that *Vegas* interested him more than *The Rum Diary.* I can't say anything definite on this, because the bastard has been "off his game," as it were, ever since he got here. No point trying to explain this by mail; it would only get dangerously tangled.

There are numerous other possibilities in this area, but I think I should push them a bit further before you get excited. One of the main difficulties, right now, is that I refuse to rent my guest house, for the winter, to Mike Burns (Schneider's protégé), and this has led to a scurvy hellbroth of personal recriminations, etc.

36. Ian Ballantine was publisher of Ballantine Books, now a division of Random House.

What I *may* do, however—since the Washington gig seems definite by now—is rent the guest house to Burns, provided BBS takes a 6-month lease on the main house (mine). I'll see about that tomorrow.

In any case, both Rafe & Schneider seem to be tied up for the next 6 months to a year—and so am I, for that matter: Once I get locked into the '72 presidential campaign, I don't want to have to be dealing with a film-script with my left hand on my off-hours. (Rafelson's first comment on *The Rum Diary*, about 2 months ago, was "Can we do it before September?" Obviously we couldn't . . . and his later comments led me to believe he knew that, when he said it. But when he began mumbling about Vegas. . . .)

And so much for all that, for now. I'll let you know just as soon as I smell a break . . . although the fact that I'll be tied down in Washington for the next year doesn't leave me open for seizing on anything quick. So let's leave this one hanging for the moment. . . .

Another thing to consider is that *not* going to Saigon blows that verbal contract I made with Rinzler for giving me an extra $5K for letting *RS* put my Vtnm articles into a book that would also be pub. by Random House. (When I say "contract" here, I refer to that brief conversation that I told you about, in which I said: "Yeah, that sounds OK to me, but of course you'll have to talk to Lynn before anything is definite.")

Loss of the Vietnam book leaves us with maybe a good possibility of going the same route with my Washington/Campaign gig. I'm not sure how this would work out in terms of Ballantine, RH, etc., but maybe it's worth considering . . . although *RS* would have a definite claim to this one, whereas they don't have any hold at all on the Vegas book . . .

. . . particularly not after going ahead with including the first Battle of Aspen piece in their anthology, or whatever it's called. Probably it won't make any difference, but I think we should hurry Silberman inre: that $5000 that comes with the "first third" of the politics book. As I said in the outline/letter, as far as I'm concerned he has the First Third now. He could argue that—claiming it's only bulk copy—but in any case he has enough so that we can start thinking about where to draw the line for that $5K.

Another big factor, in that area, is that this "politics" (AD/BA) book has been in limbo for so long that forcing a decision on the First Third/$5000 question would put definite pressure on both me *and* Silberman. In view of the time factor—the necessity to get it published by next summer—I think some heavy fiscal pressure would be a definite impetus. I get the feeling, from talking to him, that he's still thinking more in terms of an *idea* than a *book*.

That transition has to be made immediately, or we'll blow all our lead time—which is already getting narrow. I know, from experience, how hard it is to make Random House move fast on *anything*. They already have about $10K in the book (about half of that toward my travel expenses), and I think another $5 grand might be just what Jim needs to get his adrenaline up for a fast finish . . . and some heavy pressure from his end is about the only thing that will force me into the kind of feverish concentration that I'll need to get the book done . . . a Forced March, as it were: that's the only way I *ever* get anything big done. (He doesn't have any experience with this, because it was Shir-Cliff who dealt with it on the Hell's Angels book. On the basis of far less than Silberman has now, S-C gave me the second & third leg of my Advance in a $3000 lump sum—because I said that's what I needed to "get the book done"—and along with the money came an ominous warning that if he didn't get a finished ms. on the specified date I could start looking for a newspaper job, because I'd be finished in book publishing . . . and what happened "is history," as they say: After nine months of fucking around I had about half the book done—and then with only 2 wks to go before the deadline, I moved to a motel and wrote the second (better) half in four days. Selah. . . .)

Anyway, the point of that story is grossly evident. I'm definitely going to need some pressure from RH—and preferably from somebody like a copy editor who knows precisely what copy I'm talking about, rather than Silberman, who only knows about the *idea.* I tend to work only as hard as I think I have to work—and what gets me in gear is a *serious* deadline & people screaming at me on the long-distance telephone about *specifics*—like, "We *must* have the ending to Chapter Seven by Friday, or the printers are going to sack the whole goddamn book."

I have a history of never missing a *real* deadline—and Silberman has (wisely) never given me one, if only because neither of us understands exactly what book I was supposed to be writing. But now I think I understand it. God only knows what he thinks about it. But if he can handle that outline I sent, then he should stop fucking around and start setting deadlines . . . and he should assign somebody to the book who will prod me unmercifully, in the same way a copy editor named Margaret Harrell kept me locked to the daily grindstone on the Hell's Angels book.

Maybe I'll try to locate Margaret. The last time I heard from her, she'd married a Flemish poet & was living over a water closet in Algiers. But that was a year or so ago, and possibly she's back by now. If so, she's definitely the Missing Link. I'll see if I can find her.

And that's about it for now . . . except to clarify my statement, today, that I wasn't "desperate for money." Which is true, because I got that royalties (*HA*) money—and I hope you'll remember this moment of addled honesty in the future. But my failure to Cry Wolf doesn't mean you shouldn't pursue that "First Third/$5000" with all your zeal and talent. I need that. Not only for the dollars, but to escalate the (mutual) level of commitment to the book.

Ciao,
Hunter

TO MARGARET HARRELL:

To sweeten the appeal to his trusted Hell's Angels *copy editor for help on his new book, Thompson attached a darkly funny essay blaming movie icon John Wayne for everything that had gone wrong with the American Dream.*

August 12, 1971
Woody Creek, CO

Dear Margaret . . .

Where are you? And why? I've lost track completely. My last definite word was from a water-closet in Algiers.

Anyway, I'm sending this on the odd chance that you might have bounced back to the U.S. since I last heard anything. If so, I've been hassling Silberman severely to assign a "Margaret-type" copy editor to this goddamn book that I finally seem to be on the verge of getting together. But god only knows who he'll assign . . . and it worries me, for all the obvious reasons.

The bastard has to be finished by Nov 1, because that's my date for moving to Washington, DC, to become the Chief Political Correspondent for *Rolling Stone*—a contract job for one year: Nov '71 to Nov '72. The book is now titled "The Battle of Aspen," but the main thrust is toward the idea of translating our Aspen "Freak Power" tactics into the national politics arena—so it will have to be out by the summer of '72.

If you're anywhere loose & within hailing distance of Random House, I think I could recommend you for a job there—beginning almost immediately, although the pressure won't get serious until around Sept 15 or maybe even Oct 1. That's when I'm going to need somebody who can deal with the book without having to waste 2 months "getting to know me." I am not encouraged by memories of the other copy editors I met there . . . but if dragging you back is absolutely out of the question, maybe you know somebody who could handle it????

This deadline is real, I think. I had most of the bastard written last spring, but then I went out from LA to Vegas to do a "Quick caption" for *Spts. Illustrated* . . . but I got so involved with the place that the caption is now a book, incorporating what Silberman thought would be the final section of the "big" book. (He's been a little nasty about letting the Vegas chunk go for a separate book, but I think he's finally agreed. Last week—after about two months of haggling.)

So what I'm looking at, right now, is *two books*. Vegas is almost finished. It's called: "Fear & Loathing in Vegas: A Savage Journey to the Heart of the American Dream—by Raoul Duke, Doctor of Gonzo Journalism."

If you hurry, you can deal with that one, too. I've promised to have it all finished by the end of August. Jim already has about 35,000 finished words, with a maximum of 25,000 more to come. I'd prefer to keep it down to 50,000 or so, but I don't think I can. It's a boomer—a spontaneous outburst that almost wrote itself.

Let me know where you are & if there's any chance at all of tracking you down to help out on the Battle of Aspen. I'm not worried about Vegas, but the other one makes me very nervous. I suspect I'll need a friend to make the bastard work & beat the deadline. Send Word at once, from anywhere. Even if you can't make it, I'd like to know where you are & what you're doing, thinking, feeling, etc. Ciao . . .

Hunter

(Attached)

JOHN WAYNE/HAMMERHEAD PIECE:

This country is so basically rotten that a vicious, bigoted pig like John Wayne is a great national hero. Thomas Jefferson would have been horrified by a monster like Wayne—and Wayne, given a shot across the time-span, would be proud to pistol-whip a "radical punk" like Jefferson.

John Wayne is a final, rotten symbol of everything that went wrong with the American Dream—he is our Frankenstein monster, a hero to millions. Wayne is the ultimate & perhaps final "American." He beats the mortal shit out of anything he can't understand. The brainwaves of "The Duke" are like those of the Hammerhead Shark—a beast so stupid and irrationally vicious that scientists have abandoned all hope of dealing with it, except as an unexplainable "throwback." The Hammerhead, they say, is no different today than he was in One Million B.C. He is a ruthless, stupid beast with only one instinct—to attack, to hurt & cripple & kill.

There is no evidence in modern science that the Hammerhead Shark had any ancestors—and no descendants, either. But science is at least half-wrong on this count. Like many another species, the Hammerhead survived by moving to a new habitat. The most advanced of them came out of the sea and learned to walk on land. They learned to speak American—despite their tiny brains—and a few of them moved to Hollywood, where they found themselves much in demand as extras & even as heroes in hundreds of "cowboy" films.

The New Hammerhead was a perfect cowboy. He was vicious & stupid & ignorant of everything except his own fears and appetites. He beat the mortal shit out of anything that made him uneasy, for any reason at all. The Hammerhead was a perfect warrior. He defended the flag. Any flag. He learned to understand words like "orders" and "patriotism," but the secret of his success was an ancient taste for blood. He thrived on action. But he was brainless; he had to be aimed.

The Hammerhead was the one you hired when you wanted to kill Indians. He was also available to whip Niggers. And then to hang Wobblies. He was given a badge and a club, and by 1960—or maybe even 1860—the Hammerhead Ethic *was* the American Dream.

The press created a whole pantheon of Hammerhead Heroes: J. Edgar Hoover, John Dillinger, Audie Murphy, Joe McCarthy, Ira Hayes, Lyndon Johnson, Juan Corona[37] . . . but the king-bitch stud of them all was "The Duke," John Wayne, a cowboy movie actor whose only real talent was an almost preternatural genius for brainless violence. The Duke wasn't satisfied with just killing people; he beat them into bloody, screaming hamburger.

Which made him Number One at the box office—the ultimate Hammerhead, a total American Hero. Thomas Jefferson was a useless artifact at this point, and even Horatio Alger was little less than a convenient myth. By 1960 John Wayne was more American than Studebaker;[38] he had the whole Dream in his fists.

And it was just about then that the Duke took his gig to Vietnam. Both the Negroes & the Indians had been beaten to jelly; the Beatniks were finished, the Hippies were on the ropes . . . and only the Gooks remained.

(historical pause)

The rest is history, as they say. The Duke *ate it* over there in The Nam. And he took all his relatives down with him: Westmoreland, McNamara, Bundy, Rostow, Rusk, Taylor,[39]

37. J. Edgar Hoover was director of the Federal Bureau of Investigation from its founding in 1924 to his death in 1972; John Dillinger was a notorious gangster responsible for sixteen killings in the Midwest in 1933–34; Audie Murphy, America's most decorated soldier in World War II, became a Hollywood leading man in the 1950s; Ira Hayes was one of the U.S. Marines who raised the American flag at Iwo Jima in February 1945; and labor contractor Juan Corona was sentenced to twenty-five terms of life imprisonment after being convicted of the murders of twenty-five Mexican migrant workers in Yuba County, California, in 1970–71.

38. Studebaker was a popular make of American car throughout the mid-twentieth century.

39. General William C. Westmoreland was U.S. commander in Vietnam from 1964 to 1968 and U.S. Army chief of staff from 1968 to 1972; Walt Rostow, a close adviser to Presidents Kennedy and Johnson, played a key role in planning the U.S. intervention in Vietnam; Dean Rusk was U.S. secretary of state from 1961 to 1969; and General Maxwell Taylor, U.S. Army chief of staff from 1955 to 1959, was U.S. ambassador to Vietnam from 1964 to 1965.

LBJ—a whole generation of King Hammerheads went down with the Duke in Vietnam . . . and by 1971 the only real question was whether or not Nixon, whom even the Hammerheads scorned, was stupid enough to link his name forever to some kind of horrible, nightmare echo of Dunkirk[40] . . . an army of wild junkies, fleeing in terror along some broad and bloody highway that Texas contractors built with personal Income Tax money from Saigon to that beach on the South China Sea . . . and then wading, under fire, into the timeless surf toward a handful of broken lifeboats.

A nation of Hammerheads going back to sea. A panic worse than anything lemmings ever dreamed of . . . an indescribable tragedy for those who will die there, with lungs full of blood and seawater . . . but not for the Main Hammerheads; they will toss another log on the fire down in Texas, and polish their gold-plated memoirs.

The filthy truth is that 50 years from now our grandchildren will be herded, by law, into stylish jail/bunkers that will still, even then, be called schools . . . and they will be forced to buy millions of expensively bound "history books," which they will study under the watchful eyes of a new generation of enforcers who will still, even then, be called "teachers" . . . and they will learn from their texts and their teachers that men like Richard Nixon and Lyndon Baines Johnson were "American Statesmen." And other names, like Agnew and Humphrey—along with Rusk, Rostow, and [JFK/LBJ national security adviser McGeorge] Bundy—will fade away into footnotes.

That is the horror of it: That in 1995 the standard/text high school history books will not say that America in the 1960s was ruled and effectively gutted by a gang of cheap thugs who also happened, for reasons of political necessity, to be Mass Murderers. The history books will not say that Lyndon Johnson was more vicious than Mussolini and more stupid than Hitler.[41] They will not say that Robert McNamara's hands were so bloody that after five years he forgot what blood smelled like . . . and that

40. Dunkirk, a seaport in northern France on the English Channel, was the site from which 337,000 trapped World War II Allied troops were evacuated between May 27 and June 4, 1940.
41. Benito Mussolini was the Fascist dictator of Italy from 1924 to 1943; Adolf Hitler was Germany's Nazi dictator from 1933 to 1945.

the ranking Generals with "honored West Point names" like Taylor & Westmoreland & Abrams[42] were still screaming, all the way to the end, for more blood and bombing and fire . . . and that even in 1971, with the awful truth so obvious that even Senators could see it, the ranking fixers who still ruled the U.S. Congress were threatening editors of *The New York Times* with "prosecution for Treason" because they finally published documented proof of what a whole generation of young Americans had been screaming in the streets for five years—while fifty thousand others died senselessly to protect a dozen or so wealthy dope-dealers who were also Generals and occasionally Presidents of that cancerously corrupt little finger of Asia called "South Vietnam."

These dirty truths will not appear in the history texts of 1995. The hired fixers will take over just as soon as this undeclared war is unofficially finished—just as soon as the last shark is called off and brought home for an angry rest. And not one of these blood-hungry Hammerhead scumbags will ever be nailed to the final whipsaw judgement they all deserve.

Not because of what they did. But because they did it in the name of a Dream & a Human Possibility that was fragile from the start, but strong enough to survive almost every abuse and cruel failure that human beings were capable of . . .

. . . except the Hammerhead Ethic, and the beasts who rode it to power. These were the swine who found their model in a brutal freak like John Wayne.

If it won't salute, stomp it. Break it. Destroy the goddamn queer dirty thing. Rip its lungs out . . .

Then nail that coonskin to the wall, like LBJ said. If there is any real justice in this world or the universe, God has already dug a special hole in Hell for LBJ and the Duke—a pit full of rancid blood & fang-leeches, which the bastards will never escape from.

But there is not much evidence in history of either God or Justice. The best we can hope for is Truth. Not often, and a pretty thin gruel even then. The Hammerheads get all the meat.

42. General Creighton W. Abrams was commander of U.S. troops in Vietnam from 1968 to 1972.

TO JOE ESZTERHAS, CLEVELAND *PLAIN DEALER:*

In 1969, Hungarian-born Cleveland Plain Dealer *reporter Joe Eszterhas had lucked into one of the biggest scoops of the Vietnam War when an old college friend turned Army photographer asked if he'd like to see some gruesome shots of the 1968 massacre of hundreds of South Vietnamese civilians at My Lai. Eszterhas became disenchanted with his own triumph, however, when his employer proved determined to profit from the atrocity by selling the images to other publications at outrageous prices, and in September 1971 he excoriated his own newspaper in a fourteen-thousand-word article, "The Selling of the My Lai Massacre," in the tiny, liberal* Evergreen Review*—upon which he was immediately fired.* Rolling Stone *hired him soon after he lost the wrongful dismissal case he filed against the* Plain Dealer*; he would write several searing articles for the magazine before trying his hand in Hollywood, so successfully that he stayed there. Eszterhas made his screenwriting debut in 1978 with the Sylvester Stallone vehicle* F.I.S.T., *and in 1992 received a reported $3 million for his script for Sharon Stone's star-making* Basic Instinct.

August 31, 1971
Woody Creek, CO

Joe . . .

I just finished your My Lai piece in *Evergreen,* and it reminded me once again to bitch at Jann Wenner (*Rolling Stone*) for not offering you a fat contract of some kind. I thought your things on Kent State and The Biker War at Polish Hall were two of the best pieces *RS* has coughed up this year. I was especially taken with the biker thing, because I could almost smell every fucking detail . . . and when I read it in galleys I thought, shit, I'd better hustle, because here's a bastard who can write this stuff almost better than me.

Anyway, I just sent a note to Wenner, reminding him that I told him to hire you about two months ago. If a gig like that interests you, send him a note & don't worry about references. *RS* could use a hell of a lot more of the kind of stuff you do best.

And if you get to Washington D.C. anytime after Nov 1, ask info. for a *RS* phone number and give me a call. At the moment it looks like I'll be there all winter, fucking with national politics.

Best,
Hunter S. Thompson

TO JANN WENNER, *ROLLING STONE:*

Thompson was dragged once again into the tradesman chores of freelancing.

September 10, 1971
New York, New York

Jann . . .

I tried to call you the other nite—& even during the day—& Stephanie [Mills] finally told me you were in NY. I considered the idea of tracking you down—more or less as an exercise—but under the circumstances I decided against it. All I really wanted was a bit of talk about the preliminary trip to NY & Washington—along with some kind of non-vague understanding about whether or not all my expenses would be covered. This is a problem because [Carte Blanche] hasn't yet officially reinstated my card, and I'm still waiting for a $5000 check (less $500) that Lynn somehow drilled out of RH.

In other words, I'm penniless now and without a *sure* credit card. But if necessary I can borrow the $500 or so that I'll need to make the trip—and after giving that idea some thought, I decided to go ahead, rather than try to deal with [David] Felton or anybody else at the office. (What this situation underscored, once again, I might add, is the yawning abyss in authority at *RS* when you're out of the office. I don't know enough about the individuals there to offer any suggestions—and I've never been one to knock "equality"—but in truth it's a fucking bummer to call there & know that I've hit a goddamn dead end if you're not available.) We should talk about this, when there's time. There's no fucking way you can be a good editor, effective publisher, world-traveling personage & beleaguered family man all at once.

Which reminds me about that note I sent inre: Joe Eszterhas in Cleveland. He strikes me as having excellent instincts, along with a pretty firm head and decent work-background.

But fuck all that. What I was calling about was the NY/Wash trip—and as of now I plan to leave on Tuesday, for NY, to see Sanders inre: The Process & also to hassle with Silberman . . . which brings up another aspect of the thing that suddenly mushroomed on Wednesday, when I called Lynn to demand money. She informed me that Silberman was "not interested" in publishing Vegas in tandem with *anybody*—which resulted in a lot of yelling, from me, and then a quick bit of harsh explanation from her . . . which is something else we should talk about, when there's time. Because it involves Silberman's opinion—for good or ill—of the entire St. Arrow book operation.

Anyway, I told Lynn that *she* would have to call Alan. I refused to. And about three hours later she called back to say everything was fine—but that word came thru Sandy, because I wasn't here to talk with her (Lynn). In any case, I'm assuming that the word I got was valid . . . and I'm sure I'll learn more about what happened when I get to NY. Actually, I already know what happened—&

I can't even feel guilty about it, because I have a taped conversation that makes it absolutely clear that I actually effected, *at one point*, a *RS*-RH joint publishing agreement, at least for one book. But of course this is meaningless, except as a sort of object lesson—along with that other one I mentioned earlier: The ugly truth that Silberman was quick-witted enough to buy *control* of Vegas, in book form, by paying all expenses for both trips, without even asking for a breakdown. The bill I sent him was about three lines long: One figure of $500-plus for the Mint 400 & another $500-plus for the Drug Conference—and then a total of $1000-plus. He never even asked what the money went for. He just sent the check and jotted down "Vegas/Thompson" on his list of RH futures.

You'll recall that I warned you about this at the time. And you'll also recall that the situation developed because whoever sent me that $500 in Vegas made sure that it went against my retainer, instead of "expenses" . . . which gave Silberman his opening.

Maybe something can still be worked out. If possible, you should track me down for a phone talk before I leave NY. For instance I have no idea how to deal with Sanders inre: his Process material. And unless I hear something definite from you, I'll go ahead & deal with him as a free-lance writer.

I figure on getting down to Washington by the weekend (18/19), then renting a car and sort of looking the place over. But I can't see much real good coming from it unless we can talk, first, about what I'm looking for. I've worked the DC thing out into two separate categories—and the root-difference between them works out to the difference between a "Washington bureau" and a "contributing editor based in Washington." This is also the difference between looking for a house on Capitol Hill, and a safe apt. in Georgetown. I can probably scout both possibilities while I'm there, but I can't do anything definite until after we've talked.

Meanwhile, I've settled the deal with Stranahan & have tentatively leased both houses until June '72—but I can't sign the contract for this one until we arrange something definite inre: Washington. (I realize that I'm laying all this gibberish on you at a bad time, and I wish there was some kind of suprawisdom I could spray it all with . . . but the truth is that if I had any wisdom for you, I'd have let you know a long time ago. I wish I did, but . . .)

Anyway, call me when you can. And in the meantime, I've taken a definite liking to the Randy Agnew story. I think that would be a nice way to kick off the Washington gig—so I'll get onto it during the scout visit, if possible. Greene[43] might be useful as a leg man, but the tone of his letter indicates a pervasive lack of brain-speed & essential curiosity—along with a full belly, which means we probably shouldn't count on him. Okay for now. Send word ASAP. . . .

H

43. Dan Greene was a young Washington correspondent for *The National Observer.*

TO BILL CARDOSO:

Thompson's friend from the 1968 Nixon press bus had given up his post as editor of the Boston Globe Sunday Magazine *for a job in the Azores.*

September 10, 1971
Woody Creek, CO

Billy . . .

My health is excellent, although failing in various critical areas that I choose to ignore. For some peculiar reason, your letters always seem like a shout from the far shores of sanity. Your current gig sounds good . . . as a matter of fact I've been thinking about it all afternoon, since your letter came, and it occurs to me that maybe Sandy & I could lash out there for Xmas. Weird, eh? You can always count on your friends to fuck you around when you find something good. It never fails. . . .

Anyway, current plans say I'll be moving to Washington (for a year—no more) on Nov 1, as the Chief Political Correspondent for *Rolling Stone.* I'm going there in a few days to look it over & try to find a house . . . then back here for a month of steady work on *another* book. I just finished one. *Rolling Stone* will publish it in two parts, beginning in October, and then Random House says they'll put it out in book form. The *Stone* version will list "Raoul Duke" as the author, but RH insists on going with HST—which will make life difficult for me in Washington, because the book is a first-person account of an incredible string of felonies committed in Vegas. (But more on this later; I've just finished the bastard, and I'm "high as a fucking pigeon."—L. Buckley.)

In any case, this Washington gig looks definite. For the first time since that heinous political fuckaround, things seem to be going fast & hard for me. I just managed to buy 2 houses and 128 acres in Woody Creek for no money down, & there are also signs that I'm learning how to beat the NY money machine . . . and on the basis of all this, I think it would be entirely fitting for me & my bride to spend Xmas in the Azores. Could you handle it?

One possibility is that you might work out—or at least put me onto—some kind of free-ride hookup with whatever airline services that filthy place. What better way to get right smack in the middle of the Hip Map than inviting the Sports Editor of *Rolling Stone* out for a visit? With one fell stroke, I could make Funchal the "in" place to go this year. Maybe you could check out that crowd at the Hilton on this.

But what the hell? We have plenty of time for that gig. I'm serious, though. We could leave the kid in Florida, with Sandy's mother, and rip out there with a satchel of fine mescaline—which would definitely be worth a story. I'll be writing a *column* out of Washington, in addition to the normal stuff, so I figure I might as well ride this trip all the way out—for a year; why not?

Let me know at once. It's possible that I could actually pay my own way, but shit, nobody else does, so why the fuck should I? And it seems to me that the Funchal Hilton could use just about *any* publicity they can scrape up. Selah.

On other fronts . . . your tale of [William] Kennedy's visit sounds well nigh intolerable, and all your observations seemed dead on. That thing about "too late hipped in life . . ." is worth stealing. I guess the fucker has gone a bit wild with his new status. Although in fact we had considerable trouble with him out here during the election. He came out to cover it for *Harper's* (this was before his *LOOK* gig), and since he was "an old friend" I gave him total access—denied to all other press. So he went immediately nuts & developed into a hell of a problem. We ended up making him stand guard duty outside the house in 12 degree cold with a .30-.30—on the 3 to 5 a.m. shift. And no dope, because we told him he had to be *alert,* in case the vigilantes attacked.

And so much for that. I'll get on him for dragging a bunch of creeps into your place. No excuse for it. He *is* an old friend, but I suspect you're right about his head. Selah.

Inre: Your piece for *RS*—I sent it immediately to the *wrong* editor. But I didn't understand this until a week or so ago. I thought the guy was a heavy, but it turns out that he's about to be fired. The weird thing is that—although he never acknowledged receipt of your piece until I finally yelled about it—he actually went to Boston, looking for Avatar, and came back to SF with all kinds of variations (featuring you, personally) on that piece you wrote. When I sent it on, I made no guess about whether or not it was true, but he came back from Boston muttering about the "mythical freak, Cardoso." And he never put his rumors together with the story he had on his desk . . . which is shitty, but the truth is that most of the people at *RS* aren't much better than what you had at the *Globe.* Their hair is longer & they smoke a few more joints, but so what? This cocksucker (the editor in question) didn't even acknowledge 2 hits of mescaline I sent him . . . so you see what I'm dealing with.

I am, however, getting this *RS* trip under control. I even have Raoul Duke on the masthead as a "contributing editor." When I go to Washington I'm going to promote Duke into my spot as Spts. Ed. . . . so I can use him to spew out my pure gonzo stuff. (You'll want to read my Vegas thing; it's a must. Let me know if you have any problem getting *RS* out there; maybe I can get you a free sub. I've never tried that, but maybe I can convince Wenner that it's important for *RS* to be *seen* in the Azores. I think I can. Send a note & remind me.)

OK for now. Everything in your letter gets my head moving. I definitely want to make it out there for Xmas. Check the free-ride thing and let me know if it's possible. I can lean on somebody over here, if you send me a name.

Ciao . . .
Hunter

FROM OSCAR ACOSTA:

Acosta had been arrested.

October, 1971
San Francisco, CA

Hunter,

I hung around Frisco with Henry for two more days with heavy dope and his constant babble after I left you in the dust with The Blue Mustang. I took another peek in the city for a pad then played the game all the way out and looked around Berkeley to please Marco. Knowing all the time I'd not find my *sitio* in any place where there is danger. I had become so paranoid I even secretly accused you of many evil things. (Fortunately I kept it all to myself so I got no apologizing to do.)

Saturday I picked up Marco, talked to his mother and auntie for a couple of hours and nearly went out of my skull with the fear that I was actually hung up on something so out of my league. She still likes opera, Pepsi and [Adlai] Stevenson, probably in that order.

It worked well, however, because that was the last push in the butt I needed to get out of sin city. I came back to my parents' house in Modesto, kicked my old man out of his room, painted it a funky red-green-gold&pink and am now a writer in residence. I haven't felt this good, safe and open since 1968.

I have nothing but memories here to haunt me and even those seem trivial. It sure beats the shit off the fucking banging around I've been getting the past year. That whole trip was so bizarre I'm afraid it'll take even a heavier writer than you or me to make any sense of it. Not that either of us will actually try, but I'm going to take a stab at it.

Then Monday we returned to L.A. for my court bit. First my old man's station wagon completely broke down at the foot of the Grapevine and we had to hitch it in to the land of fear. Then my lawyer got sick and I had to go to court all alone, with Marco as my bodyguard. They've put one of the heavy D.A.'s on the case and he started in on me right away. I was dressed like when you last saw me. And in no mood to play the lawyer anymore. He refused, that's right, refused to arraign me. . . .

"You've been charged with, etc. . . . How do you plead?"

"Not guilty."

That's what the entire hearing consisted of, legally that is. He argued with the judge that I was a defendant like any other one, and that since this was a felony I had to have a lawyer present. The judge reminded him I, me, was a lawyer. . . .

"I see no reason to treat him differently than any other person charged with a crime," the bastard argued.

The judge says, "But, counsel, this is a special case."

I finally got into it and thought I might end up in jail again. "This is a special case." The D.A. charges everyone else with a misdemeanor, but on me he files a felony.

Anyway, the motherfuckers are really after me. They want my ass so bad it drips all over them.

I really felt like pleading guilty and getting the fucking thing over with. Do my time, pay my fine and then get into what the fuckers really want . . . my license.

My lawyer and I spent a long time talking about the case and we've decided it's going to be as weird as The Biltmore.

We found out that the guy in the car who told us he dropped it, apart from his fantastic inconsistencies, lied through his ass to position his friend, my ex-client in the Biltmore case . . . to make a long story short, I am now convinced he is totally useless and in fact dangerous as a witness . . . we are paranoid as hell because the only way we can use him is if *he* testifies differently than *he* remembers . . . which is perjury . . . which, if we encourage it, is subornation of testimony and conspiracy on our part . . . and it would completely knock out our main defense, which ultimately is: I didn't have it & the cops know I didn't, and based on their own statements about the whole reason for tailing me for three hours, the chances are that they planted it on me. . . . So, as of today, we are not planning to call him.

I picked up the transcript of the testimony of the feds & sheriffs and it is a real doozy.

I really felt strange in that court room. It ain't paranoia no more. But no one believes me. How is it that a folk hero such as I was in East L.A. this past year is suddenly without a single fucking supporter? I who taught them how to make points off the man by whopping it up in his face, who defended perhaps 100 dudes, never had a client sent to jail, got 100,000 votes, t.v.'s most popular kid in L.A. . . . I mean, how would you feel if they were out to get your union card so that you'd never be able to write again?

The sickness, the real wretchedness comes from the realization that I'll neither be found guilty or innocent. So I can look forward to perhaps two or three trials. And if there is a conviction . . . perhaps three years of appeals . . . and then the fun begins. The action to take away my license could last five years.

Do you hear me, boy? If you do, you and Neil [Herring], my lawyer, are the only two in town who do. But I seriously doubt that you do. You are so much into the Vegas thing, *R/S* & D.C. that you fail to see which side your bread's buttered on and it's getting all over you . . . fuck it, I may as well run it all down.

When I called you last September on the Salazar case we made an agreement that from here on out things would be on something more than a personal basis. Each would have some voice, some control, a piece of the action . . . excluding bread. Although we spoke of 50/50, I told you that wasn't my bag nor my need. After a hell of a lot of work on both our parts we got it out. The final piece you wrote and I put my complete trust in you . . . and I have no regrets, you came through like a champ. But if you read the piece carefully, you'll notice that a good half [of] the info, the stuff on which you base your opinions, art, etc. . . . would not have come from your pen *as it did* had I not been around. Can anyone in his right mind believe that Rudy, Benny, & Frank[44] would have talked to you without me? Or that you picked up all those paragraphs on the Chicano Movement from someone other than me & the gang?

To a lesser degree, much vaguer on details, the Vegas thing was no different.

As a result of Salazar, I got booted out of the gang. My life threatened, etc. In your large head you think it was the writing. In your racist head you think it was cause they hate white people. Quite simply, it was a matter of personal loyalties. It was because I told them you were my *camarada* that the axe fell. If I'd said, "Man, I'm just *using* this honkey fool to get my picture in the paper and maybe a contact with a publisher. . . ." Shit I'd still be on top. . . . Instead, I got no friends, they took my fucking grant away from me and I ended up doing the Biltmore without their support. And now I got to do my own case with nothing but me & Neil.

Do I indulge myself? Sure would be easy to simply lay it down to paranoia, wouldn't it?

So what am I bitching about? I got my picture in the paper, didn't I? And, as you've strongly hinted, I got a contract from Wenner—Not Alan—through you.

And I can hear you right now . . . I told you I didn't want to write about friends. You knew what you were getting into.

. . . ultimately, I've had absolutely not one iota of control except that which I've sneaked in over your head; i.e., I've had a measure of influence into what ultimately went into the work by my mere presence and godlikeness.

What, do I want recognition? Perhaps a little footnote that says, this idea came from Oscar?

If that is what you think—and I think you do—then buddy you don't know shit about your subject.

All I want is for you to quit playing the role that I'm some fucking native, a noble savage you discovered in the woods. I mean, your Frisco-*R/S* action this time was a bummer.

Like, did you even so much as ask me if I minded your writing & printing the Vegas piece? Not even the fucking courtesy to show me the motherfucker. No, I don't control what you write or what anyone prints . . . but as a friend, *pendejo*,[45] as a friend who has *already* suffered the pangs of purgatory because

44. Rudy Sanchez was Oscar Acosta's "quiet little bodyguard"; Benny Luna and Frank were fellow Chicano activists.
45. *Pendejo* is Spanish for "fool."

of your first piece, one would think my old buddy would say, Here it is, what do you think, and do you mind? Your only statement on the subject, which I tried very hard to raise on several occasions . . . "Your name's not on it."

Jesus Christ, can one change history—facts—by merely calling it a different name? Even the lesbian knew better than that.

I forgot, you told Wenner it was all *fiction*. And you told me you knew how to write good dialogue before we went to Vegas.

Holy Mary, you sound like Abbie,[46] Mailer & Wolfe all in one.

My thoughts are not exactly flowing smoothly because I'm really getting worked up as I write this shit.

. . . and then you say, I *think* we might use the picture.

. . . and then David says, I don't think we'll use the picture.

Oh, sure, late at night, with everyone gone, you finally said, What do *you* think?

It was too late and too little.

But the best line of the whole week was, "I'm *thinking* of going down for your trial. *Maybe*, if I can swing it. I haven't talked to Wenner yet."

You dumb cocksucker, you talk to *me* first. Your fucking arrogance has really gone to your head. Could it be it's because you're becoming successful? On the staff of *R/S* and all that?

Fuck it. If you ain't got the message by now.

TO OSCAR ACOSTA:

October 18, 1971
Woody Creek, CO

Oscar . . .

Just read your last letter over again, and agree with Sandy that the most merciful way to deal with the thing would be to ignore it. The letter was a mess, and I doubt if I'm the only one getting tired of that paranoid, self-pity, Hey look at me, I'm Oscar trip . . . and all I know about your book contract is that *nobody's* going to publish a lot of weepy gibberish about how nobody knows how important you are. You don't know how fucking lucky you are that I didn't run into you cold, as a stranger, on something like the Salazar story—because, with an act like yours, I'd have crucified you on general principles. Shit, you're *lucky* the LA press is a bunch of lame hacks; anybody good would screw you to the fucking floor.

He might regret it later, once he "got to know you," but that probably wouldn't happen anyway. If you mean to continue that Belli trip, you'd better

46. Abbie Hoffman was a leader of the radical Youth International (Yippie) Party and an outspoken opponent of the Vietnam War.

give up on the idea that the press is going to love you for it. Not unless you're dealing with somebody who can shrug it all off and talk to you later, with all the psychic cameras gone. There is a certain gut contradiction in knowing that the press is a gang of assholes and expecting them to love you & make you famous in spite of themselves—and you'd better figure that out if you intend to keep on practicing public law.

But fuck all that. It's 7:13 a.m. here & I want to go to sleep, but probably I won't be able to because I feel so fucking guilty about what I did to you with that Salazar piece. It won't happen again, and the only way you'll get me to your goddamn pill trial is to subpoena me—which I assume you'll do, if you think I can be any help. And if I can, I will—but only as a witness, not a writer.

As for Vegas, I refuse to let you or anybody else edit the fucker—no more than I'd have let you edit Salazar, and for a lot better reasons, this time. The Caesars Palace photo won't be used without your permission; I told you that a long time ago, and at this point I think it would clash with Steadman's drawings . . . so as far as I'm concerned, we won't use it.

Talk to Wenner if this deletion offends your sense of justice—and if you insist on being identified as "my attorney" in the text, I guarantee you'll regret it. This is *my* book. There *is no editor* on it—not at *RS* or Random House either. RH hasn't even assigned a copy editor to it. (There is, however, the chance that I'll want to use that CP photo of you & me on the *back jacket* of the RH book version—probably without *any* ID, just the photo. Let me know if you plan to object. Or maybe you'll want an ID. Is that possible? If so, let me know & I'll make the proper arrangements . . . and god's mercy on your ass if you try to turn this book into a personal publicity trip.)

That's about it for now. I'm deep into packing for the move to DC. The house is torn all to pieces. Millions of goddamn boxes; packing everything I own into two basement rooms & then renting it out. My address in Washington is c/o *Rolling Stone,* Room 1369, National Press Building, Wash DC 20004. No phone yet. . . .

In closing, let me leave you with a straight verbatim echo of a thing that my old (& now dead) friend Lionel Olay sent me a few years ago when I was complaining about all the personal/mechanical problems that were keeping me from finishing the Hell's Angels book. You've probably seen it on my wall:

"You better get back to that machine, mister. You can con those guys out of front bread once, but *only* once. . . ."

There's more, but I think the point is made. You'd better write that fucking book. A $2500 advance is about $1000 more than most first/unknown book writers get these days, and the truth of the matter is that I had nothing to do with it. The book thing is between you & Alan, and although I don't know the guy at all I get the feeling that he attaches considerable importance to it—for himself, as well as you, and if I felt like tossing idle guesses around I'd guess you'll have a hard time conning another publisher if you blow this one. But that's only a personal guess . . . and I'm sure you'll take it that way, for whatever it's worth.

In the meantime, for fuck's sake get off the acid. There's too much paranoia in it—especially for you, because you seem to enjoy cultivating it, and that's suicide. There's too much good in your head—and all the rest of you, for that matter—to bog it all down in sick gibberish like that last letter to me.

As for details . . . I'm waiting for RH to send me some money before mailing you that $200, but I *can* send it immediately if you need it. And I could probably go $300 more, if necessary, so let me know. And if you think I could do you any good on the stand, let me know on that, too. Ciao . . . H

"INSTRUCTIONS FOR READING GONZO JOURNALISM"

November, 1971
Washington, D.C.

• Half-pint, 10-inch hypo-needle (the kind used for spinal taps & inoculating bulls)
• Fill this full of rum, tequila or Wild Turkey & shoot the entire contents straight into the stomach, thru the navel. This will induce a fantastic rush—much like a ¾ hour amyl high—plenty of time to read the whole saga.

Gonzo Journalism—like quadrophonic 4-dimensional sound—exists on many levels: It is not so much "written" as performed—and because of this, the end result must be experienced. Instead of merely "read."

Beyond that, it should be experienced under circumstances approximating—as closely as possible—the conditions surrounding the original performance. For this reason, the editors have agreed to pass the author's "reading instructions" along to all those who might want to "experience" this saga under the "proper conditions." We offer them without comment—& certainly without recommendation.

To wit: Read straight thru, at high speed, from start to finish, in a large room full of speakers, amplifiers & other appropriate sound equipment. There should also be a large fire in the room, preferably in an open fireplace & raging *almost* out of control.

(alternative, hot tub & vibrator)

The mind & body must be subjected to extreme stimulus, by means of drugs & music.

TO JANN WENNER, *ROLLING STONE:*

Thompson installed himself in the nation's capital on behalf of Rolling Stone *on November 1, 1971.*

November 18, 1971
Washington, D.C.

Jann . . .

I'm interrupting *VORTEX/Washington* #1 to whip off this quick note inre: timing, deadlines, priorities, etc. What I've written so far is a slag heap of spotty gibberish with no real subject at all, and it suddenly occurs to me that I'd rather miss an issue than send something bad and/or useless.

What happened during the past three days was that Dave Meggyesy came into town to promote his book via Radio/TV & newspaper interviews, and since he was staying here at the house I found myself bashing around from scene to scene with him and doing about half the talking. In a nut, I've been on the DC promo circuit, talking mainly about the Youth Vote (that rotten phrase again) & why *RS* is "opening a Washington bureau."

It never occurred to me that so many media people in Washington would know who I was. I went into the city room of the *Wash/Star* today, to cash a check (my checks are totally worthless here & I have no cash), and suddenly found myself socked into a long Q&A session that eventually became a formal interview for a series the *Star* is doing on "Intellectuals & Sports." None of these people had even read the Vegas stuff; their interest stemmed entirely from the HA book & two things in *Scanlan's*. As it happens, the spts ed. of the *Star* just came from the *SF Examiner* & is staffing his whole section with freaks (see attached memo for two gratis subscriptions). He offered the facilities of his office for anything I needed: phones, typewriters, work, etc.—so I now have a second office.

There are so many things happening that I can't even sleep. Coming out of Woody Creek into this scene has jacked me into a brutal adrenaline trip—compounded by the shock of finding myself treated like a public figure of sorts. Given this odd visibility factor, I suspect the new fact of a *RS* "bureau" in D.C. will soon be viewed more as a lobby gig than a news operation because I'm already locked into the idea that I'm here to write a column with one hand and whip up a giant anti-Nixon Youth Vote with the other. There's no escaping it; my history is too public—so for christ's sake let's *create* that vote. We have a tremendous amount of latent sympathy (& potential energy) among young heads in the media. They seem puzzled at the idea that *RS* is "getting into politics," but they all seem to like it. Shit today I got my first Job Application, which I'll forward as soon as I xerox it. Within a month or so, I suspect we'll be needing that extra room in Prisendorf's office[47]—more for political [reasons] than anything journalistic, and now that I think on that I suspect we

47. Thompson shared office space in Washington, D.C., with *New York Post* reporter Tony Prisendorf.

should be pretty careful. The point, however, is that a hell of a lot of people seem to want to "help" me. Too many, I think, but at this point I don't want to turn anybody off.

On more specific fronts, I'm already gearing down to make "The Real Nixon" *VORTEX/Washington* #2 (that name is off the top of my head & might not last, but let's use it for now as a sort of working title. It conveys a certain amount of urgency and bogus drama that fits in nicely with the activist side of this gig). In truth, I feel a bit like Victor Louis. From here on out it's going to be hard to defend the notion that I'm here to merely write a column.

OK for that. #3, I think, could combine "Youth Vote" & "Candidates" by running a flash survey on how various candidates view the possibility of a youth vote. That way, I could run a series of quick interviews with *all* the candidates, on the basis of a single question—then come back to the ones we want, after using the survey to sort of introduce myself.

I think, however, that we *have to* get away from that phrase "Youth Vote." It leaves out about two thirds of the people we're talking to. Ideally, we should come up with something about halfway between "Youth Vote" & "Freak Power." Something to embrace both the latent (& massive) Kesey-style voter with the 18–21 types.

***

Now a few important details:

1) My rent checks should be made out to:

J.M. Ely . . . and sent on the first of each month to that name & acct. #, c/o the SURBURBAN TRUST CO., Hyattsville, Md.

2) I've had a long talk with the mgr. of the newsstand next door to the Nat. Press Bldg (see enc. note with name of big boss for all six UNIVERSAL NEWS stores) & the man in store says *RS* invariably sells out "in a few hours." I told him I wanted it there the next time I came around, so he gave me this man Siebert's name—which you should pass along to the distributors. I got the note on the doubled-up distribution & according to the man at Universal, they'll all sell. Maybe not, but he had no reason to bullshit me.

OK for that. I haven't seen a copy of *RS* for sale since I got here—and that makes life unnecessarily difficult for me. There is—now that I think on it—a first-class FM rock station here that reaches almost the entire young/music type audience. I'll get the name & send it along. A few spots on it might work wonders. I'll check around for other possibilities & let you know.

Right now I have to get to bed. It's 6:30 a.m. & I have to get up before noon, in order to buy a bed & a TV set. Today is Saturday. (My private phone number just got activated yesterday. It's 726-8161). Don't give it to anybody; not even on the master Rolodex. The *RS* number—882-2853—rings here in the house; that should be enough for all but the critical few.

The point is that I want to have one phone I can always answer, without fear of being fucked around by lunatics . . . and the first time I start getting hassled on *that* number, I'll change it. So don't give it to anybody except Max, Stephanie, etc.

Well . . . now that I have all this space I'll include the two names I want to lay gratis subscriptions on:

1) Dave Bergen, Sports Editor
   Washington Evening Star
   225 Virginia Ave. SE
   Washington, DC 20003
2) Kiki Levathes
   1280 21st St. NW
   Washington, DC 20036
   (this is the girl who's doing the "Intellectuals/Sports" series for the *Star.*)

Actually, since I'm paying $5 a hit for these subs, I see no point in explaining *why.* So from now on, just deal with the names & bill me & assume I know what I'm doing.

This would work nicely as a sort of General Rule, for that matter—except that right now it's not entirely true. What I'm doing at the moment is feeling my way around & trying to cope with all these unexpected reactions to my gig. The problem, oddly enough, is that things are working out better than I expected . . . but at the same time I'm swamped with vicious little details. The phone man, for instance, got here at 10:00 and left at 4:30. He's just back from Vietnam, & for a number of reasons that need no explanation it took him six hours to drill through a stone floor & then a stone wall, in order to put two phones in the Fear Room. And then he came back this morning: to check the phones, he said, but what he really wanted was a copy of #95. Not for Vegas 1, but because of that story on Sly.[48] "I been wonderin why that sonofabitch is always late," he said . . . then he said he's been reading "the *Stone*" for 2 yrs in Nam. I figure he'll be around again—which is okay, I think, because in a city that's 72% Black it might be nice to have a sharp black friend. When the bastard came back today he was wearing a hat that would have freaked even Sly.

And that's it for now. Hopefully, I'll get a column in by Tuesday—but I'm not optimistic about its potential coherence or heaviness. If it looks bad I'll simply hang it up and make the nut with something else. Don't worry, either way. This is going to be a good & extremely active gig, but I'll have to get grounded first. (I assume, by the way—based on the schedule you sent me—that the *real* deadline for *VORTEX* #1 is Dec 1, instead of Tuesday 11/22. Is that right?)

Send word,
HST

48. In 1967, rock music producer Sylvester Stewart took the name "Sly Stone" and formed the "psychedelic soul" group Sly and the Family Stone.

TO JANN WENNER, *ROLLING STONE:*

Thompson found that settling into the Washington political scene was no easy task, given his notoriety and limited resources. Among other things, he wanted an assistant to spare his wife, who was pregnant once again, from the chaotic pace.

December 9, 1971
Washington, D.C.

Jann . . .

Just a note to get this stuff out of the way before I get down to putting #1 together . . . jesus; it's 3 hours since I hung up the phone after our talk & I'm still getting things straightened out enough to do any writing (making dinner & reading today's *Post* & *Star* took most of that time; the *WSJ* & the *NY Times* are still unread—along with *Newsweek* & a whole In-box full of other magazines).

Which brings up the question of hiring some kind of assistant for these things. (We may as well face the fact that Sandy is absolutely useless on this front. Between the doctor, Juan's school and setting up the house, she has about 2% of her time left for the sort of secretary-act that she was doing in Woody Creek . . . and this is proving to be a hell of a lot more of a problem than I might have thought, if I'd given it any thought: because I've grown accustomed to letting her deal with my day-to-day reality & keeping the fucking weasels off my back.)

We had a terrible hassle, for instance, about that seemingly quick little thing of picking up that shit from the Moroccan embassy. She finally did it, but I'll never ask her to do anything like that again . . . pregnant women are very touchy; and especially pregnant women who are very tense about being that way, like Sandy is.

Anyway, the point of all this is that I find myself having to cope with all kinds of minor-detail bullshit that I'm not used to even thinking about. . . .

Which brings up the question of an assistant.

Valliere is a possibility, but that raises various problems: 1) I'm not sure if anybody who takes himself seriously as a "heavy young journalist" (as Valliere seems to) could handle all the maddening bullshit I'd necessarily be laying on him. What I mainly need is something like a very bright secretary-type to stand between me and the world of daily detail-madness—and to do all the stuff that *must* be done, by somebody, but not by somebody who has to *write,* too. In other words, I need somebody to do most of the things I've spent most of my time doing since I've been here—like trying to find a fucking copy of *RS* & taking it out to the Capitol press gallery because they wanted it for my credentials trip . . . or talking to these lunatics who keep calling the *RS* number and asking weird questions . . . or getting things xeroxed, or etc. etc. etc.

2) Valliere wants to write, not get into slave-work, and I suspect he'd be more valuable as a sort of regular back-up man for stories I think are important but not quite important enough to cover personally—especially when I won't be in town. The other thing is that Valliere has a job in the Nat. Press Bldg. that pays his rent for about 2 & a half days work, per wk, and he's very eager about *writing*, which means he'd probably work—for a yr. at least—on a regular piece-work basis, with maybe a monthly or weekly minimum & anything he can make on top of that on a per-word basis.

3) This would leave us the option of hiring a sort of halftime secretary & general non-writing assistant, which is what I really need. This should be a girl, I think—if only because Prisendorf would like that, in the office, whereas he couldn't handle some eager young sport whose very presence would be a put-down to his own assistant. (In other words, a male writer-type assistant would mean getting another office—and I'd hate to lose the bundle of odd advantages of working in a scene with a guy whose job requires him to stay on top of every breaking big story & who also has an assistant, a wire ticker, vast files, many contacts & considerable prestige on the DC press front. I can go in there at 4:30, for instance, and get a quick, authoritative rundown on everything important that has happened since dawn . . . and even when I don't go in, I can count on either Tony or his assistant calling me at home if something heavy comes up.)

This is too good a thing to write off—in addition to the hassle of finding another office, somewhere, and then paying for it. I haven't seriously pushed the idea of sharing a part of the rent; I mentioned it once, but Tony shrugged it off. He's clearly more interested in whatever side-benefits might come from having the *RS* operation in there with him—like the *RS* refrigerator ($72.50, delivered), and also whatever free records might come with having the DC bureau on the "record-reviewers" list. That kind of stuff, plus a bright & hopefully decorative *girl* assistant around the corner, would probably work very nice & not even cost much.

In any case, we're going to have to do *something* about the non-writing aspects of this gig. There's no way I can hide from them. People know I'm here, & to some extent I'm a bit of a public figure—but I also have to work, and that means I need a human buffer to keep well-meaning people from driving me fucking nuts. I no longer have the protection of an unlisted phone in Woody Creek, Colorado; I'm now in the belly of the beast, as it were, and if things keep up like they have been, I see no hope for any sort of concentration . . . unless I do something like move to some fishing village on Chesapeake Bay & take a different name.

There is also that quote from Max about *RS* making so much money that it's almost obscene . . . which I promise not to tell anybody if you hire me some decent assistance. Otherwise, I'll pass it on to Lee Berry & tell him to flail you with it.

Another point, inre: your filthy comment on my "batting average" vis-à-vis my friends. By my count it's at least .500—rather than the .333 you mentioned. I recall pushing you for 3 or 4 months to hire Eszterhas, & I also recall having to lean pretty heavily on you to even hire Steadman for one shot. Your first reaction to his Dog Book, as I recall, was something like . . . "who needs this kind of cheap Steinberg?"[49]

But . . . well, yes . . . there *was* Ed Sanders, and Lucian [Truscott]. And also [John] Clancy, I guess, whose value remains to be toted up; that will come around Apr 15 of next year, I think—for both of us.

Anyway, I insist on .500—and the only problem about Dan Greene, for that matter, is that the *Observer* pays him about twice what I get (on the salary front, anyway), and since he lives in a city where he never sees *RS* for sale anyway, he didn't see where he stood much to gain by writing for it.

That exposure problem goes far beyond mere sales figures. A writer wants to think he's being read—and people who talk to writers want to think they'll see themselves in print. And in that context, I might as well be the DC correspondent for *EARTH* [Straight Arrow's short-lived environmental magazine] . . . and I want you to understand that this is a fucking, flat-out bummer to have to work with.

But fuck all that. I realize the problems & I have total faith that they'll all be dealt with—but I want you to keep in mind that *RS* looks a hell of a lot different from out there in that corner office on Third st. than it does to people here. We are not what you'd really call Big in this town—except with a handful of young journalist types who might, if this White House press hassle goes right, be precisely the ones who can give us the leverage we need here. So for christ's sake get rid of your notion that we should tell our tiny handful of allies here to Fuck Off. That would be a terrible mistake, & it would put me in a very bad hole. (And keep in mind that you *did* say that—"tell them to fuck off.") So if you get any calls from the *Post, Star, NY Times,* etc. about the White House press hassle, keep in mind that these bastards are in a position to make my life very difficult if you treat them like scum. The real issue is far larger than a simple little matter of whether or not I get a White House press pass. The important thing is whether or not people think it's worth their while to even talk to me, and on this score we couldn't ask for anything better than a clash with the White House with the DC press on our side. Fuck the credentials; what we need is a front-page argument with Ziegler.[50]

OK for now, and so much for all that. The only other thing is the question of that phone-xerox machine. I already have the sending half of the action in the office; so all we need, on your end, is the receiver—which rents for $50 a month, according to Prisendorf, and which could also be used for NY copy.

49. Saul Steinberg was a well-known cartoonist for *The New Yorker.*
50. Ronald Ziegler was the Nixon administration's White House press secretary.

That would mean cutting our copy-transmission time down to three or four minutes per 300 words instead of 3 or 4 days by mail. I could finish a story at noon and have it on Charlie's[51] desk, ready for final editing, by 2 p.m. . . . or finish it at 6 a.m. and have it there by dawn, SF time.

This would also work for NY stories. The fucker will even transmit photos. Tony sends *all* his stuff to the *Post* on the thing. It would virtually eliminate the mail/deadline lag . . . and, given the tax problem with all those obscene profits, you could probably get the net-transmission cost down to almost nothing.

Anyway, you should definitely check it out. There's no fucking reason in the world why I should have to kill the last four days before deadline time with an air-mail scene—when the whole thing could be easily solved by a relatively cheap machine. Shit, they even make them in *portables*—so I could walk into any phone booth in Chicago and transmit the whole thing, comma for comma, in less than 30 minutes. These things are common equipment even for sportswriters. . . .

(Good God, I feel a vomiting fit coming on . . . cold sweats & all that, so I'll hang this thing up and go outside for some air.)

Ciao . . .
H

TO RALPH STEADMAN:

British artist Ralph Steadman's illustrations for Rolling Stone*'s "Fear and Loathing in Las Vegas" articles—published in the magazine's November 11 and November 25, 1971, issues—exactly captured the Gonzo spirit, and Thompson knew it.*

December 16, 1971
Washington, D.C.

Dear Ralph . . .

Thanx for poking Thames TV for the campaign film; they said "fuck off," but that won't be the end of it. I'll take the problem from here—now that you've put them on record.

On other fronts, the Random House deal seems fixed—at whatever price your agent can grind out of them. If the price seems low, keep in mind that *my* book contract with RH (for the Vegas book) says that it will include "drawings by Ralph Steadman; cost to be borne by the publisher." So for fuck's sake don't settle on *any* price before you talk to me . . . because it's already in *my* contract that the book will include *your* drawings; which puts us in a very comfortable bargaining position, and as far as I'm concerned (which is only *my* opinion and

51. Charles Perry, *Rolling Stone*'s brilliant, multilingual copy editor since 1968, had been LSD guru Augustus Owsley Stanley III's roommate when both were students at the University of California at Berkeley.

general outlook), you shouldn't settle for anything less than at least $5,000—which is a bit less than half what they've agreed to pay for the writing, and I figure that's just about fair. I feel the drawings are necessary to the book—but what we have to keep in mind is that Silberman (RH) seems to feel the drawings are a sort of indulgence to the author; and he's hinted here & there that he'd just as soon publish the book with no art at all.

The kicker here, however, is that everybody now involved with "Vegas" is on record, unofficially, to the effect that I should never have gotten involved in a piece of shit like that in the first place. My agent advised me against even *going out there* for the Mint 400, *Rolling Stone* refused to pay my expenses for either trip, and Random House refused to even *consider* the ms. *for a book* until I arrived in NY with the bastard totally finished.

So on that score we have them all. (This is a long story & I'll let it hang for the moment; I'll fill you in when you get over here in January.)

I'm absolutely certain I can sell that trip to the Super Bowl over here for a nice chunk of $, or at least as a package with other, more political stories—there's a paddlewheel steamer leaving St. Louis two days before the game (a steamboat trip down the Mississippi) and I told Wenner tonight that he had 72 hrs to say Yes or No; leaving me free, if he won't pay fat for it, to sell the whole spectacle to somebody else. (Wenner almost cried at the idea of paying your expenses to come over here for one story—so I told him we could bring you over in January and then keep you around for the entire Presidential campaign. In other words, to do *all* the illustrations for my bi-monthly coverage (a regular column called Fear & Loathing in Washington), and also for the book, which is already contracted to the *Rolling Stone* book division.

You should give this idea at least a serious thought. For one thing, there's a definite chance (better than 50/50, I think) of a film on the book—and one of the main ideas right now is centered on that animated drawings idea that I mentioned on the phone. We should know the prospects on this by the first of next year.

In the meantime, for christ's sake don't make any agreements with anybody to do *anything* over here in the U.S. Obviously—if somebody offers you a hell of a lot of money to illustrate something you should probably go ahead & do it . . . but you should balance any offer you get against the idea that by June of '72 *we* (the Steadman-Thompson coverage, etc.) are very likely to be worth more than the sum of our parts. In other words, we can probably earn twice as much together than either one of us could earn separately. (I'm not totally *sure* of this, but I'd be willing to bet on it. That Vegas saga has had a massive impact among the sort of in-group, writer/editor clique—and I think if we wait till the Random House book comes out we'll be in a position to sign a really staggering contract, for almost any story we want. . . .)

Keep this in mind. We really cracked the buggers with this one; we drove them right down to their fucking knees . . . and the most fantastic thing about it is that the thing is really flat out fucking *good.* It's a genuine fucking classic; the overall reaction to the thing has put me seriously off balance . . . people are reading far more into the story than I ever intended to write. And god only knows what will happen when RH floods the bookstores with the hardcover version. (You should, by the way, tell your agent to negotiate some kind of agreement that will make you more money if the book becomes a best-seller, which is not unlikely. . . .) In other words, the idea that you might make *more* by asking *less* in front is entirely feasible. Give that one some thought, too.

OK for now. The thing to do, right now, is really to sit back & wait until the book comes out—and also to let me know if you're up to coming over here in early January & staying a few months. Maybe six—possibly nine; all the way up to election day, doing the whole fucking campaign . . . think on that a while & let me know. But remember that riverboat trip down to the Super Bowl; I think that's a *must.*

Ciao . . .
Hunter

TO IAN MARTIN, THAMES TV:

London's Thames TV production company had sent a crew to Aspen to film Thompson's 1970 campaign for sheriff for the British news show This Week.

December 21, 1971
Washington, DC

Dear Mr. Martin:

You cheap, half-wit asshole. What the fuck do you mean, "We cannot normally make them (film-prints) available to people who *have taken part* in programmes"?

I realize that you've just answered a complaint according to the RULES of the network, and of course you're not to *blame* for anything . . . and beyond that I don't expect this letter to have any effect over there, because I understand quite perfectly that you executive types can't be held responsible for agreements made by your film crews when they're across the water.

But just for the sake of history I want to clear up a detail or so. That was *my* campaign for sheriff that your clumsy eight-man crew swarmed onto in Nov of 1970 . . . and they were only *allowed* to cover it after lengthy conversations between Peter Ibsen & Udi Eichler for your side—and several of my campaign managers, representing me. It was a horror to have those fuckers around, with all those lights & cables & other assorted garbage everywhere we went; but we figured we stood a good chance of winning, & for that reason we also thought it would be good to have the story on British TV.

To this end, after lengthy negotiations, both Ibsen & Eichler agreed to furnish us with $100 for the campaign-headquarters beer-pool *and* a print of the film, as soon as possible. This was accomplished only after long hassling with several members of my staff who felt it would be a terrible mistake to lay that kind of trip on the locals—huge banks of lights & 8 people yelling with heavy British accents at every public gathering at the climax of a brutally emotional campaign in a treacherously unsophisticated Rocky Mountain community.

This proved to be a mistake as we thought, and the reaction came almost immediately—but since we had made the agreement & also because we had more important things to worry about, we tried to ignore Eichler's crew and assumed that they were at least serving *some* purpose by getting the campaign on record.

Another factor here is that, a month or so after the campaign, I called Ibsen at the ITV office to ask about the film, and he assured me it was "coming very soon."

But now I understand. They never had the authority to make any agreements, anyway, so how could we have been so goddamn foolish to have taken them seriously in the first place?

How indeed?

Well, Martin . . . perhaps one of these days, in my travels, I might have the opportunity to discuss this problem with somebody from Thames TV. We have another campaign over on this side of the water, this year, and perhaps you'll be wanting to cover it.

I plan to cover the entire campaign—including most of the primaries and both conventions—for *Rolling Stone,* and somewhere along that ugly trail I'm sure I can be of some assistance to your people; like maybe helping you arrange a bit of coverage, or something like that. Don't hesitate to call on me. I'd welcome an opportunity to do a bit of translating for you, with the locals.

You scurvy, lying pigfuckers deserve all the help you can get, right?

Right.

Just ring me up anytime, Martin. I'll be traveling a lot, but if you can't find me anywhere on the campaign circuit you can always reach me thru *Rolling Stone* in San Francisco.

My name is

Hunter S. Thompson

1972

FREAK POWER GOES TO WASHINGTON, STRATEGIC RETREAT INTO NATIONAL POLITICS . . . MADNESS & VIOLENCE ON THE SUNSHINE SPECIAL . . . GETTING TO KNOW THE WHITE HOUSE, LEARNING TO FEAR RICHARD NIXON . . . FALLING IN LOVE ON THE ZOO PLANE, FAREWELL FOREVER TO INNOCENCE . . .

(Cover by Tom Benton)

Hunter and Juan Thompson at home in Washington, D.C., 1972.
(Photo by Ellsworth J. Davis)

California campaign trail, 1972.
(Photo by Annie Leibovitz)

Dr. Thompson and George McGovern on a train in Nebraska, 1972.
(PHOTO BY ANNIE LEIBOVITZ)

Democratic National Convention, 1972. Front to back: HST, Pat Caddell, Warren Beatty, Tim Crouse.
(PHOTO BY BOB MCNEELY)

TO JANN WENNER, *ROLLING STONE:*

Throughout 1972 Thompson was so engrossed in covering the presidential campaign for Rolling Stone *that he found little time for private letters—but his editorial correspondence with Jann Wenner proved so politically astute that much of it would be published in his next book,* Fear and Loathing: On the Campaign Trail '72.

January 3, 1972
Woody Creek, CO

Jann . . .

I fucked around with the Chicago/Youth Vote thing for about five hours & didn't get a hell of a lot done, but I think it looks okay for getting finished this week. I'll definitely plan on that. So I can get up to N.H. next week with George McGovern.

No point hanging around here any longer. I'm taking off today at 2:30 on TWA. It's 6:00 a.m. now & my brain is too tired to keep humping along on this thing . . . but I think it looks okay for a finish in 3 or 4 days. That's not a promise, but I see no reason why I can't get it done by the weekend and then move north.

I feel much better about the gig now. For some twisted reason, my head is a lot straighter today than it was when I got here—despite all apparent evidence to the contrary. (The fucking CFIP got me again last night & put me thru the roadside acrobatics trip again. Incredible! Twice in 4 days. How could it happen?)

Anyway, I'm heading east on the assumption that we've cured whatever was trying to kill me—but not necessarily on the basis of what we talked about that afternoon (thurs.) on the balcony. After the meeting-talk, I decided that we'll have to make the column a separate gig—keeping it fairly short, with the same title, in order to keep my opinions from becoming a problem for everybody else . . . and also to croak any conflict that might arise vis-à-vis my corporate identity (that columnist vs. editorial writer thing, which tends to haunt me in a way that I can't even rationally explain. But it's real, so we may as well deal with it).

All in all, I think we have the thing under control. I'll get on that secy/researcher thing at once, & also call Tim Crouse, Landau & Tim Ferris[1] so I can organize the eastern front ASAP. Hopefully I can check thru NY next week, en route to Boston & then to N.H.

I can't figure out what the fuck makes me think the Big Sur gig was an unquestionable success, but as far as I'm concerned it was. (Except for Felton, that treacherous little fart. Why not send him to open a Lima bureau & then stop payment on his expense checks? That would sure as hell teach him a lesson, eh?)

On balance, I think we somehow managed to chop the Great Gordian knot. If the week served no other purpose, it at least gave Duke a stay of execution, & I think that's Important. Sorry we didn't get to talk more, but what the fuck? The important thing was to croak my Hate Trip, & that worked out. I feel definitely Up about things now, and I was impressed with the general style & tone of the crowd you've managed to put together. Whatever problems we have now seem minor.

As far as I'm concerned, we should plan on two distinctly separate trips inre: DC—one, the column, which is mine, and, two, the political coverage, which is *Rolling Stone*'s. We'll have to figure out the technical aspects of the format, but that should be easy. I'll call before shoving off for NY & Boston.

There remains, of course, the problem of my attorneys. What can I say? Oscar's trial begins on Jan 5—and as far as I'm concerned Clancy's should have been yesterday. I have changed my mind about the Death Penalty.

The only other problem that comes to mind is Janey [Wenner]'s muddleheaded notion that I'm a decent person with right & proper instincts but I think maybe I managed to solve that one, too. Probably you shouldn't mention my thing with Carol Doda,[2] but I guess that bastard Felton let the pig out of the bag anyway, so fuck it.

OK for now. This no-sleep trip is beginning to wear me down. I think I'll go over & pack my rhinoceros skin bag & hit the road. Thanx for a good week.

HST

TO JANN WENNER, *ROLLING STONE:*

Thompson chose Rolling Stone *staffer Timothy Crouse—a Peace Corps veteran, Harvard graduate, and son of Pulitzer Prize–winning playwright Russel Crouse—as his assistant on the '72 campaign trail, an apprenticeship Crouse made the most of. His book* The Boys on the Bus: Riding with the Campaign Press Corps, *published by Random House in 1973, became a critically ac-*

1. Boston-based Jon Landau was *Rolling Stone*'s chief music critic; Timothy Crouse and former *New York Post* reporter Timothy Ferris were among the magazine's writers.
2. San Franciscan Carol Doda was a pioneering recipient of silicone breast implants.

claimed best-seller that The New York Times*'s David Halberstam called "the best writing about journalism I have ever read."*

January 14, 1972
Washington, D.C.

Jann:

Here's the general outlook for political coverage for issues #102 thru #106—mainly in terms of coordinating things between me & Tim Crouse vis-à-vis the N.H. & Fla. Primaries.

The only serious problem looks to be issue #105, which will be going to press just about the time the deal goes down in New Hampshire. The election there is on Tues, March 7, which puts us in a bit of a bind . . . and which will also determine what kind of coverage we schedule for issues #104 and possibly even #103.

The main question, I think, has to be whether Tim should do an overall N.H. wrap-up piece for #104/#103 or try to file a last-minute "results piece" for #105—keeping in mind the *real* distribution & mail delivery dates for #104, which would get a N.H. wrap-up to *most* readers about a week before voting time in N.H.

On the other hand, this would make things very difficult for Tim—having to wrap the fucker up two weeks before it happens. But maybe he could do this with a sort of Question–Issue piece for #104, and then me filing a last minute thing from D.C. when the N.H. results are final around midnight EST (using the xerox).

That's one option. The other would be for me to go up to Manchester, with the xerox transmitter, and help Tim file a last-minute "results" piece for #105. This *could* be a real nightmare, if the results are still hazy by midnight; we might find ourselves going to press on #105 with the *real meaning* of N.H. still up in the air. The only essential questions up there concern the *size* of the vote McGovern and McCloskey[3] will pull—and this figure could hang until noon the next day. (There is, of course, the unlikely possibility that either George or Pete will jump off to an early lead and then hold it—in which case we'd *have* to wait, as long as that possibility existed.)

Anyway, you see the problem for #105. Ponder it and let me know, because what we do with that one will have a definite influence on my own plans for #103–4–5 and #106.

On #102, I'm pretty clear. I'll cover the Mass. Rad/Lib Caucus[4] on Sat 1/15, then move across the border to spend a few days with McGovern & then file a

3. Republican congressman Pete McCloskey of California, who had won the Navy Cross, Silver Star, and Purple Heart during the Korean War, sided with the liberal antiwar stance on Vietnam.
4. The "Rad/Lib Caucus" in Worcester was organized to unify Massachusetts liberals in anticipation of the state's April 25 Democratic presidential primary; George McGovern bested Eugene McCarthy in the informal ballot by nearly three to one.

piece on his stance & general outlook in both Mass & N.H. (If the Mass Rad/Lib caucus rejects him, however, the Young/Left vote has to make a choice among 3 or 4 candidates. The winner will be ahead not only in Mass., but all over the country in terms of long-range publicity.)

Tim is also pretty clear for #102. He's onto McCloskey. We'll meet in Manchester on Monday and figure out the details from there—but it's already definite that we have two separate pieces for #102: McCloskey, and McGovern against the background of whatever happens in Mass. on Sat.

The problems begin with #103—mainly because of the problem with #105. I'll talk to Tim & get his ideas, but whatever he has in mind won't much affect the question of whether I should do my "Lindsay in Florida" thing for #103 or #104. In any case, I'll plan to leave N.H. in time to get down to Florida so I *can* do a Lindsay piece for #103—although it might be better to save it for #104, which would leave me free to do a D.C. piece (maybe "the Real Nixon," etc.) for #103, then Lindsay in Fla. for #104, then a last-minute "results" piece on N.H. for #105 . . . and then back to Fla. for an "election nite & what now?" piece from Florida, combining the N.H. & Fla. Results—with the added advantage of having 3 days between the election & the Fri 3/17 deadline to get the piece in via Xerox.

Actually, this piece would seem almost mandatory, either way . . . so the question is how to space out my movements for #103–4 and #105 . . . and this depends on how we plan to handle #105, vis-à-vis the 3/7 voting date in N.H.

I assume all this is at least tolerably clear. The only gut problem is how to handle #105 . . . and my own inclination would be to have Tim do his final N.H. piece for #104, then have me do a last-minute thing on the N.H. results for #105 from DC, instead of N.H. Personally, I don't much give a fuck. I'd just as soon take the transmitter up to Manchester & do a Results story with Tim for #105—but I think this would be very risky. On the other hand, we're going to have problems with #105 no matter how we try to fuck with it. If we spring for the last-minute Results story, for instance, that will leave Tim on the loose for #103 and #104. But if he does his N.H. wrapup for #104, that would leave him loose for #105 and a very belated analysis thing on "The effect of the Youth Vote in N.H.?" for #106—along with my Fla. wrapup.

On balance, however, I think I would argue for this. The fuckup possibilities of trying to get the N.H. results & analysis into #105 are immense—unless Tim can somehow do a sort of "overnight" wrapup that we could lash together at the last moment, and hope to sweet jesus that the final results go according to form. (The only upbeat note, here, is that we should both—Tim & I—know a lot more about how N.H. looks by the time #102 goes down: so maybe there's solace in that. But not much . . . keep in mind that I spent a month in N.H. in '68, & even with my pro-McCarthy bent I was *stunned* by the size of his vote; and I can't really recall anybody up there who was more optimistic about McCarthy's chances than I was . . . so we may as well assume that any attempt to predict '72 is subject to at least a 30% error factor—which is all either McG. or McC. needs to claim a "victory.")

OK for all that. The only *immediate* question, for right now, is whether I should plan to file from Fla. on Lindsay for #103 or #104. I'll go down there anyway, after N.H., but let's keep in mind that we'll have a valid chance for filing a DC-datelined piece on something like "the Real Nixon" for #103, then doing a long & fairly well-written piece on Lindsay in Fla. for #104—which would still leave me loose for whatever we need for #105, then back to Fla. again for a final for #106.

Shit . . . no point in scrambling this up any more than it already is. I have it all charted out, but I refuse to send my only copy of the chart & I still can't get the Xerox people to deliver the machine. I've already signed a contract & given them a deposit of $18 for the delivery fee, but they refuse to be definite about *delivering* the fucker. If it's not here by the time I get back from N.H. I'll get another brand. According to [consumer crusader Ralph] Nader, Xerox is not the best, anyway . . . but what the hell? The point here is that you'll have to make your own chart of this "#103 thru #106 coverage" problem.

Right after I talked to you tonight I had a long chat with Tyler Knapp, Nader's Volvo raider, & as of now I get the feeling he's ready. I'm leaving him with about six projects, including the writing of a "story" on the "Volvo Myth," based on his own massive research. What he does for Nader, he says, is usually prepare lengthy "research memos" that Nader usually edits for speeches or personal presentation in one form or another. So I told him to do one for *RS* on "What's Happened to Volvo." And, in addition to that, I left him with about five fairly prickly problems to solve . . . so I should know about that when I get back, & I'll let you know at once.

OK for now. I'll check in with Landau on Sat nite or Sunday, & then meet Tim at McGovern hq. in Manchester at Monday noon. McGovern will be in N.H. until noon, Wed. & at that point I'll head back here—then down to Fla. But I'll talk to you before then.

Ciao,
HST

TO BERNARD SHIR-CLIFF, POCKET BOOKS:

Convinced that Fear and Loathing in Las Vegas *would be a hit, Thompson lobbied Shir-Cliff to buy the paperback rights.*

January 30, 1972
Woody Creek, CO

Dear Bernard:

I was shocked & deeply saddened by the general style & tone of your talk the other afternoon. It was bad enough to find out that you didn't know

Rolling Stone from the *Journal of Addictions*—which explains your failure to notice a new work by Raoul Duke—but even after long thought on the subject I can't see any graceful way for you to explain that gibberish about having to catch the Next Train to West Egg,[5] or whatever, and maybe we could have a drink around lunchtime whenever I came up with something that might pass off as a legitimate lunch/talk expense.

It was a bummer, Bernard . . . a stone bummer.

But I decided to send you this thing anyway—mainly because you're the only paperback editor I know in a personal sort of way who can also sign big checks. And also—in what has now become a peripheral consideration—I'm assuming there must be something left of your sense of humor.

I could lay a lot of heavy advertisements and flashy endorsements for this thing on you, but I figure you should just sit down & read the bugger first—because it runs its own interference. In football terms, Bernard, *Fear and Loathing in Las Vegas* is what us fans call a Naked Reverse, which means that the offensive blockers all move in a false direction, forcing the defense to roll with them, and then the ball-carrier—usually a flanker—suddenly takes off in the opposite direction with no blockers at all, depending entirely on his own speed & strange moves to turn the corner & go long.

But this is getting a bit heavy, eh? But you want to keep in mind that I've spent the last two months in the shadow of the White House, where Jimmy the Greek[6] takes his cocktails.

Anyway, read the fucker and then call me for the corporate checkbook before you ring up Silberman. When I first called you the paperback price was $100K—but 4 hrs later, when you failed to call back, it was up to $110K. And by the time you get this letter, Bernard, god only knows what it might be when you finally get around to reading it. My guess is that we could maybe settle for $125K if you can come up with a cashier's check by this Friday.

But what the fuck, Bernard? Why worry about money? This book is pure fucking gold. There are only two kinds of people who could lose money on it: a fascist waterhead publisher, and a fascist anal-retentive distributor . . . but in either case they would need the help of an ignorant, humorless, fascist, anal-retentive editor.

None of which is likely. Things are well under control at the moment. I've already taken care of all of those problems we had with the *Hell's Angels* gig—things like advance publicity, legal squabbles, film sales, preparing the market, lashing the ms. into final galleys, art, the whole nasty trip . . . it's all been taken care of, Bernard; we're home free.

Which explains the price, eh? A flat-out fucking bargain at $150K . . .

5. "West Egg" was F. Scott Fitzgerald's fictional *Great Gatsby* version of Long Island's posh Westhampton.
6. Gambling expert "Jimmy the Greek" Snyder was a Las Vegas newspaper columnist.

. . . which reminds me that you once sent me a book called *A Clockwork Orange* and asked me what I thought about it, and I remember telling you it was one of the best things I'd ever read . . . which immediately caused you & Ian [Ballantine] to dump the fucker and let poor Burgess piss away his film rights for $10K.[7]

But to hell with all that. I've never been one to get ugly about past blunders, or to hold grudges any longer than absolutely necessary . . . and it might also be worth mentioning, at this point, that in the long run I have almost never been wrong.

I say "almost" out of modesty, Bernard. But the really terrifying truth is . . . well . . . shucks . . . let's save it for later.

In the meantime, read *Fear and Loathing in Las Vegas,* then crank out a check for $175K. About the only guarantee I can make you right now is that you'll take any ties; that's for old time's sake.

I never forget my friends, Bernard. And I know you feel exactly the same way. But keep in mind that if I don't have your check by Lincoln's birthday you'd better put a fucking wolf-lock on the door to your office, because I'll be sending my attorney around to find out what your problem is.

Sincerely,
Hunter

TO MARK LEBEAU:

Thompson sent an encouraging reply to a young fan from Minneapolis who had written of his disillusionment with the upcoming presidential election.

February, 1972
Washington, D.C.

Dear Mark . . .

Thanx for the note & the cheerful upbeat flash that came with it. When you talk about voting, however, keep in mind that it's no real trick to vote for "the best" of a bad lot. You'll get a little tired of that after you've voted a few times. I've tried it, & my feeling now is that the compromise/lesser-of-2-evils game doesn't seem to be getting us anywhere.

So I'm looking for something in the way of candidates or ideas that might really *change* the institutionally corrupt nature of politics in this country. So don't mistake anger for pessimism. I believe the democratic process *can* work in America—but not as long as the Major Parties keep forcing us to choose between double-negatives.

7. British author Anthony Burgess's satirical novel *A Clockwork Orange* was published in 1962; director Stanley Kubrick's movie version was released in 1971.

Anyway, keep an open mind. There's still a chance that something Right could happen in this election . . . & who knows? You might even want to vote for it.

OK,
Hunter S. Thompson

TO JANN WENNER, *ROLLING STONE:*

This is the first of many dispatches Thompson would send Wenner from the '72 campaign trail.

Late February, 1972
Washington, D.C.
Campaign Trail

Dear Jann—

Jesus, what's the other one? Every journalist in America knows the "Five W's." But I can only remember four. "Who, What, Why, Where" . . . and, yes . . . of course . . . "When!"

But what the hell? An item like that tends to pinch the interest gland . . . so you figure it's time to move out: Pack up the $419 Abercrombie & Fitch elephant skin suitcase; send the phones and the scanner and the tape viewers by Separate Float, load everything else into the weightless Magnesium Kitbag . . . then call for a high-speed cab to the airport; load on and zip off to wherever The Word says it's happening.

The public expects no less. They want a man who can zap around the nation like a goddamn methedrine bat: Racing from airport to airport, from one crisis to another—sucking up the news and then spewing it out by the "Five W's" in a package that makes perfect sense.

Why not? With the truth so dull and depressing, the only working alternative is wild bursts of madness and filigree. Or fly off and write nothing at all; get a room on the edge of Chicago and shoot up for about sixteen straight days—then wander back to Washington with a notebook full of finely-honed insights on "The Mood of the Midwest."

Be warned. The word among wizards is that [Maine senator Edmund] Muskie will have the Democratic nomination locked up when the votes are counted in Wisconsin . . . and never mind the fact that only 12 percent of the potential voters will go to the polls in that state. (The Arizona pols—using bullhorns, billboards, and fleets of roving Voter Buses—managed to drag out 13 or 14 percent.)

This ugly truth is beginning to dawn on the big-time Demos. They commandeered a whole network the other night for a TV broadside called "The

Loyal Opposition"—featuring Larry O'Brien[8] and all the top managers discussing The Party's prospects for 1972.

It was a terrible bummer. Even though I am paid to watch this kind of atavistic swill, I could barely keep a fix on it. It was like watching a gaggle of Woolworth stockholders, bitching about all the trouble they were having getting the company to hire an executive-level Jew.

Whatever O'Brien and his people had in mind, it didn't come across. They looked and talked like a bunch of surly, burned-out Republicans—still wondering why Hubert Humphrey didn't make it in '68 with his Politics of Joy.

Jesus, what a shock it was! The Hube always seemed like a Natural. But something went wrong . . . What was it?

The Democrats don't seem to know; or if they do they don't want to talk about it. They had a big fund-raising dinner for "the candidates" the other night at a ballroom in downtown Washington, but the people who went said it sucked. No candidates showed up—except Humphrey, and he couldn't stay for dinner. Gene McCarthy was introduced, but he didn't feel like talking. Ted Kennedy stayed for dinner, but nobody mentioned his name . . . and when the party broke up before midnight, the chairman was still looking for somebody who could *say something meaningful.* But nobody seemed to be ready—or none of the regulars, at least, and when it comes to party affairs, the regulars are the ones who do the talking.

People who went to the party—at $500 a head—said the crowd got strangely restive toward the end of the evening when it finally became apparent that nobody was going to say anything.

It was very unsettling, they said—like going to a pep rally with no cheerleaders. One report said Ted Kennedy "just sat there, looking very uncomfortable."

And so it goes. One of my last political acts, in Colorado, was to check in at the Pitkin County courthouse and change my registration from Democrat to Independent. Under Colorado law, I can vote in either primary, but I doubt if I'll find the time—and it's hard to say, right now, just what kind of mood I'll be in on November 7th.

Meanwhile, I am hunkered down in Washington—waiting for the next plane to anywhere and wondering what in the name of sweet jesus ever brought *me* here in the first place. This is not what us journalists call a "happy beat."

At first I thought it was me; that I was missing all the action because I wasn't plugged in. But then I began reading the press wizards who are plugged in, and it didn't take long to figure out that most of them were just filling space because their contracts said they had to write a certain amount of words every week.

8. Lawrence O'Brien was chairman of the Democratic National Committee.

At that point I tried talking to some of the people that even the wizards said "were right on top of things." But they all seemed very depressed; not only about the '72 election, but about the whole long-range future of politics and democracy in America.

Which is not exactly the kind of question we really need to come to grips with right now. The nut of the problem is that covering this presidential campaign is so fucking dull that it's just barely tolerable . . . and the only thing worse than going out on the campaign trail and getting hauled around in a booze-frenzy from one speech to another is having to come back to Washington and write about it.

Ciao,
Hunter

FROM ALAN RINZLER, STRAIGHT ARROW BOOKS:

In July 1970, major publisher Macmillan Co.'s pop-culture book editor, Alan Rinzler, had packed up his family and left New York for San Francisco, lured by Jann Wenner's risky offer of the number-two associate publisher slot at Rolling Stone*—plus stock options and control of the company's fledgling Straight Arrow Books division.*

March 3, 1972
San Francisco, CA

Dear Hunter:

I sent you those figures because you asked for them. Nobody's selling your contract. Find your enemies where they are, and do not thinkest evil unto your friends.

Kisses to you,
Alan Rinzler

TO ALAN RINZLER, STRAIGHT ARROW BOOKS:

Oscar Acosta had threatened Rolling Stone *with a libel lawsuit over Thompson's heavily fictionalized portrayal of the attorney as a drug-crazed "300-pound Samoan" in* Fear and Loathing in Las Vegas.

March 7, 1972
Woody Creek, CO

Alan:

No evil thinkest. But what I asked for (perhaps not too respectfully) was a *breakdown*—not just an amount. (I need to know where the $$$ is going.)

I assume you have some figures. Otherwise [Doug] Mount couldn't accuse me of spending "most of it for records."

That's what bugged me: not the letter (especially since I only recall *one* record purchase of $53 or so—at Tower in SF with Oscar).

That situation is looming very ugly. I spent today in NY with Silberman & the R.H. house lawyer, Joe Kraft—who is not inclined to either take risks or publish Libel. Nor is he inclined to pass the Vegas book until he knows what Oscar really wants.

I see no need to stress the potentially brutal fallout that would come from a cancellation or even a postponement of the book itself. The only way I can get this thing straight is to *talk* to Oscar.

Do you have an address or phone number for him? I'd appreciate a quick answer on this—& also a copy ASAP of the "Brown Buffalo" galleys.

Thanx,
HST

TO JANN WENNER, *ROLLING STONE*:

It wasn't the rain that left Thompson forlorn and poetic in his Miami hotel room on the eve of the Florida primary: on February 21, 1972, Richard M. Nixon had gone to China and opened U.S. relations with the Communist giant, a masterstroke of both foreign policy and domestic politics that further tightened the president's virtual lock on reelection.

Late March, 1972
Miami, FL
Campaign Trail

Dear Jann—

Cazart! . . . this fantastic rain outside: a sudden cloudburst, drenching everything. The sound of rain smacking down on my concrete patio about ten feet away from the typewriter, rain beating down on the surface of the big aqua-lighted pool out there across the lawn . . . rain blowing into the porch and whipping the palm fronds around in the warm night air.

Behind me, on the bed, my waterproof Sony says, "It's 5:28 right now in Miami. . . ." Then Rod Stewart's[9] hoarse screech: *"Mother don't you recognize your son . . . ?"*

Beyond the rain I can hear the sea rolling in on the beach. This atmosphere is getting very high, full of strange memory flashes. . . .

"Mother don't you recognize me now . . . ?"

Wind, rain, surf. Palm trees leaning in the wind, hard funk/blues on the radio, a flagon of Wild Turkey on the sideboard . . . are those footsteps outside? High heels running in the rain?

9. Gravel-voiced "mod" rock singer Rod Stewart.

Keep on typing . . . but my mind is not really on it. I keep expecting to hear the screen door bang open and then turn around to see Sadie Thompson[10] standing behind me, soaked to the skin . . . smiling, leaning over my shoulder to see what I'm cranking out tonight . . . then laughing softly, leaning closer; wet nipples against my neck, perfume around my head . . . and now on the radio:

"Wild Horses . . . We'll ride them some day. . . ."[11]

Perfect. Get it on. Don't turn around. Keep this fantasy rolling and try not to notice that the sky is getting light outside. Dawn is coming up and I have to fly to Mazatlán in five hours to deal with a drug-fugitive. Life is getting very complicated. After Mazatlán I have to rush back to San Francisco and get this gibberish ready for the printer . . . and then on to Wisconsin to chronicle the next act in this saga of Downers and Treachery called "The Campaign Trail."

Okay,
Hunter

FROM ALAN RINZLER, STRAIGHT ARROW BOOKS:

Straight Arrow Books published Oscar Acosta's Autobiography of a Brown Buffalo *in 1972.*

April 13, 1972
New York, NY

Dear Hunter,

Here is Oscar's book. You are referred to throughout as Damon Duke. Have a look and see if there's anything offensive or grossly inaccurate that you'd like us to change. Time is of the essence, naturally, so call me if there's any problem whatsoever.

Kisses,
Alan Rinzler

TO OSCAR ACOSTA:

Acosta's threats of a libel action continued to hold up publication of Fear and Loathing in Las Vegas.

April 15, 1972
Washington, D.C.

Oscar—

You stupid fuck; send me a mailing address so I can explain what's happening because of what you've done.

10. Sadie Thompson was the oft-drenched South Seas island trollop in W. Somerset Maugham's 1928 short story "Rain."

11. Quoted from the Rolling Stones song "Wild Horses," written by Mick Jagger and Keith Richards.

All talk of film sales *stopped,* for instance, the minute word got around that *Vegas* was tied up by some kind of mysterious legal problem. Nobody is especially curious about learning the details—all they know is that "the property is not free," or whatever terms they use.

At the moment I'm not sure what can be done about this—it's like being labeled, by Agnew, as "a known communist" while you're running for office. There's no way to spike it—because nobody wants to argue.

At least not for the record—although there is a fairly unanimous private agreement that the name Oscar Acosta now ranks alongside the name of that shithead who blew the whistle on Willie Sutton.[12]

You're a credit to your race, Oscar—just like they said at La Raza.

Anyway—the R.H. version is coming out with the original foto on the back—*Just like I had it laid out from the start.*

In other words, all you've managed to do is turn a possible best-seller into a "spooked property" that nobody wants to be a part of. And this is going to cost me about a year's income even on the book side—not counting whatever a film sale might have brought in.

I assume you had some excellent, long-stewing reason for doing this cheap, acid-crippled paranoid fuckaround. Remind me to make sure you're in the same cage with Clancy the next time I get into politics.

On other fronts, I want to assure you that your long-awaited autobiography will no doubt crack the literary world wide open. You'll get all the help you deserve when the time comes.

Good Luck,
HST

MEMO FROM THE NATIONAL AFFAIRS DESK:

An underdog even among the Democratic presidential aspirants of 1972, liberal South Dakota senator George McGovern eked out a surprising early victory in the April 4 Wisconsin primary, with George Wallace finishing second, ahead of Hubert Humphrey and Edmund Muskie.

April, 1972
Milwaukee, WI
Campaign Trail

Dear Jann—

I am feeling a little desperate about getting out of this hotel. Eight days in the Sheraton-Schroeder is like three months in the Cook County jail. The place

12. Colorful bank robber Willie Sutton nabbed an estimated $2 million by bluffing his way into bank vaults in guises including fireman, Western Union messenger, and policeman. Despite his many successful jailbreaks, Sutton spent most of his life behind bars.

is run by old Germans. The whole staff is German. Most of them speak enough English to make themselves understood in a garbled, menacing sort of way . . . and they are especially full of hate this week because the hotel has just been sold and the whole staff seems to think they'll be fired just as soon as the election crowd leaves.

So they are doing everything possible to make sure that nobody unfortunate enough to be trapped here this week will ever forget the experience. The room radiators are uncontrollable, the tubs won't drain, the elevators go haywire every night, the phones ring for no reason at all hours of the night, the coffee shop is almost never open, and about three days before the election the bar ran out of beer. The manager explained that they were "runnig oud ze inventory"—selling off everything in stock, including all the booze and almost every item on the menu except things like cabbage and sauerbraten. The first wave of complaints were turned aside with a hiss and a chop of the hand, but after two days and nights of this Prussian madness the manager was apparently caused to know pressure from forces beyond his control. By Friday the bar was stocked with beer again, and it was once more possible to get things like prime rib and sheep's head in the dining room.

But the root *ambience* of the place never changed. Dick Tuck, the legendary Kennedy advance man now working for McGovern, has stayed here several times in the past and calls it "the worst hotel in the world."

Ah yes . . . I can hear the Mojo Wire humming frantically across the room. [Tim] Crouse is stuffing page after page of gibberish into it. Greg Jackson, the ABC correspondent, had been handling it most of the day and whipping us along like Bear Bryant, but he had to catch a plane for New York and now we are left on our own.

The pressure is building up. The copy no longer makes sense. Huge chunks are either missing or too scrambled to follow from one sentence to another. Crouse just fed two consecutive pages into the machine upside-down, provoking a burst of angry yelling from whoever is operating the receiver out there on the Coast.

And now the bastard is beeping . . . beeping . . . beeping, which means it is hungry for this final page, which means I no longer have time to crank out any real wisdom on the meaning of the Wisconsin primary. But that can wait, I think. We have a three-week rest now before the next one of these goddamn nightmares . . . which gives me a bit of time to think about what happened here. Meanwhile, the only thing we can be absolutely sure of is that George McGovern is no longer the hopelessly decent loser that he has looked like up to now.

The real surprise of this campaign, according to Theodore White[13] on CBS-

13. Theodore H. White wrote the seminal *Making of the President* series of presidential campaign books.

TV last night, is that "George McGovern has turned out to be one of the great field organizers of American politics." But Crouse is dealing with that story, and the wire is beeping again. So this page will have to go, for good or ill . . . and the minute it finishes we will flee this hotel like rats from a burning ship.

Hunter

MEMO FROM THE NATIONAL AFFAIRS DESK:

McGovern's campaign strategy relied on the reforms that came out of the Democrats' bloody 1968 Chicago convention. The party's new delegate selection process, which McGovern had helped devise, ensured greater representation of African Americans and other minorities, women, and the new eighteen-to-twenty-one-year-old "youth vote," while limiting the clout of local party bosses, unions, and other political pros. Because the reforms also prompted more states to hold primaries to select their delegates, McGovern focused on getting the nomination by mobilizing a fresh grassroots coalition in those new primary states. The idea was to worry about taking on Nixon later—but charges by rival Democratic candidates Hubert Humphrey and Washington senator Henry "Scoop" Jackson that McGovern was soft on "amnesty, acid, and abortion" soured the party regulars whose support the eventual nominee would need in the general election.

May, 1972
Campaign Trail

Another Wednesday morning, another hotel room, another grim bout with the TV Morning News . . . and another post-mortem press conference scheduled for 10:00 A.M. Three hours from now. Call room service and demand two whole grapefruits, along with a pot of coffee and four glasses of V-8 juice.

These goddamn Wednesday mornings are ruining my health. Last night I came out of a mild Ibogaine coma just about the time the polls closed at eight. No booze on election day—at least not until the polls close; but they always seem to leave at least one loophole for serious juicers. In Columbus it was the bar at the airport, and in Omaha we had to rent a car and drive across the Missouri River to Council Bluffs, which is also across the state line into Iowa. Every year, on election day, the West End bars in Council Bluffs are jammed with boozers from Omaha.

Which is fine, for normal people, but when you drink all day with a head full of Ibogaine and then have to spend the next ten hours analyzing election returns . . . there will usually be problems.

Last week—at the Neil House Motor Hotel in Columbus, Ohio—some lunatic tried to break into my room at six in the morning. But fortunately I had a strong chain on the door. In every reputable hotel there is a sign above the knob that warns: "For Our Guests' Protection—Please Use Door Chain at All Times, Before Retiring."

I always use it. During four long months on the campaign trail I have had quite a few bad experiences with people trying to get into my room at strange hours—and in almost every case they object to the music. One out of three will also object to the typewriter, but that hasn't been the case here in Omaha. . . .

(PROPOSED PHOTO CAPTION)

Sen. George McGovern (D—S.D.), shown here campaigning in Nebraska where he has spent 23 hours a day for the past six days denying charges by local Humphrey operatives that he favors the legalization of Marijuana, pauses between denials to shake hands for photographers with his "old friend" Hunter S. Thompson, the National Correspondent for Rolling Stone *and author of* Fear and Loathing in Las Vegas, *who was recently identified by* Newsweek *magazine as a vicious drunkard and known abuser of hard drugs.*

A thing like that would have finished him here in Nebraska. No more of that "Hi, sheriff" bullshit; I am now the resident Puff Adder . . . and the problem is very real. In Ohio, which McGovern eventually lost, by a slim 19,000 vote margin, his handlers figure perhaps 10,000 of those were directly attributable to his public association with Warren Beatty,[14] who once told a reporter somewhere that he favored legalizing grass. This was picked up by that worthless asshole Sen. Henry Jackson (D—Wash.) and turned into a major issue.

So it fairly boggles the mind to think what Humphrey's people might do with a photo of McGovern shaking hands with a person who once ran for Sheriff of Aspen on the Freak Power ticket, with a platform embracing the use and frequent enjoyment of Mescaline by the Sheriff and all his Deputies at any hour of the day or night that seemed Right.

Ciao,
Hunter

TO JANN WENNER, *ROLLING STONE:*

Thompson's original plan had been to road-test a "genuinely hellish" Vincent Black Shadow motorcycle during his "off hours" while covering the California primary—"but serious problems developed." They had for McGovern, too: after leading Humphrey in the polls by as much as twenty percentage points just a week before the California vote, the South Dakota senator would come out on top by only five percent in the winner-take-all primary (for 271 delegates of the 1,509 needed to win).

14. Movie actor Warren Beatty organized fund-raising concerts by the Grateful Dead, Simon and Garfunkel, and Peter, Paul and Mary that brought some $1.5 million into George McGovern's 1972 presidential campaign.

June, 1972
Los Angeles, CA
Campaign Trail

Dear Jann—

Ten days before the election—with McGovern apparently so far ahead that most of the press people were looking for ways to *avoid* covering the final week—I drove out to Ventura, a satellite town just north of L.A. in the San Fernando Valley, to pick up the bugger and use it to cover the rest of the primary. Greg Jackson, an ABC correspondent who used to race motorcycles, went along with me. We were both curious about this machine. Chris Bunche, editor of *Choppers* magazine, said it was so fast and terrible that it made the extremely fast Honda 750 seem like a harmless toy.

This proved to be absolutely true. I rode a factory-demo Honda for a while, just to get the feel of being back on a serious road-runner again . . . and it seemed just fine: very quick, very powerful, very easy in the hands, one-touch electric starter. A very civilized machine, in all, and I might even be tempted to buy one if I didn't have the same gut distaste for Hondas that the American Honda management has for *Rolling Stone.* They don't like the image. "You meet the nicest people on a Honda," they say—but according to a letter from American Honda to the *Rolling Stone* ad manager, none of these *nicest people* have much stomach for a magazine like the *Stone.*

Which is probably just as well; because if you're a safe, happy, *nice,* young Republican you probably don't want to read about things like dope, rock music, and politics anyway. You want to stick with *Time,* and for weekend recreation do a bit of the laid-back street-cruising on your big fast Honda 750 . . . maybe burn a Sportster or a Triumph here & there, just for the *fun* of it: But nothing serious, because when you start that kind of thing you don't meet many *nice people.*

Jesus! Another tangent, and right up front, this time—the whole *lead,* in fact, completely fucked. What can I say? Last week I blew the whole thing. Total failure. Missed the deadline, no article, no wisdom, no excuse . . . Except one: Yes, I was savagely and expertly duped by one of the oldest con trips in politics.

By Frank Mankiewicz,[15] of all people. That scurvy, rumpled, treacherous little bastard . . . If I were running for President I would hire Mankiewicz to handle the press for me, but as a journalist I wouldn't shed a tear if I picked up tomorrow's paper and saw where nine thugs had caught poor Frank in an alley near the Capitol and cut off both of his Big Toes, making it permanently impossible for him to keep his balance for more than five or six feet in any direction.

15. Frank Mankiewicz joined the 1972 McGovern campaign as press secretary.

The image is horrible: Mankiewicz gets a phone call from Houston, saying the Texas delegation is on the verge of selling out to a Humphrey/Wallace coalition . . . he slams down the phone and lunges out of his cubicle in "McGovern for President" headquarters, bouncing off the door-jamb and then grabbing the Coke machine in order to stay upright—then lunging again into Rick Stearns'[16] *office to demand a detailed breakdown on the sex lives and bad debts of every member of the Texas delegation . . . then, trying to catch his breath, gasping for air from the terrible exertion, he finally lunges back down the hall to his own cubicle.*

It is very hard to walk straight with the Big Toes gone; the effect is sort of like taking the keel off a sailboat—it becomes impossibly top-heavy, wallowing crazily in the swells, needing outriggers to hold it upright . . . and the only way a man can walk straight with no Big Toes is to use a very complex tripod mechanism, five or six retractable aluminum rods strapped to each arm, moving around like a spider instead of a person.

Ah . . . this seems to be getting heavy. Very harsh and demented language. I have tried to suppress these feelings for more than a week, but every time I sit down at a typewriter they foam to the surface. So it is probably better—if for no other reason than to get past this ugly hang-up and into the rest of the article—to just blow it all out and take the weight off my spleen, as it were, with a brief explanation.

Morning again in downtown Los Angeles; dawn comes up on this city like a shitmist. Will it burn off before noon? Will the sun eventually poke through? That is the question they'll be asking each other down there on the Pool Terrace below my window a few hours from now. I'm into my eighteenth day as a resident of the Wilshire Hyatt House Hotel, and I am getting to know the dreary routine of this place pretty well.

Outside of that pigsty in Milwaukee, this may be the worst hotel in America. The Sheraton-Schroeder remains in a class of its own: Passive incompetence is one thing, but aggressive nazi hostility on the corporate level is something else again. The only thing these two hotels have in common is that the Sheraton (ITT) chain got rid of them: The Schroeder was sold to a local business magnate, and this grim hulk ended up as a part of the Hyatt House chain.

As far as I know there was no pool in the Schroeder. Maybe a big grease pit or a scum vat of some kind on the roof, but I never saw a pool. There were rumors of a military-style S&M gallery in the basement with maybe an ice water plunge for the survivors, but I never saw that one either. There was no way to deal with management personnel in the Schroeder unless your breath smelled heavily of sauerbraten . . . and in fact one of the happiest things about my life, these days, is that my memories of life in the Sheraton-Schroeder are becoming

16. Rick Stearns, in 1972 a twenty-eight-year-old Rhodes Scholar out of Stanford, was a top McGovern campaign strategist.

mercifully dim. The only open sore that remains from that relationship is the trouble I'm still having with the IBM typewriter-rental service in Milwaukee—with regard to the $600 Selectric Typewriter I left behind the desk when I checked out. It was gone when the IBM man came around to pick it up the next morning, and now they want me to pay for it.

Right. Another contribution to the Thousand Year Reich: "We will march on a road of bones. . . ." Tom Paxton wrote a song about it. And now I get these harsh letters from Milwaukee: "Herr Docktor Thompson—Der Typewriting machine you rented hass disappeared! And you vill of course pay!"

No. Never in hell. Because I have a receipt for that typewriter.

But first things first. We were talking about motorcycles. Jackson and I were out there in Ventura fucking around with a 750 Honda and an experimental prototype of the new Vincent—a 1000-cc brute that proved out to be so awesomely fast that I didn't even have time to get scared of it before I found myself coming up on a highway stoplight at ninety miles an hour and then skidding halfway through the intersection with both wheel-brakes locked.

A genuinely hellish bike. Second gear peaks around 65—cruising speed on the freeways—and third winds out somewhere between 95 and 100. I never got to fourth, which takes you up to 120 or so—and after that you shift into fifth.

Top speed is 140, more or less, depending on how the thing is tuned—but there is nowhere in Los Angeles County to run a bike like that. . . . I managed to get it back from Ventura to McGovern's downtown headquarters hotel, staying mainly in second gear, but the vibration almost fused my wrist bones and boiling oil from the breather pipes turned my right foot completely black. Later, when I tried to start it up for another test-run, the backlash from the kick-starter almost broke my leg. For two days afterward I limped around with a golfball-size blood-bruise in my right arch.

Later in the week I tried the bastard again, but it stalled on a ramp leading up to the Hollywood Freeway and I almost broke my hand when I exploded in a stupid, screaming rage and punched the gas tank. After that, I locked it up and left it in the parking lot—where it sat for many days with a MCGOVERN FOR PRESIDENT tag on the handlebars.

George never mentioned it, and when I suggested to Gary Hart[17] that the Senator might like to take the machine out for a quick test-ride and some photos for the national press, I got almost exactly the same reaction that Mankiewicz laid on me in Florida when I suggested that McGovern could pick up a million or so votes by inviting the wire-service photographers to come out and snap him lounging around on the beach with a can of beer in his hand and wearing my Grateful Dead T-shirt.

17. Future U.S. senator Gary Hart was McGovern's 1972 campaign manager.

Looking back on it, I think that was the moment when my relationship with Mankiewicz turned sour. Twenty-four hours earlier I had showed up at his house in Washington with what John Prine[18] calls "an illegal smile" on my face—and the morning after that visit he found himself sitting next to me on the plane to Florida and listening to some lunatic spiel about how his man should commit political suicide by irreparably identifying himself as the candidate of the Beachbums, Weirdos, and Boozers. . . .

How long, O Lord, how long? Where will it end?

All I ever wanted out of this grueling campaign was enough money to get out of the country and live for a year or two in peaceful squalor in a house with a big screen porch looking down on an empty white beach, with a good rich coral reef a few hundred yards out in the surf and *no neighbors.*

Ciao,
Hunter

TO JANN WENNER, *ROLLING STONE:*

In his 1977 autobiography, George McGovern cited his quip to the Washington press corps' annual Gridiron Club dinner in 1973: "Last year we opened the doors of the Democratic Party, as we promised we would, and twenty million Democrats stalked out." Then he added: "For years, I wanted to run for President in the worst possible way—and I'm sure I did!"

June, 1972
Campaign Trail

Dear Jann—

One of the first people I plan to speak with when I get to Miami is Larry O'Brien: shake both of his hands and extend powerful congratulations to him for the job he has done on the Party [as chairman of the Democratic National Committee]. In January of 1968 the Democratic Party was so fat and confident that it looked like they might keep control of the White House, the Congress, and in fact the whole U.S. Government almost indefinitely. Now, four and a half years later, it is a useless bankrupt hulk. Even if McGovern wins the Democratic nomination, the Party machinery won't be of much use to him, except as a vehicle.

"Traditional Politics with a Vengeance" is Gary Hart's phrase—a nutshell concept that pretty well describes the theory behind McGovern's amazingly effective organization.

"The Politics of Vengeance" is a very different thing—an essentially psychotic concept that Hart would probably not go out of his way to endorse.

18. Chicago-based folksinger and songwriter John Prine has thrived as one of rock's wittiest lyricists and most musically sophisticated composers.

Vehicle . . . vehicle . . . vehicle—a very strange-looking word, if you stare at it for eight or nine minutes. . . . "Skulking" is another interesting-looking word.

And so much for that.

The morning news says Wilbur Mills[19] is running for President again. He has scorned all invitations to accept the Number Two spot with anyone else—especially George McGovern. A very pressing bulletin. But Mills must know what he's doing. His name is said to be magic in certain areas. If the Party rejects McGovern, I hope they give it to Mills. That would just about make the nut.

Another depressing news item—out of Miami Beach this time—says an unnatural number of ravens have been seen in the city recently. Tourists have complained of being kept awake all night by "horrible croaking sounds" outside their hotel windows. "At first there were only a few," one local businessman explained. "But more and more keep coming. They're building big nests in the trees along Collins Avenue. They're killing the trees and their droppings smell like dead flesh."

Many residents say they can no longer leave their windows open at night, because of the croaking. "I've always loved birds," said another resident. "But these goddamn ravens are something else!"

Ponder the meaning,
Hunter

TO JANN WENNER, *ROLLING STONE:*

Before covering the Republican National Convention in Miami, Thompson advised Wenner to be straightforward in dealing with first-class writers such as himself.

August 2, 1972
Washington, D.C.

Jann . . .

OK, I got the Fontainebleau reservation and also the GOP credentials letter—so I plan to be in Miami again on Aug 18 or 19, until the 25th . . . or maybe the whole weekend, so I can write the piece before leaving. I suspect it might be disastrous to try and lose a day or so travelling, then write it someplace else. So I'll take the Mojo with me and plan on filing from Miami.

Let me know about Findlay. I'd like to have him along. He won't be much help to *me,* but I think he'd be a plus for *RS*. Especially if there's any violence—which is just about impossible for *one* person to cover. If I took the inside & Findlay took the outside, we could probably handle anything that comes up.

19. Arkansas Democrat Wilbur Mills was chairman of the U.S. House Ways and Means Committee from 1958 to 1974.

Regarding the questions of expenses: I'll take my chances with this Miami thing, on the assumption we can work out something on paper, inre: Who'll pay my tab for covering the rest of the campaign. Alan tells me I've already spent $18,602 of my own money—and I frankly don't see where I have much to gain by picking up my own tab the rest of the way . . . and I doubt if I'd have much trouble getting somebody else to pick it up, although bringing in a wild card at this point might lead to a certain amount of trouble vis-à-vis the Book. I could do it without violating the contract—7500 words a month, etc.—but probably not without creating some nasty legal problems with regard to the book.

I'd rather avoid this, but if we're going to have trouble on it, I'd rather have it sooner than later. So if we're heading for a nut-cutting scene, let's schedule it right after Miami. You're already on a nasty collision course with your notion that you can hire first-class writers and then treat them like junkie cub reporters. I've talked to enough people to get a pretty widespread feeling that *RS* is on the brink of a serious confrontation with itself—and although I feel nicely insulated from any flak or fallout when the crunch comes, I also share what appears to be a general concern for *RS*'s future good health . . . so it might be worthwhile to sit down sometime soon and have a sort of second annual WC Future Concepts conference.

Or maybe not. Whatever's Right . . .

Other items: I want the original *Vegas* manuscript for my permanent papers collection . . . and also that Stearns/Beach tape,[20] along with the un-edited transcription. I saw that notice on the B/Bd about how all staff-tapes must be turned in to the *RS* library, but once again the fact that *RS* pays none of my expenses on these stories makes me immune to all those Big Brother edicts. (Like they say, You Get What You Pay For—and, looking back on our relationship for the past year, I figure I've carried my end of the bargain pretty well—and all I can say to those lame cocksuckers who think my stuff is wasted space and a bad drag on their dinner schedules, is that I don't have the time right now to discuss their problems in print, but I expect to find as much time as I need sometime around December.)

Well shit . . . I see I'm getting a bit on the nasty side, here, so I'll cut the thing off.

Except for one more matter: I don't recall exactly when we agreed on that *salary raise* from $12K to $15K, but I remember it was a week or so before the Calif. primary, & when I added it up at the rate of $50 a week—it came to exactly $1000 as of Nov. 7. (Five months at roughly $200 per—which means you

20. Thompson's "Stearns/Beach tape" of his conversation with Rick Stearns and fellow McGovern confidant Bill Dougherty was recorded in Miami on Saturday, July 15, two days after the close of the 1972 Democratic National Convention. A near-verbatim transcript appears in the July 1972 section of *Fear and Loathing: On the Campaign Trail '72*.

already owe me $400, with $600 to come.) I'm not especially anxious to have it all right now, but I'd like a letter from you, confirming the agreement.

There's also the matter of how that Fla/Boohoo segment turned up in Charley's book without permission from—or either credit or payment to—the author, but I guess we can let that one slide for a while.

Anyway . . . sorry to sound so testy, but the current atmosphere seems to call for it, and I think it's better to deal with these problems while they're still minor; and also while I can still afford to admit that I've fucked up a few times, myself. My head is fairly well balanced these days, and I'd just as soon keep it that way.

OK,
Hunter

MEMO FROM THE NATIONAL AFFAIRS DESK:

The July 10–13 Democratic National Convention in Miami had gone wrong in many ways, and things got worse for McGovern from there. His choice of Missouri senator Thomas Eagleton as his running mate turned disastrous within two weeks, when imminent press reports forced the vice presidential candidate to announce that he had indeed spent time in mental hospitals on three occasions, twice receiving electroshock therapy. McGovern made matters worse by declaring that he stood behind Eagleton "a thousand percent," even while scrambling to dump him. He dropped Eagleton in favor of Kennedy-by-marriage Sargent Shriver, the former head of JFK's Peace Corps and LBJ's Office of Economic Opportunity, who was so inoffensive that Republican president Richard Nixon had let him stay on as U.S. ambassador to France until 1970.

August, 1972
Campaign Trail

Indeed. It made fine sense, on paper, and I recall making that same argument, myself, a few months back—but I'd no sooner sent it on the Mojo Wire than I realized it made no sense at all. There was something finally and chemically wrong with the idea of Ted Kennedy running for *vice* president; it would be like the Jets trading Joe Namath to the Dallas Cowboys as a sub for Roger Staubach.[21]

Which might make excellent sense, from some angles, but Namath would never consent to it—for the same reasons Kennedy wouldn't put his own presidential ambitions in limbo for eight years, behind McGovern or anyone else. Superstar politicians and superstar quarterbacks have the same kind of delicate egos, and people who live on that level grow accustomed to very thin, rarified

21. 1969 and 1972 Super Bowl MVPs respectively, Joe Namath played quarterback for the New York Jets and L.A. Rams from 1965 to 1977, Roger Staubach for the Dallas Cowboys from 1969 through 1979. Staubach was the NFC's leading passer five times between 1971 and 1979; Namath never was, in either NFL conference.

air. They have trouble breathing in the lower altitudes; and if they can't breathe right, they can't function.

The ego is the crucial factor here, but ego is a hard thing to put on paper—especially on that 3 × 5 size McGovern recommends. File cards are handy for precinct canvassing, and for people who want to get heavy into the Dewey Decimal System, but they are not much good for cataloguing things like Lust, Ambition, or Madness.

This may explain why McGovern blew his gig with Kennedy. It was a perfectly rational notion—and that was the flaw, because a man on the scent of the White House is rarely rational. He is more like a beast in heat: a bull elk in the rut, crashing blindly through the timber in a fever for something to fuck. Anything! A cow, a calf, a mare—any flesh and blood beast with a hole in it. The bull elk is a very crafty animal for about fifty weeks of the year; his senses are so sharp that only an artful stalker can get within a thousand yards of him . . . but when the rut comes on, in the autumn, any geek with the sense to blow an elk-whistle can lure a bull elk right up to his car in ten minutes if he can drive within hearing range.

The dumb bastards lose all control of themselves when the rut comes on. Their eyes glaze over, their ears pack up with hot wax, and their loins get heavy with blood. Anything that sounds like a cow elk in heat will fuse the central nervous systems of every bull on the mountain. They will race through the timber like huge cannonballs, trampling small trees and scraping off bloody chunks of their own hair on the unyielding bark of the big ones. They behave like sharks in a feeding frenzy, attacking each other with all the demented violence of human drug dealers gone mad on their own wares.

A career politician finally smelling the White House is not much different from a bull elk in the rut. He will stop at nothing, trashing anything that gets in his way; and anything he can't handle personally he will hire out—or, failing that, make a deal. It is a difficult syndrome for most people to understand, because few of us ever come close to the kind of Ultimate Power and Achievement that the White House represents to a career politician.

The presidency is as far as he can go. There is no more. The currency of politics is power, and once you've been the Most Powerful Man in the World for four years, everything else is downhill—except four more years on the same trip.

Ciao,
Hunter

FROM JOHN CHANCELLOR, NBC NEWS:

NBC News correspondent John Chancellor had a minor quibble with something Thompson had written in his August 17, 1972, Rolling Stone *piece on the Democratic Convention, "Fear and Loathing in Miami: Old Bulls Meet the Butcher."*

August 11, 1972
New York, NY

Dear Hunter,

Because we share a fear and loathing for things which aren't true, I point out that it ain't true that I was taken in by the McGoverns on the South Carolina challenge in Miami Beach.

While they were still switching votes, I said on the air that they might be trying to lose it deliberately. We had the floor people try to check this out and they ran into a couple of poolroom liars employed by McGovern who said yas, yas, it was a defeat, etc., but a little while later Doug Kiker[22] got Pat Lucey[23] to tell it all. (Lucey called headquarters for permission, first, as Kiker waited.)

We were pleased that we got it right. Adam Clymer of the [Baltimore] *Sun* called the next day with congratulations. I think the reason most people thought we blew the story is that CBS blew it badly. I guess I should have gone through the night pointing out what happened, but we got involved in the California roll-call and a lot of other stuff, and suddenly it was dawn.

Other than that I enjoyed your convention piece and let's have a double Margarita when we next meet.

J. Chancellor

TO JOHN CHANCELLOR, NBC NEWS:

Thompson replied to Chancellor regarding the unorthodox behavior of certain members of the '72 campaign press corps.

September 11, 1972
Woody Creek, CO

Dear John . . .

You filthy skunk-sucking bastard! What kind of gall would prompt you to write me a letter like that sac of pus dated Aug. 11? I checked your story—about how NBC had the South Carolina trip all figured out—with Mrs. Lucey (Pat wouldn't talk to me, for some reason), and she said both you & Kiker were so fucked up . . . that you both kept calling it "the South Dakota challenge," despite her attempts to correct you. She was baffled by your behavior, she said, until Mankiewicz told her about you. . . .Then, about an hour later, Bill Daughtery (sp?)[24] found Kiker on his knees in the darkness outside McGovern's command trailer, apparently trying to choke himself with his own hands . . . but, when Bill grabbed him, Kiker said he was trying to un-screw his head from what he called his "neck-pipe," so he could "check the wiring" in his own brain.

22. Douglas Kiker was a political correspondent for NBC News.
23. McGovern supporter Pat Lucey was the governor of South Carolina.
24. Longtime McGovern adviser Bill Dougherty was South Dakota's Democratic lieutenant governor.

But I guess you wouldn't remember that episode, eh? Fuck no, you wouldn't! . . . I'm heading east in a few days, and I think it's about time we got this evil shit cleared away. Your deal is about to go down, John. You can run, but you can't hide. See you soon. . . .

Hunter S. Thompson

TO JANN WENNER, *ROLLING STONE:*

After two weeks at home recuperating from the Republican National Convention in Miami in late August, Thompson began bracing himself to "go out on the campaign trail with Richard Nixon, to watch him waltz in—if only to get the drift of his thinking, to watch the moves, his eyes."

September 11, 1972
Woody Creek, CO

Jann . . .

I was ready for all the standard-brand Secret Service bullshit. The only thing that worried me was that maybe some of the SS boys might have seen the current *Rolling Stone*—which was available that week at newsstands all over Washington. It contained, along with my calm and well-reasoned analysis of the recent GOP convention in Miami, some of the most brutal and hateful caricatures of Richard Nixon ever committed to print, in this country or any other.

That crazy bastard Steadman! Why is it that it's always your friends who cause you to be screwed to the wall? What do you say when you go across town to the White House to apply for press credentials to cover the Nixon campaign as the National Affairs Editor of *Rolling Stone* and the first thing you see when you walk through the door of the press office is one of Steadman's unconscionably obscene Nixon/Agnew drawings tacked up on the bulletin board with a big red circle around Ralph's name?

"Well . . . ah . . . yes. Ho ho, eh? My name is . . . ah . . . . . . Thompson, from *Rolling Stone,* and I'm here to pick up my credentials to fly around the country with President Nixon on Air Force One for the next month or so."

Cold stare from the man at the desk. No handshake offered.

"Well . . . Ho ho, eh? I can't help but notice you've been admiring the work of my friend Ralph Steadman. Ho ho, he sure has an eye for it, eh? Sure does. Good ole Ralph." Sad smile and shrug of the shoulders. "Crazy as a loon, of course. Terminal brain syphilis." Keep smiling, another shrug. "Jesus, what can you do, eh? These goddamn vicious limeys will do anything for money. He was paid *well* for these rotten drawings. My protests were totally ignored. It's a fucking shame, I say. What the hell is the world coming to when the goddamn British can get away with stuff like this?"

Ciao,
Hunter

TO RALPH STEADMAN:

British artist Ralph Steadman had turned in a series of particularly apt and hideous drawings of the President to illustrate Thompson's September 28, 1972, Rolling Stone *coverage of the Republican National Convention, "Fear and Loathing in Miami: Nixon Bites the Bomb."*

September 11, 1972
Woody Creek, CO

Ralph . . .

You illiterate bastard. I had to send your letter to an interpreter to figure out what kind of "ecology book" you were talking about. Needless to say, I'd like to work with you on it—but anything involving a lengthy text is out of the question for at least six months. I have a '72 Campaign book due on Jan 1, and after that another book for Random House. But if you can get by with a series of captions, instead of a full-length text, I can probably manage to do it—providing you can arrange to have me flown over to London for at least two weeks, so we can lash our ideas together.

To that end, I spoke with Jim Silberman—editor in chief at Random House—about your ideas, and he said he would contact Jonathan Cape[25] & see what they had in mind. I've also mentioned it to my agent, Lynn Nesbit . . . and between them they should be able to make sense of the thing.

As for Straight Arrow (*Rolling Stone*'s book publishing arm), I would not at this time be inclined to deal with them under any circumstances—with the possible exception of a huge advance in the form of gold bullion. I suspect Alan Rinzler and Sidney Zion were weaned on the same ugly tit, and Wenner acts more & more like Hinckle with every passing day.

Under the circumstances, I don't want to go into detail on this—but until we can talk personally I advise you to be very wary of making any long-term contract agreements with either one of them.

OK for now. I assume you'll hear something shortly from Cape, inre: Silberman & Random House. Meanwhile, that Nixon stuff was a first-class horror from start to finish . . . and the center-spread was so bad that I'll no doubt be barred from coming anywhere near Nixon for the duration of the campaign.

But what the hell? I only have to do 4 more columns, and then 6 weeks on the book . . . and then a nice rest. But I like the *idea* of your twisted ecology book, so why not send me some details? Or at least one. OK for now . . .

Hunter

25. Jonathan Cape was Steadman's prospective British book publisher.

TO PAUL SCANLON, *ROLLING STONE:*

Low-key former Wall Street Journal *reporter Paul Scanlon was managing editor of* Rolling Stone.

September 11, 1972
Woody Creek, CO

Paul . . .

I just talked to Gary Hart again, & now he wants to *rent* my car until election day, instead of buying it. Last week he was ready to spring for $2250, quick cash. Should America's top political reporter read anything into that switch? Would you?

Anyway, Hart's disturbing turnaround removes my most pressing reason for flying to Washington today. (Crouse will be there tomorrow, to pick up the car & put it into a garage until I can get there in a few days.) My other pressing reason—the idea that I might beat the Steadman centerfold to the White House—has also gone by the boards. The deskman at the *NY Times* D.C. bureau had already either seen or heard about it on Saturday, which means G. Warren[26] can't be far behind. So I assume there's no hurry now; the bastards will be ready for me when I show up—waving the goddamn thing in my eyes.

I have a new plan, but it's too complicated to explain now, so I'll call ASAP. Meanwhile, I think what I'll do is write a short sort of Pause & Reflection piece for this issue—2500 to 3500 words—and then go to Wash. this weekend for a 5 or 6 day visit with the Nixon crowd & a long piece for the issue after this one. The Crouse/Press job should be just about enough politics this time, anyway—and if that won't make the nut, you can always ask Alan to tap The Creator of Gonzo Journalism for a few thousand sparkling words. (My only real regret, at this point, is that I never got around to conning Alan into publishing a book on Volvos by Tyler Knapp.[27] Considering his now-legendary tapeworm-appetite for swill, Knapp's tome would have been a natural for him—resulting in massive lawsuits that would have caused Straight Arrow to explode like a lump of magnesium in firewater. . . . Ah, these missed opportunities; but perhaps I can make it up to him in a few months.)

Anyway, considering the circumstances I think I'll take it easy this week. Figure on a (printed) page or so by the weekend, but nothing serious. As for art, I think we can get off with one photo: it appeared in that post-convention issue of *Newsweek*—a shot of Nixon doing the Humphrey handshake with one of his youth freaks. Call me if you have trouble locating it.

OK for now. Tell Findlay I thought his Miami piece was excellent; it's about time *RS* had some first-class real journalism, instead of all this crazy bullshit. . . .

26. Gerald L. Warren was deputy press secretary in the Nixon White House.
27. Dapper and gentlemanly Tyler "Ted" Knapp was the Scripps-Howard newspaper chain's innocuous top political reporter and a onetime Ralph "Nader Raider."

And the next time you worthless sybarites feel the need for a whipping boy, I suggest you look around for somebody besides [David] Felton. He's not only the best writer on the SF staff, but also the best editor. He did a hell of a job putting that monster of mine together. One of these days somebody out there is going to have to confront the question of why all the best talents who've ever worked for *RS* have either quit in a rage or been fired.

Nothing personal here. I'm just talking off the top of my head at 7:26 A.M. Let me know when you'll be in Aspen. I'd like to talk about some of these things. OK . . .

Hunter

MEMO FROM THE SPORTS DESK:

Toward the end of Fear and Loathing: On the Campaign Trail '72, *Thompson would concede of McGovern's effort that "If George gets stomped in November, it will not be because of anything Richard Nixon did to him," but because the candidate went along with the conventional wisdom that he had to abandon the mostly young, antiwar grassroots coalition that gave him the nomination and "swiftly move to consolidate the one he'd just shattered: the . . . senile remnants of the Democratic Party's once-powerful 'Roosevelt coalition.'"*

September, 1972
Washington, D.C.

From: Raoul Duke
To: Hunter S. Thompson
Subject: CAMPAIGN '72

Dear HST:

I've been meaning to write this note for a long time, but numerous financial problems have made my life difficult & until yesterday I didn't have time for fucking around with dilettante sports like Politics. But yesterday I came across a three-day-old copy of *The Washington Post* (9/7/72) and I was jolted to the point of bad craziness by a headline on page A6 that said:

"McGovern Plans Touring in Tandem With Party Stars"

The nut of the story had to do with McGovern's new campaign plan—apparently lashed together by Fred Dutton[28] and Frank Mankiewicz—to spruce up his crippled campaign by making a series of joint appearances with what *Post* reporter Bill Greider called "other big stars of the Democratic party."

28. Washington lawyer Fred Dutton, a close adviser to Robert F. Kennedy in his 1968 presidential campaign, was a top aide to McGovern in 1972.

The only one currently under contract, as it were, was said to be Ted Kennedy, who agreed to campaign with McGovern in "nine industrial cities of the Midwest and East." I caught his act on the *CBS Evening News* last week: He was in Albany, NY, making fun of Nelson Rockefeller.[29] But he looked and sounded so much like Sargent Shriver that I didn't even realize it was Kennedy until the news spot was over and [CBS anchorman Walter] Cronkite did the ID. Granted, I have a cheap set & the picture's a little ragged—but I still could have sworn it was Shriver. I don't recall much of what he said, but I think most of it had to do with getting rid of Nelson—or maybe it was Nixon.

But what the hell? That wasn't what I wanted to ask you about, anyway.

The thing that really horrified me was a paragraph in Greider's story that said: "After (Kennedy), McGovern's campaign organizers hope to arrange similar dual schedules with some other big names—Sen. Hubert Humphrey, Sen. Edmund Muskie and perhaps Sen. Thomas Eagleton, the man who was dropped as McGovern's running mate."

Jesus!

What the hell is McGovern thinking about?

According to the *Post,* he plans "to appear with Humphrey in California, where the two men were at each other's throats last June when they were campaigning in the California primary." Mankiewicz seemed to like the idea, calling it "a great crowd gatherer" . . . and Dutton defended it on the grounds that "the pluses are overwhelmingly stronger than the minuses."

Well . . . Mankiewicz has nursed his strange act through many hazards this year, but now he is pushing his luck right out to the edge. Only a fucking lunatic, or worse, would talk publicly about going into California with a McGovern-Humphrey routine. It sounds like a scene out of *The Magic Christian.*[30] A word like "demented" is not strong enough for it. The idea of George McGovern and Hubert Humphrey necking in front of big crowds up and down the West Coast goes beyond dementia to the brink of obscenity and stone sickness.

Here is one of the three states McGovern must win—along with New York and Illinois—and also one of his potentially strongest states, because of the massive College/Youth vote . . . so his California strategy is to seize those electoral votes by blitzing the state "in tandem" with Hubert Humphrey, the one politician in America more despised than Richard Nixon among anti-war College/Youth voters.

Hubert is big in Omaha, Philly and St. Petersburg—but in California he

29. Nelson Rockefeller, governor of New York from 1959 to 1973, was an unsuccessful candidate for the Republican presidential nomination in 1960, 1964, and 1968. Gerald R. Ford would appoint him vice president in 1974.

30. *The Magic Christian,* starring Peter Sellers, was British director Joseph McGrath's hilarious 1969 movie adaptation of Terry Southern's manic novel.

sucks wind. His role, in that primary, was to function as a sort of transvestite stand-in for George Meany and Richard Nixon. If George Wallace had been on the ballot in California—and if he'd been able to campaign there like he did in Wisconsin and Michigan and Pennsylvania—Humphrey would have finished a bent third, instead of second.

Even in California his strength was deceptive. He pulled just over 40%—but it was essentially an anti-McGovern vote, not pro-Humphrey. With the help of his friend Lorne Greene,[31] he managed to convince thousands of elderly Jews around Los Angeles that McGovern planned to send them to The Showers the moment he got elected . . . and with the help of the old union bosses, he convinced more thousands of insecure aerospace workers that a McGovern victory would put them on permanent welfare.

This was the Democratic "fear vote"—a disorganized *negative* mass, hunkered down in the suburbs and screeching fearfully at each other: "No! No! If it's anything new, we don't want it!" These useless slugs would have voted just as readily for Judge Crater as they did for Hubert Humphrey . . . but the Judge was not on the ballot, and Hubert was; so the California vote came down, in the end, to a sort of unspoken trial run for the same ABM ("Anybody But McGovern") movement that Humphrey himself led at the convention in Miami, a month later.

***

So what will be the effect of a brief and awkward McGovern-Humphrey alliance, against Nixon, in California less than six months after that savage primary? Will Hubert's appearance somehow deliver the Jews and the riveters back to McGovern? Or will the shameless hypocrisy of the George & Hubert Show cause McGovern's original hard-core supporters to wonder what in hell the primary was all about in the first place?

Perhaps Dutton and Mankiewicz are right about Humphrey's latent pulling power in California, but I doubt it. Their theory derives from LBJ's 1964 idea that any contest between the Right and the Center automatically co-opts the Left voters for the "centrist."

But that is no longer necessarily true. It worked nicely for Johnson in '64, but in '68 it failed. Not entirely—but enough to cost Humphrey the election. Most political wizards agree that George Wallace was the man who made the '68 election such a cliff-hanger. His 15% (check this figure)[32] came mainly from Nixon's nut, they say. And no doubt they're right. But the Cleaver/Gre-

31. Canadian actor Lorne Greene starred as Ponderosa ranch patriarch Ben Cartwright in NBC's TV Western *Bonanza* from 1959 to 1973.

32. American Independent candidate George C. Wallace won 13.6 percent of the popular vote for president in 1968.

gory vote—roughly 2% (?)[33]—took just enough votes from Humphrey to put Nixon into the White House, whether that was wise, etc. . . . ?

***

(Jump to McGov staff reaction against press . . . then to real reasons . . . NJ girl Joe Kraft[34] Hump quote . . . the problem with McGov is that he might sink the idea of the New Politics without ever really representing it . . . like Lindsay (recall Morgan comment about my advice)[35]

TO JANN WENNER, *ROLLING STONE:*

Top McGovern campaign strategist and pollster Patrick Caddell had come up with new data he claimed showed the Democratic cause might not be as hopeless as it looked. He wrote up his analysis and gave it to Thompson to consider for publication in Rolling Stone.

September 17, 1972
Woody Creek, CO

Dear Jann:

I have just finished Caddell's article & agree with Paul [Scanlon] that it's essentially a piece of unconvincing propaganda—but I think we should print the fucker anyway. Pat is a key figure in the McGovern machinery, so his thinking—right or wrong—is definitely worth having.

Whether we agree with it or not is beside the point. The Stearns-Dougherty tape had a lot of stuff in it that I didn't agree with, but I think it was an important document & definitely worth printing.

Further, I think we should offer McGovern a full page, *free,* in every issue between now and the election. As far as I'm concerned he has a pretty weak goddamn case, but I think we should give him a chance to make it—especially in *RS,* because everything he's done since Miami has been subject to criticism by various *RS* writers, including me, and I suppose it's possible we've all been wrong.

So why don't we just give him a "house ad" in every issue from now until Nov 7? Let him do whatever he wants with it: solicit funds, denounce drugs, praise Muskie, etc. . . . whatever he wants.

Needless to say, we'll reserve all rights to comment, whenever necessary, on the content of the ads . . . Or at least *I* will.

33. Left-fringe 1968 presidential candidates Eldridge Cleaver and Dick Gregory—both representing the Peace and Freedom Party—tallied 0.01 and 0.06 percent of the popular vote, respectively.
34. Joseph Kraft was a syndicated Washington-based newspaper columnist.
35. Tom Morgan, New York mayor John Lindsay's press secretary, told Thompson late in the summer of 1972, "We all admired that stuff you wrote about the Lindsay blueprint. But there was one thing you didn't know—there was no Lindsay blueprint. There wasn't even any Lindsay strategy. We just winged it all the way from the start."

Anyway, let's print the article. If nothing else, it might serve as a good evidence/exhibit after the election. It also might work in the book . . . so somebody should probably check on getting the *rights*, etc.

OK for now. I have no plans to come to California anytime soon—unless McGov follows thru on his rumored plan to campaign out there with Humphrey. If that happens, I'll definitely make the trip. A horror like that would just about wrap the thing up for me, I think. With a little luck, maybe they'll bring Al Barkan[36] along, too. I look forward to that one.

Hunter

TO JANN WENNER, *ROLLING STONE:*

Dissatisfied with his treatment at Rolling Stone*—and particularly his relegation to the lesser media's raucous but remote "Zoo Plane" throughout the 1972 presidential campaign—after the election Thompson resigned from the magazine, and took Raoul Duke with him.*

November 27, 1972
Woody Creek, CO

Dear Jann:

For a variety of reasons too tangled to explain at this time, this letter is my official resignation from the staff of *Rolling Stone*—effective immediately (Monday, Nov 27, 1972). It is also the official resignation of Raoul Duke, whose name—along with my own—should be removed from the masthead at once, beginning with the first *RS* press-date in December '72.

Don't read any malice or strange fit of drug-anger into this; it merely formalizes the existing situation and confirms my status as a free-lance writer, vis-à-vis *RS*. My resignation (and Duke's) from the staff will have no effect on the Final Campaign article or the Campaign '72 book for Straight Arrow.

Perhaps we can come to some *contractual* work agreement for 1973. If you have any ideas on this score, by all means send them along—to me, John Clancy, Lynn Nesbit, or all three.

OK for now,
Hunter S. Thompson

TO MORTON DEAN, CBS NEWS:

Morton Dean was a respected political correspondent for CBS News. Richard Nixon had been reelected in a landslide with 60.7 percent of the popular vote, carrying forty-nine states and winning 521 electoral votes to George McGovern's 17. The "youth vote" the Democrats had counted on failed to turn out: fewer

36. Al Barkan was right-hand man to AFL-CIO chief George Meany.

than half of America's newly enfranchised eighteen to twenty-one-year-olds voted, and those who did split evenly between Nixon and McGovern.

December 17, 1972
Woody Creek, CO

Mort:

The closest I've come to NYC in recent weeks was last Thursday when Mankiewicz & I spent 20 minutes circling Times Square in a tiny chartered plane with a pilot who kept saying "Hell, as long as we're stuck in the pattern let's have some fun, eh?" I was sitting up in the cockpit with him, so I dug it. We came so low on TSq that I felt I could reach down & touch people. Very weird. Frank was back in the cabin & not especially happy with our standing on the wing & buzzing junkies, etc. . . . but what the fuck?

Anyway, I'm desperate right now to get some Election Turnout figures for Nov 7, & I understand CBS did a survey that's available to the public. My book deadline is Jan 15 & one of the most crucial unanswered questions in my mind is *Whether or Not the Potential McGovern Vote Came Out.* I figure this has a huge bearing on any future "new politics" campaigns . . . and I need some help on these FIGURES. Can you send me anything? I'll consider it a huge & repayable favor. Let me know ASAP.

I've been dealing with Desmond Smith & Hughes Rudd in re: a piece of some kind on me or at least something vaguely connected with me for the past few weeks, but I don't know enough about what's happening to tell you anything. In any case, I'll call when I get to NYC in January.

Thanx—
Hunter

TO SANDY BERGER:

Samuel R. "Sandy" Berger was a McGovern speechwriter who had stayed with the campaign since the South Dakotan's surprising showing in the Florida primary back in March 1972. Berger would go on to become a member of Jimmy Carter's administration and White House national security adviser under the next Democratic president, Bill Clinton.

December 17, 1972
Woody Creek, CO

Sandy . . .

Sorry I didn't get hold of you in the 2 or 3 days after our tequila dinner at La Fonda . . . but I was heavily preoccupied in various ways, including a postmortem talk with McGov & then missing the plane to fly out to SD with him.

So I fucked up . . . but what the hell?

Anyway, it just occurs to me that if you're looking for someplace to practice law for a while you might give a thought to Colorado—and specifically Aspen. We just elected our only two friendly anti-establishment lawyers to the County Commission, so now we're faced with a sort of implied conflict of interest every time we have to deal with the power structure; or anything else, for that matter, since both these poor bastards are still identified with my Freak Power campaign.

In other words, we need a new & at least apparently neutral mouthpiece. I couldn't guarantee you anything for starters except instant action & a weird clientele. Aspen is heavily over-stocked with lawyers & always has been, but personal madness & professional incompetence are the only dominant characteristics of the whole lot & most people understand this.

Success has fucked us, in a way; it's hard for me to cope with the idea that my personal attorney & erstwhile mescaline dealer is now a County Commissioner.

Which is neither here nor there, for right now. Just a weird idea you might want to think about . . . and there's also the fact that I'm thinking seriously about running for the Senate against Dominick[37] in '74. In a week or so I'll drive over to Denver for a chat or so with Gary Hart & Dick Lamm,[38] among others, about how to handle a weird gig like that. I have a feeling it's about time somebody rammed the fat straight into the fire on the national politics level: no more of this coalition/compromise bullshit—just offer up the symbol of The Hammer & say "OK folks, here it is, & if you're too fucking lazy or stupid to use it in your own interest, then bend over & grab your ankles & don't bitch about what happens after that."

The only people I've talked to at any serious length about this (Senate race) gig are Rick Stearns & Carl Wagner,[39] who both seem sort of abstractly interested & that means to me I'm about 40% home . . . the other 60% would be you, Eli & Pokorny.[40]

(& just for the record, that's *my* list of five)

But what the fuck? It's 5:17 A.M. right now & the radio says McGov is calling Nixon a liar in re: Vietnam . . . a fearful surprise, eh? Who would have guessed it?

I am coming more & more to grips with the notion that getting on the Zoo Plane permanently fucked up my life—and the only way to redeem myself is by seizing a seat in the U.S. Senate.

So what all this boils down to, as always, is a sort of crab-wise move in the direction of self-interest—which is only another definition of Politics, as I see

37. Republican Peter Dominick was one of Colorado's incumbent U.S. senators.

38. Colorado Democrats Gary Hart and Richard Lamm would be elected U.S. senator and governor, respectively, in 1974.

39. George McGovern called 1972 campaign aide Carl Wagner "one of the best field organizers in the business."

40. Gene Pokorny, who had worked for Eugene McCarthy's 1968 campaign, and Eli Segal were two of McGovern's key managers in 1972.

it—so if the idea of moving to Aspen & becoming the local Freak-Lawyer interests you, let me know & I'll pursue it a bit further.

If not, keep me posted as to your movements (write c/o *Rolling Stone* in San Francisco or this Owl Farm Address) . . . and let me know if I can crank up any personal highs on whatever you get into . . . Which still strikes me as the only true definition of What It's All About.

As for my own gig, I seem to be on the verge of signing another one-year contract as the National Affairs Editor of *Rolling Stone* . . . but this time with total control over whatever stories I choose to do (when, where, etc.), which means I can go just about anywhere I want to, for any reason that seems right, and work out on any asshole I can fix in my sights . . .

. . . and that's not a bad gig, considering what's available.

So . . . let me know what kind of drift you get into. If coming out here interests you at all, I'll do everything I can to make it work . . . but if not, well, I figure whatever you get into should be worth a look from time to time . . . so I figure we'll be crossing paths one way or another sometime soon.

On balance, I figure the McGov thing was A Botch. We can do a lot better. The Weight is out there, just waiting to be picked up & focused. If you have any good ideas, let me know. I figure my basic education is just about complete now . . . & I'm ready for The Main Crank. Kilroy died a long time ago. When the graffiti freaks start getting it on 10 years from now (or even 5) I'd like to think they'll be writing "Thompson Was Here."

Right. Even if we lose in the end, I want to leave the bastards a scare they'll never forget . . . when they reach down to scratch their swollen stomachs, I want them to feel a long blue lump with an itch that won't go away. The idea of losing doesn't bother me particularly, but the next time we lose—& I wouldn't even be thinking about running for the Senate if I thought we couldn't win—I'd like it to be for the right reasons, & not in the kind of confused haze that still haunts the McGov campaign.

If we really are a Nation of Pigs, let's make the bastards admit it. No excuses, no cop-outs—just back the bastards into a corner and make them say it.

If nothing else, it would be a king-hell Bitch of a campaign—one of those special gigs where you could always look back & say "Yeah, but there was *one time* when we really got it on."

Shit . . . I seem to be lapsing into a stone politics pitch here, and that wasn't what I had in mind when I started.

So I'll quit & go to bed; hopefully in time to get up & do some cross-country skiing before the sun goes.

Meanwhile, let me know how you're thinking. Call my home phone, but don't give the number to anybody . . . and especially not to Ted Van Dyk,[41] be-

41. Ted Van Dyk was another earnest young McGovern campaign staffer.

cause I'm about to libel that worthless pimp bastard in the heaviest language I can conjure up & still stay out of court.

OK for now. Hello to Susan & good luck with the baby. If you feel like stopping out for a look at the place, feel welcome anytime after Jan 15 or so. Until then I'll be locked into total speed-work on the campaign book (Number 21, as I recall) . . . but as I look around at the competition I don't feel especially bothered.

Cazart,
Hunter

MEMO FROM THE SPORTS DESK: FROM HUNTER S. THOMPSON
TO: JOHN CLANCY AND JANN WENNER
IN RE: 1973 HST/DUKE WRITING CONTRACT WITH *RS*

Too shrewd to accept his star writer's resignation, Wenner had instead offered Thompson the upper-masthead title of National Affairs Editor of Rolling Stone.

December 19, 1972
Woody Creek, CO

In general I think we're about settled on all the main points, but one or two questions remain—and one of them seems at least potentially central to my whole relationship with *RS*, to wit:

1) I'm assuming the $80 per diem expense arrangement applies to the 13 proposed columns as well as the Six Main stories—if only to give me the option of de-escalating (or perhaps even escalating) the proportions of a story once I've gotten into it. Needless to say, if I fly off to Chicago on the basis of a seemingly reliable rumor that Mayor Daley will be burned alive the next day on that Picasso sculpture in the Loop—at a guaranteed $80 a day—and when I get there I find it was really Mike Royko[42] who was scheduled for burning that day & he failed to show up due to over-weening drunkenness, I'm going to feel in a bit of a bind if I'm faced with a choice of filing 7500 words for $2000 & $80 a day, or scaling the thing down to realistic proportions for $350 that probably wouldn't even cover my real expenses for the trip. My entirely reasonable reaction under those circumstances would be to hang around Chicago long enough to get 7500 words—or, if we couldn't agree on that, to find *another* Chicago story & sell it to the highest bidder (other than *RS*) who would sure as hell pay more than $350, plus all expenses . . . but the very *last* thing I'd be inclined to do, under those circumstances, would be to slink back to Woody Creek at my own expense and zap off a fine, ho-ho big readership

42. Mike Royko was a populist columnist for the *Chicago Sun-Times*.

column for $350 . . . & then get a bill on my own Carte Blanche card for $415 for the Chicago trip.

An exaggerated circumstance, of course. Probably even paranoid. In any case, it's something I want to be sure of—on paper—before any final agreement.

2) The reason I see this as "potentially central to my whole relationship with *RS*" has to do with the question of Personal Autonomy . . . whether I'm a free-lance writer with certain sharply-defined obligations to a pop-music magazine in San Francisco called *Rolling Stone,* or whether I'll be functioning more or less full time as the "National Affairs Editor" (or "National Correspondent," as the case may be) for a "new" San Francisco–based national magazine that has only recently come to be taken seriously by the vanguard of a potentially massive readership that doesn't give a flying fuck what the Jackson Five[43] eats for breakfast, but which—to a degree that surprises even me—has suddenly come to take *RS* seriously as "a voice" for/of something that nobody quite understands yet, but which even Stewart Alsop has cited (in his *Newsweek* column) as a voice to be reckoned with.

Which may or may not be true. I don't know, myself, and I seriously doubt if anybody else now on the staff does either—including Jann. *RS* was born in a cultural vacuum that no longer exists. In 1968 Bob Dylan could have run for president and—given the same organization Gene McCarthy had—probably done as well or better than McCarthy himself. But in 1972 Dylan would have run neck-and-neck with Sam Yorty[44] in the New Hampshire primary . . . at 3% or so.

"How does it feel . . . to be out on your own . . . ?"

How indeed?

What the fuck *is Rolling Stone* in 1973? Where do we go from here? Why do we even exist?

None of which is especially pertinent to this memo, except that these are the questions I get hit with every time I find myself wandering around in public as a representative—not just a writer or editor—of *Rolling Stone.* Maybe other *RS* writers get this kind of thing; I don't know (except for Tim Crouse, who repeatedly fouled his own nest—as persons of Germanic ancestry often will, in times of stress—by allowing himself to be trapped into defending not only *Rolling Stone* but the madness of the national affairs editor as well). . . .

But what the fuck? I seem to be wandering. The point I was leaning into was that there's a hell of a difference between being "a writer from *Rolling Stone*" in a familiar sympatico scene (say, a mood piece on a Boz Scaggs[45] concert in

43. The Jackson Five were a bouncy five-brother pop group inducted into the Rock and Roll Hall of Fame in 1997.

44. Samuel W. Yorty was mayor of Los Angeles.

45. William "Boz" Scaggs was a San Francisco Bay area rock/pop/soul singer and rhythm guitarist who played on two Steve Miller Band albums in 1967 and 1968. His 1969 solo album *Boz Scaggs* was produced by Jann Wenner. Scaggs would achieve greater success with his more disco-oriented 1976 album, *Silk Degrees.*

Berkeley) and being a writer for a "rock & roll magazine" that nobody's ever heard of in a relentlessly hostile environment (like trying to get a seat on the Nixon/Agnew press planes—or even getting into a McGovern "situation room" on the night of a primary when the only other press person allowed through the door is John Chancellor).

1973

THE GREAT SHARK HUNT . . . MARLIN FISHING IN MEXICO, KILLING TIME WITH THE OAKLAND RAIDERS . . . ROOKIE OF THE YEAR IN WASHINGTON, RUBE OF THE YEAR IN HOLLYWOOD . . . WAITING FOR WATERGATE, HATCHING THE PLOT TO CROAK NIXON . . . THE CURSE OF SUDDEN FAME . . .

National Affairs Desk,
Key Biscayne, 1973.
(Photo courtesy of
HST Archives)

Hunter, Juan, and Sandy, Woody Creek, 1973.
(Photo by Michael Montfort)

Cozumel, 1973.
(Photo by Sandy Thompson, courtesy of HST Archives)

Smith & Wesson Model 29 .44 Magnum.
(Photo by Michael Montfort)

FROM JUAN THOMPSON:

Holed up at San Francisco's Seal Rock Inn to finish Fear and Loathing: On the Campaign Trail '72, *Thompson got good news from home from his eight-year-old son, Juan.*

January 25, 1973
Woody Creek, CO

Dear DAD,
I Did everything You Told
Me. And Now I Am The Most
Popular Kid in the County.

Thanks For The Suggestions.

Love Your Son

TO KAY AGENA, *PARTISAN REVIEW:*

Kay Agena of the conservative Partisan Review *had written to tell Thompson that he had finally become respectable enough to be given a low-risk tryout with the magazine—which Thompson described as run by "a rigid cluster of right-wing neofascist intellectuals in the pay of the CIA."*

January 26, 1973
Woody Creek, CO

Dear Kay . . .

This is a very difficult letter for me to write. But, after giving it a lot of thought (inre: your letter of Jan 19), I've decided that it would not be a good thing for me or anyone else if my name somehow showed up in "*PR*'s table of contents."

Nothing personal; I assure you of that . . . and I thank Sweet Jesus that there is still room in this world for gentlemen of taste & insight like [Agena's fellow contributing editor] Dick Gilman. I admire his talents no less than his tolerance, but I think he's biting off more than he can righteously chew when he says my "rhetoric can be gotten around."

Ah, Kay . . . I hate to say it . . . but not even Gilman can get around my Rhetoric. It's too heavy, too rude, too weird & with too many sharp edges . . . and besides all that, I like it.

Which is a horrible thing to say, I guess . . . but it's true: I get a real boot out of writing that crude & unconscionable gibberish. It's fun, in a strange kind of way . . . Jesus, maybe I shouldn't put this in writing, eh? Especially to the *Partisan Review* . . . Holy fuck!

Have you checked out these rumors about Hubert Humphrey having leverage of some kind with the *PR* editorial board? He's never liked me, and this may be his way of trying to burn me on what he naturally assumes is my own turf . . . God *damn* his treacherous ass! Who'd have guessed that a useless atavistic dingbat like Hubert would have zeroed in on my one weakness?

So . . . save your energy for better things & stop trying to crash my byline into *PR*. I'd just as soon save that for when I get a lot older and can't get it up . . . when I start sounding like Norman What's His Name & those people. But not now; it would be like wrapping me into a nine-numbered strait-jacket.

Meanwhile, I plan to spend as many afternoons & evenings as possible in the Jerome bar. Say hello the next time you stop in. I'll be the one writing poetry with the blood from my own fingers on the mirror behind the booze racks.

As for your friends . . . Well, you can bring Gilman, but for christ's sake leave the other ones back there where they belong.

OK . . .
Hunter

TO JIM SILBERMAN, RANDOM HOUSE:

Eager to begin his next writing project, Thompson wanted to settle the outstanding American Dream book he had agreed to write for Random House before Fear and Loathing in Las Vegas *and* On the Campaign Trail '72.

February 20, 1973
Woody Creek, CO

Dear Jim:

I keep making plans for a trip to NY—but I keep putting it off because I can't quite focus on what I plan to say when I get there. I keep saying to myself, "Yeah, I should definitely get to NY sometime soon & talk to Silberman about that book" . . . but in the meantime things are happening all around me; the phone rings incessantly, & every time I answer it there's somebody else yelling about something that *must be done now,* and damn the expenses . . . and consequently I keep postponing that trip to NY, because if only by contrast it strikes me more & more like a sort of Duty Trip, for dealings with a gang of anal-retentive Seconal addicts.[1]

1. Seconal is a prescription barbiturate.

Your letter of 1/16 is . . . . . . a . . . . . . nice . . . . . . example . . . . . . of . . . . . . what . . . . . . I . . . . . . mean . . . . . . I guess.

"Let me know when you're going to turn up." That's a quote from your closing line (1/16/73).

Well . . . I can "turn up," as it were, just about any time I can find a good reason or even a reasonable excuse for calling the travel agent & asking for a RT ticket to NY . . . or I can stop by in connection with another trip, if necessary. I have to fly to Cambridge in a week or so, for instance, to speak with the Nieman Fellows.[2] And in mid-March I have to go to the Univ. of Chicago for some kind of speaking trip . . . and whenever I can get a few loose days I have to go to Washington for 3 or 4 reasons.

What will we talk about if I stop in NY? A book? The old "American Dream" contract? A new and/or different book for Random House? Or will we just sit around & wring our hands stylishly in some expensive french restaurant?

I've finished the Campaign '72 book. It went to press this morning . . . and I'd like to get on with something else. (I recall saying almost exactly the same thing to you when I finished the Hell's Angels book in the spring of 1966—remember that phone call from Alpert's[3] house, when I said I wanted to do a book on that gang of freaks who were eating this stuff called "acid" & hanging around the house? No hope for that one, eh? Much too esoteric.)

Yeah . . . I thought I'd jab that one in again, just for laughs. . . . Haw, haw. We shore blew that one, eh?

But what the hell? It was only five years—and I did, after all, survive.

Indeed. But I don't plan to go that route again. It's too high a price to pay for a peaceful, prestigious slab in the Random House morgue. I have no intention of waiting five years before writing another book . . . for good or ill; two books in two years is one too many, I suspect, but my instinct said it was better to go with the circumstances & on balance I think it worked out.

In any case, I want to get started on another book *immediately.* Before the adrenaline boils off & I get sunk into pig-ranching again.

So if you want me to write another book for Random House, let me suggest very respectfully that we get the bastard settled at once. Otherwise, we should make arrangements for me to pay off that old contract & then maybe write a book for somebody else . . . a foolish & irresponsible notion, no doubt, but that's the way I'm feeling these days & I figure it'll be about a year before I come back down to that other level.

Ah . . . madness, madness . . . where will it end, eh?

2. The Nieman Fellowships are awarded annually to a small group of working journalists deemed worthy to spend a year in Cambridge, Massachusetts, pursuing the studies of their choice at Harvard University.

3. Richard Alpert, who later changed his name to Baba Ram Dass, helped his colleague Timothy Leary set up the International Federation for Internal Freedom at a mansion in upstate New York, where they experimented with psychedelic drugs and dabbled in Eastern mysticism.

Where indeed? All I can say for sure is that I have every intention of signing another book contract as soon as possible and if you can work up any interest in that subject, I think we should talk about it very soon.

As for subjects, that "Welcome to Texas" thing looks good, but I simply can't tolerate the idea of moving to Dallas right now . . . and I think that's the only way to do it.

Maybe in six months or so . . . but in the meantime I'd like to spend most of my time between trips out here in Woody Creek, finishing off a short, *Vegas*-type novel called "Guts Ball," a saga of madness & terror in the first-class compartment of a DC-10 on a midnight coast-to-coast flight from Washington to Los Angeles. I have it all lined out, a kind of cranked-up sequel to the Vegas book . . . ah, but maybe it won't work; the plot is set, but the characters are still 2-dimensional, so I'll have to give it more thought.

In the meantime, why don't you sit back at your desk and stare fixedly, as it were, at the nature of our relationship and then let me know what . . . you . . . finallllllly . . . deecciddde . . .

OK?

TO GARY HART:

McGovern campaign manager Gary Hart was about to enter Colorado's 1974 U.S. Senate race.

February 22, 1973
Woody Creek, CO

Gary:

I assume you have your advance copy of my book by now; let me know when you get your lawsuits ready. Otherwise, I hope you can choke a few laughs out of it.

On other fronts, I hear you've decided to bite the bullet, as it were, inre: The '74 Senate race. It should be a real bitch, eh? I already have some posters done up.

I'm lashing things together on this end—& sometime soon maybe we can have a drink (or a sarsaparilla, eh?) & have a look at the situation. I've had a lot of calls from Washington about it . . . indicating a sort of . . . *abnormal interest* . . . yes, I guess that's the term.

Anyway, see you soon.

HST

TO JANN WENNER, *ROLLING STONE:*

After two years of furious writing, deadlines, and debt, Thompson opted to take a break from his arrangement with Rolling Stone.

April 22, 1973
Woody Creek, CO

Dear Jann . . .

Since I haven't heard from you inre: Suspension of my $1000 per month retainer, it occurred to me tonight that I should probably suggest it myself. I was surprised to get the check for this month, in fact—because of the 90-day "failure to produce" clause in the contract—and the only reason I deposited it was the fact that I'm currently working on the Kissinger/Acapulco story,[4] which should be in your hands by May 1 or so.

At that point, presuming the story works, we can get back on something approaching a normal schedule . . . but my gut feeling at the moment is that we should probably keep the contract in a state of limbo until I have time to sit back here on the porch and re-assess my commitments, which seem to be getting more & more out of hand. The central horror of my (and Sandy's) life at the moment is that I seem to have somehow set myself up for a travel/writing schedule in 1973 that looks very much like a replay of 1972—which would no doubt be as intolerable for the people in the *RS* production dept. as it would be for me. I get no more pleasure out of putting people like Charley & Dan & Paul[5] to the wall than I do out of those painful subhuman speed runs of my own at the Seal Rock Inn—& especially now that we're reduced to weird & unpredictable speed. That last trip was too ugly all around for any replay. . . .

As for money details, my understanding of the contract is that once my monthly $1000 is "suspended" I won't be into you for any more dollars until I deliver something printable—which is better all around, I think, because my adrenaline reserves are too low at the moment to maintain the same kind of ball-busting schedule we somehow (more or less) sustained for the past 18 months. Looking back on it, I see that I've produced two books in two years, which is sort of like a woman having two babies in the same amount of time—and with the same kind of results in terms of physical, mental & emotional drainage, to push it any further at this point, I think, would be coming pretty close to trying to squeeze blood out of last year's corpse.

As for "expenses"—phone credit card & Air Travel—my own preference would be to keep both of those and not use them until I get back to legitimate *RS* work . . . but if you'd feel more comfortable with cancellation on both fronts, well . . . I suppose that should be worked out with [John] Clancy in the context of the contract.

4. While vacationing in Acapulco in 1972, then national security adviser Henry Kissinger had been called upon by Mexican foreign minister Emilio Rabasa, who presented his country's case that excessive salinity in the Colorado River waters flowing into northern Mexico from the United States violated a treaty between the two countries signed during the FDR administration in 1944.

5. *Rolling Stone* chief copy editor Charles Perry, traffic coordinator Dan Parker, and managing editor Paul Scanlon.

As I've said, I'd prefer to just declare a state of limbo on the whole thing. At the moment I feel like I've pushed myself—& been pushed—just about as far as I can stretch for the time being. One of the central tenets of my concept of chemical "speed" is that it is not energy in itself, but merely enables the brain & the body to tap *latent natural energy resources,* which amounts to willfully trading—on a two or three to one basis—time Now for time Later.

And I'll still make an argument for that notion, but only up to a point, and that's the point where I find myself right now. I think it's about time I get back in the habit of writing at least a *second draft* of my gibberish, instead of lashing all this last-minute lunacy into print for no reason except to fill space or justify some ill-conceived headline in *RS.* I definitely appreciate the Exposure you've given me, but after checking (at great & far-flung length, as always) with my sources, I'm hard pressed to feel any great & overweening guilt about having taken cruel and/or exploitative advantage of you.

But what the fuck? It's morning here and I'm tired. Seven days of almost continuous sleep haven't cured me entirely of whatever's ailing me, but I figure the funk has to pass very soon; I've never been through one quite this long.

My current plans include making it to D.C. for the *More*[6] party, but only if I can work it out in conjunction with a story of some kind. I've already worked out a plot with [Frank] Mankiewicz to use his address in order to get a new House/Senate press card for '73—but I suppose we should put that in limbo along with all the other stuff, for right now. I still have that Random House book contract to deal with, along with a few other loose ends, and my instinct is to take them one at a time—at my own pace, for a change, instead of somebody else's.

OK for now. Why don't you brood on this for a day or so, then give me a call. In the meantime, I'll assume my $1000 a month retainer is shut down & I'll refrain from using my *RS* phone & Air Travel cards except under situations of genuine need, in which case I assume we can work those details out against payment for incoming work. (One of the main focal points of my energy at this time, in fact, is a sort of multi-pronged effort to get some new credit cards of my own—but we apparently still have a ways to go before the statute of limitations runs out on that goddamn *Scanlan's* nightmare.)

In the meantime, we're about 18 hours away from a total split with El Rook's candidate for Mayor of Aspen. . . . Unfortunate, but it looks to be inevitable. Benton, Edwards, Solheim & I have spent the past 48 hours probing for viable alternatives, but we finally came down to The Dirk.

Horrible, eh?

Good news is scarce these days.

In any case, don't be in any hurry to respond to this rambling screed. All I can tell you for sure is that whatever it says is exactly the way I feel right

6. *More* magazine was a hip but short-lived national journalism review of the early 1970s.

now . . . and it seems to me that a state of edit/contract Limbo is the best solution on all fronts.

But maybe not . . . and if that's the case I'm sure you'll come up with your own solution before the next full moon. Chances of seeing you in D.C. look about 50–50 right now. I have some definite reasons to go east, sometime soon, but I'm not sure a 3-day drunk in Washington has any real priority unless I can get something real out of it.

In closing, however, please find enc. my check for $20—which should cover that $5 tab for the B-12 shot and also the $13 plus for those two color-contact sheets. My attorney has advised me not to discus that $90 fraud inre: Damage to the hood of your car by some drunken thug in the dead of night, so I assume that's still up for grabs . . . and that's just fine with me; it's always best to have at least one nasty loose end snapping around.

Cazart,
Hunter

TO VIRGINIA THOMPSON:

Thompson was ready for a break from his rigorous writing schedule.

April 23, 1973
Woody Creek, CO

Dear Mom . . .

I thought you'd get a boot out of my new stationery; it arrived about 10 minutes after I mailed off my official resignation to *RS.* The prospect of spending another year under that fiendish deadline gun was more than I could face—especially after finishing my second book in two years, which is not my pace at all.

The new (Campaign '72) book is already involved in one of those bureaucratic nightmares that seem to track me around and might—for the benefit of future generations—eventually explain why I could never pay my rent, despite all outward appearances of fame & fortune. The publisher for this one is *Rolling Stone*'s book division, Straight Arrow—instead of Random House—and the editor called a few days ago to tell me that they'd "refused to accept" all but about 500 copies of the First Printing (10,000) from the printer, because of "inadequate inking." God only knows what that means, except that most of those 500 copies were sent out, automatically, to book reviewers all over the country—while the other 9500 copies are still stacked in a warehouse in Reno. Sometime soon, and perhaps even now, a second "First Printing" will start filtering into the bookstores, libraries, etc. . . . but in the meantime the only copy I can get my hands on is the one that got sent to the *Aspen Times* book reviewer. The sales mgr. at St. Arrow says a carton (18 books) of the new reprint edition is on its way to me, but so far I haven't seen it—which makes me feel a bit strange when I pick up the new *Saturday Review* & read a back-slapping commentary/review of the goddamn thing. The publisher of *Harper's* mag. called the other day to say that they were scheduling a big, complimentary review by [novelist] Kurt Vonnegut for sometime in the late spring . . . but it's hard for me to relate to a book I can't even get, despite the fact that I wrote it.

Anyway, I thought I should send a note & explain why you haven't received or even seen a copy. I'll send you one from here as soon as my official "carton" arrives, which should be within a week.

On other fronts, things are going okay & I look forward to as many months as possible of sloth & unemployment. My next project is a weird novel for Random House, around 1975 or so, but between now & then I have no plans at all—except maybe to run for the U.S. Senate from Colorado, but at the moment that's only a threat.

OK for now. Call when you get the book. No need to say anything nice about it, but I'd like to be sure it got there.

Love,
Hunter

TO SID GRIFFIN, ATHENAEUM LITERARY ASSOCIATION:

The coeditor of Louisville Male High's 1973 yearbook had written to the most distinguished alumnus of the school's Athenaeum Literary Association for permission to excerpt some of Thompson's prose in that year's Spectator*—and to sell him an ad in it.*

May 3, 1973
Woody Creek, CO

Dear Sid . . .

I get a lot of weird letters I never answer, but yours as of (whatever the fuck date it was) was so unnaturally bizarre that I figured I had to reply. I've never quite seen myself as a typical ALA "old grad," but there's no denying the strange fact that I am—so here's $5 for the ad, and if you need any fillers for this year's *Spectator* feel free to lift anything you need out of any one of my books you can lay hands on. If you do this, however, I trust you'll be guided by my long-time personal motto: "Moderation in all Things." In other words, I suspect you could steal up to 1000 words without disturbing the publisher, but anything more than that might bring a nasty but meaningless letter from the House Counsel.

In any case, by all means send me a copy of this year's *Spectator.* I spent a lot of time with Porter Bibb, putting the 1955 issue together, and I'm curious to know what the product looks like now.

OK,
Hunter S. Thompson

TO IAN MARTIN, THAMES TV:

June 1, 1973
Woody Creek, CO

News & Documentary Dept./Ian Martin
Thames TV, 306 Euston Rd.
London NW1 3BB

Gentlemen:

A recent effort to straighten out my desk turned up a letter from you, dated 10 Dec 71—in proper military fashion. In any case, it dealt with Ralph Steadman's effort to force you to honor your agreement (made by somebody named "Udi," as I recall) to send me a print of a film you made in Aspen, Colorado when I was running for Sheriff of Pitkin County.

The agreement—& I'm sure I recall it correctly—let your film crew cover all aspects of my campaign, in exchange for $100 worth of beer for the headquarters & a print of the film when Udi finished it.

Your letter of 10 Dec 71 was quite clear in its statement that nobody working then or now for Thames TV had the authority to promise me a print of any film made by your people. To wit: "We do sell our films to other television companies for transmission on their channels, but we cannot normally make them available to people who have taken part in programmes."

In light of this, I was taken a bit aback when I got an invitation, several weeks ago, to attend a "private showing" of the above-mentioned film at the (local) meeting hall of the Aspen Institute. My wife & I paid $2 each—along with many others—to have a look at the film. The doorkeeper explained that it was being shown by its "owner," one of the main shareholders in the local AM radio-station, who had brought it back from London.

She ran it for several nights, charging $2 a head at the door, and I assume it made a nice profit.

So much for your bullshit letter of 10 Dec 71, eh? Why didn't you just come right out and tell me how much you wanted for a print? I am not entirely without funds—and, despite the flat-out lies of your producer/director, I would probably have paid for a print . . . since the sale of same was never a matter of "policy" at all, but only a matter of money.

All I'd like to know is How Much? I am sending a copy of this letter to my London literary agent, Deborah Rogers, who will be in touch with you shortly. I trust you can shuck off your devious bullshit long enough to deal with her in a straight fashion and sell me a print of a film that covers an episode in my life that remains very close to me—despite the lame/corporate interpretation your people managed to put on it.

In any case—since you're obviously selling prints of the film—I can't imagine any reason why you wouldn't sell one to *me*. My agreement with your producer/director is obviously defunct, so we might as well get down to straight dollars.

Tell me how much you want for a print (the title, as I recall, is: "High Noon in Aspen") . . . and I'll send you the money.

Sincerely,
Hunter S. Thompson

cc: Deborah Rogers

TO JOSEPH DOLAN:

Thompson had encountered Joseph Dolan—another Democratic candidate for Colorado's U.S. Senate seat in 1974—at an Aspen cocktail party.

June 2, 1973
Woody Creek, CO

Joe . . .

Thanks for the letter & the obvious good instincts.

And just for the record, by the way, I assumed you knew who I was when I slouched into Diane's apartment—since she'd formally invited us, and we'd called at least twice to say we were coming. There was no malice in the "grilling" you mentioned. The people with me were some of the activists in my sheriff's campaign, and they merely wanted to know if you were any different from the other politicians . . . and in all fairness I should add that they were not immensely edified by your Presence, your answers, or the symbolic alternative you posed to Politics as Usual.

Also, in fairness, I know Gary [Hart] well enough to assume he wouldn't have fared much better under the same circumstances. The kind of people I spend most of my time with—friends, readers, constituents, etc.—tend to share my uneasy conviction that Democrats are no better than Republicans.

As for my own political plans, I'm entirely unsure at this point—but if I decide to do anything serious, I'd like to talk to both you & Gary about it, before I crank up. I have no "political ambitions," per se, but I think we have a very flux situation in Colorado & it may be one of the few states in the country where we can make a start on the drastic structural changes that we all know will sooner or later be necessary, if we have any honest hope for the survival of the democratic process.

My quarrel with you & Gary is that neither one of you seems to understand that [GOP candidate Peter] Dominick is not the real enemy—and not even a symbol of the real problem. You could scour the noontime streets in Denver & come up with one person out of every ten who would be a better Senator than

Dominick . . . but so what? That's like calling for a national referendum on the question of whether Haig is a better Nixon flunky than Haldeman.[7]

Which is drifting off the point, I think. Maybe you should risk a trip to your local bookstore and spend some of that massive fortune I understand you recently piled up for a copy of my book on the '72 campaign. It won't cure what ails you, but it might save us a lot of useless haggling.

You might also take a long look at your advance-staff. Anybody running for the U.S. Senate who can be hassled for almost 2 hours by a potential opponent & four of his henchmen without any idea who's hassling him would appear to be in serious trouble when the going gets heavy.

Jesus, I went out of my way to be *nice*. What if I'd come there to really fuck around with you?

Maybe we can talk about this when I get over to Denver in the next few weeks. If nothing else, we can have a drink or so and try to get things focused.

Cazart,
Hunter

TO FRANK MANKIEWICZ:

Frank Mankiewicz had been a lawyer in L.A. and director of the Peace Corps under LBJ before he was hired as Robert F. Kennedy's campaign press secretary in 1968. Four years later he joined George McGovern's staff in the same capacity, quickly rising to campaign manager and then political director of the 1972 Democratic effort—"The Man Behind the Man," as Thompson put it.

June 4, 1973
Woody Creek, CO

Frank . . .

It's snowing heavily out here for the third straight day, and after watching the *CBS Morning News* I've about decided to make the big move to the Washington Hilton and start fucking around with the Watergate story. Lynn [Nesbit] says you could use some competent help on your book—getting the facts straight, etc.—and there seems to be pretty general agreement in NY publishing circles that I'm the help you need.

But first I have to finish off this goddamn *Playboy* article[8] & nail down a New Deal with either Random House or somebody else for the new book—a sort of neo-novel, more on the order of *Vegas* than the *Campaign '72* thing.

7. General Alexander M. Haig, Jr.—whom President Nixon had elevated to four-star rank in January 1973, just four years since then Colonel Haig had joined Henry Kissinger's National Security Council staff—was named White House chief of staff after H. R. Haldeman was forced to resign the post on April 30, 1973.

8. *Playboy* had commissioned Thompson to write about a shark-hunting competition in Mexico in April 1973.

Meanwhile, however, I have to make at least a lame stab at writing something for *Rolling Stone,* and Watergate is about the only thing that interests me right now, so I'll probably see you in D.C. sometime around the middle of June. Until then, I'm counting on you to cause a gross public upheaval by displaying the poster I'm sending you under separate cover. . . . I expect you to crash it right into the Hearing Room, using Josh [Mankiewicz, Frank's son] to fight off the cops while you explain your (our) position to the TV cameras. A scene like that might go a long way towards atoning for all your media-crimes during the campaign.

Yeah—speaking of Josh—tell him I tried to get his threat to kill me into a footnote for the second printing, but I was too late; it went down the tube along with the 422 other major corrections I've been trying to insert ever since the first galleys came back. Hopefully, I can get at least some of them into the third printing, which is set for July. Selah.

On other fronts, my '74 Senate campaign is picking up a fearful head of steam. Both Gary & Joe Dolan are trying to head me off somehow (pleading letters, phone calls, emissaries, etc.)—but I get Muskie-style flashes off both of them and I suspect it's all over. Neither one of them seems to understand that what I'm doing is for the Greater Good, as always.

For the moment it's all I can do to keep control of my supporters, who want to croak both Hart & Dolan at once & then do a Godzilla-trip on Dominik (sp?). Shit, I can't even spell his name—but then I could never spell "sheriff" either. In any case, I don't want to peak too early. But you should probably start getting your affairs in order, because when we move it'll be like a fucking whirlwind & I'll want you well-rested.

Okay for now . . .
Hunter

FROM WILLIAM J. KENNEDY:

Kennedy enclosed galleys of a friend's new novel for Thompson to endorse.

June 9, 1973

Hunter . . .

The last time I talked to you you were much younger. I don't know how this communication gap developed. Have you stopped writing letters or have I?

The occasion for this is somebody else: Valerie Petersen, wife of Don Petersen, the author of *Does a Tiger Wear a Necktie,* a play. Valerie is going by the alias of Kohler Smith in her novel, which is coming out from Dial in the fall. I helped her get into Dial and am trying to get her some recognition with it. I think it's one of the funniest novels I've read in years. Almost as funny as *Fear and Loathing in Las Vegas.* If you feel up to it and also magnanimous, send a blurb on the book to Donna Schrader, the publicity girl at Dial. If not, not.

I met Kurt Vonnegut for dinner about a month and a half ago and he talked of your book, full of praise. Said you were due east one of these days, which I presume now has come and gone. I assume you no longer communicate with easterners.

I'm about to go to Ireland for some magazine pieces, one for the *Atlantic* and one for the [*New York*] *Times Magazine* and maybe some travel stuff to cover whiskey expenses.

I seem to be finishing my novel, which is about as much as I want to say about it at the moment. More later if I ever see you.

I can't afford to buy your book but have read much of it as it went along and recently eulogized you and Gonzo in a journalistic summary I wrote for Empire State College, quoting the new book. You've done well for an upstart. I can't say the same for all those *Stone* writers who are also riding the gonzo trail.

I see [Bill] Cardoso's name in print out there. Give him my best when you see him.

I had a good visit with McGarr in New York about six months ago. First time we ever really talked to one another, it seemed.

Maybe you heard from Peggy [Clifford] the news I wrote her about Lee & Laurie [Berry]'s house burning down; they stayed with us about a month or more and are now in a friend's summer house, building a new place near the old site. They had some insurance. Talked to Rosalie [Sorrels] this week. She's got a new record coming out, all songs about the '50s. She's living at Saratoga with Lena, or maybe by this time is sharing a place with Bruce Phillips. Dana has opened two clothing stores, Grand Rags Ltd., in partnership with a friend & help from her tycoon brother. Doing nicely but no family profits yet. All right. And is the senatorial race real?

Kennedy

TO JIM SILBERMAN, RANDOM HOUSE:

June 18, 1973
Woody Creek, CO

Jim . . .

Yeah, I'm definitely serious about buying the remaining copies of *Vegas*—but my seriousness is based on what I assume is a mutual understanding that the best you can do with them is a mass Remainder-Rack Dump at about 30 cents each, or more like 19 cents . . . let's use 22 cents each as a working standard.

If this is the case, I'll have to make some fast logistical arrangements—inre: Storage, etc.—before I can tell you anything definite. My notion would be to Buy Low and Sell High in a pretty quick time-span. Like egg futures. . . . Anyway, before I can do anything I'll have to know what I'd have to pay you for the mass of unsold copies: $10 or $12 thousand, as I understand it.

(On the other hand—now that I think on it—there might be a high & definitely perverse kind of satisfaction in *sticking you* with them, and forcing you to sell the whole bunch at patently ridiculous prices . . . tacitly admitting a bad botch on the sales front, eh?)

Sometime soon, by the way, I plan to force a readjustment in my long-time status (or role)—from RH's House Freak & Subsidized Looney to the role of an actual, profit-churning *Writer.* It's been fun all around—no argument about that—but I get the feeling it's about time we tried to establish a serious relationship. (Which is not to say that I plan to start taking *myself* seriously; all I'm talking about here is my *work,* as it were. . . .)

Anyway, you should let me know how many *Vegas* books you have on hand, and how much you want for them. . . . Then I'll make you an offer.

And, yes . . . Inre: the Guts Ball tape, please return it to me ASAP. I promised Rinzler a valid shot at the book before signing any contracts with you, and that tape is about as close as I plan to come to anything resembling a Real Outline. I should have made a dupe before I sent it to you, but I didn't . . . so I'd like to have it back pretty quick, in order to make a few copies.

Okay for now. I came back from LA on a DC-10 & saw the whole story unfolding right in front of me. I also saw massive possibilities for the Video tape gig I tried to sell you on about 3 years ago . . . but this time I'll do it on my own and then *sell* it to you, when you finally figure it all out.

Yrs. in Sloth &
Complacency . . .
HST

TO JOHN HOLDORF, A. L. JOHNSON LIBRARY, UNION COLLEGE:

Washington Post *national affairs reporter William Greider would join the* Rolling Stone *staff as a political columnist in the summer of 1982.*

June 18, 1973
Woody Creek, CO

John Holdorf
A. L. Johnson Library
Union College
Cranford, N.J. 07016

Dear John:

Bill Greider of *The Washington Post* has pulled himself together long enough to forward (to me) your letter of 5/25 . . . and he also sent along a copy of his letter to you, in re: The Meaning of the word "Cazart."

Surprising as it might seem to those of us in The Trade, as it were, Bill's definition of the word is essentially correct. His dim Appalachian background has been both the curse & the catapult of his career at the *Post.* There is also a thin

Princeton influence, which probably explains why he missed the root *meaning* of the word. . . .

"Cazart" goes beyond Greider's surface definition of mere shock & surprise; it also implies an almost doom-rooted *acceptance* of whatever grim situation has suddenly emerged. Bill's Ivy League/Foggy Bottom background probably explains the missing dimension in his understanding of the word—to wit: "I took the meaning to be roughly 'holy shit.'"

Which is nice, but not enough. "Cazart" goes far beyond mere shock, outrage, etc. If Bill had a better grip on semantics, he would have told you it meant: "Holy shit! *I might have known!*"

Fatalism, I'd say. It's a mountain word, but not commonly used—one of those finely-honed words (or expressions) more common to Brazilian Portuguese (the Mato Grosso, in particular) than to everyday English. In contemporary terms, we might compare it to the first verbal outburst of a long-time cocaine runner who knew he was bound to be nailed, eventually, but when it finally happens he instinctively shouts "Cazart!"

I hope this will clear the thing up—and, in addition to all that, your note that "none of the standard dictionaries list this word" will soon be remedied. I am forwarding your letter to Jim Silberman, Editor-in-Chief at Random House, and I'm sure we'll see "Cazart" in the next edition of the *RH Dictionary*.

Sincerely,
HST

TO WILLIAM J. KENNEDY:

Thompson expressed his thanks for the gift of a stranger's galleys to read.

June 20, 1973
Woody Creek, CO

Bill . . .

Thanx, you scurvy pigfucker. All I really wanted for my birthday was another goddamn Uncorrected Galleys of another stranger's book. I'm being driven fucking mad by them. I didn't even know the fucking things existed until last month (I've never seen one of *my own* books in that form), but all of a sudden my box is full of the goddamn things, from people I've never even heard of.

About 2 wks ago I finally read one of them (from Holt, Rinehart, etc.) and sent a thought-out one-page comment to the editor—who swiftly denounced me, by return mail, as a useless asshole because I failed *to understand the entirety*, or some such bullshit, of his product. Actually, I *liked* the book—and tried to say so, in my way—but it didn't seem to work out.

That's the third time I've tried it, and the third failure. The other two cost me two friends—George Kimball & Charles Kuralt. Luckily, this last one only caused me to know hatred for a stranger. . . .

In the meantime I am, as you've noted, much younger. Not many people have noticed that, but I figured you would. As for my rumored trip to the east, it never happened and I doubt if it will anytime soon. I have come to agree with [Arizona senator Barry] Goldwater that NY should be chopped off and sunk in the Newark Lagoon. The entire east coast from Miami to Boston is a petrified scumbag.

It is now 5:18 A.M. on a Wed. morning and I'm trying to finish my annual reject/effort for *Playboy.* I quit *Rolling Stone* about 2 months ago, but they . . . well, fuck that . . . we should keep that stuff in the family, as it were.

Anyway, I'll try to crank myself up for reading that goddamn thing you sent—but it better be good.

On other fronts, I have very little to say. My next gig will be what looks like a massively unsaleable novel that will keep me busy—regardless of whether or not anyone buys it—for at least the next year: Flying back & forth from Washington to LA on a DC-10. I was supposed to spend the summer covering Watergate for *RS,* but I couldn't live with the horror of all that time in D.C. and it's better on TV anyway.

As for my Senate race, it's mainly a threat—but not entirely. By next fall I might be unnaturally hungry for a new adrenaline rush. But I'm not really planning on it.

I'll let you know if & when it jells.

Saw Cardoso in LA last wk; he's doing some stuff for *RS* & I'm leaning on Wenner to make him The Man in LA—for good or ill. That ugly news about Lee's house was a bummer; he seems to have more than his share of bad luck. I live in fear of that (fire) thing happening out here. I finally bought the place, but it's not insured for anything & the taxes are ungodly. Save up some money so I can borrow it from you next year. I have a powerful feeling that I'm about to shit in my nest again. OK . . . and hello to Dana . . .

HST

TO HUGHES AND ANNE RUDD:

CBS Morning News *correspondent Hughes Rudd and his wife, Anne, had sent Thompson a clipping of one of the many glowing reviews of* Fear and Loathing: On the Campaign Trail '72.

June 21, 1973
Woody Creek, CO

Hughes/Anne . . .

Thanx for the weird *NY Post* clip. This book seems to be settling nicely into the mold of the other two—incredibly "good" but disastrously-ignorant reviews and less than half the minimum-sales anticipated by the editors. (The R. House version of *Vegas* never got above 18,000, they tell me, and Straight Arrow says we'll be lucky to hit even that with the Campaign book.) I'm not sure just what kind of a book you have to write to Sell Big in this country but all I can say for sure is that *I'll* never write it.

Meanwhile, however, I'm sitting out here in stone poverty—having taken a "leave of absence" from *RS* about 3 months ago—and juggling an outline for a novel (Jesus, what kind of lunatic would try to sell *anybody* a goddamn novel at this foul stage in our history???) . . . but the flip side of my perverse refusal to cover Watergate seems to be the idea that I should finally write A Novel; I'm fucked if I know why but there's damn few things I ever really understood anyway, so why worry about this one?—(shit, this goddamn [IBM] Selectric typewriter won't work anymore—but I bought it from extremely dubious sources, so I can't turn it in for repair; which means I have to go out and get another one on the same dark market).

Well . . . nevermind. It's been a weird night and I've been dealing with a head full of something rumored to be LSD-25 for the past six hours, but on the evidence I suspect it was mainly that PCP animal tranq, laced with enough speed to KEEP the arms & legs moving. The brain is another question, I think, but I keep hoping we'll have it under control before long . . . along with this goddamn rotten typewriter.

Anyway . . . I just woke Sandy up to ask if we have any copies of the Campaign book in the house; after a long struggle I finally got them to send me a Box (18 copies) and the only others that got sent out went to names on the various presidential campaign press lists, the press rosters I stole off ALL those hq. hotel bulletin boards. Consequently, things like the *Mountain Gazette* and the *Topeka Daily Screed* got maybe two review copies each—and you got none. I hope to remedy this situation very soon, but not until I can get at least another box of 18 for myself. And that'll take another two wks, at least.

Wups . . . Sandy emerges from the darkness with a book in her hand, cursing me for a worthless dope addict as she hurls it my way, then spins on her naked heels & disappears back toward the bedroom . . . Yes, here it is. Guard it with your fucking life.

OK, I'll be in Washington sometime soon to fuck around with the Watergate team & Other Strange Thugs. With luck I should get wrapped up here and make it east by July 4 or so.

OK for now . . .
HST

TO DAVID BUTLER, *PLAYBOY:*

"The Great Shark Hunt," Thompson's article about covering an international deep-sea fishing tournament off Cozumel, Mexico, in April 1973, appeared in the December 1974 issue of Playboy.

June 22, 1973
Woody Creek, CO

David . . .

Shit . . . I was just sitting down today to start a tentative second draft that might lash together the 30/40 rough pages I've already croaked up inre: Cozumel. . . . Indeed, ready to get right into it, no more fucking around (and also with the jangled euphoria from an unexpected handful of righteous blotter acid last night in the Jerome bar) . . . yes: make some sense of the fucking thing . . .

But just as I was finally shaking off the last of the acid horrors about ten this morning, Sandy came back with the mail, which included, along with your $700+ expense check, a copy of Wolfe's *New Journalism* book[9] . . . which didn't tell me a hell of a lot except that I used to be a lot more coherent writer than I seem to be now. Or maybe just hungrier. Or more vengeful. Who can say for sure?

Anyway, it's now 3:11 p.m. & I'm sitting on the porch under a blazing goddamn sun with the Allman Brothers on the portable Sony speakers just like they were, down there in Cozumel (for the vibes, the gut rhythms, etc.) . . . and I just got off the phone with Lynn Nesbit, who called to say that Acosta rang her up yesterday afternoon to announce that he was suing me for gross fraud, massive damages & obstruction of justice or some such bullshit inre: The sale of the *Vegas* book for a film . . . which won't faze the film rights, because I have a xerox of Oscar's release of all claims, etc. tacked inside on the kitchen wall, but in the short run it will undoubtedly croak any hope of immediate delivery on the $7500 option-money: film mongers are not normally eager to acquire properties even vaguely rumored to be in litigation. (One half-mad letter from Oscar's "attorney" very nearly caused Random House to suspend publication of the *Vegas* book. . . .)

All of which might or might not explain why I'm writing you this letter, at this time, instead of sending the revised first half of the first draft, etc. that I thought I'd be finished with today . . . but I thought I should write & let you know that I haven't just disappeared on you. I've been working on the goddamn thing as steadily as my psychic circumstances allow(ed) for the past few weeks, and although I still don't see the main skeleton in it, I've finally begun to see where it's heading—not necessarily *going;* just heading.

To this end, in fact, I might zip into town pretty soon and xerox a disconnected clump of enough pages to give you some idea what's happening. . . . (Jesus, I should have known better than to try to work out here in the open on this goddamn porch. About six people have come & gone for a variety of odd reasons since I got into this letter. In one case, the Co-Op gas truck came into

9. Tom Wolfe's *The New Journalism, with an Anthology Edited by Tom Wolfe and E. W. Johnson,* was published by Harper & Row in 1973. Included was a fifteen-page excerpt from Thompson's *Hell's Angels.*

the driveway & I thought *hot damn,* here's 300 gallons of gas for my big red farmers' tank—but what I got out of the truck was an 18-yr-old girl hitch-hiker from Takoma Park, Md. (read, D.C.) who's still here, fencing a bit delicately with my wife, and chasing the peacock around in the field while I try to get this letter finished. . . . But no gas for my empty tank.)

Then, just a moment ago, after spending half the afternoon on the phone with Lynn Nesbit about the unexplored option for madness & violence in the up-coming book-contract negotiations, and then talking to my *new* attorney in SF about attaching $506.01 of Acosta's book royalties . . . when all that was ended, the goddamn phone rang again and after 22 minutes of brainless jabbering I found that I'd agreed to define the word "corruption" for *Harper's,* in 500 words or less within 48 hrs and for $100.

Why not? I should be able to go right to the mat with that one—no trouble at all. Just dash the fucker off.

And . . . yes . . . It's now 5:38 & I just had to tell Sandy to cancel my flying lesson at 6:00. My only hope for physical survival now lies in fleeing this peaceful wooded hideout and rushing into town for a swim in the Jerome pool. Ten lazy laps in cool water is all that stands between me & hysterical disintegration at this point.

. . . although between now and then I'll try to jerk out a few pages of the Cozumel first-draft for your perusal—or really just because I'm beginning to feel guilty about not sending you anything heavy, incisive, etc. after so long a time. Don't view the shit as anything except loosely-constructed notes; but even in that form you might get some idea what kind of a spineless-saga I'm grappling with. I have the usual amount of ultimate faith in it—along with the usual sense(s) of futility, hatred and despair . . . and the trick, as always, is in refusing to even read the accumulated pages until they're ready (or at least typed cleanly) for mailing.

Right . . . and that's one of the main real values of the Mojo Wire: Once you feed a page into that bastard it's gone forever—no frenzied editing or anal-compulsive rewrites.

Which is neither here nor there, right? I'll lash a few pages together & send them along under separate cover tonight. Probably we should talk about this thing pretty soon, just to keep me honest & not lose whatever thin dose of ersatz momentum we might have going here. . . . Okay for now:

Hunter

—Thanx for the quick action inre: expense check.

TO KURT VONNEGUT:

Renowned author Kurt Vonnegut's partly autobiographical 1969 novel about the World War II bombing of Dresden—Slaughterhouse-Five, or the Children's

Crusade—*had been made into a big-budget movie directed by George Roy Hill in 1972.*

June 28, 1973
Woody Creek, CO

Kurt . . .

I've been meaning to send you a note about your review (in *Harper's*) of my *Campaign '72* book ever since Russ Barnard[10] told me about it on the phone about 3 months ago. As you've doubtless seen, Straight Arrow has used your words mercilessly ever since—and I suppose I should apologize for that, because it seems a bit greedy & grasping. For good or ill . . . although in retrospect the "ill-factor" seems negligible.

Only the *intent,* eh? Like Nixon.

Anyway, I thought I should tell you that I have about 500 reviews of my books lying around the house, here (most of them astoundingly positive, for all the wrong reasons), but if I had to pick an epitaph, right now, out of all that gibberish—the one paragraph that cuts through it all & comes closest to what I'd like to think I was saying was your closing graph in the *Harper's* review—inre: "Hunter Thompson's Disease."

No point jabbering any further about it, except to emphasize the good, high feeling that came on me when I read it.

I was planning on having a drink with you in Miami, but things got weird. Maybe we can make a human connection when I come east in mid-July to have a look at the Watergate situation. I'll be mainly in Washington, but my hustlers tell me I have to come up to New York for a few days, on the breaks. If you'll be in town around then, maybe you could call Kirstin White at Quick Fox (the distribution arm for Straight Arrow) and leave a phone number where I can reach you. She'll have a vague fix on my movements. . . .

Okay for now. In closing, let me assure you that my health—at least for the moment—is extremely good, on paper. I just went through a *total* physical examination, and the doc was baffled at the lack of ominous signs, symptoms, etc. The findings seem to insult everything he spent 12 years learning . . .

. . . Which gives me a boot, of sorts, but as a Doctor I know better. He just hasn't found the right combination of tests, yet. The D. Gray syndrome is not in his books.

Which gives me a bit more time, if nothing else. If you drift west, let me know in time to invite you to pass some time out here on the Owl Farm. Meanwhile, thanx again for the good eye & good instinct.

Hunter S. Thompson

10. Russ Barnard was the publisher of *Harper's Magazine*.

TO U.S. SENATOR GEORGE McGOVERN:

George McGovern had returned to his seat in the U.S. Senate after losing the 1972 presidential election.

June 29, 1973
Woody Creek, CO

Dear George . . .

Thanks for the good words (about my *Campaign* '72 book) and the fine lift you gave Sandy when you called out here the other day. She was stuck in Washington throughout the campaign, and your call almost made up for it . . . Not quite, of course, but the Watergate hearings on TV are rapidly covering the rest. My personal projection for the end of the summer is definitely *up*. (As a matter of fact I recently made a $1000 bet in L.A. that Nixon will offer his resignation by Labor Day.)

Bad craziness, eh? But remember—they laughed at Thomas Edison. And also keep in mind that David Broder[11] wound up owing me $500 after the '72 primaries . . . Selah.

Anyway, whatever instinct prompted you to pick up the phone & make the call yourself was exactly what caused me to vote for you last November—the first time I'd voted for a major party presidential candidate since 1960. And it was perfect that you talked to Sandy instead of me. She had a crush on you from the start, and—as the local (Aspen) campaign manager for our ex-Democrat county commissioner candidate last fall, she was one of the prime architects of the jangled coalition that won Pitkin County (Colo.) for you and our local "extremist candidates."

If you recall our conversation on the Monday night before election day—aboard the *Dakota Queen II,* en route from Long Beach to Sioux Falls—you asked how it looked in Colorado and I said I couldn't speak for the state but you were safe in my district; which proved out to be true—Pitkin was the only county you won in Colorado. (No, there are rumors of another (rural Chicano) county in the SE corner of the state that went for you, but nobody can name it for me . . . and you know how us Objective Journalists treat rumors.)

Anyway, thanx again for the call. I thought about returning it, but—as both Frank & Gary can attest—I'm not at my best on the telephone. So I figured I'd wait and drop in on you personally when I get to Washington around July 9 or so. I want to be there for [former Nixon attorney general John] Mitchell's appearance, and Frank will know how to reach me. I'll call him & check in, just as soon as I get to town.

11. David Broder is a veteran national affairs reporter and columnist for *The Washington Post.*

Sandy may be with me, and—if you have a loose hour or so, some evening—maybe we can have a drink or some dinner. The only restaurant in Washington I can tolerate is a Mexican place at 17th & R, as I recall . . . but what the hell? After 10 months on the campaign trail, I can eat anywhere.

In any case, I'll call you at the office when I get there. Despite all the foul things I had to say about your pragmatism, I look back on your campaign as one of the high points in my life and one of the most honest & honorable efforts in the history of politics, including my own, I might add . . . and that's rarified air to be fixed in.

Ok for now. See you in 10 days or so.

Cazart . . .
Hunter S. Thompson

TO PATRICK J. BUCHANAN, THE WHITE HOUSE:

Future syndicated columnist, TV pundit, and perennial conservative presidential candidate Patrick J. Buchanan remained at his post as a White House speechwriter and Nixon stalwart all the way through Watergate until his president's resignation in August 1974. Thompson arranged for Buchanan to receive a complimentary subscription to Rolling Stone *at the White House.*

July 9, 1973
Woody Creek, CO

Dear Pat . . .

I'm sure you've heard rumors, by now, of my plans to retire from journalism & seek a career in politics. But I'm having a bit of trouble deciding whether to jump in on the electoral or appointive levels, and that's why I'm writing you.

As you know, I've long been interested in the Governorship of American Samoa. Larry O'Brien, in fact, once led me to believe I was all set for that part—but for reasons never adequately explained, he failed to follow through.

I mention this to you because I plan to be in Washington very soon (probably by the time you get this letter) and it occurred to me that you might like to discuss the situation. Maybe some night over a half-gallon of Wild Turkey in that dungeon where Stearns lives. One of my prime reasons for coming to Washington is to hire Rick for my Senate campaign in Colorado, in case this Samoan gig looks lifeless.

In any case, I'd like to have a drink with you and maybe some talk—on whatever terms you want. My feelings about The Boss haven't changed any since we talked that night in Boston 5 years ago and I doubt if yours have, either . . . which reminds me that I never thanked you for your help in setting up that interview in '68, or for whatever aid you might have rendered in clearing the way for my brief & predictably unfriendly excursion with the Nixon campaign last fall. I appreciated the mixed feelings I knew you had in both cases. You'd be hell on wheels if you had good (political) sense to match your good instincts—but Rick says there's no hope for that, so why nag at it? We spent a lot of time talking last year, and if anybody on the McGovern staff had overheard the things he said about you, he'd have been banished to Butte, Montana.

Which is neither here nor there, for right now—but it gives me a sense of real optimism about the ultimate health of the political system in this country to know that people like you and Rick can beat each other like gongs in public, then sit down at night as friends and human beings.

Jesus! I seem to have wandered far off the point here. All I meant to do—behind all the filigree—was to warn you that I'll be back in Washington for most of late July & probably August, and to say I'd enjoy a human talk with you, if things work out.

If not . . . well, I won't take it personally. It strikes me that your schedule might be a bit tight at the moment. I can offer my condolences—but not much else—at least not in public. Can you imagine what it would do to my image if I were seen chuckling in a pub with you?

Anyway, say hello to [fellow Nixon speechwriter] Ray Price for me when you see him. He deserved a better fate than this bummer. But so did we all, I think—and that's the real tragedy.

Sincerely . . .
Hunter S. Thompson

TO DAVID BUTLER, *PLAYBOY:*

Thompson assured Butler that he would focus on the Cozumel article now that he was back from Washington.

August 16, 1973
Woody Creek, CO

David . . .

Here's another chunk—probably the last big one. What I have to do now is lace the shit together and try to cut it down to size. In any case, we now have at least the raw material (with the tapes and this END section) for the "middle and the end" that were missing.

I'm feeling increasingly guilty about the long delay on this thing—but there's been no way to avoid my ever-deepening involvement in the Watergate story. It's just too damn big and critical to keep anything but a total fix on. I've spent 5 of the past 6 weeks in Washington, and despite my best intentions I haven't done much of anything on this Cozumel story.

Now—after stumbling off the plane & sleeping for 48 hours—I think I can get this thing under control in a week or so. Jesus, I have to. Because I have a 10,000 word Watergate wrap-up due by the end of August.

The main problem here was my original/disastrous decision to try to do *anything* in tandem with Watergate. It's been like trying to write both the *Vegas* &

the *Campaign '72* books at the same time—not only 2 different things, but 2 different sets of mind. It's damn near impossible to go out to dinner with Dick Tuck, Adam Walinsky[12] & Wisconsin congressman Les Aspin for a long argument about impeaching Nixon, and then come back half-drunk to work on a story about drug-madness in Cozumel.

But I'm trying, David . . . trying.

And in my spare time, as it were, I'm dealing with a federal drug blitz on Aspen that has already subpoenaed 10 or 12 of my friends for a Grand Jury gig in Denver—and which is likely to reel me in at any moment, on general principles; or maybe just on the basis of the Vegas book. Now I know what Pat Buchanan meant last week when he told me—sitting at a table beside the Watergate pool—that working in the White House was like living from moment to moment in "The Bunker."

But fuck all that. None of it excuses my failure to get this goddamn thing done. I'm amenable to any crisis solutions you deem necessary, but I think I'll wait until we're definitely into a crisis before I suggest any. . . .

Christ . . . here I am trying to write this letter and watch the *CBS Morning News* at the same time; the same kind of split/vision focus that's been driving me nuts all along.

Anyway, take a look at this stuff, then see how it fits with the rest and tell me what you think.

As for Mailer, I think Sandy told you I couldn't find him in Washington and I don't have a home phone number for him. Beyond that, I haven't been able to crank up a hell of a lot of enthusiasm for the idea of a *mano a mano* gig with Norman . . . and Lynn Nesbit's reaction to the idea was that Mailer should write a piece about me. (That was *her* idea, not mine.)

But what the fuck? One thing at a time, eh? Barring the very real possibility of a nark-swarm on my house at any moment, I'll spend the next few days on this Cozumel article and get it finished. My idea, as of now, is to treat it more as an editing job—rather than do any more bulk-writing—and just get the bugger into printable form as soon as possible.

I'll be here for the next month, I hope, so give a call whenever you feel up or down to it. Okay . . .

Hunter

MEMO FROM THE SPORTS DESK, AUGUST 16, 1973:

From: Raoul Duke
To: Jann Wenner
Subject: Article on Sam Brown's birthday party; *RS* #142, Aug 30

12. Adam Walinsky had been Robert F. Kennedy's head speechwriter both in the U.S. Senate and in his 1968 presidential campaign.

This is a difficult memo for me to write, because I am trying to speak for both myself and Dr. Thompson—who called tonight from Washington in a fit of snarling rage, inre: the Sam Brown article. I share his feelings on this subject, so the rest of this comment will have to speak for both of us.

Hopefully there is no connection between Joe Eszterhas's appointment as News Editor and the appearance—in the middle of the Aug 30 news section—of a watered-down version of a bitchy little slap that not even the Denver society-page editors would print.

The original version of that article—as Eszterhas must have known, since he got the carbon copy—appeared in a local (Denver) gossip-sheet run by wealthy Humphrey-style Democrats who've considered Sam Brown a serious menace ever since he moved to Denver and brought his style of political-organizing with him.

It was Sam and his friends who put together—last November—the ballot-box veto of Gov. John Love's Big Money/Big Tourism proposal to hold the 1976 Winter Olympics in Colorado. That was a bitter & unexpected defeat for both the Nixon/Love Republicans and the Humphrey-style Democrats who stood to make the same kind of money off the '76 Winter Olympics as some of them still hope to make off the strip-mining development of Colorado's (publicly-owned) western-slope oil shale acreage by major oil companies. The names of these people are a matter of public record—not only on the deeds involving oil shale ownership, but also as the publishers of the same local paper that bent over backwards, as it were, to sandbag Sam Brown. They published the original themselves—a classic of lame bitchiness—and then they sent the carbon to *RS*.

And we printed the goddamn thing disregarding the fact that the *RS* version was offered under a different name than the author of the original, and including a stupid libel on Dick Tuck: "He will probably be best remembered," according to both the *RS* and Denver gossip-sheet versions, "for having cut short a *McCarthy* whistle-stop speech by disguising himself as a railroad worker and signaling for the train to depart."

We can try to forgive the lame prose—by somebody who called himself "Ron Wolf" in the *RS* version, and "Freddy Bosco" in the original—but it is hard to forgive the ignorance that would fix one of Tuck's finest shots in a campaign *against Gene McCarthy,* instead of the 1960 Kennedy-Nixon campaign where it actually happened.

Or where the story and the legend were born, in any case. It is hard to know, with Dick—but that's beside the point: Anybody careless, ignorant or even stupid enough to publish an article saying Tuck ran that trip on McCarthy, instead of Nixon, has no business editing political articles for a national magazine. It is one thing for a hired hack in Denver to write that kind of swill for 66 readers at the Cherry Hills Country Club Bar—and quite another when he can send the carbon to *RS* and have it published all over the country, on the same page with Steadman and Ralph Gleason.[13]

There is still a very clear line—and I'm sure Dr. Thompson will agree with me on this—between brutal subjectivity and bitchy ignorance. The Supreme Court's historic decision on libel (*NY Times* vs. *Sullivan*—date? [1964]) gives us a lot of room to work with—but not the kind of room where a "writer" using a pseudonym (sp?) and an editor far gone in either carelessness or ignorance, or both, can frivolously re-write political history by giving some yo-yo from the Denver cocktail-circuit two columns in *RS* to run a sick Suzy Knickerbocker[14] trip on one of the straightest and most effective organizers in American politics.

It's easy enough to understand why a clutch of rich Democratic dilettantes in Denver would want to zap Sam Brown—but I'm fucked if I understand why *Rolling Stone* would get into that kind of game . . . and the real purpose of this memo is to make it absolutely clear that neither the Sports Desk nor the National Affairs Desk had anything to do with that cheap, inaccurate, libelous piece of shit about Sam Brown's birthday party.

Sincerely,
Raoul Duke

TO ANTHONY BURGESS:

English writer Anthony Burgess had authored several respected satirical novels, including his 1962 best-seller about a corrupt and violent future society, A Clockwork Orange, *which director Stanley Kubrick made into an initially X-rated movie in 1971.*

August 17, 1973
Woody Creek, CO

Dear Mr. Burgess:

Herr Wenner has forwarded your useless letter from Rome to the National Affairs Desk for my examination and/or reply.

Unfortunately, we have no International Gibberish Desk, or it would have ended up there.

What kind of lame, half-mad bullshit are you trying to sneak over on us? When *Rolling Stone* asks for "a thinkpiece," goddamnit, we want a fucking *Thinkpiece* . . . and don't try to weasel out with any of your limey bullshit about a "50,000 word novella about the *condition humaine*, etc. . . ."

Do you take us for a gang of brainless lizards? Rich hoodlums? Dilettante thugs?

13. *San Francisco Chronicle* columnist Ralph J. Gleason was the cofounder of *Rolling Stone*.
14. Suzy Knickerbocker was a popular syndicated gossip columnist.

You lazy cocksucker. I want that Thinkpiece on my desk by Labor Day. And I want it ready for press. The time has come & gone when cheapjack scum like you can get away with the kind of scams you got rich from in the past.

Get your worthless ass out of the piazza and back to the typewriter. Your type is a dime a dozen around here, Burgess, and I'm fucked if I'm going to stand for it any longer.

Sincerely,
Hunter S. Thompson

TO KATHARINE GRAHAM, *THE WASHINGTON POST:*

Katharine Graham was publisher of The Washington Post, *in which reporters Bob Woodward and Carl Bernstein uncovered and exposed the Watergate scandal from the break-in at Democratic National Headquarters on June 17, 1972, through President Nixon's resignation on August 9, 1974. Graham's Washington Post Company also published* Newsweek *magazine.*

August 23, 1973
Woody Creek, CO

Dear Ms Graham:

I definitely appreciate your offer inre: the editorship, as it were, of *Newsweek*—but for a variety of personal reasons I cannot accept at this time. My doctor has warned me, however, that I'll be dead within three years unless I find a more sedentary line of work, so perhaps we can deal with this matter at some time in the foreseeable future.

Meanwhile . . . I'm enclosing my blank check for whatever amount your subscription dept. failed to mention when they sent me this menacing ("will stop soon") notice/bill/money demand with regard to my Air Mail subscription to the *Post.* I trust you will fill in the proper amount and forward my check to the sub. dept. When I ordered the subscription I never asked about the cost, so I have no idea how much the bastards want from me. I merely asked Bill Greider to arrange for the *Post* to be sent to me in Woody Creek by the fastest possible method . . . which he did (I get Sunday's *Post* on Monday, for instance), but in order to pay the bill I'll need at least a hint of how much this high-speed subscription is worth.

To this end, I'm enclosing my cheque, in hopes that you can fill in the proper amount and get the bugger cashed.

Okay for now. In closing, however, I'd like to congratulate you on the king-hell job the *Post* has done on the Watergate story. If you keep up this kind of coverage, you'll put me permanently out of work—which I'd consider a real favor at this point, so keep hammering the bastards.

Anyway, next time you get to Aspen, give me a ring if you feel like having a drink without [Aspen Institute President] Joe Slater in attendance. . . . Or [at] Tom Benton's gallery; or my floating office in the Jerome Hotel bar. Cazart . . .

Hunter S. Thompson

TO HUGHES RUDD, CBS NEWS:

The CBS Morning News *had just debuted the pairing of veteran network correspondent Hughes Rudd with former* Washington Post *Style section reporter Sally Quinn, who had never done TV news before. Rudd became solo anchor early in 1974.*

September 11, 1973
Woody Creek, CO

Hughes . . .

Six A.M. now, watching you, Sally & some geek named Jeffrey St. John. Heavy duty. And it occurs to me now that we've passed the point—in terms of fairness—where I can refrain from discussing my life-long blackout on CBS News.

I am, as always, open to opposing points of view. This is one thing I want to make very clear. There are, no doubt, many true & excellent reasons for my failure to make the nut with CBS—just as there are true & excellent reasons for my long-standing problem with *Time.*

In any case, I want you to know that there'll be nothing personal—if & when I might or might not indulge myself with a lash or two at CBS. There are, in fact, *other* reasons—ranging from CBS's lame refusal to indulge in "instant analysis" to CBS's lame/camera coverage of pro football games. Cheap shit on all fronts, eh?

But fuck all that. I just wanted to get this memo sent & noted (& especially now that I'm watching Laird beat your people to jelly on the screen) . . . but what the fuck? We've made all those points before, right, so why worry?

Good luck in your new job.

Cazart . . .
HST

TO JANN WENNER, *ROLLING STONE:*

Thompson wrote to Wenner with the usual criticisms of his business practices as well as suggestions for future writing projects.

September 14, 1973
Woody Creek, CO

Jann . . .

Inre: yr. $$ memos of Sept 7, 10, etc. . . . I think we should suspend *all* dealings until you & Clancy can get the problem settled. I have every intention of remaining totally calm and quiet about this thing—which is why I'm turning it over to Clancy, with instructions to keep the hassle completely out of my life until it's settled.

As for the Dom. Rep. thing with Kirby, I cancelled it tonight. Or at least *my* part in it. I also mashed my plans to go back to D.C. for Phase 2 of the hearings . . . along with Phase 3 . . . and even Phase 4, a deep-boiling story about the Strauss/Connally[15] Connexion prior to June 17 '72 that will, if it proves out, be a Z-bomb in the boiler-room of the Demo party in '76, if not sooner.

As for the Princess Anne wedding[16] gig, Steadman is proceeding with the various arrangements for coverage & I plan to make that trip & write the story for *RS* or whoever wants it. You can send Bibb[17] to report on the "Perfect Master" gig in Houston. I like the Iquitos idea[18]—along with maybe a "Rio Revisited" piece after cruising down the Amazon—but we'll have to stabilize our relationship somehow before getting into that stuff. I am tired beyond the arguing point with this insane haggling over every goddamn nickel, dime & dollar. . . .

. . . Ralph put his finger on it very nicely, I think, when he said: "Jann doesn't seem to realize that every dime he screws somebody out of today might cost him a dollar tomorrow."

Maybe not, and that's a risk you'll have to take. But the haggling is getting pretty goddamn old, I think, and the most depressing aspect of it all is that we never seem to make any progress.

For the past few years I've been playing with the idea of opening a pawn shop in Aspen, but I could never find the right person to run it . . . until *now;* but don't worry about getting in touch with me—when the time is right, I'll call you. We have to do some groundwork before hanging out the balls.

OK for now. Talk to John, and when things are calm on that end we'll talk again.

Cazart,
HST

15. Texan Robert Strauss was chairman of the Democratic National Committee and special trade representative under President Jimmy Carter, and U.S. ambassador to the Soviet Union under President George Bush; John B. Connally, Jr., was governor of Texas from 1963 to 1969, and U.S. Treasury secretary from 1971 to 1972.

16. Great Britain's Princess Anne married Captain Mark Phillips in the autumn of 1973.

17. Former *Newsweek* executive and Thompson high school classmate David Porter Bibb III had been named publisher of *Rolling Stone* early in 1972. Jann Wenner fired him before the end of the year.

18. Iquitos is an Amazon River port in northeastern Peru.

TO DAVID BUTLER, *PLAYBOY:*

September 17, 1973
Woody Creek, CO

David . . .

OK, I'm focused entirely on the Cozumel piece now—although my current state of mind shows (above) with the unfortunate Jan. . . . no—September . . . dateline. The only hopeful sign is that I *caught* it pretty quick.

The need for a middle/fishing section is as obvious as it is depressing—but I hope to be able to do something with the Shark-hunt tapes you had transcribed. My thanks to Bonnie & the Kelly girl on that score. . . .

I couldn't tell from your letter (8/31) whether you were mainly worried about the lack of a coherent middle/fishing section, or whether the whole style & tone of the piece turned you off. I got the impression you wanted a completely new lead (something properly fishy & colorful), in addition to the purging of all *F&L in Vegas* type material.

If so, this tends to confirm my worst fears about this assignment—that somewhere out there in the Great Darkness beyond Woody Creek is a cabal of editors who still believe that my talent is still salvageable, and with the proper discipline & direction I can still learn to write like Bob Considine.[19]

I wouldn't write this kind of thing to most editors, David, but since we've always dealt pretty straight with each other I feel comfortable in telling you that I'm pretty well hooked on my own style—for good or ill—and the chances of changing it now are pretty dim. A journalist into Gonzo is like a junkie or an egg-sucking dog; there is no known cure.

And so much for all that. What I need to know now is my *space limit* in terms of actual words. Let's get this settled at once. As for the style & tone, I suspect you'll just have to live with whatever I send—and if it won't go, what the fuck? I've been through that before, right? So don't worry about hurting my feelings.

Send word when you can. Thanx . . .

Hunter

FROM WILLIAM J. KENNEDY:

September 24, 1973
Woody Creek, CO

Hunter . . .

I tried to call you the other day and found you had re-listed and clandestinized your number. What the hell is it?

19. Syndicated news-in-brief columnist Bob Considine wrote his "On the Line" newspaper bits from 1933 until he died in September 1975.

I'm reading your book with much old and new pleasure and am closing in on the final phase of my own. Truly the final phase after many rewrites.

I write also to wonder about your response to Valerie [Petersen, aka Kohler] Smith's book, *The Rape of the Virgin Butterfly.* Maybe you never cracked it. She's a good friend as I told you and I liked the book. It's wild and funny. In New York you said you'd make a comment without looking at it, but I don't want to ask that. But if anything you say is going to be meaningful, it should be in hand within a week or less. For what it's worth to you, John Lahr, the *Voice* theater man, and Dotson Rader[20] both have given it blurbs which go on the jacket. One sentence will do, and the jacket is about to go to press. A wild look at McCarthy era crazies.

If you're not up to this bullshit it's all right with me; I'm only conveying a need of a neurotic but worthy friend. I'm not up to date with *Rolling Stone* so if you're in there with a Watergate piece I haven't yet seen it.

Both my brothers-in-law are on the way to being millionaires. I don't know what that means.

That was a good visit in New York with you and Sandy, but as usual too crowded. I never got to talk to you about your proposed novel. All I heard was tape recording . . . Silberman . . . fifty grand. There's probably more to the story.

Okay. Send the blurb to me if you decide to write one.

Kennedy

FROM KRISTI WITKER:

A dust-jacket blurb from Thompson was obviously a prized commodity.

September 24, 1973
New York, NY

Dear Hunter,

I hope you will remember that during an off-guard moment over the barbecue fire at Dick Tuck's a couple of weeks ago you told me that if you didn't have to read my book you would give me a quote for it!

It's called *HOW TO LOSE EVERYTHING IN POLITICS Except Massachusetts* and it's the story of my rapid downhill spiral after accepting Frank Mankiewicz's offer to become Deputy Press Secretary on the [McGovern] campaign and how I wound up instead carrying [JFK press secretary] Pierre Salinger's laundry to the Laundromat. I have gotten three very good responses so far—[humor columnist] Art Buchwald said it was very, very funny, true, insightful, etc.—so I promise you the book is not a total dog.

If you could find it in your heart to say something unincriminating like "the truest book I've ever read about a political campaign except my own" or "a

20. Dotson Rader was a well-known drama critic of the 1960s and '70s.

must for anyone who has ever worked in or considers working in a political campaign in the future," etc. I would love you forever! One columnist said "Hilarious! The funniest book I've read in a very long time . . ." so I've got that angle covered. Really, I know this is a draggy request but with some 25,000 books coming out this winter I need all the help I can get, especially a quote from the master political writer of them all.

My publisher is desperate to get something as soon as possible, so I am facilitating your effort by enclosing an airmail self-addressed envelope. Of course, if you want to READ this great work I could have it sent out—Thank you, thank you, thank you. I am exceedingly grateful. Best to Sandy.

Very sincerely,
Kristi Witker

October 1973

"FEAR & LOATHING IN THE DOLDRUMS"

by Raoul Duke

"Who is this that darkeneth counsel by words without knowledge?"

—Job 38:2

Who indeed? What kind of irresponsible bastard would do a thing like that? Poor Job must have been thinking about his lawyers when he uttered those words. They definitely laid some dark and ignorant counsel on him, and he suffered badly because of it . . . boils, madness, many deaths in the family. . . .

The Lord was testing his faith. Job never understood that he was a very important test-case. He was God's white rat, and in that role he established a lasting precedent . . . he Kept The Faith, and if his lawyers knew what was happening they had enough sense to keep their mouths shut.

Dark and ignorant counsel.

When times get weird and madness starts closing in, I always turn to the Bible. I was brought up on it. Some of my earliest memories hark back to those hot Kentucky mornings when I was three or four years old and my grandfather—God rest his troubled soul—used to lash me to the hitching post with strips of wet rawhide and order the field-darkies to throw handfuls of sharp gravel at me while he read from the Good Book. He identified very strongly with Job, as I recall, and he wanted to toughen me up for the harsh & brutal times that he knew I would sooner or later come to grips with.

I was thinking about this the other afternoon as I sat in the Jerome Bar, sifting through my mail and listening to a man who said he had just been released from federal prison. He had some very ominous things to say about the machinations of the U.S. Attorney General's office. "Once they get hold of you it's all over," he was saying. "You're completely at their mercy; they'll just grind you under their thumb until you break."

I nodded, pausing to call for another beer before ripping open the third of a half-dozen large envelopes that had showed up in my mailbox that day. . . . The things he was saying were true; I knew that, but I also remembered that the last stranger who showed up in Aspen to warn me about "the ruthlessness of the pigs" turned out to be an undercover agent from the U.S. Treasury Department in Denver. He thundered into town on a big chopped [Harley-Davidson] Hog, wearing a Hell's Angels costume, and offered to sell me "as much dynamite and as many M-16's" as I needed. But the city police arrested him for carrying an illegal sawed-off shotgun before he could do any serious damage. "You can't bust me," he told them. "I'm a federal agent. The sheriff called me in to get the goods on this evil bastard, Thompson." The sheriff admitted it. He was up for re-election, at the time, and I was running against him—so it was only natural, he explained, to ask the feds in Denver to send over an informer/provocateur to help him keep tabs on the opposition. The sheriff never explained why his undercover man was so eager to load dynamite and automatic weapons into my campaign headquarters. . . .

But what the hell? All that happened two years ago, and two of the top strategists in that infamous Freak Power campaign were just elected to the three-man board of County Commissioners . . . which doesn't prove a hell of a lot, but on the other hand it's hard to argue with the idea that, in a "majority rule" situation, two out of three is a nice place to start from, especially on those once-a-year days when The Sheriff has to go before the Board of County Commissioners and request enough tax money to pay his own salary & operating expenses for the next twelve months.

None of this was passing through my mind as I sat there in the Jerome Hotel bar the other afternoon, opening my mail and listening to this man who said he had just been released from the federal pen. Since the end of the '72 presidential campaign, the Jerome Bar has become the de facto *Rolling Stone* National Affairs Desk. I do most of my business there, because of the comfortable atmosphere. There is something about the whole scene at the Jerome that is strongly reminiscent of the McGovern campaign, and after sixteen months in that feverish vortex I am having a little trouble slowing down. And besides, the Jerome is a good place to open the mail—which is becoming heavier & heavier, for some reason, and so consistently unpredictable that it's nice to have witnesses when I start ripping into the packages.

About a week ago, for instance, I received a hard plastic tube about six feet long. My old friend Mike Solheim, the proprietor, eyed it nervously. "Don't open that goddamn thing in here," he said. "Take it outside; get down in the deep end of the pool, where there's plenty of ice."

"Don't worry," I said. "I think I know what it is."

"So do I," he replied. "It's another one of those goddamn blowguns."

Which proved to be true. The tube contained a six-foot aluminum blowgun, with a package of needle-sharp darts. There was also an instruction sheet; "WARNING!" it said. "TAKE CARE NOT TO BREATHE IN DART WHEN INHALING FOR AIR!!!"

No, none of that. These buggers were five inches long. "When needle sharp, your SAFARI darts will easily penetrate one-half inch plywood, auto tires and tin cans," said the instruction sheet. "Then think what these darts will do in the bodies of their victims! They will bury themselves to the dart head every time. They kill without poison! The SAFARI blowgun is so accurate that a beginner can easily hit a two-inch bulls-eye at 30 feet."

"Bullshit," Solheim muttered.

I inserted a dart—taking care not to inhale—then aimed the blowgun at a life-size portrait of [nineteenth-century heavyweight boxing champion] John L. Sullivan at the other end of the bar and drilled him straight in the chest. THONK! A table of ski-tourists immediately paid their bill and left the bar. The dart had buried itself so deep in the oak paneling that we couldn't pull it out . . . but the instruction sheet explained this: "Always carry a small plyers with you when shooting the blowgun," it said, "because you cannot remove SAFARI darts from wood without a plyers."

Al Romanowski, the Polish ski champion, had been watching us curiously. "Jesus Christ!" he said. "One of those things could penetrate a human skull!" He grinned. "How much do you want for it?"

FROM OSCAR ACOSTA:

Acosta was wrong about Thompson having a movie deal for Fear and Loathing in Las Vegas.

October 11, 1973

Hunter:

We can do it amicably—through lawyers—or hand to hand. You choose the weapons. But you are not going to get off Scott [sic] free. I promise you that.

I've been silent on the subject for almost two years because of the blackmail threats from both you and Jann that ultimately my book could be stopped. Well, old pal the book is out now and I'm coming after you. You cocksuckers have been ripping me off for a long time.

You are really getting bum advice my boy. I can stop the fucking movie and sue both Cohen and Zimmerman for simply *passing around* the script. I never gave you or anyone else the right to libel me *in a movie,* stupid! And your contract with IFA or Zimmerman must have a movie clause in there saying that you warrant the story to be free from libel as well as from any other claim. Don't you realize I can get Clancy in serious trouble with the bar for stealing that "release" from me?

It must be that you guys have planned to settle with me right from the start because you haven't got a chance in court . . . about as much as you do of becoming a U.S. Senator.

Believe me, man—I am dead serious. Call me or my agent—Robert Henry *muy pronto* and make an offer. It would be better for all if we settled it and forgot it. Besides you can afford it now.

your old ex-friend
Oscar

TO KRISTI WITKER:

Thompson did not disappoint: he sent several colorful blurbs for the jacket of Witker's campaign book.

October 17, 1973
Woody Creek, CO

Kristi . . .

I just got back from testifying at a rape trial in Fresno & found this goddamn letter inre: COMMENT on your book, and I remember promising to send something if I didn't have to read the text, or whatever.

Jesus . . . what can I say? And is it too late? Probably not, because publishers always lie about deadlines . . . so, well . . . let me think for a moment . . . not long . . . and I'll come up with something . . . maybe. . . .

Yes: how's this?

"This book will blow the balls off all the atavistic geeks like Frank Mankiewicz and Ted Van Dyk who've been running big-time politics in this country (in the Democratic crypt, at any rate) for so long that any right-thinking society would have had them locked up in the Women's House of Detention at least 10 years ago, when it still existed. . . ."

—or—

"If Kristi Witker is right, Frank Mankiewicz should be castrated."

—or—

"This book is the best argument I've ever read for getting women out of politics and into sex and drugs where they belong."

—or—

"A disgraceful indictment of the sexist swine who ran American politics. Nothing short of selective castration on a massive scale will right the wrongs Mz. Witker outlines here. . . ."

Cazart: I think that should do it. You can use my name with any one—or any combination—of the quotes I've chiseled out here. I want to remain on record, however, as a firm advocate of the theory that no quote (or blurb) ever sold more than 13 copies of any book in hardcover, and no more than six in paperback.

OK for now. Good luck with the fucker. It's bound to be at least the second-best book written on the '72 campaign.

Hunter

TO U.S. SENATOR GEORGE McGOVERN:

Thompson, who had grown close to both candidate George McGovern and his wife, Eleanor, during the '72 campaign, was in the early stages of planning a high-level, invitation-only conference on politics under the sponsorship of Rolling Stone.

October 17, 1973
Woody Creek, CO

George/Eleanor . . .

Here are two copies for your shelf. I was going to send two copies of the Campaign book (to replace the two I sent to your office earlier), but at the last moment I decided to substitute a copy of my *F&L in Vegas* for Eleanor. It's a much finer & purer effort, and if I had to make a choice between the two—strictly on artistic & literary merits—the Vegas book would win easily.

But that's only my taste, eh? And I leave any judgements on that to you—out of politeness, if nothing else, because I have total faith in it when the deal goes down.

OK for now. As for the Senate race in Colo., I'm holding back & maybe backing off; it's hard to say for sure right now, because I can't get a fix on either Gary or Dolan . . . and I'd hate to jump in & accomplish nothing more than re-electing Dominick. Sometime very soon the Two/One-party system will have to be seriously challenged, but I'm not sure Colorado in '74 is the right time & place to do it. If you have any hard wisdom on this score, I could definitely use it . . . so call any time; preferably as late as humanly possible (it's 3:06 A.M. now, & I'm just getting the typewriter warmed up). On normal nights I'm up until 7 or 8 EST.

On other fronts, I have a relatively complicated subject to discuss with you (George)—having to do with a conference or maybe just a compilation of publishable statements centering on the possibility of a genuine New Politics in the immediate future. *Rolling Stone* has agreed to foot the bill for a sort of low-key "ignition conference," and for starters I've been trying to get Carl Wagner and Adam Walinsky together to thrash out an agenda. I figure if I can force those two cranked-up freaks to agree on something, the rest will come easy. (This is the opposite, you'll note, of your '72 campaign strategy: Crack the hardest nuts first, instead of later.)

Anyway, don't mention this to anybody until we have a chance to talk about it. (Max [Palevsky], by the way, is no longer connected with *Rolling Stone* except as a minority stockholder; I don't know the details of the split, but it had heavy overtones—strongly reminiscent of that Wed. afternoon in Miami when I tried to convince him that he was making a mistake by leaving the Doral in a rage.)

In the meantime, I've de-activated the National Affairs Desk for the time being & am going back to sports . . . which is another subject I'd like to talk about, vis-à-vis [team owner] Joe Robbie and the Miami Dolphins. I understand he's a family friend, and if that's the case I wonder if you could introduce me to him and let me make a case for my covering the Dolphins for the remainder of this year like I covered your campaign. (I understand the implications of this, so feel free to back off, if that's your instinct—but if you'd feel comfortable in effecting a human introduction I'd certainly appreciate it.)

That's about it for now. I've been hunkered down for a while, trying to recover from 2 yrs of steady work—a feeling I suspect you'll understand without much trouble. In any case, I'll call sometime soon.

Cazart . . .
Hunter

TO JIM SILBERMAN, RANDOM HOUSE:

Thompson had been asked to write another dust-jacket blurb—this one for his Rolling Stone *colleague Joe Eszterhas's new book,* Charlie Simpson's Apocalypse.

October 17, 1973
Woody Creek, CO

Dear Jim . . .

Jesus, I was amazed to get a human coherent letter from you; I thought the failure of *Vegas* had put me permanently on the RH Non-Person list.

Anyway, I'll take your subjects in order:

1) I got the *Vegas* royalty statement and was naturally shocked—not only by the original sales failure, but also by the lack of any attempt to recoup by tying *Vegas* in with the relative success of the Campaign book.

2) As for *Hell's Angels,* it appears to be permanently out of print. A writer for the *Wall St. Journal* came out here last week to do a piece on "gonzo journalism" and said he couldn't find a copy of *HA* anywhere in Los Angeles. The Campaign book was prominently displayed everywhere, he said, and he was able to pick up a paperback copy of *Vegas*—but not even Pickwick [bookstore] had a copy of *HA* . . . so I look forward with real interest to whatever papers & records you can dredge up from the Ballantine files, inre: sales figures, printings, earnings, etc. All I know is that I've received some $1100 in royalties during the past 3 years, but last spring I found a copy (the first one I'd ever seen for sale) in the San Antonio airport and it was part of the *ninth* printing . . . and the last printing I got any money for was something like the third, or pos-

sibly the fourth, but I was never aware of a *fifth* printing, much less a ninth. (*HA* cover #3, by the way, was even worse & more un-focused than *HA* cover #2, both of which now make your original cover seem like a piece of inspired art on a level with van Gogh's ear.)[21] One of these days I'm going to get pissed off enough about that *HA* ripoff to sit down and compile a really brutal "*Hell's Angels* Log," which will be good for a lot of laughs in some circles, and maybe even among those who pocketed the money from it.

But what the hell? Like you said that time on the phone, when I signed the *HA* contract, "it was the only game in town." Which was true, at the time—just like Ehrlichman[22] used to have leverage—but I think this goddamn Rebozo[23] syndrome has been pushed just about to the brink. If necessary, I'll hire an independent auditing firm to deal with the *HA* royalties. Even if I gave the bastards 50% of whatever monies they recover, I figure I'd still come out way ahead.

Indeed. But I see we've fouled the agenda here; that *HA* bitch was supposed to come *last,* and it was definitely not aimed at you. At least not personally.

3) Mankiewicz's claim that he bought a copy of *Vegas* for 19 cents, at some unspecified store in Washington: Which I must admit I never verified—or even pursued, for that matter—because at the time I was frankly appalled to hear a thing like that, and since it was said in a group of some sort (at McGovern's house, as I recall) I wasn't especially eager to make a scene about it.

But he definitely *said* it, and in a way that gave me no reason to think he was lying . . . although maybe he was; Frank has a weird sense of humor.

In any case, I was surprised to get your version of the meeting with Doug Mount—who was definitely empowered (during a long phone talk on the night before he came to your office) to act as my agent & partner in a deal that would take all remaining copies of *Vegas* off your hands at 22 and a half cents each. But when I talked to him a day or so later, he said you'd been something less than receptive to the idea, implying that I was bit wiggy for even sending him to see you in the first place. At this point, while he was half-accusing me of sand-bagging him, I got the distinct impression that you had sand-bagged me—by offering to sell me the books at the price I suggested, then disowning the deal when Mount appeared in NY to consummate it.

Whatever actually happened, I'm still interested in buying the books—so, in order to avoid any further confusion, you should let me know in writing just exactly what *you* have in mind. Once I know that, I'll crank up something serious on my end. The original proposal, as I recall, was for a mass-purchase, by me or somebody acting in my behalf & probably with my money, of *all remaining copies* of *F&L in Las Vegas* for 22 and a half cents each. I was under the impression that you'd agreed to this, which is why I sent Mount to see

21. Dutch postimpressionist painter Vincent van Gogh cut off part of his left ear in a fit of pique in 1888.

22. Nixon's White House domestic policy adviser John Ehrlichman.

23. Florida businessman Charles "Bebe" Rebozo was President Nixon's closest friend.

you—but the two of you apparently had a communications breakdown, so it will probably take a while to get our figures together again. I assume, however, that my offer will be substantially the same—give or take a penny or so—and I'd like your response in writing ASAP. Thanks.

4) This one is tricky, and it was actually the real reason for my writing this letter in the first place (I haven't done a letter this long in 2 years) . . . but anyway, we now get back to whatever you want me to say about Joe Eszterhas' book, presumably for use somewhere on the jacket or at least in the advertising. You've never told me what you really want, but I assume it's something like that one Tom Wolfe had on the inside flap of the *Vegas* book . . . the one that made *Vegas* such a fantastic seller . . . right, you remember that one: "Scorching and Outrageous . . ." as I recall. . . . It was a good quote (excerpted from a letter from Tom to me, as an outgrowth of some conversation we'd had earlier in San Francisco about the nature of "new journalism," and I remember feeling guilty & apologizing to Tom for so obviously putting his words to my own commercial use—or at least what *seemed* like a commercial use at the time; the fact that we were grossly disabused of that notion very shortly in no way reflects on the spirit of Tom's original letter).

Which brings me now to the subject of Joe's book, and my apparent inability to write a proper sales pitch for it—a problem that has caused me more personal anguish and cost me more friends in the past two years than anything else I can think of. For a while I was getting maybe three or four books a year to read, evaluate & put in a selling capsule of 20 words or less . . . but in the past six months I've been getting on the average of one book a week, and sometimes I get 3 or 4 a week. Just tonight I sent off a handful of unuseable quotes (no publisher has ever used anything I've sent, despite the fact that I usually labor and groan over the fuckers) for a book on the McGovern campaign by a girl named Kristi Witker; I also, tonight, sent a letter to some editor who wanted me to endorse a book by Kenneth Anger[24] that he hadn't bothered to send me (he said he'd send me a batch of copies "for my own use" in exchange for a selling blurb); and also, tonight, I sent a guilty letter to a friend of mine who'd sent me the galleys of his girlfriend's first book, along with a note saying her whole future depended on my publishable comments on her work . . . but I dashed off a letter calling him a rotten bastard for putting me in that kind of a position and saying I refused to read her book under any circumstances, or any other book he might send in the future.

I'm telling you all this just to warn you about my current state of mind—which has been badly bent, of late, by a goddamn torrent of people who not only want to come out here and move into my house, but also into my head &

24. Independent filmmaker Kenneth Anger's *Hollywood Babylon,* which exposed the salacious sides of some movie stars' private lives, was first published in France in 1959 and reissued by Straight Arrow Books in 1975.

my crotch. On a recent Saturday we had twelve (12) applicants for my Senate campaign appear in the driveway between the hours of nine and six. Fortunately, Steadman was here to speak with them—because I have a firm rule now about *never* answering either the phone or the door, which has put an ever-increasing burden on Sandy's nerves. Every time the phone rings we just stare at each other for a while, then her eyes get narrow and her shoulders curl down and she jerks the bastard off the hook and says Dr. Thompson will not be available, for any foreseeable reason, at any time in the near or distant future.

Our only hope now is that Juan can soon take over. He seems to enjoy talking at length with these strangers, even the kinkiest, and he's developing a real talent for it.

But, again, this has only a peripheral bearing on the Eszterhas book problem—which, due to your last letter, has now become a major psychic burden for me. I have no real idea what you want or need from me, or how you plan to use it—but the only thing I'm absolutely certain of, right now, is that my failure to produce this thing is going to haunt me for years to come and probably scar me for life.

And I *will* fail. There's no doubt at all about that. Just as I've failed in every other attempt to write blurbs for other friends' books. Not one has *ever* been used, Jim. Not one fucking word, by anybody—and I've invariably put more work into the goddamn things than I normally put into 5 or 6 pages of a complex political article. A particularly galling example occurred about 3 months ago when a set of bound galleys arrived, with a note from some editor I'd never heard of . . . and for some strange reason I took the thing to bed with me one night and read it straight through. The next day I sent the editor a note full of king-hell quotes, saying it was one of the meanest & fastest-moving stories I'd ever read; I recalled several scenes that I described as "crazed and fantastic violence," and I closed the letter with a brief graph saying that all I missed in the book was a certain sense of dimension, complexity, reality, etc. in the protagonist. It was the kind of complaint a "creative writing" professor would toss into an otherwise high-bouncing gold-hatted critique. Because *all* books are flawed, of course—either horizontally or vertically—and since they'd sent me this book to read and comment on, I felt that classic sort of reviewer's compulsion to whack it at least once, if only to lend a suggestion of balance & perspective to all the good things I'd said about it.

Well, Jim . . . it didn't work. About 3 weeks later I got a letter from the editor who'd sent me the galleys in the first place—a total stranger to me, just like the author—and he spent a whole single-spaced page moaning about how sad it was that I couldn't find it in my heart to acknowledge real talent when it was laid out right in front of my eyes, and how he'd perhaps made a mistake in sending me the book in the first place, along with random dollops of gibberish here & there about "success" and "failure" and god only knows what else . . .

and the net result of the whole thing was, if that mush-minded cocksucker ever sends me another book, by anybody, I'm going to soak it in two quarts of epoxy glue and send it back to him, COD, in a box made of oak logs. . . .

As I told you in an earlier letter, you can sign my name to almost anything short of disgraceful madness. (A recent review of both *Fear & Loathing* books, for instance, said the *Vegas* epic was "possibly the best book since The Bible.") I would not be willing to go quite that far with Joe's book, but I *would* say, for instance, that it's "one of the best and most brutally truthful pieces of American journalism since *Maggie: A Girl of the Streets*."[25] Or that "Eszterhas explodes the myth of the 'new journalism' by showing what 'old journalism' could have been, all along, in the hands of a fine writer."

But none of that shit will sell books, will it? No more than Wolfe's fine words sold any copies of *Vegas*—or at least not enough to matter—and it occurs to me now that there is something not quite right or reasonable that Random House writers should be burdened with the obligation to sell each other's books. What the fuck do you pay all those salesmen for? How about the Publicity dept? The promotion people? All those wizards in the editors' offices who'll make twice as much this year as either me or Eszterhas? My gross salary last year was $12,000 and I paid every goddamn dime of my campaign coverage expenses out of my book advance—approximately $32,000, or slightly more than my half of the paperback sale . . . and now, with both of my RH books out of print in hardcover and my royalty statements a series of foul testaments to some kind of baffling stagnation that nobody including me seems able to understand . . . now, in the shadow of all this, you're leaning on *me* for some kind of instant wisdom to help you sell Joe's book! . . .

None of this matters at the moment, however. The first three points should be easy enough for you to deal with, but #4 is a real bastard. I can write the flap copy and ads for my own books, but my experience with trying to do it for other people has been extremely grim. Maybe we could lash something together real quick on the telephone. If you want to try it, I'm game—and we could probably come up with something right in less than 10 minutes. Give me a ring some afternoon if you feel up to it. Cazart . . .

Hunter

TO GARRY WILLS:

Respected magazine writer Garry Wills raised Thompson's hackles with his lukewarm review of Fear and Loathing: On the Campaign Trail '72.

25. Stephen Crane's 1893 novella *Maggie: A Girl of the Streets* tells the sad tale of a young girl degraded by the squalor of her life in the tenements of New York City's Bowery district.

October 17, 1973
Woody Creek, CO

Garry . . .

Jesus, it came as a bit of a shock to get beaten so savagely for two typos . . . but I guess you have all those notes & other bullshit by now, so there's no point working it over again. As a final note, however, I think your total misunderstanding of my argument about "what McGovern should have done . . ." might be worth arguing about over a beer or nine someday. I never equated "new politics" with "moving left." That connection was made, quite predictably, by establishment columnists.

This is one of the subjects I like to bash around with Pat Buchanan. He's one of the few hit-men in that crowd (or any other, for that matter) that I can really enjoy getting it on with. We disagree so violently on almost everything that it's a real pleasure to drink with him. If nothing else, he's absolutely honest in his lunacy—and I've found, during my admittedly limited experience in political reporting, that power & honesty very rarely coincide. I never tried to absolve Pat of Nixon's crimes & cruelties; all I said was that he didn't mind talking with me about them . . . and considering the things I've said about "The Boss," I have to respect Pat's willingness to invite me over to his apartment and deal with me as a friend . . . even when I'm sitting there, half-drunk in the sun, telling him that somebody could do the world a big favor by dragging [former Nixon White House aide Charles] Tex Colson down Pa. Ave, at the end of a 40-ft. rope.

Can you imagine sitting down for beers with Ehrlichman and telling him a thing like that? (In the winter of '71?) Give that one some thought & then see if you still think it's so rotten for me to sit down and spend an afternoon of flat-out verbal arm-wrestling with Pat Buchanan.

In any case, and just for the record, I disagree savagely with at least 92% of Pat's political views—but I like the bastard and I intend to keep on drinking with him, from time to time, and anybody who doesn't like it can suck wind.

On other fronts, I can understand how you might have gone a bit off the edge when you saw [George F.] Will's theory attributed to you[26]—but I guarantee your reaction was mild, compared to mine. Ever since I began writing politics for *RS,* my main problem has been that most of the editorial staff—who've never even seen me—tend to take my image absolutely seriously; which apparently makes it hard for them to believe I can even spell my own name, much less anybody else's. (At last count—as the 4th or maybe 5th edition of my Campaign book went to press—I was still fighting to correct 422 serious errors in the text—but at $3 a character (in the line-count), that's a hard argument to win on the phone, 1500 miles away from the printer.)

26. Liberal magazine writer Garry Wills was occasionally confused with conservative syndicated columnist George F. Will.

But fuck all that. The bad rap you laid on me regarding the typos will die easy—but if you want to push that thing about "what McGovern should have done," the least you can do is get straight on what I said. And if I didn't make myself clear in the book, I think it's important enough to talk about before we do any more arguing in print. Sincerely . . .

Hunter

TO GEORGE STRANAHAN:

Thompson's neighbor George Stranahan still owned much of the land around Woody Creek.

October 19, 1973
Woody Creek, CO

George . . .

I've been thinking for the past few months that we should get together for a long rambling talk about what's happening and going to happen in this valley . . . but I never seem to get myself focused enough or to find you loose & alone, at the right time, and meanwhile things seem to be happening very fast all around us. I went (almost by accident) to the last meeting of the Woody Creek Caucus and got involved in a nasty crunch about the future of Gravel Pits in WC . . . I meant to go as a pure Observer but with C. Vagneur and D. Barry running one side of the gig, I yielded to my weakness and got involved.

In any case, the geeks in Lower Woody are getting their plans together & I think it's unhealthy for you not to be involved in some way—if only because I want to know what the fuck you're thinking about doing with your land.

Right. My interest is totally selfish. I remember a Bobby Kennedy press conference in Rio that I went to about 10 years ago (it was '62 & JFK was still president) . . . and I remember Robert's words pretty well, if not with exact precision: In answer to some question that no longer matters, he said . . . "The United States, as always, will look primarily to its own interests."

This has stuck in my head for a decade, and that memory has served me fairly well, I think, in terms of journalism and various other areas . . . and the reason I mention it now is that I assume our interests still mesh, with regard to what's happening in W.C. If so, I think we'd be doing ourselves a favor by getting together and articulating them, some evening . . . and, if not, I've spoken with [Joe] Edwards about arranging some kind of "buy-out" addendum to our land contract, which—in return for a sum of money—would leave me free to sell out to the highest bidder, if circumstances dictated.

Another alternative (which just occurred to me about 96 seconds ago) is that you could sell me the pasture *in front* of my house (under the most restrictive of all possible circumstances) and we could then use my "land-bridge" over the county right-of-way to effectively seal off the valley from here to Lenado. That would have three immediate & obvious benefits: 1) The pasture in front of me would remain in its natural state, 2) The county road would have to run *through* one land-holding (instead of between two different ones, as it is now), and 3) . . . well, shit, now that I give it some thought I see various loose ends; not many, but enough to spend at least another hour or so thinking about it.

The nut, however, has to do with the long-term future of Woody Creek . . . and I get the feeling that those people down on the river are sort of teetering on the brink, right now—between selling out & hanging tough—and one of the main factors in their confusion seems to be whatever plans (or lack of them) you and Stanley might have for "Upper Woody."

In other words, there's no point in them spending time & money fighting the Slag Heap, only to have another nightmare develop *above* them. (T. Garth, for instance, mentioned the possibility of a copper mine above his place . . . and nobody has the vaguest fucking idea what you're up to, including me. . . .)

So I think we should talk about this—and preferably in some human atmosphere free of savage accusations, etc. I'm essentially concerned with what you have in mind, and how it might affect me, in the long run . . . and very soon, I think, a lot of other people (whose interests at the moment are hovering between the short-term & the long) will be coming to that same conclusion. There is not much doubt in anybody's mind that you have it in your power to alter or *not* alter the whole complexion and reality of Woody Creek.

This is something that goes far beyond my own personal interest, financially or any other way, in the land I currently occupy here. If I controlled enough acres to be able, by a personal decision, to turn the tide in terms of land-use, I'd be in the kind of situation I think you're in right now . . . which is a kind of cat-bird seat, whereby you can de facto guarantee the sanctity of other people's land by the way you decide to use yours . . . and from what I've seen & heard from the others, there's not much doubt about this. The real horror of land use in Woody Creek, up to now, has been the example, in a vacuum, of Wink Jaffe. He has set a very aggressive tone—not just selling his land, but grinding it up into gravel & piecing it off by the truckload.

On the generally-accepted spectrum, Jaffe's blind greed has made your own dealings seem philanthropic and far-sighted . . . but there's no point kidding ourselves about that, is there? How many more mesas will you have to sell to those corporate butt-fuckers at The Institute? But do you really want to sell the whole valley to absentee-owners and New York–based landlords? Addled-brained shitheads like Slater & Nielsen?[27]

27. Waldemar A. Nielsen was Aspen Institute president Joseph E. Slater's right-hand man.

Shit, I have other things to write—for money, to pay off the mortgage—so I'll chop this off here & hope I've made at least a bit of a point. Call ASAP & let's get together for a talk. . . .

OK,
Hunter

TO VIRGINIA THOMPSON:

After two years of nearly nonstop work, Thompson found that his bank account had not grown at the same rate as his reputation.

October 20, 1973
Woody Creek, CO

Dear V . . .

I never liked "Mom," and "Virginia" seems too formal . . . and since I sign "H" on letters to my friends, maybe V will serve with you . . . I feel more comfortable with it, at least in writing. . . .

A quick answer to your letter of today is that there is no news from me, Sandy & Juan. Nothing except the dullest & most mundane activity has afflicted this place since the long-suffering end of the Campaign '72 book and my half-involved summer in Washington at the Watergate scene. I seem to be in the grip of a deep/dark letdown after spending two years at top speed on the *Fear & Loathing* books. At the moment I feel physically and mentally & emotionally drained. . . . I can't even get excited about what I think is the imminent demise of Nixon. I tried to go hunting the other day, but—standing around the campfire about midnight before the hunt—I realized I would never pull a trigger the next day, so I drove a jeep down the mountain & crashed it into a boulder so violently that it destroyed the front end, and I spent the next 2 nites sleeping out in the weeds of a river-bottom on the western slope of the rockies . . . looking up through the limbs at the jet-trails 33,000 feet up in the sky on the run between New York and LA, and knowing that on any other night I could be up there in one of those planes . . . but feeling very nice down there in my sleeping bag like a totally anonymous person or maybe even an animal. All alone. Not a human being within ten miles in any direction . . . I'd forgotten how it feels to be absolutely alone for more than brief moments here & there.

Anyway, I find myself getting "famous," but no richer than I was before people started recognizing & harassing me almost everywhere I go. The Vegas book, for instance, was a drastic failure on the money front—only 10,000 sales out of a 30,000 first printing. That's bad for the editor, very bad—which explains why my next book will be published by Straight Arrow instead of Random House.

The Campaign '72 book is doing better than expected; it looks to be more along the lines, financially, of the Hell's Angels book, which has so far netted a bit over $25,000—spread out over five years.

But things seem to be working out. The one benefit of "fame" seems to be a big expense account—but that only works when I'm traveling, and the net is always zero. I'm beginning to feel like Joe Louis[28] when he was wallowing in all those dollars for so many years, but none of them stuck to his fingers & when the deal went down he couldn't even pay for his taxes. But no—it's not that bad. I have all manner of geeks from TV shows and lecture agencies calling me at *Rolling Stone,* and I suppose I could make a wad of money if I returned the calls—but I tried the lecture circuit for a week last spring and it came close to destroying me. I made a drunken fool of myself at places like Yale, Harvard & the University of Chicago, and when we added up the bills I was somehow about $600 in the red, due to unexplained expenses on the road.

The only TV thing I've agreed to do this time around is a one-hour argument of sorts with Dick Tuck on NBC next week in Los Angeles. It's a new show called *Tomorrow,* which comes on around one in the morning, following *Tonight.*[29] We're scheduled to tape our gig on Oct 24, for the Thursday Oct 25 program. If I can keep a straight head for the taping, the result might be worth watching. Check the listings on Oct 25—*Tomorrow,* NBC, in the early morning hours.

As for that "running for the Senate" trip, that's just another case of trapping myself in my own rhetoric—and the idea that I should "ambush" Dominick in the GOP primary was Pat Caddell's wishful thinking: He'd already signed on to do the polls for Gary Hart in the Democratic primary (for the Senate), so he tried to pass me (his other client) off as a dingbat Republican.

Politicians are pigs—but the people who make their living off of politicians are beyond description.

And so much for all that. What was that madness about getting me into a lawsuit in Memphis about some estate I never even heard of? I assume it was some spin-off from Uncle Garney—but, Jesus, what a nasty shock to suddenly find myself named as a plaintiff in some goddamn lawsuit in Shelby County, Tennessee, or some such place. I have enough real lawsuits on my head, without having to grapple with people I never even heard of. (At the moment, Oscar Acosta—the Chicano attorney whose behavior was the genesis of "my attorney" in the Vegas book—has an apparently valid claim against me for $25,000, which would worry me considerably if there was any way he could get it, but even in a money vacuum he's managed to kill any chance of a film-sale by his constant threats of a libel suit.)

28. Joe Louis was heavyweight boxing champion from 1937 to 1949.

29. NBC's late-late-night interview program *Tomorrow*, hosted by veteran radio talk-show host Tom Snyder, aired weeknights from October 1973 through January 1982.

So in essence nothing has really changed much—except that I'm now making mortgage payments, instead of rent, and that's a big difference psychologically, if nothing else. Juan is fine, Sandy's teaching reading at the Community School, and I'm doing nothing at all. NOTHING. And that's the way I like it—for now, anyway.

Love,
Hunter

TO JEROME GROSSMAN:

In February 1972 Thompson had gone to Worcester to cover the "Rad/Lib Caucus" organized to unify Massachusetts liberals before the state's April 25 Democratic presidential primary. George McGovern beat Eugene McCarthy nearly three to one in the informal ballot: "To make things worse," Thompson wrote in Fear and Loathing: On the Campaign Trail '72, *"one of the main organizers of the Rad/Lib Caucus was Jerry Grossman, a wealthy envelope manufacturer . . . and a key McCarthy fundraiser in the '68 campaign," who after the event "went far out of his way . . . to make sure McCarthy was done for" by immediately endorsing McGovern.*

October 20, 1973
Woody Creek, CO

Dear Jerome:

I am going through your long letter of Sept 11 for the third time, tonight, and I'm damned if I know how to answer you. Some of your points are so hard & true that they snap me up short with a sense of humility—the backed-off "journalist" vs. the totally committed "activist"—and some are such pure, petty gibberish that I wonder if getting into politics on a national level is worth the horror of putting up with this kind of bullshit, or even existing in the same arena with it.

But what the hell? Let me read the goddamn thing again, and maybe after that I'll be able to deal with it on that level—undetermined, as yet—where it was conceived or at least written.

In the meantime, however—and despite any ugly outbursts that might come your way in the future—I should probably say here, while there's still time, that every milligram of energy that you've put into politics since I first heard your name up at the Wayfarer in '68 is a milligram I envy & have to admire. And whatever description of you in my book that seems to have offended you was, after all, just a quote from one of your local politics wizards. If I zapped you personally, I don't recall it—and if I was ever that careless I should probably apologize. One of my continuing fears is that a combination of rampant ego and fun with the language might result in the flaying of innocent people . . . but I try to be careful, and a backwards glance at the evidence leaves me feeling pretty clean.

Which is not to say that I might or might not have maligned you, accidentally, in my account of the '72 campaign Mass. Rad/Lib Caucus, or perhaps in some other area. Contrary to the assumptions of many book reviewers, I began & continued my coverage of the '72 campaign with the idea that a totally ignorant person might learn a lot more than somebody with a bag of old ideas.

Your claim, however (referring, as you do, to pg. 65 of my book) that the Mass Rad/Lib Caucus was not conceived as a launching pad for McCarthy in '72 reminds me that I would never even have known about the goddamn thing if somebody working for McCarthy hadn't called me at my house in Washington to tell me about it—which is why I went there, for starters—and I also attended the McCarthy rally at Holy Cross the night before the caucus, where Gene made some very strong statements that were not supported by his showing when the deal went down some 15 hours later. I listened to [Democratic political strategist Richard N.] Goodwin speak that day, I listened to Gruening speak, and I was out on the floor when Reuther[30] was counting his votes . . . and it was brutally clear to me, even before the vote was announced, that Gruening & Reuther had you & Goodwin beaten stupid.

I was a bit shaken by the outcome, as I said in the book, but after a time I managed to overcome my shock—and also that memory of McGovern arm-in-arm with Hubert at the Stockyards in '68—and by the time of the California primary I was able to feel a sense of at least journalistic unity with *the troops* in the McGovern campaign.

It was not until a month or so later that I realized that this was not quite the same as feeling a sense of unity with McGovern's top command . . . but at least I admit my mistake on that score, and the deadly weakness I see among You People is that you never understood what was happening (or failing to happen) in '72. All anybody has to do, to understand why Nixon is Our President today, is lock himself in a motel room, overnight, with Marty Peretz,[31] Adam Walinsky and Al Barkan. After eight hours of that, *anybody* would vote for Nixon—or even Agnew *now.*

This is the horror that I see in politics today—a pack of self-righteous hyenas feeding on an unexpected carcass, and getting bloated too fast on all that sudden meat.

I can rail & shout against this, but it won't mean shit in the vacuum of energy & ideas we're all flailing around in right now. As painful as it might be for you, we have to admit that McCarthy was a fraud and Sam Ervin is worse, and

30. Former Democratic senator Ernest Gruening of Alaska, one of the two U.S. senators to have voted against the 1964 Gulf of Tonkin Resolution granting the president free rein in the conduct of the Vietnam War, was eighty-five years old and McGovern's official spokesman at the Massachusetts Rad/Lib Caucus in Worcester in February 1972; fellow speaker John Reuther was the nephew of late UAW president Walter Reuther.

31. Martin Peretz owned *The New Republic,* a small but influential liberal weekly policy magazine.

that McGovern, for all his faults, was a potentially viable presidential candidate in '72 if he hadn't splintered his constituency (or if people like you & Peretz hadn't splintered it *for* him) and that at least a part of his root problem lay in the turned-off "if you're not a virgin you're a whore" syndrome that emerged from the Worcester caucus. This attitude was either an excuse or a reason for much of McGovern's staff-thinking throughout the campaign—and I doubt if he understands, even now, why Mass. was the only state he won.

Jesus . . . I only meant to send a note saying I'd answer your long letter at some later date, when I had time to cope with it. But I see I've gotten into some of the meat; not all, certainly . . . and now that I think on it for a moment I don't see much point in haggling with you over the *details* of what went wrong in '72 . . . because the Main Drift is painfully apparent.

Anyway . . . I'm sure you've noted by now that my stationery stash contains no second sheets. (Herr Wenner feels very strongly about titles and letterheads. . . .)

And I'm sure you've also picked up on the fact that I haven't responded to the main thrust of your letter . . . which struck me, frankly, as a classic of Linthead Thinking, but which was so artfully and aggressively presented as to demand an answer in the same vein. . . .

And in all truth, Jerome, I'm just not up to that right now. It's almost dawn and I have a lot of things to deal with—everything from digging holes to planting two 16-ft. blue spruce trees in my front yard to organizing a local land-use referendum and re-writing the 13th draft of my statement explaining why I can't muster enough adrenaline to run for the U.S. Senate in Colorado this year.

Colorado is a long way from Massachusetts, and at the moment I'm about 8000 feet higher than you—which may or may not affect the tenor of our talk, but in any case it gives me a sense of wasted energy with regard to this letter. It is more than what I intended, and much less than what I'd planned . . . but, considering the possibilities, maybe it's just about right.

In closing—from one politics-junkie to another—I feel pretty safe in assuming that you'll keep hammering the swine from your own stylish mountain-top. You might not believe this, Jerome, but the truth is that I'm really on your side. . . . What worries me now & then is that you might not be on mine.

Cazart . . .
Hunter S. Thompson

FROM U.S. SENATOR GEORGE McGOVERN:

October 22, 1973
Washington, D.C.

Dear Hunter:

The books arrived with the inimitable Hunter Thompson inscriptions, wrappings and trappings. They are warmly appreciated by Eleanor and me. Thanks so much, too, for the two delightful posters which were mailed earlier. We will treasure them.

Enclosed is a copy of my letter to Joe Robbie, recommending that he agree to your suggestion. I think it would be a good mutual arrangement. With regard to the New Politics matter, I will await your call on that sometime in the near future. I think you are probably a better judge of the Colorado situation than I am, but if I get any brainstorms, I will give you a call.

Love to you and Sandy.

As ever,
George McGovern

Eleanor was pleased that you remembered her with the *Las Vegas* book inscription. I will read it too.

FROM KATHARINE GRAHAM, *THE WASHINGTON POST:*

Graham sent her personal thanks for Thompson's subscription and payment.

October 25, 1973

Dear Mr. Thompson:

Thank you for your enthusiastic appraisal of the *Post* and for backing it up with lovely $. I only hope we fulfill the promise, which the paper shortage is making us look at rather hard.

I am an admirer of yours and don't want to put you out of work. But I would like to have that drink. Since Aspen looks pretty remote, please let *me* know if you can come East.

Tell your doctor that *Newsweek*'s editors edit standing or even running.

Sincerely,
Kay Graham

TO JANN WENNER, *ROLLING STONE:*

Thompson was forging ahead with his plans for a Rolling Stone*–sponsored summit of the nation's best political thinkers.*

November 27, 1973
Woody Creek, CO

Jann . . .

Both my typewriters are fucked now, so this will have to be "handwritten," as it were—the required memo inre: plans, budget, etc. for A-76.

I talked for about an hour with Dick Goodwin tonight & also with Adam Walinsky this afternoon—& at this point I feel I've gone as far as I can without some kind of *formal, written* commitment from you. Without it, I fear the vicious embarrassment that would come to be called "Thompson's Folly" or "The *Rolling Stone* Political Nightmare" if I get the thing half-organized & then let it drop for lack of funds, interest, understanding, etc. on your part.

So far, we have Adam, Goodwin, Wagner, & Dave Burke[32] tentatively agreed on a *small* meeting (& the *necessity* for it) sometime in *January.* Dick & I agreed on a target number of nine (9) participants—which probably means eleven (11) in the end. But right now we're aiming for nine, as a very manageable number.

This memo, in addition to the copies you already have of Wagner's outline & my letter of 11/10 to Adam, should give you enough information for a DECS/COMM (decision commitment) ASAP. I absolutely *need* this before I can go any further on my own. Given the obvious fact of my own inability to finance the thing—& also my somewhat nebulous connection with the *RS* empire—I feel the need for some firm footing before I get locked into this gig any further than I am now.

So . . . here's the way I think we should do it.

1) Organize the whole thing, on paper, in the form of a book contract with S/A [Straight Arrow]—along the same lines as my C-72 book. The contract would essentially be between me & S/A—or, rather, between S/A & HST plus 10, 11 or 12 "John Doe's" (names to be filled in later, for royalty purposes). By this means, all expenses for putting the conference (& the book) together would be covered by an *advance,* with all profits beyond the advance (15%) going in equal amounts to the "authors."

2) Under this arrangement, I would be personally responsible to S/A for delivery of the book—which would not only *focus the responsibility,* but spare us both the apparently interminable & energy-sapping money squabbling that seems to be part of any working arrangement with *RS.* It would also require a credit card & a *separate* phone credit card (like the C-72 book contract) that would allow for separate accounting and budgeting.

3) It would also require a lump sum payment to me—for organizing the whole thing & writing the introduction—along the lines of the C-72 con-

32. David Burke was Massachusetts senator Edward M. Kennedy's chief of staff.

tract . . . probably a $10K payment on delivery to me, with another $20K as an advance against expenses . . . for all "author/participants."

(Cazart! It's 5:57 A.M. now & the Aspen FM station is howling "White Rabbit"—a good omen, eh?) ". . . Feed your head . . ."

. . . & starve a habit; that's what I've always said. . . .

Anyway, the A-76 project would also require the services of a more or less full-time ex-secy to keep the lines untangled. You may have somebody in mind; if not, & with considerable luck, I might be able to arrange for somebody out of my own vast experience. I figure the whole project—from DECS/COMM to publication—will take about a year . . . but if it works out right, we'll have a landmark book for '76 & a steady seller until 1999.

The main problem lies in the selection of the people—Goodwin is going to call in a few hours with *his* list: Adam & Carl have theirs—& then, of course, there's mine. All of which now amounts to 25 or 30 names so far (we've already vetoed JK Galbraith, and any use of the word "Democratic" in the title, for instance—just to give you an idea how the thing is beginning to mesh. . .).

So . . . we should have a long (& perhaps taped) phone talk very soon, then we'll need a D/C & a Contract, which Lynn can arrange, I think, after proper instruction. Personally, I like the C-72 contract as a working model—it allows for maximum freedom, minimum hassle, total reimbursement of all expenses, & potentially unlimited returns.

Any pre-pub. excerpts in *RS* should be treated as a separate matter, I think . . . once again, like my C-72 arrangement.

Overall, I see no real problems unless we create them ourselves. Goodwin & I can handle the personnel problems & a good ExSecy can do the tangible organizing—travel, location, communications, etc. (Dick's function, as I see it, will be to keep me from stacking the thing with wild-eyed radical freaks—& mine will be to keep Goodwin from turning it into a Kennedy for President & organizing seminar. . . .)

As for you . . . well, when your nerves get so bad that you have to be doused with a fire-smothering agent, for your own good. . . . I hate to say this, but institutionalization is not always a bad thing.

In any case, I'll probably see you over there in a few days. I'm planning to make the Houston trip with the [Oakland] Raiders this weekend . . . so give this thing some thought ASAP so we can get it settled quick.

Thanx
H

FROM OSCAR ACOSTA:

Acosta was also a bit of a "politics junkie."

November 29, 1973
Los Angeles, CA

Hunter—

For the past six months I've tried to find a job as a writer, lawyer, clerk, laborer, etc. . . . I am blackballed everywhere—in Frisco & L.A.

I've lived on food stamps and petty theft. As you know, counter-culture "legends" don't pay off in cash. Ass & dope are always plentiful, but no one seems to care about my room & board.

Despite all messages & nightmares to the contrary, I still am looking to you as my only serious white connection for the big contract . . . the way it looks from here, I'd even settle for a small one.

Send immediate seed money to discuss the possibilities of forming a political alliance between your freaks and my *cucarachas*. . . . If I had the bread, I could—without doubt—be elected to the offices (one) of City Council, Assembly, Judge and probably Congress. A new "chicano" district has just been ordered by the Calif. Supreme Court.

If you're still serious about running for Senate, you are going to need Corky.[33] I am back with the boys in East L.A. The "commies" who drove me out 2 years ago are now stone nazis (pl.). I ran into César[34] at the press club and he gave me his blessings in front of the politicos who would be my only opponents.

I am very aware that all this sounds like a repeat of my early letters of '68—but the truth is that things have gotten more deadly serious—much more than in those days when it all sounded like pipe dreams.

e.g.: 1) "chicano"—i.e., power is now officially accepted—2) The deputy Mayor (Aragon, former CIA in Brazil) told me to give him a call if I needed anything—3) The press all came at my command—all I said was I'd written an exposé of the CLF, etc. & they came but were too embarrassed to ask if it was fiction or journalism—etc.—4) And East L.A. (part of unincorporated county) will soon be incorporated, which would automatically give me at least city attorney, if not chief of police. . . .

My only "drawback" is the status of my taxes (9 years no file) but it will actually raise all those good American issues once again, "No taxation w/o rep., etc."

Why don't you set up a meeting with May? After all, I can probably even make trouble for [L.A. Mayor Tom] Bradley, his boy. In a close race, I am the best spoiler candidate in town.

33. "Corky" Gonzales was a prominent Chicano activist who was arrested on dubious robbery charges during the riot that ensued upon the news of Ruben Salazar's murder by a Los Angeles County sheriff's deputy.

34. Mexican-American labor leader César Chávez founded the United Farm Workers of America.

At the very least, send my share (you did say 20%) of the film rights to *F/L*—Clancy said you got $7500.00 . . . deduct my loans from you to me and wish me well, as I do you.

The bill for the car, assuming you had to pay for it, should be sent to [associate editor] David Harris at *R/S* since he used it for that week. (I *didn't* get to fuck Joan)—or—you can consider that my fee for holding your hand all the way *into* the fucking airplane.

Money-wise, I am desperate. Send help to above address, quick . . . thanx.

Oscar

TO OSCAR ACOSTA:

By late 1973, relations between Thompson and Acosta had deteriorated to the point of this scathing missive.

December 4, 1973
Woody Creek, CO

Dear Oscar:

Your mail has been getting through—for good & mainly ill, as it were, so I thought I should send you this note inre: your request of Nov 29 for "seed money."

Or any other kind, for that matter. What in the fuck would cause you to ask me for *money*—after all the insane bullshit you've put me through for the past two years? Why don't you try to collect "your 20%" of that $7500 Clancy said I got for the film rights to *Vegas*? A gig like that should keep you busy for a while.

Right . . . put your legal skills to work; work in your own vicious shadow for a change, and see how it feels. The ugly truth, Oscar, is that there *never was* and as far as I know *never will be* a fucking penny for the film rights to *Vegas*—not for me, or you, or Savage Henry (sic) or the Hitch-hiker or your LA lawyer or anybody else. The book has been rendered totally unsaleable for film, for reasons I suspect you understand far better than I do . . . and the only satisfaction I get out of telling you this comes with knowing that you need that 20% a lot more than I need the 80%. I can still make a living by *writing*, old sport—but all you seem able to do is burn your ex-friends. (Yeah . . . I *paid* that goddamn $258 rental-car bill, & Wenner laughs at the idea that Harris used it for working on a *RS* story.)

Anyway, good luck with your grudge. No doubt it'll make you as many good friends in the future as it has in the past.

As for me, my attorney advises me that I can at least deduct something around $10,000 for *losses* you caused me in '73. In the meantime, why don't you write a nice movie? Or a book? You shouldn't have any trouble selling the fucker, considering all the people you've fucked over & burned. . . .

Good luck,
Whitey

TO MAX PALEVSKY:

No longer associated with Rolling Stone, *Max Palevsky had written to Thompson that he was calling in a ten-thousand-dollar personal loan he had made to the writer.*

December 4, 1973
Woody Creek, CO

Ah, Max . . . sometimes I wonder about you.

Your last letter was, as always, a joyous thing to receive. It confirmed my life-long belief that "there is no such thing as paranoia." Only ignorance, naïveté, sloth & the ever-present danger of allowing one's affairs to fall into the hands of toothless ten-percenters.

Which means—and I suppose this was inevitable from the start—that I'll have to come down there and deal personally with this goddamn thing. All my hired surrogates come back with different stories—which might surprise me if I didn't know you—so I figure the only way to understand what shorted out is to talk on a human basis. Or at least as close to that as possible, given these newer & cheaper circumstances.

In any case, I'll call in a day or so from SF. That should give you adequate time to consult with the charred remnants of your conscience.

Cazart,
Hunter

TO MAX PALEVSKY:

Fear and Loathing in Las Vegas *was finally made into a movie—directed by Terry Gilliam, starring Johnny Depp, and screened at the international Cannes Film Festival—in 1998.*

December 25, 1973
Woody Creek, CO

Max . . .

I'm sure you're aware that anything I write or say to you right now—with regard to that $10K & the *Vegas* film rights—is subject to certain constraints and essentially aggressive advice from other quarters—all of which I *pay for,* for good or ill, and which (for that reason, if no other) I'm inclined to take seriously.

And the nut of this advice, for right now, is that *somebody other than me* has fucked up vis-à-vis the *Vegas* film gig. I have not—to my knowledge or even in the realm of accusation—done anything weird, wrong or disruptive in that area . . . which leads me to feel, on balance, that I should not logically bear the brunt of other people's mistakes. I have never backed off from paying my own dues—but at the same time I feel a genuine reluctance to write a cheque for other people's fuck-ups.

I suspect you understand this—just as I hope you understand that I appreciate your loan of $10K & have every intention of repaying it. But you should also understand that I can't just freak out & disregard all the professional advice I pay for, the essence of which is that I'm being ripped to the tits for no reason.

I was hoping, on that afternoon that I drove Linda [Palevsky] and Janey [Wenner] out to the airport, that we could cope with the problem on a human basis & thus get it off both our backs . . . but that was clearly impossible under the circumstances . . . so we're still in the pit, and every solution proposed to me seems more distasteful than the last—but it's also a fact that the logic of the moment seems entirely on my side, for good or ill.

So—in answer to your last letter—let me assure you once again that I have every intention of repaying that $10K loan. The only question, right now, is *how* it should be repaid. And that involves what I regard as an essentially *ethical* question vis-à-vis the *Vegas* film rights . . . just as I regard the $10K loan as an ethical question, with the onus on *me.*

For that reason, the repayment of the $10K loan should be the least of your worries. The question I have to deal with now is *how*—and to understand that I have to get straight on the facts of that goddamn film deal, which at the moment are not within my grasp, but which in the final analysis will have a drastic effect on my personal finances.

So don't take it personally, Max, if I seem to be a trifle less than eager to abandon all hope on this matter—which has suddenly assumed a complexity far beyond the simple matter of a $10K personal loan. But, whatever happens, I'd like to keep it on a friendly human basis. If not . . . well . . . I've never been averse to a good fuckaround, especially in the face of the odds we're looking at here . . . but, even then, I'd rather not get personal.

I'm sure, in the meantime, that either you or your lawyers will be in touch with IFA, on one level or another. So let's leave it at that, for now. Shit . . . we might even have some fun with this thing; maybe even a good story of some sort.

Cazart . . .
Hunter

TO JANN WENNER, *ROLLING STONE:*

December 25, 1973
Woody Creek, CO

Jann . . .

Here's a copy of a thing I just sent to Walsh.[35] My feeling at the moment is that neither he nor you nor anyone else at *RS* can really help me on this (given

35. Former *Newsday* sports editor John Walsh was briefly managing editor of *Rolling Stone.*

the dim results of Walsh's best efforts to lean on the Raider management) . . . so I think we'll all be better off if I just deal with the bugger myself, & hope for the best. (Walsh, however, can be critical in any dealings that might arise inre: my press credentials for the Super Bowl) . . . but beyond that, I think we've pretty well shot our wad vis-à-vis *RS* & the Raider management, and any further "pressure" from *RS* will only piss them off & prejudice whatever's left of my human connection over there.

I'm assuming, for now, that I have valid (& 1st class) press credentials for the Super Bowl in Houston—and, to that end, I think we should ask for photog credentials for Raoul Duke, in addition to the normal "press" bullshit for HST. That way—as a compromise solution in line with the one you've already suggested . . . I might be able to work incognito as a photographer. Which might work out at least as well as it did on that Cozumel/*Playboy* assignment.

OK for now. I hope to fuck you've left the "A-76" trip intact enough for me to cope with it personally. Otherwise, I doubt if there's any point in wasting either of our time & effort on a '74 writing contract. As far as I'm concerned, my recent visits to SF inre: the Pro Football story & other gimcracks constitute the "fair & reasonable trial period" we informally agreed on during my quasi-violent Halloween visit . . . and I doubt if anyone who lived thru the last one would urge any further extension of the trial period.

My feeling about *RS,* at this time, is that we'll all be better off if I stay as far from the day-to-day operations as humanly possible—and if you called for a staff-vote, I think the results would agree with me. (I want to be on record, however, to the effect that I remain genuinely & personally concerned inre: the direction *RS* appears to be drifting toward at this time—and if there's anything I can do to have a *real* effect on this drift, I'm still interested enough to lend a bit of crank to it.)

Otherwise, I think we'll all be better off if I work directly with St. Arrow on a contract basis—like last year—& leave you & yrs. free to do whatever you want with the "book." Every once in a while, perhaps, we might find something mutually excerptable from my book-work, & on these occasions I assume we can work together on an "article" not subject to either editing or expense-hassles.

In the meantime, pls. keep me advised on the status of "A-76." It's the only project we're mutually involved in at this point that seems to have any real future.

Cazart,
Hunter

TO GREG JACKSON, ABC NEWS:

Thompson's love of pro football went unrequited, due to the reputation that had grown up around him. Jackson had become a close friend of Thompson's on the campaign trail.

Xmas morning 1973
Woody Creek, CO

Jackson . . .

It's 1:22 A.M. here & I just got yr. thing in re: J. G. Dunne[36] & Las Vegas—which started out fine & sharp & personal, then fell back on itself in the end (maybe due to bad editing) . . . so I guess I'll have to wait for the book.

I met him & his wife about a month ago, incidentally, at a dinner party at Palevsky's; they seemed like inordinately *quiet* people. Or maybe it was just because of my own standard-brand behavior—drunk, speedy & raving.

Anyway . . . thanx for the clip.

On other fronts, how do you like [Tim] Crouse's trip? I feel like the illegitimate father on a trip that would have to include you as the mid-wife . . . and in the wake of all that campaign fever & bullshit, I feel a strange sense of angst and dis-jointed emptiness about "journalism." The past year has been a total waste of time & everything else, to my mind . . . and tonight is my last chance to finish a piece for the Jan 1 *NY Times* Op-ed pg. on "the meaning of '73," or whatever.

Which is a hard thing to write—because (despite the wild breakthrough of Watergate, etc.)—'73 has been as dull & rotten a year as I can remember. I have a $50K book/novel contract to fulfill by July of '74—and I suppose I'll have to do it; but all that really interests me now is the '76 Campaign.

In the meantime, seize any chance you get to stop by the Owl Farm & do *nothing* for a week or so. That's all I can offer at the moment. My only gig for the past 3 months has been a long and psychically complicated "pro football" story—which unexpectedly terminated last week when the Oakland Raider management suddenly informed me that I was barred—because of my "personal involvement in the drug scene"—from any contact with the team in public or private. There was no explanation, to me or the editors of *RS,* and right now I'm waiting for official word that I'm barred from even attending the Super Bowl in Houston.

It's the Ziegler trip all over again, but this time I'm dealing with pros. When the NFL comes down on you, it's like the NKVD[37]—they make the White House hacks look like amateurs.

Anyway, if you get to the Super Bowl in Houston, I'll be there—and probably under the same ugly circumstances that characterized my arrival on the '72 primary scene in Florida. Which might be fun, or at least a reasonable facsimile, so why don't you try for a sort of auxiliary coverage gig at the Super

36. Novelist John Gregory Dunne and his wife and frequent collaborator Joan Didion wrote the scripts for the 1971 movie *The Panic in Needle Park* and 1972's *Play It As It Lays.* Dunne also wrote the novel *Playland,* chronicling the harsh life of onetime child star and nymphet Blue Tyler.
37. The Soviet Union's Narodnyi Komissariat Vnutrennikh Del, or People's Commissariat of Internal Affairs.

Bowl—using a peg like "the socio-political aspects of pro football," or whatever you can make of it.

OK for now. I have to get back to struggling with this goddamn thing for the *Times*.[38] If you can't get out here in the next few months, I'll see you in either Houston or NY.

Cazart,
Hunter

38. Thompson's political commentary "Fear and Loathing in the Bunker" ran in *The New York Times* on January 1, 1974.

1974

BACK TO WASHINGTON, BACK TO WORK, BACK TO THE HALLS OF THE EVIL WATERGATE HOTEL . . . COLLAPSE OF THE NIXON EMPIRE, REVENGE OF THE BRUTAL FREAKS . . . CONSTANT TRAVEL, CONSTANT PLOTTING, SUMMIT CONFERENCE IN ELKO & FATEFUL FIRST MEETING WITH JIMMY CARTER . . . SENATOR THOMPSON FROM COLORADO? . . .

Studebaker Society, 1974, clockwise from 6:00: Little Richard, Dick Goodwin, Adam Walinsky, Dave Burke, Carl Wagner, Pat Caddell, Rick Stearns, Sandy Berger, Jann Wenner. (Missing from photo: Doris Kearns and Hunter Thompson.)
(PHOTO BY HUNTER S. THOMPSON)

Jann Wenner and Doris Kearns, Elko Conference, 1974.
(PHOTO BY HUNTER S. THOMPSON)

Pat Caddell and Sandy Berger, Elko, 1974.
(PHOTO BY HUNTER S. THOMPSON)

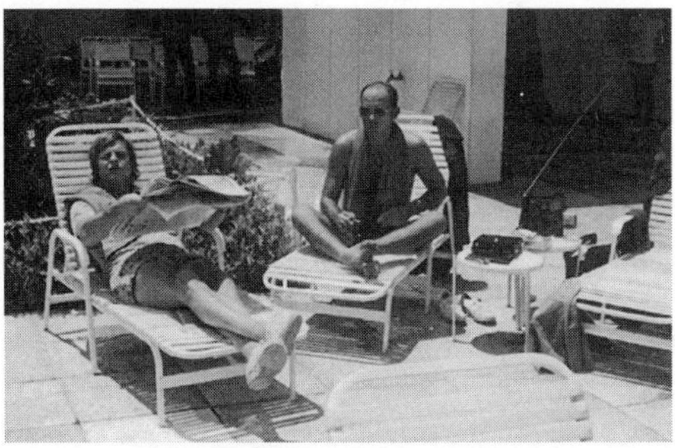

Zaire, 1974, with George Plimpton.
(PHOTO BY RALPH STEADMAN)

Leaving Elko, 1974. Left to right: Pat Caddell, Dick Goodwin, Jann Wenner.
(PHOTO BY HUNTER S. THOMPSON)

With Ralph Steadman in Zaire, 1974.
(PHOTO BY RALPH STEADMAN)

TO PATRICK J. BUCHANAN, THE WHITE HOUSE:

After newsstand sales proved the popularity of Thompson's 1972 campaign-trail articles, the National Affairs Desk was encouraged to expand Rolling Stone*'s political coverage.*

January 3, 1974
Woody Creek, CO

Dear Pat:

Why is it that every time I pick up a magazine or newspaper I see your name? More often than *mine,* even. And on top of that, my dubious & beer-stained relationship with you has "lent," as it were, a certain onus to my reputation.

In any case, it occurred to me tonight—in my semi-retired capacity as Nat. Affairs Ed. of *RS*—that you might get a boot out of writing a real hammerhead screed for us, something to jerk the dope-addled *RS* audience off its ass and generate some of that old-fashioned fear & loathing that we all came to know & love in the old days.

More specifically, I'm thinking about your prognosis vis-à-vis the health & future of "conservatism" in American politics—given the current . . . ah . . . uneasy circumstances. As you know, I've always felt a certain twisted sympathy for your (personal) stance—if only because of what strikes me as its basic integrity, along with a stylistic brutality that I can appreciate for reasons I see no need to discuss at this point in time.

As for the chance of your doing a screed for *RS,* I'm thinking about something between 2000 and 4000 words, which would be either one or two pages in the magazine (with heads & white space) at about twice the money you get from the *NY Times* Op-Ed gang.

Or maybe more. I don't want to be put in the position of negotiating for yr. wisdom on a sleazy commercial basis. I am, as you know, above that sort of thing—and besides that, Jann Wenner (the editor) has the final say on fees. Just between you & me though, I wouldn't take anything less than a grand for anything substantial.

My reason for mentioning length-limits is that if you run over 2K you're into another page—which is no real problem, but I've always found things more congenial if you can seize a whole page (or two) for yourself, which means shooting for either 2 or 4 thousand words, just in order to clear the decks.

I can't guarantee your *audience* reception, but as far as any editorial interference is concerned, I'll make damn sure that whatever you write gets printed—or at least that you'll have the final cut on any editing; and our format's so flexible that I can't see any likelihood of that.

So . . . give it a thought. I think we're all a bit nervous, these days, about what's coming next, and I'm personally curious as to how *you* see it—for good or ill. Shit, for all I know, the *RS* readers might lock right into yr. trip. That would scare me a bit, but what the hell? Let me know how you feel about doing the piece.

Meanwhile, hello to Shelley . . . and also I want to get together with you and Nick[1] when I get back to DC in early spring—to cover the impeachment proceedings. OK. Say hello to the boys in the bunker for me.

Cazart . . .
Hunter

cc: Jann Wenner

TO TERRY COOK, *HOT ROD:*

Hot Rod *editor Terry Cook had asked Thompson, a longtime car-racing fan, to consider covering a California road race for his magazine.*

January 4, 1974
Woody Creek, CO

Terry . . .

Thanx for the good letter; I'm not much on answering mail, but yrs. hit a friendly nerve & I thought I should rip out a note in the few remaining hours before cranking off to Houston for the Super Bowl festivities.

Fortunately, I've never had the time to sit back & really think about what I've been writing—but if it has anything even remotely resembling that Lewis & Clark[2] effect you mentioned, I figure it can't be all wrong . . . and, despite the assumed limitations of yr. own gig, why not give it a whack now & then, and see what happens. You'd be surprised what even real pigs will swallow when they're looking down the barrel of a brute-deadline and the first 10 pages of the book are still empty.

Anyway, thanx for writing & I hope you'll keep me posted (thru Dave Felton at *RS*) on whatever we have to do to get posted for the next Cannonball

1. Pat's wife, Shelley Buchanan, and Nixon advance man Nick Ruwe.
2. Meriwether Lewis and William Clark, with the help of their Indian guide and interpreter Sacagawea and at the behest of President Thomas Jefferson, made the first overland American expedition to the Pacific Northwest coast, starting out from St. Louis, Missouri, in 1804 and returning there in 1806.

Baker classic. Given the nature of the fucker, I suspect Nixon's 55 mph speed limit should only make it more interesting . . . and it's hard to see much difference between 90 and 110 past the cop-house in Needles.

Fuck Nixon; he doesn't even have a driver's license.

In any case, I'm eagerly awaiting post-time, etc. for the CB classic. Cazart . . .

HST

cc: Dave Felton

TO ALAN RINZLER, STRAIGHT ARROW BOOKS:

Thompson had convinced Jann Wenner to have Rolling Stone *sponsor a gathering of the best liberal thinkers from the staffs of the 1968 and 1972 presidential campaigns of Robert F. Kennedy, Eugene McCarthy, and George McGovern for a four-day political symposium in February 1974. The idea was that these Democratic gurus would hash out an issues agenda for America's future, which Straight Arrow would publish in book form and distribute to the nation's decision-makers.*

February 2, 1974
Woody Creek, CO

Dear Alan:

Enc. pls. find two documents: 1) My original memo to Jann, dated Nov 27 '73, on the A-76 gig . . . and 2) My altered version of the stupid & insulting contract you sent me inre: the same subject.

Or at least I assume we were talking about the same subject, despite the lack of evidence in that pawn-shop contract you sent. I talked to Jann on the phone last night & told him to strike my name from any connection with the planning end of the project . . . and his suggestion, at that point, was that I should "amend," as it were, the contract you sent . . . which is the purpose of this hopefully brief memo.

So, let's take it page by page—although the two main changes I have in mind deal with pages One & Two.

On Pg. #1)—I have no plans to *ever* sign a contract of any kind that lists me as co-author with *anyone* else, and certainly not in a situation where the contractual "author" is responsible not only for delivering a book comprised mainly of the works of at least 10 other people (most of them lawyers & writers with agents of their own), but where the contractual "author" is clearly responsible for use & disbursement of the $20,000 Expense Budget. The nature of this project—and we should all understand that unless it works first as a *project,* no book worth reading or even publishing will ever come out of it—makes it absolutely imperative that *one person* has enough control over the project to accept responsibility for delivering a finished ms.

I don't really give a fuck who the author of record is—in the contract or on the book jacket—because my original conception of both the project & the book effectively precludes the likelihood of anybody except the publisher making any significant amount of money from it. My original concept was essentially communistic with regard to royalties—with the lone exception of a $10,000 "author's" fee to me, for lashing the whole thing together and working like a bastard to create some kind of significant ms. out of it.

That $10K figure seems eminently fair to me—and if it strikes either you or Jann as extravagant, I suggest you find somebody else to handle the bastard. I have other money-projects, as you know, and the only reason I'm involved in this one is that it was my idea in the first place & also that I think it's an important thing to do.

That same feeling, I think, is the prime motivation for the others' participation. Nobody thus far—except whoever designed that rancid, cheapjack contract—has viewed this thing in terms of personal gain.

Well . . . I seem to be too angry to continue this fucker in any rational or detailed sense; and besides that I have a chartered Cessna 210 waiting for me at the Aspen airport for a flight to Salt Lake City to pick up Jann, then to Elko to check out the conference site, make all reservations & arrangements, then back to Aspen for a two-day haggle with Jann before leaping over to Denver on Wednesday for the [Bob] Dylan concert.

So let's get to Pg 2 at once: The only serious problem there has to do with the $20K Expense provision. . . . Under no circumstances will the "contributors" be paid out of the expense fund, as long as I have anything to do with this project. If you & Jann are prepared to run a flagrant rip-off on people like Dave Burke and Adam Walinsky, I can't even wish you good luck. All you'll succeed in doing is getting yourselves in the same psychic category with Ralph Ginzburg[3] & Sidney Zion—and I intend to do everything necessary to disassociate myself from an ugly trip like that.

In any case, my suggestion of a $20K expense fund was arbitrary—and will be subject, no doubt, to the same factors that affected the expense-budget for my C-72 book. But that contract *worked,* I think, and that's why I used it (in the Nov 27 '73 memo) as a model for this one. It made me responsible for delivering the book, as well as making me responsible for paying off all expenses incurred in a year of unpredictably-expensive research that eventually came to over $32,000—every fucking dime of which was repaid, you'll recall, within 2 or 3 months of publication.

Right . . . and I think this memo should end very soon. The two main & essential changes in the contract I want to make are: 1) *No co-authorship*—for reasons of edit. & organizational control, more than any concern about whose name appears on the book jacket. If I'm the "author," then I'll organize the

3. Former *Esquire, Eros,* and *Fact* magazine editor Ralph Ginzburg.

thing and deliver the *ms*. . . . Or if you think Jann should be the "author," then he can handle all that & I'll either quit the whole gig or limit my participation to writing about the thing, if it happens. The only other contract change I can think of at this point is a small jump in the author's fee—to $12,500, instead of $10,000, in order to cover two days of extreme mental anguish for the originally-designated author and also his agent's fee . . . and also a provision for one-half of the "author's fee" ($6,250) to be paid on signing of the contract . . . to be paid, in the usual manner, via Lynn Nesbit c/o IFA in New York . . . and no reference shall be made in the contract, in any way, to any presumed or implied obligation by the author to the IFA corporate entity.

OK for now. I think this memo takes care of my central points & objections vis-à-vis the sub-human contract I received in yesterday's mail.

For reasons that I've halfway explained to Lynn, any detailed conversation on this subject should be directed to *me*—for reasons involving the absolute necessity for privacy on this project, until we can get it properly organized. Any prior publicity or even press-gossip could cripple the whole thing beyond repair.

Right . . . and now I have to pack & catch that goddamn little beach-ball of a plane for the ride to Salt Lake & Elko.

Cazart,
Hunter S. Thompson

TO PAUL SEMONIN:

Thompson claimed to his old friend Paul Semonin that a week before The Realist *had mentioned "the assassination of President Nixon," he himself had interviewed someone who claimed to know something about an alleged plot.*

February 10, 1974
Woody Creek, CO

Paul . . .

I just got the new issue of *The Realist* & noticed on page 3 (top-right) a reference to "the assassination of President Nixon."

This was an odd thing to see, coming as it did less than a week after interviewing a person who popped up more or less out of nowhere with a flat-out "incredible" story about how people were being screened for that job. It was a hard thing to believe, at first—& especially with no hope of corroboration—but your note about Packwood[4] suddenly gave it some flesh.

Maybe we should get our heads together on this sometime soon. I'm leaving for Boston in a few hours, and just in case my plane crashes with Gordon

4. Republican Robert Packwood of Oregon held a seat in the U.S. Senate from 1969 to 1995, when he opted to resign rather than face expulsion for his grab-ass approach to virtually every woman he came in contact with professionally as well as personally.

Liddy's[5] god-son on the passenger manifest, I've left the details of my volatile contact (above) with Wenner . . . and I've also contacted Carl Bernstein at the *W/Post* to see if he knows anything about this weird connexion.

In any case—regardless of how this thing gets dealt with in the big-time press—I think I'm onto something worth pursuing; by you, me, the *Post,* or anyone else who can run it down for real. Because if what this bastard told me was true, it's going to be a sellers' market for bullet-proof vests very soon. But in the meantime, let's keep it out of print until we can put these things together.

Sincerely,
Hunter

TO JANN WENNER, *ROLLING STONE:*

Following his 1962 fiction debut One Flew Over the Cuckoo's Nest *with the equally acclaimed novel* Sometimes a Great Notion *two years later, Ken Kesey had abandoned writing for a while to tour full-time with his band of "Merry Pranksters" on their psychedelic bus* Furthur. *By 1974, Kesey had turned to grassroots politics in Oregon.*

February 15, 1974
Woody Creek, CO

Jann:

Inre: Kesey's note on how the BITR Council should be covered by *RS,* I suspect his long-camouflaged penchant for news-management has finally crept out in the open.

He may or may not have been right, originally, about my "coming on too vitriolic." (Although this was totally contrary, as you know, to the spirit of all our previous talk about how to cover & deal with the thing. . . .) But now that he's actually said it, I have an ominous feeling that his Fear might turn out to be Father to the Fact . . . and to that end I think this one should be removed from the realm of the NA desk and assigned from the SF end. I could make some suggestions, but since I'm sending a copy of this letter to Ken, I figure anybody I'd mention would be automatically prejudiced when he/she showed up in Oregon.

In any case, this (BITR Council) is the only state-level gig I've heard about that seems to be heading in the same direction as the one we've been talking about nationally—and because of that, I'd definitely like to know what comes of it. The press release "proposal" is somewhat hazy . . . but then so was the original announcement for the first SF acid test in Longshoreman's Hall, so I'm

5. Former FBI agent and Watergate burglary co-coordinator G. Gordon Liddy refused to plea bargain and was sentenced to twenty years in prison for his activities on behalf of the Committee to Re-Elect the President (CREEP).

inclined to suspend any judgement on this one until we see what Kesey & his people can do with it.

As a final shot: As much as I like both [Paul] Krassner and [Tom] Wolfe, personally, I'd be strongly inclined to avoid whatever temptation there might be to assign either one of them to this story, if only because of the potential news-management problem I've already cited (above). If Kesey wants to understand *realpolitik* & be his own press secretary at the same time, God's mercy on his ass . . . and (although I say this with a sense of genuine reluctance) I think we have to view him with the same hard eye we've used all along on Nixon/Ziegler.

On balance, however, this is a fairly minor point. Both the idea and the potential should be taken very seriously in terms of a possible breakthrough on the state/local political front . . . and I hope the bugger can make it work: But if he can't, I think whoever covers the thing for *RS* should feel just as personally free to say *why* it didn't work (& to name all the necessary names) as he/she should be to celebrate the success & to name names on that end, too.

Personally, I hope he can make it work. I just came from Ann Arbor, where things are not going nearly as well as they were 2 years ago, and tonight I read a piece in the *Wash/Post* on what seems like a similar downhill drift in Petaluma. The Berkeley situation is beyond my ken at this point, but here in Aspen we're facing a serious backlash very much like the Petaluma & Ann Arbor scenes . . . and all these hung together might be worth a story in itself.

Let's talk about this ASAP . . . and if there's anything we can do to help the Oregon thing, let's do it; but I don't think assigning somebody to do a friendly, in-house white-wash will help Kesey, us, or anyone else.

Cazart:
Hunter

cc: Kesey

TO KEN KESEY:

Thompson applauded Kesey's decision to take on the political establishment by its own rules.

February 15, 1974
Woody Creek, CO

Ken . . .

Here's a carbon of a thing I just sent to Jann, inre: the BITR Council & possible *RS* coverage. If it seems harsh or "vitriolic" by yr. standards, that's not the way I meant it. But, let's face it—assigning Wolfe & especially Krassner to cover your debut in politics would have a pretty obvious touch of the Fix in it.

Jann might disagree, but your implied restrictions on press coverage put me in a position where I should probably stay clear of the whole thing & just see what happens.

I'm not quite sure just exactly what you have in mind, but I hope it works and if I/We can be of any help in the way of organizing & logistics, let me know what you need and I'll try to put you in touch with some hired guns up your way.

If not, good luck with the thing. If you do it right, it could definitely be the kind of model you want it to be.

Anyway, it's good to hear you're coming back to Main Street, if only for a visit. It's a rotten place to live, but that's where they set all our prices—so we should give the bastards a whack in the kidneys from time to time, just to remind them that it's our world, too.

Okay for now,
Hunter

—if you feel like calling anytime in the late afternoon or night, do . . . but if I start getting strange anonymous calls from Oregon I'll do the same thing you'd do if . . . well, shit . . . why go into that? Cazart . . . H

TO LUCIAN TRUSCOTT, *THE VILLAGE VOICE:*

After an awkward gap in communication, Thompson reconciled with his friend Truscott.

February 15, 1974
Woody Creek, CO

Lucian . . .

I suspect there's something more than a natural-accident factor in the odd fact that the fine shirt you sent me was size "M," instead of the "XL" I usually wear. (On rare occasions—when we're dealing with finely-tailored dress shirts, etc.—I can wear a size "L." But as a rule of thumb I go the "XL" route, for good or ill.)

In any case, thanx for the shirt & also for the good-spirited note that came with it. Needless to say (or maybe not, I guess) . . . I'm as sorry as you are about last year's "horror show." But, just for the record, I never saw it as a "falling out." Just a bummer. But I agree with you (& have for a long while) that it's "gone, over & forgotten." So let's hear no more about the fucker. Your letter (long ago) on the subject made more sense than most of my gibberish—but I was not entirely rational at that time, for reasons I assume you'll understand as well as I now understand how you got caught in the middle of the thing.

Okay? No more, eh?

Anyway, I just finished your piece on the Dylan concert & given the fact that I've doubtlessly missed a few, it strikes me as maybe the best thing you've ever done—a really fine fucking piece. I went to the Denver concert & came away with a nervous sense of angst that I couldn't explain & for which I took a lot of shit from the others who went & worshipped (including Wenner), but until your piece showed up in today's mail there was nothing I could point to & say "Okay, here's at least *one* other person who agrees with me"—which you did, almost straight down the line & all the way to the end—so, although I doubt if it changed anybody's real opinion of the concert or the myth, it at least made me seem a little bit less like a brute & a bigot.

I was supposed to write a "column" for *RS* on the Denver gig, for that matter, but I refused to either write it or explain why I wouldn't. . . . But maybe later, eh? When the gold dust settles.

Anyway, your stuff has been looking better & better—especially in the context of trying to deal with Nixon on one hand and Dylan on the other, which requires a bit of . . . ah . . . *range;* is that the word? If not, send me a note & tell me what they call it in NY. I need to know these things.

As for you . . . well . . . . . . as you know, I've always been opposed to the concept of marriage except for myself and a few other people who can handle it, and the evidence of late appears to be on your (& Peggy's) side . . . so what the fuck; why not?

Don't invite me to the goddamn wedding, but send a line as to where you'll be living . . . and stop by for a visit if you get out this way. (But check first, because I'm here about half the time: I just got back from 2 "speeches" in Buffalo & Ann Arbor, for instance, and I'm off in 3 days for points west to deal with the NA desk.)

Okay for now. Thanx again for the shirt, which fits Sandy just about right—& I think that's appropriate. Hello & good luck to Peggy. Cazart . . .

Hunter

A-76
Memo #XO1
Elko, Nevada
Organizing Conference: Feb 21–24, 1974

Thompson selected the unlikely venue of Elko, Nevada—population 8,617 at the time—for Rolling Stone*'s cabal of sharp liberal strategists to sort out the future of American politics. Before the conference began Thompson distributed the following memo to his fellow participants: sponsor Jann Wenner; RFK '68 campaign veterans Dave Burke, Richard N. Goodwin, Doris Kearns, and Adam Walinsky, and '72 McGovern operatives Sandy Berger, Patrick Caddell, Rick Stearns, and Carl Wagner. Unfortunately, Thompson would pronounce the summit meeting's results not only unpublishable, but "gibberish."*

This is a first-draft, last-minute attempt to lash together a vague preamble, of sorts, with regard to the obvious question: What the fuck are we doing here in Elko, Nevada, in a corner of the Stockmens' Hotel about 200 feet from the Burlington & Northern RR tracks on a frozen weekend in late February—

sharing the hotel with a state/sectional bridge-tournament—at a time when the rest of the country seems to be teetering on the brink of an ugly, mean-spirited kind of long-term chaos that threatens on an almost day-to-day basis to mushroom beyond anything we can say, think or plan out here in this atavistic sanctuary with nothing to recommend it except the world's largest dead Polar Bear and the biggest commercially available hamburger west of the Ruhr. (Both of these are in the Commercial Hotel, across the RR tracks from our plush hq. in the Stockmens' Motor Hotel.)

Indeed . . . This is a valid question, and in the next 48 hours we will not have much else to do except try to answer it. Or maybe just hang weird at the gambling tables & try to ignore the whole thing. Both the bars and casinos in Elko are open 24 hours a day, in addition to several nearby whore-houses staffed by middle-aged Indian ladies, so anybody who doesn't feel like getting into politics has a variety of options (the train doesn't stop here, and all departing flights are fully booked until Sunday) to while away these rude and lonesome hours until we can all flee back to our various sinecures in those bastions of liberalism where hired guns and dilettantes are still honored.

In any case, the original impulse that led to this gathering bubbled up from a conversation I had in Woody Creek last summer with Adam Walinsky, in which I expressed considerable reluctance vis-à-vis my long-neglected idea about running for the U.S. Senate from Colorado. I had, at that point, received several hundred letters from people who wanted to work in "my campaign," and the notion of backing off was beginning to fill me with guilt—which Adam nicely compounded by saying that, if I decided not to run, I'd be one of the few people in the country who could honestly say that he had the Senator he deserved.

Which is *not* true, of course—given the gang-bang nature of the '74 Senate race in Colorado—but after brooding on that remark for many months I find it popping up in my head almost every time I start thinking about politics. And especially about the elections in 1976—which, until the unexpected demise of Spiro Agnew,[6] I was inclined to view in very extreme and/or apocalyptic terms. Prior to Agnew's departure from the White House and (presumably) from the '76 presidential scene, I saw the 1976 elections as either a final affirmation of the Rape of the "American Dream" or perhaps the last chance any of us would ever have to avert that rape—if only temporarily—or perhaps even drive a stake of some kind into the heart of that pieced-off vampire that Agnew would have been in '76, if "fate" had not intervened.

But things have changed now. Agnew is gone, Nixon is on the ropes, and in terms of *realpolitik* the Republican Party is down in the same ditch with the Democrats—they are both looking back into their own loyalist ranks for

6. Vice President Spiro T. Agnew resigned his office on October 10, 1973, pleading no contest to tax-evasion charges dating to his governorship of Maryland from 1967 to 1969.

names, ideas & possibilities: The GOP has been stripped all the way back to 1964, with Goldwater/Reagan vs. [Republican New York governor Nelson A.] Rockefeller & maybe Percy[7] on the outside . . . but in fact Nixon's mind-bending failure has effectively castrated the aggressive/activist core of the GOP (all the Bright Young Men, as it were), and barring totally unforeseen circumstances between now & Nov '76, the GOP looks at a future of carping opposition until at least 1984.

This may be good news for professional Democrats, but it is not likely to be viewed as a Great Victory by those of us who share what seems to be a very active and potentially massive sentiment among the erstwhile "youth generation" (between ages 25 & 40 now) to the effect that *all* career politicians should be put on The Rack—in the name of either poetic or real *justice,* and probably for the Greater Good.

This sentiment, reflected in virtually *all* age, income & other demographic groups, is broad & deep enough now—and entirely justified, to my mind—to have a decisive effect on the '76 elections, which *might* in turn have a decisive effect on the realities of life in America for the next several generations, and also on the life-expectancy of the whole concept of Participatory Democracy all over the globe.

As a minor & maybe even debatable forerunner of this, we can look back at what happened in South America (in the time-span of 5 or 6 years) when it suddenly became obvious in the mid-1960s the new Democratic Administration had scuttled the Alliance for Progress,[8] in favor of the war in Vietnam. In half a decade, we saw a whole continent revert to various forms of fascism—an almost instinctive reversion that was more inevitable than programmed, and which will take at least five decades to cure.

Ah . . . that word again: "Cure."

Manifest Destiny.

The question raised by the ostensibly complex but essentially simple reality of what happened in South America in the late Sixties—and also in Africa and most of Asia, for the same basic reasons—is only now beginning to seriously haunt the so-called "civilized" or at least "industrialized" nations in Europe and the northern Americas. President [Ferdinand] Marcos of the Philippines put it very bluntly about a year ago in a quote I can't find now—but I think it went something like this: "Your idea of 'democracy' was right for *your* development, but it's not what we need for *ours.*"

I've been meaning to go to the Philippines to see what kind of working alternative Marcos had in mind, but I haven't had the time.

7. Republican senator Charles Percy of Illinois.

8. The Alliance for Progress, instituted by JFK in 1961, was a federal program designed to boost the social and economic development of the twenty-two Latin American countries that joined the United States in signing the Charter of Punta del Este.

Maybe later. If we decide even tentatively here in Elko that Marcos was *right,* I want to spend some time over there very soon—because, regardless of what happens in the Philippines, the question Marcos raised has a nasty edge on it.

Was Thomas Jefferson a dingbat?

Ten days before he died, on July 4, 1826, Jefferson wrote his own valedictory, which included the following nut:

"All eyes are opened or opening to the rights of man. The general spread of the light of science has already laid open to every view the palpable truth, that the mass of mankind has not been born with saddles on their backs, nor a favored few booted and spurred, ready to ride them legitimately, by the grace of God. . . ."[9]

President Marcos would probably agree, but he would also probably argue that Jefferson's reality was so different from what was happening 100 years later in Russia or 200 years later in the Philippines that his words, however admirable, are just as dated and even dangerous now as Patrick Henry's wild-eyed demand for "liberty or death."[10]

Ah . . . madness, madness . . . where will it end?

I think I know, with regard to the way I live and intend to keep on living *my own* life—but as I grow older and meaner and uglier it becomes more & more clear to me that only a lunatic or an egomaniacal asshole would try to impose the structure of his own lifestyle on people who don't entirely understand it, unless he's ready to assume a personal responsibility for the consequences.

When the price of liberty includes the obligation to be drafted and have your legs blown off at the age of 22 in a place called Veet-Naam for some reason that neither Democratic nor Republican presidents can finally claim to understand, then maybe death is not such an ugly alternative. Thomas Jefferson kept slaves, but there is nothing in history to indicate that he routinely sacrificed any of their lives & limbs for the sake of his fiscal security.

Jesus, here we go again. Is there anyone in this star-crossed group with access to a Doctor of psychic-focus drugs? If so, please meet me in the northwest corner of the Commercial Hotel casino at dawn on Saturday.

Meanwhile, I want to wind this thing out & down as quickly as possible . . . and, since I asked most of the other people here to bring some kind of Focus-Document for the rest of us to cope with, I think this will have to be mine, if only because it's Wednesday morning now and I've already sunk six pages into what seems like a single idea, and it also strikes me as an idea (or question) that rarely if ever gets mentioned at political "conferences."

9. Thomas Jefferson actually wrote these lines in a June 24, 1826, letter to his friend Roger C. Weightman.

10. In a speech to Virginia's second revolutionary convention on March 23, 1775, Continental Congressman Patrick Henry proclaimed: "Is life so dear or peace so sweet as to be purchased at the price of chains and slavery? Forbid it, Almighty God! I know not what course others may take; but as for me, give me liberty, or give me death!"

This is the possibility that maybe we're all kidding ourselves about the intrinsic value of taking politics seriously in 1970s America; and that maybe we (or the rest of you, anyway—since I'm a doktor of journalism) are like a gang of hired guns on New Year's Eve in 1899. Things changed a bit after that, and the importance of being able to slap leather real fast at High Noon on Main Street seemed to fade very precipitously after 1900. A few amateurs hung on in places like San Diego and Seattle until The War came, but by 1920 the Pros took over for real.

Which is getting off the point, for now. What I want to do is raise the question immediately—so we'll have to deal with it in the same context as all the others—as to whether Frank Mankiewicz was talking in the past, present or future when he said, in the intro to his book on Nixon, that he learned from Robert Kennedy that "the practice of American politics . . . can be both joyous and honorable."

Whether or not Frank still agrees with that is not important, for now—but in the context of why we're all out here in this god-forsaken place I think it's important *not* to avoid the idea that reality in America might in fact be beyond the point where even the most joyous & honorable kind of politics can have any real effect on it. And I think we should also take a serious look at the health/prognosis for the whole idea of Participatory Democracy, in America or anywhere else.

That, to me, is an absolutely necessary cornerstone for anything else we might or might not put together—because unless we're honestly convinced that the Practice of Politics is worth more than just a short-term high or the kind of short-term money that power-pimps pay for hired guns, my own feeling is that we'll be a lot better off avoiding all the traditional liberal bullshit and just saying it straight out: That we're all just a bunch of fine-tuned Politics Junkies and we're ready to turn Main Street into a graveyard in the name of anybody who'll pay the price & even pretend to say the Right Things.

But we don't want to get carried away with this Olde West gig—except to recognize a certain connection between politics/campaign Hit Men in 1974 and hired guns all over the West in 1874. It's just as hard to know for sure what Matt Dillon[11] thought he was really doing back then as it is, today, to know what the fuck Ben Wattenberg[12] might claim as the "far, far better thing" he has in mind.

One of the primary ideas of this conference, in my own mind, is to keep that kind of brutal option open—if that's what we seem to agree on. Maybe tilting at windmills really *is* the best & most honorable way to go, these days. I get a

11. Marshal Matt Dillon, played by James Arness, was the hero of the long-running CBS TV Western series *Gunsmoke.*

12. Sociologist Ben J. Wattenberg, co-author with Richard M. Scammon of 1970's *The Real Majority: An Extraordinary Examination of the American Electorate.*

definite kick out of it, myself—but I have a feeling that my time is getting a bit short, and I'm getting unnaturally curious about how much *reality* we're really dealing with.

This is what the rest of you are going to have to come up with. My only role in this trip, as I see it right now, is to eventually write the introduction to some kind of book-form statement that the rest of you (& probably a few others) will eventually crank out. We are dealing with a genuinely ominous power-vacuum right now, in terms of political reality. Both major parties seem to be curling back into an ill-disguised fetal crouch—and the stuporous horror of a [Scoop] Jackson–[Gerald] Ford race in '76 is as easily conceivable as the barely-avoided reality of another Nixon-Humphrey contest was in 1972.

There is no way to get away from names and personalities in any serious talk about the '76 election—but if that's *all* we can talk about, I think we should write this whole project off, as of Sunday, as a strange bummer of sorts that never got un-tracked. We'd be better off at the crap tables, or watching the Keno balls, than haggling over who should be given command of a sinking ship.

On the other hand, I don't think we're here to write some kind of an all-purpose Platform for a (presumably) Democratic candidate in '76. There are plenty of people around who are already into that.

What we *might* do, I think, is at least define some of the critical and unavoidable questions that *any* presidential candidate will have to deal with, in order to be taken seriously in '76. We have a long list of these goddamn things to deal with, in the very short space of two days, and the best we can do for right now is: 1) Decide if the patient is worth saving . . . 2) What's basically wrong with the patient . . . and 3) If the saving is worth the effort, how to define & begin dealing with the *basics*.

At the same time, we want to keep in mind that a really fearful (or "fearsome") chunk of the voting population is in a very vengeful & potentially-dangerous mood with regard to national or even local politics. If George Metesky, the infamous "Mad Bomber" who terrorized New York in the 1950s, decided to run for the Senate in NY against Javits[13] this year, I suspect he would do pretty well. . . .

And, for the same reason(s), I'm absolutely certain I could fatally cripple any Democratic candidate for the U.S. Senate in Colorado by merely entering the race as a serious Independent . . . but that would only guarantee Dominick's re-election, I think, and besides that I have a great fear of having to move back to Washington.

Which is neither here nor there. My only real concern is to put something together that will force a genuine alteration of consciousness in the realm of national politics, and also in the heads of national politicians. Given the weird temper of all the people I've talked to in the past year, this is the only course

13. Liberal Republican Jacob K. Javits of New York held a seat in the U.S. Senate from 1957 to 1981.

that could possibly alter the drift of at least a third of the electorate *away* from politics entirely . . . and without that third, the White House in '76 is going to become the same kind of mine-field that Gracie Mansion[14] became about 10 years ago, and for many of the same reasons.

Okay for now. I have to get this bastard xeroxed and then catch the bush-plane for Elko in two hours. The *agenda* will have to wait—not only in terms of time, but also for people who will hopefully have a much better sense of priorities than I do.

If not, you bastards are going to wish you never heard the word "Elko."

Sincerely,
Hunter S. Thompson

FROM PATRICK J. BUCHANAN, THE WHITE HOUSE:

Thompson had proposed that Buchanan write an article on the future of American conservatism for Rolling Stone.

March 2, 1974
Washington, D.C.

PERSONAL

Dear Hunter:

Sorry I haven't been able to get back to you sooner; but all leaves and furloughs have been canceled for the last sixty days, on orders of the General Staff. At the appropriate time, I may well deliver myself of the recommended "hammerhead screed," but I must say I was disillusioned to learn that *Rolling Stone* had exercised the bad judgement to throw away three good pages on Richard Goodwin. As the Old Man said in the final days of that wonderful year, 1968, it is "getting down to the nut-cutting." Tell your liberal friends we expect to be treated with all the deference and respect as outlined in the Geneva Conventions on the handling of prisoners of war.

Best,
Patrick J. Buchanan
Special Consultant to the
President

MEMO FROM THE SPORTS DESK:

On May 9, 1974, the U.S. House Judiciary Committee, chaired by New Jersey Democrat Peter J. Rodino, would open impeachment hearings against President Richard M. Nixon.

14. Gracie Mansion is the official residence of the mayor of New York City.

April 17, 1974
Woody Creek, CO

TO: H. THOMPSON
FROM: R. DUKE
INRE: IMMEDIATE PRIORITIES / NIXON IMPEACHMENT

The returns from Michigan's 8th Congressional District are in now, and tonight is as good a time as any to schedule our work for the rest of the year. We had a bad stroke of luck last night when Nixon's numbwit palace guard let the press get a fateful step on them in the interpretation of (Demo) Bob Traxler's 3% victory over (Rep) James Sparling in that special election in Michigan's 8th district. By 8:00 a.m. EDT it was all over & Nixon had lost his last chance to deflate the notion that his administration—and his continuing presence in the White House—is a disastrous millstone around the neck of the GOP in the upcoming elections, 1976 as well as '74.

So we might as well figure, now, on spending most of the rest of this year in and out of Washington. As a result of last night's GOP loss in Michigan being interpreted as a deathblow to Nixon, & his value to the party, it seems almost certain that the Rodino committee will hand up (or out, or whatever) a bill of impeachment for the House to deal with in late May or June. The impeachment vote in the House will presumably be public & televised—but you should find out immediately from Louise Crow (Senate Periodical Press) if you'll need *special credentials* for any impeachment proceedings. Hopefully, Mankiewicz can handle this & keep us ahead of any credentials crunch. If not, he should be fed to the sharks.

The tentative schedule right now looks like Impeachment in June or early July, then a 6 to 8 week lull while Nixon prepares his defense, and then a Senate Trial in early August or September. With any luck at all, we'll get most of July & August off, while Nixon prepares for the crunch.

Without luck, the cheap bastard will slip the noose and resign on some kind of sloppy pretext between now and July. If this happens, it will blow one of the best stories of the last 200 years because The Impeachment Of Richard Nixon, if it happens, will amount to a de facto trial of the whole American Dream. Because the importance of Nixon now is *not* merely to get rid of him; that's a strictly political consideration. . . . The real question now is: Why is the American political system being forced to impeach a president elected less than two years ago by the largest margin in the history of presidential elections?

So, with the need for sleep coming up very fast now, we want to look at two main considerations: 1) The necessity of actually bringing Nixon to trial, in order to understand our reality in the same way the Nuremberg trials forced Germany to confront itself . . . and 2) The absolutely vital necessity of filling that vacuum that the Nixon impeachment will leave, the lanced boil—and the hole that will be there in 1976.

TO ALAN RINZLER, STRAIGHT ARROW BOOKS:

Thompson was tossing around the possibility of writing a book on his coverage of the Nixon impeachment proceedings.

May 18, 1974
Woody Creek, CO

Dear Alan:

I'm not at all sure what kind of a future we're dealing with here, but I suspect we ought to come to grips with it sometime soon. At the moment I'm trying to balance the (potential) impact of "Guts Ball" against the apparent necessity of covering Nixon's Impeachment & the concomitant possibility of getting a book out of that.

And, just to keep things straight, I've spoken with Silberman about the latter—although at the moment we're not beyond the "hot damn!" stage, and I haven't even talked to Lynn about it.

I have, however, kept Jann advised of everything I'm either into or thinking about.

No decisions (or no mutual ones, at any rate) have been reached on any front—except for the obvious necessity of my gearing down *tonight* to write that goddamn introduction for Ralph's book. Which I'm trying to do at the moment. . . .

And so much for the moment; call when you feel like it.

Cazart,
Hunter

TO RICHARD N. GOODWIN:

Dick Goodwin was probably the heaviest hitter at Rolling Stone*'s Elko Conference in February 1974. Beneath his rough bluster, Goodwin had an impeccable background in liberal politics: he had graduated first in his class at Harvard Law School in 1958, clerked for U.S. Supreme Court Justice Felix Frankfurter, written speeches for Presidents John Kennedy and Lyndon Johnson, and established himself as a "player" in mid-1960s Washington, one of many such Democrats without portfolio in the Nixon years.*

May 18, 1974
Woody Creek, CO

Dear Dick:

This is to confirm—as per Jann's implicit request—my absolute & wholly instinctive (if not entirely thought-out) decision that you're the best person to deal, from now on, with whatever evolves from the "Elko" or née "A-76" situation. It seems to me that the thing is now on a level that is far more in tune with your lifestyle, abilities and connexions, than mine—all of which should be no more prohibitive to continuing neo-active participation in the project than to the inescapable responsibility of composing my own Minority Report, if I ever feel up to it. . . .

In the meantime, I took delivery tonight on the evil tool we spoke of on the phone several nights ago. It's a *de-activated,* M-3, .45 ACP grease gun, and the barrel that came with the gun is welded stone shut—which, according to my attorney, means I can ship it across state lines at my whim. It's too bad we don't have an open M-C barrel & about 300 rounds of .45 ACP ammo, in order to have some fun with the bugger, eh?

But that's how the world runs, I guess. In any case, I'll see you up north—for good or ill—around the middle of June.

OK,
HST

TO JANN WENNER, *ROLLING STONE:*

Thompson's article "Fear and Loathing in Washington: The Boys in the Bag" ran in the July 4, 1974, issue of Rolling Stone.

June 7, 1974
Woody Creek, CO

Dear Jann:

Here is the bill for "The Boys in the Bag"—$4000 for four *RS* pages at (jesus!) $1000 each, disregarding any and all copy-cuts, for whatever reason, on your end.

Given all the realities—tangible, personal and otherwise—that I considered in arriving at this figure, it seems both fitting & reasonable at this time. . . . And if Walsh feels that *RS* can't afford to have me cover the Nixon Impeachment Saga at these rates, I'd appreciate a memo to that effect *from John,* along with yours. And we will naturally want all pertinent correspondence *in writing,* as you've noted many times in the past.

As for the future—given our awkwardly obvious failure to arrive at any mutually-advantageous, long-term relationship vis-à-vis my writing, rates & relationship, etc.—I think $1000 a page should be just about right from now on. If we're heading for a terminal haggle, I think we should at least do it on righteous terms, eh?

Like you always said: If we *must* argue, why argue about nickels and dimes?

Why indeed?

So here's the fucking bill—$4000. With a side-winder's salute to Tom Rush.[15]

15. Boston-based folk musician Tom Rush had "gone electric" in 1966.

In any case, if I seem to be grinding down a bit hard in this area, I want to assure you that this is precisely what I mean to be doing, for good or ill, and not without giving adequate thought to the whole situation.

Cazart,
Hunter S. Thompson

PS/Note: I talked to [Carl] Wagner today about Elko one and a half, or whatever, and as a result of that talk I decided that I'll definitely attend that July meeting in Maine. I won't have anything special to add, personally, but I have a tape I want to play . . . and I'll also make *all* my own travel & lodging arrangements.

Okay for now,
H

TO JANN WENNER, *ROLLING STONE:*

Thompson again attempted to sort out his financial terms and future projects with Wenner.

July 4, 1974
Woody Creek, CO

Jann . . .

With dawn coming up on what is always a vicious day in this valley, I want to get off a note on the general action.

One, I'm leaving for DC tomorrow—you can reach me at either the Hilton or c/o Dick in MacLean (?sp?) [McLean, Virginia]. Anyway, I'll be there for a week or so—it might be worthwhile to talk about the possible result . . . since at the moment I see no focus at all, beyond the result of the 7/8 Sup. Ct. arguments on Monday, which Dick has hopefully got me accredited for.

Inre: Armstrong[16] . . . I'll get him together with Dick this week, & we'll see what happens.

Whatever other stories might or might not be brewing in DC are beyond my ken right now. Lacking any idea of who's doing what, I think I'll run my own course & check with Dick for anything new, weird or different. According to our earlier talks, for instance, the Ehrlichman trial is being covered by Szulc.[17] (I got a xerox of a Kissinger piece from SF—but, like almost all the xeroxes I get from out there, it was virtually unreadable. Beyond that, there was no byline, so I can't say much about it.)

As for Chris and/or the question of a secretary in Aspen, Sandy has effectively made that decision for me, to wit: Given the reality that she has to deal with anything of any importance (to me) anyway, I figure we may as well put

16. Joe Armstrong was *Rolling Stone*'s advertising director at the time.
17. Tad Szulc was a foreign and national affairs correspondent for *The New York Times.*

her to work on a serious basis and pay her, accordingly, for her time . . . which would amount, on balance, to a lot less than anybody I'd have to hire and cope with. As for money, I think $10 an hour is about right, which would rarely run—I assume—to even $200 a month. That strikes me as the best of all possible worlds, given all our ominous possibilities. If nothing else, Sandy is the only conceivable "secretary" I could hire that I'll feel free to lean on—or even trust on a personal level, for that matter, so I assume that problem is solved.

One that isn't solved, however, has to do with that missing $500 (already listed as "paid" in yr. overall accounting statement for '74), and the $200 basic expenses in connexion with the Freud book.[18] I feel I have a pretty wide latitude on that one—beyond the $200—but I have no intention of getting seriously into it (beyond the enclosed) until I get something *in writing* from you.

Enclosed, meanwhile, is the tape I mentioned & also the typed translation of a 15-page outburst I lashed together on a night when I was probably as deep in the throes of cocomania as I'll ever get. My idea was to get as crazed as possible on the stuff, then try to write something . . . and these 6 (enc.) pages are the result.

Strange, eh? I was long past the point of being able to talk into the tape recorder when I wrote this stuff—and it's absolutely unedited, except for the red marks on this carbon copy.

So . . . we should think on the question of a relatively long & serious cocaine piece . . . and also on the question of covering Impeachment vs. getting on with "Guts Ball."

I assume Walsh is taking care of my credentials for the Ali–Foreman fight in Zaire around mid-September.[19]

Beyond that, I don't have much to talk about—except to say you better hope that missing $500 gets to me before I find an occasion to do any talking—on the air or for print—about my general relationship with *RS*. That was a cheap, street-dealer's kind of rip-off & depressingly reminiscent of Sidney Zion.

OK for now,
Hunter

TO WARREN HINCKLE:

July 4, 1974
Woody Creek, CO

Dear Warren . . .

I just finished reading & clipping your 7/1 piece on "4 Nixon Justices . . ." The box-score for the Nixon court, as it were . . . and I thought I'd send a sort

18. Viennese neurologist and psychoanalysis founder Sigmund Freud's book of essays on and case studies of cocaine use, *The Cocaine Papers*, had been reissued in 1974.

19. Muhammad Ali and George Foreman would fight for the world heavyweight boxing championship in Kinshasa, Zaire, on October 30, 1974.

of general "thanx note" or whatever for the help you've unwittingly given me over the past two or three years, by means of this same kind of backed-off, main-focus story—on The Court, a Campaign, the Press or anything else.

As I've said repeatedly, as an essentially polemic and/or adversary-type writer, I figure I have the best leg men in American journalism working for me, whether they want to or not . . . and your 7/1 piece on The Court is a perfect example of the kind of story I couldn't possibly do, myself, but which I also can't do without.

Anyway, I figure I've been stealing from people like you and [David] Broder for so long that I should at least acknowledge the debt in writing. On the more tangible side, I'll probably be hanging around the Impeachment scene this summer, so if you notice me hunkered down in a corner somewhere in the capital, give me a prod and I'll buy you a drink. Ok for now . . .

Hunter S. Thompson

TO WILLIAM FARR, *LOS ANGELES TIMES:*

Fellow journalist William Farr went to jail for refusing to surrender his "reporter's notes" in a highly publicized court case. Thompson sent him a few words of encouragement.

July 4, 1974
Woody Creek, CO

Dear Mr. Farr . . .

I'm enclosing an obviously token $100 personal check to help buy your lawyers some lunch while they haggle over various strategies to get you out of jail.

I wish there was something heavier I could do to help—but I'm not that rich and I'm not even sure I can pass this on to *Rolling Stone* as a legitimate "business expense," although to my mind it's one of the most legitimate kind of expenses anybody in journalism could put in for.

Anyway, I assume the *Times* is paying your tab—for whatever that's worth, considering what you've been through personally—and I figure this check won't mean much except to let you know that a lot of people understand that you're doing time for all of us. The next time I see Fred Dutton (who I assume is still a UC [University of California] Regent) I'm going to tell him he's the gutless asshole I always thought he was unless he can establish a William Farr Chair [in] Journalism at UCLA or maybe Berkeley.

Meanwhile, it's nice to know that there are at least a few people in this business with stone brass balls . . . and if there's anything else I can do to make your gig a bit easier, let me know what it is and I'll do what I can. (You can always reach me via the *Rolling Stone* office at 625 Third St. in San Francisco.)

OK for now, and thanks. Sincerely,

Hunter S. Thompson

FROM CARRIE NEFTZGER (TO *ROLLING STONE*):

Thompson's Gonzo style apparently displeased a ninety-one-year-old accidental reader of Rolling Stone, *whose letter was forwarded to him by the magazine's subscription manager, David Obey.*

September 18, 1974
Carbondale, IL

President Richard Irvine
of *Rolling Stone*
625 Third St.
San Francisco, CA 94107

I did not subscribe for your *Rolling Stone* magazine so you can quit sending it to me as it is embarrassing to me to have it deposited in my mailbox. It is a dirty, low-down, barnyard language sheet that is very offensive to me, so quit sending it.

It first came while I was on vacation and to-day the Oct issue came. So you see that I get no more of that trash.

Your writer Hunter S. Thompson, who himself is so ignorant that he doesn't know that people with adequate vocabularies and something worthwhile to say do not need to resort to such obvious means of gaining attention and that profanity is a "crutch for conversational cripples." I am a 91 yr. old woman so vulgarity isn't smart with me.

Mrs. Carrie Neftzger

TO CARRIE NEFTZGER:

September 27, 1974
Woody Creek, CO

Dear Carrie:

David Obey at the main *Rolling Stone* office in San Francisco has forwarded your letter of Sept 18 to me—the one where you canceled your subscription to *RS* because of my "vulgarity."

. . . and I also want to tell you right now that I *never* answer mail from readers; but I couldn't resist talking back to a 91-year-old lady full of zip—and despite the prevailing ignorance of your letter, that zip came thru in every line. If I ever get to be 91, I hope I'll be as mean as you are.

In any case, I'm enclosing the most recent *RS,* with my compliments—and despite your nasty language about me, I'm sure you'll read it. You've lived long enough to know that words are just *tools,* for a writer, and when I write about Richard Nixon I'll use all the tools I can get my hands on, to make people like you *think* about why Richard Nixon was elected by a landslide in 1972. My primary idea, whenever I sit down to write, is to *get the attention* of people like you, and make you *think*—and your letter of cancellation to Obey tells me I was successful in your case.

If you read the enclosed piece ("The Scum Also Rises") with any kind of wit, you'll see that what you react to as "vulgarity" is only a prod to make you *listen* . . . and if you disagree, well . . . I've done what I can, eh?

You can run, Carrie, but you can't hide . . . not even after 91 years; and if you voted for that cheap, thieving little bastard, then you deserve what you got.

If not, I guess you're on *my* side—but I doubt if we'll ever meet. Anyway, I admire your balls in canceling your subscription to *Rolling Stone*. . . . But I get a lot of letters from people with balls, and not many from people with brains.

Why don't you read the enclosed article and write me one from your *head* next time?

Sincerely,
Hunter S. Thompson

FROM U.S. SENATOR WALTER F. MONDALE:

October 16, 1974
Washington, D.C.

Dear Hunter:

Many thanks for your nice note of October 8 and for your support of my assessment of Ford's economic proposals. I'll be glad to put you and Dick Goodwin on my mailing list and look forward to hearing from you again if one of my statements strikes you one way or another.

In the meantime, my Press Secretary Ernie Lotito and I will look forward to having that drink during one of your visits to Washington.

Keep in touch,

Sincerely,
Walter F. Mondale

FROM ANNIE ACOSTA:

Oscar Acosta, the controversial Chicano lawyer Thompson had befriended and corresponded with for years, had mysteriously disappeared in the spring of 1974. What happened to him remains unknown.

October 22, 1974

Dear Hunter—

I am Oscar Zeta Acosta's sister Annie—

Oscar has not been heard from since April—'74. Yes—it is unusual as wild as he is; I know & love the big baby & should have heard something—anything, which I have not. He said he was on his way here!

Two ugly rumors—he was *shot* and on a yacht doing a bit of smuggling! Well Hunter—I am desperate and seriously fear for his life. He has been sought after by too many ugly *gabachos* & I dare them to think it may have ended, if you know what I mean! Oscar always thought the world of you—hopefully it works both ways. Could you possibly think of something that could be done—I have written & phoned just about everyone here in California that he may possibly have had contact with . . . nothing.

I have read & re-read all of his past years of correspondence, hopefully covering *all* possible contacts—

Please R.S.V.P. as soon as possible—

Thanks,
Annie

FROM ROSCOE C. BORN, *THE NATIONAL OBSERVER*
(TO HUGH M. HEFNER, *PLAYBOY*):

Roscoe C. Born, vice editor of The National Observer, *for which Thompson once freelanced, wrote in to comment on the writer's claims in a* Playboy *article of his "bitter dispute" with the* Observer. Playboy *wanted to run Born's letter along with a response from Thompson.*

November 6, 1974

Dear Mr. Hefner:

We all love our legends, and far be it from *The National Observer* to try to rob Hunter S. Thompson of his (The *Playboy* Interview, November 1974). As a fascinating figure flitting about on the periphery of journalism, Hunter has a certain value as long as he is not taken too seriously.

So we don't object if Hunter wants to believe and say that he had "just quit and been fired almost at the same time by *The National Observer*" because we wouldn't let him cover "the Free Speech thing at Berkeley." We think most readers would understand that, well, that's just Hunter talking.

But to have *Playboy* accept Hunter's statement as fact, as you did in the introduction to the Hunter Thompson interview, is another matter. Your intro states that Hunter quit the *Observer* "in a bitter dispute with his editors over coverage of the Berkeley Free Speech Movement." Now that's *Playboy* talking, not Hunter, so we must object.

In fact, Hunter was not fired, nor did he quit. He was never hired. He was a free-lance, never an employee. As a free-lance, by definition, he was free to cover anything he wanted to cover and to sell to anybody who would buy. If he had a "bitter dispute" or any dispute with anybody here about covering the Free Speech Movement, nobody here can remember it—and a dispute with Hunter Thompson, I should think, is likely to be remembered.

The files disclose this reference to the Free Speech Movement in an Oct. 12, 1964, letter from Hunter:

"The U.C. Berkeley story had a lot of meat to it and I can't help regretting I didn't work on that. . . . Your printed version was too much like a wire-service wrapup—a good one, to be sure, but there was a lot more to it than our writer had space for."

That's all. It doesn't sound much like a bitter dispute, or any dispute at all. And nobody here (including the editor who worked directly and patiently with Hunter) can recall any discussion with him about the Free Speech Movement. In fact, Hunter continued to send us pieces after the Free Speech episode at Berkeley.

Perhaps Hunter's lifeview is enriched by imagining some such dramatic event with the *Observer,* but it didn't happen.

Sincerely,
Roscoe C. Born
Vice Editor

TO LUCIAN TRUSCOTT, *THE VILLAGE VOICE:*

An incensed Thompson aired his objections to what he considered a whiny article.

November 15, 1974
Woody Creek, CO

Lucian . . .

Here's the first "letter to the editor" I've written since I was 19 years old. Could you see that it gets printed *intact,* or not at all—and if "not at all," I'd like to know whose name to put on The List. OK, & thanx. . . .

I just got back from London & Africa, a hideous nightmare that I doubt will ever see print. In any case, I'm heading into the Jerome in a few hours for the Monday nite *futebol.* Let me know if you get any hot stock market tips. . . .

HST

LETTER TO THE EDITOR, *THE VILLAGE VOICE:*

November 15, 1974
Woody Creek, CO

Herr Editor . . .

I sympathize very deeply with Brock Brower's "Walking Nervous Breakdown," as described in your issue of Nov 7 . . . but I also wonder what kind of presumptuous and gratuitous kind of self-serving bullshit led him to include *me* in the pantheon of sick crazies he name-dropped in the opening graf of his lame confession about how he couldn't quite make it in this world by living in Princeton, N.J. and sitting on a log in the woods wearing a hand-loomed irish-balladeer sweater and $55 ascot saddle-strollers.

Mr. Brower might do his own mental health a good turn by understanding that not all of "us" live that way. I don't know what Robert Pirsig[20] had in mind when he aimed his bike toward Montana, or what John Gregory Dunne was looking for when he went to Las Vegas . . . so I can't speak for *them.*

As for myself, however, I went to Las Vegas for reasons that would even now be understandable to any nickel & dime agent or editor on Mr. Brower's NY luncheon circuit . . . and those reasons were 1) Money, and 2) A chance to Get It On, on somebody's corporate tab. It's entirely possible, I suppose, that I had a "walking nervous breakdown" in the process—but if I did, I wasn't aware of it, and if that's what happened I'd just as soon do it again, because it was an extreme kind of high & I dug it.

Again, I want to emphasize that I've always considered Brock Brower (or is it Bower?) as one of the dozen or so writers whose name in any table of contents would usually cause me to buy whatever magazine it appeared in; he has always struck me as a generally sane & perceptive writer. . . .

. . . until now, when I open the Nov 7 *Voice* and see where he decided to take me, Dunne and Pirsig with him when he apparently went down the tube, lo, those many months ago. How would Brower feel if I flipped his coin in print and included his name among those writers who had inadvertently joined me on the long slide to terminal brain damage from drugs?

Which may or may not be true—and I frankly don't give a fuck either way—but if the day ever comes when I decide to publicize my own failure & blame it on drugs, I hope I'll have the grace to ride that rail alone, just like I started.

I'd also like to remind Mr. Brower that the pieces in Scott Fitzgerald's *Crack-Up* were written *after* he'd written one of the technical masterpieces of American literature and one of the cleanest, saddest statements in the English language.[21]

In a nut, Brower's piece reminded me of the same editorial instinct that prompted your cheap & vicious attack on George Plimpton several weeks ago . . . and although I don't want to include Brower personally in this flash at what appears to me to be a sort of bitchy/neurotic editorial bent, I just want to make it clear to him and to you that if I'm going mad, I'll goddamn well do it on my own terms . . . and I suspect Dunne & Pirsig feel the same way.

Brower may be right in assuming that a lot of writers just want to "sit tight and not move off (their) butts," but he should do a little research west of the

20. Robert Pirsig wrote the best-selling 1974 book *Zen and the Art of Motorcycle Maintenance.*
21. The essays in F. Scott Fitzgerald's collection *The Crack-Up* were serialized in *Esquire* magazine beginning in November 1935—a full ten years after the publication of *The Great Gatsby.*

Hudson before he starts naming them, just in order to lend weight to his own lame confession.

Almost everybody who goes to the mats gets beaten, one way or another, but not all of us get broken.

Sincerely,
Hunter S. Thompson

cc: Lucian Truscott

TO GEORGE V. HIGGINS:

Duke University had refused to compensate Thompson for an October 22 speaking engagement, claiming that he had arrived forty-five minutes late and was belligerent toward the audience (calling them "beer hippies and pig farmers" and throwing a glass of bourbon in the air from the podium). Thompson refused to speak at Florida Atlantic University because of contract stipulations that he appear at a press conference and reception afterward.

November 17, 1974
Woody Creek, CO

Dear George:

Here is the lean meat of my APB [American Program Bureau] file, with emphasis on our lack of an original agreement and the Duke fiasco—along with the Fla. Atlantic Univ. botch that I aborted because of that contract-rider that *Novotny signed for me,* in absolute defiance of a statement I made in a meeting of APB sales reps at their Boston office & under Walker's aegis. In other words, Walker invited me out to Hq., and had me sit down in a meeting with his salesmen & explain my act . . . that was almost two years ago & every date since then has gone off pretty much according to *my* book, to wit:

I said very firmly that I detested these fucking things & that since I felt I had nothing to say I refused to even pretend to make a speech. I would, however, answer any and all questions from the audience—preferably in the form of a pile of 3 × 5 cards submitted in advance, although I specified in advance that any person designated by the speakers' committee or any person appointed by them could select the questions. . . . In other words, I wasn't trying to dodge anything; all I wanted was some help in sorting out the bullshit, so I wouldn't have to do it on stage—which was *not done* at Duke, a fuck-up (considering that they had 45 minutes to wait for me, they claim) that contributed very strongly to the chaos that resulted.

I also specified, during my talk with the salesmen at APB—with Walker listening in—that I would in *all* cases insist on drinking my own beverage while speaking & that it would be either Wild Turkey or something stronger. They were not required to provide the booze, but ice and a large glass were part of the deal. In all other cases, however, I've been provided with so much Wild

Turkey, prior to speaking, that I ended up giving quarts away before leaving town.

There was also the "Cocaine Proviso," which I enunciated quite clearly at the APB salesmen's meeting: I would, I said, agree to knock $100 off the speaker's fee (mine), if the "hosts" provided me with a gram of coke for my own use while in town. This was said with my tongue about halfway in cheek, but the first two schools they laid it on took it seriously . . . and things went very nicely, all around.

What I'm getting at here—since APB so politely accepted Duke's refusal to pay me, and since *they* signed a contract-rider for the Fla/Atlantic U. trip the night before that would have guaranteed non-payment—is a certain feeling on my part that APB owes me the full amount for both the Duke and the Fla/A.U. appearances, plus about $100,000 for gross damage to my reputation . . . and possibly to my earning power as a campus-speaker in the future, in light of Jann Wenner's mumbling today about a "blacklist" inre: "problem speakers."

In fact—due to this hassle with APB over the Duke non-payment—I was forced to cancel two appearances this week: On Nov 19 at the State Univ. of NY at Albany for $1250 plus expenses, and at St. Lawrence Univ. on Nov 20 for $1250 plus expenses.

These two losses amount to at least $3000, in addition to another $3000 inre: Duke & Fla. Atlantic . . . so that's $6000, plus incalculable damage to my reputation and my future earning-power as a speaker.

I figure $506,000.00 as a proper amount to claim from APB. How about you? $6K actual & $500K punitive.

Let me know.

OK,
Hunter S. Thompson

TO MAX PALEVSKY:

Thompson offered Palevsky a settlement to resolve the matter of the $10,000 loan.

December 5, 1974
Woody Creek, CO

Max,

My instinct tells me you're hunkered down out there in a state of fear & confusion vis-à-vis your lawsuit against me—& God knows, Max, I hate that vivid image. . . .

Whereas, in fact, *I'm* the one who's laid out—with malaria, strep throat, & god knows what else.

Anyway, I have a carbon of the letter Sandy sent to you while I was getting re-educated in Africa—and I think that pretty well covers it. We can end this whole wretched farce by my sending you a check for $2500—is that right?

I forget the terms & details, but I think that's what it was. Neither IFA [International Famous Agency] nor Clancy is aware of these letters between us—except in the most general sense—& I'd just as soon keep it that way. I'll tell them that weasels deal on one level, & humans on another. And that there's no real need for them to understand it anyway.

Meanwhile, you vicious Polish bastard, Clancy is dunning me for $3500 in fees connected with this nightmare. I'm sure you'll get a nice laugh out of that . . . but what the fuck? The simple fact of the loan puts me in a position where I can't get righteously angry at you—so we'll let this one pass.

My only consolation is that the mesa above my house that you could have bought for $50K, more or less, when you saw it, is about to be zoned for 2-acre "ranchettes," which makes the current price around $500,000. . . .

Jesus—what consolation is that, for me? All it means is I'll have to sell my 100 acres & move to Bel-Air.

Ah, Max—*there is no victory.* Neither fame nor fortune is worth a shit these days—the only thing worth clinging to is a sense of humanity.

Anyway, I'll call soon—but in the meantime I assume we're essentially even (I'll send the goddamn check).

OK,
H

TO ROSCOE C. BORN, *THE NATIONAL OBSERVER:*

December 6, 1974
Woody Creek, CO

Ah, Roscoe . . .

How nice to hear from you again . . . after all these years.

Just a bit more than a decade, isn't it? Ten years? Eleven? Twelve? You were a "senior editor" then, & now you're a "Vice-editor." Jesus, I can almost smell that gold watch they're saving for you, up there at the Dow-Jones morgue on Wall St.

Which is not the kind of thing I'd normally want to get into with somebody I don't really know & never liked anyway—& that feeling was always mutual, wasn't it?

Roscoe, old sport, are you still with me? Don't slink off; I want to establish the essentials of our relationship before I get into the main gum of your complaint—which was not entirely wrong. . . .

It was like receiving a scolding letter from Hubert Humphrey, or from Richard Nixon's favorite law prof. at Duke University—establishing a level, as it were, & now that we've done that I want to say that I got a fine boot out of the spectacle of a Dow-Jones lifer giving the back of his mossy hand to "free-lance" writers . . . & a "vice-editor" of the *Nat. Obs.* talking contemptuously about "the periphery of journalism." Those were genuinely off-the-wall strokes, Roscoe. I was stunned.

Can you smell the rank humor in that spectacle, Roscoe—even though your charges are not without merit? Can you hear me laughing out here in the Rockies, as I write this? Because you are going to *remember* this dispute, Roscoe—Just like you said in paragraph four of your complaint.

And now to the charges—not necessarily in the order you raised them:

1) That I was never fired because I was never "an employee." OK. We both know *why* I was never a formal time-clock employee—don't we, Roscoe? Right. Because I refused to work in that Silver Spring (Md.) office where you've been fighting the good fight in the mainstream of American Journalism for the past 11 years. And we both know—don't we, Roscoe?—that I was offered & repeatedly urged to accept your style of employment by (then) managing ed. Dan Carter & (then) executive ed. Bill Giles.

And we both know that I refused to work under those circumstances, don't we? And that I came to lunch with you & all the other heavy editors at the National Press Club & said I'd just as soon continue as I had for the previous year or so in South America—as the *Observer*'s highest paid non-staffer, but now working out of Colorado & California . . . as a de facto roving correspondent—essentially the same kind of relationship I've maintained with *RS* for the past few years . . . and I kind of like it, Roscoe, shameful as it might be in the eyes of people like you to be denied the privilege of punching a time clock.

And as I recall, Roscoe, you were still trying to be a writer, then—why don't you go back, once again, to your files & count up which one of us had more front-page pieces in the *Observer* during the period of my *active* "free-lancing" . . .

. . . as opposed to my "inactive period," which brings us to your point about the "bitter dispute" that finally ended my relationship with the *Observer.*

Are you ready for this one, Roscoe? If not, you'd better call on Cliff Ridley—"the editor who worked directly & patiently" with me during this difficult & angst-ridden period—which ended, after 2 good years & one bad one, in a dispute that might not have seemed "bitter" by your corporate standards, but Ridley's absolute refusal to speak to me under any circumstances for the past 10 years would seem to justify the word "bitter," in my own context.

But you were *right,* Roscoe, when you said this "bitter dispute" did not arise directly from the *Observer*'s refusal to assign me to cover the first flarings of the Berkeley "Free Speech" Movement. That was more an open sore than a "dispute," because once Ridley made it clear to me that "the Berkeley story" was being taken care of (for the *Observer*) by a moon-lighting reporter from the *SF Chronicle,* I naturally let it go—at least for the *Observer,* although I wound up writing it for *The Nation* & later for my Hell's Angels book.

So, Roscoe . . . (you are right, on that point). The "bitter dispute" that ended my relationship with the *Observer* erupted at almost the same time as my running argument with Ridley about the Berkeley story, but the real crunch came in the wake of the *Observer*'s refusal to publish my (very favorable) review of Tom Wolfe's first book (*The Kandy-Kolored Tangerine-Flake Streamline Baby*). This dispute went down *by telephone,* Roscoe, so your files will not yield it up. I spoke with Ridley from a phone booth in the midst of a Hell's Angels freakout in Bass Lake, Calif., in the summer of 1965 & was told that my review would not be published because "somebody with leverage" at the *Observer* had worked with Wolfe at the *Wash. Post* & didn't like him—which had already resulted in Wolfe's being turned down when he applied for a job at the *Observer,* & now accounted for this rejection of my favorable review of the book.

I recall saying, at that point: "Clifford, we've been friends for a long time & I've never even seen this bastard, Wolfe—but on the evidence this is stone chickenshit, right?"

He agreed—but refused to tell me who it was in the *Observer* hierarchy that was blackballing Wolfe on all fronts—from employment as a writer to favorable reviews of his first book.

So I hung up the phone at Bass Lake & went back to the Hell's Angels orgy at Willow Cove, to work on my book. . . .

But I was *pissed off,* Roscoe. It was the first time in 3 years that the *Observer* had actually *rejected* something I'd written—& I had written a lot of extremely weird things, Roscoe, which thank christ you were not in a position, then, to spike . . . but this blatant murder of a book review, for reasons that Ridley freely & apologetically admitted on the phone, made me angry.

So I went back to San Francisco—after the madness at Bass Lake—and sent Wolfe a carbon copy of my review of his book, along with a cover letter explaining why the *Observer* had refused to publish it.

Then I sent a carbon of my letter to Wolfe back to Ridley at the *Observer*—& it was *then* that our "bitter dispute" erupted.

Ridley was not happy with me for having told Wolfe why the *Observer* wouldn't publish my review of his book; he accused me of willful treachery, betrayal of "our family relationship," & that sort of thing.

And I just happen, Roscoe, to have a copy of that letter in *my* files—along with my own reply to Ridley, which turned out to be my last official communication with *The National Observer.*

And all that happened 10 years ago, right? Christ, I was content to let sleeping snakes sleep, Roscoe—what kind of lame madness caused you to poke them awake?

You have stepped in shit, my man—Herr Vice-Editor—and before you start foaming at that pale slit you call a mouth, I'd suggest a chat with your vice-cohort Cliff Ridley, in order to get yourself properly grounded before you pick up the axe-handle again for another one of those ill-advised free-lancer stompings, on the "periphery of Journalism."

And that's about it from this end, Roscoe. What else can I say?

Except that I enjoyed working with Ridley & for the *Observer* during that time, & I'm also glad that I quit (stopped, failed, ceased, terminated, or whatever word you like) precisely when I did.

Maybe someday, if tragedy strikes, I will limp back to mainline, time-clock journalism. But until that ugly moment, I guess I'll just have to flit around out here on the periphery of Journalism with all those other neo-serious "freelancers"—geeks like Wolfe, Mailer, Vonnegut, Halberstam, etc.—who can't measure up to the standards of big-league newspapers like *The National Observer.*

Yours in perpetual humility,

Hunter S. Thompson
National Affairs Desk
Rolling Stone

FROM U.S. SENATOR GEORGE McGOVERN:

December 11, 1974
Washington, D.C.

Dear Hunter:

I fear that we have struck out on your request for the Gerald Warren press briefing of July 18th in Laguna Beach.

After receiving a tardy interim reply from GSA,[22] indicating they were forwarding our request to the White House, the White House Counsel's office phoned to say that as with each succeeding President, they have no access to President Nixon's papers. The papers are evidently further under an embargo until the various court cases and final disposition is made.

I am sorry that we were unable to get the transcript for you, Hunter.

Sincerely,
George McGovern

22. The federal government's General Services Administration.

1975

LAST DANCE IN SAIGON, END OF THE WAR IN VIETNAM, CONVERSATIONS FROM THE GARDEN OF AGONY . . . TOURING THE ORIENT FOR MONEY, SEX & VIOLENCE IN HONG KONG, LAST MEMO FROM THE GLOBAL AFFAIRS DESK . . .

Buy the ticket, take the ride—Saigon, 1975.
(Photo courtesy of HST Archives)

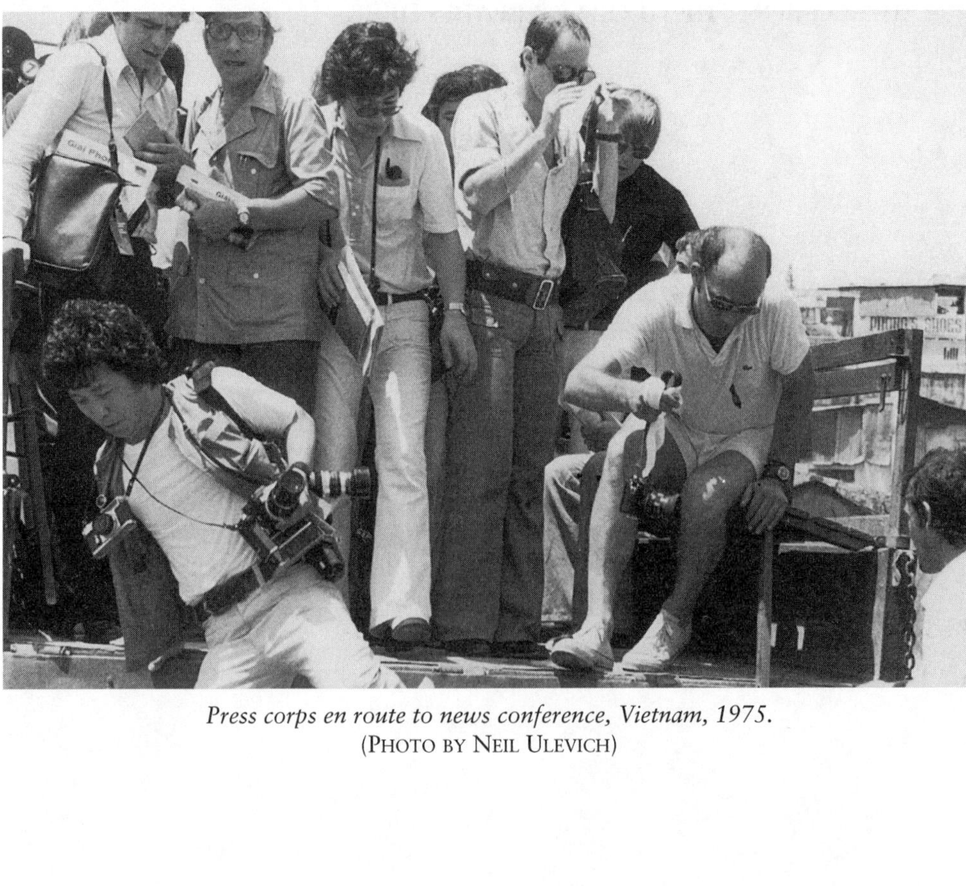

Press corps en route to news conference, Vietnam, 1975.
(Photo by Neil Ulevich)

Buffett's wedding, 1975. Left to right: Jimmy Buffett, Roxy Rodgers, Jane Buffett. (PHOTO BY ALAN BECKER)

Sign outside the Rolling Stone *Global Affairs suite, Hotel Continental, Saigon, 1975.* (PHOTO COURTESY OF HST ARCHIVES)

San Francisco, 1975. (PHOTO BY EDMUND SHEA)

FROM GOVERNOR JIMMY CARTER:

Hunter S. Thompson had admired Jimmy Carter since he heard the Democrat's Law Day address at the University of Georgia on May 4, 1974. In fact, he would write, "I have never heard a sustained piece of political oratory that impressed me any more than the speech Jimmy Carter made on that Saturday afternoon." Nearly two years before the 1976 election Thompson began acting as an informal adviser to the Georgia governor's nascent presidential campaign.

February 5, 1975
Plains, GA

To Hunter Thompson:

We'll contact your friend Dixon.[1]

Maybe I'll see you while campaigning, unless you've graduated to favorites & are traveling with Scoop.[2]

Everything looks good so far. It's a great country & I am enjoying the campaign & intend to win.

Come to see us.

Jimmy

TO JANN WENNER, *ROLLING STONE:*

Thompson was frustrated by his undefined relationship with Rolling Stone.

March 10, 1975
Woody Creek, CO

Jann . . .

I've been trying to get into the Coors memo for about two hours & I just figured out why I'm having so much trouble getting started on it—to wit: I am

1. Attorney William Dixon was a senior Democratic investigator for the U.S. House Judiciary Committee.

2. U.S. senator Henry "Scoop" Jackson of Washington state was one of Carter's early rivals for the 1976 Democratic presidential nomination.

immensely fucking pissed off about that vicious sandbag job you laid on me vis-à-vis the C-76 book contract. I've spent the past 72 hours skiing, shooting & eating acid in a deliberate attempt to keep my mind off the whole stinking business—but now that I'm back at the machine I feel like I'm sitting in a bathtub full of pus and my sense of humor is still locked in reverse.

I haven't talked to either you or Lynn since Thursday night, so I have no idea if *or* whether there are any new developments or possible solutions . . . which would be nice, but I can't conceive of *anything* right now that could effectively remove the memory of you sitting out here in my living room with the fire & the music & the coke (and even Bangkok Fred), acting like a human being while we worked over that proposal of yours . . . and then going back to San Francisco & driving a stake through the heart of the whole relationship so casually that you only saw fit to mention it as an afterthought in an hour-long conversation when I happened to bring it up about 10 days later—which still leaves me wondering when you might have gotten around to telling me about the tragic & unforeseen "death of the book division" if I hadn't asked specifically about that contract you said you were going to send.

. . . and there is the ugly nut of it: not that money problems or other, more ominous factors forced the demise of the book company, but that you came out here and laid a near-perfect con job on me while wallowing in an atmosphere of friendliness and hospitality that might be hard to revive on your next visit. The next time you feel like accusing ex-*RS* editors of "taking advantage," think back on your recent vacation out here.

Anyway, by the time you get this I assume we'll be into another round of haggling—which depresses the shit out of me, but I can't see any way around it unless we just take a goddamn public hammer to the whole relationship and let the bone chips fall where they may. I am frankly not in favor of this course, but I've given it enough thought to feel pretty certain I'll survive the worst that can happen if you want to seriously get it on.

Meanwhile, I am sitting here on a massive pile of work projects (pending visits to Carter, Harris,[3] Chicago, etc., plus Coors, Zaire, the Brown-Davis tapes, the HST anthology tapes, "Guts Ball". . . Jesus, there's no end to it) . . . and I still have no focus or framework for any of it, except that hazy one-page contract that has never—as we both know from long experience—been anything more than a reference point for that "spirit of the contract" that I've tried to explain to you as long and persistently as you've refused to even recognize it.

God's mercy on your ass when your time comes to explain yourself to the Lords of Karma (sp?), but in the meantime we should make some kind of legally & financially binding agreement as to my professional relationship with The Empire, however arthritic it may or may not be at this point. At the mo-

3. Former U.S. senator from Oklahoma Fred Harris was a Democratic political consultant.

ment, we have the existing "contract," which [John] Clancy assures me is valid inre: fees & expenses—but which we both know is useless in a fog of either personal *or* professional animosity. No doubt there are numerous ambitious typists who'd be happy to "cover politics" on the cheap for *RS,* and if that's what you think you need, why not just write me a letter and say so? There's no need to skulk around like Sidney Zion; just send a memo down to Baker[4] and have me declared a non-person . . . and then send Cockburn[5] a note about what a flaky greedhead I am.

Until then, however, I have to proceed on the assumption that I'll be covering the '76 campaign, more or less, for *RS* and also for a book of some kind, for somebody. To the best of my recollection & taking all the obvious risks into consideration, I think we agreed that you're prepared to pay for twelve (12) relatively short articles, one each month throughout 1976, in exchange for a $25K salary and a $30K expense budget . . . which is okay, I guess, but without a book contract it leaves me in a fairly obvious no-profit situation—due to a heavy cut in fees because of the shorter articles and also an expense budget $2500 short of what I required in '72 and so clearly on the low side that not even you, thus far, have argued that it might be adequate to cover my real expenses.

But I can live with that, just as long as we get the details in writing—so we won't spend the whole goddamn year haggling about whether I *really needed* a red convertible to cover the Texas primary or whether my reimbursement for out-of-pocket expenses depends entirely on the printed word-yield from every conversation with any candidate or staffer, regardless of the circumstances. This puts me in a position, for instance, of having to pay my own way if I want to spend three days raving drunk with Fred Harris in Nova Scotia—a situation I obviously couldn't use in print, and therefore wouldn't get paid for. Only an editor with cheap shit for brains would put me, of all people, into that kind of a crippling bind; it not only robs us of all the natural edge I built up during the '72 campaign, but it puts me in a position of having to carefully censor my copy for *RS* and save vast chunks of otherwise inimitable copy for the pages of some book that may or may not ever see print. The only parallel that comes quickly to mind is that week I spent in Chicago in August of '68, filling notebooks for some book that never happened and with no magazine assignment for a story I still regard as the heaviest thing I ever covered . . . and if I wanted to get genuinely ugly on this point, I could look back in the bound copies of *RS* and find the *RS* pre-convention "coverage" on Chicago. It was, as I recall, very much like your pre-Woodstock coverage a year or so later.

4. Tom Baker was vice president of Straight Arrow Publishers, Inc.

5. Alexander Cockburn, then a *Village Voice* political columnist, was hired to cover the 1976 election for *Rolling Stone.*

And so much for all that. I have to think you've divined the nature of what I've been trying to say for the past hours. . . . No doubt there are areas where I seem to misunderstand the essential truth & beauty of your real intentions, and if so I'm prepared to apologize when you pinpoint my errors. But before you get started on that chore, let me remind you once again that for the purposes of this letter I've systematically discounted all verbal agreements or once-natural assumptions that may or may not have previously seemed to exist between us. I have listened to too many tapes of our other summit meetings (remember the "Half-Moon Conference"?) and scanned too many hand-scrawled notes from your recent visit to have any faith, for now, in anything but legally binding documents.

And we are stark fucking naked of those, with regard to C-76. What, for instance, is the status of the "Paris provision" at this point? Or where does a thing like my "Billy the Geek" odds-making feature fit into *RS*'s C-76 coverage? If it turns out that Scoop Jackson is heavily into Kitameen [*sic*][6] during the primaries, will I be allotted (and paid for) enough space in *RS* to deal with that? Or will it have to be saved for the book? Or sold quick to somebody else? I don't mind keeping those elegant tangents off the *RS* Mojo Wire, but I sure as hell don't intend to disregard them just because you want tighter & cheaper copy. If you want *Time* & *Newsweek*–style squibs on the '76 campaign, I understand former *Newsweek* political reporter Dick Stout is out of work & I could almost certainly get you his phone number.

Jesus . . . it's 6:44 on Monday morning now and I still haven't touched all this Coors garbage stacked up to the left of the typewriter. But I haven't written a real *letter* to anybody in a while, and I think it's sort of nice to have this one for the record, if nothing else. I don't have the slightest fucking idea what you'll make of it, and until I hear from you I'm going to keep on acting like a writer who plans on covering the '76 campaign for *RS* . . . but not on credit cards, old sport. I've been down that dirty road before.

The one thing you can be sure of, though, is that I'll have a room at the Wayfarer Motor Inn during the New Hampshire primary, and I'll be writing for *somebody.* In the words of my associate, Herr Bloor: "When the going gets weird, the weird turn pro."

Either way, we should get this thing *firmly* settled very soon. No doubt you've already spoken with Lynn, and if that fails you'll be hearing from Clancy . . . and then Bloor. I never expected to find myself writing you a letter like this; but then life is full of surprises, eh? I think Bob Dylan wrote a song about it.

Cazart,
HST

6. Ketamine is a general anesthetic administered intravenously or intramuscularly, usually to large cats or small apes.

TO PAUL SCANLON, *ROLLING STONE:*

Thompson traveled to Southeast Asia in April 1975 to cover the fall of Saigon and its aftermath for Rolling Stone.

April 21, 1975
Saigon

Paul the phone lines are temporarily out of order here and I can't call so here is how I see the situation. I will file another 2000/ two thousand or maybe a bit more if possible, which should start reaching you Monday afternoon or Monday night and Tuesday morning. If you don't have room for that much or my timetable is wrong, you must repeat must telex me back here immediately so I can adjust. Also I must repeat must know something definite from you about my arrangement with Palmer[7] who is already working so this is important. Thanx, Hunter.

TO COLONEL VO DAN GIANG, PROVISIONAL REVOLUTIONARY GOVERNMENT OF VIETNAM:

Colonel Vo Dan Giang was spokesman in Saigon for the PRG, or Vietcong.

April 22, 1975
Continental Palace Hotel
Suite 37
Saigon

Col. Vo Dan Giang, PRG
c/o Ton San Nhut Airbase
Saigon

Dear Colonel Giang . . .

I am the National Affairs editor of *Rolling Stone*, a San Francisco–based magazine with offices in New York, Washington and London that is one of the most influential journalistic voices in America right now—particularly among the young and admittedly left-oriented survivors of the anti-war Peace Movement in the 1960s. I'm not an especially good typist, but I am one of the best writers currently using the English language as both a musical instrument and a political weapon . . . and if there is any way you can possibly arrange it in the near future, I'd be very honored to have a private meeting with you and talk for an hour or so about your own personal thoughts right now.

We would need the help of one of your interpreters, because my French is a joke, my Spanish is embarrassing and my command of Vietnamese is non-

7. Laura Palmer also covered the fall of Saigon on assignment for *Rolling Stone*.

existent. I came to Saigon two weeks ago, just after the panic at Da Nang, because I wanted to see the end of this stinking war with my own eyes after fighting it in the streets of Berkeley and Washington for the past ten years.

And the reason I'm writing you this note is that I was very much impressed by the way you handled your Saturday press conference the first time I attended, on the Saturday before last. That was the one in which you made three or four specific references to the dark fate awaiting "American military advisors posing as journalists"—and each time you mentioned that phrase, you seemed to be looking directly at me.

Which is understandable, on one level, because I've been told by my friend Jean-Claude Labbe that I definitely look like that type. But we both know that "looks" are very often deceiving, and almost anybody among the American press in Saigon today will tell you that—despite my grim appearance—I am the most obvious and most well-known politically radical journalist in your country today.

In any case: Shortly after leaving your press conference I called my associate, Tom Hayden, at his home in Los Angeles and asked him what he knew about you. Tom, as you know, is married to the American actress Jane Fonda, and they have both been among the strongest voices in the Peace Movement for the past ten years. Tom Hayden is also an editor of *Rolling Stone,* as you can see by the enclosed masthead . . . and when I asked him about you on the phone, he said I should make every effort to meet you because he considered you one of the most intelligent and humane leaders of the PRG. He also said you have a sense of humor and that I'd probably like you personally.

I had already picked up that feeling, after watching your press conference, and I am writing you now with the hope that we can arrange a brief and informal private meeting very soon. I think I understand the political reality of the PRG, but I'm not sure I understand the Human reality—and I have a sense that you could help me on that latter point. You might be surprised to know how many of the American journalists in Saigon today admire you and call you their friend.

I understand that a letter like this one puts you in a difficult position at this time, so I won't be personally offended if you decide against having a talk with me . . . but I trust you to understand that, as a professional para-journalist, I am in the same situation today that you were as a para-military professional about three years ago . . . and if you have any serious doubts about my personal and political views, please ask one of your friends to stop by the Hotel Continental, #37, and pick up a copy of my book on the 1972 presidential campaign in America. I will give the book to anybody who asks me for "the book for Che." Or I'll bring it to you myself, if there is any way you can invite me into your compound out there. . . . And, as a matter of fact, if there is going to be any real "battle for Saigon," I think I'd feel safer out there with you and your people than I would in the midst of some doomed and stupid "American Evacuation Plan," dreamed up by that senile death-monger, Graham Martin.[8]

If you think it might be of any help to you to have a well-known American writer with you out there in the compound when the "battle" starts, I'll be happy to join you for a few days in your bunker. . . . But that is not the kind of arrangement I can make on my own; it would require some help from you, to let me pass quietly through the checkpoints outside your compound . . . and I give you my word that I'll do that, if you can make the arrangements and let me know.

Okay for now. I hope to see you soon . . . but even if I don't, allow me to offer my personal congratulations for the work you've done and the very pure and dramatic victory you've accomplished. I can only feel saddened by all the pain and death and suffering this ugly war has caused on all sides . . . but your victory, I think, is a victory for all of us who believe that man is still capable of making this world a better, more peaceful and generous place for all our sons and daughters to live in.

This is the kind of thing I'd like to talk to you about—not such things as "battle strategy" or your current political plans. That is not my style—as a journalist or a human being—and besides, you'll soon be getting all the questions you can handle on those subjects. No pack of jackals has ever been more single-mindedly obtuse in their hunger for news/meat than the army of standard-brand American journalists who will soon be hounding you for wisdom and explanations. I can only wish you luck with that problem, and I hope we can have a quick and friendly private visit before you get caught up on that tiresome merry-go-round.

As for me, I won't stay in Vietnam much longer, unless I hear from you in the next few days. I may return in a few months, but I am homesick for the peace and quiet of my log-house in Colorado and I want to get back there as soon as possible. My home address in America is Owl Farm, Woody Creek, Colorado 81656—or you can reach me in care of any one of the *Rolling Stone* offices listed on the enclosed masthead. I am also a friend of Senator George McGovern, Senators Gary Hart and Ted Kennedy, and former Senators Eugene McCarthy and Fred Harris . . . so if I can be of any help to you as a friendly contact in Washington, feel free to communicate with me at any time and I'll do whatever I can . . . but in the meantime, I hope you'll let me know, by whatever means you think best, if there is any chance for us to get together: perhaps even here in the Continental for a quiet bit of drink and talk with a few of your friends in the American press. I have a feeling you'll be a welcome guest in this place fairly soon and I think you'll enjoy it.

8. Graham Martin was the last U.S. ambassador to South Vietnam, from 1973 through the fall of Saigon in the spring of 1975.

And that's all I have to say at this time. It is five minutes before six in the morning and I need to get some sleep, so I'll end this letter now and take it around to my friend who plans to deliver it to you.

Very sincerely,
Hunter S. Thompson

TO JANN WENNER, *ROLLING STONE:*

Uncomfortable, unproductive, and eager to leave Vietnam, Thompson was outraged by the lack of communication from his employer—especially after Rolling Stone *canceled his insurance policy and reneged on paying his expenses in Indochina. This missive marks an ongoing dispute between Thompson and Wenner that remains a source of contention.*

April, 1975
On the Road, somewhere
in Indochina

Jann your most recent emission of lunatic, greed-crazed instructions to me was good for a lot of laughs here in Saigon . . . especially among people who are being paid war-risk salaries, operating with unlimited war-risk expense-budgets and whose employers are paying their special seventy-five dollar a day war-risk life insurance . . . while my own life insurance policy was automatically cancelled on the day I got here and your obviously deliberate failure to reply in any repeat any way to my numerous requests by phone, cable and carrier for some clarification vis-à-vis what the fuck I might or might not be paid for whatever I'm doing out here makes a stupid, dimesucker's joke of your idea that I'm going to lounge around out here in the middle of a war at my own expense and with no idea as to what I might write, on spec, about your mythical chopper evacuation and my notes on my summer vacation in "tent city" at Subic Bay. You ought to read my copy from last week before you start jabbering about what I should do next. Or did you ever receive my copy from last week?

Anyway, my current plans are still to do whatever's right, according to my own judgement at the time, and at the moment that means I'll be leaving here on Saturday if the current calm holds and you can ram Subic Bay far up into the nether reaches of your lower intestine. I have all the material we agreed I should have on quote the last days of the American presence in Saigon unquote and now I'm going somewhere to write it. The only round-eyes left to evacuate from Saigon now are the several hundred press people who are now trying to arrange for their own evacuation after the U.S. embassy pulls out with the last of the fixed-wing fleet and leaves the press here on their own. Needless to say, if that scenario develops it will involve a very high personal risk factor.

. . . and also big green on the barrel-head for anyone who stays, and unless the 130s [U.S. military C-130 transport planes] start hitting Saigon before Saturday that is the outlook. If you wonder why I can't explain this situation any further right now—well, you'll just have to wonder, because I can't. You could check with Klein at *Newsweek* and see what Loren [Jenkins] says about his own situation and cash needs, and maybe that will tell you something about my repeat my situation. Cash will definitely be a factor, and since I realize your feelings about the high cost of a telephone call to me here at the hotel in Saigon, I am not optimistic about the prospects of getting any more expense money . . . unless I get a call or a cable from Lynn repeat from Lynn, confirming some up-dated money arrangement she might possibly have made with you. Our original agreement, as you know, did not include a press-evacuation coverage or six unpaid months of house-arrest when Saigon finally falls. [Tim] Crouse said he might like to handle that aspect of the story; I hope you forwarded my wire to him yesterday.

As for me, I have a piece to write and I figure that sooner or later you'll find some cost-cutting method for communicating the deadline-day to me c/o *Newsweek* in Hong Kong. Meanwhile, unless you can arrange on your end some way for me to buy into the post-embassy evac plot, my options are so limited that at the moment I have no choice but to leave Saturday and ponder my next move from wherever I can get a flight to. In closing I want to thank you for all the help and direction you've given me in these savage hours, and about the only thing I can add to that is that I genuinely wish you were here. Cazart. Hunter.

MEMO ON SAIGON

Thompson kept a journal throughout his stay in Southeast Asia. This unfinished entry describes his experiences during the U.S. evacuation of Saigon the day before the South Vietnamese government officially surrendered to North Vietnam's forces.

April, 1975

Balls. If I wanted to go to Subic Bay, I'd join the goddamn navy. That dime-sucking fool has already seen my copy & my description of the hopeless madness of the Embassy's evacuation plan—21 Hueys,[9] holding 7–8 people each, are now available to lift us off the rooftops & out to the 3 main pickup points where the Jolly Green Giants can land—and, as Alan Carter at USSS pointed out yesterday in his office—with Jerry Ford's picture off the wall & ready to be flown out—"all they have to do is shoot down one chopper" & that will end that phase of the plan—leaving anybody still in downtown Saigon to get out on his own.

So I am off to Laos on Saturday—while I still have enough cash to function—& then back to Hong Kong & Bali—where Sandy will supposedly meet me.

9. "Huey" is the nickname of the American UH 1-B armed helicopter.

Even lame strangers & non-journalists who can help out with red tape, etc. are getting $50 a day in green out here, plus expenses—and as far as I know I'm not getting anything at all.

Sitting in Brinks Up Town Club for breakfast again—for the past two hours I have been the only person in the dining room, but now a few journalists are beginning to drift in—but the building is virtually empty.

Outside the air-conditioned restaurant, the outdoor theatre where they used to show American movies at night is deserted & stripped of equipment—there is no more toilet paper in the bathrooms—either Ladies or Gents—but the wooden rollers are still locked in place with solid brass locks & nobody knows or cares where the keys are.

On the street below, two dozen tiny Vietnamese construction-workers are still working steadily on a 6-story apartment that is half-finished—heavy steel-reinforced concrete, faced with orange tile bricks. Only a direct hit will have much effect on that building, & the new Chinese (Hong Kong) owner was apparently willing to gamble on that, because he's still paying his crew—although in brutally inflated piastres. (The official rate remains 750p = $1.00 US, but the Bank of India is giving 2800—$1.00 today, up 500p since I changed $200 for the Rolex on Tuesday, while ordering my tailor-made TV costumes at 20Kp each. I am the only person in the press who still has his clothes & equipment lying un-packed around his hotel room—& still ordering clothes from the tailor. All the others have sent everything out, except what they can carry in one "running bag.")

My second arrival at the Continental was a strange sight—bringing in so much luggage that I needed three bearers to get it into the hotel—and one leather red chinese suitcase that was so heavy I had to carry it in myself—a morale-building move, I thought—but it was widely interpreted as the act of a doom-seeking lunatic—especially the idea of bringing in a new 240V electric typewriter that wouldn't work at all in the hotel's 110V sockets—until Mr. Dang, *Time*'s fixer, managed to wire it into the air conditioner with a crude 6-inch "extension cord" made of stripped lamp-wire & scotch-tape.

Dang now has every credential I own—my passport, my press card, my *RS* air travel card. . . . How many out-going tickets will he charge on it? And what will I say if he tells me it *got lost*?

Nothing—or at least no more than I'd say if the white-pajama hall-boys began looting my room, with bayonets in their teeth. Right. Just help yourselves, boys; don't mind me. Can I help you with that packing?

Yesterday morning I saw a drunk ARVN soldier[10] wandering around the halls of the Continental for the first time. Not armed—or at least not with an M-16—although he might have had a knife or a pistol . . . and who would I

10. Army of the Republic of [South] Vietnam.

have turned him in to . . . after a fight . . . And he would definitely be back—with some friends, to wreak vengeance on the Global Affairs suite.

Yes—the fuse is burning down here; the air is almost electric with fear & blind anticipation of something awful that could start happening at any moment . . . although this nervous waiting for the end could last for months, or at least a few more weeks. The fate of Saigon is now *entirely* in the hands of the VC/NVA (PRG)[11] top command—and they now have 16 divisions massed in a ring around Saigon to underline their bargaining position—while the ARVN is destroyed & even a quickly-formed emergency coalition government in Saigon would have little or no leverage at the bargaining table. Maybe a *"third force"* govt. here could offer Hanoi a peaceful & gradual transfer of power without destroying Saigon in the process. Sort of a new version of the old American axiom: *"We had to destroy Saigon in order to save it."*

TO JANN WENNER, *ROLLING STONE:*

April, 1975
Global Affairs Desk,
Suite 37
Hotel Continental Palace
Lam Son Square
Saigon

Jann don't pay any attention to any of the bullshit you see in the newspapers or the newsmagazines, or on TV about how savage and ugly things are out here. I was roaming all over downtown Saigon about three hours after curfew tonight with a drunk South Vietnamese teenager carrying a funky old M-1 carbine and all we saw worth shooting was a gaggle of huge rats around the base of the gigantic and insanely ugly statue of two drug-crazed marines pointing a bazooka at the National Assembly building, where the bats used to live. I also made three new friends today, Jann. Isn't that wonderful? I also bought a forty-five with two full clips but it was stolen before I could seize it and then a gin-crazed Flying Tiger pilot ran amok with a loaded thirty-eight in the Caravelle bar and got into an argument with a gang of pinko limeys about the relative merits of British versus American colonialism. The Flying Tiger then stomped the limey three times on the bar-rail and as the English pig went down for the third time he shouted: "At least we left them railroads!"

That was about the extent of this week's violence in Saigon—except for several bombs that went off yesterday and killed three people in a public market about a five-minute walk from the Continental and the explosion of a nearby ammo dump that rattled my windows and caused nausea & vomiting at Doctor Chang's final opium party in the Continental basement.

11. Vietcong/North Vietnam Army (Provisional Revolutionary Government).

In any case, I think I am leaving for Laos today, which is Saturday, despite the consensus betting that our Ambassador will pull the plug today and send all the press to Guam, where I definitely do not want to go because I almost got in a fight with the ex-governor of Guam on my flight coming out here. On the other hand, I might have to visit the new CIA concentration camp in Bali, where the hard core political mavericks are being taken for terminal interrogation behind a shroud of silence. I learned about this today from a pilot I met in the ruins of Saigon American Legion Post No. 34, which is now officially in exile along with the Shanghai Am/Legion Post No. One, which has been officially in exile since 1949. And I, for one, am extremely bitter about this. . . . So bitter, in fact, that I am leaving immediately for Laos and then Bali, on the track of a story that will blow your goddamn gizzard right out of your body when you realize the implications.

Meanwhile, I am leaving the Global Affairs Suite here in the hands of Laura Palmer. She is extremely weird and flakey, but what the hell? After six months in a tent city on Guam she might not be quite so uppity and abusive vis-à-vis the expense account. She maintains about four huge rooms here in the Continental, so you might have to ring around a bit if you want to reach her by phone.

I will of course be on the road for the next few weeks, but you can reach me, as it were, through the Hong Kong *Newsweek* office. My personal contact there is Mr. Hay-Chung, who handles my affairs.

And if possible I'll file something fairly short for the current issue, but I need to know the deadline . . . and so does Laura, just in case she has to file from Guam in a few days. My own dateline for next time will be either the Lane Xang hotel or the White Rose orgy & opium den in Vientiane. Ok for now; Send more money ASAP. Expenses are awful out here in the East.

Cazart,
Hunter . . .

TO TIM CROUSE c/o PAUL SCANLON, *ROLLING STONE:*

Crouse was slated to take over Rolling Stone's *post–Vietnam War coverage after Thompson left Southeast Asia.*

April 23, 1975
Saigon

Paul please pass this on verbatim to Tim ASAP. Message: Tim, the time has come to start packing for the long trip to Saigon. If you can get here by Saturday, April 26/twenty-six, you can take over the Global Affairs Desk here in Suite 37. We'll have a formal changing of the guard ceremony down in the garden on Friday night after curfew—just before I leave for Laos, Hong Kong,

Bali, and Colorado. As usual, I've had to play the icebreaker role and establish our credit, credentials, style, contacts, etc. out here and I had a powerful sense of déjà vu all the while I was doing it . . . but the situation is stabilized now and I see no point in staying on to watch that part of the action that you said you were interested in; mainly because it is going to take too much time and I have other business that needs tending immediately. The fear and loathing orgasm came yesterday, in the 12/twelve wild hours before Thieu[12] resigned . . . and now the boil seems to be lanced. I'd like to stay here for the victory parade down Tu Do street, but I'm afraid that might be too long a wait . . . and by "too long" I mean even one more week, mainly because I can't get any reply out of the home office, as it were, with regard to the nature of my assignment or how much I can expect to be paid for whatever I'm doing. These are things you should get absolutely straight before you come out here, because once you arrive in this fine little madhouse of a city you're fucked in terms of any communications with the outside world. I still have no idea, for instance, if the four-thousand words I managed to file by telex yesterday reached San Francisco before the deadline. Jann is off skiing somewhere in Utah with Gordon Strachan,[13] and nobody in SF seems to understand that a telex works in both directions . . . or maybe it's another budget-cutting move, but in any case I don't feel like staying out here in the bunker any longer on pure, paranoid spec. So I'm getting out soon and you're welcome to my suite in the Continental—which is, by the way, one of the world's very special hotels. I will actually feel very sad to leave it. When it comes to adrenaline in the proper atmosphere, this place makes the Wayfarer seem like a nursing home in Queens. And that's it for now . . . except that you must repeat must call Sandy and read this whole message to her because I haven't been able to get through by phone for three days and I know she's worried. So please do that and also tell her to see if she can change her plane ticket for a round-trip to Bali, where I can meet her for a week or so of beach time on my way back to the U.S. She can leave word inre: Bali with Loren Jenkins' wife or the *Newsweek* office in Hong Kong. Okay and cazart . . . Hunter

TO JANN WENNER, *ROLLING STONE:*

As the situation in Saigon rapidly deteriorated, Thompson suggested to Wenner from Hong Kong that Rolling Stone *print evacuation accounts as soon as possible.*

12. South Vietnamese president Nguyen Van Thieu.

13. Gordon Strachan, who had been chief of staff H. R. Haldeman's assistant in the Nixon White House, had helped run CREEP's 1972 dirty-tricks campaign.

May 1, 1975
Repulse Bay Hotel No. 205
Hong Kong

HST/Endgame

FEAR & LOATHING IN HONG KONG

"AT LEAST WE LEFT THEM RAILROADS"
or
"BYE BYE MISS AMERICAN PIE"
and
"WELCOME TO HO CHI MINH CITY"
by Hunter S. Thompson

zip Jann I trust we can use at least one of the above heads, although I can't say which one will fit until I see how the piece turns out. As we discussed on the phone it will be more in the form of a memo on what to expect in the "final & savage analysis" to come later; just a series of points, ideas & memories that it will take me some time to develop but which I think we should get into print ASAP, if only as a gaggle of vignettes. I also think we should get something personal from Laura Palmer on the close-up details of how she managed during the evacuation. I gave her 200 dollars for four days work and another 150 thousand piastres for expenses just before I left Saigon, with the understanding that she would pick up my photos and cover for me until I returned, so I assume she plans to write her own version of the final rout and that you'll get at least a short piece from her to run along with this one. Meanwhile, I have tentatively arranged for a piece from one of those who stayed behind & also some photos, but I can't confirm this yet because all wires out of Ho Chi Minh City were interdicted around noon today & we can't be sure if any messages are getting in . . . but I'll let you know on this ASAP. As for art, I would send Annie[14] down to Camp Pendleton[15] to look for gangs of hookers and ex-generals with belts made of gold-link bars. . . . Marshal Ky's[16] wife is presumably still in the Bay Area & she might be worth a shot or two on her own. As for wire & agency stuff, look for some of the helicopter evacuation stuff or wild mobs attacking the embassy or possibly a shot of the UPI staffers whose car got swarmed en route to the embassy because that was the one thing we all feared and they apparently got it full bore. OK for now; I'm just going to let it run and see what comes out—beginning with a verse from your favorite song, to wit: zip.

14. *Rolling Stone* photographer Annie Leibovitz.
15. Camp Pendleton is a U.S. Marine Corps base near Oceanside, California.
16. Nguyen Cao Ky, South Vietnam's vice president, was accused of several forms of corruption, including involvement in the heroin trade, but Ky denied the charges.

"So bye bye Miss American Pie; drove my Chevy to
the levee, but the levee was dry . . .
Them good ole boys were drinkin whiskey and rye,
singin this'll be the day that I die . . .
This'll be the day that I die . . . "[17]

I had never paid much attention to that song until I heard it on the muzak one Saturday afternoon in the roof-top restaurant of the new Palace Hotel, looking down on the orange-tile rooftops of the overcrowded volcano that used to be known as Saigon and discussing military strategy over gin and lime with London Sunday *Times* correspondent, Murray Sayle. We had just come back in a Harley-Davidson powered rickshaw from the Viet Cong's weekly press conference in their barbed-wire enclosed compound at Saigon's Ton San Nhut airport, and Sayle had a big geophysical map of Indochina spread out on the table between us, using a red felt-tipped pen as a pointer to show me how and why the South Vietnamese government of then-president Nguyen Van Thieu had managed to lose half the country and a billion dollars worth of U.S. weaponry in less than three weeks.

I was trying to concentrate on his explanation—which made perfect sense, on the map—but the strange mix of realities on that afternoon of what would soon prove to be the next to last Saturday of the Vietnam War made concentration difficult. For one thing, I had never been west of San Francisco until I'd arrived in Saigon about ten days earlier—just after the South Vietnamese army (ARVN) had been routed on world-wide TV in the "battles" for Hué and Da Nang. This was a widely-advertised "massive Hanoi offensive" that had suddenly narrowed the whole war down to a nervous ring around Saigon, less than fifty miles in diameter . . . and during the past few days, as a million or more refugees filtered steadily into Saigon from the panic zones up north around Hué and Da Nang, it had become painfully and ominously clear to us all that Hanoi had never really launched any "massive offensive" at all, but that the flower of the finely U.S. trained and heavily U.S. equipped South Vietnamese Army had simply panicked and run amok. The films of whole ARVN divisions fleeing desperately through the streets of Da Nang had apparently shocked the NVA generals in Hanoi almost as badly as they jolted that bonehead ward-heeler that Nixon put in the White House in exchange for the pardon that kept him out of prison.

Ford still denies this, but what the hell? It hardly matters anymore, because not even a criminal geek like Nixon would have been stupid enough to hold a nationally-televised press conference in the wake of a disaster like Da Nang

17. Quoted from Don McLean's 1971 hit song, "American Pie," about the deaths of pioneering rock musicians Buddy Holly, Ritchie Valens, and the Big Bopper in a plane crash in Mason City, Iowa, on February 3, 1959.

and compound the horror of what millions of U.S. viewers had been seeing on TV all week by refusing to deny, on camera, that the 58,000 Americans who died in Vietnam had died in vain. Even arch-establishment commentators like James Reston and Eric Sevareid[18] were horrified by Ford's inept and almost cruelly stupid performance at that press conference. In addition to the wives, parents, sons, daughters and other relatives and friends of the 58,000 American dead, he was also talking to more than 150,000 veterans who were wounded, maimed and crippled in Vietnam . . . and the net effect of what he said might just as well have been to quote Ernest Hemingway's description of men who had died in another war, many years ago—who were "shot down and killed like dogs, for no good reason at all."

My memories of that day are very acute, because it was the first time since I'd arrived in Saigon about ten days earlier that I suddenly understood how close we were to the end, and how ugly it was likely to be . . . and as that eerie chorus about "Bye bye, Miss American Pie" kept howling around my ears while we ate our crab salad, I looked out across the Saigon River to where NVA howitzers were hitting sporadically in the distant rice paddies and sending up clouds of muddy smoke.

MEMO FROM THE GLOBAL AFFAIRS DESK:

As more American journalists fled from Saigon to Hong Kong, Thompson worked to capture the chaotic climate in his article drafts.

May 2, 1975

HST/Endgame

(cont.) "The day the music died . . .
So bye bye, Miss American Pie . . .
drove my Chevy to the levee, but the levee was dry
Them good ole boys were drinkin whiskey and rye,
Singin this'll be the day that I die . . .
This'll be the day that I die."

zip Jann it's been 24 hours since I wrote the stuff above, and I've been running around the city half mad on Reactivan, dealing with the first wave of press refugees from Saigon with all their nasty stories and also watching the first "fall of Saigon" films coming in from the fleet . . . but I am not supposed to have seen any of this film or talked to any of these people, for the record, so in the following text I'll attribute most of what I picked up today to my private sources at the Mongol/Transworld News Agency (see below) and my time is getting so short now that I can't afford to do any more legwork if I want to get

18. Eric Sevareid was a distinguished CBS News commentator.

this in for the current issue, so from now on it will have to read like a hastily-composed memo . . . although once I get this done I can go back and squeeze some of these sources for what appears to be a vast amount of good detail and gonzo-style material for the main piece. Also, according to the people I spent all of tonight with, Laura Palmer will probably not be able to file anything substantial for this issue because she is said to be trapped with all the others.

(cont.) "The day the music died . . .
So bye bye Miss American Pie; drove my Chevy
to the levee, but the levee was dry . . .
Them good ole boys were drinkin whiskey and rye,
Singin this'll be the day that I die . . .
This'll be the day that I die."

There was not much music in the last days of Saigon, but what little there was died very suddenly and violently in the last few days of April, 1975 when the eleventh-hour cease-fire agreement that was supposedly on the verge of being ratified by both sides blew up and disintegrated in a frenzy of bombings, street-fighting and heavy artillery blasts that turned the long-delayed American evacuation into a nightmare of panic and confusion . . . and most of the good ole boys in the Anglo-American press corps who'd been sitting around drinkin whiskey and rye in the hotels around Lam Son square for lo these many months are now steaming across the South China Sea toward Manila, aboard U.S. aircraft carriers. They were hauled out of Saigon by CIA pilots and U.S. Marine helicopters, and we will hear their collective story soon enough.

It will not be especially pleasant—but not nearly so weird and ugly as the stories that we will probably not hear for quite a while, of those who were left behind in the panic to flee what is now called Ho Chi Minh City. Saigon is no more.

On the day after the final "American evacuation" from Vietnam, I was sitting on the long, open-air balcony of the dining room at the Repulse Bay Hotel in Hong Kong, brooding over a late breakfast of bloody marys and crabmeat . . . reading the front page of the *South China Morning News* while a heavy monsoon rain pounded down on the small fleet of blue rowboats tied up on the beach in front of the hotel. The beach had been crowded yesterday, but now it was empty and rain-swept as the hotel balcony, which had also been crowded yesterday at this lazy hour of the morning . . . but there is nothing gentle about a monsoon rain in Hong Kong, and just before noon a rising wind began lashing an occasional sheet of warm water across the red linen table cloths on the balcony and a busload of Dutch tourists who had just arrived for lunch were herded inside to the dining room. They went eagerly, happy to get out of the rain and staring in obvious puzzlement at me and the only other person on the balcony who refused to leave.

He was a young-looking American with damp blond hair and blue eyes, wearing Levi's, cowboy boots and an olive-drab Air America[19] pilot's jacket. We were both sitting at tables right next to the railing when the wind began lashing gusts of rain across the balcony, and when the waiters started herding the Dutch tourists inside they left both of us alone. He was drinking a San Miguel beer and writing very intently on a red-white-and-blue striped Air Mail letter tablet; the only sign he gave of acknowledging the rain was to move his chair about a foot closer to one of the tall concrete pillars and into a position precisely downwind from the weather, where he signaled one of the Chinese waiters for another bottle of San Miguel and kept on writing in his tablet.

By this time my newspaper was getting too wet to read, and I saw him glance up briefly when I moved my two bloody marys and my silver pot of coffee to a table about six feet away from the railing, to a table that was not so exposed to the storm . . . and from that half-dry vantage point I could watch him still filling his damp red-white-and-blue pages while I read the *South China Morning News*'s account of how U.S. Marines had used their M-16 rifle butts to smash the fingers of desperate South Vietnamese trying to climb over the barb-wire topped wall into the American Embassy compound in Saigon yesterday, trying to get aboard the Air America helicopters evacuating the last of the journalists, businessmen, U.S. Embassy staffers and other American refugees out to waiting aircraft carriers, just off the Vietnam coast.

Neither one of us had been a part of that final, nightmarish scene—because it was impossible, as we both knew, for anybody who'd escaped from Saigon on Monday to be on the balcony of the Repulse Bay Hotel in Hong Kong as early as Tuesday. The U.S. Marines' refugee flotilla was still somewhere out in the South China Sea, probably headed for the U.S. Navy base at Subic Bay in the Philippines.

MEMO FROM THE GLOBAL AFFAIRS DESK:

May 4, 1975
Laos

I have finally arrived in Vientiane, after a long and torturous five-day journey from Saigon, via Hong Kong and Bangkok. When I walked into the Lane Xang Hotel last night, sometime around two-thirty in the morning in a drenching monsoon rain, the man at the desk first refused to let me register because he said I had no reservation . . . which may or may not have been true, de-

19. Air America was a CIA subsidiary headquartered on Taiwan and used for covert U.S. air operations across Asia.

pending on which view of the understandably scrambled Indochinese mind one subscribes to in these menacing times—but in fact I *had* sent a cable from Hong Kong, requesting a large room with a king-size bed, quick access to the pool and a view of the Mekong River, which flows in front of the hotel.

After a fairly savage argument, the night-clerk agreed to a compromise. He would give me the best suite in the hotel for as long as I wanted, provided I gave him twenty green American dollars at once for the company of his daughter for the rest of the night. He described her as a "young and beautiful student—not a bar girl" who spoke excellent English and would certainly have no objection to being awakened at three in the morning and hauled over to the hotel by taxi in a hellish rainstorm, just in order to make me happy.

"Look," I said. "You are dealing with a very tired person. The only thing I need to make me happy is a long sleep in a big bed with nobody bothering me. I have nothing against meeting your daughter; I'm sure she's a wonderful person—but why don't I just give you twenty dollars and never mind about waking her up tonight. If she's free around noon tomorrow, maybe we can have lunch at the White Rose."

The man winced. Nobody's "daughter" goes near the White Rose. It is one of the scurviest and most infamous *bangios* in all of Indochina—even worse than "Lucy's" in Saigon—and the moment I said that name and saw the man's face I knew I'd said both the right and the wrong thing at the same time. He was grievously insulted, but at least we understood each other. . . . So he had one of his assistant pimps carry my bags up to #224, a rambling suite of rooms half-hidden under the top flight of wide white-tiled stair/ramps that rise out of the middle of the Lane Xang lobby. When I first went into #224, it took me about two minutes to find the bed; it was around the corner and down a 15-foot hallway from the refrigerator and the black-leather-topped bar and the ten-foot tan couch and five tan easy chairs and the hardwood writing desk and the sliding glass doors on the pool-facing balcony outside the living room of #224 . . . and at the other end of the hallway, half-hidden by the foundation of the central stairway, was another big room with a king-sized bed, another screened balcony, another telephone and another air conditioner, along with a pink-tiled bathroom with two sinks, a toilet and a bidet, and a deep pink bathtub about nine feet long.

"We normally charge fifty dollars a day for this one," he said. "But in your case, I'll sell it for forty."

"You must be sick," I said. "I had a better suite than this at the Continental in Saigon for twenty—with two beds and a ceiling fan."

He stared thoughtfully at the ceiling and sucked on his gums for a moment, then looked me in the eye and said: "Okay, I'll sell it to you for twenty-five."

I shrugged. "Why not?" I walked over to the refrigerator to get some ice, but there was none. Both he and his henchman were baffled . . . until I had a look at the wiring and saw it was not plugged in. None of the lamps were plugged in either—along with both air conditioners and the hot water heater in the bathroom. Suite #224 had obviously not been used in quite a while.

I asked the night-clerk if he would get me a bucket of ice. Somewhere in the bowels of my luggage I had a film-can full of extremely powerful Cambodian red, along with a quart of Jack Daniel's I'd just bought in Hong Kong, and the prospect of a few iced drinks along with a pipeload of paralytic hallucinogens seemed just about right for that moment . . . followed by fifteen or sixteen hours of stuporous sleep.

But my new buddy, the bashful pimp, had not yet tied the knot in *his* half of the bargain. "Very good," he said finally. "I will order your ice when I go downstairs to call my daughter."

"What?"

"Of course," he said. "You will like her. She is very beautiful." Then he smiled and held out his hand. "Twenty dollars, please . . ."

I hesitated for a moment, listening to the rain pounding the palm trees outside my window, then I reluctantly pulled out my wallet and gave him a twenty-dollar bill. I had seen enough of Vientiane on the drive into town from the airport to know I'd be in very grave trouble if I got thrown out of the Lane Xang at three-thirty in the morning in the middle of a blinding monsoon, hauling an electric typewriter and a soft-leather suitcase, with no currency except U.S. and Hong Kong dollars, and not speaking a word of Laotian or even enough French to beat on somebody's door and ask for directions to another hotel. . . . No, I couldn't stand that; but I wasn't sure I could stand the kind of nasty scene I suspected this humorless, fat little hustler was planning to lay on me, either. As he opened the door to leave I said, "That money is for ice, okay? Just bring me a bucket of ice and keep the money yourself. I'll talk to your daughter tomorrow."

He paused for a moment, looking back at me, but his eyes were blank and I could tell his brain was busy with other matters. Then he pulled the door shut behind him and left me alone in the room. I slumped back on the couch and opened the bottle of hot bourbon, propping it up on my chest and my chin so I could drink with only a slight movement of my lower lip while I listened to the rain and tried not to think about anything at all. . . .

FROM JANN WENNER, *ROLLING STONE:*

Thompson finally received a response from Wenner.

May 6, 1975
(Cable & Wireless)

GOT YOUR LETTER MONDAY ALL IS UNDERSTOOD AND GENERALLY AGREEABLE LAURA FILED EXTREMELY GOOD LAST NIGHT IN

SAIGON AND THE RIDE TO GUAM PIECE WHICH WE'RE JAMMING INTO THIS ISSUE SHE'LL BE WELL COMPENSATED FOR ALL HER WORK REST ASSURED ITS UP TO YOU TO TAKE AS MUCH TIME AS YOU WANT IN THE SOUTHERN PACIFIC I AM JUST CONCERNED THAT DURING THAT TIME THAT YOU CONTINUE WRITING SO THAT THE STORY KEEPS GOING ON IN YOUR MIND YOU'RE THINKING ABOUT IT MAKING PROGRESS AND HAVE IT ACTIVELY UNDERWAY WE ALL WANT THIS TO BE A GREAT ONE I DO HAVE IN MIND FINISHING UP THE ANTHOLOGY WHEN YOU GET HERE BUT THERE'S NO HUGE RUSH I WILL BE OUT OF TOWN ANYWAY UNTIL MAY 16 AND NATURALLY WOULD LIKE TO SEE YOU THROUGH SAN FRAN WHEN I'M THERE I DID REMEMBER OUR DISCUSSION ON THE POLITICS SECTION AND WOULD NOT HAVE SO PLACED THE PIECE EXCEPT THAT IT WAS THE VERY LAST DAY AND IT WAS THE BEST OF THE FEW SOLUTIONS WE HAD THE NEEB PHOTO WAS SENT BACK TO YOU IN HONG KONG C/O NEWSWEEK IF YOU COULD GET BACK INTO SAIGON IT CERTAINLY WOULD BE WORTHWHILE WAITING AROUND OR VACATIONING IN A PLACE WHERE YOU WOULDN'T BE TOO FAR AWAY BUT IF NOT SELAH THE ONE THING THAT MIGHT BE WORTH DOING ON THE WAY BACK TO SAN FRAN IS TO STOP IN GUAM FOR A DAY OR TWO AND SEE THAT REFUGEE CAMP AND PICK UP ALL THE STORIES THAT THE GIS WILL START TO TELL ABOUT THE FIRST DAYS OF SAIGON WHICH THE OTHER PRESS WILL HAVE MISSED SINCE THEY WILL ALL HAVE MOVED ON I ANTICIPATE NO HASSLE ABOUT YOUR EXPENSES JUST AS LONG AS YOU SUBMIT THOROUGH ACCOUNTING ACTUAL EXPENDITURES—YOU WILL BE REIMBURSED ON THE ACCOUNTING YOU PROVIDE HAVE A GOOD TIME SERIOUSLY CONSIDER THAT GUAM STUFF IT MIGHT BE JUST PERFECT IN TERMS OF LITTLE SAIGON LOOK FORWARD TO SEEING YOU IN SAN FRAN CALL ME IN NEW YORK IF YOU HAVE ANY QUESTIONS

JANN

TO DOUG SAPPER:

Doug Sapper was a former Special Forces operative in Southeast Asia.

June 1, 1975
Woody Creek, CO

Doug . . .

This is just a quick note to say thanx again for The Help, as it were, in Bangkok. At 50 cents a hit, that shit is the cheapest miracle on the market—except maybe for that 25 cents a pound weed those dope-addict bastards were smoking up in Laos.

Anyway . . . I remember you saying you were thinking about heading for Africa, so I thought I'd send a note and not lose track of you. I'll be here most of the summer, but after that I can't say—although you can always reach me at the Owl Farm or c/o (Tom) Benton's Studio, Box 1561 (I think) in Aspen . . . or c/o the Jerome Hotel Bar in Aspen. . . . As for *RS*, my relationship with them was plunged into ugliness when I got back here and learned that the owner/editor had cancelled my health/medical insurance—without telling me—just before sending me to Saigon.

Shit . . . and you thought *you* were working for useless assholes.

But I'll still be writing for *RS*, and what interests me right now is the idea that you might be able to do a relatively short (1000–1500 words) piece on your own views of the realities and general relationship between the U.S. press/media/etc. and the U.S. military & politics establishment in Southeast Asia during the past 10 yrs. . . . In other words, a personal commentary on how *you* viewed the press, for instance, when you worked with the Special Forces (with *Examples, Names, Details, weird stories,* etc.) and then bringing it all up to date with any stories & examples you might recall from Saigon, Cambodia, Laos or Bangkok—with a special eye on the question of whether or not the U.S. (or any other) press knew what was going on, *at the time,* and how they treated that knowledge. . . . The same kind of focus, more or less, that Tim Crouse and I brought to the coverage of the press in the '72 campaign. Nothing especially brutal or heavy, but just a relative press outsider's opinion of how hip the press was to the realities of the moment.

I have no idea what you might or might not do with this idea, and I don't recall ever discussing it with you—but it seems to me that you have a definitely unique kind of vantage point, when it comes to watching the U.S. press in combat & under pressure. We could handle the thing any way you want: From a bylined first person piece, to a completely anonymous critique—but either way I think it should be in the first person, and I'd frankly prefer your byline, if possible—although I'll guarantee your anonymity if you think it's important.

Let me know on this ASAP, because I'm laboring mightily to bring forth something big & heavy for publication by the end of June. In terms of money, I can guarantee you $500 for a 1500 word piece *if they use any part of it*—which usually puts them in a sort of untenable position where they have to pay for anything I commission; the only hook in this, however, is a nasty story on today's *Wash. Post* wire about my mano a mano gig with the *RS* editor.

Well . . . "When the Tough get going, they should first know the lay of the land. . . ." Who said that? I think it was that vicious, half-mad but germ-free lunatic. . . .

Hunter

TO GEORGE C. BLUESTONE:

George C. Bluestone, an attorney for a debt-collection agency in New York City, had written to Thompson regarding his unpaid London hotel bill from the previous autumn.

June 1, 1975
Woody Creek, CO

Dear George . . .

I hate to be the one to lay this on you, old sport, but I have a feeling that you've stepped in some very weird shit this time. I have no idea who you are, or what kind of law you practice—but I suspect I'm in a pretty good position, George, to assure you that this one is going to be different.

And when I say "this one," George, I refer to your letter of April 28, in which you threatened me with "legal proceedings" unless I quickly send you a personal cheque for a $1,075.00 bill at Brown's Hotel in London—which, as you specifically noted, "was arranged through *Rolling Stone* of London, England."

I also want to thank you for the xerox copy of *Rolling Stone* (of San Francisco) editor Jann Wenner's letter to you, which very specifically states in paragraf #2 that "Mr. Thompson's expenses incurred in London during November, 1974 do not come under our jurisdiction." (sic) I was particularly happy to get this copy of Mr. Wenner's letter, since I was unable myself to elicit any explanation at all from him, vis-à-vis *Rolling Stone* (of London)'s failure to honor whatever agreement they may or may not have made with Brown's Hotel with regard to the occupancy of any (or perhaps all) of their rooms by one (or perhaps many) *Rolling Stone* writer(s). I just came back from Hong Kong, Bangkok and Singapore, George—so I think you'll know what I mean when I say there is ample evidence in this world to suggest that your typical British hotel-keeper is capable of almost anything, in the context of "making arrangements."

But that is hardly the point, eh? We were talking about an unpaid hotel bill, "arranged through *Rolling Stone* of London, England." Well . . . at this point, George, and unless things change pretty drastically with regard to this matter, I frankly have no intention of ever sending you a fucking dime, for any reason at all. I have not had extensive experience in the debt-collection business—or at least not on your end of it—but I've had enough to know that only a goddamn waterhead would try to enforce a money demand on the basis of a non-existent agreement. Even the Hell's Angels, George, had a valid piece of paper in their hands when they went out on the streets of Oakland to mash the teeth and stomp the fingers of those unfortunates who had fallen behind in their payments for autos and TV sets.

Which is neither here nor there, of course, because I am far more interested in securing any knowledge you might have with regard to the connection (if any) between this London hotel bill and a series of extremely savage & defamatory criminal charges that were made against me by a British newspaper reporter, writing for a New York weekly paper called *"The Village Voice."* These charges appeared in the *VV* of May 19 '75 (Vol. XX No. 20) and involved allegations of attempted and/or forcible rape; actual or threatened assault with a deadly weapon; wanton use and dissemination of cocaine on the streets of London, by means of a "switchblade knife" (the same weapon allegedly used in my numerous rapes & assaults); and a variety of other felony charges that, for our purposes of the moment, might just as well be grouped under the heading of Gross Public & Private Insult: These include Threatened and/or Attempted Murder, Rape, Dismemberment, Trespassing, Obscenity, Depravity, Brutality and attempting to force an elderly Italian woman to gratify my lusts in exchange for a bowl of spaghetti . . . and all this, George, was allegedly done at the point of a "switchblade knife."

So . . . now we come to it, eh?

But we lack a few crucial details . . . and I think you can help me on this, George; if only to establish a tangible connexion (if any) between your blatantly misdirected money-demand on me, and this malevolent spate of felony allegations made against me in *The Village Voice.* Unfortunately, neither you nor that star-crossed fop who sold all those charges to the *Voice* made any reference to dates, names, places or other specifics that could irrevocably link these two problems in any kind of *time-context.* I must assume, however, that—since I have only visited London once in my life and hope never to do so again—both your money-demand and these ugly rape, drug & assault charges are somehow connected to that visit Mr. Wenner refers to as "during November, 1974," when "Mr. Thompson's expenses (did) not come under (his) jurisdiction."

Indeed . . . and before I get into this next shot, George, let me assure you that there is absolutely *nothing personal* with regard to my feelings about you or your law practice . . . and I also think you should know, if only for your own peace of mind, that this same Mr. Wenner who suggested that you try to put the squeeze on me and gave you my address so you could track me down (or up) to my lair out here in the mountains of Colorado, is the same treacherous asshole who (in his role as both editor and majority stockholder in *Rolling Stone* of San Francisco *and* London, George) not only sent me on assignment to London last November & now refuses to pay a hotel bill that I had no part in arranging & certainly no intention of paying . . . but Mr. Wenner is also the same owner/editor of *Rolling Stone* who recently sent me to cover "the last days of Saigon" while at the same time removing me from the *Rolling Stone* payroll and officially canceling my health & medical insurance without ever mentioning it to me—not even while I was working in Saigon under conditions that most of the world press called a terminal "siege" and what every insurance company in the world called an extremely dangerous "war zone."

My own (personal) life insurance policy became invalid the moment my Air Vietnam jet touched down at Ton San Nhut airport in Saigon, but I naturally assumed I was still covered under *Rolling Stone*'s group policy (No. G16780) with "the Lincoln National Life Ins. Co." of Fort Wayne, Indiana. But I was wrong, George. By his decision to remove me from the *Rolling Stone* payroll—without either written or verbal notice, or even *mentioning* his decision to anybody except the company comptroller, who quietly effected it—Mr. Wenner was also removing me and my family from any benefits under "hospital expense policy #G16780." And I might *still* be ignorant of my loss, George, if I hadn't decided to call Mr. Wenner on the occasion of my recent return from a six-week tour of every goddamn war zone in what the British used to call Indochina. . . .

And I hope with all my heart, George—because I feel no hatred for you—that you are not the U.S. collection agent for any British-owned hotels in the Orient: the Repulse Bay in Hong Kong, for instance, or the Hotel Erawan in Bangkok. Because those are only two of *many* Asian creditors who will soon find themselves bogged down in nickel & dime court battles with your friend, Mr. Wenner.

Are you beginning to get the picture, George?

I sure as hell hope so, because I'm getting goddamn tired of writing these letters to people like you, who seem to think I travel around the world at my own expense and write long articles for *Rolling Stone,* just for the fun of it. . . . Yes, and now that we've hit on this vein, I wonder if you might know anything about the recent rash of rumors (published in *The Village Voice, New Times* and other U.S. outlets) that I somehow wasted anywhere from $10,000 to $28,000 of *Rolling Stone* (of San Francisco)'s money in connexion with a heavyweight (boxing) scam that occurred last fall in Zaire.

I seriously doubt that you had any part in that kind of vicious and defamatory libel, George—but since you're teetering right on the brink of it with this lame bullshit about "my" bill at Brown's Hotel in London, let me use these last few lines to discharge what I regard as the last of my ethical obligations in this cheap, familiar and always-degrading kind of quarrel by reminding you that not everybody in this world feels the same kind of bilious contempt and repugnance that throbs in my body like nine gallons of rancid blood when I stare once again at your letter and know that politicians are not alone in their belief that "there is no such thing as *bad* publicity." Some people actually like it, George—especially if it sells their newspapers.

But we live in bad times, old sport, and I don't own any newspapers. I don't own much of anything, in fact, and with any warning at all—maybe five or six hours—I can slip across the border and pick up my passport from the fast-growing nation of Joad, where every citizen is judgement-proof, and every creditor is fresh meat.

Ah, George, what have we done to be plagued by these hellish fantasies? These menacing sinkholes in our lives? These devious swine and greedheads who keep people like you in business? . . .

Which is probably not a fair assumption to make, because I know nothing about you, George. Mr. Wenner neglected to introduce us when he sicced (siked? sicked? how is that goddamn word spelled?) you on me . . . and for all I know you're a fine ambitious & idealistic young man, fresh out of law school and just trying to make a decent living by leaning on anybody stupid enough to think they have to protect their Personal Credit by paying off every geek and shyster who writes them a money-demand letter.

But if all that is true, George, it means we think very differently . . . and it also means I don't want to hear any more of this bullshit about rape, brutality, assault, hotel bills in London or some editor's libelous fantasies about me running up massive expense bills.

I'm an extremely old person, George; and I'm also far past the point of even half-worrying about what suckfish like you can do to me. My credit is rotten, and it has been for 20 years. But I've learned to like it that way, and I've also learned the real meaning of "Poisson's Formula of Discontinuous Disturbances."[20] There is not enough space to reproduce it for you here, with only a simple typewriter, but if you're interested let me refer you to page 193 (Volume Five) of *The Scientific Papers,* by Lord Rayleigh, aka John William Strutt (1842–1919).

Lord Rayleigh was not into violence, and as far as I know he never advocated the radical application of Poisson's Formula that has enabled me to travel constantly around the world, from one brutal rape-orgy to the next, while maintaining the lavish style so often attributed to me by editors, fops and comptrollers.

But Rayleigh never dealt with these swine, and certainly never with bogus creditors, so he never saw any need to expand Poisson's Formula to the point where I found myself forced to expand it almost 20 years ago.

Let me give it to you in a nut, George. My life, for the past two decades, is a scarred but healthy monument to the concept of Terminal Extremes as regards the application of Poisson's Formula—which means that Discontinuous Disturbances *need not be tolerated,* and that nowhere in the language of physics is there any provision for an equal/opposite reaction when a Discontinuous Disturbance is whipped, crushed or terminated, by any means at all.

20. Siméon Denis Poisson (1781–1840) was a French mathematical physicist who proposed formulas for defining integrals, probability, and electromagnetic theory.

Ah . . . but the rest should be left up to you, because it may in fact change your life. But in the meantime, a sort of free and functional translation—in the terms of this malignant little relationship that fate has set up for us—would boil up to a friendly suggestion that you take another look at this scumbag of global treachery you're about to step into by getting yourself involved in an extremely complex & heavy argument over expense-payments between me and Mr. Wenner.

But the choice is clearly yours, George, and I don't give a flying fuck which way you decide to go—just as long as you don't bother me. You can write all the letters you want; hell, I know how it is with your type of client . . . but if you want to mail anything else to me, please address it to my attorney, John Clancy, at Suite 2130, Crocker Plaza in San Francisco, 94104.

I don't particularly want to get to know you any better than I already do. You should feel free to write me, of course, but don't expect me to answer . . . and if you want to pursue this matter to the point where I can get a nice handle on your head, you'll wish to hell you'd never heard of me, London, *Rolling Stone,* switchblades, expense accounts or anything else connected with this degrading bag of pus.

Unless you can tell me something about that connexion I mentioned (above) . . . and in that case I think you and Mr. Clancy can make a deal. I'll call him tonight and give him all the details.

Or you can keep after me, George, if you're into that kind of action.

Hunter S. Thompson

TO JANN WENNER, *ROLLING STONE:*

With his status at Rolling Stone *still in question, Thompson demanded a written explanation from Wenner.*

June 18, 1975
Woody Creek, CO

Jann . . .

I certainly appreciate your sending me that copy of [Ralph J.] Gleason's ugly letter to you in 1968 . . . and although I'm sure you must have had some shrewd & devious motives in doing so, I'm damned if I can figure out what they are (or were). It struck me as an almost meaninglessly demented act—sort of like Nixon sending an autographed transcript of one of his most damaging tapes to John Dean.[21]

I was impressed, however, with the integrity of Ralph's instincts & also his economy of expression—since he managed to put down on one page the same feelings it took me six pages to line out in my letter to you [of May 30, 1975]

21. Former White House counsel John Dean was a key witness for the prosecution in the U.S. Senate Watergate Committee investigation.

in which I expressed the same repugnance vis-à-vis "the assumptions on which you operate."

But what the hell? I'm getting extremely tired of this cheap, neo-public bullshit—and also extremely tired of being drastically misquoted by all these "straight journalists" who keep calling me. That asshole [Tom] Zito—the man who wrote your puff-piece for the *Post*—ran off a classic example of what I mean when he substituted "unwillingness" for *willingness* . . . and I choose that example deliberately, because of its flagrance & despite the fact that what I actually said gave you more of a break than what Zito wrote . . . and I leave you to figure out where it all fits.

Meanwhile, I need a *written* explanation from you at once, with regard to my payroll status at *Rolling Stone*—which, as you know, affects not only my medical insurance, but also my tax status and my eligibility for unemployment insurance. You might think it's funny to "unilaterally suspend my retainer" with a word to [Straight Arrow vice president Tom] Baker on the inter-office phone, but the federal bureaucracies of this world we have to live in like to have things in writing.

And so do I—because until I get some kind of written notice from you, I consider myself still on the *RS* payroll (according to the masthead) and if I have any tax, medical or unemployment problems resulting from your capricious failure to clarify my situation, you can be goddamn sure they'll bounce back on you—in court, in person, and every other way that seems appropriate.

In the meantime, I'm sitting here with about 100 pages and 200 pounds of Indochina stuff—awaiting some word from you (thru Lynn) with regard to its ultimate destination.

Okay . . .
Hunter S. Thompson

TO U.S. REPRESENTATIVE JOHN BURTON:

On May 12, 1975, the U.S. merchant ship Mayaguez *was seized by Cambodian forces in international waters in the Gulf of Siam. Over the next sixty-five hours, U.S. Marines attacked Kho Tang Island while American planes bombed the transgressors' air base until the Cambodians surrendered the ship and its thirty-nine crewmen on May 14. Although forty-one American servicemen were killed during the rescue operation, the public deemed it such a success that President Gerald R. Ford's approval rating jumped eleven percentage points.*

June 22, 1975
Woody Creek, CO

John . . .

Thanks for the material you sent inre: the *Mayaguez* incident. But before I do any writing about it I want to check this one very powerful impression with you—an impression I've picked up from the gross input I have from you, your staff and the combined news agencies of both the eastern & western worlds . . . to wit:

That nobody in the U.S. Congress, the U.S. press or any other professional grouping in this country outside whatever office Ford & Kissinger[22] do their business in has *any* hard facts or real information at all with regard to what actually happened in, over or around those islands off Cambodia on whatever date those events occurred (no dates were fixed in either H. Res. 536 or in the official press release inre: the "Joint Statement" (Resolution of Inquiry on *Mayaguez*) dated June 11, 1975).

I was impressed by the breadth, scope & thrust, etc. of the 14 questions you & your 28 cohorts posed to the president on 6/11, and my initial impression from news reports as well as the resolution itself was that you people had at least a bluffing semblance of an information base with regard to the questions you asked—but I have since been given to understand that neither you, your staff nor your 28 cohorts have any more hard information on the "*Mayaguez* incident" than I do . . . and, jesus christ, John, I was somewhere between Bangkok and Bali when it happened, reading papers like the *Bangkok World* and the *South China Morning News,* which carried nothing but a hash of UPI bulletins and a few shots of local copy . . . and if you & 28 other congressmen don't know any more than I do about this goddamn wretched thing, there is something seriously wrong with the machinery . . . because I was *on vacation* at the time & not even trying to pull it all together.

If I'm wrong on this, please correct me at once, because I get a very distinct feeling—reinforced by the clips [Eli] Segal sent me from [*Congressional Quarterly*] 4/26—that the U.S. Congress is a totally useless & fearfully expensive backwater that might just as well be abolished as soon as possible.

I don't know about you, John, but if I'd gone to law school I'd probably remember that gibberish that almost everybody picks up in their first course on trial law—which says, "never ask a question you can't answer yourself." Or something like that, but any way you say it the point is still there—especially when it comes to asking fourteen (14) *major* questions of "the President." Mother of babbling god! I just got beaten like a fucking gong by the tax-man

22. Henry A. Kissinger was U.S. secretary of state in the Nixon and Ford administrations from 1973 to 1977.

and I know that at least some of that money goes to pay "my congressman's" salary—and although we both know *you* are not *my* congressman, I think we both understand why I called you, instead of the puffball who allegedly represents me, when I wanted some hard information vis-à-vis *Mayaguez*.

I know you probably agree with most of what I'm saying or at least implying here & I'm honestly not trying to hassle you on this thing . . . but, jesus, the larger implications are root-ugly: Here we have a disastrously stupid (in the eyes of almost everybody I talked to until I got back to the U.S.) and potentially terminal "military operation" set in motion by Nixon's appointed President and Nixon's appointed Secy of State, endorsed in spades by a mean & immensely wealthy thug appointed by Ford to the vice presidency[23] and also clearly endorsed and planned by whoever in hell the "Joint Chiefs" happen to be at this moment . . . and the best information either one of us can get on the goddamn thing (you as a U.S. Congressman & me as a journalist) is no more than a mixture of newspaper wisdom that appeared shortly after the fact . . . and yet we both *know* beyond any doubt and even from "the record," as it were, that the whole *Mayaguez* gig is hagridden from start to finish with lies, conflicts, at least 41 senseless deaths and god only knows what else—and that it also stands, along with the American evacuation of Saigon, as a stinking monument to what appears to be a serious loophole in Public Law 93-148 (the "War Powers Resolution" of Nov 7, 1973).[24]

In other words, I get a definite impression that the White House—now occupied by a president and potentially by a vice president that nobody ever voted for—has a de facto carte blanche to order up a full-bore, top-secret military operation by U.S. Marines on any country in the world whose government happens to cross "the U.S.A." at any given moment, even by accident or a set-up.

This might be a good thing for us to talk about when I get to Washington, because I have a feeling we're going to hear a bit more on the subject, for good or ill, during the next year.

Meanwhile, if you're up to it, I could probably make good use of any written reply you might want to make to this screed full of wild & ominous accusations—all of which I'm beginning to take quite seriously. But maybe I'm just paranoid, eh? Or drunk & bent . . . and if that's the case, I hope you'll clear it all up for me as soon as possible—on any basis you feel comfortable with: confidential, off-the-record or anything else—at least until we talk again & come to a better understanding; the same assumption that led me to write you instead of Jim Johnson will serve, for now, as a presumption of confidentiality.

23. Nelson A. Rockefeller.

24. On November 7, 1973, the U.S. Congress overrode President Nixon's veto of the War Powers Resolution, which curbed the chief executive's power to deploy U.S. troops in potentially dangerous situations abroad without congressional approval.

I'm far more concerned with getting coherent answers than I am with whipping up a headline for *RS* or anyone else. OK for now . . .

Hunter

TO FRANK MANKIEWICZ:

Prodding his friend to run for president in 1976, Thompson threatened to do so himself otherwise.

July 14, 1975
Woody Creek, CO

Frank . . .

I'd planned to discuss this subject with you at lunch last week in Washington, but you brought so many uninvited guests that it was impossible to speak freely or even intelligibly, given the wretched circumstances. . . . Jesus, it seems to me that anybody who's lived in Washington as long as you have should know The Rules by now . . . but what the hell???

Anyway, my quick survey of who's doing & thinking what vis-à-vis '76 led me to the almost intolerably weird conviction that you should kick out the jams and get your campaign organized *at once* . . . and if you think I'm kidding, just ask around; if you keep a straight face, like I did, you might be surprised at the answers you'll get. . . .

And don't give me any of your kinky shit about *"what campaign?"* Because the next time we talk I'm going to ask you, for the record, just exactly why you might or might not lack the courage of your convictions. And you should also consider Josh; the poor bastard can't get a job—and neither can I, for that matter—unless you do The Right Thing, and you know what that means.

Consider your friends, Frank; you've always been a selfless person & a lot of people are counting on you now, in this grim & desperate hour, and also consider that if you don't do it, I might . . . and from what I've seen & heard thus far, I'm half-inclined to jump in if you don't . . . which might mean that you'd be forced to *ask me for a job* in January. Either one of us could win the New Hampshire primary (and probably most of the other linchpins, for that matter), and I doubt if we'd even need those matching funds to do it.

But of course I *might* be wrong, Frank. You'll want to look back on the record before you make a decision on this . . . but current circumstances have forced me to give it quite a bit of thought and I have a feeling that 1976 will be the Year of the Geek.

Let me know on this ASAP . . . and while you're at it, remember that they laughed at Thomas Edison, too.

Cazart,
Hunter

PS—thank Marilyn for the help inre: Udall;[25] her scheduling worked out & I got all the time I needed with him.

Selah.

TO LOREN JENKINS, *NEWSWEEK:*

In July 1964, fresh out of the Peace Corps and armed with a Ph.D. in government, fellow Aspen-area resident Loren Jenkins had appealed to Thompson for advice on becoming a successful journalist. A decade later Jenkins—now a close friend as well as a foreign correspondent for Newsweek*—had proved quite helpful throughout Thompson's travels in Southeast Asia.*

July 14, 1975
Woody Creek, CO

Loren . . .

Jesus christ the shitbog I fell into here, immediately on my return, makes everything I bitched about in Asia seem like a picnic-vacation by comparison. If I'd had any sense I'd have stayed in Laos instead of coming back to this nightmare—most of which involves a personal war with *Rolling Stone* (Wenner) over his unannounced decision to fire me (& thereby cancel my medical/health insurance) *while I was en route to Saigon.*

Yeah . . . I know that sounds beyond the pale, but it's true, and he very reluctantly admits it, which effectively destroys our whole relationship and puts me in the ranks of the broke & unemployed.

Jesus, it's dawn & I have a dentist appt. in 3 hours, so I'll write a real letter either tonight or tomorrow—but in the meantime I note you're "leaving for India," but you don't say when & I don't want you leaving without doing something with that goddamn typewriter . . . and I suppose the best thing is to send it over here by the cheapest possible means that will still make sure it arrives. If you can sell it there for anything near the purchase price, give Jeannie 10% of whatever she can get—but if that won't work, just send the bastard along to Woody Creek & I'll try to sell it here. OK for now; I'll sleep for a few hours & give you a better outline either tonite or . . . or . . . shit, all I'm really sure of is that I'm getting out of journalism as soon as possible. All the humor has gone out of that "fear & loathing" logo.

Hunter

TO LYNN NESBIT:

Still uncertain of his status with Rolling Stone, *Thompson sought advice from his agent about which writing project to focus on next.*

25. Arizona congressman Morris K. Udall was in the top tier of candidates vying for the 1976 Democratic presidential nomination.

July 15, 1975
Woody Creek, CO

Lynn . . .

If it's any comfort to you, I just finished 15 (almost) publishable pages on my (last) week in Washington & my opening impressions of the '76 campaign—which would normally be sent to *RS* under the title "Fear & Loathing on Embassy Row," but which under the circumstances will probably be held for inclusion in the *Playboy* piece—if for no other reason than I'm sure Geoffrey[26] will pay for them.

And my only reason for telling you this is to reassure you that I do actually write things (pages)—and that they come as easily as they always have when I'm convinced I'm writing for money instead of an argument.

Which raises the issue of Jann's mention of his "contract" with me in that coke-jangled letter of July 1 (see pg. 2, graf #1). Perhaps we should try to determine just exactly what "contract" he has in mind, because if it exists I don't know anything about it and my (possible) ignorance might cause me some serious trouble when it comes to dealing with the bastard for money. Any off-the-wall reference to "a contract" from Wenner should not be ignored, because his instinct is to disregard contracts of any sort on the assumption that the lawyers he keeps on retainer from PM&S can outlast the lawyers any plaintiff can keep hired on a fee basis, and that in the long run any writer, editor, etc. with grounds for legal action be worn down & terminally discouraged by the simple expedient of dragging out the legal process for so long that nobody operating with limited money-resources can afford to hang on to the end—which is usually true, but his record in cases that have actually gone to trial suggests that it pays to hang on.

I mention this only after finishing 15 good pages and because I think I should know precisely what he's talking about when he mentions "a contract" with me—because if I was working under some kind of contract when I went to Saigon, it seems odd that he'd be able to fire me without any kind of notification at almost the same time he was calling me about the assignment.

Or maybe the "contract" he refers to is the one he mentioned in that cable that was printed in *More*—which puts him in a queer position if he claims the cable was real & tries to sue them for stealing it. If it was a phoney cable he can't sue them, and if it was real (& it was) he owes me $5000 for almost anything coherent I send him, on top of the stuff I sent from Saigon . . . so keep this in mind & try to determine what he meant by his reference to his "contract" with me, because if he can take me off the payroll and cancel my medical insurance & cancel all my *RS* credit cards & still keep my name on the

26. *Playboy* editor Geoffrey Norman.

masthead without breaching whatever "contract" he thinks he has with me, I'm in serious fucking trouble and Clancy just bought a Magnum-load of grief.

On other fronts, could you try to find out from Pop. Library how the Campaign '72 book is selling? I've never received a dime from there for either that one or *Vegas* (as far as I recall without asking Sandy, who's asleep) and I'd like to have some money-figures from C-72 before I make a final decision on either a book or articles or both for C-76.

What I'm looking for here is some kind of a financial comparison between *Vegas* and C-72 (*F&L: On the Campaign Trail '72*)—in order to arrive at some sort of at least tentatively reliable judgement on the relative merits of "Guts Ball" vs. C-76. The prospect of having to work with Jann for a whole year of intense campaign coverage pretty well cancels out the high of being personally involved in a campaign—or at least any campaign except Frank's—so the question of covering C-76 then boils down almost entirely to money, and without any figures for the C-72 book (keeping in mind that I paid $32,500 of my own expenses) I can't make a proper judgement on the value of getting myself locked into this next campaign.

As far as I can tell, *Vegas* was a financial bust . . . but I can't be sure of this without some help in the translation of these goddamn "statements" that appear in my mail from time to time. I don't understand them . . . so could you possibly give me a written opinion as to the money earned from each, so I can have a solid basis for deciding whether to do "Guts Ball" or C-76?

Thanks,
Hunter

TO SANDY BERGER:

Thompson sought the counsel of Sandy Berger, his attorney friend from the McGovern campaign, on dealing with Washington Post *Style section writer Sally Quinn's serious misquote of him in her new book, which was excerpted in the August 1975 issue of* Esquire.

July 22, 1975
Woody Creek, CO

Dear Sandy . . .

Please take a look at the Aug. issue of *Esquire* (pg. 124) & tell me what kind of legal position I'd have vs. *Esquire*, Sally Quinn or her book publisher (the book is due for publication either very soon or maybe it's already out, in which case the problem is worse . . .) vis-à-vis her false, unattributed & entirely unverifiable "quote" to the effect that I've said "only" (or "at least") "45% of what I write is true." I'd rather not get into any lawsuit on this, but as a professional writer/journalist I think I have to do *something*, because a libel like that could not only cripple my income for the rest of my life, but also cause extreme damage to my reputation even after my death.

I fully expect you to bill me for any time you put into this, but before we do anything formally I'd like to see what Sally can do about either changing the quote (see enc. carbon of my letter to her) or just knocking it out of the book. I've been through this shit many times with Random House, and I know they can change *anything* in any edition of a book not already in the bookstores—but only if they're convinced it's necessary, because it's very expensive to change words once they're engraved on the plates and the editors will fight any changes unless the company lawyers lean on them—and that means the threat of a serious and money-meaningful lawsuit they can't win—and this one is a flat-out loser, I think, because of the genuinely crippling (to me) nature of the false quote & also because I've *never* said a thing like that, not even as a joke. I've mentioned various percentages (see enc.) at times when I've been asked about my Vegas book, but always in very vague terms and always to confuse the issue of fiction and/or non-fiction in a book so potentially incriminating that I'd *never* claim it was 100% true.

But I've never even considered the idea of percentages when I've talked about my political journalism. I've explained things like my Muskie/Ibogaine fantasy by simply pointing out that anybody who reads carefully will see that it's *worded* as a fantasy (or a "rumor"), but this bullshit about "45% truth" is likely to haunt me for a hell of a long time—and especially when it comes out right now, when I'm in the midst of negotiations for a book on the '76 campaign that Wenner (before Straight Arrow folded) had already agreed to pay $150,000 for . . . and I wouldn't blame any book publisher or editor who didn't know me personally (as Wenner did) for not understanding my prevailing sense of humor and getting very nervous about signing a book contract for a $150,000 advance to a writer quoted in *Esquire* & in god knows how many thousands of books on the market *right now* as saying "at least 45% of what (he) wrote was true." Shit, *nobody* would pay a writer for 55% lies—not even in the Style section of the *Post*.

In any case, I'm getting goddamn tired of being libeled, mis-quoted and generally discredited by these fucking hacks in the *Post*, the *New Times*, *The Village Voice* and now *Esquire*, who call themselves "straight" reporters—like that asshole from *The Wall Street Journal* who couldn't even get his figures right when he was told, first-hand, by a sane & reliable participant in our vote at AV's on the Demo nominee . . . or maybe Rick got it wrong, but that's beside the point & this one doesn't matter anyway.

The real point is that I can't sit back & ignore this kind of nit-picking bullshit about my *credibility as a journalist* much longer, without making a public example of somebody & getting into some public show & tell about "truth percentages." There are a lot of *levels of truth*, as we both know, in almost any story, and my argument with the so-called "straight" journalists is that I tend to deal on levels (or areas) that "straight" journalism can't handle because you can't always find two "reliable sources" to verify what you *know* is true—and that's the fork in the journalistic road where I parted company with those bastards a long time ago.

It might be interesting, in fact, to force some of these "straight" yo-yos into a position where they have to match their own "truth percentage" with mine . . . and unless we can get Sally to take appropriate & satisfactory action vis-à-vis that "45%" figure in *Esquire* (& also in her book), I'm inclined to stop smiling about all these "gonzo jokes" and kick a few people in the balls.

Anyway, I'm serious about taking legal action on this *Esquire*/Quinn business, if only to stop the drift of what I consider a very dangerous tendency that will ultimately discredit me as a journalist & thereby stunt the growth of a journalistic breakthrough that I can't really define or even claim to represent, except that I know it should be defended at least in principle . . . which is not a hell of a lot different from the kind of breakthrough we're still looking for in politics.

Yeah . . . and so much for philosophy. What I need at the moment is a change or deletion in Sally's book, and if that means stopping the presses or yanking the goddamn thing out of the bookstores, so be it—because unless you tell me I'm wrong on legal grounds, page 124 of the August issue of *Esquire* contains one of the most actionable libel suits I've ever looked at, and my mood right now is to kick out the jams & make somebody answer. Or pay. And on that front I'd just as soon jerk *Esquire* out by the roots, along with Sally and her book publisher—because there's no possible way they can defend that "45%" gig without hiring perjured witnesses. I've been accused of a lot of things that weren't entirely true but which I saw reason to ignore, but this is *not* one of them.

Call me ASAP on this. And if you don't want to handle it, please put me onto somebody who can—or tell me why I'm wrong.

Thanks,
Hunter

TO SALLY QUINN, *THE WASHINGTON POST:*

Explaining the disastrous repercussions her misquote of him could have on his career, Thompson politely asked Quinn to set the record straight.

July 22, 1975
Woody Creek, CO

Dear Sally . . .

Jesus christ, I thought you always preened yourself with the notion that you always bad-rapped people on purpose, instead of by accident—or at least I assume that false & brutally defamatory quote (in the current *Esq.* excerpt from your book) about me once having said that at least forty-five percent of what I write is true *must* have been an accident, because it didn't fit at all with the generally humane & friendly context of the other things you said about me . . . which I appreciate, & thanx. . . .

But Sally, let me ask you to put yourself in *my* place for just long enough to wonder how you'd feel if you were a professional free-lance journalist & no editor wanted to fuck you and you got stuck with a completely unattributed and unverifiable quote to the effect that "at least 45% of what (you) wrote was true." That's a very nasty rumor for a journalist to have to live with, right? And it could have a very nasty effect on my income for the rest of my life, right? And if I didn't consider you a friend I wouldn't be writing you this letter, asking you to knock that alleged quote out of the book, right?

Yeah . . . I'd sue you, *Esquire* & the book publisher for immense damages to my reputation & my future income . . . because I never said that to anybody: I may be crazy, Sally, but I'm not stupid. If you were an editor, would *you* pay for serious political copy from a writer who'd allegedly said a thing like that?

Your "quote," I suspect, is a bastardized, fourth or fifth hand version of an answer I usually give to people who ask me *how much* of my book *Fear and Loathing in Las Vegas* is *true*—and for reasons that should be perfectly obvious I usually reply with a figure ranging anywhere from 60% to 80%, and I've answered that question so often that I'm sure various versions of my answer are floating around so extensively that you probably caught one of them from somebody who heard it from somebody else who told it to a "straight" journalist who then passed it on as 100% fact—like "straight" journalists always do.

Anyway, enough of this shit. I don't know what stage of publication your book is in, but I hope there's still time for you to get hold of the page proofs and either correct that sentence so that it deals specifically with the Vegas book, or knock it out entirely—because otherwise the whole American book market (including many editors) is going to be flooded with an extremely damaging and entirely false "quote" regarding the alleged inaccuracy of my work, which we both know is just as false as that thing about Edith telling me I needed a bath when I was standing in your make-up room at CBS demanding to take a shower so I could get myself at least halfway in shape for the interview after the news show. . . . Jesus, and you're complaining about the ugly press you got: In the past few months I've been accused of mass-rape in London, running up a $28,000 expense tab in Africa, working for the CIA in Saigon, and now I pick up a relatively friendly piece in *Esquire* and see myself labeled as some kind of smelly freak who has to be forced to take a bath at CBS and who insists that "at least 45%" of what he writes is true.

Like you said, Sally, this "celebrity" gig can be a goddamn nightmare, and sooner or later you get a little tired of just sitting back & gritting your teeth and saying "publish & be damned" like the Duke of Wellington[27]—who apparently didn't give a fuck what was written about his personal life, but I suspect he'd have raised a very intense & painful kind of hell with anybody who falsely quoted him as saying that he won at least forty-five percent of his battles.

And that's enough for now. For christ's sake, do us both a favor and make that one simple correction. . . . I'll even trade you that "need a bath" libel for the "45%." The last thing I need right now is a goddamn lawsuit to ruin my summer, but I really can't just sit back and let a false & potentially disastrous "quote" like that one go by. It's just too goddamn heavy to ignore—and hopefully so easy to cure that neither one of us will have to ever mention it again.

In any case, let me know how things stand ASAP. Call me here—or you can reach me through Lynn Nesbit or Sandy Berger at his law office in Washington.

Sincerely,
Hunter

TO GORDON LISH, *ESQUIRE:*

Thompson was undecided about how he would cover the 1976 campaign.

August 12, 1975
Woody Creek, CO

Dear Gordon . . .

There are about 49 good reasons why I haven't gotten back to you vis-à-vis whatever you were calling about (which I assume had something to do with a Campaign '76 book, because of Clancy's letter), but it would drive you fucking mad if I started telling you about a long summer of brutal struggling over things like water rights, septic tanks, crossover circuits, bad debts from London & Saigon, or anything else like that . . . so let's just say I've been waiting for my focus to restore itself, more or less, in order that I might speak decently with people not accustomed to my day-by-day gig, which is Chaos.

But it's 4:00 a.m. now & I have time to write a note, so I thought I'd write & ask what you have (or had) in mind, because one of the things that is definitely *not* in focus for me right now is what I plan to do about "covering" the '76 campaign . . . and one of the main X factors in that area has to do with the possibility and/or advisability of committing myself to write a book about it.

My own feeling at the moment is very down . . . but I've been poking & prodding for almost six months, and I find that somewhere just under the sur-

27. Arthur Wellesley, first Duke of Wellington, leader of the final defeat of Napoleon at the 1815 Battle of Waterloo, and Britain's Tory prime minister from 1828 to 1830, is said to have sent back a blackmailing letter from the prospective publisher of courtesan Harriette Wilson's *Memoirs*—which included Wellington's letters to her—with the words "Publish and be damned" scrawled across it.

face of my own pessimism about the '76 campaign is a tough nut of suspicion that it ain't gonna be what me or anybody else can foresee right now; because what we have right now is such an obvious power vacuum in the challenge area that all we can be sure of is that Nature (human or otherwise) will move into it, if the politicians don't . . . and this is the kind of reality that keeps me thinking in terms of sudden changes that could lead to something genuinely savage, like a Kennedy-Rockefeller race. That was my public prediction about a year ago, and although recent events would seem to have made me a fool, I'm still willing to bet $100 at 20–1 on it happening. . . .

Yeah . . . you'll notice I changed those odds from 10 to 20, and even at 20–1 it seems generous; so if you want to pick up an easy $100, let me know and I'll sign on . . . or I'll go 10–1 that both TK and Rocky will be announced or at least real candidates before the gig is over.

So you see my area of interest, which is the only thing that keeps me tuned in to the ugly machinations of the race. And with that in mind, along with the unhappy truth that I'll almost certainly be covering it anyway, I think maybe the wisest way to go would be to sell a non-returnable $20 grand *option* for a book, just in case the bugger erupts into something genuinely berserk—at which point the option could be converted to a $20K advance against something like $150,000. That's a Seven and a half to One bet, which is just about right, considering the odds on a really memorable and dramatic campaign.

Give me a call or a note on this, either way. I have no idea what your role would be in the arrangements, but if anything develops I'll put you in touch with Lynn Nesbit, who maintains my link with financial reality in these matters . . . and meanwhile, say hello to Sally Quinn for me, if you see her. Okay . . .

Hunter

TO DON ERICKSON, *ESQUIRE:*

In a similar letter to his onetime Esquire *editor, Thompson requested a full retraction of the false quote in Sally Quinn's book excerpt.*

August 25, 1975
Woody Creek, CO

Dear Don . . .

No, we are *not* agreed; no, it is *not* OK; and, no, you did not work *with* me on a magazine excerpt of *Hell's Angels.* As you know, I was not consulted in any way inre: the *HA*/excerpts that ran in *Esquire*—any more than I was consulted, called or checked with to verify that ugly "45% true" quote in the Aug. issue.

Jesus! *This thing* again.

I realize, Don, that I'm extremely naive to think a simple mistake can always be simply corrected . . . but, for reasons of my own, this is a basic, sort of geometric belief that I'd prefer to hang on to . . . because the human mind is not capable of handling the geometric realities implied in the notion that a simple mistake might logically require a *complex* correction and/or solution . . . and once we accept that, even the slightest deviation from a one-to-one gear ratio, we have to abandon the idea that man is capable of either governing himself or correcting his own errors, because once we accept that imbalance, it is a mathematical certainty that our capacity for mistakes will at some point outrun our capacity for solutions . . . a sort of metaphysical check-kiting (sp?) that would drive us all mad if we thought about it long enough, and right now I'm not in the mood for it.

I want to thank you for your letter of Aug. 22, but I don't really think that yr. publication of a letter from me—particularly your own version of any said letter—will make the point that I know you understand as well as I do *should* be made: just a simple fucking admission that *Esquire* & Sally Quinn quoted me as saying something I never said or even thought, and which—if taken literally—could cause me considerable grief as a political journalist, and also have a nasty effect on my income in that area.

But this is not the thing we're arguing about, is it? Jesus . . . Sally says she doesn't know where she picked up the quote, you say "it's right to correct the record" . . . so why don't we just *correct the record?* And you know as well as I do that a grumbling letter from me won't do it.

Hunter S. Thompson

TO JANN WENNER, *ROLLING STONE:*

The Rolling Stone Press anthology of his work that Thompson refers to here would be published in 1979—through Simon & Schuster's Summit Books division—as The Great Shark Hunt: Strange Tales from a Strange Time—Gonzo Papers, Vol. 1.

August 28, 1975
Woody Creek, CO

Jann . . .

I talked to Lynn tonite about your reaction to Alan [Rinzler]'s submission of the anthology and I got a drift in the talk that I don't think we need right now—to wit: The assumption of compound treachery on all fronts, mine, yours and everybody else's; a massive juggling of contacts, contracts, plots, plans, back-stabbing, etc. . . . and although none of this came from Lynn, in so many words, I got a definite impression that she was confused as to which one of us was lying to her (or maybe 3rd or 4th parties compounding the lies) . . . so just for the record, I'll send a carbon of this letter to Lynn. I'd like to focus your head on reality in terms of just a few points, and if they get a bit tangled in the telling, just keep in mind who's sitting at this typewriter (which is *not* the one, incidentally, that you sent me via Parker in exchange for $458—that one is useless & I've been offered $199 for it by the local IBM man, so I'm back to using this one, which I got from Oscar for $200. . . . I think Oscar's ominous disappearance is a story we have an obligation to do . . .).

. . . I am thinking very abstractly here, and perhaps even cosmically—but then I just came back from a long night with [musician Jimmy] Buffett & Rafelson—and I want you to be certain that no vision of you and/or yours has crossed my mind in many weeks, until I talked to Lynn today and heard you were withholding payment on the book on the basis of a clause that was already in the contract . . . and it was at that point, Jann, that I felt my chain slipping on the teeth.

So let me suggest this procedure, for now: 1) I have an *immense* personal investment in the anthology, far beyond any $10K advance, and I want to get the bastard en route to *publication*, not litigation, as soon as possible—and, as evidenced by my emergency editing run to Berkeley 10 days ago, I've put a very high priority-rating on it . . . because I will have to live with the bastard for *years,* and it's a very different kind of book than anything I've ever published before; it's a far more personal book (if you've read even the raw transcripts of the interview) than anything I've ever done; and its involvement in a stupid, paranoid squabble is the last conceivable thing I'd want for it right now . . . and I'm fucked if I can understand why you're treading water with it, bitching about a clause that's already in the contract (according to Alan & Clancy). Jesus, the very nature of the goddamn book makes it obvious that I'll do everything even halfway necessary to be sure it gets published in the right way . . . ah . . . fuck . . . *why? why? why?*

Why indeed? Which gets us back to The Procedure . . . and that leads back to the anthology, which Sandy informed me earlier tonight cost me another $800-plus for the 4/5 day editing rush in Berkeley. . . .

So I think all you have to do right now is decide whether or not you want to publish the bugger—and if you don't, just tell Lynn right away and that's that . . . but if you want to publish it under whatever kind of imprint you have in mind, the first order of business will be to send me that $10K check . . . because once I get paid the advance, I'll at least know the bastard is on its way to the printer (somewhere, somehow) and I think you know me well enough to know I'm going to brood & bitch over every comma & column breaker all the way to the press—which is not a thing either one of us should be overly concerned, at this point, with pointing out to any potential copy editor; because some poor, unsuspecting woman, unknown to either of us right now, is going to have her hair turned cotton-white on this one . . . and now that I think on it, the only person I know who could naturally handle a nightmare like this is a girl who used to work for Random House who did all the editing on *Hell's Angels;* her name is Margaret Harrell, and Silberman could probably find her if necessary. As a matter of fact, she's the only editor I can think of right now that I could work with on a book like this in total confidence . . . she married a Flemish poet a few years back & went off to Morocco, but her forwarding address is Margaret Harrell c/o Harrell Family, Greenville, North Carolina. . . . I once recommended her to Alan, but that one went by the boards like all the others. . . .

In any case, yes . . . The Procedure . . . which means that if you want to "publish" the anthology then you're going to have to pay the $10K advance immediately, and at that point you or anyone you choose to "assign" will have my total cooperation . . . and if you don't want the book, I'd be inclined to look with a very ugly eye on any attempt by you to hang it up in cheap niggling, because at that point I would start taking the situation very personally.

Which is exactly what I'm trying to get away from now. The only reason you don't have huge (& I mean fucking *huge*) chunks of "Siege of Laos" on your desk today is that I don't want to risk sending anything less than a total ball-buster, for fear you'll use my otherwise-normal, scrambled submissions as an excuse for refusing to pay off the expenses—mainly the phone & the AmExp cards—which are causing me endless grief; for reasons I *know,* from experience, will seem small & silly a year from now, but at this moment in time they are causing me PAIN, *constant goddamn pain,* and everybody in town who'll still speak to me is feeling the rotten effects of it. . . .

And that about takes care of The Procedure, I think—at least in terms of The Anthology; and if you want to fuck around with that, I have more than enough pages of Saigon/Laos to send, in order to demand at least the $5K you agreed to pay for it . . . but if we're going to have to fight over that one, too, then I think we may as well take the axe to the whole goddamn relationship right now, for good or ill . . . although not without a settlement on the Saigon-Laos piece.

And I suppose that's okay, too, but I'm getting a little bit tired of it . . . and, once again for the record, the *only serious change* I've been talking about recently, with [*Playboy*'s Geoffrey] Norman or anyone else, is the flat-out, mathematical impossibility of making a living by means of serious journalism . . . and, needless to say, your name has become part of the formula; because it seems to me that if a local plumber can come out here while I'm in Berkeley and scare the shit out of Sandy with physical threats over a $488 bill that's about 39 days overdue, then the past ten years of my life has amounted to nothing at all—because that's precisely the kind of shit I've spent most of my life trying to get away from.

Yeah, I fully understand that you have a different viewpoint—the larger view, as it were—but not all of us live out our lives from the red-leather driver's seat of a big white Mercedes sedan, and not all of us keep a team of PM&S attorneys on retainer to deal with leaks in the system. . . . Which is a cheap shot, and I'll admit that much, but since we've begun this system of third-party communication I've been severely impressed by how far apart our basic stances really are, and how little you seem to understand that difference.

Jesus . . . where the fuck did that come from? I think I was talking about The Procedure, which by my lights means an instant payment of $10K for The Anthology, in exchange for a total and perhaps onerous cooperation from me on the book, all the way to the printer. Or, failing that, I think the thing for you to do is sign off on any personal or professional obligation inre: The Anthology, and Lynn can take it from there. At $10K, I think we can probably sell it quick, so either way you can't lose—at least not on the balance sheets.

And so much for all that shit. This is another wasted night in terms of work and this constant expenditure of angry energy is useless to both of us. . . . What I am mainly looking for at this point is some indication that will open the bottleneck that began when I learned I'd been fired (or "Arbitrarily Removed from the payroll," as you put it) while en route to Saigon, which still strikes me as one of the most monstrous acts in the history of journalism . . . but my anger over the thing has resulted in the crippling of one of the best stories I've ever smelled, much less been a part of, and it's also been financially ruinous.

So there is something very basically wrong here, and perhaps my anger is a main ingredient—because journalism, after all, is a business like any other, and perhaps I misunderstood that truth all along . . . but whatever I might or might not have misunderstood in the past, I'm getting awful goddamn tired of not writing for print & payment, and I mean to chop that knot just as soon as I can. My writing income for this year has been zero, and my tax bill—which I paid, for some insane reason that embarrasses me now—for '74 was almost $15K, so the figures alone should tell you why the Owl Farm has been gripped, of late, with a serious high-tension angst. There are so many goddamn things I *must* deal with, that I can't deal righteously with any one of them.

But this bullshit has gone on too long; it's getting light outside & I almost wish I was stuck in some hellhole like the Sheraton-Schroeder, in the belly of some corrupt & doomed campaign . . . or back at the Lane Xang Hotel in Laos, where life was extremely direct, if nothing else.

Ah . . . the stories, the madness, the sheer fucking strangeness of that trip are like foam on the brain . . . and I would definitely like to get that piece done, particularly right now, since Laos has finally & officially gone under.[28] The truth, of course, is that it went under about three days before I left—but it couldn't be official then, because David Andelman of the *NY Times* had not yet arrived to take over the Global Affairs Suite in the Lane Xang, when I left. An-

28. Neutralist, U.S.-supported Laotian premier Prince Souvanna Phouma capitulated to the Vietcong-backed Pathet Lao in May 1975; the Lao People's Democratic Republic officially assumed control of the country on December 3, 1975.

delman is one of those people you'd automatically choose to be plunged into a vat of aboriginal clap-spoor, just to test the effects . . . and as I was emptying my money belt to leave the hotel, he was screeching heavily at the manager to make sure "the *Times*" got my room—#224: remember that secret number if you ever go to Laos, because it's a "private" suite, and not on the list.

OK. OK. OK . . . we *must* end this. And what have we solved? You have a massive goddamn ms. for the anthology, and I have a massive goddamn cash shortage, along with constant pain in my life because of it . . . so I think, on almost any standard, that an immediate decision and/or cash on that one is not unreasonable, and that means *before* you take off for Europe . . . and a $10K check would free me to make a final rush on "The Siege of Laos," another $5K and the breaking of the Siege of Woody Creek, which might turn out to be my swan song in journalism . . . but I'm not really looking at that.

Ah, fuck—this Kent State verdict on the *CBS Morning News*; we are pushing the Midnight Hour, I think, and the '76 Campaign story will not be what we're looking at now. . . .

As for the Coors memo and your recent letter, I'll do it as soon as I can—which means, in effect, that if we can settle this anthology thing quick, I can focus on things I have to write instead of grappling with creditors, but in any case I think it has to be done (the Coors memo). The main thing at the moment is not to fuck around or kill any more time. Or if that's what you want to do, you should do it out front and not even try to be polite about it—because I've wasted as much time as I can afford to on this bullshit, and I don't really have any choice now except to get rolling, in whatever direction where I can see some light on the tracks. The best sequence, as I see it, would be 1) a firm decision on The Anthology, 2) Coors Cunts & the Straight Press memo, 3) Laos, in extremis, which means a long and ragged piece—probably as weird as anything since the first "Vegas" hit, 4) A decision of some kind, if only an option for interim coverage, on the '76 campaign . . . and we can wait as long as we have to for that summit conference you've mentioned; I've been through enough of those to know what they mean, come sunrise. And that's it for now; here's Rocky on TV, butchering "the liberals" in S.C. How long, O Moloch,[29] how long . . .

HST

TO U.S. SENATOR GEORGE McGOVERN:

There is a special poignance in Thompson's longing for F. Scott Fitzgerald's "fresh green breast of the new world" via the governorship of American

29. Moloch was a Semitic god to whom children were sacrificed by the ancient Ammonites, according to seventeenth-century English poet John Milton's *Paradise Lost* (book i., 392–398).

Samoa: after all, he made the plea to George McGovern, who had been trounced in the 1972 presidential race and wasn't even running in 1976.

September 5, 1975
Woody Creek, CO

Dear George . . .

I don't know how *your* mail is running these days with regard to these foetid rumors about a Humphrey-McGovern ticket in '76, but mine is getting pretty goddamn nasty . . . and since I haven't been reading Dorothy McArdle recently I don't know your thinking, but my mail is piling up and pretty goddamn soon I'm going to have to explain to these people, in print, what I think is going on. . . .

Because I simply can't answer all these letters, George. I don't have a machine like you do—and besides, the kind of people who write me would run amok if I started sending out form letters, especially in response to mail that is drifting more and more into the realm of personal abuse.

God knows, it never occurred to me back in '72 that I'd one day be called to account for your behavior on the national stage, but that's what's happening and I'm getting very unhappy about it . . . for a variety of reasons, but mainly because I don't know what to tell these people.

We talked, as you recall, about your feeling and/or personal connexion with Hubert in '76, and unless memory fails me I think you dismissed it as a bad joke . . . but if you've changed your mind on that subject, I don't feel it's out of line for me to ask you as a friend just exactly why I'm being plagued by these hideous rumors of a Humphrey-McGovern alliance in '76, and how I might explain it.

Because at some point, George, I will *have* to come to grips with this rumor, if only to clear my own name . . . and if you can give me help on this score, I'd greatly appreciate it. We can do it either on or off the record, by mail or in person. I'll be in Washington for most of the first week of October, staying in the sleazy but venerable National Affairs Suite at the Washington Hilton . . . or you can find me via John Holum or Sandy Berger.

Maybe we could have dinner sometime in that week, perhaps with Sandy or Carl Wagner, if he happens to be in town—and get ourselves grounded at least well enough to survive this ugly rumor.

Maybe it's this goddamn isolation I live in. And it has been a wretched year . . . but, my friend, you don't know what wretched slime *is* until you put yourself in my shoes and try to look forward to a campaign year that could end with Ford&Rocky vs. Hubert&George. I just heard that Bill Greider is taking '76 off, going to Europe to write a novel—and that knowledge gives me the fear, because Bill has good instincts.

Indeed . . . and now is as good a time as any to mention this: It's an ugly hustle, but why not? 1976 might well be the year of the Ugly Hustle, and you know how I like to stay ahead or even sometimes beyond things . . . so let me just ask you flat out, and even for the record, if necessary, if you can do anything to remove that psychotic basketball coach from the Governor's Mansion in American Samoa, and put me in it. I've been lusting after that job for many years, George, and nobody in his right mind will argue that I'm not eminently qualified.

Under any other circumstances, I'd be far more subtle. Certainly you understand this. But we are dealing, in this case, with an appointment that, from time immemorial, has been visited on some of the most lame, savage and demented yo-yos this side of the long-armed jacket . . . and the underlying reason for all their appointments has always been to get them out of the country, for reasons that have never been bandied about in public.

Which is not to suggest any downbeat parallels or comparisons . . . Because when I think of Samoa, George, I think of the last Jeffersonian frontier, a slow-paced agrarian democracy where no man need fear the bent tangents of his neighbor, or the twisted frenzies of local winos, cannibals and politicians. . . . Yes, a fresh green breast of the new world, that same enchanted island that once pandered in whispers to the last and greatest of all human dreams.

Ah, think of it, George: The Green Light, the orgiastic future that year by year recedes before us . . . With Greider in Europe and me in Samoa, there'd be nobody left on The Bus with the balls to properly express the kind of monumental repugnance that I fear awaits us on the campaign trail next year.

I trust you'll give it some thought between now and the first week in October, when I get to Washington . . . but in any case please let me know.

Thanks,
Hunter

TO JANN WENNER, *ROLLING STONE:*

In a particularly high-spirited letter, Thompson asked Wenner to take care of Rolling Stone*'s bills. Wenner had sent Thompson a check.*

September 7, 1975
Woody Creek, CO

Jann . . .

I hardly know what to say, and frankly it's very difficult for me to even type this thing because I've been crying most of the night & I can barely see . . . and when I talked to Lynn a few minutes ago she was crying too and goddamnit Jann *I won't have you abusing that poor woman* . . . and why the fuck is Tom Wicker calling me three & four times a day to bitch about that money you owe him? Why in the name of god can't you just pay these people what you owe them? Hell, you know I'm not concerned for myself; Baker's been sending me the checks right on schedule—but what kind of perverse instinct makes you pick on decent people like Lynn & Tom?

You dirty racist bastard: One of these days they'll pop you, and don't come running to me for help.

Yeah . . . and I just picked up a rumor that you actually sent Lynn a check. But I told her not to cash it, because it's not made out to me—and I also want that evil pigfucker from American Express to have a chance to work out on you for a while, with regard to that $1620 you owe them for the cataract operation on that transvestite you hired under false pretenses . . . and why the fuck am I getting bills from Hong Kong? You know I always pay cash in Hong Kong. I got a bill for 700 HK dollars the other day for those ice-picks you asked me to send to Murray Gart. . . .

Ah, Jesus . . . I can't keep it up. Nothing intolerable has happened to me for three (3) consecutive days, and I can't handle it. The peacocks have hatched, the Crop has come in, my incredibly expensive maze of underground water spouts is working for the first time in a year, and the two grisly rake-murders in Snowmass remain unsolved.

The Siege of Laos creeps along, but unless you stop payment on the book-check I suspect we are through a very nasty bottleneck and I figure I can now afford the risk of sending a few chunks, rather than sit here and brood on the whole goddamn thing. It also helps that the *NY Times* has finally declared Laos a fallen country, which finally gives me a stable time-frame for the thing . . . although I will, of course, have to return to Laos for a few weeks to update my notes.

Jesus, it's taken me all afternoon to write this goddamn page. The phone rings constantly. Many offers. Sally Quinn wants me to write a musical comedy with her for $500K, but I'm afraid of her so I can't do it. Ed Williams has offered me the presidency of the Redskins when he quits next year, but I'm afraid of George Allen so I can't do that either.[30] The one offer I've accepted, however, is the position of Drug Consultant to Doctor Nork, who is now at the Aspen clinic.

And that's just about all the news from here, Jann. . . .

No, wait a minute, I just noticed your extremely queer letter of 8/12, which seems to indicate that we can actually do the Coors memo *before* Laos, so I think I'll get to that while I'm still in the proper mood.

In any case, I'm feeling too weird to continue with this. My intake has finally leveled off at six to eight Quaaludes and about 30 whites a day, which seems about right for doing business . . . and speaking of business, I'm enclosing a letter I sent to McGovern earlier today. I think we are going to have to treat this campaign nightmare with extreme caution.

30. High-powered D.C. attorney Edward Bennett Williams owned the National Football League's Washington Redskins; the team's then-coach, George Allen, still ranks fifth-highest all-time in winning percentage (at .681) among NFL coaches.

(Now, several days later, I think I'll just send The Above gibberish along, for the record . . . and, yes, speaking of records, I just got the check from Lynn and also a copy of the ms. for the anthology, which I'm now looking at for the first time & also in light of Lynn's comment (when I asked what you plan to do with it) that you were "sending it to Silberman.")

Jesus, the copy of ms. that *I* have is in no condition to send to anybody—mainly because of that goddamn interview that still exists only in the form of *raw transcripts*, and I have to wonder how we're going to cope with the fucker, now that you have no editorial machinery & no people to deal with a monster like this, which still needs a hell of a lot of work if we stick with the original plan of weaving the interview around the pieces . . . so I think we should talk about this thing ASAP; satisfying the conditions of the contract is one thing, but publishing an embarrassing book is something else again (for both of us, I would think . . .).

We should also ponder the '76 campaign, for good or ill. I still plan to "cover" it, but without a book advance that would make it worthwhile or even the prospect of a sharp-edged campaign, I'm beginning to get a bit concerned about a year in that hell-hole . . . and I think we should talk ASAP on this one, too. . . . In any case, thanx for the cheque. I guess it's my turn to act decent now, so I'll give it a try. OK,

Hunter

TO DICK DRAYNE, PRESS SECRETARY TO U.S. SENATOR EDWARD M. KENNEDY:

Thompson suggested interviewing Senator Kennedy for a Rolling Stone *piece.*

September 9, 1975
Woody Creek, CO

Dick . . .

I don't know how me & EK got on the same mailing list(s) for all these nuts, but the one I got most recently (from a "Robert J. MacDonald" in Ketchum, Idaho) strikes me as worth noting. The style & tone of the two letters he sent me by Certified Mail to the *RS* office in DC—along with copies of one to Teddy & another to Weinberger[31]—had a quality of aggressiveness and perverse competence about them that caused me to put them in a different pile from the rest of my mail. There was nothing explicitly quotable from either one, but the tone was distinctly menacing, and I don't get many like that—although I *do,* in fact, get threatened with a fairly consistent regularity, and I also get a lot of letters "from prison," etc. like the last one I sent you.

31. California Republican Caspar W. Weinberger, a former director of the Office of Management and Budget in the Nixon administration, was U.S. secretary of health, education, and welfare from 1973 to 1975.

But this last thing from MacDonald in Idaho had a very sharp edge to it, and if EK has been getting the same kind of stuff from him, I just thought we should compare notes.

It also occurs to me that a good story might lurk in the twisted depths of EK's daily mail—a sort of weird compendium of all that gibberish you get; perhaps in connection with a *RS* interview, or maybe on its own.

And in case you don't know, Ketchum, Idaho is the town right next to Sun Valley, where EK has been known to spend some winter time in the past & where I know some people . . . but I'd prefer to tread very lightly when it comes to using my friends as potential intelligence sources for anything connected with the government, so unless it seems absolutely necessary I'd rather not get involved in evaluating the potential threat of crank letters by questioning friends about somebody they may or may not know . . . but if you see a good reason, let me know and I'll do what I can.

OK for now. I'll be in DC for the first week in Oct. I'll try to stop by for a drink or six. See you then. . . .

Hunter

TO SANDY BERGER:

Once again Thompson sought Berger's counsel on a potentially actionable case of libel—this time cartoonist Garry Trudeau's addition of the drug-addled shyster "Duke," a character clearly based on Thompson's public persona, to his popular Universal Press Syndicate comic strip, Doonesbury. *Trudeau won the 1975 Pulitzer Prize for Editorial Cartooning.*

September 10, 1975
Woody Creek, CO

Sandy . . .

Jesus, am I doomed to spend the rest of my life in a maze of demented litigation? First Sally Quinn & now this (see enc.) from that dope-addled nazi cartoonist . . . where the fuck will it end?

Thanks for the (copy of) the letter to *Esquire,* and I hope the rest of that action goes smoothly; because frankly, I'd like to get back to work . . . and if I don't, you can forget about sending me any bills.

Anyway, this shit in the comix may or may not raise an interesting legal possibility with regard to the definition of a *public figure.* I think I mentioned a recent decision in Chicago during one of our recent phone talks, where a man who *had been* a public figure (looking at *NY Times* vs. *Sullivan*) was deemed to have lost that status—thereby *winning* his libel action—when he quit politics & retired. . . . I have a copy of the opinion (or decision) here somewhere, so if you haven't heard about it, let me know and I'll send it along when I find it.

There might also be a very real possibility of *malice* in this comic strip stuff, although I'm damned if I could point you to any tangible reasons, since I've never seen the cartoonist and don't know him at all. . . . Or, if we want to give paranoia full rein we could assume this is Wenner's way of getting back at me for some of the things I've said about him, by using Trudeau's strip as some kind of *Rolling Stone* mouthpiece.

But that's about as close as I can come to a shrewd guess . . . and the only way I'd want to get involved in any litigation on this is if you (or [Merrit] Prettyman, or whoever) might see a firm handle on it, both financially & in terms of case-law. With the legal definition of a public figure a bit hazy now, this comix assault strikes me as playing with fire . . . or maybe I'm totally wrong & I can be whacked just as heavy in the public prints as I whacked Hubert in '72; and if that's the case I sure as hell don't want to get tied up in a money-ulcer lawsuit that'll drive me mad. . . . But from the standpoint of my own work, as well as that of others, I think it's important for me (both as a working journalist & a victim) to know exactly what the definition of a *public figure* is, and right now I don't, and I'm not sure the papers who publish Trudeau do either. I've talked to Mike Howard (of Scripps-Howard renown) at the *Rocky Mountain News,* and he says his lawyers have told him the "public figure question" is now a grey area, in the context of libel suits, and that the Chicago decision I cited earlier might have a serious hedging effect on *Times/Sullivan*—provided it's upheld, if & when. . . .

Anyway, just in case you don't have much else to think about these days, I thought I'd lay this one on you for some mental exercise. . . . Because I think any case that re-defines a "public figure" in terms of potential libel actions could have as much effect on (at least *my* kind of) journalism as the Nixon-era "new crime code" or whatever they call it that Ford would apparently like to pass—the one that would allow reporters & editors to be locked up for publishing "classified" information, a sort of U.S. version of the British "state secrets" law.

I'm just talking off the top of my head here, and I may be wrong on a point or a memory here & there, but as I get the drift of things, it looks like the kind of journalistic freedom that a lot of us have enjoyed for the past decade might be on the verge of a drastic re-structuring.

Or maybe not . . . But if the question of doubt exists, then so does the question of risk, and I've argued with enough pub/lawyers to know they *always* win if they can raise a real question of risk. Hell, not one of the three books I've published would have gone to press if the pub/lawyers had prevailed with their initial objections . . . but until now, I've always had a pretty good nuts & bolts grasp of the libel laws.

That's what's worrying me now: I'm no longer sure just where the line is, and I get the feeling that nobody else is either. . . . Which gives us all something to think about, eh?

Anyway, ponder the meaning of these comix & tell me what you think. If this kind of shit is legal, then I don't think I have to worry about any libel actions against *me,* because I've never pushed my luck this far, not even with Hubert. If this comix stuff is libel, then of course I'd like to sue for at least $20 million in damages. . . . And if it's not, then it gives me a new sense of freedom in my own work.

I'll be at the Hilton for the first week of October & we should definitely connect early on, before I run amok. Did you call George about dinner? And if you & Susan feel like coming out here for a visit anytime soon, let me know & I'll have the guest room re-assembled. That's a serious invitation, and I'll see you in a week or so.

Okay . . .
Hunter

Enc: *Doonesbury* of Sept 8 & 9, *RMN,* Denver

TO U.S. SENATOR GARY HART:

Former McGovern campaign manager Gary Hart had won Colorado's 1974 U.S. Senate contest.

September 11, 1975
Woody Creek, CO

Dear Gary . . .

I am trying to get this written quickly, between a constant barrage of sonic booms, zoning wars, attacks on my water source by armed thugs, and crazed junkies on my porch . . . along with another demented assault on everything I stand for by that nazi yo-yo of a cartoonist in the *Post.*

So, without delay—let me first request a copy of S.1 from you; and in addition to that, I'd like to know *how* you plan to vote on it, and *why.* It looks to me like a newer, leaner version of the ill-famed "Tom Charles Huston plan,"[32] and needless to say I'm very concerned about it, along with a lot of other people.

I'll be in Washington for the first week of Oct., and if you have any time I'd like to have a beer and ponder a few things. You can reach me thru the *RS* office in DC, or at the Washington Hilton; if I'm not in the N.A. Suite, try the pool.

Shit, the pool won't be open, will it?

God *damn* that rotten town. I think you should sponsor a bill to move the national capital to Los Angeles; tack it onto S.1 as a rider, and that way . . . No! What the fuck am I saying? If thousands of politicians were sud-

32. Conservative former White House adviser Tom Charles Huston, who helped formulate the notion of a "New Federalism" that President Nixon advanced in his 1971 State of the Union Address, is better known for coming up a few years later with his unabashedly illegal "Huston Plan" for U.S. counterespionage operations.

denly moved to LA, they'd have to close the pools for health reasons. . . . So never mind that one.

Anyway, I get a feeling that this S.1 vote is going to get a lot of long-term attention, and my feeling at the moment is that anybody who votes *for* it should be castrated. . . . But maybe I'm wrong; that possibility always exists, eh? So I'm looking to you, My Senator, for wisdom on this question . . . and unless I hear from you to the contrary, I'll expect to have a beer (or a sarsaparilla) with you when I get there to make my various speeches.

Cazart,
Hunter

TO DICK TUCK:

The shenanigans of Democratic prankster Dick Tuck—who had become notorious for his silly disruptions of opposing candidates' campaign appearances (known as "black advance" or "ratfucking")—didn't seem so amusing once Tuck made Thompson his target.

October 4, 1975
Woody Creek, CO

Dick . . .

You have already done me serious harm by your handling of that MacArthur/Hollingsworth tape that you got from my house the night before you left. God only knows what made you take it to NY & play it for a *Newsweek* writer (Steele), but I've spent about $200 so far in accepting collect calls from Hong Kong and taking some very unpleasant abuse from people I used to call friends. Despite my best efforts to dismiss all the bullshit that developed in the *Newsweek* hierarchy after you fed the thing to Steele, I've been accused of all kinds of sneaky, cheap madness, including "ruined careers" and almost everybody who was in Saigon with me is now convinced that *their voices* were on that tape and that Kosner is now holding it . . . and since I can't get hold of you, I have no idea where the tape is or what further damage it's causing. Nick Profitt[33] in Beirut has already taken some shit from *Newsweek* about it, and also Loren Jenkins in Hong Kong . . . and since I can't call Kosner, for fear of making it worse, I can't spike the rumors . . . so for christ's sake send the cassette back to me immediately, *without dubbing it* for any further cocktail entertainment. As I told you out here, the copy you have was a raw trial run for the Hollingsworth/MacArthur cassette I sent to Aspen, so his version is harmless—but I'm getting that one back too, just to be sure nothing volatile is floating around.

33. Nick Profitt had been a *Newsweek* correspondent in Southeast Asia.

It makes no difference that the stuff on the tape you have is harmless. . . . What matters is that I'm being pilloried all over the fucking world for taping confidential conversations in Saigon and then sending them to *Newsweek* and butchering people's careers . . . and if this is your idea of humor, it sure as hell isn't mine, and needless to say I'd never have given you that thing if I'd had the faintest fucking notion that you were going to use it to make a worldwide asshole of me . . . and for all I know you're playing the bastard all over Europe right now, and there's no possible way I can ever kill all the stinking rumors it's caused, because I'll never even hear some of them . . . but anywhere I go, from now on, people are going to run from me when I bring out a tape recorder . . . and every time that happens, Dick, I'm going to think of *you*.

All I can do at the moment is *ask* you to send the fucker back to me and try to mend any damage you've already done with it, by rumor or otherwise . . . and if I keep hearing stories about how you're "amusing" people with a tape that I duped for you in good faith and without the slightest notion that you'd put it to this kind of use, you might as well plan ahead and buy a plot in the cemetery next to your Aspen house for those dogs of yours, because I'll come into your yard and blast those little fuckers into hamburger right in front of you. Two of them bit me last summer, and I see no reason to tolerate that shit any longer . . . so the next time they menace me I'll kill them.

Okay for now . . .
Hunter

TO GEOFFREY NORMAN, *PLAYBOY:*

Playboy *subeditor Geoffrey Norman had commissioned Thompson to write a nuts-and-bolts article on the increasingly interesting 1976 presidential campaign.*

October 4, 1975
Woody Creek, CO

Geoffrey . . .

If we are coming up on any kind of crunch on this Campaign-76 piece, I should be made aware of it in a very direct way. The only thing I've heard since I saw you out here was some kind of paranoid gibberish from Tuck about "uncertain plans" and "flux situations" and "two issues at once," but none of it made any sense and I've been expecting to get some word from you, for good or ill.

My own situation is that I've been deliberately waiting as long as possible, before committing *anything* to print on a 3-month lead time. . . . Although I have enough pages so I can do a forced march on the bugger whenever the whistle blows. . . . And meanwhile I'm running up huge phone bills to Washington, keeping myself current on things like [Sargent] Shriver's entry & who's working for whom, etc. . . . but things change almost daily and I'm never sure where or when I'll have to cut off the input and just write on the basis of whatever I have.

The only development that seems real since I saw you is Shriver's entry, which was conceived mainly as the Demo "left's" last hope of stopping ["Scoop"] Jackson in New York, which is beginning to look like *the* key primary, because it's now on the same early date as Wisconsin . . . April 6, I think, but it's almost dawn here & I don't have a calendar so I can be absolutely certain. . . . But in any case, if Jackson wins New York, he'll be the unquestioned frontrunner until the finale in California, and both those states have that massive Jewish vote that he's been playing with for years . . . and according to the wizards, a Jackson win in NY will have a domino effect in California, which will bring him into the convention with enough delegates to either win or dictate . . . so Shriver's decision to go for NY is a major development, particularly since he'll have a lot of the old Kennedy clout. Teddy even gave him his press secretary, Dick Drayne, and that's definitely a serious move—so serious, in fact, that I'm beginning to get nervous mutterings from my personal braintrust, the people you met in Chicago; they don't like Shriver, but they'll never in hell cross Kennedy, and that's how it stands, as of now. If Shriver can keep Jackson from winning big in NY, I'd bet on a Kennedy-Shriver ticket in November. . . . And in fact I'll do $100 on that ticket right now, at 10–1, which is entirely reasonable at this stage of the game. Let me know if you're up for it.

And also let me know about whatever deadline we're facing. I'm leaving for Washington on Oct 10 . . . and if there's any real rush I can come thru Chicago on my way back here, and finish off the piece because by then I'll have a grip on what's happening. In any case, send word ASAP, so we don't drift into an emergency. Okay . . .

Hunter

TO PETER HAAS AND HOWARD LEARNER, UNIVERSITY OF MICHIGAN ACTIVITIES CENTER:

Thompson generally found public speaking engagements more trouble than they were worth, in every sense.

October 4, 1975
Woody Creek, CO

Dear Haas/Learner:

You scurvy bastards. I might have been a trifle bent when I spoke at Ann Arbor last time, but I wasn't blind—and when I looked out from the podium I saw a fucking madhouse *full of people,* and at least half of them were crazier than me. That was one of the most berserk situations I've ever been plunged into. . . . But I dug it and on balance I had a good time, so rather than toss your lame money-offer into the fire along with the rest of the junk mail, I gave it a second thought and came up with a possible compromise, to wit:

I'm not sure exactly what I got paid last time, but I think it was around $1200, which means I got about $800—due to the agency's 33% cut. And I know there were more than 1000 people in that place, so unless you're embezzling heavily from the Future Worlds speakers budget, why don't we dispense with this poor-mouth talk about my not making the nut last time. . . . Unless all those people came in through the windows, which wouldn't surprise me but I can't feel real guilty about it either. Security is not my gig.

Anyway, my personal feeling about these "appearances" is the same as it was then: Nine out of ten are bummers, and I don't do them often enough to affect my income much, either way, so there's no way in hell that I'll deal with that madhouse again for less money than I got the first time—and on that one we also had a few amenities tossed in, which worked out very nicely, but my natural bent for discretion militates against putting those kind of specifics in print, so we'll have to leave them for later, if we ever get that far.

For now, however, we have two options: I can forward your letter to the *Rolling Stone* lecture bureau and you'll get a call from Patty Morrisey, asking you for (at least) a $1500 certified check 3 days in advance of my appearance there, plus a round-trip plane ticket from Aspen to Ann Arbor, also in advance . . . and frankly I'd just as soon do it that way, because it spares me the hassle of writing letters like this one, when I should be working. . . .

The other option, which should only apply if you really are cramped for money (or embezzling), would be for me to explain your heart-rending quandary to Patty & then deal directly with you, based more or less on the decent relationship that emerged from the last trip. In this case, you would have to send *me* a certified check for $1000 (the same minimum I'd net if we worked through any agency), along with a pre-paid RT ticket from Aspen to Ann Arbor (or Detroit). And we could look at a date in the second week of April, like the 9th or 10th. The whole goddamn spring of '76 is riddled with presidential primaries, so I'll have to be pretty precise about dates for this kind of thing.

In any case, by the time you get this letter I'll be in Washington—staying at the Washington Hilton from Oct 6 thru 10, so you can give me a ring there if you're up to it. And if I don't hear from you by Oct 17, by phone or mail, I'll send your letter on to Patty and she'll give you a quick lesson in contemporary economics. Okay for now . . .

Hunter S. Thompson

TO MARY McGRORY, *THE WASHINGTON STAR:*

Political reporter Mary McGrory has written a lively liberal column for The Washington Post *since* The Washington Star *folded in the early 1980s. Thompson had shared the stage with McGrory at a forum on politics at Washington, D.C.'s John F. Kennedy Center for the Performing Arts.*

October 12, 1975
Woody Creek, CO

Dear Mary . . .

I meant to apologize personally for that weird situation that I inadvertently plunged you into when I showed up late for the Town Hall thing last week. I wish I could have handled it better than I did . . . but then I have that feeling about a lot of things these days, and wishing hasn't helped me much in the way of finding a cure.

Anyway, I assume it was obvious to you that I had no idea at all what I was doing on-stage in the concert hall of the Kennedy Center at that hour of the morning (I came over there thinking we were going to tape a quiet PBS radio show with a studio audience of about 20 shills hired by [Fred] Dutton . . .) and I was totally un-hinged to find myself in a set that seems in retrospect like something arranged & organized by Albert Speer[34] . . . and my only real thought when I blundered into the back of the hall and saw [*New York Times* political reporter R. W. "Johnny"] Apple talking up there in front was that if I didn't get up on the stage *quick* that I'd never in hell be paid for whatever I was expected to do . . . so I just made a blind & greedy rush for the mike, if only to establish my physical presence, for the record, so Fred couldn't claim I hadn't showed up . . . and I had no idea I was displacing you until the situation was explained to me (by Pat Oliphant, as I recall) several hours later, although by then it was too late to apologize for putting you in a weird situation that neither one of us had any reason to anticipate. But apologies are cheap, so I won't dwell on this one . . . but the first time I get a chance to balance it out in some tangible way, I'll do it, which is something you'll just have to take on faith, for good or ill. I haven't quite come to grips yet with the odd realities that seem to have overtaken me in the past few years, and the notion of being both a journalist *and* a public figure (sic) still confuses me, particularly when I have to grapple with it in public and with no warning about what to expect.

Anyway, I owe you one . . . and thanx for being so decent and competent in the way you handled that scene. Given my strung-out condition at the time, you could have reduced me to a confused & gibbering wreck by merely keeping your seat & raising your eyebrows a bit.

Indeed . . . and so we beat onward, boats against the current (sic)[35] . . . and never really learning much except how to express it a little bit better, now & then; bluff, blunder & filigree, all of it firmly anchored on the Great Skyhook.

34. Adolf Hitler's close aide and official architect Albert Speer organized the Nazis' slave labor camps, for which he was sentenced to twenty years in Spandau Prison at the 1946 Nuremberg war crimes trials.

35. Quoted from the closing line of F. Scott Fitzgerald's 1925 novel, *The Great Gatsby:* "So we beat on, boats against the current, borne back ceaselessly into the past."

Jesus . . . what am I saying? This is not the kind of thing a front-runner should be even *thinking* at this point, much less putting in print, but what the hell? When the going gets tough, the tough get going. [1950s New York's Mad Bomber] George Metesky said that. . . . OK,

Hunter

TO TOM DOWLING, *THE WASHINGTON STAR:*

Tom Dowling was among several Washington Star *political reporters who encouraged Thompson to run for president himself in 1976.*

October 12, 1975
Woody Creek, CO

Tom . . .

Needless to say, it never occurred to me that meeting you for breakfast that morning would have such weird & ominous consequences. The combined efforts of you & Pat [Oliphant] & [Dave] Braaten have complicated my life very severely; I have spent the past 72 hours sorting & pondering applications from wizards, hit-men, seers, zealots and other action-junkies, all of them seeking positions of leverage & influence in my '76 campaign . . . and if this madness keeps up you can expect a steady diet of calls no earlier than 2:00 a.m. . . . Indeed; remember Dr. Frankenstein, who also reaped the fruit of his labors.

On another, more serious & relatively human level, thanx for handling the thing the way you did: You've clearly mastered the first and only main rule of political journalism—which as far as I know has never been written down by anybody, including me . . . but that's another story & we can talk about it later, once you get the hang of your new job.

Okay for now; see you on The Trail, eh?

HST

TO DAVE BRAATEN, *THE WASHINGTON STAR:*

Known for his smart tongue-in-cheek columns in The Washington Star, *David Braaten joined the groundswell at the newspaper behind a 1976 Hunter S. Thompson candidacy for president.*

October 12, 1975
Woody Creek, CO

Dave . . .

Well, you dumb fuckers stirred up a genuinely weird and electric sort of talent/hornets' nest with that full-bore treatment you laid on me in the twisted wake of my last visit to DC. . . . I've been swamped for the past few days with calls, cables, mail, etc. from people who want to get on the train before it erupts out of the station; thanx to you & Pat & Dowling, I am now in a position to assemble a genuinely awesome campaign staff, merely by sorting through the numerous applications here on my desk. (There is an element of healthy humor in all this, but there's also an undertone of something a bit heavier and definitely kinkier than meets the general eye—which means, I think, that the whole matter should be dumped on the cruel & meaty shoulders of my Public Affairs Consultant, Dr. Oliphant. Rank assaults on the public consciousness are nothing if not his specialty, so I think we can leave the next step to him . . . and meanwhile I'll be back in D.C. on Nov 4, 5, or 6 for another dog-dance, and if the chance comes up I'll pull the ripcord on Bellows, just for the hell of it . . . and I also want to be there for the public crushing of Pat's left hand, which I've already contracted for, so I guess I'll see you somewhere in all that madness. . . .)

Anyway, it was a nice, sharp kind of piece, and if it hadn't been for the stinking art that went with it, I'd offer to buy you a beer or so next time around. As it is, however, we'll have to wait & see. . . . OK,

Hunter

FROM GOVERNOR JIMMY CARTER:

The Georgia governor welcomed Thompson's entry into the 1976 presidential campaign.

November 17, 1975
Plains, GA

To Hunter Thompson:

When I heard you had announced I started to withdraw. However, with the faint hope that you may still be interested in the higher office of sheriff, I'm going to stick around & try to fill the vacuum you may leave.

Your friend,
Jimmy

TO JIM SILBERMAN, RANDOM HOUSE:

November 18, 1975
Woody Creek, CO

Jim . . .

Your letter of Nov 10 arrived in the same mail that carried mine of Nov 15 off to you—which, if nothing else, seems to establish a new, five-day mailing time between Manhattan & the Owl Farm. (In the good ole days, before Free enterprise took over the Postal Service, it was three days: Selah.)

Which reminds me that you should tell Selma [Shapiro] to be alert, on Nov 23 or 24, for a bulky, lightweight package in a padded book-envelope with a Quadrangle Books mailing label on it—just in case the two of you ever want to visit the Rainbow Room again, on your own. And just in case she can't cope with the complexities of the enclosed Shure stylus, she can call my friend Tim Ferris for expert advice . . . (and just for the record, you rabbit-punching bastard, I left The Tie in Ferris' hands, for delivery back to you; Tim's agent, as you know, is Erica Spellman, who works with Lynn . . .) and the next time you lay a shot like that on me, get ready for a few collect-call editorial queries at four or five in the morning; I am getting mean & merciless in my old age, Jim, and just because I chose to ignore your comment up there in the Rainbow Room about Asians not having the same respect for human life as we do, doesn't mean I won't remember it. . . .

And so much for all that, eh?

Which is not the point of this letter, anyway.

There are, in fact, two points: 1) I won't be getting back to NY on Nov 21, & probably not for a few weeks after that, because I suddenly have two critical magazine deadlines to meet before Dec 1; Wenner is threatening to sue me (again) for outstanding expenses, so I have to get an Indochina piece to him immediately, which will keep me busy for another week . . . and,

2) I hate to formally temper my enthusiasm for the idea I presented so feverishly with regard to the Texas book—but I agreed with Bob Rafelson that I would do the initial research *for a film, instead of a book*. I think you'll agree that I should go ahead and do it that way—for a variety of good reasons, but mainly because the gun-running aspect of our back-burner Texas-book notion was a thing that Bob & I developed mutually in a conversation out here about a month ago, it seems right to keep it on that track until Bob has a chance to either get into it or reject it as a film, instead of putting him in the position of being offered the chance to buy it in book form, later on. I assume all this makes sense, or at least reads coherently (jesus, I just found that Selma's package has a TWA mailing label, still in a padded book envelope—so forget that Quadrangle business, and if it gets lost, don't look for it . . .).

Anyway, back to the Texas gig—which probably doesn't make any difference anyway, because by the time you'd get around to grappling with the idea, Bob and I will no doubt have settled the film aspect anyway, for good or ill. And besides, your 11/10 letter was considerably less encouraging about the idea than your talk that Thursday afternoon in your office. . . . So the next time we get together, this will definitely be a main topic, because by that time I'll have spent two or three weeks in Texas and I'll know a lot more about it, and probably be a lot more into it—because the only difference in my root feeling about the Subject, since we first discussed it about two years ago, has been the ever-changing focus in each of our priorities (& connexions), along with my three visits to Dallas, Houston, & Austin that mainly served to confirm my most savage suspicions. The only thing that could turn me around on this one, now, would be a sudden & overwhelming conviction that I was headed for terminal violence—and I suspect we both have our doubts about the effect of even that, eh?

In any case, I can't see where a film-priority at the moment should have any effect on the book idea except to postpone the final decision for a month or so. I told Bob to arrange for a summit-meeting at the Royal Biscayne hotel across the bay from Miami at Super Bowl time, and by then we'll both know enough to make a decision on the film. I may or may not get to NY before then (unless you convince me it's necessary), but I'll definitely be in touch by phone, with both you & Wilcox . . . and if this letter puts you off balance in any way, for christ's sake let me know, because that's not my intention. I didn't realize how much I liked the idea of working with you and Selma again until I got into your office and put on my tie. Getting famous in 49 states wasn't half as much fun as I thought it would be, especially since it didn't make me rich and drove Sandy half-mad in the process . . . so if I have to play writer for a living, I figure I may as well do it in decent company.

And so much for all that, too. On other fronts, please be sure to send me those books I left in the office—and definitely send me Frank Gannon's[36] book; that's an extremely weird twist, and as much as I hate to pursue it somehow, I feel I must . . . because it just occurs to me that Gannon probably knows Judith Campbell.[37]

(cut to pg. Three—48 hours later)

Ah, yes . . . sweet Judy: They warned me she was bad company, and I knew she had heavy friends . . . but I was young & foolish then, and how could I have known that when she wasn't with me she was off with Sam and/or Jack?

It hurts, Jim—so please never mention it to me. Like Mr. Gatsby said, it was "only personal," and I'd just as soon not talk about it, except for something like $400,000, and even then I might lie to you.

●●●●●●●●●●

Zang! How do you like them column-breakers? Do you have a key like that on *your* typewriter?

Anyway, we talked today and that naturally changes the tone of this letter. I have a strange feeling that I've out-flanked myself on this Texas gig; it flowered so fast that I never had time to put a price on it . . . but all the best ones seem to happen that way, so what the hell? The main question, as always, is who's going to pay for education.

Jesus, where has Clancy been on *that* one? Why the fuck should a geek who was expelled from high school for rape have to pay taxes on monies advanced

36. Frank Gannon had been an aide to Nixon White House press secretary Ron Ziegler.
37. Judith Campbell Exner was revealed to have been romantically involved with both reputed mob boss Sam Giancana and President John F. Kennedy in the early 1960s.

to him for the purpose of furthering his education? I think those bastards at the IRS owe me a hell of a lot of money . . . and it occurs to me now, once again, that lawyers are the real police-class in our society, because their minds are fixed on precedent, which is another word for laws.

When Brown's Hotel of London tracked me all the way up here to the Pitkin County courthouse for an unpaid $1000-plus bill that Wenner refused to pay, my Aspen lawyer asked me what kind of defense we should try to run on them & I said "Insanity." And he said, "You can't plead 'insanity' in a civil case," and I said "Why not? I was insane. Only a lunatic would have gone to London & torn up a suite in Brown's Hotel & expected Wenner to pay for it. Indeed—*prima facie* Insanity; we can even subpoena Wenner and force *him* to testify in my defense. . . ." So we may have a precedent coming up on this one; nobody has ever even *tried* to plead insanity in a civil case, but I have nothing to lose . . . and the case comes up on Dec 3; I'll keep you posted. We might rattle a cage or two on this one. . . .

And so much for all that. On the basis of our talk today (11/20) I think the new password is "Galveston." And now I think I know how MacArthur felt when he first thought of that Inchon landing,[38] coming out of his bed one midnight and seeing the full moon and the rising sun at the same time, one in front of each eye and about three feet away . . . leaping out of the khaki sheets like some kind of killer jack-in-the-box and thinking: Hot damn! Wait till they hear about *this* one, back at The Point! Stone silence on The Plain, a shudder of true madness in the Long Gray Line . . .

Hell, I could do that one better, but I don't have the time right now. I've been listening to MacArthur's speeches, and let me tell you, he stomped on the terra. There's nobody in politics today who could stand on the same stump with that crazy bastard. I gather, from some of the people I've talked to who were there when it happened, that there's a fiendish drama in the Senate hearings where Russell[39] ambushed MacArthur and put him on the record as a madman. . . . The book on those hearings would be hard to get, but I suspect it would be worth some effort; I'll lean on my end if you'll lean on yours, and maybe we'll come up lucky: What we want, I think, would be the testimony of Gen. Douglas MacArthur at whatever hearings Sen. Russell, D—Ga. (is that right?) was conducting just after Mac came back from Japan/Korea to deliver his "Old Soldiers Never Die" speech. That was Apr 19, 1951, so the hearings were probably in late '51 . . . just in time to derail MacArthur's presidential express in '52.

38. One of the greatest victories of U.S. Army General Douglas MacArthur's long and flamboyant military career—the September 15, 1950, amphibious landing he commanded at the South Korean port of Inchon near Seoul—put U.S. troops 150 miles behind the North Korean enemy's lines.
39. Democrat Richard Russell of Georgia was then chairman of the U.S. Senate Armed Services Committee.

Yeah . . . and speaking of generals, I've been talking to Carl Wagner about Napoleon and his logistics. Carl is the best political organizer in the country, according to people who should know . . . and if the name seems familiar, he's the one Jann wants to edit the Elko book, and Carl called me the other day to ask what it all meant . . . so I told him I'd ask *you,* rather than Jann, and get back to him. Which is entirely logical, since I was the one who conceived the Elko meeting & put it together—a secret meeting of ten of the country's heaviest politicos at the Stockmen's Hotel in Elko, Nevada (Dave Burke, Dick Goodwin, Adam Walinsky, Rick Stearns, Carl, etc.). It was supposed to be a blueprint meeting for a flat-out takeover in '73, and Jann paid for it, but nobody ever followed up & I regard it now as one of the great Lost Opportunities of our time . . . and if you see any kind of a book in it, you should definitely talk to Carl, if only to see where the future lies. But he's leery of Jann's offer to be the "editor," and I can't really say that I blame him—if you see even the seed of a book in "Elko" (or even if you don't), you should at least talk to Carl and get to know him. If I were running for President, he'd be the first person I'd hire . . . so it would probably be worth your while to call me and pursue this connexion a bit further, because one of these days you're going to be calling me to get his private number at the White House. Selah.

And . . . yes . . . it's about time to end this bugger, eh? So . . . . . . 1) I talked to Wilcox today, after we had our chat, and I think he's doing fine on the Anthology . . . and 2) I'll send a copy of all this to Lynn, so she can straighten out my affairs while I have a look at the Texas border, & after that, we can talk about making me rich . . . and meanwhile I'll settle the film-situation with Bob, so that next time we talk I'll know what I'm doing inre: Galveston . . . which is not to say I don't know already, but there's always the problem of finding the right legal words for it.

Okay for now . . .
Hunter

TO GOVERNOR JIMMY CARTER:

Thompson sought to correct Carter's impression that he was actually running for the presidency by offering political advice to the real candidate.

November 24, 1975
Woody Creek, CO

Dear Jimmy . . .

Thanx for the note inre: my "announcement"—but, just for the record, I'd like to make one thing perfectly clear: I was careful not to say I was *running* for president, but only that I refused to take myself out of the running, as long as the nomination of Hubert Humphrey remained a possibility. And I saw McGovern saying almost exactly the same thing on the news tonight, which indicates a change for the better in his thinking because less than two months ago he was thinking seriously (although he refused to admit this to me) about a Humphrey-McGovern ticket as a possible solution to a deadlocked convention. My advisers in Washington keep me on top of these shifts, and what they're telling me now is that we should get ready for the spontaneous eruption of a McGovern-Thompson ticket. (At first they said "Thompson-McGovern," but I felt that would be speaking too soon, so I've instructed them to deny everything except my reluctant availability for "a place on the ticket," but only if it becomes absolutely necessary. I'm sure you can appreciate the wisdom of this stance, and for reasons of personal friendship I thought I should tell you about it. Selah.)

Also—despite my conscious refusal to get physically involved in the campaign until Jan 1—I've been watching it pretty closely and talking to a lot of people, and the only real change I've sensed in the past few weeks is that the people I talk to have suddenly decided to take you seriously . . . and one of these you should know about and talk to *personally,* if possible, is Carl Wagner, who works for the Municipal Workers Union in Madison, Wisc. (At least I think that's what he's doing right now, officially, but what he's really doing is looking for the right campaign to get into, and if I *were* running for president, Carl would be one of the first three people I'd hire.) If I were you I'd call him, because it probably wouldn't take much more than that to get him involved in the Florida primary. We talked a few days ago and agreed that you might actually be the front-runner by mid-March (or close enough to act like one) if you can finish at least third in N.H. and then convince the national press that Wallace needs 60% of the vote in Florida for a real victory. My own feeling, after watching Wallace on *Meet the Press* last Sunday, is that it's entirely possible for you to win in Florida—especially if you can break Wallace's grip on the "Richard Petty[40] vote." In any case, there's no way the bastard can get 60% down there. In '72 he pulled about 42% or 43%, and that was against a crowd of dumb zombies. My main impression of the '76 Wallace on TV, however, had to do with his tendency to lose his temper, even under the most passive kind of questioning. And if I were running against the bugger down there, I'd try to get on the same TV screen with him as often as possible, hopefully in a Q & A situation with some fairly aggressive press people, and let him beat himself. . . .

But what the hell? I'm slipping out of my journalistic role here, and I think it's a bit too early for that. Some of the things I've said about you have already been interpreted as a mystic endorsement of some kind, so I have to be careful—or at least act that way, for now, because I'm still not sure what role I'll be playing in this campaign, if any . . . although I've already made reservations at the Wayfarer in Manchester and the Royal Biscayne in Florida.

40. Stock-car driver Richard Petty won both the Daytona 500 and the NASCAR national championship seven times between 1964 and 1981.

Indeed, and on the Florida front you might be able to do me a favor. My reservation at the Royal Biscayne is from Feb 15 to March 13, but they say they can't guarantee me a ground floor room near the beach, which is very important to me—especially if I have to stay there for almost a month. If you have any leverage with those people (it's a Sheraton/ITT property—or at least it *was*) through your hq. in Florida, I'd appreciate it if you could nail down a ground floor room near the beach for me. Or maybe a beach-front room at the Silver Sands, next door to the Royal Biscayne . . . The Key is only 10 or 12 minutes from downtown Miami, but in terms of pace & privacy it seems a hell of a lot farther.

Another small favor has to do with the renting of a convertible, which are no longer available from the big rent-a-car companies—but which can be had fairly easily via the yellow pages (car rentals) in the Miami phone book. The last time I was there I got one from a used-car lot, but that's a little chancy unless you have time to look around; so if there's somebody in your Miami hq. who can locate & reserve a convertible for me (any make), I'd appreciate that, too . . . but neither one of these things is a serious problem & I don't mean to lean on you with them, but what the hell? If they're easy, why not do it that way? And while we're at it, another thing I've always had trouble with in Miami is renting an IBM *Selectric* typewriter. . . .

Hell, this is awful. All I really meant to do was answer your note, not ask a gaggle of favors—but again, what the hell? If it's easy, let's do it. If not, I'll be there anyway, and I'm definitely looking forward to it.

In the meantime, say hello for me to Rosalynn and all the other Carters. I got a note from Jack recently & he sounded like he was ready to move right into the White House. Sandy thinks you're all crazy for wanting to live in Washington, and I tend to agree . . . but good luck anyway, and I'll see you in New Hampshire.

Hunter

1976

JIMMY CARTER & THE RISE OF THE ROCK & ROLL VOTE . . . MARIJUANA GOES TO THE WHITE HOUSE . . . CRIME IS THE LONG-TERM ANSWER . . . PREFERENTIAL TREATMENT FOR JOURNALISTS . . . BUY THE TICKET, TAKE THE RIDE . . .

With Darwin,
Woody Creek, 1976.
(PHOTO BY
MICHAEL MONTFORT)

Juan and Darwin,
Woody Creek, 1976.
(PHOTO BY HUNTER S.
THOMPSON)

The Reader's Chair—
Owl Farm, 1976.
(PHOTO BY
MICHAEL MONTFORT)

Taking instructions from Hughes Rudd in New York, 1976. (PHOTO BY JILL KREMENTZ)

Key West, 1976. (PHOTO BY N. A. LUKAS, COURTESY OF HST ARCHIVES)

Fire Ball: HST and Jann Wenner celebrating Jimmy Carter's Democratic presidential nomination at a Rolling Stone *party, 1976.* (PHOTO BY ED BRADLEY)

TO JANN WENNER, *ROLLING STONE*:

As he prepared to set off on the 1976 presidential campaign trail for Rolling Stone, *Thompson wrote to thank Wenner for sending him a "mojo wire": his term for a Xerox telecopier, sort of a first-generation fax machine.*

January 2, 1976
Woody Creek, CO

Jann . . .

The goddamn mojo wire arrived by UPS (right to my front door) on Xmas eve . . . Jesus, what a wonderful present!

There is, of course, the matter of the traveling case—an extremely crucial item for any sort of road-work . . . and, speaking of road-work, we should have a talk ASAP about how to handle the early primaries. Canceling the *Playboy* piece left me with a grand or two in rudimentary, out-of-pocket expenses—mainly phone calls, lunches in Washington, etc.—that I've incurred during the long watch-and-wait period since last July. None of these are legally yours, but since all that background material will turn up somehow in the early pieces on the campaign, I assume we can charge most of it off to expenses, not all, but I'll have to check with Lynn on the amount. . . .

Okay for now. [David] Felton called me from either SF or NY inre: "Laos," but his call came in the midst of a 3-day frenzy and when I tried to call him back, the people in NY said he was in SF, and the people in SF said he was in NY. I'll try again today—which reminds me that I don't know where you are either, so I'll send a carbon of this note to NY.

There is no question but that "Laos" must be finished at once: It is going to cover a hell of a lot of ground—from Saigon to Beirut and Angola, to Manchester and Orlando. . . . A sort of "hello again" piece, with tangents all over the globe. The impression I got from both Felton & Erica is that you want to pay my expenses to come out to SF for 3 or 4 days, to finish it off with Felton, but before we do that I think we should at least talk about the bastard on the phone, so we all understand where we're heading on it. The opinions are pretty broad: We can either do a relatively terse, retrospective piece on the Last Days of American Empire in Indochina . . . or we can do a long and speedy re-cap of the whole year, from Kinshasa to Plains, Georgia to Saigon, Laos, Bali, Hong Kong, and also a bit of Washington and a kick-off look at the primaries. . . .

But this matter of *focus* is something we should get straight *before* we start a blitzkrieg with Felton; because without a focus, we'll all go mad trying to force it all together.

2 hours later:

And so much for all that; I think we just dealt with almost everything pertinent in the course of the (just-completed) Saturday morning phone call. I'll proceed along the lines we discussed inre: Laos—Part One in the form of a long, rambling up-date Memo from the NA desk, and then to Part Two as Travelogue from Indochina (along with some notes & comparisons on & from Africa, using Zaire as a route to some brooding on Angola & the CIA) . . . and then when we have the first two parts at least roughly finished, I'll do Part Three from either New Hampshire or Florida.

All of this is likely to get a bit complicated on the money front, and sooner or later we'll have to cope with that angle. I dread it, but there's too much cash in the balance to ignore, and right now I'm extremely cash-poor and I'm laboring very strongly under the impression that I'm writing this thing for *money.* If we're heading for another hassle or even a "failure of communication" on this score, I think we'd be doing ourselves a favor by getting the entire money situation straight immediately, so we don't wind up nursing a boil that might eventually have to be lanced. Writing for a living is hard enough, but arguing for a living is un-acceptable. I don't know about your time, but mine is way too short for any more of the kind of cheap, ingrown bullshit we've been wallowing in for most of the past year . . . so let's *confront* the money situation up front & get it settled. I'm still under the impression that a normal HST-style piece based on the Saigon trip will net me $5K, plus reimbursement of all legitimate expenses above the $3K you advanced. Our original agreement, you'll recall, had it $5K plus expenses for anything I wrote if I went beyond Hawaii . . . but rather than hark back to old wounds, let's just agree on what kind of money we're talking about now. I've more or less adjusted to the shock of a massive income-loss for the year, and I'd frankly prefer to forget the whole thing, rather than get into another money-hassle.

Jesus, I feel a pall of depression coming down on me just mentioning this stuff—but under the circumstances I think it's necessary, just to make sure it won't fester and blow up on us later. The next hassle will be the last one.

And on that ominous-sounding note, I'll close and get back to whatever comes next. The cash-crunch here is very real: not so much a crisis as hellish inconvenience. . . . Having given up the notion that even a "famous" writer can make a decent living by means of journalism, I tend to view it now as a kind of morbid self-indulgence that—with a lot of luck and constant skilled management—should more or less pay for itself. [*The New York Times*'s] Harrison

Salisbury might be onto something, but I don't get the feeling it's going to do me any good.

There may be some kind of mid-range salvation in writing books, but I'm not sure of that either. Crime, I think, is the long-term answer . . . but in the meantime I'm heavy into the buying and selling of strange gimcracks. For $1000, for instance, you can have a full-bore stereo cassette of the classic "Goodwin's Breakdown," a guaranteed, money-back ball-breaker when played at the proper volume on suitable machinery. . . . For another $1000, for instance, you can have a bronze plaque from the door of the Global Affairs Suite in Saigon . . . and for another $1000 each you can have both of [Mike] Solheim's thumbs. . . .

Human thumbs, incidentally, are among my fastest-moving items. I just closed a contract for one of Bob Arum's[1] thumbs for $3000 cash in advance, and Arum himself is about to close a $10K deal for a Jack Nicholson thumb. . . . The fee for tattooing (or "engraving," as it were) the name of the former owner on each thumb is a mere $100 extra, but serious collectors are turning more and more to the thumb-necklace concept, and for this the tattoos are a must.

So let me know well ahead of your expected delivery date. And mum's the word, of course; once these buggers get wind of what's happening, they become extremely hostile to strangers, or even friends. When the going gets savage, The Savage buy bolt-cutters . . . right?

Right,
Hunter

TO RICHARD N. GOODWIN:

Thompson had attended the recent wedding of his friends and fellow Elko conferees Richard Goodwin and Doris Kearns.

January 2, 1976
Woody Creek, CO

Dick . . .

I've been talking to Arum & Pierre[2] on a strangely regular basis since the wedding (jesus, only a madman would have brought that kind of weird human chemistry together—and under the roof of the Colonial Inn, at that) . . . but anyway, the A/P axis says you & Doris are back, that the book situation is fa-

1. Robert Arum, a former lawyer (for *Scanlan's Monthly*) turned boxing promoter, had urged Thompson to cover the October 30, 1974, Muhammad Ali–George Foreman heavyweight championship fight in Kinshasa, Zaire (now the Democratic Republic of the Congo).
2. Pierre Salinger had been JFK's campaign and then White House press secretary.

vorably settled, and that life in general is at least momentarily calm. . . . Which is all we can reasonably ask for, in these wretched downhill times.

And which brings me to a brace of items that must be dealt with at once: 1) Sheehan[3] needs $150 for his PPK, and since I paid you by check for both pistols at once, I guess you owe Neil the money. Let me know about this, so we can finally get that situation behind us. . . . 2) I need that TEAC tape deck at once, or at least as soon as you can arrange a trade for the Uher. I have some potential buyers out here for $300-plus, but since the machine is there and so is your TEAC dealer, I'd prefer to go with the same deal we discussed when I was there for the wedding; which, as I recall, left me paying between $200 and $250 for the trade. . . . Jesus, this leaves me taking a bad beating on the Uher, but under the circumstances I figure I need the TEAC *now* more than I need a good deal later: So tell your man to ship it at once & I'll pay his bill when I get the machine. OK? Okay . . .

Strange note here: I just talked to a guy named Dick Parker, who owns a store called the Racquet Shop in Concord (it's a tennis & ski-wear shop, I think) and he has your cane—the one I think I recall stealing from your house. Anyway, he did us a huge favor by giving us a ride to Logan Airport when there were no cabs available, and I left your cane in his car. He's holding it for you at the shop in Concord, so stop by and pick it up.

On other fronts, what are we going to do this year? My own situation is flux to the point of madness: Immense wealth hovers just beyond my grasp, but legal & contractual confusion is driving me to the brink of suicide. . . . On Xmas Eve the United Parcel truck rolled into my driveway with two packages: One contained three sets of monogrammed (red, black & gold) satin sheets, and the other box contained a brand new xerox telecopier (mojo wire) from Wenner. . . . And we both know what a "Christmas present" like that means: *Nobody* gives a mojo wire as a *present,* right?

In the meantime, I can't even pay my bar bill at the Jerome. My decision to take the month of December off, at *any* cost, has had the obvious repercussions—especially in the ledger of a free-lance writer who effectively took the whole year ('75) off, for reasons of foreign travel, rare drugs, and random tangents into exotic and always expensive styles of sensuality that can only be supported by a bottomless pit of wealth.

Within two weeks, however, I'll have necessarily signed to do either a novel, a film-script, or monthly coverage of the '76 campaign. This is going to have to be a working year, for good or ill. Do you have any money-fat ideas in this area?

3. Foreign and defense correspondent Neil Sheehan, who in 1971 had obtained the Pentagon Papers for *The New York Times,* would have his scholarly memoir, *A Bright Shining Lie: John Paul Vann and America in Vietnam,* published by Random House in 1988.

Jesus goddamn sweating christ! I see the sun coming up and I know that means I have to deal with a plethora of strange situations in the next 12 hours. Bobby & David are here, along with R. Reagan's son & numerous other human wild-cards . . . but what the hell?

I also have to finish the Indochina piece for Jann, then cover the Super Bowl for *Playboy*. . . . So I ain't resting.

How about you? Let me know ASAP inre: the PPK & the TEAC, so I can get those out of the way . . . and before I forget, let me tip my hat, or whatever, once again, to the finely muted style and precision of the wedding. It was a work of art from start to finish, and thanks for inviting us. Your wedding present is still at the taxidermist's down in Rifle, but it should reach you around Feb 15 or so.

OK for now. I have to work, before the deluge hits me once again . . . and since I'm on the subject of wedding presents, let me remind you once again that the honeymoon outfit I found in the airport was a *two-part,* sort of interim, gift: The top was for Doris and the pants were for you. I wasn't sure that split was entirely understood in the confusion of the wedding. (If you get a chance, send me a shot of you wearing your half—I'll mount it on the wall.)

Cazart,
Hunter

P.S. Visit here anytime—give warning, etc.

TO LOREN JENKINS, *NEWSWEEK:*

In the process of dubbing some audiocassettes he had made in Southeast Asia, Thompson found himself in need of the typewriter that he left in Hong Kong. He also lamented to Jenkins, who was now stationed in Rome, that Aspen was becoming too much of a tourist trap.

January 15, 1976
Woody Creek, CO

Loren . . .

I'm sitting here listening to you and Tuohy[4] whooping it up in the Continental garden; for some odd reason, you and Bill and Nick [Profitt] tend to dominate my tape-record of the last days of The War . . . and consequently about half my tapes sound like they were made at a New Year's Eve party in the alcoholic ward of a sort of international insane asylum. Your raving (tele-

4. *Los Angeles Times* Vietnam correspondent William Tuohy won the 1969 Pulitzer Prize for international reporting.

phone) gig with the *Newsweek* photo editor is a definite classic . . . and, yes, now that I look back at your recent letter I see a possible trade-off, to wit:

I'm now in the process of dubbing all my Indochina cassettes on big reel-to-reel tapes, for the ages . . . and from these reels I can make high-quality cassette copies of any tape you might want for yourself, and then mail them to you in Rome.

Which brings us to the matter of that goddamn Olivetti electric typewriter, and also the nasty fact that there is no way I can effect delivery of the thing from Hong Kong to here. . . . But with all the massive & world-wide logistical machinery at your command, *you* should be able to get it to me somehow, or maybe sell it to somebody in HK by putting a notice on the bulletin board at the Fgn. Corresp. Club. I'm still offering a 10% commission to Jeannie or whoever sells it for anything over $150. If memory serves, I paid slightly more than $200 for the brute.

In any case, there's damn little I can do about it on this end, so I'm leaving the problem in your hands, for good or ill. I'd naturally be more inclined to get these tape-copies to you in conjunction with a satisfactory solution of the typewriter problem, but of course I'm not making it conditional on that . . . and if the hellish truth be known, once you get the thing to Rome I'll be happy enough to give it to Nancy as a tool for her own use at home, provided she'll let me use it whenever I get there. That way, I'd always be sure of having my own typewriter when I arrive to cover the Fall of Rome—which is bound to happen sometime soon, given the current fate of Beirut & other one-time outposts of empire.

The only aspect of the typewriter gig that bothers me is the idea of just leaving the bastard in HK as a total loss. If you can get Ron to bring it to Rome, just hang onto the bugger and consider it a down-payment for the inevitable hospitality you'll have to extend when I get stranded there, myself.

My travel plans at the moment are vague, but I have a feeling I'll get to Angola or maybe S. Africa sometime soon . . . although in the next few months I won't be going much further than Florida, Texas or L.A. I've been trying to get a contract for a novel or a screenplay this year, but in the meantime I've been roped back into covering another goddamn campaign, mainly because I'm stone fucking broke. I'm leaving for Florida next week, if only to get away from my creditors and this rotten snow.

Aspen no longer seems salvageable. At one point during the recent Xmas rush, the local CC [Chamber of Commerce] figured there were 30,000 tourists in town. Thirty thousand, including a whole new element from Hollywood café society: Diana Ross, Warren Beatty, Truman Capote & all of John Denver's[5] friends. . . . Jesus, I'm beginning to think seriously about putting the Owl

5. Singer Diana Ross fronted the 1960s Motown trio the Supremes; writer Truman Capote's works include the novella *Breakfast at Tiffany's* and his "nonfiction" crime novel *In Cold Blood;* Aspen resident and pop singer John Denver wrote and recorded such wholesome songs as "Rocky Mountain High."

Farm on the market and looking around for another base. The multiple costs of living here are getting almost too high to pay—particularly for somebody who hates cold weather as much as I do.

We had a bit of excitement last weekend, however, when Tom Benton & Billy Noonan maced a whole restaurant full of people, including the mayor and the city manager & their wives. They were detained & held just long enough to have a good alibi for the moment, about 2 hrs. later, when some lunatic fired a marine emergency "parachute flare" in the front door of the Jerome, just as two cherry bombs went off inside the back door . . . and in the ensuing uproar, a visiting skier was shot in the back with a 50,000 volt electric dart gun called a "Taser." Clarence Kelley, that geek who runs the FBI,[6] has been telling anybody who'll listen that 1976 will be "a year of violence" in this country; he hasn't said why yet, or where he's getting his tips, but if Aspen during the first week of January was part of the pattern, I suspect Kelley might be onto something—and maybe I won't have to travel, after all.

Speaking of violence, how is Phil Caputo?[7] I heard he was wounded a while back in Beirut. Is Nick Profitt still there? And what about Tony & Claire? We got a letter from them on St. George's Hotel stationery, but it got here six months late and by then the hotel was no more. . . . I assume Tuohy managed to avoid the violence, as usual, by stealing bits & pieces of "eyewitness accounts" from anybody crazy enough to drink with him after midnight.

(Before I forget, I'm reading a book on War Correspondents called *The First Casualty* by Phillip Knightley. You should definitely have it, so if you can't get a copy over there, let me know and I'll send one.)

Jesus, it's getting light here & I have to get some sleep. But before I quit, I think a word of congratulations is in order with regard to your new duty station. That's worth about five Niemans, I'd say—and it also establishes you as one of the few master craftsmen in your field. I'll visit ASAP, but in the meantime Sandy & Juan say hello.

Salud,
Hunter

TO TED SOLOTAROFF, *THE AMERICAN REVIEW:*

Thompson passed on reviewing Tom Robbins's new novel Even Cowgirls Get the Blues.

6. President Nixon appointed Kansas City chief of police Clarence Kelley as FBI director in July 1973.

7. Philip Caputo, a former Marine Corps platoon leader who became a Vietnam correspondent for the *Chicago Tribune,* wrote the 1977 memoir *A Rumor of War.*

February 3, 1976
Woody Creek, CO

Dear Mr. Solotaroff . . .

I've spent about three hours trying to write you a letter to say why I can't send the kind of "words of welcome" I suspect you want in re: *Even Cowgirls Get the Blues*. But everything I've written so far would almost certainly sound rude and cynical & arrogant on your end, so I figure it's best to just junk all the earlier drafts and tell you, in this one, that I spent a few years as a part-time book reviewer and almost ten years, now, reading reviews of my own books . . . and on the basis of all that evidence, I think I'll pass on the chance to render any judgement on other people's books.

There are, of course, exceptions: When I first read *Dog Soldiers*,[8] for instance, I recommended it to friends with the assurance that I'd reimburse them for the price of the hardcover if they didn't like it . . . and on the other end of the scale, where rancid bullshit lives, I am forced from time to time to comment on the Works of "Werner Erhard."[9]

In any case, I wish to hell you'd never sent me the galleys or proofs or whatever of *Cowgirls*—but since you did & I tend to trust yr. judgement for a variety of reasons that would take too long to list or even think about here, I'm inclined to lend you the use of my name (since I assume that's why you sent me this goddamn thing in the first place) to say—and to reproduce in any & all forms—any combination of English-language words amounting in total to less than 20, to say anything you deem fitting with regard to the merits of *Cowgirls*. You can say, for instance: "A weird & stunning work," or "Sooner or later a book like this was bound to be written." And sign my name to anything you compose.

I just got back home from 3 wks. in Miami & LA, and I'm not in the mood to read a book that begins with an apology by the author for his use "throughout this book" [of] "third person pronouns and collective nouns in the masculine gender"—or any other gender, for that matter. . . . And I also opened the book, as is my wont with unknown manuscripts, to a page somewhere in the middle: and in this case I hit on pages 160 and 161, where I found the style & tone or whatever of the writing to be not in my taste . . . which doesn't mean this is anything but a wonderful book; but that's *your* business, since I assume you're somehow involved as an editor, and because of that and what I've heard about you I figure you're in a far better position to judge this book than I am . . . and for that reason I'll trust your judgement (in twenty (20) words or less) to say anything you want about the book, and to use whatever you want

8. Robert Stone won the 1975 National Book Award for fiction for *Dog Soldiers*, his brutal novel about smugglers of heroin from Vietnam to California.

9. Werner Erhard was a "self-improvement" guru who in 1971 launched Erhard Seminars Training (est), a pricey, psychobabbling series of long and demeaning behavior-modification sessions that preached the virtues of selfishness.

to say in my name for any purpose you think is right; I can't imagine that anything I'd say would make the slightest difference in any way, but if you think it might, seize this opportunity & kick out the jams. For any & all legal, promotional & esthetic purposes, I hereby appoint you my spokesman for any combination of up to 19 words you can lash together.

For good or ill;
& Good luck,
Hunter S. Thompson

TO BILL MACAULEY, UNIVERSITY OF NOTRE DAME, CLASS OF 1976:

Thompson was flattered to have been selected as a finalist for the renowned (and Roman Catholic) University of Notre Dame's Senior Class Fellow Award, an honor each graduating class conferred upon an individual "the majority of the seniors feel closely expresses their understanding of life."

February 6, 1976
Woody Creek, CO

Dear Bill . . .

I just got back from two weeks or so on the road to find your letter of Jan 5, regarding the Senior Class Fellow Award . . . and although I'm still not sure what the hell to make of it, I want to thank you for the letter as well as what I can only regard as a combination of high madness and generous instincts that caused it to be written. The idea of victory in the "final election" is more than I can come to grips with right now . . . but in the unlikely event that such an awesomely weird thing should come to pass, I wouldn't want to miss the chance to be part of it.

As for the dates you mentioned, the schedule of presidential primaries that more or less governs my movements this spring seems to leave me relatively free during the last week of March, the later the better, and I should probably warn you now instead of later that I look forward with genuine Fear & Loathing to the notion of "delivering an address" to any senior class, anywhere, for any reason at all . . . and in saying this I want to emphasize that my reasons for trying to avoid any speechmaking are entirely impersonal, non-sectarian and absolutely across the board, with no exceptions at all . . . and if I were in the mood to indulge any personal preference I suspect that ND would have an edge on almost *any* other university, if only because of the generally humane & intelligent response to my only other appearance on your campus;[10] which occurred sometime in the spring of 1975, under the sponsorship of the Civil Rights center, or whatever it is that Michael Wise is connected with. If Michael

10. The University of Notre Dame's campus is in South Bend, Indiana.

is still around, let me suggest that you check with him on the advisability of conferring this honor on me. . . . Because he'll understand all the hooks and reefs and strange implications, and I'll be inclined to go along with his judgement as to whether this is a good thing for all of us to get involved in . . . and as a matter of fact, let's leave it at that: If Michael Wise thinks this is a right & proper thing for me to be a part of, I'll do it with no worries or reservations at all—and if I do it on that basis, you'll have no worries, because I'll definitely do it right.

Indeed, but now we're getting into the realm of wild and heavy assumption, and that's always risky—especially since I'm still on the "maybe" list. But regardless of the outcome of the "final election," I want to thank you for your letter and whatever thinking led you to write it. My only other experience in this realm came last spring when I lost a run-off election against my old buddy M. Ali for the "honor" of addressing the senior class at Harvard. That was my idea of life & reality finding its own level, all the way down to the finest and meanest subtleties . . . but if you play in that league I guess you have to be ready to win, instead of losing closely and comfortably, but always with grace & style. OK for now. . . .

HST

TO BOB ARUM:

Thompson had designs on the helicopter landing pad in front of former President Richard Nixon's house in Florida.

February 6, 1976
Woody Creek, CO

Bob . . .

On the recommendation of the gentleman from Mobile, I'd like to retain you at this time—provided we can come to some agreement on the fee—to handle a job for me in Key Biscayne.

I want to buy the large concrete helipad in front of Richard Nixon's house on Bay Lane. I was down there last week, making inquiries, but [Bebe] Rebozo wouldn't talk to me and when I started asking around I got the impression that the natives weren't entirely sympathetic to my cause. . . . So I think the transaction should be handled, as it were, by a person or persons not openly & publicly hostile to Nixon and everything he stands for. I haven't asked Pierre if he has any specific contacts on Key Biscayne who could handle the transaction, but Sandy tells me he's in England & won't be back for a while . . . so I thought I'd go ahead and lay it on you, at least until Pierre gets back.

The opening, I think, lies in the 99% likelihood that the helipad, which sits about 100 feet off-shore from the two Nixon-owned houses he's been trying to sell for a while, was built with U.S. govt. monies and is therefore owned by the

GAO[11] and not by Nixon—which makes it govt. property and not subject to any sales-terms negotiated by Nixon with regard to the houses. I couldn't ascertain this for sure when I was down there, because my interest in the helipad was regarded with genuine suspicion by the few people I questioned. One of these, an attorney/friend of Rebozo's, had already told me of the numerous efforts (presumably made by Rebozo) to sell the helipad to Dade County, various state of Fla. agencies, local marinas, etc. . . . and thus far nobody wants it.

Jann Wenner, yr. buddy at *RS*, has offered to fund the project, but we had only one conversation about it and although he mentioned a figure of $25,000, we didn't get around to defining any terms, except to vaguely assume it would be a 50–50 deal, with me arranging the purchase and him putting up the money.

At the moment I'm awaiting a call from Washington that will hopefully tell me whether or not the GAO actually owns the helipad; and if the answer is a definite *yes,* all I'll have to do is make an official bid on a govt.-owned property . . . and in this case I think Pierre should do the bidding, provided he can handle it discreetly. Or wants to. . . .

So your own role, for now, is unclear . . . and for the moment you should just hold this letter as background, until I can call you with a few concrete facts. I suspect, however, that I'll get no firm answer vis-à-vis ownership (of the helipad) from my initial inquiries at the GAO, and I'm not at all certain Pierre will see enough humor in this gig to want any part of it . . . so I figure we'll be talking seriously in a week or so.

Meanwhile, on the gambling front, Sandy says you're under the impression that you lost $20 each on the playoff games . . . but according to my own hazy recollections, we broke even. It seems to me that I had Dallas & Oakland with five points each, but there's always the hopeful possibility that I'm wrong. Did you make any notes on the bets? I did, but I can't find them . . . so I can't say for sure, except that anybody as broke as I am right now would almost certainly not forget two winning bets in a single afternoon . . . and if I *did* forget, that's almost more ominous than actually losing, because it augurs ill for the future. In this case, I'd prefer breaking even to the specter of failed memory. Because that would hint at brain damage, and $40 is cheap if it gets me off that ugly hook.

OK, I just got the call from DC in re: The Helipad—which is owned or at least controlled, apparently, by the GSA, and not the GAO. (GAO is govt. accounting, and GSA is govt. services.) In any case, I'll know in a few hours if the property is biddable, or even remotely on the open market . . . and if it looks good I'll call you right away.

OK for now. I have to write some bullshit for today's deadline, so no more gibberish. . . .

HST

11. The General Accounting Office (GAO) is a U.S. congressional agency.

TO FRANK GANNON:

Thompson had formed an unlikely friendship with former Nixon White House press aide Frank Gannon, but failed in his bid to go along on the ex-president's controversial private visit to China February 21–29, 1976—the fourth anniversary of Nixon's historic first trip to Beijing by a U.S. president.

February 9, 1976
Woody Creek, CO

Dear Frank . . .

Sorry to be so long in getting back to you in re: the deep & lengthy socio/political conversation we planned, but I have a new idea that might allow us to touch all those strange bases at once, and under circumstances that most people would probably call awesomely weird. . . . To wit:

I'd like to go along with Mr. Nixon on his trip to China . . . and if I can work the logistics out with *Rolling Stone,* I'd like to bring Ralph Steadman along with me . . . but at the moment I don't even know if Ralph is free to travel, so let's consider this letter a formal request (or informal, if that's a better way to handle it) in re: the details and probability of getting me [in as] a press-member of The Tour.

We both know I can't offer you much in the way of guaranteed blue-chip publicity when I write about the trip . . . but we also know (or at least we should) that there is nothing in the long history of my relationship with Mr. Nixon to indicate that I'd write or say anything contrary to any agreement or understanding we might or might not arrive at, beforehand. My only valid reference on this score is Pat Buchanan, but I figure that's enough.

The whole idea of this trip puzzles and fascinates me, for all the obvious reasons. . . . Which I see no point in detailing here, but if you want to talk about them I'll be happy to come out to San Clemente for a chat, ASAP.

But in any case, please let me know something in time to make my own arrangements for the trip. I've already asked the *RS* office in Washington to apply for a China visa for me, and I assume you'll let me know if there's anything else I need.

Thanks,
Hunter

FROM GROVER LEWIS:

Brown Power activist Oscar Acosta had disappeared from Los Angeles in early 1974. Some speculated that he "went underground" to evade various authorities, but his friends were alarmed, including Thompson and Texas newsman Grover Lewis, a former Village Voice *writer and associate editor of* Rolling Stone *from spring 1971 to summer 1973.*

April 17, 1976
Kanarraville, Utah

Dear Hunter:

I've heard from several sources that Oscar Acosta is dead, the murder victim of drug traffickers.

For my own peace of mind, I intend to get to the bottom of the matter, find out if the rumor is true or false. Do you know anything about it?

I'd be most appreciative if you'd be in touch with me on this.

Best wishes,
Grover Lewis

TO LOREN JENKINS, *NEWSWEEK:*

April 24, 1976
Woody Creek, CO

Loren . . .

You thieving scumbag. I never heard of anybody named John Select and I never even mentioned the idea of recovering that typewriter from Hong Kong to anybody but you . . . so now that your hench-people have dealt with it in the most obvious kind of HK style, you owe me $200.

Never let it be said that an old Indochina hand like me can't recognize a classic Saigon-scam, especially when it comes with the imprint of an infamous Tu Do St. moneychanger glaring out from between every line.

You pig. You couldn't be satisfied to let the thing fall (or drift) gracefully into the hands of your own wife. . . . No, you have to fall back on the habits of an ill-spent lifetime and sell the bugger for profit to some HK dope addict. One of these days I'll probably get a thank you note from Denis Cameron, written on my own typewriter from some ugly dungeon in Egypt. I understand Denis had a pretty active TV talk with Sadat.[12] Was Rokoff behind the camera?

Anyway, you picked a perfect time to rip me off—because I've been sitting here for the past week or so, trying to figure out where to go for my next busman's holiday, and all of a sudden you just solved my problem.

Indeed, why not Rome? For six or seven weeks . . . Hang around the better cafés & get a feel for the place, change some money, catch a few diseases, and of course I'd have to spend a bit of time each day in the office, *on the typewriter.* And the *telex.* Many *phone calls* to Doug Sapper in Rhodesia; or to my man John Select at *Rolling Stone,* making inquiries with regard to the fate of your various articles. . . . Just the other day, in fact, Wenner was asking me where to send your check, and I told him I'd deliver it personally, just as soon as I finish this goddamn article on the Campaign. At this point, I am sitting on

12. Anwar al-Sadat was president of Egypt from 1970 until he was assassinated in 1981.

something like $14,000 worth of out/pocket expenses, covering almost everything from all-nite naked cycle rides in Laos to cocaine orgies in the National Affairs Suite that I finally retired (permanently) about three weeks ago—but not before I gave it one last, long run that will not be soon forgotten; nobody ever covered a presidential campaign like I covered the first six weeks of this one. From New Hampshire to Miami, we kicked out the jams and brought not only the style and tone of the Lane Xang and the Continental garden but also the brute substance of both, right straight into the heart of the Campaign Trail . . . and when I say "we," I refer to at least two mutual friends from the boom-boom days, but for reasons that need not be mentioned here except to say that Dick Tuck still lives, these people will not be named by me, in print or any other way. But let me tell you it was worth all the rotten, low-life agony that goes with covering this silly campaign to be sitting in the bar of some Holiday Inn up there in the snows of Manchester and looking up to see some wild-eyed fucker wearing a Hong Kong tailor-made jacket with only two buttons and a $2000 gold Cambodian chain bouncing on his chest & a gold Rolex on his wrist and yelling "Fuck All These Bums, Doctor O and his people are holding a press conference in 216 about fifteen minutes from now, and there is definitely no *press* allowed."

But that act couldn't last. Nobody had ever seen an out-front plague of dope addicts on the campaign trail before, and the Secret Service couldn't handle it. By the end of the Florida primary, most of the loonies had been retired or sent back across the water . . . and that was when I quit, too. It was not worth the effort. If anybody ever tells you to come back over here and get "promoted" to some shit-eating gig like covering the White House, run like hell for Angola; and if all else fails, go into business with Sapper . . . or even that filthy degenerate, Tuohy. But don't let them lure you back here; there is a powerful stench of doom and desperation in the air, and when things get that tense it doesn't even matter who's president. All the people who said I'd finally caved in to terminal brain damage when I started betting on Jimmy Carter two years ago are now brushing up on their scripture, just in case the "new Hubert Humphrey" won't sell any better than the old one did. If I had to make my final bets right now, I'd have to go with Carter to get the nomination and beat Ford—but I'm still not sure what to make of it, except that all the alternatives seem a hell of a lot worse, and I honestly doubt if the outcome of this election will make any real difference to anybody. The die is cast, the fat is in the fire, and if the Grim Reaper wants to come on like Jesus, so be it.

But shit, I guess you read all this stuff in *Newsweek*, so I'll quit and get back to work. I have one final article to do, then it's down to Texas to work on a novel about gun-running and the smack trade . . . but before I get seriously into a novel, I think I'll need a vacation.

And meanwhile, just in case that ratbastard John Select shows up in Rome with my typewriter, seize it immediately and have the bastard killed. Or hold him until my agent Semmes Luckett III shows up to handle matters. He is the only person authorized to deal in my name on the Continent, and I expect he'll be seeing you soon.

Tell Nancy how sorry I am that you saw fit to sell my gift to her, but I guess you filthy journalists are all the same.

OK,
HST

TO JANN WENNER, *ROLLING STONE:*

Thompson's article on Jimmy Carter—"Fear and Loathing on the Campaign Trail '76: Third Rate Romance, Low-Rent Rendezvous"—ran in the June 3, 1976, issue of Rolling Stone.

June 16, 1976
Woody Creek, CO

Dear Jann . . .

Your un-dated letter in re: your decision to pay only 40% of my expenses on the "Carter" article arrived today—but I had a hard time following all the disallowed expenses you referred to, because the "enclosed accounting" you repeatedly mentioned was not, in fact, enclosed. Whether it exists or ever existed is an interesting but academic question at this point, because we both know how useless any further argument would be.

We both know, too, what an immensely treacherous beating I took on the Carter article expenses . . . and we both know there's not a fucking thing I can do about it, because our agreement inre: expenses was verbal and not in writing. It was kind of you to note, as Lynn has, that "We undoubtedly should have been more specific, via Nesbit, in front. . . . "

Indeed. But then we never would have had an article, eh?

Have you tried golf yet?

Anyway, $4000 expenses and a $4500 fee means that effort cost me $1500 and one credit card—which is bad economics for a free-lance writer, but not nearly as bad as it might have been for me if I'd had a leg blown off in Saigon, with no medical insurance. . . .

So I guess I should count myself lucky, eh? I was having such a good time down there in Key West that I guess I didn't hear you when you were telling me to go back home and write the article because you weren't going to pay my expenses, but I'm still a bit confused about who sent that Xerox tech-rep over to the Santa Maria Motel to fix my mojo wire so I could keep sending pages to that office in San Francisco.

In any case, you've made yourself eminently clear on this matter . . . and, like you say, " . . . that's that on expenses."

How many other writers have gone to the pawn shop with that phrase (from you) ringing in their ears?

Hunter

TO BOB RAFELSON:

Thompson sent movie director Rafelson a rough sketch of his ideas for the Texas arms trading screenplay he planned to turn to after the 1976 election.

"GALVESTON" MEMO

June 23, 1976
Woody Creek, CO

Bob Rafelson
Outov Inc.
933 N. LaBrea
Hollywood, CA

Dear Bob,

After talking to you earlier today I looked at the 5-page handwritten letter I wrote you from the Trinidad Hilton and found that it related almost entirely to *revision and refinement with regard to characterization* vis-à-vis the film/plot/story tentatively titled "Galveston" that we've been discussing on and off for the past six months. . . . And since the letter was essentially a wild-eyed, pre-dawn memo *to you*, it contained little or no mention of the plot or the story itself, and hence would be of little use to you for any purpose except as a tangible reassurance that my head is very much into the project—even while grappling desperately with thieves, thugs, cops, and other bloodthirsty scumbags in Trinidad and Tobago, from which I escaped by a series of incredible maneuvers that still cause me too much pain for any kind of written description at this point. In a quick nut, however, the bastards took my money, my wallet, my credit cards, my press credentials, my acid, my weed, my mescaline, my vacation, my sense of humor and whatever was left of my unsupported and generally unsupportable faith in the "better instincts" of the human race . . . and then they chased me off the fucking island(s) like some kind of a crippled rat.

Conrad was right: "Exterminate the brutes."

Or was that Mistah Kurtz talking?[13]

We'll never know, eh? And it don't make no never mind anyway, right now, except to explain why the memo I scribbled to you in my last frenzied hours on that stinking island was not entirely satisfactory in terms of context, back-

13. The exact quote of Kurtz's command in Joseph Conrad's 1902 war novel, *Heart of Darkness,* is: "Exterminate all the brutes!"

ground, plot lines, etc. It focused entirely on a new and sudden understanding of the characters in the Galveston story that came to me for reasons I'd just as soon never understand—in the foulest and darkest depths of personal despair.

Rather than send you that frantic gibberish, however, I am going to run the risk of trying to translate it onto the typewritten page, and hopefully in some kind of context that will give you something a bit more tangible than a few pages of admittedly brilliant character development in a story I referred to only by accident in the letter, since my only purpose in writing it was to tell you that I felt I'd suddenly solved what I felt was the Main Problem with the Galveston story—which was WHO the characters were and WHY they were tangled up in this ugly & disastrous gun-running trip. The general outline of the plot has always seemed pretty clear to me, but until that hideous night in Trinidad I had never seen the characters in any kind of focus—never really seen them at all, for that matter, and if we are going to proceed, as I normally do, on the notion that Character is Destiny, there is no way to write a convincing story about people neither one of us feel we *know.*

I have that feeling now, but at this point I have no more idea than you do whether I can make any coherent sense of that feeling in two or three pages on very short notice . . . and it's also possible that this "feeling" I dredged up from the bowels of my own rage & terror is nothing but a crude & pitiful delusion that won't make the slightest fucking sense to anybody, including me.

But what the hell? I got the impression from our phone talk earlier today that you were anxious to see something tangible from me on this Galveston story, and that a crazed memo about characters and motivations would not make the nut, on your end . . . so, not entirely in accord with my better judgement, I figure I might as well sit down at this wretched machine and try to get a few basic things down on paper—so we'll at least have something to look at, for good or ill.

And for christ's sake don't give me any cute nazi bullshit, like last time, about the stilted language of this letter. My sanity is hanging by a thread at this point, and I can't stand any abuse. . . . About 30 minutes before you called today, I learned that Juan had accidentally disposed of $4,000 (that's FOUR THOUSAND DOLLARS) while I was in Tobago/Trinidad. Gone. Sent off in the goddamn mail. He has spent the last 24 hours hiding somewhere in town, and Sandy won't tell me where. . . .

Anyway, I'm trying to put this down in a form that might make sense to somebody besides you & me, so you'll just have to live with this High English I tend to drift into whenever I see a sheet of carbon paper in my typewriter. Selah.

And now . . . well . . . let's see what I can make of this fucker: From here on, I'm just going to wing it & hope for something coherent . . . but it might dissolve into gibberish at any moment, and if that happens I'll send it anyway. . . .

For the record, I'm still thinking purely in terms of "a story," without trying to make any distinctions in my own mind or on paper between film or print, although probably I'll be seeing the story as a book, because if I start trying to see it through the eye of a camera I'll go mad in 20 minutes—and that's something I've wanted to do for a long, long time: ZANG! With a running start I could be around that Final Bend before *anybody* caught on that this time I was really making a run for it. . . .

Yeah . . . but let me give a bit more thought to this thing, first. I'm not sure why, but I'm broke again and I have to do something, so why not this?

One thing I've already taken care of, for instance, is the music, the sound track. The name is Russell Smith, and before you argue, go out and buy a new album by the Amazing Rhythm Aces, called *Too Stuffed to Jump*. Listen to it *twice,* by yourself, sitting in a totally dark room, and that should take care of the music.

As for the story . . . well . . . shit. Let's keep on calling it "Galveston" for now, although we could just as well call it "Brownsville" or "Beaumont" (no, scratch "Beaumont"). . . . But there is a finality about "Galveston," to me at least, that matches my sense of the story. I want to make sure that every human being who sees or reads this thing will be haunted by it for the rest of their lives. That's why I want the title to be a word that will keep popping up—on maps, in *Time* & *Newsweek,* in random conversations, on the network news, in jigsaw puzzles . . . I want to make the word "Galveston" completely synonymous in the American language with absolute and inescapable *doom.* I want to make it the *Guernica,*[14] a dark and ominous word that can never be said with a smile. . . .

Indeed . . . and in order to do that we will need three very believable characters that at least 50 million people between the ages of 25 and 45 can somehow identify with: Not freaks, not bikers, not psychotics or politicians or bodybuilders or hookers or perverts or rich or poor or black or crazy or powerful . . . but three people—one male aged 34, one male aged (aged? is that a word?) 41, and one female aged 27. All three will be just a little bit brighter and prettier and more adventurous and more successful at coping with life than the people around them. . . . But only a little bit, because I want them to be mirrors, not comets, because the only way to lure the reader or the viewer into this hellbound train is to make sure they first identify in some personal way with the characters . . . and then, after setting the identity hook, we offer these three characters an opportunity to make a lot of money by doing something just risky enough to be genuinely dangerous, but not so dangerous that most viewers/readers wouldn't at least think they might be capable of doing it

14. *Guernica,* Pablo Picasso's famed painting of the Basque town in northern Spain destroyed by German planes fighting for anti-republican General Francisco Franco in the Spanish Civil War in 1937, hangs in Madrid's Reina Sofia Museo Nacional Centro de Arte.

themselves—like quietly dropping out of their own separate realities for two or three weeks and delivering a 2-ton U-Haul truck full of M-16s from a warehouse in Salt Lake City to a dock in Galveston, for a quick and seemingly foolproof profit of $100,000. Maybe more, maybe less; these are the "details" I'll have to deal with under the heading of research. And the reason for research is to make a fictional story with fictional characters appear to be true—at least for the life of the story, and hopefully for the next 300 years. I want to know exactly how many M-16s will fit in a 2-ton truck, exactly how much a truckload of M-16s stolen from the Army will cost in Salt Lake City, and exactly how much they will sell for on a dock in Galveston—not because the numbers or figures themselves are so important, but because every small truth in a fictional story makes it that much more believable, and unless the first half of this story is irresistibly believable, the second half will seem like a bad joke . . . but anybody who believes that the first half could easily be true is going to take a brutal hammering in the second half, to wit:

The kink in the story is the same one we've talked about, although not in much detail: Everything goes according to plan until the trio reaches Houston, where they find themselves two days ahead of schedule. They have to be at the dock in Galveston at exactly 6:00 p.m. on Friday—so on Wednesday afternoon they check into a motel on South Main that is near a congenial roadhouse called The Blue Fox, owned by a friend of a friend, etc. . . . and on Wednesday night one of the three pulls the pin in the story by saying something half-serious about their "truckload of machineguns. . . ." Right, and on Thursday night their truck disappears out of the motel parking lot. Stolen. No clues, no way to report it, no way to get it back—a U-Haul truck full of M-16s stolen from the U.S. Army and paid for in Salt Lake with *fronted money.*

(Goddamnit, Bob, the mail goes out in exactly 46 minutes and there's no way I can finish this thing by then. . . . So I think I'll do as much as I can in the next 30 minutes, then mail this, and then go into town and xerox the Trinidad letter and mail that in Aspen. . . . So you'll be getting *two* letters & they *might not* arrive in the same mail, but the second will be just a few hours behind the first . . . and it's going to take me another day to weave this thing together anyway, so for now I'll just do what I can and we'll talk on the phone when you get both letters. . . .)

Anyway, the terror begins when they realize the truck has been stolen. They (and the reader/viewer) are 99% sure the owner of The Blue Fox (somebody a bit like Bob What's-his-name who owns Galena Street, a clean-cut criminal who is also into Houston politics) had the truck stolen or at least knows who stole it, but at this point he is also their only possible hope for getting it back . . . and it is at this point that all three of them begin to understand (one at a time) that they have moved outside the world of "law" and relatively civilized behavior that has both restricted and protected them all their lives. . . . It is free-fall now, the law of the jungle, the tooth and the fang, etc. . . . and their first move, once they understand how helpless they are, is to turn the girl over to the owner of The Blue Fox. The girl for the guns, right?

Wrong. The girl is the first to understand what's happening, and by noon on Friday she has clearly gone over. The 34-year-old protagonist (see enc.—goddamnit I'll just send the whole packet at once—you rotten bastard! How did you get me into this madness? The goddamn mail leaves in 13 minutes & I'm still down here in the basement & not even started on the characters . . .).

The 41-year-old ex–dope dealer from LA is not far behind the girl, but he is the one who got the front money from "the mafia" and he knows he can run but he can't hide—and his friend (let's imagine J. Buffett at 34, bored with success and looking for some money-action) wants to stay and force some kind of solution. I haven't figured out what kind of madness he might want to try, but whatever it is, it's doomed. But for about two hours on Friday afternoon it looks like his plan might work—and then, with no warning at all, he opens a door somewhere in Galveston and gets his spine severed with a .357 Magnum. Paralyzed forever.

They drifted into The Deep End.

And now I have six minutes to get to the WC store with this fucker. OK for now. Call me when you get work.

H

TO JIMMY CARTER:

Thompson had interviewed Carter several times over the preceding two years, but now found himself in the awkward position of covering the 1976 campaign for Rolling Stone *after having advised the Democratic candidate.*

June 29, 1976
Woody Creek, CO

Dear Jimmy . . .

In case I haven't reached you by telephone before you get this letter, let me explain what I'll have in mind whenever I *do* reach you by phone—so I won't have to waste a lot of time explaining why I'm calling.

Due to circumstances beyond my control, I've agreed to do another long *Rolling Stone* article on Campaign '76—which means, in effect, that I'll be covering the Demo Convention in NYC and then writing a long article right afterwards; and since I can't *count on* the convention itself to generate the kind of adrenaline-action that I need to get me to the typewriter for another long bout with political journalism, it occurred to me tonight that the sanest, easiest, most mutually comfortable and in fact the most potentially meaningful thing I could do at this point would be to sit down with you in some kind of relatively relaxed situation and have another one of our more or less "annual tape talks."

Looking at the calendar, I see that my first encounter with you was on the first Saturday in May, 1974 (the Law Day speech), and my second was almost exactly a year later—after you'd made your candidacy official—when I came down to Plains in May of 1975.

. . . And now, looking back on the past two years and all the things that have happened since we first met, it occurs to me that we both have a sort of esthetic debt to history to keep this strange movie rolling as long as we can, or at least as long as it's comfortable . . .

. . . and that, of course, would be a significant turn in the story-line, regardless of which fork it took. Unlike *Time,* I don't see anything especially "bizarre" in our relationship as one decent human being to another, but I might as well admit that in almost any other public or private context I can see why there are a hell of a lot of people—including some of my best and most intelligent friends—who are honestly puzzled by what they perceive as a weird and neo-ominous "alliance" between two people who *seem* to represent two of the most extreme & opposite poles on the socio-political spectrum. People like Alan Baron and Dick Goodwin, for instance, are genuinely baffled by most of the things I've said about you—and the main reason for their bafflement, I suspect, is that I've never properly explained why the obvious difference in our private lifestyles and political backgrounds doesn't necessarily preclude either a personal friendship or a real mutuality of interests when it comes to presidential politics.

This is a thing I'd like to be able to explain and get down on paper, once and for all—and in order to do this, I think we need another good, relaxed and wide-ranging (taped) conversation about whatever seems important at the time.

That would amount to the Third Annual "Carter/HST Live & Random Conversations" vis-à-vis an era in U.S. history that I think will prove out, in history, to be one of the most interesting, meaningful and historically critical eras this nation will ever go through.

I could, of course, be wrong. I have been wrong before, but not very often—and right now I'll match my published, on-the-record outbursts of political "wisdom" against anybody else in the business, including Apple and Broder and Germond[15] and that crowd. . . . So I'm riding pretty high right now, but just between you and me, I'm not quite as sure of the reason(s) for my success as I'd like to be. . . .

. . . And that's why I'd like to sit down and have another fairly long and relaxed talk with you. The last year I backed a winner in presidential politics was 1960, but that time it was mainly a matter of being sure *who I was against*—

15. *Washington Star* political columnist Jack Germond and his partner Jules Witcover would write the 1981 campaign-analysis book *Blue Smoke and Mirrors: How Reagan Won and Why Carter Lost the Election of 1980.*

which is always a lot easier and more defensible than being *for* a candidate; and let me tell you, my friend, that you have given me more than one anxious moment in the past six months. . . .

. . . And no doubt there will be a few more, but what the hell? For a variety of strange reasons that neither one of us ever really encouraged, I now feel saddled with a personal stake (with regard to my own judgement & credibility) in your candidacy, your views, and in the success or failure of what I've been telling people for the past two years is the very likely prospect of your presidency. I am stuck with you now, for good or ill—and although I'm not nearly as worried with that prospect as a lot of my friends tell me I should be, I feel a very powerful obligation to at least understand who and what I'm stuck with. It makes me nervous to feel responsible for the actions of any person except myself—especially if that person happens to be the President of the United States—and that's precisely why I think it's time to tape Chapter Three of this "bizarre" and unlikely saga.

We would need a framework of about 24 hours, to do it right—either another visit to Plains or maybe a long talk during the convention in NY—but, if absolutely necessary, I could probably do it with 12 more or less consecutive hours in either Plains or NYC, provided we could spend *at least half of those hours* (6) in relaxed and mutually comfortable circumstances, with time to talk at length about whatever aspects of a Jimmy Carter presidency most concern both of us. In 1972, my "story" on the Demo convention in Miami turned out to be a very long & detailed (taped) conversation with Rick Stearns on the real, bottom-line mechanics of how McGovern's strategists managed to clinch his nomination on the first ballot. . . . And that's the same sort of thing I have in mind for my Demo '76 story, except that this time the conversation will have to be *with you,* instead of one of your colonels. . . .

. . . Or even a general, for that matter, because the dramatic tension of the story (and the reason why it's worth $5000 to *Rolling Stone*) lies almost entirely in my personal relationship, such as it is, with you, and not with "the Carter Campaign."

So . . . I assume you see what I'm talking about; and just in case there's any misunderstanding, let me say here & now that what I am *not talking about* is another jury-rigged travesty like that "interview" we had to cope with—courtesy of Pat and Hamilton[16]—on the plane from Orlando to Chicago on the morning after the Florida primary. I had serious problems with *Rolling Stone* about justifying that trip for expense-account purposes. That was the time I had to get off your plane in Chicago and fly at once back to Tampa for one of my "speeches" inre: "the real meaning" of Campaign '76 . . . and, yes, that was also the time I tried to burn Ham out of his room in the Carleton House.

16. Carter's pollster Patrick J. Caddell and campaign manager Hamilton Jordan.

We don't need any more scenes like that one; the stakes and style of this drama have escalated quite drastically since then, and I doubt if your Secret Service detail would see much humor in the spectacle of the Democratic nominee's campaign manager getting immolated by a crazy, fire-breathing journalist in the lobby of New York's Americana Hotel. . . . So, if it's okay with you, I'm going to try to orchestrate *this* Talk/Conversation/ Etc. as painlessly as possible, and I urge you to approach it the same way.

After all the strange water that's passed under both our bridges since my first appearance at The Mansion in May, 1974, I think we owe ourselves the luxury of a visit we can both have some fun with. . . . And if your new realities make a thing like that impossible; well, then I guess *that's* the story . . . but in any case I've come to the point where I need either an ending or a new chapter for this tale, and just as soon as I finish this letter I'll mail it and then get on the phone to Ham, Jody[17] or Pat, to get the thing set up . . . so if you start getting messages that I'm trying to reach you, at least you'll know what I want.

Okay . . . My schedule these days is a lot looser than yours, but my July 24 (or possibly July 31) deadline is a very serious matter to me, *Rolling Stone,* and my loan officer at the Bank of Aspen. . . . So please let me know, as soon as possible, if and when you'd feel comfortable having me join you for an afternoon or evening, or both, of the same kind of informally serious talk we've done in the past. . . . And if you think that's not feasible, let's talk about *why.* All I need, real quick, is an answer, so I can tell *Rolling Stone* what sort of an article to expect for the post-convention issue.

Either way, I'll see you in New York. . . . Which is not a thing I look forward to, and in a sense it's *your fault* that I now have to spend a mid-July week in the bowels of Manhattan; but since it now seems inevitable, I might as well come out of it with a good, valid and historically meaningful story—which means I'll need some private, un-hurried time with you, in Plains or New York.

I can see how this might be a problem for you, in terms of schedule & priorities—but, in the context of our personal & professional relationship over the course of the past two years, it seems like a problem worth solving—in your interest, as well as my own. There are still a hell of a lot of decent, intelligent people "out there" who are not yet convinced that you're human, and that's a problem I think we can and should solve by smiting them hip and thigh, as it were, with another long JC/HST interview/talk/conversation about some of the things that concern them.

Indeed . . . So it looks like a worthwhile project, and one that we both might enjoy; or at least that's how it looks to me, and I hope we can find enough time to do it right.

17. Jody Powell was Jimmy Carter's 1976 campaign press secretary, the same job he would hold in the White House.

Let me know, as I've said, ASAP. You can call me here at home, or by asking Jody to track me down through Ed Bradley from CBS, who just left here to pick you up in Milwaukee. Ed and I have been brooding and haggling about you since those very early days up in Manchester & Boston when he was covering Birch Bayh, and ever since he got himself assigned to you we've been comparing notes and impressions at least three times a week . . . and, for whatever it's worth, you're still ahead on real points.

Zang! This letter is getting too long, so I think I'll quit right now. Anything else I have to say can wait until later. . . .

. . . Sincerely,
Hunter S. Thompson

TO U.S. SENATOR GARY HART:

Thompson intended to see to it that his friend Gary Hart, who now represented Colorado in the U.S. Senate, was working for him in Washington.

July 1, 1976
Woody Creek, CO

Dear Gary:

I missed you at the Pomegranate in Aspen and also at the Demo "convention" in Denver . . . but if you get to NY for the love-in, I'll probably see you there.

In the meantime, however, could you bring me up to date on the progress (or fate) of S.1 . . . That's S.1, which you assured me quite a while ago would never pass. . . . But I keep hearing ominous talk about it, and I figure it's time for an update. If S.1 is likely to go anywhere at all, I want to come to Washington and make sure it doesn't slip by without some fear & loathing attached. So please send me a progress report, to date, and then we can talk. Thanx. . . .

Also, I just caught an item on the *CBS Morning News* to the effect that the Senate just voted to end price controls on . . . What? Natural Gas? Gasoline? It went by so fast that I didn't catch the details, but the main thrust was painfully obvious . . . and with that in mind, I wonder if you could supply me with a list of Yes and No votes in the Senate on this thing. Or was it a secret ballot?

The enclosed material vis-à-vis my current problem with the Williams Energy Company should be self-explanatory, and I wonder if you can get a better explanation of their pricing-practices out of them than Sandy could by writing their office in Grand Junction. As far as I know, these bastards have a total monopoly in this area (Aspen is on natural gas, but us ranchers are stuck with propane), and $13.50 per day is a goddamn outrage—but to get a memo like this in response to a polite request for an explanation is like having your insurance man triple your rates and then set fire to your house when you complain.

I haven't given you a hard time about anything you have or haven't done since '74, but I think it's about time you started earning your salary & this thing is too savage & obvious to ignore. The bastards should at least be forced to explain themselves, right? Let me know ASAP.

Thanx,
Hunter

TO FRANK N. DUBOFSKY, AMERICAN CIVIL LIBERTIES UNION:

The state chapter had sent Thompson a long and wandering appeal for "a substantial contribution to the Colorado affiliate of the A.C.L.U. . . . above and beyond your A.C.L.U. dues."

July 6, 1976
Woody Creek, CO

Frank N. Dubofsky
ACLU of Colorado
1711 Pennsylvania St.
Denver, CO 80203

Dear Mr. Dubofsky,

Your letter of March 29 just turned up in a pile of mail from *Rolling Stone* readers who want me to do everything from setting myself on fire to running for President. . . . And since I only subject myself to this kind of ordeal (reading the *RS* mail) once a month, I failed to see or read your letter until last night.

And now, after reading it again, I am still a bit hazy what you want from me or why you wrote the letter. . . . Which is not entirely reassuring: If I were going to hire an attorney for anything important, I would be reluctant, as it were, to retain somebody who can write eleven paragraphs on two single-spaced pages and either fail to say what he means, or succeed in saying something so trivial as a request for money that could just as easily have been made on a 3 x 5 postcard. . . . You might at least have wasted a twelfth paragraph to say how much money you want.

In any case, if all you want is money, you'd have been smarter to write somebody who has some. If I wrote a check for a thousand dollars today, it would probably bounce—and I have no savings account. I could perhaps double my annual contribution of (approx.) $50 to the ACLU, but on the evidence of your

3/29 letter to me I wouldn't have much trouble concluding that *any* money I sent you might very likely be spent to pay the salaries of however many typists you need to write more letters to more people, asking for more money.

And so much for that, eh?

If I were you, I'd try to figure out some slightly more imaginative way to get money out of me. . . . Three or four of these come to my own mind immediately, but if I have to line them out for you, it raises a definite question of confidence vis-à-vis what use these monies might be put to. I have been a member of the national and/or N. Calif. ACLU for almost 15 years, so there is obviously no lack of interest on my part. . . . But I think it's reasonable for me or any other member to wonder what my money is being used for, and who is spending it. Cazart . . .

Hunter S. Thompson

TO DAVISON THOMPSON:

Writing to his brother, Thompson tried to reconcile his acceptance of a recent small inheritance with his earlier stance that "inherited wealth" should be abolished.

July 7, 1976
Woody Creek, CO

Davison . . .

Congratulations. I have a letter here from one Jim B. Johnson in Memphis, saying I finally won my long and savage "complaint" against Howard P. Pritchard, Executor of the estate of Velma H. Ray, et al.

Needless to say, I feel a bit like the Lonesome End on the "et al." team—especially since I long ago tried to quit the squad altogether & split my share among the other "et al." members—but, as I explained to Mom on the phone quite a while ago, my offer (to quit & split, as it were) became null & void when it was judged to be legally non-feasible. That seemed fair to me then, and it still does. . . .

Which leaves me sitting here with this letter & xeroxed "settlement and decree" from Johnson, saying that all I have to do in order to collect $6000 is sign a receipt and send him my Social Security number. . . . But he didn't enclose any receipt and I can't tell whether I should send my SS No. to him or to you.

Johnson's letter also comes at a time when I'm feeling nervous about re-paying a loan from Noonan for an amount not much less than my share of the "et al." settlement. . . . So if you're sitting there wondering if I really want the money, the answer is yes; not so much because I want it or even feel I deserve it, but because I now *need* it. Juan recently disposed of $4200 by an accident of logistics so incredible that it would take me three pages to explain it, but the bottom line is that I just got back from a nightmarish vacation in Tobago to find that my "Summer of '76 Money Cushion" had been cut, in my absence, from $5000 to $800. . . .

But what the fuck? None of this gibberish really matters right now, does it? I've assured Noonan that his money is currently en route from a weird & mysterious source, and if it's at all possible I'd like to end this thing, receive & distribute my share of the funds, and get enough out of debt to quit writing about politics and get to work on a new novel that's due in Sept.

So please let me know what I must or should do, in order to get my hands on the money. I still feel like a drooling greedhead because of my part in this gig—mainly because one of the main points in my "tentative platform" when I was thinking about running for the U.S. Senate back in '74 had to do with my plan to abolish the whole concept of "inherited wealth" in this country; but now that I'm on the legal/public record in the Chancery Court of Tennessee as a complainant in a lawsuit over a contested will, I figure I might as well take the money.

As a Senator I could have skimmed $6000 a month with no trouble at all, for at least the next six years. . . . But now I guess I'll have to get by on my own, which means I have to keep a sharp eye on the trolling lines, for good or ill. . . . So it's back to the drawing boards and to hell with politics.

On other fronts, life at the Owl Farm remains much the same as always—a never-ending chain of crisis-peaks and occasional peaceful valleys. If I'd had any sense I'd have been a goddamn lawyer, but I'm a bit too old for that now, so I guess I'm stuck with whatever I am.

Right . . . and now I have to go into town to file a massive lawsuit against [George] Stranahan about my water rights, so I'll finish this and leave the next step with you. If I get a check in today's mail for the movie rights to *Vegas* (or any other unexpected windfall), I'll re-assess my position vis-à-vis my share of the settlement. The simple reality of *being able* to turn the money down would be a tremendous high for me—but right now that's a high I can't afford.

And to hell with all this. After 20 years of practice, I've developed a certain talent for affording un-affordable highs, and maybe I can deal with this one, too, in time. My latest news bulletin on your situation was decidedly upbeat, so I assume you're still holding the fort on your own terms—which is the best any of us can hope for in this world, I think; but every once in a while I get a powerful urge to abandon everything, change my name, and become a terminal wino in some rotten skid-row town like Galveston or Pittsburgh.

If you have any better ideas, let me know ASAP.

Zingo,
Hunter

DEMOCRATIC CONVENTION NOTES—2 HRS. BEFORE LEAVING WC FOR NYC:

Thompson composed this elegant reflection after a late-night swim two hours before he had to leave Woody Creek to cover the 1976 Democratic National Convention in New York City.

July 10, 1976
Woody Creek, CO

A full moon tonight, and a cold bright sky above the long pool behind the Jerome Hotel. The Milky Way looking down from so close that it looks like a madman with good reflexes could shoot the stars out of the sky, one by one, with something like a .264 Magnum or maybe a .220 Swift. The pool is warm, the bar is closed, Main Street is empty except for an occasional cop zooming by in one of the red Saabs they use. No cars on fire in the parking lot behind the Jerome tonight, no dope addicts lurking around in the darkness under the tent, no red-tipped cigarettes glowing suddenly back in the darkness where white iron lawn tables, wet on the tops from cold mist & dampness, sit under the big cottonwood trees behind the old *Aspen Times* building. . . .

Easing into the pool around 3:30, no racing dives at this hour of the morning when a 200 pound body hitting flat on the water would echo for three blocks . . . just quick & naked over the side and into the cold deep end, then pushing off fast to neutralize the cold, and then the burning energy takes over . . . cruising along with no sound, looking up at the stars and the blue-black infinity so close to my eyes now stinging from the first hit of chlorine . . . 21 laps with no sound but rippling water and blow-hole breathing like a whale. Marty Nolan[18] once told Sandy that I swim "like a school of whales." And Craig Vetter described my "rodent-like crawl." The only other animal who swims like me is the Stoat, but his reasons are different. The stoat wants the best possible combination of speed and silence; he is not especially concerned about "exercise." But I want the feeling of muscles pulling, stretching, pulling, relaxing—every muscle from the thin layers under my scalp to the tendons down in my toes, and this is the only stroke I know that pulls *every* muscle; and if I feel one that isn't working I can roll over on my side or kick vertically instead of like a frog, until I feel the lazy one come alive. . . . Pulling deep with the arms, almost straight down like rowing with muffled oars, fingers tight in a web/cup, legs intensely rigid at the end of each deep stroke to get the best possible glide, and then a moment of total relaxation just before the next stroke, when the energy of the glide starts falling off. This is a home-made stroke, mainly for ocean swimming because the face can be tucked down on the chest and the waves break *over* the head instead of into the face, and that mo-

18. Martin Nolan was a reporter for *The Boston Globe*.

ment of total relaxation between strokes lets the lymph glands/nodes empty, so the muscle fatigue of each stroke has time to dissipate instead of building up.

This is as close as I can come to peace—out in the middle of a big olympic-size pool at 3:30 in the morning; nobody can get to me out here, no phones ring, nobody can interrupt to, say, ask me about Jimmy Carter, to offer me drugs, to call me a bastard, or ask me why Claudine *really* shot Spider.[19] I am moving too fast to hear anything but the sound of moving water and the pumping of blood through my body and my own sputtered blasts of breathing between the long slow strokes. The Jerome is a 10-stroke pool, which means I can cut it to nine if I concentrate totally on every stroke—and if I keep my toes completely straight and my fingers straight and tight against my body at the end of every stroke, I can make it from end to end in eight strokes. But if I don't pull deep enough or fail to concentrate all the way to the end of each stroke, (or if I fuck up on my breathing) the Jerome can be an eleven or even a twelve-stroke pool.

Three extra strokes per lap for 21 laps is 63 extra strokes: 252 strokes to cover the same exact distance that I'd cover with 189 strokes if I concentrated on maximum thrust & glide, with minimum resistance in the water: the idea is to move like a torpedo instead of a terrified squid. . . .

Jesus! I am thinking like Jimmy Carter again—adapting the language of physics to the inefficient realities of everyday life, thinking in terms of the Power Train, concentrating on minimizing the ratio between energy and effect. The energy that goes into 63 wasted strokes could be used for writing these pages, for instance: 63 strokes would cancel at least three pages, and at my normal rate of one page an hour, that is the main part of a night's work at the typewriter. . . . Or maybe three delegates, in the context of presidential politics.

The language of physics and the language of law have always fascinated me; they are not the same, because the ends and antecedents are different, but there is a sameness in the precision and the efficiency, although the language of physics is bent to solving problems, while the language of law can be just as precise and efficient when used to create problems, or obscure them, or even to alter the nature of problems and create the appearance of a solution. . . . But there is no room for an adversary relationship in physics, because that in itself is a problem and a barrier.

Right . . . and to hell with all this. I wanted to sit down and write a few pages about what I *expect* from the next few days at the Democratic Convention in New York. I had not planned to go until last week, when I realized that Juan's incredible expenditure of $4200, along with Wenner's refusal to pay $5000 or so of my expenses for the Carter article, had put me deep in another

19. French pop singer Claudine Longet shot and killed her boyfriend, champion skier Spider Sabich, in 1976.

money-hole . . . and then came the idea for another annual conversation with Carter, whose reality has changed so drastically since I first met him that the most amazing thing about the change is that it now seems entirely logical. . . .

But I mainly want to get down *what I expect* to find in NYC, or at least what I plan & want to find—so I can have these pages as a baseline, when it comes time to write, exactly seven days from now.

What I want and expect is at least a good talk with Carter, and to be with him in his Americana hotel suite on the night of his nomination. We will need a day or so later, in Plains, for the sort of conversation that we had last May. And I expect to get that too. This is the first time I've ever asked for flat-out preferential treatment as a journalist. Jody Powell says there are a hell of a lot of journalists who want private time with the next president; he has a long list of requests, or even demands in some cases. . . . But my feeling about that is Fuck Them; where were they when there were no lines at Jimmy Carter's door? There was plenty of room last year on Jody's list of Requests for Interviews. In May of 1974 when I first met Carter—by accident, while covering Ted Kennedy—he was so hopelessly obscure that I turned down an invitation to spend the night at the Governor's Mansion in Atlanta with Carter and Kennedy . . . and in May of 1975 when I went down to Plains to have a personal talk with him about his just-announced candidacy, I called him at home and wound up spending the next two or three days with him at home, "sleeping" in the guest room over the garage . . . and the only other journalists I ran across during that time were two from *The Atlanta Constitution,* which had strongly opposed Carter before, during and after his term as governor. . . .

So this time I don't see any need to "be fair" when it comes to getting in line with the National Press. They had all the time and opportunities they needed to qualify for preferential treatment . . . and besides that, I have been sitting out on a very uncomfortable limb like a treed raccoon for the past year, while Carter was using my name at campaign appearances and the national press gents were telling each other that I'd finally gone over the hump into terminal brain damage, and while Dick Tuck was betting $100 at 50–1 against Carter's nomination, with me giving Tuck the same bet on Hugh Carey.[20] That bet is on video tape in Aspen, but—unlike sports bettors—politicians and journalists rarely pay off when they lose. Like Broder betting $500 with me on Humphrey against McGovern in the '72 California primary. . . . Yes, and it's now 7:55 a.m. in Woody Creek and my plane leaves at 10:00, and I haven't even started packing. Bill Dixon is in town at the Jerome and I have to meet him at the airport or maybe at the Holiday Inn for breakfast. He is going to the Convention and maybe we can finish these preliminary notes on the plane, on tape. . . . We get to Kennedy at 5:40. Carter arrives at 4:00, and I want to talk to him

20. Democrat Hugh Carey was governor of New York state.

tonight—mainly to say hello and have some fun with that Carter peanut bag I got last year in Plains.

There is also the VP problem, which looms crucial because it is the first thing Jimmy has come to grips with since he announced that has put him in a position where *any* choice he makes will force him out in the open to make a decision that will define himself in the eyes of a lot of people—including me—who are still not sure what kind of a *president* he will make. If he's already made the choice there is nothing I can do to change it, but if he hasn't and if he's still considering Glenn or Jackson over Church,[21] then I want to get to NY early enough to say whatever I can for Church. A Glenn, Jackson or even Stevenson choice will put me in a position where I will feel a nervous slippage in my footing inre: my stubborn support of Carter and my own confidence in him as a president . . . and since my deadline for the article is next Friday, I won't have time to "carefully consider" my reaction to a choice that strikes me as an ominous indicator, but only to write on the basis of instinct & what I already know, which means Carter could put me in a position of having to stomp on him in print in the article next week—if only to cover myself. This is the first time I have ever backed a winner in national politics, except for 1960 when I couldn't vote, and now I am stuck with Carter: And he is stuck with me. Selah. And now it's time to pack . . . (end).

TO PAUL GORMAN, WBAI-FM:

As Jimmy Carter's presidential campaign really began to take flight, a number of media organizations asked Thompson for copies of the interviews he had taped with the now-Democratic nominee in 1974 and 1975, back when the rest of the national press were calling Carter "Jimmy Who?"

August 1, 1976
Woody Creek, CO

Dear Paul,

RS forwarded to me what appears to be an undated "letter to the editor" from you, regarding various tapes of my conversations with Jimmy Carter in 1974 and 1975 . . . and since the nut of your letter seems identical with similar complaints I've received from *Time* and other magazines, I figured I'd try to answer all you dumb cocksuckers at the same time, rather than deal with these complaints individually. . . . To wit:

I have been a working journalist for at least ten years, dealing with all kinds of publications and all kinds of editors—but this is the first time any national-media editor(s) with an I.Q. above 66 has ever suggested that I have some kind

21. Ohio freshman senator John Glenn, the first U.S. astronaut to orbit the Earth, in February 1962; veteran Washington senator Henry "Scoop" Jackson; and Idaho Democrat Frank Church, chairman of the U.S. Senate's 1975–76 investigative hearings on the CIA and its activities.

of inherent obligation or duty to work for no money at all. In the last graf of your letter to *RS*, for instance, you ask, "Would Hunter be willing to turn (These Tapes) over to us voluntarily?" So that you, *Time,* WBAI and all other interested parties "could share these experiences and thus be comforted."

Well . . . Let me assure you, Gorman, that I have never felt any overwhelming need to make either you or the editors of *Time* magazine "comfortable." That is not my business. And as a matter of fact I don't give a flying fuck if you live or die—or what you think about Carter, or me, or my opinions about Carter, or his opinions about me; or anything else, for that matter. . . . Nor do I feel any obligation or need to "comfort" the editors of *Time,* Ron Rosenbaum[22] or Jann Wenner by working for free. I don't know how you pay your rent, but I pay mine by *selling my work*—and since my work as a journalist almost always involves the use of at least one and sometimes three or four (of my own) tape recorders, I am genuinely baffled at any suggestion from an editor or *any* professional journalist that I should "voluntarily turn over" my tapes, notebooks, photographs or even my random opinions to the editors of *Time,* WBAI, *Rolling Stone* or anybody else who clearly plans to use *my work* for their own personal, professional and/or commercial benefit.

If you, Jann, *Time,* or anybody else wants to *buy* either tapes or transcripts of my conversations with Jimmy Carter or anyone else, all you have to do is send me a check—and the price, to you, is now about $2000 per cassette (90 minutes each), or you can have *any three* of the twelve (12) for $5000.

And if you think that's high, consider that the price to *RS* is exactly double what I'm quoting to you—and the price to *Time* is exactly double the *RS* price. (These price quotations are at least ten times higher now than they were six months ago, and they are not going to get any lower—so the question now is how much it is worth to you, *Time* or Wenner to "be thus comforted." And the price covers all rights to the unedited originals, FOB the office of my agent, Lynn Nesbit, in New York.) If *Rolling Stone* had chosen to publish the transcripts of any of these tapes during the past year, all Wenner had to do was pay for them—and if you or *Time* want them now, the same condition applies. As a free-lance writer, I feel I have a definite obligation to myself and my family to *get paid for my work,* and no amount of public or private abuse from assholes like you or the editors of *Time* is going to alter my position on that point.

As for the Carter "Law Day speech," the entire transcript was scheduled to run in the same issue of *RS* that carried my article on Carter that Wenner chose to label an "endorsement," and nobody has ever explained to me why it didn't. If you want an *edited version* of that one, all you have to do is spend 13 cents on a letter to Hamilton Jordan at Carter headquarters in Atlanta . . . and if you want an *unedited* version, which is something like 36 minutes long, send my agent a check for $1500 before September 1, and I'll send you a broadcast-

22. Ronald Rosenbaum wrote on politics for New York's alternative weekly *The Village Voice.*

quality cassette by air express, at my own expense. On Sept. 2, the price (to you) will be $3000; on November 3 it will be $6000, and on Jan. 1, 1977 it will be $15,000.

And that's about it for now, Gorman. I don't know what you do for WBAI, but I assume you get paid for it—and if you get paid for your work, what the fuck makes you think I shouldn't get paid for mine? I don't recall seeing you or any other media gents standing in line outside Jimmy Carter's door when I first went down to Plains to ask him why he was running for president. You and *Time* and all the others had about 18 free months to ask him anything you wanted to, and he had plenty of time to answer. . . . But I guess you were busy with other matters then, just like Carter is busy with other matters now. . . .

And so am I, old sport—but I'm not so busy that I can't take a little time off to do business with people like you and the editors of *Time*. I'm not really looking forward to it, but I'm getting a little tired of this Manhattan cocktail-party bullshit about all These Tapes you people seem to think I should "voluntarily" turn over to you, just so you can "be thus comforted."

Jesus, Gorman, my heart bleeds for you—but if you want any comfort from me and the work I did while you and your ilk were begging for interviews with Hubert Humphrey, it's going to cost (you) $22 a minute—and if that seems expensive to you, just wait until the next time you ask.

Sincerely,
Hunter S. Thompson

cc:
—*Time*
—Jimmy Carter
—Jann Wenner
—Others as needed

TO CAPTAIN VITO ADAMO:

A Rolling Stone *reader from Las Vegas had written to Thompson alleging that there had been more to the 1975* Mayaguez *incident than the national media had reported, or the Ford administration let on.*

August 1, 1976
Woody Creek, CO

Capt. Vito Adamo
5204 Koa Ave.
Las Vegas, Nev. 89122

Dear Captain Adamo,

Your (undated) letter to me was forwarded by the *Rolling Stone* office in San Francisco & apparently arrived here while I was "covering" the Democratic

Convention in New York. No doubt I am late in replying, but this goddamn election year has taken up most of my time and focus for the past six months and I have let a lot of things slide that I should have dealt with a long time ago.

Your letter was one of these, and I can only apologize for my tardiness in getting back to you . . . and I will get in touch with you again just as soon as I can evaluate the possibilities of using the material you sent me in the context of a story on "the *Mayaguez* affair," which is something I've spent a lot of time on, but never quite put together.

The problem—as always in journalism—has been the reluctance of editors to pay for my research on a story that I can't guarantee will result in a newsstand blockbuster. I was in Bangkok when the *Mayaguez* thing happened, and I knew at the time that it was not what it seemed, but I have never been able to find that one hot handle that editors need to make them reach for their checkbooks . . . and although the material you sent has re-kindled my own interest in the story, I have gone over it several times without finding any single (and necessarily simplistic) idea, fact or connection that would give me the kind of leverage to convince a money-editor to pay for the time and research it would take me to link your situation with that of "the *Mayaguez* affair." The fact that you and I and a lot of other people (including several Congressmen) are convinced that the whole thing was a set-up is not enough, unfortunately. What I need is at least one fact or even a believable allegation that I can use as a can-opener for what is obviously a strange can of worms . . . and if you can give me that, in one or two paragraphs that I can use as a sort of ice-breaker to convince my publisher that there *really is* some light at the end of this tunnel, I think I can take it from there.

What we have here is a story that nobody really believes or understands, but which so far lacks that one key link (like the testimony of the photographer who took the My Lai photos) to put the journalistic machinery in gear. . . . And if you can search your memory, your perceptions or even your valid suspicions and give me the can-opener, I think we can raise some much-needed hell on this one.

Okay for now. I hope to hear from you soon.

Sincerely,
Hunter S. Thompson

FROM U.S. SENATOR GARY HART:

Hart replied promptly to constituent Thompson's concerns.

August 2, 1976
Washington, D.C.

Dear Hunter:

Let me first apologize for my tardiness in replying to your July 1 communiqué. Each time I've tried to respond, the sight of the *Rolling Stone* letterhead has made me misty, taking me back to that night on the East Side when our throng of irate—but unified—Democrats milled about outside the week's most prestigious fête. My present avocation, of course, requires prudence in all matters. And knowing New York's streets to be perilous after sun-down, I retired to more congenial surroundings—P. J. Clarke's.

Now, turning to the concerns of my constituents . . .

Senate Bill S.1 has been kept at bay, at least for the present. At the next session of Congress, Senators Kennedy and McClellan[23] intend to introduce a compromise measure which hopefully will eliminate the Bill's most offensive provisions. The concept of a federal criminal code is a sound one, but I will continue to oppose any version that poses a threat to civil liberties. In the meantime, fear and loathing would probably be premature.

The news item you refer to was related to decontrol of middle distillates. They are a form of home fuel oil, but not the type you consume with such abandon.

Duke, I'm not one to moralize, but all that propane can't be good for you. What you do in the privacy of your home is your business, but cheap thrills can break you. I'll say no more about that.

Natural gas decontrol was a hotly debated item this winter. I supported that measure in conjunction with efforts to deconcentrate the oil and gas industry. I am convinced that deconcentration will restore vigorous competition and thereby reduce costs to the consumer. Even ranchers. Enclosed are summaries of the Senate votes on that issue.

In a first step toward restraining the predations of your propane supplier, I have forwarded to our Denver office a copy of the Hooley Memorandum and your frightening response. Hapless Hooley is out of his league.

Until we succeed in bringing the likes of Hooley to their knees, we must all do our best to reduce the wanton consumption of propane and other central nervous system stimulants. I fear we Americans may all be getting soft. It is well to remember that our forebears endured winters far more harsh than last year's, snug in their wickiups and calmly awaiting eternal Spring's first bloom.

Sincerely,
Gary Hart

TO U.S. SENATOR GARY HART:

Of the current religious drift among politicians, Thompson remarked: "Being on Nixon's 'enemies list' was one thing, but being on God's is something else entirely."

23. Longtime Senate Appropriations Committee chairman John McClellan of Arkansas.

August 6, 1976
Woody Creek, CO

Dear Gary,

You continue to amaze me, old sport: I always knew you could dance—but now it looks like you think you can sing, too (viz: your letter of Aug 2).

Where will this madness end? Maybe I should check my Chinese calendar and find out what year this is: The Year of the Preacher? The Hyena? The Stoat? There must be *some* reason for this sudden frenzy of brazen ambition and assertiveness in the religious community. What do you people *want,* anyway? Is there any connection between this New Wave of power-crazed preachers and a full-page photograph in the July issue of *The Cross and the Flag* (Vol. 35, No. 4) that shows God stroking confidently across the finish line, far ahead of his challengers, in the annual River Styx, 8-mile freestyle "Contest of Champions"?

Probably so. With Gerald L.K. Smith leaking photos like this one, I have to assume—since I am, in fact, one of the shrewdest political journalists of our time—that God is in fact on the "terminal list," and now that the word has finally filtered down to the Lay Preacher level, you buggers are going to subject the rest of us to some kind of brutish power struggle, to see who will take over and fill that awesome vacuum. . . .

Indeed. I saw this hellish situation developing back in 1973, when I was still seriously pondering my Senate bid. As a Doctor of Divinity, a native Southerner and a natural power-junkie of the first rank, there was never any question that I could knock *you* off and win the seat easily—but Sandy and Juan, as you know, refused to move back to Washington under *any* circumstances; and when I had Caddell take a poll in Colorado on my chances of winning, with the slogan, "If Elected, I Will *Not* Go to Washington," the numbers came out almost exactly 50–50, against Allot . . . and then I remembered all the trouble I used to have with the Executive Protection Service when I would go out in Rock Creek Park and shoot the .44 Magnum at rabid squirrels so I figured, "What the hell? Gary needs the work, so I'll let *him* go to Washington, while I pursue my own lust for power in stranger and far more arcane ways. . . ." Which I did, and now you see what I'm stuck with: Some knotty little cracker who (allegedly) told Mike Howard the other day that he "sees little difference between the Warren and Burger (U.S. Supreme) Courts."[24]

Goddamnit, I *knew* I was taking a nasty risk by making even a tentative and temporary exception to my basic Scorched Earth Policy with regard to politicians—but the foul spectre of Hubert Humphrey and a gambler's natural af-

24. Chief Justice of the United States Warren E. Burger, appointed by President Nixon in 1969, led the Supreme Court back to a more conservative approach than the judicial activism of his predecessor Earl Warren, the former Republican governor of California appointed to the Court by President Eisenhower in 1953.

fection for one of his own, hand-picked long-shots must have taken a serious toll on my better, more savage instincts. . . .

Whoops! I write so few letters these days that every once in a while I tend to forget who/whom I'm writing to. . . . But what the hell? If you can leak *my* letter, I guess it's only fair that I can leak *yours*—along with all those thinly-veiled references to your propane habit & other weird predilections. If you own any propane stock, I suggest you get rid of it immediately. . . .

I'll take it off your hands for 22 cents on the dollar. Should I send you a check, or bring the cash to Washington in a brown paper bag? Let me know on this, ASAP. . . .

And now, with regard to more tangible matters . . . I am going to count on you to keep me advised on the progress of S.1. Do you have any idea how Carter feels about it? His (alleged) remark about Burger vs. Warren may be the tip of a very ugly ice-berg . . . we are not knee-jerk civil libertarian here; on the basis of my own experience with Jimmy, I get the feeling that his tolerance of other people's quirks, sins and wrong-minded personal behavior is rooted more in his Baptist concept of "grace" than any intellectual commitment to civil rights. (Just because Jesus refused (allegedly) to judge the Fallen Woman in public doesn't mean he was wiping her slate clean, eh? Being on Nixon's "enemies list" was one thing, but being on God's is something else entirely. . . .)

And in the case of my own (alleged) civil liberties, the question of the moment seems to be whether I'll be set up and busted by the "President Ford Committee" *before November,* in an effort to embarrass Carter—or whether I'll get a pass from Ford & Specter,[25] and then get busted by Carter, perhaps at his own Inauguration, on direct orders from God. How many motes can a Righteous Man tolerate in his own eyes, before he has to blink?

Which brings us to the matter of my recent unpleasantness vis-à-vis the Williams Energy Company and the now-infamous "Hooley Memorandum." On my return from that ill-fated trip to NYC for the Big Party you couldn't crash, I found a long and detailed letter from somebody in the Williams hierarchy. [Enclosed is a] xerox copy of same explaining that the above-mentioned "S. Hooley" was in fact a hapless wretch of a clerk whose name is Mrs. Sandra Hooley, and whose figures (in the memorandum) were as faulty as the apparent intent of her language. In any case, she has taken a temporary leave of absence until her husband has settled my hash, and in the meantime my debt to Williams has been temporarily stabilized at $99 per month, on a year-round "balanced-payment" basis. . . . So let's hold any action on that one in limbo, until I can get a better fix on the realities of this goddamn, increasingly-menacing fuel-cost situation.

25. Republican senator Arlen Specter of Pennsylvania was a top staff lawyer on the 1964 Warren Commission, appointed to investigate the assassination of John F. Kennedy; then congressman Gerald R. Ford of Michigan was a member of the commission.

According to various "resident experts" on Solar home-heating, my house is almost ideally situated and constructed for easy conversion to solar heating. . . . So I think I'll ignore Williams until they jack up their prices again—or until I catch S. Hooley's husband creeping around the Owl Farm at night with a Bowie knife in his teeth—and concentrate in the meantime on converting to solar heat. Can you give me any specific leads, names or engineering information on this subject?

Your votes inre: Gouging & De-Regulation continue to haunt me, but I know better than to hassle you on any question I don't already have all the answers to, so I'll postpone any drastic action on that one until we can talk about it.

And . . . yes . . . speaking of "talk," I just made an arrangement with Wenner that will allow me to "cover" the GOP convention on TV, instead of going to Kansas City . . . and it occurs to me that we could probably have some fun if you wanted to come out here and watch the thing with me: A sort of "guest commentator" gig, as it were.

Ye gods! I just found this letter in the typewriter and I thought it was mailed three days ago. . . . How has my organizational discipline gone so lax? . . . And why? That one is the larger question, eh?

Indeed . . . and since I need time to ponder it, I think I'll chop this letter off right here and get back to work: And since the letter is so delayed, I'll probably talk to you on the phone before you get it. . . . But meanwhile, consider the idea of coming over here and watching the GOP brawl with me on TV. (The Owl Farm is an Equal Opportunity Resort—Women & Children are Welcome. . . .)

Let me know on this ASAP. I'll need at least 48 hours to prepare myself, metaphysically, if I'm going to have a politician on the premises. . . . Yeah, and that's it for now:

Hunter

MEMO FROM THE SPORTS DESK: NO. 3/0076108

Music has always acted as a tonic on both Raoul Duke and Hunter S. Thompson.

August, 1976
Woody Creek, CO

To: The Editor
From: Raoul Duke
Subject: The Agonies of Dr. Thompson

Pursuant to your query of August 1, I am forwarding the entire file vis-à-vis Dr. Thompson's recent Unpleasantness with the Liberal/Elitist Media. That is the Doctor's phrase, not mine. To me, they are just a gang of flatulent Jews who took the "D" train by mistake. . . .

. . . once again; And you have to wonder just how many times a fragile intelligence can make that sort of mistake, which results in a high-speed, seemingly endless sprint through the sewers, all the way from the Village up to Harlem at 125th (is that right? Or is it 110th? Jesus—does the "D" train still exist?). . . . Anyway, I know from experience that nobody except a certified egomaniac or the purest kind of *idiot-savant* can make that mistake more than twice without suffering an irretrievable loss of self-confidence. There are a lot of small and meaningless mistakes a person can make in this world, but taking the "D" train by mistake is not one of them. Somewhere around the middle of Central Park, about 200 feet under the zoo, a cold and sudden flash that feels like a 40-pound water rat gnawing the coccyx bone off the base of your spine causes every muscle in the lower back to seize up and the knees to feel like rubber bands along with extreme pain—every thirty seconds from spasms of the bladder and the mouth goes slack like the sun-rotted lips of a dead walrus and the bile wells up in the throat and drools viscously out of the cracks between clenched teeth and down on the chest and the shirt in long wet foul-smelling stains and when the brain is finally able to stabilize itself from the first wave of seizures long enough to articulate some kind of dim and desperate emergency-message to the medulla. . . . When the spasms finally slow down to one every 60 seconds instead of one every 30 and you can finally take a breath between the mindless screams of pain and terror that kept erupting out of the blood-choked throat in long blasts of noise and reddish sputum, you finally hear a voice that you know is your own saying, "Ye fucking gods! I've done it again! This thing is . . . yes . . . the goddamn "D" train, and the next stop is Harlem: Millions of wild niggers, and all of them crazy with hate. Should I abandon all hope and just fall out when we get to 125th and hope to god I can get to the third rail before the niggers get hold of me?"

. . . Ah, *hit it* Russell! You twisted little bastard. ". . . Let me see you dance, ooooooohhhhhh baby, let me see you dance. . . . " *Stomp* on that bastard! Whip on it!

Excuse me. Yes. This kind of objective journalism is a hard thing to mix with the Amazing Rhythm Aces and that ballbuster love song that Mr. Smith and Mr. Brown put together . . . so let's have a truce for just a minute or two while I get across the room and fuck with those knobs. I have 80 speakers in this room and I can crank 210 big McIntosh/Nakamichi watts into every one of them. . . . But my work tends to suffer when I weaken and go for The Knobs; there is something in this wild and elegant combination of music, memories, blood-lust and that awesome mass of electronics over there in the corner that tends to knock the edge off my classical training . . . and I am still not sure what it means; probably it is brain damage; nobody with good sense would try to work under these frenzied circumstances. Every time Russell leans into one of his long, mournful curls I feel a great pressure in my balls and somewhere up in the front edge of my brain I hear a voice that I never even recognize except between two and six in the dark & quiet hours and it's telling me to get the hell away from this electric pimp and jump across the room to wallow in that maze of hot wires, Azimuth Alignment Beacons and Pitch Control Screws. . . . Yes, and the big silver Gain Control knobs, the "A" and "B" slope-adjustments on the Frequency Energizer . . .

Ah, jesus, here we go again. . . . "Standin beside the ocean, lookin across the bay . . . Lights are flickerin all along the shore: People dancin there, but I don't dance no more. . . ."

And then, BOOM! the afterburner kicks in, The Crank, and every log in the house rattles with the jackhammer screech of [James] Hooker's piano, the palm fronds tremble, the big thermopane windows start to bulge, and that pompous brute of a peacock out there on the porch starts screaming and Lazlo the 100 pound waterhead Doberman is trying to get through the wire mesh, un-hinged by the primitive, demented intensity of the peacock's hellish screams. . . .

Madness, madness . . . But there is still a bit of room at the top; there is still about a half-inch of slack behind the Output knob on the Nakamichi; we could pump about 20 more decibels into this situation by screwing that one all the way over, and with a delicate touch on both Gain Control knobs we could peg the VU needle and add maybe 10 more decibels. . . . Which would get the whole gig humming along at something like 105, ten or fifteen points above the pain threshold, and by killing all the filters and flogging the bass and treble knobs all the way over, we can move things up to 110 without breaking the windows. . . . One of the bass speaker boxes is starting to emit smoke; or maybe that acrid-smelling blue haze is coming from one of the Universal 3-Way Dividing Network boxes. . . .

But to hell with the smoke; the first time this happened, I panicked and shut down the whole system—but when I took the back off the speaker box I realized that it was only the insulation burning, which is not a serious matter when you have 80 speakers in one room. According to the human cinder who built this system and then left town without ever giving me a schematic to show me how to put it back together in case some dope addict falls into the wiring, I can afford to sacrifice at least ten speakers to fire and smoke without any serious fall-off in sound quality. The break-point, he says, would be somewhere between 15 and 20. At that point—with 15 or 20 speakers burned into cinders, disappearing one after another in balls of blue smoke—I would start getting some fuzz on the low end, and also a loss in the clarity.

Which is not what I want. It has taken me too long to lash this monster together to just sit here and watch it go up in smoke for no reason except to drive that goddamn brainless Doberman into such a frenzy that he will hurl himself right through the wire and into the peacocks' turf. . . . I have been trying to push Lazlo around that bend for about two years now, but he still resists. He will sneak in there and suck an egg once in a while, but only when some kind of full-moon kinkiness like blueballs or meat-hunger has lured the Main Squeeze off his perch and out into the fields to look for something to eat, kill, penetrate or maybe just rip into shreds for no good reason at all.

I have lived with a lot of mean, weird animals in my time, but I have never seen anything even half as mean and weird as a male peacock when he finally gets a fix on whatever it is that looks like an obstacle between him and whatever he wants to do. A peacock might brood for three days about whether or not to walk across the driveway and eat a wild strawberry—but once he has pondered all the factors, weighed all the risks, measured the distance and analyzed every centimeter of the terrain between him and the strawberry that he has watched long enough to be sure it is really there and that he really wants to eat it, the only two beasts on this earth that *might* be crazy or vicious enough to deliberately try to prevent the peacock from getting to the strawberry would be a wolverine or a hammerhead shark.

Lazlo, the brainless Doberman, will jump out of a speeding car and run right through a glass door to get his teeth around the eyeball of a 200 pound Great Dane—but somewhere deep in his twisted Prussian genes is at least one wise and rational chromosome that short-circuits all his natural instincts whenever it looks like he might be on a collision course with the peacock. There is a vast potential for treachery and genuine savagery bred into the brain of most Dobermans: One of the problems with using them as guard dogs, for instance, is that you can never be sure that a Doberman—unlike a German Shepherd—will bark or even snarl at a human intruder before he gets the target lined up and springs off like some kind of noiseless, black torpedo on that final eight or nine yard sprint that ends with a long, silent leap in the general direction of the head and neck area of some poor bastard who might be idly lighting a cigarette or adjusting the handkerchief shrouding his flashlight about half a second before he gets hit with what is referred to in the psycho-medical profession as "extreme trauma." Anybody who has ever been attacked by a Doberman in the darkness, with no warning at all, will spend the rest of his life feeling just a little more nervous and fearful about almost everything than he felt before "the trauma." There is a realm of psychic peace in the human brain that, once violated, is gone forever.

TO JIM SILBERMAN, RANDOM HOUSE:

Portions of this thoughtful letter to Thompson's editor at Random House were published in 1990's Songs of the Doomed.

September 1, 1976
Woody Creek, CO

OUTLINE: "F.O.B. GALVESTON" (WORKING TITLE)

A NOVEL BY: HST . . . IN FOUR PARTS, 26 SCENES, APP. 80,000 WORDS

Capsule comment & description

The spine of this story is short, tight and flexible. It has taken me about six months of brooding and plotting to lash it together—in my mind & on tape & in various notebooks—and now that I have a working skeleton, I'd like to keep this outline as short as possible. But I can make it as long as necessary, so feel free to let me know if what follows doesn't make the nut. I have a two-pound file of news clips, U.S. Treasury Dept. internal memos, confidential sources, personal contacts and five or six progressively tighter plot-lines that I can cannibalize and hurl into the breach, on short notice. . . . But, given the general nature and traditional fate of "book outlines," the only point I want to make with this one is that I am finally committed to this story on a level that I only flirted with until about two months ago. Eight years of intensely personal involvement in political journalism is a hard habit to break: There is always the tendency and/or the temptation to want to keep at least one hand in that game, if only for the promise of movement and instant action—but there is also a point of clearly diminishing returns, and I think I reached that point about two years ago, for good or ill. That was when the idea for a book set in Texas first occurred to me—but at the time I was still thinking in terms of journalism, and it was not until very recently, when I was finally faced with a choice between going to Texas to work on this story or going to Plains, Georgia to work on Jimmy Carter, that I made a conscious decision to work with both hands on a novel, instead of keeping my left hand in journalism, my right hand in fiction, and my head in a mean-tempered limbo. . . .

And so much for all that. The cord is cut now: I have quit that outpost of progress called the National Affairs Desk that I founded at *Rolling Stone,* and in the slow process of quitting I drifted so far from the backstairs complexities of national politics that I couldn't go back to it now, even if I wanted to . . . and that, I think, is a point I had to reach and recognize on my own, and for my own reasons. As long as the constant speedy lure of political journalism seemed more essential and important to me than the ugly, slow-burning reality of writing a novel, any effort to write fiction would have been a part-time, left-handed gig (like my recent journalism). . . . And in any other line of work except writing, people who try to deal with the world and life and reality off a split-focus base are called "schizoid" and taken off the streets, as it were, for their own and the greater good.

Now, after more than a week of extremely disorienting conversations regarding the ultimate fate of this story—(a novel? a screenplay? or both?)—I feel in the grip of a serious confusion, to wit: The story as I originally conceived it, more than two years ago, was a first-person "journalistic novel," set in Texas and rooted in a genuine conflict between Innocence and Violence that seemed to be the source of a unique and classically "American" style of energy that I hadn't felt since my first visit to Brazil in 1962, or to California in 1959. It was the same level of energy that I sensed on my first contact with the Hell's Angels, my first visit to Las Vegas and my first few days in the frenzied vortex of a U.S. presidential campaign. . . . But I knew that, in order to deal properly with any story set in Texas, I would have to move for a year to Houston or Dallas or Austin and actually live there; and this was the harsh reality that I wasn't quite ready to face two years ago. There were other stories to get involved in, other places to go, and the sudden millstone of personal notoriety that caused so many unexpected changes in my life-stance that I still haven't regained my balance. . . . It was one thing to slip into Texas as an anonymous young journalist with a subsistence-level book contract, and quite another to boom into a state full of boomers with a national reputation as some kind of lunatic felon, a journalistic Billy the Kid and a cartoon-character that appeared every day in newspapers all over Texas. That kind of act is known, among boomers, as a "hard dollar"—and anybody who thinks otherwise should try it for a while.

In any case, that and a few other good reasons is why I kept postponing the book on Texas. . . . But I continued to brood on it, and one of the people I brooded with from time to time was Bob Rafelson, a film director and personal friend who listened to my gibberish about Texas and violence and energy for so long that he eventually began brooding on the story himself, and finally suggested that it might work better as a film than as a book.

At that point I was still thinking vaguely about writing a book on the '76 presidential campaign and taking all the 50–1 bets I could get on my own lonely dark horse—some yahoo from Georgia named Carter—and so for all the obvious reasons that seemed at the time to mandate another HST/Campaign book, my "Texas Project" remained in an oddly-intense state of "talking limbo" for most of 1975. Rafelson was totally involved in the making of *Stay Hungry,*[26] and since there was nobody else to prod me along inre: Texas, I ignored my own fast-rising conviction that another HST/Campaign book would be a fatal mistake that would lock me for life into Teddy White's footsteps, and fell prey to the natural gambler's affection for his own long-shot—and it was not until I went up to New Hampshire to cover the first primary that I understood the finality of the choice I was drifting into. The New Hampshire results were all I needed to prove my point as a gambler and a seer, but the personal

26. Director Bob Rafelson's 1976 movie of Charles Gaines's novel *Stay Hungry,* about bodybuilding in the New South, starred Jeff Bridges, Sally Field, and Arnold Schwarzenegger.

notoriety I'd accrued since 1972 had changed my role as a journalist so drastically that even the Secret Service treated me with embarrassing deference, and I couldn't walk into a bar without total strangers wanting to argue with me or ask for my autograph. . . . And for two days after the New Hampshire primary I sat around Charles Gaines' house on a hill near a hamlet called Concoontook (sp?), trying to decide whether I should keep on covering the '76 campaign and adjust to my new persona, or to quit political journalism altogether and get seriously to work on a novel—which is something I've been planning to do ever since I finished my ill-fated *Rum Diary* almost 15 years ago. I have never had much respect or affection for journalism, but for the past 10 years it has been both a dependable meal-ticket and a valid passport to the cockpit(s) of whatever action, crisis, movement or instant history I wanted to be a part of.

And it worked, folks. Between 1962, when I was working for *The National Observer* and got the first private interview with the new president of Peru in the wake of a military takeover, until 1975 when I failed to get the first interview with the VC/NVA Colonel who orchestrated the fifth-column seizure of Saigon as the last Americans fled, I managed—by using almost any kind of valid or invalid journalistic credentials I could get my hands on—to get myself personally involved in just about everything that interested me: from Berkeley to Chicago, Las Vegas to the White House, shark-fishing, street-fighting, dope-smuggling, Hell's Angels, Super Bowls, local politics and a few things I'd prefer not to mention until various statutes of limitations expire.

Indeed. Those were good years for almost any kind of journalism; it was the main language of a very public and political decade. . . . But I suspect it will not be the main language of the 1970s, or at least not for me and most of the people I know. Very few of them subscribe to the same papers or magazines now that they subscribed to five or even two years ago, and even fewer plan to vote in the '76 general election. Not even the best and most perceptive journalists covering the presidential campaign seem to care who will win it, or why. . . . And neither do I, for that matter: After ten years of the most intense kind of personal and professional involvement in national politics, it occurs to me now that I could have left it all alone, and—except for my role as a journalist and all the constant action it plunged me into—my life would not have been much different, regardless of who won or lost any one of the myriad clashes, causes, confrontations, election brawls, chases and other high-adrenaline situations that I found myself drawn to.

Ah . . . but this is a hasty judgement, and probably not true: I can think of at least a half-dozen public realities that I managed, for good or ill, to affect by my presence, participation or journalistic advocacy—(and in retrospect I'm about 98% happy with whatever ripples I caused in the great swamp of history)—and there were also those handful of moments when my life might have been drastically changed by what did *not* happen: like dying a violent death, a fate I seem to narrowly avoid about once every year, or going to prison, or becoming a junkie, or becoming an indentured servant to Jann Wenner, or running off to Bermuda with Eleanor McGovern, or becoming Sheriff of Pitkin County, the Governor of American Samoa or a speech-writer for Jimmy Carter. . . .

Indeed . . . and on balance, my behavior as a person, writer, advocate, midnight-strategist, hatchet-man and serious gambler for at least the past ten years has been generally beneficial to myself, my friends, my wife and son, and most of the people I tend to side with, whenever the deal goes down. . . . Which is not a bad thing to look back on: and if I seem a bit cynical, at this point, or a trifle uncertain about The Meaning of It All, it is probably because of my secret conviction that a whole generation of journalists and journalism went over the hump with the Nixon/Watergate story, and that the odds against any of us ever hitting that kind of peak again are impossibly long. It was not just the Watergate story itself, but the fact that nobody who worked on the leading edge of journalism in the years between 1960 and 1975 could have asked or even hoped for a better or more dramatically perfect climax to what now seems like one long, violent and incredibly active story. When I proposed that book on "The Death of the American Dream" back in 1967 and then rushed off to cover the first act of Nixon's political "comeback" in the '68 New Hampshire primary, my instinct was better than any of us knew at the time—because the saga of Richard Nixon *is* The Death of the American Dream. He was our Gatsby, but the light on the end of his pier was black instead of green. . . . Whoever writes the true biography of Richard Nixon will write the definitive book on "The American Dream."

We should keep that in mind, because that is the book I was just beginning to scent, 10 years ago. I was hearing the music, but I am not a musician and I couldn't "put it to words," and even when I found the right lyrics, in bits and pieces of almost everything I wrote in those years, it was not until I stood in the wet grass of the White House rose garden and watched Nixon stumble onto the helicopter that would carry him into exile that I heard the music again. . . .

And I am still hearing it; but I am not quite ready to write the lyrics yet—and in the meantime I want to write a story that will leap and roll and crackle, a quick and brutal tale of *life in a world without Nixon.* What I need right now, I think, is a bit of a workout, something more along the lines of *Fear & Loathing in Las Vegas* than the Saga of Horatio Nixon & the Death of the American Dream.

NO . . . don't say it, Jim. Don't even *think* it right now. We both know what kind of pain & suffering & preternatural concentration the Nixon book will require, and I simply can't stand it right now. It's too goddamn heavy, and it would take at least two & probably three years of extremely focused research, thinking & writing; because it is obviously the one book I've been instinctively gearing down to write for lo, these many years. . . . But that one will have to wait at least until we get Nixon's own version of his ugly rise and fall, and in the meantime I think I've paid enough dues to justify another sort of busman's vacation, on the order of *F&L in Las Vegas,* which is far and away my personal favorite of the three books I've written: It was also the most fun to write, the best and most economical piece of sustained "pure writing" I've ever done, and sooner or later it will prove to be the most financially successful of the three. . . . Which is fitting, because *Vegas* is a book that no other living writer could have written. . . .

Indeed, and to hell with all that. What I'm saying now is that I think it's about time for me to indulge, once again, that whole, high-powered strata of my writer's energy that keeps bubbling up to the surface of all my journalism and confusing my standard-brand colleagues so badly that even the ones who consistently feel free to plagiarize my best concepts and perceptions seem almost personally offended by the style & stance of my "Gonzo journalism."

Which rarely bothers me—but Rarely is different from Never, and every once in a while I think it's healthy to clear the deck and lay a serious fireball on some of these bastards who lack either the grace or the integrity or both to understand that they can't have it both ways. There are numerous lame and sterile ways to counter *surface* plagarizm (sp?), but the only sure and final cure is to write something so clearly and brutally original that only a fool would risk plagiarizing it . . . and that's what I'd like to do now: If "Gonzo journalism" is essentially the "art" (or compulsion) of imposing a novelistic form on journalistic content then the next logical step in the "Gonzo process" would seem to be a 180 degree reversal of that process, by writing a "journalistic novel."

Which is bullshit, of course, because on the high end is only one real difference between the two forms—and that is the rigidly vested interest in the maintenance of a polar (or strictly polarized) separation of "fiction" and "journalism" by at least two generations of New York–anchored writers who spent most of their working lives learning, practicing and finally insisting (on) the esthetic validity of that separation.

And what the hell? I suspect it's genuinely important to them, so why not concede it? Ten years from now I might feel in a mood to force that kind of merger, but for now the formal separation works in my favor, because it gives me a straw man to beat on, and stir the buggers up. Just for the record, however—and one of these days I hope to find enough time to explain this notion properly—the only real difference between "journalism" and "fiction" in my own mind is *legalistic*: With our contemporary, standard-brand journalism as nothing more than a sloppy, lay-extension of the Rules of Evidence, rooted in the Adversary Relationship that governs our 20th century American trial procedure; and the best & highest kind of contemporary fiction or even High Novelistic Journalism with its roots in the thinking of those essentially Jeffersonian pragmatists often referred to by historians as "the great Stoic lawyers of ancient Rome. . . ."

And, mother of babbling Jesus, how did I get into this? The only point I wanted to make was that—by conceding what I consider a false distinction between journalism & fiction—I can jangle the rules even further by claiming to have made a 180 degree turn, quitting journalism and going back to The Novel, while in fact making no turn at all, and holding exactly the same course I began with *Hell's Angels*. (. . . and, yes, 10 pages of this bullshit is enough, so let's get to it . . . Selah.)

FROM U.S. SENATOR GEORGE McGOVERN:

McGovern made plans to meet up with Thompson in Washington after the 1976 election.

November 20, 1976
Washington, D.C.

Dear Hunter:

I am dictating this note over the phone to Pat Donovan since I was unable to reach you on the phone following receipt of your letter of November ninth.

I am delighted to know you will be in Washington December 9–12. It so happens that I am a delegate to the United Nations this year, but I will be in Washington on Sunday, the twelfth. Could we have dinner that night? If so, let me know where you are staying and we will work out a time and a place to get together. Call me at home, or if you can't reach me there, Pat Donovan at my office can work out arrangements with you.

Sunday night is not a good restaurant night in Washington, but I give you a couple of options—the Oak Room at the Mayflower or the Golden Palace on 7th Street—a good Chinese restaurant.

It's going to be great to see you again.

All the best,
George McGovern

SHARK/HST . . . AUTHOR'S NOTE:

Thompson composed this "Author's Note" as a draft introduction to his first anthology of "Gonzo Papers," The Great Shark Hunt.

December, 1976
Woody Creek, CO

"ART IS LONG AND LIFE IS SHORT,
AND SUCCESS IS VERY FAR OFF."

—J. Conrad

This book—if and when it finally goes to the printer—will stand like a pillar of fire as a monument to whatever strange fuel, madness or high and mysterious energy still cooks at the roots of this nation and keeps it still functioning in a world that no longer needs us.

I have done at least nine ugly things in my life that I hope I will never have to do again, and I have spent at least half my waking hours for the past twenty years trying to do things that were known to be doomed and impossible from the start; and most of them worked well enough, or at least I survived them and emerged with my body and brain sufficiently intact to insist that they all served a purpose of some kind . . . but if anybody had warned me, twenty years ago, that long before I was forty years old I would wake up in the late hours of some frozen afternoon 8000 feet high in the Rockies to the sound of telephones screeching all over my half-built log house, and then to hear the voice of some Random House editor in New York telling me I had less than forty-eight hours to write a coherent "introduction" to a book-length collection of "my work" that would be on the shelves of every library in America before the year was out, my instant reaction to such a warning would have been to bet so heavily against it that I would eagerly have sought out a notary public and signed over both balls and even my thumbs as collateral.

But that would not have been necessary or even possible, at that point—because twenty years ago I was locked up in the Jefferson County Jail in Louisville, Kentucky on a bogus "rape" charge and there was nobody in town who believed that even a three-dollar bet with both my balls and my thumbs as collateral was worth the risk on a twenty-year note. At the age of seventeen I was an infamous Juvenile Delinquent (sp?), Louisville's answer to Billy the Kid,[27] and not even my friends really thought I would live to see twenty.

Neither did I, for that matter—although if anybody had offered me even money on it, I would probably have taken the bet and felt comfortable, win or lose.

27. Billy the Kid was the nickname of late nineteenth-century Western outlaw William H. Bonney, a notorious cattle thief and murderer who was finally captured and sentenced to hang. He escaped from jail by killing two guards, but was quickly hunted down and killed by Sheriff Pat Garrett.

It was not a bad bet. The numbers were all on my side, at that age, and only a fool would have gambled like that with me anyway. My reputation as a mad-dog teen-age criminal made the prospect of winning such a bet with me almost as ugly as losing. By sundown on my twentieth birthday I would have either collected in full, or set fire to the houses of all those who owed me.

One of my last acts as a high school student, around midnight on the day of my final expulsion, was to steal a case of beer and then—with the help of two friends who had nothing better to do that evening—drive out to the posh suburb where we knew the city's Superintendent of Schools lived, and throw all twenty-four unopened bottles through every window in the front of his house. . . . I can still hear the sounds of that hellish attack: Every ten seconds there would be the shrill crash of another window shattered, then a dull wet *boom* as the beer bottle exploded on the rugs or walls or furniture inside his house. God only knows what those poor bastards in the upstairs bedrooms were thinking as they rolled out of bed and crawled desperately around in the hallways on their hands and knees, groping in the darkness for a phone to call the police . . . (according to front-page reports in the next day's *Courier-Journal* . . .).

But we knew we had plenty of time, so we set the case down on his lawn and aimed our shots carefully, putting them through the windows one at a time and laughing crazily at the sounds of carnage inside . . . and by the time the cops swarmed in, we were three miles away on the golf course in Cherokee Park, half-mad from all that adrenaline as we crouched in a sand-trap downhill from the Number One green and all three of us staggering, whooping drunk as we tried to calm down by finishing off another one of the six cases of beer we'd stolen earlier that night from The Depot . . .

Far below us, across Cherokee Lake and the steep-angled No. 5 fairway that still slants like a nasty green scar through the memories of those white-buck, haspel-cord years of my gin-soaked youth that centered so much on that park and that lake and that golf course where I spent most of my late afternoons during high school because it was the only place where I knew the probation officer couldn't possibly find me . . . and on nights when the weather was warm or at least warm enough and the dew was so thick that the greens were too wet to sit on, unless you were naked, and even the sand in the bunkers was so damp that you could roll it up in your hands like summer snowballs . . . On nights like these and especially when we knew the police were looking for us, we would flee into Cherokee Park and drive out on the golf course, with lights off, to our hideout under the oak trees near the Number One green, where we could sit on the heavy stone benches and sip from a pint of Gilbey's while we carefully constructed our alibis and stared down across the lake at the Toddle House parking lot and the back door of The Old Kentucky Tavern where we could usually recognize one or two cars that belonged to some of our friends like Sam Stallings or Bob Butler, dragging their underage girlfriends into the tavern for a Tom Collins or two in the dark and dirty "back room."

Indeed, and so much for all that—except to stress that I have lived so much longer than I or anyone else expected me to, that I made no plans or provisions for this kind of awkward longevity and the realities that keep coming with it.

My own calculations, ever since the age of fifteen when the question of my life-expectancy first became a conscious and even a comfortable subject for speculation between me and my friends, were originally based on a personal calendar that ended with age 27. I can't remember exactly how or why I fixed on that number, but I recall very clearly that—as a betting proposition—27 was as high as I was willing to go, at even odds.

Every year after that would have doubled the numbers. I would not have bet on my chances of living to collect any bets on my twenty-eighth birthday, for instance, at less than 2-1. Anybody willing to bet $100 that I would not be alive at the age of 28 would have had to pay me $200 if I was still breathing on my twenty-eighth birthday—or at least alive enough to be physically dangerous to welshers.

The price on age 29 was a *minimal* 4-1, and—even at twice those odds (8-1)—a bet against the likelihood of my ever reaching the natural age of 30 was one of history's great gambling bargains. The *real* odds on my living 30 years on this earth, I figured, were more like 20-1.

Well . . . Here we go again: Another one of these desperate, last-minute, half-sane sprints to beat another deadline . . . And, yes, it's dawn again; this time in Woody Creek, with the sun looming up very suddenly from behind those mean white peaks along the Continental Divide . . . and now, at 6:33 on this cold Wednesday morning, flashing long, laser-like beams of a light the color of white gold on the high ridge of bright snowfields across the valley . . . And yes, I have just paid another installment on my news-junkie's dues by watching my old friend Hughes Rudd do his gig once again with the *CBS Morning News*. . . .

But I found myself unable, this time, to give the morning news my full attention: There were a lot of things happening, and I recall watching part of a long and seemingly intense interview between [CBS correspondent] Bruce Morton and somebody heavy from the White House or Foggy Bottom or some other outpost of access in Jimmy Carter's world. . . . I forget who it was, or what Bruce and Hughes were asking him about, but I recall very clearly that nothing in the conversation had any effect on me at all. I felt no anger, no elation, no excitement of any kind. . . . It was like watching a Cyrus Vance[28] press conference—and for all I know, it might have been Vance they were interviewing, a sort of well-bred telephone pole in the first throes of menopause. . . . Which is not all bad, because if he handles it right he is well on his way to the kind of perpetual "senior statesman" role now occupied by such elegant fossils as Clark Clifford and Averell Harriman,[29] whose long years of "service" to the Democratic Party and The Nation—in that order—have gained them a rare and very special kind of stature that is honored mainly in the breach, but acknowledged just often enough to maintain their credibility on that level of national politics and international diplomacy that functions in the high-powered, soft-spoken, after-dark arena of Washington's social circuit: The dining rooms of

28. Cyrus R. Vance was U.S. secretary of state from 1977 to 1980.
29. Lawyer Clark Clifford was a special adviser to Presidents Truman and Kennedy, then U.S. secretary of defense under LBJ from 1968 to 1969; W. Averell Harriman, former chairman of the board of the Union Pacific railroad, served in a host of government appointments, including as U.S. ambassador to Moscow and London and as secretary of commerce under President Franklin Delano Roosevelt.

Georgetown, the lawn parties at estates across the river in woodsy McLean, and the private penthouse suites of high-rolling foreign ambassadors along Embassy Row.

So there is no rational way to explain, now, just how strange and profoundly unsettled I feel at the prospect of living to be forty years old—under *any* circumstances; but certainly not with a wife, a son, my own valley/fortress in the Rockies, and the genuinely rotten task of lashing together a book of my own writings. . . .

Which is weird, folks, so try to bear with me. I might have some trouble making a case for the bedrock-strangeness of things like having a home and a family and somehow managing to live past the age of thirty. . . . Because a lot of people have done those things and survived a lot longer than I have, for good or ill; but the factor that queers *my* equation is the one about living ten years longer than *anybody* would have bet on, in a free-falling high-speed limbo I was never prepared for, and to look back on it now and realize that I got paid *real money* all that time for just wandering around in the world and writing about whatever got in my way. . . . And *now* to have to sit down here in this goddamn soundproof dungeon that I built for myself 8000 feet above sea-level, and labor through pounds and pounds and pounds of my own "works," trying to figure out which pound or two should go into The Book, a huge tome with my own picture on both front and back covers. . . .

Well, this almost-perfect vision of Hell on Earth is my present to those knee-crawling scumbags at *Time* magazine, where I once had a job and was considered a Promising Young Man. But that was a long time ago—and when they found out what I *really* was, they fired me.

Right: "Hit the bricks, fella, you're not our type. . . ." And now they refuse to admit it. I have a letter from the *Time* personnel department—addressed to the editors of *Playboy* (who inquired)—saying I was a wonderful person and did my work well. . . . Which bothers me: First, because it's a flat-out lie, and Second, because I had to work very hard to get fired from *Time*, and the fact that I finally succeeded remains a point of personal pride, especially when I think what might have become of me if I'd failed.

We all have our private nightmares, and that is one of mine: That I might still be working for *Time*—still robbing the company of everything I could carry out of the building; still grappling with half-naked, half-drunk Vassar girls on [managing editor] Henry Grunwald's leather couch when we had to work late on deadline nights; and still telling myself that "next week" I'd go out and find some kind of work I didn't have to apologize for. . . . The man who hired me said I was an "editorial trainee," but after a week on the job I understood that I was really a Copyboy, and the only "editorial training" I got on the job was seeing what happened to the "articles" I carried from the writers' cubicles to the editors' cubicles, and then back again to the writers.

The "editing" was often so massive and humiliating that I felt personally embarrassed when I had to take it back to the writers—because *I* knew that *they* knew that I'd read the stuff coming and going; and I still remember the glazed look in the eyes of good writers like John McPhee and John Skow when I had to bring that butchered copy back to them.

Ah . . . but what the hell? Some of us survived, and in retrospect I see my year at *Time* as a sort of personal introduction to Applied or maybe Reversed Darwinism, and on the whole it was not a bad gig. In addition to subsidizing my first year of work/life in the Big City—living in the Village, beginning a first novel and running amok in every conceivable direction—my job at *Time* also forced me into daily confrontation with the world of big-time, "prestige" journalism that I soon understood was *not* what I wanted to be a success at, in this life . . . and that is a very valuable thing to be sure of, at the age of twenty-one.

So I am grateful to Time Inc. for that, if nothing else. They gave me shelter, money, time to think, and a whole rainbow of Manhattan-style fringe-benefits at a time in my life when those things were all I really needed. There were also a few lasting friendships—including George Love, the long-suffering Production Supervisor who felt far worse about firing me than I felt about being fired; and Tom Vanderschmidt, now an editor of *Sports Illustrated,* whose ill-fated idea of sending me to Las Vegas to cover the "Mint 400" resulted in total disaster for Tom and the magazine; but for me it was an accidental ticket on one of the most bizarre roller-coaster rides in twentieth-century journalism.

What began as a $250 assignment to write a photo-caption for *Sports Illustrated* ended some two years later as a book titled *Fear & Loathing in Las Vegas*—which, despite a long history of financial failure on all fronts, remains my personal favorite among all the things I've written. And it is still the lonely cornerstone of everything that has since become genuinely and puzzlingly infamous as "Gonzo Journalism."

Indeed . . . But that is too long a leap for me to make right now—in print or any other way. My fall from grace that began with a pink slip from *Time* so long ago that it seems like another lifetime was violently accelerated in the summer of 1976 when *Time* devoted a *whole page* to a harsh and hysterical assault on me and everything I might or might not stand for—written, as it were, by one of those same empty-eyed hacks[30] whose cubicle used to be one of my regular pick-up and dump-off points when I was making my daily rounds as a *Time* copyboy.

There is probably some kind of weird and perhaps even "poetic" justice in a thing like that—but the logic escapes me right now, and I don't have the time to brood on it; except maybe to fall back on that old and usually accurate piece of folk-wisdom about "knowing a man by his enemies." Which gives me a definite sense of inner peace and public satisfaction, because the three names that have hovered near the top of my own "enemies list" for the past fifteen years are Richard Nixon, Hubert Humphrey and *Time* magazine. I have dealt with them all, at close range, and my only regret is that I stomped too softly on the bastards. . . .

30. T. Griffith, in "Fear and Loathing and Ripping Off," *Time*, July 19, 1976.

The *Fear and Loathing in America* Honor Roll

Oscar Acosta
Muhammad Ali
Bob Arum
Tom Beach
Anita Bejmuk
Tom Benton
Sandy Berger
Ed Bradley
Doug Brinkley
David Broder
Pat Buchanan
Jane Buffett
Pat Caddell
Jimmy Carter
John Clancy
Tim Crouse
Louisa Davidson
Morris Dees
Bill Dixon
Donna Dowling
Bob Dylan
Wayne Ewing
Tim Ferris
Flor Flores
Jim Flug
Deborah Fuller
The Gideon Society
Gayle Golding
Gerald Goldstein
Richard Goodwin
Gary Hart
Warren Hinckle
John Holum
Abe Hutt
Doris Kearns
Bobby Kennedy
Lucy Langford
Annie Leibovitz
Frank Mankiewicz
Herbie Mann
Eugene McCarthy
George McGovern
Steve Messina
Lynn Nesbit
Heidi Opheim
P. J. O'Rourke
Tara Parsons
Beth Pearson
George Plimpton
Jeff Posternak
John Prine
Bonnie Raitt
Keith Richards
Curtis Robinson
David Rosenthal
Marysue Rucci
Shelby Sadler
Barbara Shailor

Jim Silberman
Grace Slick
Mike Solheim
Ralph Steadman
George Stranahan
Keith Stroup
George Tobia
Carl Wagner
John Walsh
Jann Wenner
Erica Whittington
Tom Wolfe
Andrew Wylie

Chronological List of Letters

Index

About the Author

Hunter S. Thompson was born and raised in Louisville, Kentucky. His books include *Hell's Angels*, *Fear and Loathing in Las Vegas, Fear and Loathing: On the Campaign Trail '72, The Curse of Lono, Songs of the Doomed, Better Than Sex,* and *The Proud Highway.* He is a regular contributor to various national and international publications. He now lives in a fortified compound in Colorado.

About the Editor

Douglas Brinkley is the director of the Eisenhower Center for American Studies and a professor of history at the University of New Orleans. He is the author of *The Majic Bus: An American Odyssey* (1993), *Dean Acheson: The Cold War Years* (1992), *The Unfinished Presidency: Jimmy Carter's Journey Beyond the White House* (1998), *American Heritage History of the United States* (1998), and *Rosa Parks* (2000). Professor Brinkley is also an American culture commentator on National Public Radio and a contributing editor to the *Los Angeles Times Book Review*.